Different Voices

Different Voices
Women in United States History

Second Edition

Emily Teipe

Restoration of archival photographs by Mark Teipe

Identification of cover photographs:

Front cover, top row, left to right
Native American woman and child
Charlotte Hartley, college student ca. 1890
Josephine Baker
Eleanor Roosevelt

Front cover, bottom row, left to right
Mildred Molesworth
Alma Ellis Caloia
WWII era woman
Latoya Thurman

Back cover, top row, left to right
Tsrigi Droma
Emma Goldman
Frances Willard
Isabelle "Belle" Boyd

Back cover, bottom row, left to right
Betty Friedan
Clara Barton
Shirley Chisholm
Abigail Adams

ISBN 978-1-56226-650-9

For Alma Ellis Caloia

About the Author

Emily Teipe was born in Baltimore, Maryland and attended the Eastern High School for Females. She received her B.A. and M.A. degrees from California State University, Fullerton and her Ph.D. from University of California, Riverside. She is professor of History and Women's Studies at Fullerton College where she has taught for twenty-three years. In 2010 she received the Teacher of the Year Award from the student body. Some of her other publications include- *America's First Veterans and the Revolutionary War Pensions; A Woman's Journal, Reading and Writing on Themes in Women's Studies;* "Will the Real Molly Pitcher Please Stand Up?" *Prologue, the National Archives:* "The Brandeis Brief"; "The British Stamp Tax", and "The Pennsylvania Society for the Abolition of Slavery 1775."

Table of Contents (Abbreviated)

Table of Contents (Detailed)

FOREWORD

The death of Betty Friedan (1921-2006) offers a poignant reminder that the second wave of feminism appeared less than fifty years ago. *The Feminine Mystique* shattered an American illusion. Why, she asked, were she and the scores of women she interviewed not the content "happy homemakers" society promised they would be? Why had they not found fulfillment in their lives as wives and mothers? Friedan described "the problem that had no name" and then she set out to find a solution. She concluded that women needed to carve out their own identities, separate from those of their husbands and families.

These revelations spawned the women's movement of the 1960s. It arrived with multiple agendas, but one critical requirement was the need to write of women's past. The efforts started slowly. Textbooks were still primarily written by and about elite white men as if only they mattered in the "course of human events." When women or minorities did make an appearance, their inclusions were tentative. Women arrived as an occasional vignette that described famous women and their particular achievements—those who fought for the vote, abolition or women's rights, perhaps a president's wife or two, and a woman here or there who performed admirable feats of courage. But these tales were more like marginalia added to satisfy the shrill voices of women's historians who were demanding attention.

Within two decades American history textbooks went through a virtual transformation. Textbook writers could no longer get away with a nod toward women; no account of America's past was possible without including women as active participants in the formation of the United States.

Different Voices is among the newest generation of women's history textbooks. While it is not the first focused exclusively on women, it carves out new terrain by devoting its rich detail to unique perspectives. *Different Voices* is multicultural and not content to describe only the rich and well born. It places women into the forefront of their own transformations. But the most exciting contributions trace the ways in which particular issues or processes go beyond discovery or change and have far broader implications and meaning. In *Different Voices*, for example, the discussion of medical science does not just treat women's diseases and the inherent political battles, it digs far deeper into the nature of women's health issues and the perceptions of women's bodies. This book pushes the story ever further on how women were and continue to be essential in American culture. *Different Voices* invites us to know how.

Sharon V. Salinger
Academic Dean, Professor of History
University of California at Irvine

ACKNOWLEDGEMENTS

I extend gratitude to my mentors who encouraged my research in American and Women's History, Dr. Sharon Salinger, University of California, Irvine and Dr. Sarah Stage, Arizona State University. I would like to thank Leslie Golden and her staff at CAT publishing for making this book possible and for their effort in making it much improved in this second edition. While I researched and wrote this edition my sons gave encouragement and help, in particular—Mark for the archival restoration of the vintage photographs throughout the book, Peter for computer systems running and upgraded and William for formatting, proof-reading and brainstorming. Inspiration was supplied continuously by my two grandchildren, Azeli and Mateo; comfort and support by my four-legged friends Molly and Princess.

Between the covers of this text are some of the women who carried the standard for women's rights and social reform. Two key crusaders, Zoe Nicholson and Professor Mary Lee Sargent, shared with me and permitted the use of their historical memoirs and photographs which filled in critical research on the failure of the ERA for ratification. On several occasions I interviewed Aileen Hernandez and it was an honor and a pleasure. Ms. Hernandez, who played a key role in the Civil Rights Movement, the EEOC, and NOW, shared with me not only her eyewitness testimony but also gave me access to her collected ephemera. I also thank the following for their help and contributions: The National Archives, Laguna Hills Branch; Dr. F. Kennon Moody, of the Franklin D. Roosevelt Library in La Grangeville, New York; Nelle Rote for reprint of letters of her aunt Helen Fairchild, a World War I nurse; Kathy Baker for the image of her great-aunt's teaching license; Thelma Schaefer for family archival photos; the Castro family for pictures of Cielo Castro's La Quinceanera; Tsekyi Dolma and Alma Ellis Caloia for use of cover photographs; Fullerton College Library for archival photography; and Fullerton Public Library for use of photographs in the Launer History Collection. This text is greatly enhanced by the archival pictures and photographs from the Library of Congress featured throughout the book and by the photo of Olive Oatman from the Arizona Historical Society. Thanks also to the *William and Mary Quarterly* for permission to reprint the research of David R. Ransome, "Wives for Virginia."

At the eleventh hour as we were finalizing the book, Mr. Bill Burger, Vice- President of Communications at Brandeis University came through for us with permission to use the photograph of Professor Anita Hill and sent us several to choose from. For all of us who admire her courage, and value her professionalism, scholarship and contribution to education it is an honor to have her photograph in chapter twenty-five. We thank Mike Lovett, staff photographer at Brandeis University for the photos of Dr Hill.

There are so many scholars whose ideas enrich this text that the Bibliography of References will have to suffice as an acknowledgement of their contribution.

In gratitude,
Emily M. Teipe

INTRODUCTION

I initially wrote this text, *Different Voices: Women in United States History*, out of practical necessity for use in my class, the History of Women in the United States, which I have taught at Fullerton College for twenty-one years. The field of American Women's History needed a survey narrative text formatted as a textbook. Although the concept sounds quite obvious, at the time no one had put together a textbook on women's history in that form. The overall plan was to compile something innovative: a women's history for a survey sophomore-level class formatted as a multidimensional textbook with primary sources, a comprehensive narrative, statistical tables, maps, photos and timelines. When initially published in 2003, *Different Voices* was the first textbook of its kind on Women's History presented with these components.

With regard to the lexicography, when quoting from historical sources, the original language and syntax have been retained wherever possible. However, for the sake of clarity in some instances, exceptions have been made and more modern usage has been substituted. Names for particular ethnic groups change over time and sources quoted here may contain phrases or words which are politically incorrect today. However, in some cases for accuracy and historical authenticity, I have retained terms used at a given period such as Black Americans, Negroes and Colored people, Indians and Hispanics. Political correctness varies by region and also by time period. In the State of New Mexico, it has been and remains appropriate to refer to all non-white persons, whether of mixed heritage (mestizo), Spanish heritage or Native American heritage, as Hispanic. For this study, in some cases, women in the Spanish colonial experience are designated Latina(s). In describing the population most affected today by Spanish conquest, Latino(s) and Latina(s) are the preferred terms because they denote a widely diverse group of people and can be more generally applied to Americans who are part of a culture where a Latin-derived language, such as Spanish, Portuguese, or French (i.e. Creole) is spoken.

The chapters include special features such as Mothers of Invention and Clio's Corner. The Mothers of Invention vignettes showcase the contributions of unique American women. Clio's Corner (named for Clio, who in Greek mythology is the Muse of History) offers a discussion of historical research, interpretation and theory by certain historians on a particular topic.

The text is divided into seven parts which are subdivided into twenty-five chapters and a postscript/conclusion. Part I, The Encounter of European, Native American and African Culture in the New World, chapters one through five, describes the women's experience against the historical background; women are featured who resided within the confines of the traditional domestic structure, or by contrast females who played a unique role which altered or affected women's status or the history of their community. In most instances, colonial women in the American experience worked and served a patriarchy whether it was English, Dutch, French, or Spanish. At the same time, Native-American, African and African-American women who were alien to and unfamiliar with European Colonial systems stand in stark comparison. African, African-American and in some cases Native American women were enslaved by European Colonials who regarded them as chattel or property. In all the colonies and under different legal systems, it was women's work that sustained the family and the greater community.

Part II, Women in the Revolutionary War and the New Republic, chapters six and seven, describes women's efforts to win the War of Independence. Overlooked in the story of America's War for Independence are the female soldiers and patriots who fought. Thousands of women who were driven from their homes by the enemy or followed husbands and sweethearts off to war, walked from battlefield to battlefield and contributed to victory. But their sacrifices were soon forgotten when the new government proclaimed that all men are created equal. In the New Republic, influential people such as Dr. Benjamin Rush, Benjamin Franklin, Charles Brockden Brown and Judith Sargeant Murray promoted education for young women but few women had access to educational opportunity. As factories were built, many young girls went to work in them for meager pay and under harsh conditions.

Part III, The Age of Reform, chapters eight through twelve, surveys an active period from 1820 to 1860, when American women were on the vanguard of all the antebellum reform movements, carving out an empire of benevolence. Reform activity, particularly involvement in the anti-slavery crusade, gave women a heightened awareness of their own inferior status. It was during this ferment of reform that the Women's Rights Movement took shape and women met for the first conference of its kind, a Women's Rights Convention at Seneca Falls, New York, in 1848. This was concomitant with western expansion. In the West, women built schools, libraries and churches. During the Civil War, women of the North and the South contributed to the defense of their cause.

Part IV, Women in the Gilded Age, chapters thirteen through sixteen, highlights the cultural experiences of women in American Victorian society, their involvement in the reform organizations after the Civil War and the state of women's health in the nineteenth century. During this period women's political activism took many twists and turns often characterized by organizing and the realignment of the women's rights campaign. As novitiates to the political process, all of this activity added greatly to their political experience and wisdom.

Part V, Women in the Early Twentieth Century, chapters seventeen and eighteen, examines the role of female Progressives and Socialists, women's service during World War I and women's steps toward winning suffrage. Women worked for legal reform and social change, and formed landmark institutions such as settlement houses, schools and clinics. One hundred years after the antebellum reform crusades, women brought social improvement once again. Working along the entire political spectrum from moderate and progressive to the radical left, women demonstrated, lobbied and labored to upset the status quo.

Part VI, Women from the Post Suffrage Period Through World War II, chapters nineteen through twenty-one, encompasses dramatic events such as Prohibition, the hardship of the Great Depression, and the horror of World War II. Changes in fashion and lifestyle affected women in the Twenties. Women were the mainstay of the family during the severe economic downturn of the Depression and even though women had always worked in industry, their work in defense plants in World War II gave them new confidence. These chapters help us gauge the progress and egress of women's status after gaining the vote.

The final section, Part VII, The Women's Experience-Mid-to-Late Twentieth Century, chapters twenty-two through twenty-five, focuses on bold changes for American society and especially women since World War II. It includes society's attempts to relegate women to the domestic space, the diverse populist movements for Civil Rights, the second wave of feminism and the defeat of the ERA. Part VII concludes with a postscript glance at the more current Third Wave/Postmodernist era which brings us into the twenty-first century.

Appendixes include the Constitution of the United States of America, the Seneca Falls Declaration of Sentiments and Resolutions, and Section 703 of the Civil Rights Act of 1964, which are essential documents for a United States Women's History Survey course. The Bibliography is arranged topically to assist students looking for books on a particular topic when preliminary research for formal papers and writing assignments is needed.

This book is dedicated to my students, whose positive response and avid interest in Women's History have encouraged me to research and write about the extraordinary women of the American past. Within the covers of this text you are about to discover your ancestors - truly heroic, inspiring and gifted women whose courage, persistence, suffering and intense labor made it possible for us to live in a manner they hoped for but could only imagine.

SPECIAL FEATURES

MOTHERS OF INVENTION

The **Mothers of Invention** vignettes showcase the contributions or roles of American women in United States History.

CLIO'S CORNER

Clio's Corner offers a discussion of historical research, interpretations and theory by certain historians on a particular topic. It is named for *Clio*, the muse of history.

Part I

The Encounter of European, Native American and African Culture in the New World

Women in the Colony of New Spain

English, Dutch and French Settlement in the New World

Dissenters, Witches and Quakers in the Colonies

The Legal Status of Women in the English and Dutch Colonies

Women's Work in the Colonies

Chapter 1
Women in the Colony of New Spain
Subject to the Monarch's Rule

Key Topics

The Role of Native American Women
The Social and Legal Status of Women

Chronology

Pre-15th century - Pre-Columbian America before European Invasion
1519 - 1521 - Conquest of Tenochtitlan by Spanish under Hernando Cortes
1565 - Spanish Establish First Colony at St. Augustine, Florida
1610 - Spanish Establish the City of Santa Fe
1769 - Franciscans Establish Mission System in California

Introduction

When Spanish explorer Hernan Cortes entered the Aztec Empire (Mexico) in 1519 with 618 soldiers and conquered it by 1521, he made Spain the envy of all Europe and established a model of conquest in the New World. Thereafter, other European states staged exploration to the New World in an attempt to match Spain's success.

The Spanish colonies in America, New Spain, included portions of what is the South, Southwest and the western United States, present day Arizona, California, Colorado, Florida, Nevada, New Mexico, Texas and Utah. In each region the Spanish crown appointed a viceroy to rule and sent Catholic missionaries to evangelize the Native Americans. Under the control of the Spanish government and the Catholic Church, each area developed with distinct features.

Spain's acquisition of territory added tremendous wealth to the kingdom. When considering the price natives paid for being discovered, revisionist historians describe European exploration and colonization as an invasion of America; other scholars go so far as to call it genocide. Their conclusion is based upon the dramatic decrease in the native population as a direct result of contact with the Spanish and Portuguese explorers. In one century, from 1492 to 1590, nearly 90 percent of the native population was annihilated by disease, warfare, and/or hard labor. The results of Spanish conquest were tragic and irreversible. As more explorers—the English, French and Dutch—came to America, the fatalities among native people mounted even higher.

Critical to the development, survival and success of Spanish colonization was the role of immigrant and indigenous women. In this chapter, we will characterize the life experiences of these women in the early Spanish colonial borderlands.

The Spanish in America

The Spanish conquistadors and priests who came to the New World for "God, Gold and Glory" intended the colony to be a permanent settlement. Exploration and settlement groups consisted of an array of people including single men, married men (sometimes accompanied by their wives), priests, native men and women as well as slaves brought by the Spanish from the West Indies. Within these groups, Spanish men predominated and a[illegible] The colonial popu[illegible] young adults rangin[illegible] and thirty year-olds.

In the New World, the Spanish were the first Europeans to experience the irony of colonial opportunity. The New World presented land in abundance but insufficient labor for agricultural production. During their invasion, native people had been wiped out by disease and warfare, leaving the conquerors land-wealthy and labor-poor. Social convention dictated that as *hidalgos*, the Spanish men could not perform manual labor.[1] Hence, workers for the *encomienda* had to be recruited elsewhere and were always in short supply.[2] The colonial Spanish government declared a policy of *repartimiento* which im[illegible]nquered natives.[3] [illegible] such as those bui[illegible] in Alta and Baja [illegible] Spain's colonial policy—to convert the natives and then to utilize them as labor. Spanish overlords using military force rounded up local natives to work at the missions, the *presidios*, and the *ranchos* but there were never enough workers to satisfy the labor demand.[4]

While the Spanish proclaimed a policy of *convivencia*, they also used coercion and cruelty to convert Native Americans to Christianity and bring them under Spanish rule.[5] For New Spain to thrive it was not a matter of deploying more soldiers from Spain or the Indies; the colony simply could not survive with the few women who came from Spain. From the onset of settlement, male immigrants cohabited freely with or sometimes married the native women since neither the government nor the church condemned mixed marriages. This Spanish pattern of settlement contrasted sharply from other European colonies. The English, for example, would first conquer and then remove native peoples in order to take and settle the land. If Englishmen forbidden by law to intermarry with Native American or African women cohabited with them, they were shunned by their kinsmen and liable for corporal punishment under English law.

Women in the Colony of New Spain

The Spanish women who came to America suf[illegible] of exploration [illegible] the first expedi[illegible]e Leon brought two Spanish women, [illegible] Juana Jimenez, to settle a place the Spanish named Florida. We know little else about these women. In 1542, one of the few women to accompany Hernando De Soto's exploration of the Mississippi, Francisca de Hinestrosa, burned to death along with her unborn child when the Spanish camp came under Indian attack. News of fatalities and dangers such as this discouraged some women from venturing to the New World but those who did displayed stamina and heroism.

During an attack from natives of the Acoma pueblo (near San Juan, New Mexico), Dona Eufemia, the wife of Francisco de Sosa Penalosa, criticized the men who talked of deserting the settlement.[6]

---

1. *Hidalgos*, noble, gentlemen of property.
2. *Encomienda*, reward to Spanish colonists from the crown, land grants as well as the privilege of collecting revenue.
3. *Repartimiento*, the distribution of indigenous people in New Spain for forced labor.
4. *Presidios,* a garrison or fortress. *Ranchos,* a ranch or working farm.
5. *Convivencia,* peaceful coexistence, under this policy the Spanish could intermarry with the native people.

The Acoma Pueblo, the site where Spanish women organized a defense for the attack on the Acoma people. (Photos courtesy of the Library of Congress.)

Dona, admired for her beauty, fiery spirit and clear thinking acted quickly and rallied the twelve wives of the company to defend their homes and protect their children. With the approval of their commandant Juan de Ornate, Eufemia and Ana Perez de Bustillo organized a women's detail to stand guard on the rooftops of their homes. After two days of fierce fighting the Spanish were victorious and attributed the defeat of the Acoma [illegible] the Virgin Mary.

Certa[illegible]ave Spanish and Native American women never included in the accounts that we will never know. But some are mentioned in the narrative, such as three wives of soldiers with Coronado's expedition who earned praise for their service. Maria Maldonado, a nurse, Senora Caballero, a native woman and Francisca de Hozes, who gathered food, cooked, tended the sick, cared for their families and laundered for the men all while marching north from Mexico City. Although they faced every danger on the journey, Francisca de Hozes dreaded more the imminent trip back to Spain because she feared the ocean voyage more than the risks of the overland trek. There were women who came to America ill-prepared for the life that awaited them on the borderlands. Dona Francisca Galinda, accompanied by her mulatta servant Isabel, arrived on the rugged frontier of San Gabriel (New Mexico) on December 24, 1600, with an extensive wardrobe of silk, satin and taffeta court dresses.[7]

Native American Women and the Spanish

Our impressions of Native Americans fail to recognize the diversity of native people. Because the Spanish conquered territory over a wide region of America, they encountered hundreds of different tribes of Native Americans. In North America alone there were at least 2,000 distinct language groups, not to mention the diversity of tribal structures, customs and beliefs. Seminoles in Florida, for example or the Choctaw, Natchez and Chickasaw of the Mississippi region had less in common with each other than Spaniards had with the English. Natives occupied various regions and ecosystems from woodland, coastal, desert, and high plains to valleys or mountainous domains. Some remained in the hunting and gathering stage, others had developed semi-permanent agricultural settlements and a few such as the Aztec had built a sophisticated empire through conquest. Throughout America tribal political structures, marriage and family practices as well as trade networks and dress were all so distinct from the other that one cannot make generalizations about them.

Although accounts of initial encounters of Spanish men and native women are anecdotal, and predominantly described by Spanish males, some such as Pedro de Castaneda's in 1541 on meeting the Teya, a tribe of Plains Apaches are informative.

> Their women are well-treated and through modesty they cover their whole bodies. They have shoes and buskins of tanned hides and wear blankets over their short underskirts made of skins tied at the shoulders, and a sort of short tunic, with small fringes reaching to the middle of their thighs.

What we know about native women is that they all shared a common destiny—to marry, (whatever form that union might take

6. *Pueblo*, a Native American village or city, a community of people extended family or tribe and the dwellings they built.
7. *Mulatta,* a person having one white and one black parent.

within their tribe) to have children and to care for their family. Before the advent of modern medicine most women had a life expectancy of thirty or forty years and about 15 percent died in childbirth. For most women—no matter what their tribal affiliation was—life consisted of domestic labor, providing food and clothing for a household, caring for children and assisting with farming chores. Among many tribes, women held a greater responsibility for agricultural production than men. Religious beliefs dictated that if women tilled the soil, planted the seeds and harvested crops, their procreative power would somehow be transmitted and make the earth fertile. Women insured the tribe's survival through childbearing, caring for their family and maintaining property.

The Taos Pueblo is a classic example of the architecture of pueblo natives of the American Southwest. This multiple family dwelling accommodates about 150 people of the Tewa tribe and has served as a continuous residence since ca.1200. (Photo courtesy of the Library of Congress.)

In some Native American tribes, a *matrilineal* and *matriarchal system* predominated, especially in those regions which are now the southwestern United States.[8] But regardless of their structure, whether *patriarchal* or *matriarchal,* once these women were taken as wives or mistresses by Spanish men they lived in the confines of a male dominated world.[9] The social, economic and political enclaves established by Spanish Conquistadors marked gendered boundaries held by men within the domain of crown, church and court, the staid structures of power and discrimination.

However, native women did not willingly submit to Spanish *convivencia.* Rape was such a common occurrence that it was rarely mentioned in the records unless as an aside or humorous incident. Columbus related one such event when he had gifted a captured naked native woman to his comrade Michele de Cuneo to be his slave and concubine. When Cuneo sexually assaulted her, she tried to defend herself by screaming and clawing at him. He eventually subdued her by beating her with a rope. Countless Native American and European women must have risked death defending themselves rather than submit to rape. One Timucuan woman, however, proved a tough match for Pedro Diaz de Herrera, a soldier in De Soto's Florida expedition. In the act of seducing her, she grabbed his genitals and held on fiercely, and Herrera, the rapist—suddenly-turned-victim—screamed for help!

Spanish men, who comprised 90 percent of the invading population, cohabited with or married native women producing a substantial *mestizo* population.[10] Communities on the borderlands consisted of various people including soldiers, vagabonds, peddlers, escaped prisoners, and a few from other places such as French explorers. These isolated enclaves often sustained themselves by adopting Indian children from various tribes—Apache, Navajo, and Pueblo orphans—into the small Hispanic families. In such a fashion they created extended families or what historian John Kessell describes as "colonies of cousins."

The Encounter of Princess Malinali and Hernan Cortes

During the Spanish conquest perhaps the most famous of the indigenous women to cohabit with Spanish men was Malinali, born in the Coatzacoalos Province of Mexico sometime between 1501 and 1504. Malinali, daughter of the Lord of

8. *Matrilineal and matriarchal,* inheritance, lineage, and rule through the mother's family.
9. *Patriarchal,* a male dominated society, through inheritance, lineage political economic and social control.
10. *Mestizo*, child born of mixed parentage, usually a European father and a Native American mother.

Painala, enjoyed a privileged life as a young girl. When her father died and her mother remarried, Malinali was sold into slavery to remove any contention over the inheritance of her newborn half brother. (Some accounts state that she was stolen by traders and then sold to the Tabascan tribe.) As a captive, she was passed on among several tribes and owners. While a prisoner of the Mayans, her life became quite tenuous. At any time, she could have been given as tribute to the Aztecs to be offered in sacrifice to the Sun God. When Cortes invaded Mexico in 1519, Malinali—by then living in a Mayan village at Potonchan—was one of twenty women handed over to the Spanish as a gift of appeasement. Bernal Diaz Del Castillo, a soldier serving with Cortes, described Malinali as looking like a princess and "of pleasing appearance, sharp-witted and outgoing." In 1522, when Hernando Cortes took her as his mistress, she bore him a son. Baptized Martin, he was one of the first *mestizo* children. Malinali converted to Catholicism and took the name Dona Marina. Cortes passed her around to be the mistress of several of his officers including Alonso Pueretocarrero.

Malinali who could speak Mayan, Nahuatl and Spanish, served as a translator and a guide for the Spanish. Cortes, in an ironic gesture gave her gold, servants and land, resources all belonging to her homeland. He also arranged her marriage to Conquistador Juan de Jaramillo, a Spanish lieutenant, with whom she had a daughter. Juan took Malinali to Spain where she was honored at the royal court. She died sometime around 1531. When Jaramillo remarried, shortly after her death, he disinherited their daughter.

In the Spanish conquest of the Aztecs, Malinali played a crucial role. When she overheard the Cholulans planning an attack on the Spanish, she immediately informed Cortes of the plan. This maneuver saved the Spanish Corps and quite likely Cortes' entire venture in Mexico. Over the course of several military disasters, such as the army's retreat from the Aztec capital, Malinali proved her loyalty and stayed with Hernan Cortes and his forces.

Because of her collaboration with the Spanish, in the History of Mexico her name became synonymous with traitor. Her legacy is a dubious contradiction since she is regarded as both traitor and mother of Mexico's *mestizos*. Undoubtedly her collaboration with Cortes was indispensable to the Spanish conquest of Mexico, for as Bernal Diaz del Castillo acknowledged, "Without her we never would have understood the Mexican language and upon the whole have been unable to surmount many difficulties." Conversely, as one of the first native women to bear a Spanish man's child, Malinche enjoys an elevated status as the maternal icon of Mexico's conquered people. Her children born of Spanish fathers were the first of the new racially mixed *mestizo* population.

In contemporary Mexican society, the name, Malinchismo, means one who sells out to foreigners. But Malinali's own experience must be considered. As a young girl, she had been forsaken by her own family, taken as a prisoner by another tribe and eventually turned over to the Spanish from whom she received better treatment than she had from her own people. Malinali, like many natives, regarded the Spanish as her liberator from Aztec oppression. It was, after all, the Aztec maltreatment of conquered peoples in Meso America which helped Cortes forge alliances with many tribes and that solidified his success.

Malinali's fame spread throughout New Spain. A generation later, when Conquistador Juan de Ornate brought 200 soldiers and their families to pacify New Mexico, he took Dona Ines, a young *Pueblo* woman who spoke several native dialects, to serve as his interpreter. He wrote home that he hoped she would be a "second Malinche."

Women on the Spanish Borderlands

By the seventeenth century as the Spanish migrated to the northern reaches of New Spain, what is today the Southwestern United States, they established more colonial settlements. But the survival of the Spanish colonies remained precarious. By 1640, the Hispanic population of outposts such as Santa Fe numbered no more than 1,000 residents.

The Colony of New Spain - this map features some of the regions of the Western Hemisphere which the Spanish had conquered by the sixteenth century. Portions of New Spain shown here later became Mexico, and the South, Southwest, and western states of the United States of America.

In 1690, the natives revolted against the atrocities and cruelty of the Spanish, and staged a well-planned attack, known as the Pueblo Revolt of all Spanish settlements near Santa Fe. This native uprising effectively wiped out all Spanish settlements in the northern reaches of New Spain. Most of the Spanish settlers who were killed must have been known to their enemies since it was natives who identified victims such as Francisco de Anaya Almazan, his wife Dona Francisca and baby. Reports of the Pueblo Revolt shook the empire. After two centuries of conquest and colonization, indigenous people had taken their domain back from the Spanish. The warfare between natives and Spaniards severely reduced the adult population and increased the number of orphans in the colonies.

In other regions such as California, after failed attempts to colonize, Spanish authorities sent a surplus of convicts and orphans there. Diseases such as smallpox and syphilis decimated the Pericues tribe, residents of the northern Baja California Coast (today the Southern California and northern Mexico region of Baja California). With their tribe facing extinction from disease, native men resorted to kidnapping Spanish immigrant women. In 1734, the Pericues killed several priests and Don Manuel Andres Romero but they took Maria Villalobos, the wife of another soldier, her two daughters and her sister as captives. They confessed to a Jesuit missionary that syphilis had claimed so many females of their tribe that the surviving men fought for mates. The Spanish viewed the Pericues plight differently. In the words of Father Tamaral, a Jesuit priest, locals were dying because people of mixed backgrounds and those of vile, mixed blood riled up the local people and led them astray.

Further settlement gradually extended throughout Texas, Arizona and California. To sustain Spanish settlements it was necessary to conscript native women who served as stoop labor and consequently the backbone of the economy. This proved beneficial to the Spanish since these women were skilled in agriculture and tending livestock. They also performed all of the household duties and cared for the children. In addition to providing farm labor, some women in these communities, known as the *anjoladores*, were skilled in home construction and maintenance, namely applying the mud plaster to the exterior of the adobe homes. Women such as the *curanderas* cared for the sick and specialized in herbal medicines; others known as *parteras*, served as midwives in their communities. The diversified skills of these native women were vital to the survival of New Spain.[11]

However, within Spanish colonial society, native women suffered exploitation and discrimination and their efforts went largely unrecognized and unrewarded. Despite harsh conditions, a few women were able to own property and businesses because Spanish law allowed them to do so. In 1730, the founder of one of the first permanent settlements near San Antonio was Maria Betancourt. Women like Maria performed the major social and economic roles for the *pueblo's* survival, from bearing and raising children to maintaining the households, working the farms and operating family businesses. In 1821, Eulalia Arrila de Perez, a native woman, came to the Mission of San Gabriel in California. For the next fourteen years, besides raising five children, she managed all of the provisions for the mission, supervised the production of textiles, oversaw the manufacturing of wine, olive oil, butter and cheese, supplied the military troops, and trained the local women in carding, weaving, and sewing.

The Legal and Social Status of Women

Spanish law allowed women to inherit, own and operate property. This proved beneficial for immigrant women who settled in New Spain because they could also receive land grants from the crown. Some of the largest Spanish, and later Mexican, land grants were given to women such as Dona Maria del Carmen Calvillo, who acquired vast holdings in Texas. This feature of Spanish law meshed with Native American tribal structures where women retained the *pueblo* or small family farm lifestyle. Their families had been matrilineal, holding to the tradition that the women owned the property and passed it on to their children. Since duty always accompanied privilege, these women were primarily responsible for sustaining the family.

Unlike their counterparts in the English colonies, women who lived in the colony of New Spain were guaranteed certain legal rights. *Latinas* had much more autonomy and independence regarding their property rights and they retained ownership of any property owned *before* marriage. Women also owned half of any property acquired after marriage. In this regard husband and wife held an equal interest. Women could sell property, as well as crops, livestock, or any products made on the *rancho* such as textiles, cheese, or butter. Women could operate their own businesses and draw up contracts in their own name and they could bring a suit to court. Women could testify in a legal proceeding, and were allowed to testify against their spouse. Unwed women with children could also seek help in the courts.

Maria Francisca de Las Rivas, the mistress of Spanish territorial governor, Francisco Cuervo y Valdes, had migrated from Mexico City to the northern frontier with her parents and siblings in 1694, when she was ten years old. At age twenty, Maria became Cuervo's mistress. He was a widower by this time and forty-six-years-old. She lived with him in Santa Fe for twenty-eight months during his governorship and bore him a son. Maria returned to Mexico City with him in 1707. They had a daughter in 1713, and Cuervo died the following year. In 1714, Maria sued in court to receive a fair share of his estate which the court awarded her. What is more significant than the legal settlement is the fact that a single mother with two illegitimate children could sue in court for her paramour's wealth. Spain also had a progressive social policy which allowed widows whose husbands had served in political or military posts to receive a government pension. The government made no distinction between a Spanish or a native wife. Both qualified and both could apply for a pension.

11. *Anjoladores,* adobe plasterers. *Curanderas,* folk healers. *Parteras,* midwives.

In other respects, colonial society imposed substantial control over women. Latinas in New Spain lived in a hierarchal society ruled by men and defined by class, race, and gender. Spanish Catholicism and Spanish laws asserted the absolute rule of the male as head of the household. This system can be traced to the *Siete Partidas*, a medieval legal code dating to the thirteenth century, in which men were defined as the rulers or monarchs of the family and women as the subjects, "The husband is, as it were, the Lord and Head of his wife." The restraints placed on women, especially those of Spanish ancestry, were accomplished through specifically prescribed roles and expectations for their sex. To maintain their domination, men maintained rigid control within their households, in the political sphere of government and the hierarchy of the Church.

Marriage, Family and the Household

Studies of families over a period of 200 years, from the seventeenth to the nineteenth centuries, illustrate how patriarchal society was firmly rooted in the concept of male *honor*. The husband and father merited respect and obedience from the family members because of *machismo*, i.e. his superior position as a male. Because property was granted predominantly to males, to insure rightful inheritance, it was crucial to ensure the legitimacy of one's heirs. Therefore, the virginity of brides and the fidelity of wives were essential to maintaining the integrity and purity of the family and a legitimate heir. This necessitated a prime responsibility for the males to protect the women in their families. Professor Ramon Gutierrez asserts that this Spanish patriarchal concept of *honor* for men and fidelity and purity for women was founded on notions of racial and moral (religious) purity related to the feudal class system. The upper class who brought this belief to the New World tried to sustain it in colonial society.

In some ways gender roles within the dynamic of the household shifted over time. After several generations of intermarriage, a number of changes took place. Historian Richard del Castillo looked first at the higher status families, where women were confined to the household, and sexual division of roles was maintained. However, as the frontier experience evolved and men and women, of necessity, worked side by side on their farms, families became more democratic. (Bearing in mind that democratic is a relative term.) There was some relaxation of roles and husbands and wives shared more of the decision making process. The father's authoritarian role, however, did not preclude a wife's powerlessness. She exercised some autonomy within the home. The mother imposed herself as the administrator of the household and her husband often deferred to her in the matter of child discipline, care and training. As the protector and provider for the family, the father dominated the perimeter just outside the home.

The key factor was the authority parents exerted on children and the reciprocal respect which children owed to parents. This system was most stringent in the colonial period, when parents chose marriage partners for their children. Among the upper class of Spanish colonial society, when choosing a mate, parents stressed honor, status, property and family. Family conflict over marriage partner choices was more frequent in the upper class because the stakes were higher in terms of social position, wealth and inheritance.

The study by Patricia Seed, "The Church and the Patriarchal Family: Marriage Conflicts in Sixteenth and Seventeenth Century New Spain," shows that in cases where parents tried to prevent a marriage, the church sided with young couples who wished to marry for love. Between 1560 and 1690, some 8,000 petitions of couples to marry in the church over the objections of their parents, show that one third of these familial conflicts involved economic differences between the prospective bride and groom. Among the other two-thirds, specific sources of conflict could not be classified, but many of these petitions revealed the use of force by parents to prevent the marriage which included threats, beatings, and incarceration in the home, a convent or jail.

In the sixteenth and seventeenth centuries in Colonial Spain, the two patriarchal institutions which exercised power over women's lives faced off. Based upon a firm belief in the right of men and women to choose their own spouse, the traditional church opposed the patriarchal family. Thus a tension existed between what parents regarded as a natural right to control their offspring and the Church's insistence that parents could not, for instance, disinherit a child for marrying against their wishes. The church regarded this kind of parental control as tantamount to sin. In practice, over time this marriage pattern among the upper class allowed some women more freedom in choosing a mate.

At the same time there was also a tendency among upper class young women in New Spain to try to avoid men of aggressive sexual appetite, a phenomenon known as "Don Juanism." There were few choices open to women but some entered the convent and found solace and escape from the constraints of marriage within the solid walls of the patriarchal church.

The Social Role and Status of Men and Women

Within the Spanish aristocracy in both the Old and New World, men were respected as the sole authority but a woman earned respect only if she conducted herself with propriety and dignity. To maintain her purity and to conduct herself as a lady, a woman must have *verguenza*, a sense of shame, or modesty.[12] *Verguenza*, a female trait, implied that in order for a woman to behave as a moral person she must realize the gravity and seriousness of shame. If she did not, a woman placed her reputation and more importantly the good standing of her family in jeopardy. Society placed a burden on women to preserve virtue and purity in order to maintain the sanctity of the family. It is apparent that the double standard was operative as well, for it was not the woman who was inherently shameful. Her father or husband was essentially protecting her not from her own shamefulness but from the advances of other males. As Gutierrez explains, this code of honor dictated that,

> Because nature created women the weaker of the sexes and rendered her helpless to the whims and sexual desires of men, male authority over them was the only means by which shame and the family's honor could be guaranteed.

In order to protect her virtue and purity, both before and after marriage, a female lived a confined existence staying within the home. Upper class women were regarded as feminine because of their virtue and submissive, quiet demeanor but other women who lived more publicly had a lower status. Both the *mestizo* and native women lacked *verguenza*, simply because they lived more openly. Occupied with farm and household work, they were not respected or held in high esteem and said to be *sin verguenza*, i.e. characterized of low morals whether they were or not.[13] This feature of Spanish morality was made more paradoxical because Spanish men married *mestizo* and native women labeled as *sin verguenza* who bore them children.

Although European and native ideas about female virtue and marital fidelity differed in belief, practice was quite another matter. Adultery was considered a moral violation by Christian standards but when Spanish men (both single and married) raped native women or took them as mistresses, it was not perceived as immoral. Some tribes offered them native women as gifts of appeasement with the most highly prized female being a virgin. In 1660, Captain Diego Romero received such a trophy from the Apache. He spent the night with a virgin in a specially prepared teepee and received a signatory white feather which he proudly wore to commemorate the event. In 1663, the Court of the Inquisition in Mexico City prosecuted Captain Romero, citing the white feather as evidence of his sins; however, officials did not charge him with fornication, adultery or violation of a young girl. The Court found Romero guilty of taking part in a covenant of heathen rites. When Juan Cabrillo's party landed at Santa Catalina Island, elder tribesman welcomed the Spaniards with not one, but ten women each. These and other

---

12. *Verguenza*, a sense of shame or embarrassment; to know right from wrong and to act accordingly.
13. *Sin verguenza*, lacking or without shame, immoral or scandalous behavior.

European accounts offer numerous examples of this kind of hospitality. However, there is equally compelling evidence to suggest that some native tribesmen held their women to a higher standard (evidently similar to the Spanish practice of a double standard). Among the Apaches (curiously the same who had welcomed Romero) observers noted they mutilated women accused of adulterous behavior.

For the women, mating practices remained a losing proposition. The Spanish could violate them with impunity and interpret the female's behavior as shameful. According to the Spanish view, because a native woman would fornicate with any man, they possessed *sin verguenza*. By comparison, the Natchez people (a Mississippi culture), who also assumed that women (not men) were licentious, had worked out a unique political scheme. Their chiefdom was hereditary but not through the son of the reigning chief. Since the chief could never guarantee that the children his wife bore were of royal blood the next chief came from the *first princess of the blood*, she being the sister of the chief. In this way the Natchez tribesmen ensured that the son of the chief's sister was of royal blood, at least on the mother's side!

The Genizaras

The demarcation and denigration of lower class women extended to slaves. Even though crown and church condemned slavery throughout the colonial period, and in 1586, the Viceroy of Mexico, Marques de Villamanrique officially forbid slavery, nonetheless colonists enslaved Native Americans and the government enjoyed the profits gained from slave labor. Natives taken captive by the Spanish were deprived of their tribal status, identity and protection. Reduced to lifetime bondage, the *genizaros* were forced to work within the *encomienda* as farm laborers, in the mines or as domestic servants[14]. When disease, warfare and harsh labor inflicted high mortality on the native population, the Spanish turned to another work force and imported slaves from Africa. Although the crown and the church also condemned the African trade, neither made any effort to enforce a policy to outlaw slavery. The status of *genizaras*, the African female slaves, was also peculiar to Spanish beliefs about gender roles. What made these women lower and inferior to the Spanish women was their lack of verguenza; they too were perceived as immoral, *sin verguenza*.

The Spanish colonials developed a rigid class system with genizaros ranking as the lowest members. This discrimination of classes left poor and slave women with little or no protection under the law. Ecclesiastical records reveal how the government categorized cases of seduction along class lines and how women were unprotected. In 1752, the crown proclaimed "a Decree on Seduction," which instructed officials on how to proceed if a maiden was seduced. The law weighed guilt or punishment in terms of which individual, the seducer or the victim, had received the most injury. However, the law further stated that if the maid had been seduced under promise of marriage but was a person of inferior status, then to legally force a marriage would cause greater dishonor to the seducer's lineage. Hence fewer dishonors would fall on the seduced woman. As the law stated, when a Duke, Count, Marquis, or Gentleman seduced a mulata, china, or coyota, or the daughter of a hangman, a butcher, or a tanner, he must not marry her because the injury to him and his entire lineage would be greater than the injury incurred by the maiden. In this case, the decree concluded that one must choose the lesser evil. The government further distinguished how to proceed when a maiden was of only "slightly inferior status."

> But if the seduced maiden is of only slightly inferior status, or not marked inequality, so that her inferiority does not cause marked dishonor to the family, then, if the seducer does not wish to endow her, or she justly rejects compensation in the form of an endowment he must be compelled to marry her.

14. *Genizaros*, slaves. Female slaves *genizara(as)*.

Mothers of Invention: Sor Juana Inez De La Cruz

One of the remarkable women of Colonial Spain, Juana Ines de la Cruz de Asbaje y Ramirez de Santillana (1651-1695), was the illegitimate daughter of Pedro Manuel de Asbaje, a Spanish Captain and Isabel Ramirez. Juana's biographer, Octavio Paz, indicates that her illegitimacy was due to her mother's refusal to marry Pedro. Evidently, Isabel, a woman of independent willful determination, passed on this trait to her daughter. At the age of fourteen, Juana had come to the attention of the Viceroy of New Spain. A child prodigy and largely self-taught she had grown into an attractive, charming young lady. Juana accepted an invitation to serve as a lady-in-waiting to the vice-regent's wife, the Marquesa de Mancera, at court in Mexico City. One year later Juana, the darling of the court, made the dramatic decision to seek a solitary life in a convent where she might be free to pursue her own intellectual interests. Juana entered the convent, and joined the Order of St. Jerome. Becoming a nun offered one of the few ways available for intellectual women to avoid marriage and devote themselves to the scholarly life. Sor (Sister) Juana explained her motive for taking religious vows:

> I became a nun, because even though I realized my state was repugnant to my temperament, given the total disinclination I felt toward marriage, it seemed the most fitting and decent thing I could do, especially since I wished to ensure my salvation.

Initially, convent life did not pose an austere standard for Sor Juana. Provided for by her wealthy, powerful benefactors, the Viceroy and Marquesa, she had her own private and very comfortable living quarters, attended by servants, and enjoyed receiving guests in a salon-like setting. Sor Juana thrived there and became a poet and playwright. She acquired some celebrity through her writing, and took advantage of her privileged relationship with the Viceroy by flagrantly challenging authorities, such as her Mother Superior and the Bishop, knowing that the Viceroy would support her.

Sor Juana is remembered not only as an intellectual but also as one of the first feminists in the western world. An outspoken woman in a society where a female's place was strictly defined, Juana constantly attacked the sexual double standard of her culture.

> Foolish men who wrongly accuse women, Without seeing that you are the cause of what you fault them for; You want with unthinking presumption to find in the woman you seek... Either love women for what you force them to be, or fashion them according to what you want them to be.

Sor Juana poses in her library of collected manuscripts. She joined the Order of St. Jerome and served most of her religious vocation as an intellectual, writer and poet. (Picture courtesy of the Library of Congress.)

Sor Juana is regarded as a pre-eminent classical scholar in the western world of the seventeenth century. From 1669-1690, she studied, wrote poetry, prose and plays. Her poems are considered some of the finest in Spanish and characterize her skill for combining the symbolism of the Aztec, Ancient Greek and Christian cultures. Juana also collected one of the largest manuscript libraries in the Spanish Colonies and dabbled in scientific experimentation in the laboratory she assembled. She also observed the stars, composed music, and painted. Sor Juana believed that scientific study could strengthen faith in God, not weaken it. As she stated, "It seems to me debilitating for a Catholic not to know everything in this life of the Divine Mysteries that can be learned through natural means."

The Spanish Inquisition—an intense investigation and persecution by church and state officials of suspected heretics—made its way to the Spanish colonies by the end of the seventeenth century. It is very likely that Sor Juana became a victim of this tribunal. By then in her late thirties, Sor Juana began to doubt her commitment to the religious life. Guilt, self-effacement and the criticism of her priest-confessor convinced her that she was not leading a pious life. In 1691, Juana yielded to the mounting pressure to reform and sold her impressive collection of 4,000 books and manuscripts and the apparatus of her scientific laboratory. After donating the proceeds of this sale to the poor, Sor Juana lived out her remaining years as an extreme penitent. Reputedly, when renewing her religious vows she wrote them with her own blood as ink, wore a hair shirt and imposed other harsh penances on herself. At this time Juana also performed acts of charity by working in a hospital. In 1695, at the age of forty-four she died while caring for victims of a plague epidemic.

Her brief but productive life personified a zealous quest for intellectual freedom. Sor Juana had found an outlet for her intellectual skills at a time when few women received an education. She was an extraordinary woman in her time: a gifted intellectual, a non-conformist, and an early visionary of feminism.

Ordering a *Mestizo* Population in New Spain: Caste, Sex, Race and Class

Despite the high rate of mixed marriages, class lines in Spanish colonial society were unusual as they did not weaken over time. By the end of the colonial period around 1800, it was more difficult for men and women of a lower rank to aspire higher socially than it had been in the early days of Spanish settlement when mestizo and native women could achieve status through land grants and/or marriage. Matriarchs such as Juana Hurtado, the illegitimate daughter of a Spanish man and a Zia pueblo woman, advantaged her birthright of a full-blooded Spanish father and obtained Spanish land grants. As an unwed independent mother, she had utilized the system and left her illegitimate children and their heirs well-heeled, socially prominent and with an espanol bloodline. Later, women of this social rank and mixed parentage would find it nearly impossible to achieve social status. Over time as the upper class grew more rigid and fewer men and women of wealth married outside of their class, society took on a caste, or *castas* structure.[15]

Although the caste system was not as rigid on the colonial borderlands of New Spain as it was in Spain, nevertheless it did restrict social mobility for lower *casta* members. Men of a lower caste found it difficult to gain political office and women of a lower caste found it impossible to achieve status in this system. In this society *genizaras* were considered the most inferior and had the lowest status.

A 1790 census of Santa Fe by caste and gender gives attention to listing the population by skin color and race with Espanoles and Spaniards ranked highest.

Caste	Male	Female
Espanoles	820	874
Color quebrado	185	195
Mestizo	101	121
Mulato	42	43
Genizaro	31	5
Indio	36	85
Coyote	2	1

15. *Casta (as)*, a society ranked by caste, with those regarded as most purebred at top and least pure at the bottom

These six categories of *castas* in Santa Fe reflected a growing population of mixed people there, with the hierarchal order determined by the people of *pureza de sangre espanola*, (pure Spanish blood). Here *genizaro* refers to a full-blooded Indian who, if not a slave, was certainly someone used for cheap labor. *Color quebrado* (color broken) denoted a generic term for anyone of mixed parentage. *Coyote* referred to a person of mixed blood—Indian and Spanish. In New Mexico, a *Coyote* was as high on the pecking order as a *Mestizo* but was from a more acceptable caste.

By 1800, the Spanish colonials progressed to another stage as they attracted people from the far corners of the globe to New Spain. Ships entered the busy harbor of San Francisco Bay from New England, and other eastern trading cities of the United States of America. Others hailed from South America, China, Russia and various Asian ports. In April 1806 Captain Jose Arguello, who commanded the Presidio in San Francisco, greeted a Russian aristocrat Nikolai Rezanov, who was beginning a six week layover in port. Rezanov clearly had designs to establish a Russian-American business enterprise in California and was instrumental in establishing a Russian outpost at Bodega Bay. During his visit, Nikolai proposed marriage to Captain Arguello's fifteen-year-old daughter Conchita. Both were Christians but Nikolai's Russian Orthodoxy required a papal dispensation from Rome before Conchita could marry him. When Nikolai left for St. Petersburg, he promised Conchita he would return with the necessary permit for them to marry. He died on the way back to Russia but Conchita, unaware of what had happened, continued to wait for his return. Over the years, she turned down many suitors and eventually became a nun and lived out her life in the convent. The story of Conchita and Nikolai, enshrined in the romantic past of Spanish California, marked a new phase in the history of New Spain. Immigrants from Asia, Europe and Latin America made entry into Colonial Spain to enrich the culture of the ever-evolving *mestizo* people.

Clio's Corner - What Have Historians Said About European-American Contact?

Spanish attempts to establish a caste system while condoning the union of Spanish men and native women was contradictory and futile to say the least. Historian Gary Nash who has studied this phenomenon notes that ironically while the interracial marriage in the Spanish colonies became commonplace by the eighteenth century, the caste system also became more complex. Classifications included a Spanish-Indian couple with a *mestizo* child. The offspring of *mestizo* and Spanish parents were designated as *castizo*. Children of African and Spanish parents were mulatto. A *chino or albino* was the child of a *Morisco* and Spaniard, but a *chino* and Indian union created a *salta atras*, literally a child who was "a step away from Spanish blood." In all of these social rankings, Native American, African, and African-American women were always placed in the lowest caste.

Professor Nash characterizes the Spanish conquest of America as creating a "zone of deep intercultural contacts." On the one hand, the attention to categories of race and color shows Spanish preoccupation with race, skin color and class. But on the other, Nash believes that officials acknowledged what had already taken place, an interracial merger of European, African and Native American people in the New World. This convergence of three cultures in America took place on a "marrying ground" not on a battleground. It was a commingling in New Spain of a tri-racial society established at the beginning of the American epic of *mestizo* history. Native American, European and African women bore *mestizo* children who amalgamated three worlds into one society, and in the process, no one escaped the colonial experience unscathed or unchanged.

Professor Magnus Morner, in *Race Mixture,* identifies what he coins a *pigmentocratic* social system where racial superiority, dependent upon one's skin color and parentage was the determinant of social and economic status. According to Professor Ramon Gutierrez, race and ethnicity were not the only criteria in the intermingling of people in the New World. Class was also important. With their obsession for maintaining family honor, the Spanish colonial upper class in New Mexico for example, created an "exaggerated moral code for personal public behavior."

The view of Historian Deena Gonzalez, *Refusing the Favor, the Spanish-Mexican Women of Santa Fe, 1820-1880,* is also useful. She cautions that to emphasize women's part in colonizing the New World based only on intermarriage presents a very limited role for them as wives, mothers, and sexual partners. Interaction between what she calls the greeting generation (indigenous people who first made contact) and the *migrating generation* (conquering and colonizing people, the Spanish and Euro-Americans) "were friendly and others were decidedly unfriendly." Professor Gonzalez contends that those who describe the colonial experience as an, "intercultural contact suggest less tension-ridden relations or imply equalities in the methods and processes and the thoughts and feelings of people confronting one another and ignore the inhibitions and sanctions that work against interracial partnerships." Using terms such as contact rather than conquest suggests harmony and accord, and ignores racial attitudes, prejudices, color codes and institutionalized discrimination.

Conclusion

In 1800, at the end of the Spanish colonial era, New Spain's population in North and Meso-America comprised a total of seventeen million people. This consisted of seven million Native Americans (through contact with the Spanish, a population reduced by 90 percent from disease and warfare), three million Europeans, one million African slaves, and six million *mestizo* people.

Clearly women played a significant part in creating the society of New Spain, in assimilating Spanish people and in amalgamating a tri-racial society and it is important to highlight their vital role in that process. The necessities for the survival of the family and community were provided by the women who lived in the villages, missions, *ranchos* and *pueblos*. Women maintained essentially every facet of life from child bearing to child caring; from planting and harvesting crops to placing a prepared meal on the table. Through women's efforts wool, cotton and flax were processed, woven and made into clothing. They assisted at childbirth and tended the sick and prepared herbs and medicines for family members and those suffering in their community. Women built and maintained homes and adorned them with comforts and style. Central figures in the family and the community, women functioned as key agents in the process of assimilation and amalgamation. These were the skills necessary to sustain civilization.

Looking at the effects of the Spanish invasion of America has both historical and contemporary implications. The establishment of permanent Spanish colonies began over 500 years ago but the settlement and relocation of people is ongoing as people migrate within or immigrate to North, Central, and South America. As immigration renews, revitalizes and replenishes these regions, one could rightly say that the Americas are a work in progress.

Descendants of the Spanish conquest of America, the *Latino* population, occupy an important place in the history and the future of the United States. In North America, this rapidly growing population echoes settlement movements. Demographers looking at population trends project that by the year 2040, the *Latino* population will become a vital majority in the United States, as they are already in southwestern states. Contrast this prediction with the 1990 Federal Census showing a *Latino* population of 23,000,000, and comprising only eight percent of the total United States population. One thing is certain, in the United States we live today with the effects of Spanish colonization.

Chapter 2
English, Dutch and French Settlement in the New World
Worse Plagues than those I Left Behind

Key Topics

English Colonization in the Chesapeake and New England
Dutch Colonization in New Netherlands
French Colonization in New France

Chronology

1585 - Exploration of Roanoke
1587 - Birth of Virginia Dare
1607 - Settlement of Jamestown in Virginia Colony
1608 - Founding of New France
1614 - Marriage of John Rolfe and Pocahontas
1624 - 1664 Settlement and colonization of New Netherlands by the Dutch
1638 - Establishment of the Sisters Freehold by Margaret Brent

Introduction

It was the English who would eventually dominate North America. They settled on the Atlantic coast first claiming land in the Chesapeake area of Virginia in 1607, then in the north in 1620 and 1630, and later in the middle colonies in the 1680s. All of these English colonies had a common heritage, but as they developed each region took on its own distinctive features. English colonists led an isolated existence on the new frontier and became quite provincial and parochial in their outlook. Some of the factors which helped influence their evolution were their regional ecosystems, the varying patterns of settlement, the immigrants themselves, their religion, their places of origin, the events in England which had impelled them to leave in the first place and the people they encountered in the New World.

After several failed attempts at colonization, the Jamestown colony at the mouth of the James River became the first permanent English settlement in North America. In the seventeenth century, however, Jamestown seemed the least likely success story. Plagued with illness, a lack of preparedness and their agitation of the Powhatan, a local tribe, the colony faced continuous threat of extinction.

In contrast, France sent the necessary people and provisions, laying claim to the interior rich farmland of the Great Lakes Region, and the Ohio and Mississippi Valleys. The Dutch, looking for trade opportunity, established the Dutch West Indies Company in their colony of New Netherlands, or what is today the state of New York. In 1638, Roman Catholic nobility under the proprietorship of Lord Baltimore took land in the Chesapeake, a colony they called Maryland. Similar to Virginia colony, estates were granted by the Crown and used for tobacco production.

Most of the English women who came to America were poor indentured servants. Under an indentured contract the poor could secure passage to the New World and work off their debt over seven years. As they settled in each of these colonies, they instilled their own customs and traditions but were also influenced by what they experienced in the America.

The English Colonization of Virginia

In 1585, a group of 120 people consisting of seventeen women, nine children and ninety-one males set sail from England and came to Roanoke, an island off the southern Atlantic coast of North America. This island and the mainland area became the colony of Virginia named in honor of Queen Elizabeth I, the Virgin Queen. That same year, Virginia Dare became the first English child born in the Americas, at the Roanoke settlement. Her grandfather, John White, Royal governor of the colony, recorded the first glimpse of America with his illustrative watercolors detailing the flora, fauna, land and people of the island. In 1587, just a few days after the birth of his granddaughter, White left for England to procure supplies and did not return until 1590. Upon his return to Roanoke, he found no trace of the English settlement, only the enigmatic carving of the word *Croatoan* on a tree. The Croatoans were a tribe living on an adjacent island. Because the colonists had been low on provisions, it was assumed that they had gone to live with the *Crotoans* in order to survive but after an exhaustive search, White never found the missing English colonists.

The lost colony of Roanoke remains a historical mystery but an event some years later offers an explanation for what happened to them. Ten years later, English explorers were met by members of the Roanoke tribe. The English noticed that among the natives some of the children had blue eyes. This suggests that some members of the lost colony must have survived and assimilated into the Roanoke tribe.

The English Colony at Jamestown

In 1607, the English attempted another settlement arriving in three ships holding one-hundred men and four boys. They landed on an island near the mainland which they named Jamestown Island, in honor of their King, James Stuart. At Jamestown colony, the first permanent English settlement in America, settlers established a camp on the James River, and built a palisade, Jamestown Fort. The following year, two women arrived, Mrs. Thomas (Anne) Forrest who accompanied her husband and Anne Burras, their fourteen-year-old servant.

From the start, Jamestown colony was so poorly planned and threatened with extinction that it barely survived the next ten years, a period known as the starving time. During the first six months fifty-one colonists died. By 1608, less than 30 percent of the English had survived. The rumors of death and suffering in the New World, which circulated back to England, made it necessary for the London Company to produce glowing advertising to recruit, transport and populate Virginia in order to sustain the colony. English courts and judges released inmates from debtors prisons (or a worse fate) if they were willing to relocate to the colony. Criminals about to be hanged could plead for transportation in place of execution. In some cases, magistrates ordered that pardoned criminals be transported to the colonies. Hence, seventeenth century Virginia society became an eclectic collection of the destitute, the desperate and the dandy with hardened criminals and the poor settling in alongside the gentry.

For those who could not afford the passage over, the London Company devised a plan. Passengers could sell themselves into a labor contract to finance the trip. This arrangement, known as an indenture, entailed service to whoever bought the contract for a term usually of seven years. Prepaid indentured servants were more inclined to mark time than work. In order to enforce a work ethic, owners treated both males and females harshly. Those who violated contracts, usually by running away, might suffer physical punishment and have their term of contract extended.

By mid-seventeenth century, indentured servitude became the common means for poor people to get to America, and Virginia's population consisted largely of white indentured servants. By 1665, nearly one-half of the members of the colonial assembly, the House of Burgesses, had formerly served an indenture. Upon satisfactory completion of their contract, indentured servants were often awarded freedom dues which consisted of food, land (about fifty acres), clothing and a gun.

Many poor women came to Virginia as indentured servants and of the entire contracted servant population in the colonies, they composed 25 percent. Nearly 75 percent of the English women who settled in the Chesapeake region, which included the colonies of Maryland and Virginia, served an indenture. One advertisement enticing females to come to Carolina boasted that:

> If any Maid, or single Woman had a desire to go over, they will think themselves, in the Golden Age, when men paid a dowry for their wives: for if they be but civil and under fifty years of age, some honest man or other, will purchase them for their wives.

Because of the critical shortage of females in the colony, many men bought up the indentured women's contracts to claim them as brides. By the time the seven years of labor had been fulfilled, many women were betrothed or pregnant and usually both. Indeed, nearly 20 percent of the indentured women became pregnant before their term of service was complete. In these cases, owners regarded a pregnancy out of wedlock as a violation of the indenture and could extend the contract for two more years.

Pocahontas, John Rolfe and the James River Settlement

Before the English arrival, Chief Powhatan had merged thirty of the Chesapeake tribes of the Algonquian people into the Powhatan Confederacy. Powhatan was determined to contain the English settlers of Jamestown even though Captain John Smith, a Jamestown colonist, had reassured him that the English had come to trade, not to settle there.

Powhatan's daughter, Matoaka, who would play a critical role in English attempts to colonize in America, ranked as the favorite among his one-hundred children. She was also called Pocahontas.[1] When the English first established Jamestown, Pocahontas was about thirteen years old, very curious about the newcomers, and frequently visited the fort. John Smith taught her to speak English, and she taught him her native dialect. He described her as, "a child of tenne yeares old, which not only for feature, countenance, and proportion much exceedeth any of the rest of his (Powhatan's) people but for wit and spirit (is) the only nonpariel [unequalled] in his countrie." In 1608, supply ships arrived with seventy more settlers and a passenger who would change her life and the destiny of Jamestown. He was twenty-eight-year-old John Rolfe, a farmer from East England who was already twice widowed.

Pocahontas saving the life of Captain John Smith. (Picture courtesy of the Library of Congress.)

When shortages threatened the settlement with extinction in the spring of 1609, Pocahontas intervened and brought food to the Jamestown settlers. But the answer to colonists' survival was right there before their eyes. What was a luxury in England, tobacco, grew wild in Virginia. Through experimentation with West Indies tobacco plants, John Rolfe produced a milder form which became the cash crop for Colonial Virginia. As the settlement expanded and tobacco farms sprang up all around the

1. *Pocahontas*, which means the playful one, was an appropriate name for her. Captain John Smith's accounts described how as a child visiting Jamestown Fort she enjoyed playing pranks on the English.

James River area, Chief Powhatan realized the English intended to settle permanently and so he set out to kill John Smith, but Pocahontas discovered the plot and raced to the Jamestown Fort to warn him.

Powhatan sent her to the Potomac country to prevent her from helping the English anymore and there in 1610, she married a native, Kocoum. With the help of the Patowomeck Indians, Captain Samuel Argall found Pocahontas and lured her onto his ship where he detained her as a hostage for ransom. Argall returned to Jamestown in April 1613, with Pocahontas and moved her to the new settlement, Henrico, which was under the leadership of Sir Thomas Dale. It was there that she met John Rolfe and they were instantly quite taken with each other. He began to instruct her in the Christian Faith and she took the name Rebecca when she was baptised.[2]

After almost a year of captivity, Sir Thomas Dale brought 150 armed men and Pocahontas into Powhatan's territory to obtain her entire ransom. Attacked by the Indians, the Englishmen burned many houses, destroyed villages, and killed several Indian men. Pocahontas was sent ashore and reunited with her family. She told them that the English had treated her well, she was in love with John Rolfe and she wanted to marry him. Her father consented and the Englishmen departed, without the full ransom.

John Rolfe, a very religious man, agonized for many weeks over the decision to take a "strange wife," a heathen Indian. But after consulting with many friends, he petitioned Governor Thomas Dale, asked for permission and convinced authorities that it was, "for the good of this plantation, the honor of our country, for the glory of God, and for mine own salvation." John Rolfe and Rebecca were married in the Jamestown church April 5, 1614. Although Chief Powhatan did not attend the ceremony, the Rolfe's was the most celebrated colonial marriage, and one of the few between an Englishman and a native woman. They settled north of Jamestown where John built their plantation home, Varina, and in 1615, their son, Thomas, was born.

Sir Thomas Dale made an important voyage back to London in the spring of 1616, in order to get more financial support for the Virginia Company. To insure spectacular publicity, he took along twelve Algonquian Indians, Pocahontas, her husband John and their young son, Thomas. Her well publicized arrival made Pocahontas the talk of the town. She was presented to King James I, the royal family, and the rest of the best of London society at a formal masque ball. Pocahontas had her portrait painted and was presented to the royal court as Lady Rebecca Rolfe. She also met with Captain John Smith, her old friend. According to John Smith's account, when they were reunited, she was at first too overcome with emotion to speak. After composing herself, Pocahontas talked of old times. Her last words to him were, "I will be for ever and ever your Countrieman."

The marriage of Pocahontas and John Rolfe at the Jamestown Church. (Picture courtesy of the Library of Congress.)

After the seven month stay, she had been exposed to many crowds of people, and a different climate. In March 1617, the Rolfes set sail but it was obvious that Pocahontas, already deathly ill from pneumonia or possibly tuberculosis, could not make the trip. The ship turned back, she was taken ashore and as this twenty-two-year-old Indian princess lay dying she comforted her husband, saying, "All must die. 'Tis enough that the child liveth." Pocahontas was buried in a churchyard in Gravesend, England.

2. *Rebecca*, another apt name which recalled the biblical mother of two nations.

John returned to Virginia without his family; young Thomas, too ill to make the trip, was entrusted to Sir Lewis Stuckley. Thomas Rolfe, who would be raised and educated in England, would never see his father again.

Pocahontas played a significant role in American history. A compassionate girl, she saw to it that the colonists received food and she intervened to save the lives of individual colonists. In 1616, Captain John Smith wrote that she was "the instrument that saved this colonie from death, famine, and utter confusion." Her marriage to John Rolfe served as a brief bond of friendship between the English and the Native Americans. The period known as the Peace of Pocahontas, from 1614 to 1622, gave the colonists the respite they needed and ensured the establishment of the first permanent English settlement in the New World.

Pocahontas, or Lady Rebecca Rolfe being presented to King James at the Royal Court during her visit to England. (Picture courtesy of the Library of Congress.)

Chief Powhatan died in 1618, and his brother Opechancanough, who succeeded him, considered the growth of the English population a threat to his tribe's survival. On March 22, 1622, Opechancanough led the Powhatan attack on English settlements along the James River. Many colonists in the Jamestown region were killed. John Rolfe died suddenly in 1622 apparently from illness. The Anglo-Powhatan Wars would continue for another decade and escalate again in 1644. This bitter conflict between the English and the Natives took its toll in death, destruction of farms and a lingering hatred of indigenous peoples. The colonial government enacted harsh policies on the surviving native population and restricted their movement, hunting rights and land use. This policy foreshadowed how all white settlements and governments would treat Native Americans.

Timing is everything in history. In 1635, twenty-year-old Thomas Rolfe returned to Virginia. Having avoided the First Anglo-Powhatan War in 1622, he survived the second in 1644. His father had secured his inheritance of land and the plantation where he was born by taking out a royal patent. His grandfather, Chief Powhatan, had left him thousands of acres along the James River.

Women for Colonial Virginia

Along with pardoned felons and indentured servants, the investors for the Virginia Colony also acquired "virtuous maids" to send to Jamestown as brides. The London Company endeavored to send women of English gentry or respectable working class families. In 1620, ships brought ninety brides to Virginia and a group of sixty arrived the following year. The women were young, averaging from eighteen to twenty-one years in age, and at least three were widows, eager to make a fresh start in Virginia.

London Company required that prospective brides provide letters of reference attesting to their virtue and honesty. The investors made it clear that the women would be expected to perform housekeeping and other demanding work in the colony. The records indicate that the 150 women possessed skills which included weaving, knitting, baking, brewing and tending dairy cattle. As an incentive, the London Company outfitted each of the women with a *trousseau* to help them set up housekeeping in America.[3] Their trunks were generously packed with gloves, a petticoat, hats, stockings, an apron, and two pairs of shoes, linens, towels, and clothes. These gifts must have added to the excitement and anticipation of the trip to America. These prospective brides acquired more luxuries than they would have received had they married and lived in England.

3. *Trousseau,* possessions such as clothes and linens that a bride assembles for her wedding

The Brides for Virginia story did not end happily. It is unlikely that many of these young women survived long enough to establish their own households. They arrived the winter of 1621-1622, and were very likely among the victims of the massacre in March 1622, when the Powhatan Confederacy attacked many Virginia settlements. At Martin's Hundred, a settlement near Jamestown, seventy-eight were dead, and at Edward Bennet's farm forty-nine were killed in the attack. Archaeologists excavating at Wollstonehometown, Jamestown and other settlements along the James River have found victims of the massacre. The records, though scanty, accurately name some of the maids as victims of the massacre, specifically Cicely Bray and Marie Daucks and link others as well. Some brides cannot be identified with certainty as massacre victims since they would have already taken their husbands' name. Chances are that if they somehow survived the attacks most of these young women died with other colonists during the following winter, the bitter starving time of 1622-1623.

Immigrants to the Virginia colony endured a series of ordeals, finding as one said, "worse plagues than those I left behind." Surviving the perilous sea voyage was one of many hardships. Native American uprisings and the massacres of 1622 and 1644—largely provoked by white settlers—took their toll on the settlements. The Virginia terrain of rivers and streams presented the extremes of freezing temperatures in winter and a hot, humid, mosquito-infested climate in summer. The English, more accustomed to cold than heat, were exposed to a climate in which diseases such as malaria, smallpox, the bloody flux and dysentery flourished in the hot, humid weather. An individual who lived through these tribulations or seasoning, as it was called, faced years of intensive labor. But for those poor people who survived the Atlantic crossing, the harsh colonial lifestyle, and the Indian wars, the Virginia colony finally offered more opportunities than existed in England.

The conditions in the Virginia colony yielded a high mortality rate and it was higher for women than for men in the seventeenth century. Exposure to disease during pregnancy, childbirth and post partum recovery left them more vulnerable. Because of the higher death rates for women, a man might marry several times in his lifetime and this created unusual marriage and family patterns in seventeenth century Virginia. Families consisted of stepmothers, stepchildren, half brothers, half sisters, in-laws and probably a few outlaws. Life in these blended families was intense with an escalated degree of sibling rivalry. The research of Lorena Walsh and Lois Carr profiles these families in "The Planter's Wife," a study of women in the Virginia and Maryland colonies in the seventeenth century. Lorena Walsh and Lois Carr found that the high death rate and frequent remarriage often left widows with younger children. In these cases, it was more common for the husband to leave property to his wife than to the eldest son. In seventeenth century Chesapeake colonies (Virginia and Maryland), a widow could inherit an estate and enjoyed more economic freedom and autonomy than her daughter or granddaughter would in succeeding generations.

The higher mortality left a disproportionate number of orphans in the population. This became so severe in the seventeenth century, that half of the children under the age of seven had already lost a parent. In the adolescent population at least 20 percent were fully orphaned by the age of thirteen. The fate of these children lay within the legal system. They were regarded as wards of the court, property of the estate and an economic liability. Children were at an economic advantage only if their parents had left them well-provided. Otherwise their only asset was their ability to work. Orphans without guardians to provide for them were bound out as indentured servants to serve an apprenticeship in order to learn a trade. As a labor force, English orphans were brought to the colony for exploitation. Records indicate that in 1618 alone, some one-hundred vagrant, poor English children were kidnapped or spirited to America to be sold as indentured servants. Since many of the poor are absent from the records, it is quite probable that many children and adults were sent to America against their will.

Brides for Virginia - Women who came on board the Marmaduke, Warwick and Tiger in 1621*

Name	Age	Name	Age
Martha Baker	20	Alice Grove	26
Susan Binx	20	Jean Grundye	21
Ellen Borne	19	Ann Harmer	21
Mary Bourdman	20	Anstie Hawkins	18
Elizabeth Bovill	20	Joane Haynes	?
Cecily Bray	25	Audrey Hoare	19
Frances Broadbottom	19	Ann Holmes	20
Elizabeth Browne	16	Ann Jackson	20
Anne Buergen	?	Alse Jones	21
Alice Burges	28	Jeane Joanes	17
Bridget Crofte	18	Lettice King	23
Sara Crosse	21	Elizabeth Markham	16
Marie Dauchs widow	26	Mary Morrise	20
Alse Dauson	18	Elizaneth Nevill	19
Mary Dauson	25	Elizabeth Pearson	19
Elizabeth Day	19	Lucy Remnant	22
Jane Dier	15 or 16	Jennet Rimmer	20
Alse Dollinges	22	Anne Richards widow	25
Mary Ellyott	19	Christian Smyth	18
Catherine Finche	23	Elizabeth Starkey	16
Anne Gibson	21	Ann Tanner	26
Alice Gaughe	28	Parnell Tenton	20
Mary Ghibbs	20	Mary Thomas	18
Elizabeth Grinbey widow	26	Fortune Taylor	18

*Adapted from David Ransome, "Wives for Virginia."

Immigrants who came to the Virginia colony in the seventeenth and eighteenth centuries were assumed to be members of the established Church of England. Whether or not they were baptized in the Anglican rite or set foot in the established church, they were required to support the church through an imposed tax. Because the Anglican Church regarded matrimony as an inviolable sacrament, obtaining a divorce or annulment was extremely difficult if not impossible.

Mothers of Invention: Margaret Brent and the Sisters' Freehold

The colony of Maryland, established by a royal charter, was granted to English Roman Catholic nobility under the feudal control of Lord Baltimore, Cecil Calvert. White indentured servants, who composed nearly eighty percent of the population of the Chesapeake colony of Maryland, were recruited to work on tobacco plantations.

As in Virginia, social class in Maryland was dramatically stratified with nobility and gentry at the top and poor white servants at the bottom. The proportion of men to women remained high. In order to encourage more gentle and virtuous women to settle there, Maryland officials offered single women one-hundred acres of land. The male population objected to this equitable land policy and pressured the Maryland assembly to restrict single women from becoming property holders. In the sub-tropical colony of South Carolina, with a climate even less conducive to the health of English men and women than Virginia, officials offered land to women who would settle there. Carolina granted female indentured servants freedom dues in the form of land granted upon completion of their labor contract.

In 1638, an enterprising woman, Margaret Brent, the daughter of Lord Admington of Gloucester, England, came to Maryland. Arriving two years before the land grant to single women was cut off, Margaret, one of 12 children, came with her sister Mary, two brothers and attending servants. Margaret and Mary were given 70 acres which they developed into a flourishing estate called *The Sisters Freehold.* Because Margaret and Mary Brent remained spinsters, they were somewhat of an anomaly in colonial society. Since English law did not recognize women as free agents and property holders, she was required to sign all legal documents as "Margaret Brent, gentleman."

To make matters even better, Lord Baltimore gave her additional land and Margaret added to her wealth through business deals. She purchased more land grants, became a productive farmer, and family members and business associates retained her as a legal advocate. In 1644, Leonard Calvert, the royal governor of Maryland, over the objections of his brother, Cecil Calvert, Lord Baltimore, appointed Margaret executrix of his will.

In 1648, taking her independence and proprietorship literally, Mistress Margaret Brent argued that her status as a property holder entitled her to representation in the Maryland Assembly and the right to vote. She is probably the first woman in American history to demand these civil rights. In 1650, after being refused an assembly seat as a voting member, Margaret sold her Maryland property and moved to Westmoreland County, Virginia, where she established another prosperous plantation.

Margaret operated as a free agent and never married. She had come to the colonies as a woman of means, and under the terms of *free holding* acquired great wealth in both Maryland and Virginia. She insured her position further by managing her colonial land investments wisely. But had she married, Margaret's status would have been altered dramatically. She would not have been able to manage the property brought into a marriage, conduct business, make contracts, or own and acquire property outright. As a resident of Maryland (a Roman Catholic colony) or Virginia, (an Anglican colony), Margaret would not have been able to obtain a divorce.

The pattern of settlement in the Chesapeake region differed sharply from that of the New England settlements. In Maryland, Virginia and the Carolinas, the majority of settlers were men who sought a better opportunity in the New World. They hoped to return to England as wealthy subjects.

The Separatists of Plymouth Plantation

In New England, entire families came to settle in America permanently. They hoped to set up independent churches where they could worship according to their own beliefs without interference from the Church of England.

Because the groups who settled in New England were directly influenced by the English Reformation, some background on this movement is helpful. Those who came to America, Puritans, were reformers within the English church who wished to further advance the reforms which the Church of England had started in the reign of Henry VIII. Puritans wished to eliminate some rituals and beliefs such as certain sacraments, the church hierarchy, and the veneration of Mary and the saints. Puritans had adopted the ideas of John Calvin, a Reformation reformer who insisted that individuals could do nothing to guarantee or secure their salvation. As Calvinists, Puritans believed that everyone had access to God through prayer and the reading of His inspired word, the Bible.

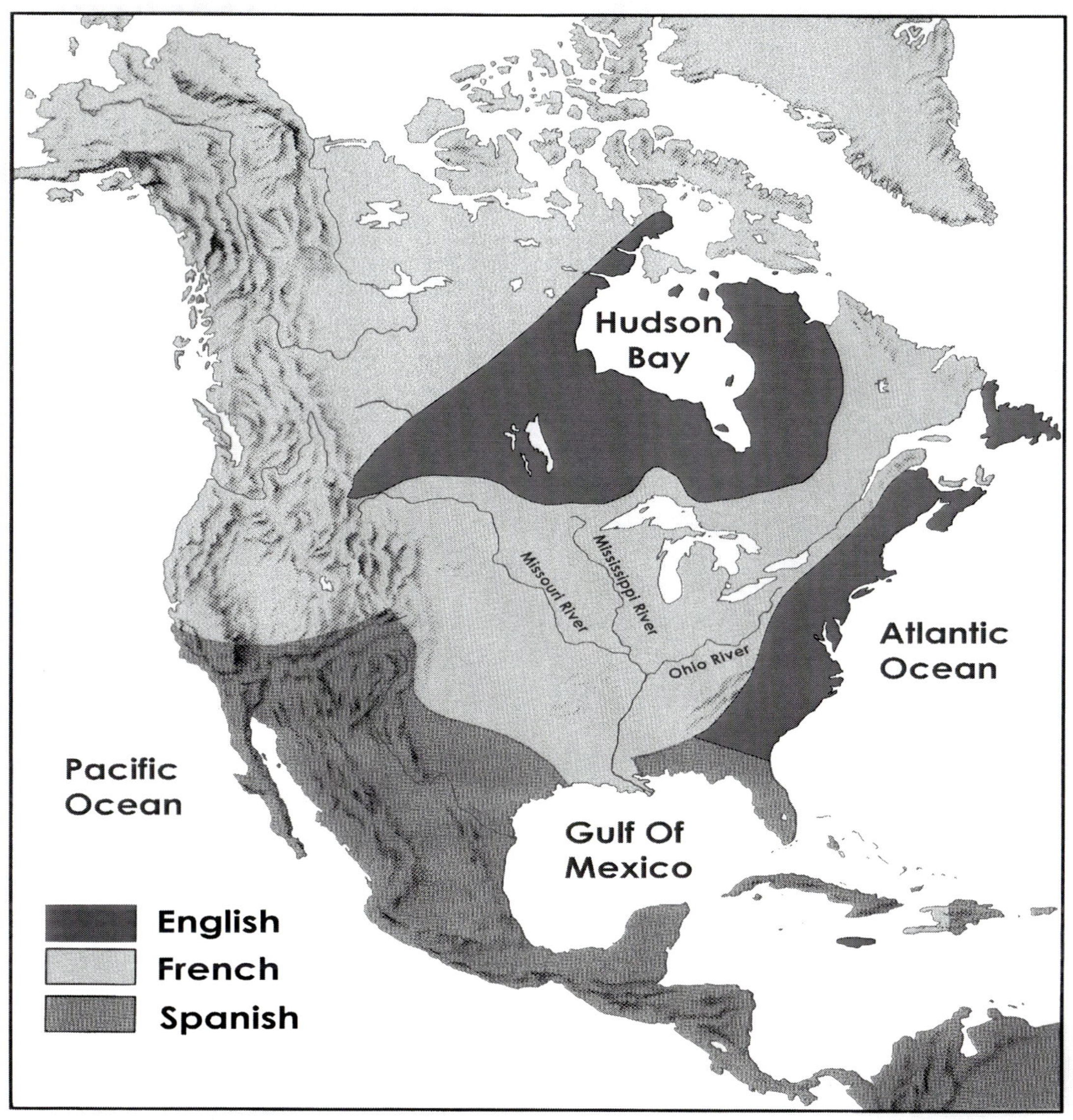

European Countries which claimed land in America and established predominant colonies were England, France and Spain.

During the Protestant Reformation, between 1500 and 1650, the population of England nearly doubled and that growth brought problems of unemployment and poverty among the working class. But in sharp contrast, the upper classes displayed more excesses of wealth and immoral behavior. In 1603, when Queen Elizabeth I died, James Stuart the King of Scotland succeeded her to the English throne. This succession affected the stability of the English church and state. The Scot Royal family, the Stuarts, had remained Roman Catholics while most Scots and many English had become Puritans.

Within the Puritan sect, one group known as Pilgrims or Separatists viewed the English church and society as irreparable, and had given up hope for reforming either. They had separated themselves completely from the Church of England. Through arrangements with the Virginia Company, in 1620, they set sail on the Mayflower bound for America. They intended to establish a permanent settlement in the Hudson River Valley but a storm just off the Atlantic coast blew the Mayflower Pilgrims way off course and they landed farther north. Before they came ashore on November 11, 1620, the forty-one men onboard signed an agreement (later called the Mayflower Compact) pledging to, "join together in a civil body politic" and to abide by "just and equal laws for the general good of the colony." Led by Governor William Bradford, 120 followers set up a colony in what they named New England at Plymouth Plantation. From the onset they faced great difficulties and many died during the first harsh winter; others during a poor harvest in 1622. Were it not for the benevolence of the local natives, no one in the colony would have survived.

The courtship and marriage of one Plymouth couple, Priscilla Mullins and John Alden, was memorialized by Henry Wadsworth Longfellow in his work of fiction, "The Courtship of Miles Standish." He relates how John Alden, a stand-in for the reticent Captain Miles Standish, proposed by proxy to Priscilla. But Priscilla Mullins accepted John's proposal instead and married him. Little else is known of Priscilla Mullins Alden. After she married John Alden, a *cooper* in 1623, they lived in Plymouth plantation until 1631, and then joined other Separatists in establishing a settlement at Duxbury, Massachusetts.[4] John Alden gained prominence serving in the Massachusetts government until he died in 1687. We assume that Priscilla Alden knew how to read but not to write. She had eleven children and settled down to the demanding life of motherhood and housekeeping.

The Separatists of Plymouth were desperate to survive and succeed. In debt to the Virginia Company, they resorted to permitting settlement to people outside of their faith. But, by 1690, they still could not make a go of it and Plymouth Plantation was incorporated into the colony of its prosperous neighbors, the English non-Separatists, or Puritans, of Massachusetts Bay, (i.e. Boston) who had settled in New England in 1630.

Under the guidance of John Winthrop, non-Separatists, or Puritans, came to America to build the model Christian community. According to Winthrop's vision,

> We shall find that the God of Israel is among us, and ten of us shall be able to resist a thousand of our enemies. The Lord will make our name a praise and glory, so that men shall say of succeeding plantations: The Lord make it like that in New England. For we must consider that we shall be like a city upon a hill; the eyes of all the people are on us.

We will take up the story of the Puritans, who developed Massachusetts Bay Colony, in more detail in the next chapter.

The Dutch Colonization of New Netherlands

In 1609, Englishman Henry Hudson aboard his ship, *Half Moon*, discovered a major seaway in North America and claimed the surrounding territory as New Netherlands and a small island at the inlet which he named New Amsterdam. Hired by a Dutch trading firm to establish a post in North America, Hudson claimed the land for the Dutch but named the River and the enormous Bay for himself. This area, a critical passageway into the interior of North America via the St. Lawrence, the Mississippi and the Hudson Rivers, was a vital tri-river causeway which would provide New Netherlands with the best harbor and transport system of all the American colonies. It also lent credence to the possibility of a Northwest Passage which explorers had searched for as the prized route from the Atlantic to the Pacific and on to Asia.

By 1624, the Dutch developed this strategic position in North America, as the colony of New Netherlands and a trading outpost for the Dutch West Indies Company. The Dutch became successful entrepreneurs engaging in the fur trade with Native Americans and hunted beaver and other highly prized pelts. In the first year of their settlement of New Amsterdam, the Dutch West Indies Company shipped out 4,000 beaver pelts and 700 otter skins for the European market. Briefly from 1630 to 1664, the Dutch dominated the African slave trade to North America. Even though New Netherlands remained primarily a trading outpost model, officials enticed families to settle permanently with enormous land grants ranging from 50,000 to one million

4. *Cooper*, one who makes or repairs wooden buckets, barrels or tubs.

acres on which holders paid little or no tax. Owners known as *patroons* sponsored family members or others to come over and work these farms in repayment for their own transport to the colony.[5]

During the Anglo-Dutch war, the English invaded and seized New Netherlands and had settled there by 1672. After conquest, the Dutch of the Hudson River Valley held on to their tradition and language for at least another century. A study of three generations of New York colonial society shows that a small Dutch population maintained a continuity and influence on the city's cultural life. In 1664, when the English captured the colony of New Netherlands, the Dutch population of New Amsterdam (New York), numbered only 1500. Over successive decades, because of the scarcity of Englishwomen in the colony, many Englishmen married Dutch women. Oddly enough, these women were more likely than the Dutch men (who married Dutch women) to sustain their Dutch culture after conquest. From 1664 to 1698, the city's population grew from 1,875 to 5,000, of which 2,161 were the children of the Dutch settler families, or what one historian identifies as *conquest/cohort families*.

Dutch Women in New Netherlands

In 1674, when Dutch schools affiliated with the Dutch Reformed Church and lost municipal support, it was the Dutch women (mostly those married to non-Dutch men) who continued their children's vocational training and perpetuated the Dutch language. Englishmen married to Dutch women testified that they learned to speak Dutch since that was the preferred language at home, (a true mother tongue)! They also deferred to their wives in matters of religious training for the children. Throughout this period it was the tenacity of the Dutch women who clung to their faith and sustained membership in the Dutch Reform church which also kept that institution strong.

Dutch immigrants enjoyed prosperity in the New World as evidenced by the finery displayed in their homes, such as the fine Delft China dishes they brought with them to grace the family table or sideboard.

Dutch colonial women, famous for their richly prepared cuisine, prepared high quality dairy products processed on their farms and in their kitchens. One well-sated visitor at a Dutch family meal wrote:

> "In the evening they made a delicious porridge of corn and in the center poured fresh milk. As we took more milk than porridge, the milk in the dish was soon consumed. We were served some meat and fresh bread with sweet butter."

Dutch women spared no calories in their baked confections. For a wedding celebrated in the Schuyler family, Mrs. Schuyler baked a wedding cake which contained twelve dozen eggs, forty-eight pounds of raisins, twenty-four pounds of currants, four quarts of brandy, and a quart of rum. All of these ingredients were mixed in a washtub, and baked in an outdoor oven. The wedding cake was enjoyed by the guests, who washed it down with 126 gallons of wine.

---

5. *Patroons*, The Dutch company granted certain members manorial rights, granting large estates to men who would pay the cost of transporting to and settling them. A bona fide patroon obtained fifty adults within a period of four years. This entitled him to have lands extending sixteen miles on one side or eight miles on both sides of a river and as far in as necessary.

One hundred years after English conquest, a visitor to New York City could still spot a Dutch colonial woman in a crowd. She was the one wearing more colorful clothing, a European headdress, large earrings and ornate gold jewelry. Dutch colonial women instituted rigorous standards of housekeeping in their colorful homes bedecked with Delft tiles and immaculate carpets. All that remains of their well-ordered lives are some stately homes along the Hudson and a few gallery portraits of finely dressed Dutch matrons.

The New Netherlanders also left a wide mark on American society. They observed the feast day of Saint Nicholas, adopted by American children as Sinter Klaus, or Santa Claus, and the Dutch winter activities of sleigh riding, tobogganing, and ice skating were embraced by American society. Dutch foods such as apple pie and chocolate became staple American fare.

French Exploration and the Immigration to New France

France also developed colonies in North America. Exploration began in the 1530s when Jacques Cartier navigated the St. Lawrence River and claimed the region for France. Samuel de Champlain followed in 1608, establishing a city and settlement at Quebec. He negotiated with the native Hurons for trading purposes and formed a defensive alliance with them to protect the settlement from the daunting Iroquois Nations. French Minister of State Cardinal Richelieu, who favored colonization in the New World, established a joint-stock venture, the Company of New France. Merchants were granted a monopoly on the fur trade and title to all the land by the government with the agreement that they would supply 4,000 settlers for the colony, provision them and also send priests.

For several reasons, despite the government's strong endorsement and support, settlers were not able to gain a strong foothold in the New World. The Company of New France could never entice enough people to immigrate or to stay in America permanently. A partial explanation lies in the difference between the development of the French and English economy. The French never experienced an *enclosure* movement like that in England.[6] Because French peasants always maintained legal rights to their farms, there was no reason for farmers to emigrate. Farming in France, a successful venture, remained so. Even though New France had fertile soil, prospects in the St. Lawrence River valley with its colder climate and shorter growing season were never as attractive.

The government itself was at cross-purposes with the colonial venture. The two groups which could have made colonization successful, young men and the up-and-coming middle class, were either discouraged or forbidden to leave the country. Because young men were needed at home to serve in the army and defend France, the government offered no bonuses for resettlement in America. The emerging middle class in France, composed mainly of Huguenots (French Protestants) were mercantile and professional people. The Catholic monarchy feared that if they allowed Huguenots to settle in New France, they might become autonomous and disrupt the colony, so they were forbidden emigration.

The Colony of New France

New France did become a vast network in the interior of North America for fur trading and missionary activity. French trappers, with the aid of Native American women, settled along the hunting trails and claimed more land for France. Louis Joliet traveled west along the Mississippi to Wisconsin and as far south on the river to Arkansas. Father Jacques Marquette, a Jesuit, accompanied Joliet and attempted to convert the natives. Oddly, agents of conversion were not the French priests or trappers but Native American women who cohabited with the Frenchmen and married them. Their earnest conversion to Roman Catholicism was instrumental in strengthening mixed marriages of Frenchmen and native women and in perpetuating French

6. *Enclosure* was a movement by landlords to drive tenants and farmers off of the land so that owners could fence up and enclose pasturage to raise sheep for the wool industry which was becoming much more profitable.

Catholic institutions throughout the region of Middle America. Exploration continued under Robert La Salle who went all the way to the Gulf of Mexico and claimed the region for Louis XIV naming it "Louisiana" in his honor.

Initially, French Jesuits made more converts than the Spanish padres because their proselytizing was less coercive and they did not impose forced labor on the natives. Ironically the few French who came to New France were enough of a critical mass to wipe out the native population but not enough to establish permanent settlement. In time, however, with increased contact, diseases brought by Europeans took their toll. By the end of the seventeenth century, epidemics such as smallpox claimed nearly 90 percent of the Native American population of New France. When prayers to the Christian deity did not protect or save them from disaster, Native Americans abandoned their newly adopted faith.

If the French government's statistical documentation can be reckoned as nearly accurate, the venture to America had been quite costly. Eventually, after 155 years of colonization, of the 67,000 men and women who came to America, about 46,000, nearly 70 percent, returned to France. Those who stayed in places like Louisiana made a lasting imprint of French customs in language, cuisine, architecture and style.

The Louisiana Colony

It was in this southern region of the Mississippi River country, Louisiana, that French attempts at colonization were most successful. Settlers in Louisiana preserved French culture and maintained ties with the Old World. There on the eastern and western banks of the river French émigrés, sponsored by investors of the Mississippi Company, established large family plantations and developed the unique *Creole* lifestyle.[7] Beginning in the seventeenth century, generation after generation of French émigrés came to the region. The French Creoles maintained extended family ties with relatives in France and êmigrés continued to come to Louisiana and marry into the founding families. Creole plantations were mapped out in long lots or strips of land which gave each property holder access to the Mississippi. The production of sugar cane and eventually the sugar granulation process made the Creoles of Louisiana very wealthy but their profits, success and lavish lifestyle were made possible by the low overhead of a slave economy. The particular slave system which developed on the sugar plantations of Louisiana was most oppressive. Sugar cane cultivation was labor intensive and machinery used in sugar granulation often caused serious bodily injury.

The Code Noir, the Black Code

Provincial records show that by 1721, the total population of Louisiana stood at 5,000 people. Of that total about 3,300 were slaves captured in Africa and 1,700 were white. In 1724, the city fathers of New Orleans enacted the *Code Noir*, or Black Code to control the predominantly black population of slaves.[8] It consisted of a series of the harshest penalties inflicted on slaves in the colony. The Code prohibited any comingling of the races, concubinage with slaves, or marriage of blacks and whites (whether or not the individuals were slave or free).[9] Slaves could be beaten, branded and otherwise severely disciplined. The Code did provide for the manumission of slaves provided their master was over twenty-five years of age

7. *Creole,* applies broadly to the following: person of European descent living in West Indies or Spanish America; person descended from original French settlers in Louisiana; person descended from Spanish or Portuguese living in the gulf states; someone of mixed ancestry speaking a Latin- based language; black slave born in America; or a Haitian of mixed ancestry.
8. *Code Noir*, or Black Code, passed in Louisiana was very similar in text and purpose with Black Codes enacted in the English colonies to control the black populations there as well, particularly in the colony of South Carolina which had a disproportionately large population of black to white.
9. The spirit of the law on cohabitation of blacks and whites in the province would certainly indicate that it was more often the case that the whites violated the codes and not slaves.

when he manumitted them. The Black Code of Louisiana also forbid the worship of any religion except Roman Catholicism and ordered the expulsion of all Jews from the province.

A Louisiana Creole Plantation on the banks of the Mississippi north of New Orleans. They operated primarily as places of business and secondarily as the family residence. Creole plantations were worked by African and African-American slaves. (Photo courtesy of the Library of Congress.)

Women for the Louisiana Colony

Many French trappers from the northern region of New France ventured to Louisiana and settled down. To populate the city of New Orleans with women, French officials deported female inmates of correction houses, prisons and brothels in France. In 1700, when a French priest recommended that all the immoral women in the colony should be removed, Louisiana Governor Lamothe Cadillac replied, "If I send away all the loose females, there will remain no women at all and this would not suit the views of the King or the inclinations of the people." Because of the shortage of unmarried French women, many men took Indian wives. Jean Baptiste Le Moyne, Sieur de Bienville, the founder of the City of New Orleans, begged his contacts in Paris to, "Send me wives for my Canadians, they are running into the woods after Indian girls."

The government issued a royal edict forbidding the transportation of persons of immoral character to Louisiana. Populating Louisiana with two distinct types of females led to the social ranking of women in the colony as either correction girls or casket girls (*filles de cassette*). *Filles de cassette* were respectable girls who came with trunks (*cassettes*) filled with their clothing and household items such as a hope chest. The Mississippi Company continued to supply casket girls for the colony at regular intervals from 1721 to 1755. Whenever a group of them arrived, however, they were guarded by nuns and soldiers until suitable husbands could be found. The matchmaking was expedited quickly for as one official coarsely stated, "This merchandise was soon disposed of, so great was the want of the country." Evidently, through some biological miracle, the casket girls must have been extremely prolific and the correction girls had no children as Louisiana families only acknowledged *filles de cassette* as their ancestors and founding mothers!

Women in New Orleans

If nature and history could have picked a less suitable place to found a colony or city, it has never been identified. New Orleans, a swamp and mosquito-infested area, was plagued by Indian raids, pirates, floods, disease and tropical storms. It was then and is today below sea-level. The Mississippi River, which has changed its course over the centuries, the Gulf of Mexico and surrounding bayou swamp (small tributaries of the Mississippi) constantly reclaim the land. Much of the credit for Louisiana's continuity must be paid to Bienville. New Orleans and Louisiana remained habitable because Bienville persisted in his dream to build a city and French culture in the area.

The religious order of the Ursulines was sent to Louisiana under contract by the Mississippi Company and established their convent on land given to them on the waterfront in the City of New Orleans. They promised to furnish six nuns to serve in local hospitals and to protect the *filles de la cassette*.

But in 1720, eighty-eight girls, inmates of *La Salpetriere,* were shipped to the colony.[10] They were placed under the guardianship of the Ursuline Sisters, the first order of Nuns to come to the French colony. With some forethought, officials also sent a midwife, Madame Doville, (nicknamed Madame *La Sans-regret*) to assist with the girls.[11] The nuns had difficulty restraining the girls. After three months, only nineteen of them had been married off. The Mississippi Company also sent girls from reputable middle class families to Louisiana and outfitted each of them with a trunk or *cassette* containing a full wardrobe of clothing.[12]

The Ursulines had agreed to give instruction to both Negro and white girls and to try to reform the "loose women and girls of bad conduct." Apparently they took this mission quite seriously; as one Sister Madeleine explained, the discipline of bad girls was to place them upon wooden horses and have the soldiers whip them. But punishment could not keep pace with the decline in morality in the town. The government also built a house of detention for abandoned females and the Ursulines were put in charge of its operation. But only ten years after the founding of the city, murder, robbery, mayhem, fighting, drunkenness, and prostitution all added to the notorious reputation of New Orleans.

Conclusion

The English Colony of Jamestown and the surrounding English plantations were saved from financial ruin by tobacco cultivation introduced by colonist John Rolfe. His marriage to Pocahontas, the daughter of Chief Powhatan, brought a temporary peace between the English and the Powhatan tribe, which enabled the English to gain a stronghold in America. Immigrant women who came to the Virginia colony under indenture, that is work contracts, labored strenuously for the colony's success. In the seventeenth century, immigrant women who could survive any number of challenges such as the harsh climate and living conditions, seasoning, labor contracts, childbirth, and warfare had a chance to improve their economic status. Briefly in that century, because of the high mortality in Virginia, officials relaxed property laws and a planter's wife who survived her husband might inherit the estate and enjoy financial independence. The risks and odds were against these women but some were able to leverage this brief window of economic opportunity.

Native American women were also instrumental in the establishment of colonies and trading enclaves in New France. Their marriages to French men and their conversion to Christianity facilitated the establishment of French culture and Catholicism in the American heartland. Women sponsored by the government and the Mississippi Company came to New Orleans, married French settlers and lived on the plantations of Louisiana which were worked by African slave labor. These French female émigrés who settled in New France developed the Creole lifestyle, a unique blend of European, African and American culture.

In New Netherlands, immigrant women sustained Dutch culture long after the Dutch had lost control of their colony to the English in 1664. Whether women lived in the culture and tradition of New France, New Netherlands, the domain of Native America, or in an English colony, they shared a common destiny: women carried the major responsibility for the survival of their family, their culture and civilization, and they did so under life threatening conditions but always within the confines of a male dominated society.

10. *La Salpetriere,* a House of Correction for females in Paris.
11. *Sans-regret*, literally without regret; an implication that the midwife would deliver babies from illicit affairs.
12. *Cassette,* in English casket. Before the nineteenth century, the term casket referred to a large storage trunk for clothing or a smaller one, a jewel casket, which contained jewelry.

Chapter 3
Dissenters, Witches and Quakers in the Colonies
Conduct Unbecoming a Woman

Key Topics

Dissenters Anne Hutchinson and Mary Dyer
The Salem Witch Trials
Colonial Pennsylvania

Chronology

1620 - Separatists Establish Plymouth Plantation
1630 - Puritans Found Massachusetts Bay Colony
1634 - Anne Hutchinson Arrives in Boston
1675 - King Phillip's War in New England
1681 - Quakers Establish Pennsylvania Colony
1692 - Salem Witch Hunts

Introduction

English Protestants who settled in the northern region of America named the area New England. They arrived first at Plymouth in 1620, and then a decade later at Massachusetts Bay (Boston). From the beginning, life in these New England colonies was rigidly monitored by church officials who dealt harshly with anyone who did not adhere to the doctrine and practices of the Puritan faith. Religious dissenters Thomas Hooker, Roger Williams and Anne Hutchinson were banished from the Massachusetts Bay colony.[1] This dissension and the controversy which led to it stripped away any semblance of Christian charity and unity. Further evidence of disharmony occurred in Salem in 1692, when residents accused their neighbors of practicing witchcraft. In the aftermath, because of the condemnation and execution of innocent people, dissension spread further. Many lost faith in the clergy and the church, and church membership dropped off sharply.

In England, the Society of Friends, or Quakers, lent their own dissension in the form of pacifism and a belief in the equality of all men and women. Under the leadership of English aristocrat William Penn, Quakers came to America in 1680, to the mid-Atlantic coastal region and founded a colony they named for their proprietor, Pennsylvania. Here William Penn established a Holy Experiment, committed to a peaceful coexistence with native inhabitants and intended to treat men and women equally.

---

1. *Dissenter,* one who refuses to accept the doctrines of the church.

Puritans in New England

Puritans, who established their colony and church in Massachusetts Bay, held to Calvin's *Doctrine of Predestination* which stated that even before one's birth, God had foreordained, or pre-destined, some to eternal life and some to eternal damnation. Yet belief in predestination left Puritans, indeed all Calvinists, unsure of their own eternal status and in a state of anxiety. They resisted the doctrine of *Arminianism* which had gained popularity in the Anglican Church.[2] Their hope for salvation lay in God's grace, an intervention of love, mercy and forgiveness known as the *covenant of grace*. Still they maintained that since salvation was predestined, only a chosen few would be saved by Divine Election. One could not be saved through faith and good work, i.e. the *covenant of works*, as Roman Catholicism professed.

A colonial goodwife would spend most of her day in household chores such as cooking, spinning, cleaning and child care. (Photo courtesy of Library of Congress)

Because not all men could serve as priests and celibates, the Roman Catholic Church had sanctioned marriage, professing that it was better for a man to marry than to die a fornicator. Puritans rebuked the Roman Catholic view that women were a necessary evil, disavowed the hierarchy of the Anglican Church and established their own structure where women were respected but subordinate to men. Puritan ministers deemed women a necessary good who shared salvation as man's joint heir, but in practice they did not regard women as equals. A common Puritan homily began, "Until a woman ate of the tree of good and evil, there was no sin in the world."

Anne Hutchinson

Anne Hutchinson arrived early to the Massachusetts Bay Colony in 1634, four years after its founding. She began to hold women's weekly devotional meetings and expressed beliefs on salvation which made Puritan elders suspicious of her ideas. Anne went so far as to say that only two of the Boston clergy were saved—John Cotton, her own minister, and John Wheelwright, her brother-in-law. This claim brought more attention to Anne and soon eighty or more members flocked to her meetings. Within a short time, more people attended the Hutchinson meeting than Sunday worship. At these gatherings Anne took predestination to its obvious conclusion, stating that if God had truly chosen the elect before birth, then there was no need for them to prepare themselves spiritually for reception of his saving grace. Staying on the straight and narrow, (which Puritans called the *Doctrine of Preparation*) and living righteously (the *Doctrine of Sanctification*) was, according to Hutchinson, delusional thinking for good works would not get a believer into heaven. The questions she raised shook the Puritan faith to its very foundation and revealed the contradiction between what the clergy taught versus what they practiced. In essence, what Hutchinson did was to accuse the ministry of the heresy of Arminianism.

Fearing schism and dissension among the ranks, Governor Winthrop took quick action to organize opposition against Anne Hutchinson. To diminish her popularity, a law was passed restricting the number of individuals who could meet for prayer to no more than sixty. For her part, Anne continued the home prayer meetings and the Reverend John Wheelwright, who took her side, continued to preach. In November 1637, the Massachusetts colonial assembly,

2. *Arminianism,* a heresy of Jacobus Arminius which rejected the Calvinist Doctrine of Predestination but believed that human free will is compatible with God's sovereignty.

summoned Anne Hutchinson and Reverend Wheelwright to court.

She was tried before a civil court in which the Governor acted as both judge and prosecutor. He accused Anne of "behavior not comely for a woman," and of "breaking the fifth commandment." (In these charges father and mother were interpreted to be the civil and religious magistrates of the colony.) Anne had attacked the core of Puritan belief by claiming that only two ministers walked in a covenant of grace and that the entire Puritan experiment was led by ministers who were incapable of determining who was and who was not saved. During the trial, she answered the questions directly and defended herself, citing specific references to scripture. Acquittal seemed obvious, then the defense took a serious reversal when Anne told the court she heard voices and saw visions. Winthrop responded "I am persuaded that the revelation she brings forth is delusion."

The following March, at the trial conducted by the church elders from Boston, the Reverend John Cotton, who had turned against her, accused Anne of spreading dangerous ideas. Professing to be a witness to Divine revelation, she was charged with A*ntinomianism*, (speaking against the law) a heresy among Puritans. The Reverend Wilson excommunicated her proclaiming, "I do cast you out and in the name of Christ I do deliver you up to Satan that you may learn no more to blaspheme, to seduce and to lie." It was reported that when Anne left the court, a crowd gathered outside and shouted insults at her. She responded, "The Lord judgeth not as a man judgeth, better to be cast out of the church than to deny Christ."

After two exhausting trials, she recanted most of her testimony. Anne and her family were banished to the island of Aquidneck in Naragansett Bay, in the colony of Rhode Island. On two occasions the Puritan officials received news which gave them satisfaction. In the summer of 1638, both Anne and her friend Mary Dyer each delivered badly deformed fetuses. Such deliveries were not uncommon then or now, and in Anne's case the description of the fetus suggests it was probably a *hydatidiform mole.*[3] The ill-fated pregnancy heightened the community's suspicions of Anne's guilt and the bizarre details fascinated Puritans in Boston. The court called in eyewitnesses of Mary Dyer's delivery to testify and trial records include this vivid description and John Winthrop's conclusion,

> God himself was pleased to step in with his casting voice, and bring in his own vote and suffrage from heaven, by testifying his displeasure against their opinions and practices as clearly as if he had pointed with his finger, in causing the two fomenting women in the time of the height of the Opinions to produce out of their wombs, as before they had out of their brains, such monstrous births as no chronicle hardly ever recorded. Mistriss Dier [sic] brought forth of a woman child, a fist, a beast and a fowle, all woven together in and without a head.

Puritans saw further manifestation of Divine justice in 1642, when news reached Boston that Anne Hutchinson and her family had been murdered during an Indian raid on their home. Magistrates interpreted Anne's misfortunes as evidence of God's judgment against her. Hearing the news of her death, Winthrop stated,

> I never heard that the Indians in those parts did ever before this commit the like outrage upon any one family. Therefore God's hand is more apparently seen herein, to pick out this woeful woman, to make her and those belonging to her a heavy example of their cruelty above all others. Thus the Lord heard our groan to heaven, and freed us from this great and sore affliction.

Anne Hutchinson had been raised in a household where freedom of expression and conscience were encouraged. Some years earlier, Anne's father, the Reverend Francis Marbury, had been imprisoned in England for attacking the incompetence of the English clergy in his sermons. In her religious convictions, Anne Hutchinson pioneered the American principles of free speech and freedom of conscience. She is remembered for her willingness to face punishment, and her courage to challenge the patriarchal powers of church and state.

3. *Hydatiform mole,* a malformed ovum.

“The Interrogation of Anne Hutchinson”

In 1637, Anne Hutchinson was charged by church officials with holding inappropriate religious beliefs. Here is an excerpt of the transcript of that proceeding. The inquisitor is John Winthrop, Governor of Massachusetts Bay Colony, one of Anne Hutchinson's chief opponents

Inquisitor: What say you to your weekly publick meeting? Can you show a Warrant for them?

Anne: I will show you how I took it up, there were such meetings in use before I came, and because I went to none of them, this was the special reason of my taking up this course, we began it with five or six and though it grew to more in future to me, yet being tolerated at the first, I knew not why it might not continue.

Inquisitor: There were private meetings indeed, and art still in many places, of some few neighbors, but not so public and frequent as yours, and are of use for increase of love, and mutual edification, but yours are of another nature, if they had been such as yours they had been evil and therefore no good warrant to justify yours. But answer, by what authority or rule you uphold them.

Anne: By Titus 2 (scripture reference Book of Titus Old Testament) where the elder women are to teach the younger.

Inquisitor: So we allow you to do, as the Apostle there means privately upon occasion, but that gives no warrant of such set meetings for that purpose and besides you take upon you to teach many that are elder than yourself, neither do you teach them that which the Apostle commands, such as to keep at home.

Anne: Will you please to give me a rule against it and I will yield?

Inquisitor: Then it is clear that it is not meant of teaching men, but of teaching in public.

Anne: It is said I will pour my Spirit upon your daughters and they shall prophesy. If God give me a gift of prophecy, I may use it.

Inquisitor: show not in all this by what authority you take upon you to be such a public instructor. [After she had stood a short time, the Court permitted her leave to sit down; Anne was expecting another child at this time].

Anne: Here is my authority, Aquila and Priscilla, [who] took upon them to instruct Apollo, more perfectly, yet he was a man of good parts but they being better instructed might teach him.

Inquisitor: See how your argument stands, Priscilla with her husband took Apollo home and instructed him privately, therefore Mistress Hutchinson without her husband may teach 60 or 80.

Anne: I call them not, but if they come to me, I may instruct them.

Inquisitor: Yet you show us not a rule.

Anne: I have given you two places of scripture

Inquisitor: But neither of them will suit your practice.

Anne: Must I show my name written therein?

Puritans and Female Literacy

By 1642, the Commonwealth of Massachusetts had passed a law requiring that all children be taught to read. Church and Civil officials endorsed literacy so that Puritans would read the Bible for their daily devotion and teach their children to do the same. Officials presented contradictory guidelines: women could only expect basic literacy, encouraged to read the Bible but little else.

Quick to point out the consequences for women who indulged in intellectual stimulation, John Winthrop responded in his journal to the news that the Connecticut Governor's wife, Anne Hopkins, had gone mad.

> .....by occasion of her giving herself wholly to reading and writing, she hath lost her reason. Her husband, being very loving and tender of her, was loath to grieve her; But he saw his error, and when it was too late. For if she had attended her household affairs, and such things as belong to women, and not gone out of the way and calling to meddle in such things as are proper for men, whose minds are stronger..... she [would have] had kept her wits, and might have improved them usefully and honorably in the place God had set her.

Puritan patriarchs argued that learning was "not a rightful nor (sic) proper place" for a woman for two reasons: (1) because it was the sole domain assigned to men and (2) women, being the weaker sex, might bring on madness and insanity by indulging in any intellectual exercise. This bias against female education would linger for centuries.

King Phillip's War and the Captivity Narratives

By mid-seventeenth century, the New England white settlements had grown to a population of 55,000. In contrast, the native population estimated at 120,000 in 1570, was barely 16,000 in 1670. To stop further English expansion, Chief Metacom, (nicknamed King Phillip by the English) leader of the Wamponoags, allied with the Naragansetts and the Nipmucks. He realized that only armed resistance of the English could save his people. Between 1675 and 1676, Metacom's alliance attacked English settlers in New England in a bitter conflict known as King Phillip's War. Natives only ceased fighting when they ran out of guns and supplies but when the smoke cleared and Metacom had been captured, the results were devastating. Approximately five percent of the colonial adult population, about 1,000 people, were dead and 20 percent of English towns in Massachusetts and Rhode Island had been burned. The natives had more staggering losses with 25 percent, about 4,500, of their people killed. Some natives who survived were sold as slaves in the Caribbean and some escaped to the backwoods to live with other tribes.

Literature written during King Phillip's War, known as captivity narratives, describes the ordeal of white settlers taken as prisoners by Native Americans. One famous narrative, *The Sovereignty and Goodness of God* was written by Mary Rowlandson, a Puritan minister's wife. On February 10, 1675, during an attack on her village, Mary was captured and held for fifteen months. Because Metacom feared English retribution, he kept the tribes and captives constantly on the move. Mary Rowlandson related how her captors moved to twenty different campsites. In captivity, Mary became the captive-servant of female warrior Wetamoo, one of Metacom's wives.

Wetamoo, who led an allied force of 300 Naragansetts and Pocasset warriors, played an instrumental role in the war. One observer described Wetamoo "as potent a prince as any round about her, and has as much corn, land, and men as Metacom, at her command." He ranked her, "next to Philip in respect of the mischief she hath done." To survive captivity, Mary bartered with Wetamoo sewing and mending clothes in return for food. She detested Wetamoo, whom she regarded as an ungodly, demanding and cruel captor. During the relocations, Mary told how she was forced to carry heavy packs of supplies and if she complained, Wetamoo would slap her.

Mary also noted the kindness and concern Native American communities had for each other and for their captives. Although she dismissed natives as savages and heathens, she was impressed with their generosity toward each other. No matter how desperate the retreat, even in the severity of winter, no one went hungry, including Mary. Her testimony contradicted white women's fears about savages and neither the captivity narratives nor any other narratives suggest that white women were ever sexually violated; on the contrary, most remarked on the natives' kindness.

Rowlandson's youngest daughter, Sarah, taken with her, died during the retreat. Her son and another daughter, captured by another tribe, were eventually released and reunited with the family. Mary wrote how the ordeal changed her life and outlook,

> I can remember the time, when I used to sleep quietly without workings in my thoughts, whole nights together, but now it is other wayes with me. When all are fast about me, and no eye open, but His who ever waketh, my thoughts are upon things past, upon the awful dispensation of the Lord towards us; upon His wonderful power and might in carrying of us through so many difficulties, in returning us in safety and suffering none to hurt us. I remember in the night season how the other day I was in the midst of thousands of enemies and nothing but death before me: It is then hard work to perswade [sic] myself, that ever I should be satisfied with bread again.

The Rowlandson family was reunited but one year after Mary's release; Wetamoo drowned while trying to elude capture. Her retrieved body was decapitated by the English and her head was displayed at Taunton, Massachusetts, for several years.

Captivity was a major concern of English officials who feared that captors would renounce their faith to live among natives. This was a particularly horrifying notion since Indians were non-Christians whom Puritans believed held covenant with the devil. Thus Puritans who fraternized with natives would jeopardize their own salvation. They also worried about possible miscegenation of Englishmen with Native American women or Englishmen with female African slaves. Consequently, laws were enacted forbidding them to cohabit or marry into either group.

The Salem Witch Trials

In the summer of 1692, terror gripped the residents of the town and village of Salem, Massachusetts, as townsfolk one by one were *cried out* by teenage girls who accused them of practicing witchcraft.[4] Before the craze subsided, 300 people were accused and arrested, nineteen were hanged, seventeen died in prison, many lost their property, one man was tortured to death, and two dogs, also accused of sorcery, were executed. The Salem incident was not the first persecution of this kind; some fifteen individuals had been executed previously in New England.

In Salem, evidence of the supernatural showed up at the minister's home as Tituba, the household slave, told the girls their fortunes. At least one adult, Goodwife Ann Putnam, knew of their activities. Goodwife Putnam, who suspected sorcery in the loss of several babies, had sent questions to Tituba via her daughter Ann. An upstanding member of the church, Goodwife Putnam's faith in fortune telling reveals something of the nature of Puritan attitudes toward the spirit world.

Seventeenth century Puritans believed evil spirits were pervasive and could be detected in many things, by an unusual birth, the loss of livestock from some unknown malady, a hen that would not lay, a cow that yielded no milk, cream that would not churn into butter, the failure of crops, a horse that went lame or had a twisted mane, a fire, a loss of family fortune or evidence of broken or missing household objects. All were attributed to the work of the devil.

In February of 1692, when two girls became ill with symptoms that resembled earlier cases of insomnia, hysterical fits and twisting and jerking, Dr. William Griggs diagnosed that

4. *Cried out*, to be accused of witch craft because the afflicted girls literally pointed or cried out the name of one they accused.

the girls had an evil hand upon them, and news spread quickly of witchcraft in the minister's home. Officials investigated and by March lst three suspects had been named: Tituba, Sarah Osborne, a reclusive, wealthy woman, and Sarah Good, a poor vagrant. Sarah Osborne, quite ill when arrested, died in prison two months later, as did the infant of Sarah Good. Officials also arrested Dorcas Good, Sarah's five-year-old daughter, when she bit one of the afflicted girls. Accused Goodwife Martha Corey labeled the girls' courtroom histrionics as antics. seventy-one-year-old Rebecca Nurse, taken from her deathbed to stand trial, had been involved in a long, drawn out dispute with Samuel Parrish over property boundaries. Also charged with witchcraft, Elizabeth and John Proctor had slighted two of the afflicted girls who worked in their home, namely Abigail Williams and Mary Warren. Royal Governor Sir William Phipps determined the cases should be tried.

English law dictated that witchcraft was a felony and punishable by execution. Witchcraft cases followed a specific procedure. After being arrested, the accused were stripped and underwent a humiliating physical examination in order to find marks of a devil's teat by which the devil or his familiar might suck their blood. Just about any kind of growth—a wart, mole, a birthmark, or flap of skin—was condemning evidence.

On June 2, 1692, the packed court opened session with more spectators than had ever graced the Sabbath meeting. Puritans were eager to hear exciting testimony. The first defendant, Bridget Bishop, who owned the local tavern was regarded by Salemites as a woman of ill repute; Bridget was found guilty and executed.

Magistrates admitted *spectral evidence*, that is, testimony from witnesses that implied the accused appeared to them in strange forms such as a specter.[5] Usually their sworn statement accused the defendant of appearing in a dream, as a spirit or animal and doing some injury to the witness. The testimony of Dorcas Good described how three birds hurt children and were her mother's *familiars*.[6] When magistrates admitted spectral evidence, Judge Nathaniel Saltonstall resigned from the case.

In July, five more women found guilty were condemned to die; Sarah Good was among them. It was reported at her execution that when the Reverend Nicholas Noyes urged her to confess, she answered loud enough for all the onlookers to hear, "You are a liar! I am no more a witch than you are a wizard, and if you take away my life God will give you blood to drink!" When Noyes died a few years later of a cerebral hemorrhage, choking on his own blood, Sarah's prediction must have evoked a chilling memory among townspeople.

By September, thirteen more victims had been executed, and fifty-five people confessed to being witches. After Martha Corey had been executed, her husband, Giles Corey, also a suspect, believed his familiarity with court proceedings would save him. A trial could not proceed unless the defendant entered a plea; however, Giles had overlooked a point of law. If a defendant refused to enter a plea, they could be tortured in order to force a confession or a plea. His execution was a slow and painful one; Giles was pressed with heavy stones laid on his chest. After two days of torture, he remained mute and died refusing to enter a plea.

Charges of witchcraft were not limited to residents of Salem. As the girls gained celebrity, they were carted about from village to village to accuse others. Based upon Tituba's testimony that, "there was an evil man from Boston, tall and with white hair, who had a book with nine witch's names in it," officials arrested John Alden, Jr. (son of the John and Priscilla Alden of Plymouth colony). Alden, 71 years of age, a respected member of his community, and a captain in the colonial militia was also a hero of the Indian wars. At his hearing, when asked why he tormented the afflicted girls, Alden asked why the court, "suppos'd he had no better things to do than to come to Salem to afflict these persons that I never knew or saw before." Some of the most damning evidence against him

5. *Spectral evidence,* witnesses described ghosts, spirits, specters, animals or other phenomenon which they testified the accused had sent to torment the afflicted girls in some way.
6. *Familiars,* in the lore of witchcraft, familiars were agents of Satan

was testimony of his "lyin with squaws." Placed under guard at his home, he managed to escape and did not return to Massachusetts until after the hysteria subsided. One of the last victims cried out was the Reverend George Burroughs.

Defendants in the Salem Witch Trials of 1692, Found Guilty and Executed

Bridget Bishop	guilty executed
George Burroughs	guilty executed
Martha Carrier	guilty executed
Giles Corey	refused to enter a plea executed by torture
Martha Corey	guilty executed (wife of Giles)
Sara Good	guilty executed
Elizabeth Howe	guilty executed
Mary Easty	guilty executed (sister of Rebecca Nurse and Sarah Cloyes) *
George Jacobs, Sr.	guilty executed
Susannah Martin	guilty executed
Rebecca Nurse	guilty executed
Sarah Osborne	guilty executed
Alice Parker	guilty executed
Mary Parker	guilty executed
John Proctor	guilty executed **
Ann Pudeator	guilty executed
Wilmot Redd	guilty executed
Margaret Scott	guilty executed
Samuel Wardwell	guilty executed
Sarah Wildes	guilty executed
John Willard	guilty executed

* Sarah Cloyes was found guilty, incarcerated for eighteen months; she sued the commonwealth of Massachusetts for the wrongful deaths of her sisters, won the case, and died shortly thereafter.

** Elizabeth Proctor, the wife of John Proctor was also found guilty but spared execution because she was pregnant.

When the afflicted girls cried out Lady Phipps, the royal governor's wife, they had gone too far. Governor Phipps terminated the trials and the hysteria abated. Since there were still over 140 suspects in jail awaiting trial, he appointed another court to continue the proceedings in January of 1693, but that court disallowed spectral evidence and none of the remaining defendants were found guilty. However, those who were released discovered that their property had been seized, and they were unable to recover their losses.

In the aftermath, some officials expressed remorse for their part in the trials. The Reverend Cotton Mather, who had taken part in the investigation reflected in his diary,

> afflicted last night with discouraging thoughts, as is unavoidable marks of Divine displeasure must overtake my family for my not appearing with vigor enough to stop the proceedings of the judges when the inextricable storm from the invisible world assaulted the country.

Witches' House, North Street, Salem Massachusetts; only remaining house in Salem with direct ties to the Witchcraft Trials. It was the home of Jonathan Corwin, a presiding judge at the trials which sent nineteen people who had pleaded innocent to the gallows. (Photo courtesy of the Library of Congress)

In 1696, twelve members of the jury from the Salem trials signed a document of contrition for their part in the condemnation of the accused. Their statements read as follows:

> We confess that we were not capable to understand nor able to withstand the mysterious delusions of the Powers of Darkness; we do hereby signify to all in general, and to the surviving suffered in special, a deep sense of, and sorrow for, our errors in acting on such evidence to

> the condemning of any person; we justly fear that we were sadly deluded and mistaken, we do heartily ask forgiveness of you all.

Within five years, most of the officials and the jury made public apology for what they had done. Throughout the colony of Massachusetts, on January 14, 1697, residents observed a day of prayer, fasting and penance for the reconciliation of the commonwealth.

So far as is known, only one of the afflicted girls, Ann Putnam, Jr., made a public apology. In 1706, Ann stood before the congregation with head bowed while the minister read her confession, "desiring to be humbled before God." Ann stated that she had not "acted out of anger, malice, or ill will." She said, "It was a great delusion of Satan that deceived me in that time." At twenty-six years of age but looking much older, Ann was already a semi-invalid who would not survive to age thirty-six. Realizing her death was imminent, she wished to make her peace with God and the people of Salem. Her confession ended, "I desire to lie in the dust and earnestly beg forgiveness of God and from all those whom I have given just cause of sorrow and offense, whose relatives were taken away and accused."

Clio's Corner - The Darkness of that Day: What Really Happened in Salem?

Because the majority of defendants and accusers were women, the Salem witchcraft trials are significant to women's history. More than 300 years after the Salem Witch Trials the mystery lingers. What really happened? Were there witches in Salem? Certainly if anyone was dabbling in witchcraft it was the afflicted girls themselves. Eyewitness Thomas Brattle spoke of the guilt of the accusers.

> ... These afflicted girls as they are called, do hold correspondence with the devil, even in the esteem and account of the Salem gentlemen; for when the black man, i.e. say these gentlemen, the devil, does appear to them they ask him many questions, and accordingly give information to the inquirer; and if this is not holding correspondence with the devil, and something worse, I know not what is....

In 1952, playwright Arthur Miller's play, *The Crucible,* attracted American scholars to this historical event. In the play, Miller expressed his outrage over the ruination of innocent people accused of being communists and dragged before Senator Joseph McCarthy's Committee. McCarthy's investigation left defendants without jobs or livelihood; many in the Performing Arts never worked again.

Historians Paul Boyer and Stephen Nissenbaum, in *Salem Possessed*, mapped out a geography of witchcraft based on a socio-economic theory of Salem. Plotting out where victims and accusers resided and property ownership before and after the trials, they determined who stood to gain when neighbors were accused and found guilty. Their research offered motive and verified what Miller had implied, a serious split in Salem's population in 1680. The congregation was sharply divided between those in favor of Rev. Parris and those who opposed him. Boyer and Nissenbaum also explained why a disproportionate number of males were accused and executed. It was because of their affiliation with the socioeconomic out group.

In *"Ergotism: The Satan Loosed in Salem?"* Linda Caporael theorized the afflicted girls were not possessed but suffering from ergot poisoning. Historian Mary Kilbourne Matossian, in *Poisons of the Past,* also attributed the outbreak to ergot which grows in rye grain. Ergot poisoning causes hallucinations, gangrene, twitching or convulsions, spasms, a weakened immune system and cardiovascular complications, symptoms which might explain the afflicted girls' histrionics.

But if ergot-laden bread was served on Salem tables in 1692, why weren't there more residents of Salem similarly affected? Perhaps there were. Symptoms of ergotism might manifest hysteria or paranoia and explain the fear that struck the community. The hysteria which began in January raged through the summer of 1692.

By September, nineteen people had been executed. It was not until mid-October when the Governor appointed another court to hear cases that the frenzy subsided. By then a fresh crop of grain would have been harvested.

In *A Fever in Salem, a New Interpretation of the Salem Witch Trials*, Laurie Winn Carlson considered climate, harvest and illness in her theory as well. She found epidemiological evidence that Salem residents suffered from encephalitis born by increased rainfall, standing water and mosquitoes. Encephalitis victims experience "convulsions, hyperactivity, catatonic stupor and eye muscle disorders." Encephalitis leaves many sufferers mentally disturbed, with severe neurological disorders, or in coma-like trances, in some cases for prolonged periods of time. Either an ergot infection or encephalitis might explain the early demise of Ann Putnam, Jr.

Raising the obvious but least-asked question, Carol Karlsen, in *The Devil in the Shape of a Woman, Witchcraft in Colonial New England,* wanted to know why women were predominantly the accused. By comparison, Professor Karlsen found that in England more poor women were accused, whereas in New England most accused women were middle-aged, and eligible for an inheritance. Townspeople and authorities perceived them as a serious threat to the established order because they challenged the supremacy of God (male, patriarchal) and society's prescribed gender arrangements. In the Puritan order of things there were only two kinds of women - good women and witches. Good women were submissive, pious and obedient but the women accused of witchcraft were assertive, angry, and dissatisfied with the status quo.

Colonial Pennsylvania

The Colony of Pennsylvania, advertised as "the best poor man's country," was blessed with fertile soil, adequate rainfall, a temperate climate, and numerous rivers. In 1681, William Penn and his followers established the Pennsylvania Colony as a Holy Experiment, a haven for their persecuted sect, the Society of Friends. Quakers, as they were commonly called, espoused complete freedom of conscience for all people. They were guided by the principle of an inner light, which they believed God granted to all as an indwelling of the Holy Spirit. Since everyone was endowed with the inner light all humans, women as well as men, were equal.

Their faith communities were the least structured of all the religious groups in America. Quakers did not build churches but gathered in a home or meeting-house. Quakers did not have a ministry or priesthood, did not celebrate sacraments and lacked a formal liturgy. At their services members meditated in silence until someone, male or female, was moved to speak.

Quakers embraced pacifism and made a treaty with the Native Americans recognizing tribal ownership of the territory which proprietor Penn claimed as Pennsylvania. William Penn purchased the land from the Delaware Tribe and maintained an unprecedented peaceful coexistence with the native people of the region.

Quakers valued the simple life. The meeting expected men and women to practice humility, speak plainly, dress simply and treat everyone with the same regard. Because William Penn's directive emphasized equality, women enjoyed more freedom of expression and experience in doing the work of the meeting than women of other colonial faiths. In Pennsylvania, women had been present from the start and maintained a traditional domestic role but those who lived in cities such as Philadelphia engaged in trade and operated small businesses. Thanks to the efforts of the colonists who settled there, Pennsylvania became one of the most prosperous colonies in the New World. As Quaker families thrived, Quaker parents instructed their children in simple tastes and prudent living, to live frugally, and "to be in this world but not of it."

As long as Quakers lived in their own colony where they controlled the government and the economy, they were secure in their religious freedom. In other colonies however, Quakers, especially females, were persecuted and often accused of heresy and witchcraft.

A convert and martyr for the Quaker faith, Puritan Mary Dyer, had settled in Boston with her husband William in 1635. Mary attended the prayer meeting at Anne Hutchinson's home and was so loyal to Anne that the

Dyer family went into exile with the Hutchinsons. They enjoyed success and prosperity in the new colony at Newport, Rhode Island, where William was appointed attorney-general. In 1652, during a trip to London, Mary attended the Society of Friends meeting and became a Quaker.

Within the Quaker meeting, a woman could preach, pray, sing or profess her faith, but within Massachusetts it was unlawful to practice the Quaker faith. Upon her return to New England, officials arrested Mary several times for preaching the word of God. In 1659, the court sentenced Mary to be executed but she received a last minute pardon while standing on the scaffold, when her son petitioned the royal governor. But the following year, when she returned to Boston, Mary was arrested again. Despite her husband's pleading to the magistrates, she was executed on June 1, 1660.

In 1681, Quakers both in England and in Pennsylvania were granted the right to hold their own meetings. The first women's monthly meeting held in New Jersey decided that female members could supervise the conduct of women, review petitions for marriage, uphold the standards of family life, visit the sick and help the poor. Resolutions passed at women's meetings were rarely questioned by the men. Quaker women's progress can be seen in a number of ways. On the one hand, the issues women discussed reinforced their traditional domestic role. But on the other, women had the latitude to express and conduct their own ecclesiastical affairs. Although unforeseen at the time, seeds were being sown among these assertive Quaker ladies for all women to take a more active part in social affairs.

Mothers of Invention: Anne Dudley Bradstreet, the Tenth Muse

Anne Dudley Bradstreet born Anne Dudley in Northampton, England, in 1612 and became America's first English speaking published poet. Due to her family's position she grew up an exceptionally well-educated woman for her time, being tutored in history, several languages and literature. We emphasize *exceptionally well educated* because most women of her time could neither read nor write or so much as sign their name. At the age of sixteen she married Simon Bradstreet. In 1630, Anne and Simon, along with Anne's parents, immigrated to America aboard the *Arabella* the flagship of the Winthrop Fleet of Puritan emigrants. The Bradstreets settled in what is now Cambridge, Massachusetts in 1632, and Anne's father and her husband served as governors of the Massachusetts Bay Colony. Her father and husband were also instrumental in the founding of Harvard University in 1636. Throughout her adult life, Anne suffered from poor health and a frail constitution; she contracted smallpox and in her later years fell prey to paralysis. She had eight children and held a comfortable and respectable social standing.

Anne Bradstreet's education gave her advantages to write with authority about politics, history, medicine, and theology. In 1650, through the sponsorship of the Rev. John Woodbridge, her book of poems, *The Tenth Muse Lately Sprung Up in America* was published in London. Despite Puritan attitudes about educating women and educated women (her father Thomas Dudley and her husband Simon Bradstreet had both presided at Anne Hutchinson's trial) Anne's accomplishments were extraordinary. She succeeded in writing poetry, having it published and being revered as colonial New England's foremost poet. While her poems were well received in both England and the New England Colonies, she did not escape criticism. In the prologue of her book, Anne Bradstreet makes reference to those who disapproved,

> I am obnoxious to each carping tongue
> Who says my hand a needle better fits,
> A poets pen all scorn I should thus wrong
> For such despite they cast on Female wits If what I do prove well, it won't advance
> They'l say it's stolin or else it was by chance

It is important to contrast Anne Hutchinson the heretic, who challenged male authority from Anne Bradstreet, the poet. Anne Bradstreet exemplified the Colonial Goodwife and the unflinching love and devotion of a woman for her husband. She never challenged male authority and her poems celebrated marital bliss,

> If ever two were one, then surely we
> If ever man were lov'd by wife, then thee;
> If ever wife was happy in a man
> Compare with me ye women if ye can

On July 10, 1666, her Andover home burned in a fire leaving the family homeless and with few belongings. Her personal library of books which was said to have numbered over 800 was destroyed. This event inspired a poem entitled "Upon the Burning of Our House July 10th, 1666." In this verse, she rejected the anger and grief that this worldly tragedy has caused her and instead looked toward God and the assurance of heaven as consolation, saying:

> And when I could no longer look,
> I blest His grace that gave and took,
> That laid my goods now in the dust. Yea, so it was, and so 'twas just.
> It was his own; it was not mine.
> Far be it that I should repine.

In 1672, suffering from tuberculosis, Anne Bradstreet died in Andover, at the age of 60. In her honor, that region where she lived in the Merrimack Valley is now named the Valley of the Poets. A marker in the North Andover cemetery commemorates the 350th anniversary of the publishing of "The Tenth Muse" in London in 1650. In October 1997, Harvard University dedicated a gate in her memory as America's first published poet, The Bradstreet Gate located next to Canaday Hall in Harvard Yard.

Conclusion

The Trial of Anne Hutchinson and the Salem Witch Trials illustrated the dilemma of the Puritan experiment. By 1634, the city on the hill intended as a model of Christian community was already cracking at its foundation. Dissenters who challenged Puritan authority and doctrine were either banished from Massachusetts Bay, or in the case of some Quakers were executed. Clearly, religious toleration and freedom were intended strictly for those of the narrowly defined Puritan persuasion.

After the initial hardships of trying to survive in the new world in the seventeenth century, English settlers of New England experienced one tragedy piled upon another. In 1678, a smallpox epidemic left thousands dead. The Reverend Cotton Mather, the prominent Boston minister, lost three children.

The fear that colonists might defect to live with Native Americans kept ministers in a constant vigil over their congregations. Those suspected of any collusion with Indians were stigmatized and condemned by their church and community. By 1690, Indian wars in New England had decimated the immigrant and native population, and nearly one-hundred towns and villages were destroyed. What effect the wars had on the children in New England cannot be imagined. Abigail Williams, one of the afflicted girls and accusers in the Salem Witch Trials, had probably witnessed the murder of her own parents during the Indian wars.

Although the Quaker founders were quickly overrun and outnumbered by other groups who immigrated to Pennsylvania, their religious concepts of equality and the dignity of each individual were firmly planted into American ideals. William Penn had created a threefold Holy Experiment: it was a haven for Quakers where they could exercise their faith and beliefs freely; he made a peaceful settlement with his Native American neighbors; and women were "equal in God's sight." In this enlightened system, women could participate more fully in the affairs of the Quaker meeting. Quaker women would become the leaven of social reform.

Chapter 4
The Legal Status of Women in the English and Dutch Colonies
In the Place God Hath Set Her

Key Topics

Courtship, Marriage and Divorce
The Legal Status of Women in the English Colonies
Dutch Women in New Netherlands
Childbirth and Motherhood

Chronology

1680 - The Dominion of New England, Restoration Government
Crown Orders all Marriages Performed by Clergyman
1765 - Blackstone's *Commentaries on the Laws of England* Published
1785 - 1812 - Midwife Martha Moore Ballard Chronicles Her Diary

Introduction

The lives of colonial women were tightly circumscribed by the patriarchal social order. In this class-conscious society, everyone paid respect or deference. No matter your social status, there was always someone above you who merited respect and honor. A bow or curtsy, a tip of the hat, honorifics in speech were just a few of the ways one expressed humility and respect for a superior. In the aristocratic planter society of Virginia or the Carolinas, the diverse middle colonies, or in New England, the social structure assigned everyone a ranking. White men of property ranked highest and slaves were the lowest social class.

To comply, women obeyed a prescribed regimen and observed the social rules carefully. One of those rules dictated that each person had a certain amount of space, a kind of invisible zone around them known as a compass. Females were required to keep within a smaller compass - a space just outlining her body. A woman's space was so minutely defined that she could not extend her arms. Maintaining a confined space insured that a woman preserved her dignity. To visualize a woman's compass, think of a stately minuet and the way in which people move on the dance floor. A women's compass never enlarged in life beyond those courtly steps. In her daily activities, the colonial woman was expected to stay close to home (within the domestic sphere) and act with restraint. Women in each of the colonies lived under a dictum of laws which did not grant them civil liberties and did not recognize them as equal partners in marriage. Depending upon their religious affiliation, married couples could or could not obtain a divorce.

Few women were literate and this helped perpetuate women's inferior status. Women's legal status varied somewhat among the colonies. Compared with the Spanish system described in chapter one, under English and Dutch laws women had a different legal status.

Colonial women were expected to marry, and bear many children. Courtship and marriage were followed by a cycle of childbirth about every two years until menopause or death ensued. Child birthing was a socially bonding experience for all women. The skill of the midwife was integral to women's health and the well-being of the community

Courtship in the Colonies

Courtship practices in seventeenth century English colonies varied with demographic regions, cultural norms and economic circumstances. In Virginia and the Carolinas, the combined factors of climate, disease and intensive agriculture meant that the adult death rate would always exceed the birth rate. The high mortality rate for newborns, infants and children further exacerbated this spiraling decline. Throughout the seventeenth and eighteenth centuries, the only way to maintain the population was through immigration not natural increase. The woman who came to America in the seventeenth century was guaranteed a husband, but courtship was a luxury and formality easily dispensed with. Consequently, with the dire shortage of women in the southern colonies, courtship was neither lengthy nor formal.

For the destitute, going to the colonies offered a whole new life. Buoyed by the prospect of a husband waiting at the docks and promising opportunity, women braved the voyage to Virginia. Poor men and women usually married at a later age after serving out an indentured contract. Among all classes, marriages were of shorter duration because life expectancy for both sexes did not exceed the age of 44.

According to the Oxford English dictionary, the word *woman* was a word synonymous with wife. In colonial and European society, the foremost objective for women was to get married and bear children. Since all women were to be married, most were in the seventeenth century. Courtship practices varied by region, by one's economic circumstance and by one's cultural background but one commonality rang true— being courted and getting married was the most important event for a woman.

Among close knit religious groups such as the Puritans and the Quakers, parents dominated courtship rites by choosing suitable mates for their children. Finding a husband of equal, or preferably better, social standing became the chief means to improving one's economic status. For many women a male prospect with landed wealth was sought and for a poor woman an ambitious man with skills or a trade was desirable.

Among the upper classes, more formal rituals of courtship played out. A young man could not just approach any young woman he wished to court. Social custom required that he first speak privately with her parents to gain their consent. This was especially true among the Society of Friends in the middle colonies. Quaker Thomas Chalkley, quite taken with Martha Betterton, was particularly impressed with her piety, virtue and modesty. He resolved, however, not to dwell on her qualities until he had secured permission from her family to court her and make a proposal of marriage.

In the southern colonies, because life expectancy was shorter, there were fewer parents who survived to help a son or daughter find a suitable mate. Historian Lorena Walsh in, "Till Death Do Us Part," examined marriage patterns in the seventeenth century Chesapeake colonies (Virginia and Maryland) and discovered the critical importance of the parents' survival in order to safeguard a daughter's future. While an orphaned female could legally inherit an estate by the age of sixteen, without a guardian to look out for her interests, she could easily be taken advantage of, swindled or deceived. Young women with both parents living had more protection and stood a better chance at making a good match. Among the young women who were already orphaned, there was a higher incidence of children born out of wedlock. Females who had lost their fathers had a higher incidence of pregnancy before marriage. The studies of southern women show not only the vital part their parents played during courtship but also how important the presence of the father was in protecting them and assuring that they would be respected.

Men courted women under the close supervision of parents but this did not hinder courting couples from seeking intimacy. Although ministers railed from the pulpit about the evils of fornication (either premarital or adulterous), the indulgence in premarital sex was quite common, and the results evident. Research shows that from the late seventeenth to the mid-eighteenth century the illegitimate birth rate and bridal pregnancy escalated. By the 1780s nearly 30 percent of all the women who married were already pregnant. Elders seemed more forgiving of consenting couples who were already betrothed, than of those sexually intimate couples who had no intention of marrying.

Privacy for courting couples was another matter, as colonial notions differed sharply from modern ideas in this regard. Privacy was closely linked to the "luxury" of personal space. Beds in homes, for instance, were usually occupied by several family members. It would have been quite common for children to grow up sleeping in the same bed or the same room as their parents, attuned to all the rhythms of life.

Courtship customarily began when young people engaged in country dances, met at family gatherings and celebrations, joined singing groups at church or attended sleigh rides and skating parties. With the labor of harvest completed, winter was the most popular season for courting. But winter months also meant shorter days and longer nights in a society where candles could not burn wastefully.

The Custom of Bundling

In New England, parents may have condoned premarital sex by allowing young people to engage in a custom known as bundling, a courtship practice which many groups brought with them from the Old World. In bundling, couples occupied the same bed without undressing. A girl's parents knew the suitor and supervised this courtship ritual to the daughter's advantage. If the young woman became pregnant, the parents knew the young man and he could be held accountable. Bundling reached a peak in popularity in the eighteenth century, concurrent with the increase in sexual promiscuity, and the rise in premarital pregnancy and illegitimate births. Bundling may have served as parental compromise. Faced with sexually active sons and daughters, parents tried to exert some control over courting couples. Historical anecdotes about the custom of bundling depict extreme practices such as placing the bundling board between male and female to prevent physical contact; or the myth that mothers supplied protective chastity garments for their daughters. Perhaps this popular verse, *The Bundling Maid,* contains some truth.

> Sometimes, says she, when she lies down,
> one cannot be encumbered with a gown.
> When maids and men favor courting,
> coats and gowns are laid aside,
> breeches take their flight,
> when time is gone, it shan't be long
> by courting candle-lite.

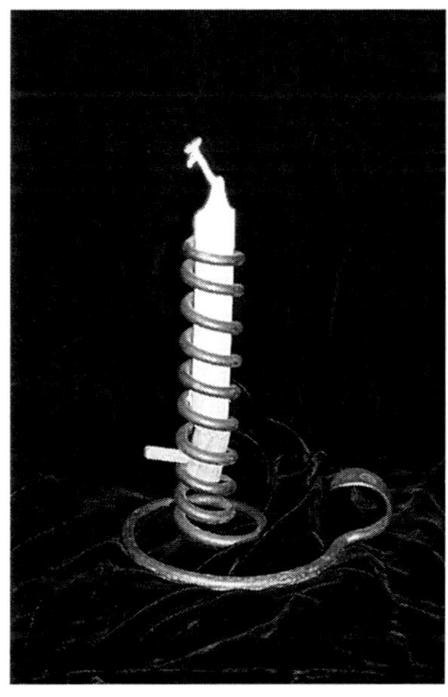

The colonial courting candle might serve as an effective means for parents to allot courting time to a prospective suitor. A favorable suitor got more time gauged by the higher candle which burned longer. The less-favored caller was assessed a shorter candle and a briefer visit.

Colonial Marriages

The Puritans praised marriage and discouraged the solitary life. In New England it was required by law that every young person without family be taken in by another family. They were usually servants or apprentices. This was particularly crucial in New England after 1670, when many young people were orphaned as a result of the Indian wars. Because Puritans appreciated the function of family in terms of companionship, support, and nurturing, concern went beyond the need to monitor young people. God had ordained that people should live together in a family, society, congregation, and community. Puritans perceived the family as a little commonwealth, a microcosm of the state. Marriage, like the government was patriarchal with rule and inheritance passed through the male line.

Ministers berated all women based upon Eve's tempting of Adam, but they considered a wife a great comfort as a helpmate and companion. Puritan ministers often preached on the benefits of marriage and wives.

> Women are Creatures without which there is no comfortable Living for man: It is true of them what is wont to be said of governments, That bad ones are better than none: They are a sort of Blasphemers then who despise and descry them and call them a necessary Evil, for they are a necessary Good; such as it was not good that man should be without.

Certainly the marriage of Anne and Simon Bradstreet belies our notion of cold, unfeeling Puritans. Anne's poem praised both the married life and her love and devotion for Simon. The union of John Winthrop and Margaret Tyndal (his third wife) exemplified wedded bliss. Winthrop, the epitome of the austere Puritan patriarch, relied on Margaret on a nearly equal par for decision making and household matters and their love letters attest to their devotion to one another. John's reference to Margaret as "My chiefe joy in this world," was countered by Margaret's salutations to her 'most sweet husband.' He attributed their successful marriage to living out the Puritan ideal, in which he functioned as sole authority and Margaret submitted to him. For, as he explained, "a true wife accounts her subjection her honor and freedom."

A young girl might embroider a sampler to practice her stitches and to learn her alphabet and numerals. More than any other group, Puritans permitted literacy for girls. Although they did not receive a formal education, most Puritan women learned to read in order to fulfill devotional scripture reading.

While making a good match granted personal gratification, one looked primarily for economic well-being in a partner, as marriage was the means whereby people passed on their inheritance to their children. A girl's parents took the upper hand in the selection of a husband because it was of critical importance for a daughter to have the guidance and protection of her parents in choosing a husband.

The actual stages of the marriage process differed in each colony, and depended upon the couple's religious affiliation. In New York, Virginia and the Carolinas, all under the established Church of England, and in Maryland under Roman Catholicism, marriage was a sacrament, usually celebrated within a Nuptial Mass. It was witnessed by clergy, family and friends, and (in the case of incompatibility) was very difficult to annul. In some faiths, mixed marriages were frowned upon. Both Puritans and Quakers discouraged their children from marrying outside of their faith, (an exogamous marriage) and Quaker meetings reported a high incidence of members being read out of the meeting for doing so. When Philadelphia Quaker

Betsy Ross, the patriotic flag maker of the Revolution, eloped and married Anglican John Ross, she was read out of the Quaker meeting and disowned by her family.

Quakers in Pennsylvania and Puritans in New England, spurning Anglican beliefs, did not regard marriage as a sacrament. Therefore they neither regarded the married state as any less blessed a calling than the religious life. Puritans treated it as a civil contract officiated by a magistrate of government. In most churches throughout all the colonies, officials required a public announcement of the upcoming marriage. This practice, known as the *banns,* was announced several times over a period of weeks before the wedding ceremony. The banns of matrimony alerted members of the community to come forward if they knew of any reason why a couple should not marry. Being already married to someone else was certainly an impediment and colonial courts heard many cases of alleged bigamy. Defendants in bigamy cases were almost exclusively the husbands.

Quakers conceived of marriage as another manifestation of the inner light, which was the core belief that a spark of the divine dwells in everyone. The solemn union of holy wedlock involved the couple, the family, and the Quaker meeting in a sacred deliberation. Once Quaker parents and the intended couple came into agreement, the meeting granted final approval before a wedding could take place. In fact, the meeting's sanction of the marriage took precedence over the parent's approval. In some cases, the meeting overruled a disapproving parent, or conversely disapproved of a union even when the parents had consented. The meeting regarded matrimony as a civil contract as well, and registered all marriages with the government. Quaker Historian J. William Frost states that the Society of Friends was very rigid in ruling on marriages and disapproved of exogamous marriages because they felt this could greatly hinder the growth of the meeting.

The Steps to Matrimony

Marriage customs, ceremonies, and celebrations also varied from group to group and colony to colony as each community honored traditions brought from the Old World and added on New World innovations. For example, Puritans established a definite rubric for matrimony, consisting of five steps:

1. Betrothal (Espousal) was the first step and depended upon the recognition and declaration of the impending marriage by both families. Celebrating and feasting, much like a modern engagement party, followed the espousal. For about the first fifty years in colonial New England, the minister officiated only over the espousal ceremony and not the wedding. He delivered a sermon to remind the congregation of the solemnity and seriousness of the couple's commitment, and reminded the couple that if either broke or violated the espousal, the other could sue for breach of promise.

2. Supplication of the Banns consisted of a series of public announcements of the espousal to inform the community of the impending marriage. The banns had to be announced a minimum of eight days before the marriage took place to allow enough time to ascertain anyone's objections.

3. The Marriage Ceremony- for Puritans a civil ceremony, for Anglicans and Catholics a sacrament celebrated in a Nuptial Mass, and for Quakers a religious and communal experience. With the Restoration of the Monarchy in 1680, English law mandated that a clergyman also perform the wedding ceremony in all instances in all colonies.

4. The Marriage Celebration - the ceremony was followed by much merrymaking among all groups and religious affiliations and included heavy imbibing of rum, and feasting. Puritans, however, did forbid dancing as that kind of enthusiastic behavior might be inspired by the Devil.

5. The Consummation of Marriage was the sexual union of husband and wife. The Puritans believed that without consummation, the marriage was incomplete.

Colonials, yes, even somber Puritans and serious Quakers, had a wholesome outlook on sex and affection in marriage and believed that wives as well as husbands should be fulfilled. There was, however, some caution given. The church reminded married couples of the importance of placing God first and foremost, lest an excess of sexual desire border on idolatry. Man and wife were admonished to express passion and love for each other, but always tempered with a greater love of God.

Divorce under English Law: Separated from the Chains of Matrimony

Under common law, two types of divorce were possible in the English colonies. The first type, *Divortium a vinculo matrimonii,* meant literally divorce from the chains of matrimony, or *absolute divorce*. If allowed, although rarely granted, it would permit either party to remarry. Supporting patriarchy, the absolute divorce law intended to protect a husband from an adulterous wife, to ensure the legitimacy of one's heirs and ultimately served English nobility. Obtaining a divorce was easier said than done. It could only be granted through an act of Parliament. In the colonies, only in New England, where marriage was a civil ceremony, did courts permit an absolute divorce.

Generally, husbands or wives could obtain another type of divorce. *Divortium a mensa et thoro*, literally, divorce from bed and board, i.e. separation from household. The law permitted this type of divorce for complaints of adultery, abandonment and cruelty. Similar to present day legal separation, the divorce from bed and board dissolved the marriage but neither party was free to remarry. In an absolute divorce the children were declared illegitimate, whereas in a divorce of household, that is separation, the children retained their legitimacy. In the English colonies, the most frequent grounds for divorce were adultery or desertion. Puritans considered the failure to consummate the marriage (usually presented in court as the husband's failure to perform) an admissible complaint. Consummation of the marriage was so important to Puritans that if sexual union was not fulfilled either the husband or the wife could petition the court for a divorce.

Quakers also allowed for *Divortium a mensa et thoro*, divorce from bed and board, in cases of adultery. Nonetheless, there are fewer Quaker divorces on record. This may be attributed to the fact that the Quaker meeting would often act as the arbiter for quarrelsome couples.

Colonial Dames in Court

1655 - This Court, considering the sad complaint of Goody Beckwith of Fairfield, in reference to her husband's deserting her do declare by evidence which hath been presented the manner of her husband's departure and discontinuance they judge that if the said Goody Beckwith, wife of Thomas shall upon oath testify to the Magistrates that are shortly to keep court at Stratford, that her husband's departure was as others have testified it to bee; and yet she hath not heard from him nor of him any ways since he deserted her, the said Magistrate may give her a bill of Divorce and set her free from her said husband.

1660 - This court orders, that in the case Sarah North hear not of her husband by the seventh year be expired (he having been absent six already) then she shall be free from her conjugal bonds.

1660 - Upon the motion of Elisabeth Vicars the late widow of Mr. Richard Price deceased, craving the benefit of the law respecting her thirds of a house and land in Boston; which was alienated by her husband Price in his life time unto Mr. John Joyliffe she not having given up her thirds. The court orders Mr. Joyliffe to set out to the said Elisabeth her thirds of the said estate, or else the court will appoint a committee for that end.

1670 - Mary Chelson being imprisoned and called before the Court to answer for her committing of fornication and having a bastard child, which she owned in court and charged Stephen Jenkins of Piscataqua to be the father of it. The court sentenced her to be whipped with fifteen stripes to pay fees of Court and prison standing committed until this sentence is performed.

1677 - This court grants Experience Shephard, the wife of William Shepherd a release from her conjugal tye to the said William Shepherd he having deserted her with a resolve never to return to his wife again.

1678 - Elizabeth Langeberry being committed to prison for her drunkeness and other misdemeanors and appearing before the Court to answer for the same. She owned that she had drank too much and that Thomas Ockerby pulled her into his lap against her will. The court sentenced her to pay ten shillings in money as a fine to the county and fees of Court standing committee until the sentence be performed.

From: *The Public Records of the Colony of Connecticut*

The Legal Status of English Colonial Women: Under His Wing and Protection

Because of differing statutes of church and government, the legal status of women in seventeenth century America varied from colony to colony. As we have seen, survival was much more difficult in the southern colonies at this time than in New England. Because of the high death rates in the South in this century, both married and single women had more opportunity to inherit an estate than in the other colonies or in England. By contrast, in New England longevity made for a much more stable patriarchal order where women remained legally subordinate to men and patrilineal inheritance was assured. There wives rarely inherited an estate because husbands lived long enough to bequeath their property to sons. Even if the husband left a portion of an estate to his widow, he usually instructed his son to manage his mother's inheritance for her.

The *Femme Couvert*

The legal status of women in the English colonies as defined by English Common Law was compiled by William Blackstone in *Commentaries on the Laws of England* in 1765, and used as a legal reference. Reflecting patriarchal will and intent, females were entitled to protection by their fathers, husbands or legal guardians. Because seventeenth century society assumed that every woman would marry, and most did, the law viewed their status as married, widowed or soon to be married. The legal status of a married female, a *femme couvert*, literally meant a woman covered. This defined the legal status of most women of childbearing years in the colonial period. *Femme Couvert* idealized one of the concepts of English Common Law, the enduring notion of the unity of person. This concept incorporated the legal partnership of man and wife into the sole entity of the husband, and regarded that unity as one person. This is evident in all marriage contracts which listed only the husband's name. Through marriage the husband and wife became one person, meaning that the very being or legal existence of the woman ceased. The wife's identity was suspended and her person consolidated into that of the husband as the law stated "under whose wing, protection and *cover* she performs everything. Since a *femme couvert*, a married woman, no longer existed as a person she could not sue, draft a will, make a contract, or buy or sell property. If she brought property into the marriage, her husband managed it and he could invest or spend her assets. All of her personal effects, including clothing, were incorporated into the husband's estate. But, if she had the means and the wherewithal, a wife might take preventive measures, by signing a prenuptial contract. This would protect her property and any inheritance she might receive from her own family. A prenuptial contract was particularly advisable in a second marriage to protect the inheritance of her children from the first marriage. Upon remarriage, without a prenuptial contract, the wife's property and her children's inheritance were assumed by the new husband/stepfather.

A married woman in New England was addressed not as Misses, (Mrs.) but as *Goodwife*, a title conveniently shortened to *Goody*. A goodwife's name was noticeably missing from legal contracts but, when necessary, she might be referred to as "Mr. John Smith, his wife. Colonial women were well aware of their limitations and status. For example, Goodwife Mary Russell of Concord, Massachusetts, in a letter to her brother, apologized for not coming to Boston to take care of some family matters, stating "I should have answered your letter long before this had I known that we were to come to Boston, but as you know I am a *femme couvert* and cannot act for myself."

The question of what a *femme couvert* could or could not do often complicated legal proceedings. An abandoned wife who had lost the "wing and protective cover" of her husband could be easily exploited. Because Elizabeth White's husband had been absent for many years, her neighbors took advantage and preyed upon the White estate. She testified in court that on the night of June 17, 1770, Lucy and Nathaniel Butler had stolen several of her sheep, mutilated and slaughtered them. The Butlers did not deny the charges of damage to Elizabeth's livestock and the court ruled that they must pay for the loss of property. The Butlers then proceeded to appeal the decision to a superior court contending the lower court should never have admitted Elizabeth's complaint. The reason stated was her status as a *femme couvert* who could neither bring a law suit to court nor sue on behalf of her husband. Thus, the court of appeals overturned the lower court's decision and ruled in favor of the Butlers. The defendants were not required to pay damages to Elizabeth. Given her legal status, the Butlers, or anyone else, were free to damage or confiscate Elizabeth's property with impunity.

The *Femme Sole*

Another legal status for women, that of *femme sole*, literally a woman alone, referred to a single woman. Females did not necessarily have to be single to be recognized as a *femme sole*; a single adult female or a married woman might acquire this legal status. For instance, a woman whose husband had abandoned her could, after a given number of years, act on her own behalf as a *femme sole;* but a married women living with her husband needed his consent to petition the court for this title. There were advantages to attaining this status. A *femme sole* could conduct business through the buying or selling of property, make contracts or bring a suit to court, and she could also be sued. A literate, informed woman versed in law found it much easier to petition for this status, and of course, then as now, the filing of legal petitions involved time, effort and the financial means to do so.

As the number of widows and orphans in the colonies increased during the Indian wars, in New England particularly, the poverty among single mothers and widows increased. As the number of poor began to mount, local officials surmised that enterprising women might better fend for themselves and their children and not be a burden on the community, or public charity. Thus, colonial legislatures passed laws known as empowering acts, which granted poor women the right to act as *femme soles*. These women joined the ranks of *femme sole* traders who could act on their own behalf and operate a business. Unlike *femme couverts*, under the protection of husbands, *femme soles* retained an identity as individuals, especially when dealing in legal matters. The case of Margaret Brent, an independent Maryland landowner, is a good example.

Some *femme sole* traders were married women who had been appointed by their husbands. In this case, a married *femme sole*, granted duties much like power of attorney, acted on her husband's behalf. Frequently, a husband occupied in fishing or a maritime trade would designate his wife to administer the household or family business in his absence. In this situation, the husband summoned a neighbor to act as a witness, and in the transaction, he designated his wife a *deputy husband*. By the eighteenth century, with the impact of the imperial wars in the colonies, courts granted widows an immediate status of *femme sole.*

Courts also distinguished the status of *femme sole* and *femme couvert* in legal decisions. A case in point is that of Rachael Wormley, a Massachusetts housewife, who had been deserted by her husband. Rachael was convinced that her husband was a bigamist. Her chief concern was not his infidelity or desertion but rather, as she explained to the court, the ambiguousness of her legal status and the ownership of family property. Under the burden of proof, the court did not render a final decision until two years later, when evidence of bigamy was deemed conclusive and the marriage was dissolved. The court declared Rachael Wormley a *femme sole* who could act on her own behalf, manage and own the property outright, and get on with her life.

A Relict or Widow

English law referred to a widow as a *relic,* or *relict,* literally something left over from the estate, much like furniture or an heirloom. Nowhere was male dominance more evident than in the court's treatment of a widow. When a wife and mother died, there was no loss to family continuity and husbands generally remarried in less than three years. But when the husband died, it meant the break up of the household. The family ceased to exist. Under the law of primogeniture, the eldest son was entitled to the estate and sons always inherited over a daughter. This law also specified that if there were no male heirs, the estate was divided up equally among the daughters. But, if a male heir to the estate died, his sisters and brothers were not entitled to any inheritance. The estate was then passed on to the children of the eldest son as his heirs.

But whether or not there was a will, a widow was entitled to one third of her husband's estate, known as a widow's third or dower rights. A few weeks after the death of the husband, Probate Court-appointed officials made a thorough inventory of the estate. Leaving no corner, niche or closet unsearched, they inventoried the contents of the household. The barn, tools, livestock and land were also inventoried. If the family owned slaves, their value as well as their modest dwellings and few possessions were appraised for the estate inventory. Records of these estate inventories show wealth or poverty and render valuable information about colonial families.

In some colonies, the widow's third might be used to pay off any debts owed by the estate. Since a husband could leave his widow more than the requisite widow's third, and/or he could specify that her eligibility for more depended upon her remaining single, a widow might forfeit her dower right if she remarried. It was more common for a man to leave a larger share of the estate to his children than to his widow. Once again, conditions which existed in seventeenth century southern colonies had created exceptions. In those places where higher mortality rates left a widow with young children, of necessity husbands willed an entire estate to the wife who was expected to manage it until the heir came of age.

The Legal Status of Colonial Dutch Women: Manus et Usus

The women of New Netherlands lived under a less restrictive legal system than did other colonial women. Under Dutch laws, women had much of the same *legal* privilege and benefit as men whether in Old or New Netherlands. First, the Dutch code, for the most part, gave women legal rights on a par with the men, and second, women could choose from among two legal options. Some of this liberality can be attributed to the Dutch economy's reliance on maritime trade which took husbands away from home. In their absence, for the sake of the family's wellbeing, husbands delegated much of the economic decision-making and responsibility to their wives. Fathers trained their daughters in financial management and bequeathed them property just as they did their sons. Furthermore, a daughter's right to inheritance ensured her economic security and independence when selecting a husband.

Unlike the English legal system, under Dutch law, women could inherit and own property. When a woman married, she freely chose either of two legal positions, a *manus* or a *usus* marriage. A wife choosing *manus* status lived much like the *femme couvert* in the English legal system, subject to her husband and completely dependent on him. Rights to her own property were suspended during marriage and if widowed, her former estate was split in half to be shared with her husband's heirs. A wife chose the *manus status* for the security her husband provided. On the other hand, if she chose the *usus status*, she lost none of her power, legal rights or property that she had enjoyed as a single woman. She could retain her own surname, engage in business, own property, draw up contracts, take legal action, and sue or be sued. Because of this legal latitude, Dutch women could make a significant economic contribution to the family and the community. Translating economic advantage to increased opportunity, it is surprising that in 1660, about sixty percent of all Dutch women were illiterate; more surprising, illiteracy among men was only slightly lower. Most Dutch colonials could do no more than sign their names. The Dutch acumen for commercial enterprise placed more emphasis on being numerate than literate.

The Legal Status of Women in New France

Inheritance is usually the key to understanding the legal rights and status of women in any given historical period or place. But it is difficult to describe or generalize women's status in New France because the legal system in their country of origin, France, was neither uniform nor standard but complex, and varied by region, custom and tradition. Laws deriving from medieval law codes often meant that women lived under the inheritance of primogenitor (compare with the English) but there were exceptions to this as well. In some places, a system of equal division of an estate between males and females developed. Noblewomen might hold land and title, and lower ranking women might operate businesses, but one can find just as many exceptions as inclusions of these provisions.

What was standard for women of Old and New France is marriage customs. All women passed from the authority of their fathers to the authority of their husbands. Both Old and New France adhered to Roman Catholicism. In each place, marriage was an inviolable sacrament which meant that divorce was difficult to obtain. The *Canon* made divorce nearly impossible except in cases of consanguinity (close relationship by blood) or adultery.[1] In cases of adultery the double standard prevailed as women were held to a higher moral standard than men. Divorce or an annulment of a marriage might take years and required that people have the economic means to pursue that legal process within the church.

In colonial provinces such as Louisiana, among Creole families where business acumen and entrepreneurship were valued, women could operate and inherit estates and run the family business (usually a plantation). This was true particularly in the absence of males (on military duty) or when the family lacked a male heir.

Childbirth and Motherhood

From girlhood on, females witnessed the travails of childbirth. Married by their early twenties, colonial women began an almost perpetual cycle of pregnancy, childbirth, and breast-feeding. They averaged twelve births and hoped at least six or seven of the children would survive. Since life expectancy for women in the seventeenth century was thirty-five years of age, most did not survive to menopause. Women who did live into menopause and displayed the symptoms of this change, were misunderstood and often labeled as aberrant, eccentric or crazy.

For the most part, women's lives were taken up with the ordeal of childbearing and perpetual child care. During pregnancy, a woman's health was particularly fragile. An expectant mother prepared for the possibility of her own death in childbirth by making a funeral shroud for herself while preparing clothing and linens for the baby. If both the mother and the newborn died in childbirth, they were customarily buried together with the baby cradled on the mother's left arm.

During the seventeenth and eighteenth centuries, the child birthing event was exclusively a female affair. Male physicians were rarely called upon and midwives experienced in delivering babies assisted expectant mothers. Childbirth was a rite of passage for women and an opportunity for all women in the community to help the mother by forming a network of support. Unwed mothers were no exception. They received compassionate attention from other women during labor, childbirth and recovery.

That same support was given to members of the community who were sick. When someone became ill, midwives and neighbors descended on them bringing food, cheer, assistance and prayers. When illness struck a family, women worked in shifts attending to the individ-

1. *Canon*, church Law.

ual around the clock. Those women who could write and keep diaries filled their memoirs with notations of nearly daily visitations to nurse the sick within their family or village. Visitors generally arrived unannounced but welcomed. People got sick, were cared for and died in their homes, and children grew up accustomed to witnessing both birth and death as normal life events.

Mothers of Invention: Midwife Martha Moore Ballard

Midwives performed their craft within the discipline of medicine and under a physician's supervision. As part of their training, they witnessed autopsies and gained useful knowledge of anatomy and disease. The midwives' journals are informative on the nature of their practice, and a significant account is that of Maine resident and midwife, Martha Moore Ballard. She managed to keep a detailed diary of her work through continuous entries for twenty-seven years, from 1785 to 1812. In its entirety, her diary recorded births, deaths, illnesses, an accounting of her housekeeping duties and expenses, the people she visited and those who called on her including physicians and legal authorities who relied on her accounting of births and deaths.

Martha Moore Ballard's diary is important as a comprehensive account of childbirth, and medical and obstetrical practices in early America. Martha began her 30 years of midwifery at age 42, when her six children (stretched out in ages from newborn to 20) were still underfoot and needing attention. Serving as an apprentice to an experienced midwife, she learned through observation and instruction how to treat illnesses and injuries using folk remedies such as homegrown herbs. A gleaning of Martha's diary reveals that she delivered a total of 996 babies, and gave birth to nine children herself.

Martha detailed the midwives' prescribed duties. They made house calls on the sick and, in an age before morticians, also prepared the dead for burial. Martha expressed sadness over the loss of her patients. "I heard that Mrs. Clayton's child departed this life yesterday, and that she is thot [sic] expiring." Next day's entry notes, "She (Mrs. Clayton) departed this life about 1 p.m. and I assisted to lay her out and laid her infant in her arms the first such instance I ever saw and the first woman that died in the childbed which I delivered." In another entry she writes, "Little William McMaster expired at 3 o'clock. Mrs. Paten and I laid out the child. Poor mother how distriest [sic] was her case, near the hour of labour and those children never very sick. Now at home, it is nine o'clock, morn and I feel depresse't. I must take some rest."

Always on the move, in one three week period alone she made sixteen medical calls, cared for her ailing husband, attended a woman in false labor, delivered four babies, took medication to a neighbor, prepared three corpses for burial, harvested herbs and made medicinal preparations. In payment for her services, like other colonial goodwives, Martha engaged in barter; she charged eight shillings per delivery but accepted payment in rum, sugar, coffee, shoes, flatirons, butter, wheat, rye, calico, linen or rice.

The prevalence of childhood diseases claimed many young children before the age of six, and many newborns did not survive beyond infancy. However, we cannot presume that because of the high infant mortality, parents were accustomed to the loss of children and did not form close attachments. Martha shared her grief over the death of three of her children to a diphtheria epidemic in 1769. Thereafter, she recorded their deaths as an annual memorial in her diary. The experiences of other colonial goodwives substantiate this. Abigail Adams related in letters to her husband, John, her grief and long bouts with depression over the loss of a baby in childbirth.

Conclusion

Whether one resided in the aristocratic planter society of Virginia or the Carolinas, the diverse middle colonies, or in New England, the social structure assigned everyone a ranking. White men of property ranked highest and slaves were the lowest social class. The lives of colonial women were tightly circumscribed by the patriarchal social order. In this class conscious society, everyone paid respect or deference. No matter your social status, there was always someone above you who merited respect and honor. A bow or curtsy, a tip of the hat, honorifics in speech were just a few of the ways one expressed humility and respect for a superior.

Courtship was brief and premarital sex commonplace among our religious forebears. Whether religious denominations regarded matrimony as a sacrament or a civil ceremony, they considered it a binding covenant and it was difficult to obtain a divorce.

Women, neither slave nor free, possessed an inferior status strictly defined by law. To maintain that inferior position whether married, widowed or single, a female kept within her compass, that small invisible space around her physical body. Women were expected to marry and most did. Within their short life span, they experienced pregnancy and childbirth in two year cycles, until death or menopause ended their fertility. Their critical role as progenitors was neither acknowledged nor respected. Women had little legal protection from abandonment or physical maltreatment. They held great social responsibility for the care and survival of their children and the operation of their household.

Chapter 5
Women's Work in the Colonies
Her Household Shall Be Clothed in Scarlet

Key Topics

The African Slave Trade in the Colonies
The Slave Codes
The Exploitation of Female Slaves
The Peculiar Institution of Slavery
Colonial Homes and Women's Work in the Colonial Economy

Chronology

1619 - Arrival of First Africans to Virginia
1640 - Earliest Documentation of Slavery as a Legal Status in Colonies
1672 - Royal Africa Company Chartered to Sell Slaves in Colonies
1694 - Dinah Nuthead, Official Printer for Maryland Colonial Assembly
1700 - Colony of South Carolina- Slaves Comprise sixty percent of Population
1700 - 1763 - Imperial Wars - Women Appointed Deputy Husbands
1738 - Elizabeth Timothy, First Woman to Publish Newspaper in Colonies
1777 - Mary Katherine Goddard, Baltimore's First Post Mistress, City of Baltimore's Official Printer

Introduction

The ultimate success of the Spanish, French, and English colonies in America can be attributed largely to the Africans whom they enslaved. Africans did not willingly migrate to the colonies. The American Colonial Slave Trade holds the shameful record as the largest forced migration in history. Bound by hand and foot and branded, slaves were forced from their native Africa. Most highly prized were females slaves who were sold for their procreative powers. At the very bottom of the colonial society, female slaves endured harsh treatment and sexual exploitation from white owners. In return, they served white families as cooks, nannies and field hands. Their labor and expertise in skills such as cookery, animal husbandry and rice, cotton and indigo cultivation helped the colonial economy prosper.

The colonial woman lived out her days and years in her home and its environs. Her domestic sphere encompassed the house, a kitchen garden, and the poultry and swine yard. In this pre-industrial world, the home was the manufacturing center. Women spun cloth, made all the clothing for their families as well as kitchen, bed and bath linens and dipped candles. In their herb gardens they cultivated medicinal plants. Their greatest effort and most of their time was spent in food production. But by the eighteenth century more women operated businesses or were engaged in trades such as printing or publishing.

The African Slave Trade in the Colonies

In 1619, it was intended that the first Africans work as indentured servants. They arrived in Virginia on board a Dutch ship. By 1640, colonial laws defined the status of Africans as permanent bondage, a condition their children would inherit. Most of them were brought from the West Coast of Africa, the Slave Coast near the Senegal and Niger Rivers. Within their tribes, women from these regions had worked customarily as merchants, traders, and farmers and held social prominence. In the Benin culture, women were respected as the preservers of the tribe's history. When they were sold into slavery and sent to America, they lost social rank and dropped to the very bottom of colonial society, and they suffered the double bind of discrimination as women and oppression as slaves.

Africans apprehended for the slave trade took extraordinary measures to resist enslavement. While being transported on slave ships for the Atlantic crossing, many jumped overboard in suicidal drowning; others simply refused to eat. From the point of capture in Africa to the final destination in the colonies, the enslavement process took a tragic toll. Historian David Eltis estimates that the trade peaked between 1780 and 1790, and from 1771 to 1811 three million slaves were brought to the New World. From 1781 to 1800, the rate of mortality for slaves in transport averaged ten percent. For the transatlantic crossing, he estimated a two percent daily mortality and mortality increased over time. After 1835, the smaller, faster ships were packed with more slaves. Captains of slave ships filled the holds to the point of slave suffocation. In 1842, the *Minerva* a ship measuring 36.5 feet in length and 10 feet in width, transported 126 children for the American slave market. They were placed in a hold with a ceiling clearance of 5.7 feet.

Onboard the ships, the captives, segregated by sex, endured the most horrible ordeal of capture—the Atlantic crossing, or middle passage. The medical journal of one ship's surgeon, Dr. Alexander Falconbridge described how slave ships, unsighted and several miles off the coast could be detected approaching port by the telltale foul stench. Falconbridge made several crossings on slave ships and described the gruesome conditions onboard.

> I saw pregnant women give birth to babies while chained to corpses which Our drunken overseer had not removed. The younger women fared best at First as they were allowed to come on deck as companions for our crew. Toward the end of the run (which lasted nearly six weeks) the mortality Thinned out in the main hold (decks below where the male slaves were kept) And some score of women were driven below as company for the males.

His observations reveal the callous attitudes toward female slaves. Even though women might be sexually assaulted by the crew, Falconbridge regarded the younger women on the open deck as "faring better." Many African women, raped in captivity, gave birth onboard the ship just as Falconbridge described, and others were pregnant by the time they arrived in America.

NEGROES FOR SALE

A Negro woman 24 years of age, and has two children, one eight and the other three years. Said Negroes will be sold separately or together as desired. She will be sold low for cash, or exchanged for victuals. Negroes for Sale a girl of about 20 years of age raised in Virginia, and her two female children, one four and the other two years old—is remarkably strong and healthy—never having had a day's sickness, with the exception of smallpox, in her life. The children are fine and healthy. She is very prolific in her generating qualities, and affords a rare opportunity to any person who wishes to raise a family of strong and healthy servants for their own use.

While the greatest numbers of Africans were shipped to South America, the slave population in North America increased significantly from about 20,000 in 1690, to a half million by the end of the eighteenth century. Import figures are not an accurate gauge of the number of slaves in each of the colonies. Although fewer slaves were transported to North America, acquiring slaves in the English colonies took on a different form. Because tobacco cultivation was an expensive venture, some colonists found it more lucrative to breed slaves than to cultivate crops. In Virginia, especially, owners transformed their plantations into breeding farms and the reproductive potential of female slaves, known as breeder women, became a selling point at auctions.

The Slave Codes

A predominant conversation among scholars of American Slave History concerns when the status of African and African-American people changed. Historians mark Virginia colonial legislation as a key turning point, when the black indentured servant's hope of freedom was increasingly being replaced by black slavery by mid-seventeenth century. In 1705, the Virginia General Assembly removed any lingering doubt about this terrible transformation; it declared and sealed the fate of Africans and African-Americans for generations to come.

> All servants imported and brought into the Country...who were not Christians in their native Country...shall be accounted and be slaves. All Negro, mulatto and Indian slaves within this dominion...shall be held to be real estate. If any slave resist his master...correcting such slave, and shall happen to be killed in such correction...the master shall be free of all punishment...as if such accident never happened.

This *Slave Code*, which would also serve as a model for other colonies, went even further.[1] Since enslaved persons did not own property and lacked the means to pay fines, the law imposed harsh physical punishments. It stated that slaves needed written permission to leave their plantation, that slaves found guilty of murder or rape would be hanged, that for robbery or any other major offence, the slave would receive sixty lashes and be placed in the stocks, and for minor offenses have his or her ears cut off. For associating with whites, slaves could be whipped, branded, or maimed.

Legal Decisions Regarding Slavery in Colonial Virginia

1662 - Whereas some doubt has arisen as to whether children got by any Englishman and a Negro woman should be slave or free, it is therefore enacted that all children born in this country shall be held bound or free according to the condition of the mother. If any Christian shall commit fornication with a Negro man or woman, the offender shall pay double the fines generally imposed for this act.

1667 - Whereas some doubts have arisen whether children slaves by birth who are partakers of the sacrament of baptism are made free; it is enacted that the conferring of Baptism does not alter the condition of the person as to his bondage or freedom. Masters may still carefully endeavor to propagate Christianity by permitting children though slaves to a greater growth in Christian charity to be admitted to the Sacrament

1669 - Be it enacted that if any slave resists his master, and by the extremity of the correction should chance to die, that his or her death *shall not be accounted felony,* and the master be acquit from molestation since it cannot be presumed that prepensed malice should induce any man to destroy his own estate.

1. *Slave Code,* Virginia colony's legislation is cited as the landmark formation of slavery in North America even though the practice probably existed before this time; the 1705 laws both formalized and legalized the practice.

Formerly, in the case of a dispute with their master, a seventeenth century slave in Virginia could be brought before a court for judgment. With the enactment of the 1705 slave codes, this was no longer the case. A slave owner who sought to break the most rebellious of slaves could do so with impunity, knowing any punishment he inflicted, including death, would not result in even the slightest reprimand.

By the early eighteenth century, slaves comprised the majority of the population in South Carolina, and at least 50 percent in Virginia. Consequently, the white population feared slave rebellions and the Slave Codes were an attempt to create a tightly controlled system. These laws restricted travel and participation in religious events such as funerals because it was during mass gatherings that insurrections could be planned or carried out. Slaves were forbidden to carry firearms, could not testify in court, or expect a trial by jury. Under colonial laws, it was inconceivable for African-Americans to enjoy the protection of the law or seek citizenship. American colonial society devised slavery as a "peculiar institution" which conceptualized slaves as chattel that is, property, not people. Needless to say, interracial marriage was forbidden and slaves could not be educated.

The Exploitation of Female Slaves

The indignities imposed by the institution of slavery affected male and female slaves differently. With a severe shortage of female slaves (there were three males to one female) slave holders sought females of childbearing years, in order to propagate more slaves. As Falconbridge attests, from the moment of capture, a female slave might be sexually exploited. Once in America, they were forced to mate with male slaves, and were subject to rape by white owners, or overseers. For their own sexual gratification, owners used the women as recreational property a "privilege" they passed on to male visitors and neighbors as a form of hospitality. One guest at Mount Vernon complained of George Washington's lack of hospitality which he expressed to a friend, "Will you believe it? I have not humped a single mulatto since I am here." Women were flogged and locked up when they refused to yield to a white master, and there were numerous cases of homicide in which a female slave killed a master who had forced copulation and abused her.

One of the most tragic cases was a pair of slaves, Peggy and Patrick, lovers who were put on trial in 1830 for the murder of their white slave master at Kent, Virginia. Because the testimony of another slave was admitted, the details of the case are known. Peggy's master had kept her confined in chains because she refused him sexual favor and he had threatened to have several men including Patrick hold her down. The witness explained that Peggy had refused to submit to him because her master was her father. In another case, Lucy, a mulatto slave, killed her master because of the sexual abuse he inflicted. Fifteen hundred slaves from adjacent farms were compelled to witness her execution by hanging. Because the law defined slaves as property and not people, if a white man raped another white man's slaves he was charged with trespassing. Rape was used only to describe a sexual crime by a black man. The laws defining rape had been enacted in every southern state to forbid interracial sex but were flagrantly violated by white men. Ironically, the statutes existed not to protect slaves but to prohibit the "pollution of the white race."

A female slave's fertility meant profits for her master but a pregnant slave never received prenatal care or the help of an attending physician for a difficult delivery. If available, a slave woman in labor might have a slave midwife. Neither their sex, pregnancy nor maternity ever exempted female slaves from heavy field work or other intensive labor. Slave owner's journals describe the kinds of work the women performed. George Washington, who maintained detailed accounts of life at his Mt. Vernon estate, explains in his farm journal the type of work he assigned to the women,

> At the Ferry set 3 plows to work- but the girl Eby to one of them. The women preparing and hoeing in the ground in front of the house. The women were hoeing the wet part of the ground between the meadows which the plows could not touch. Two men were cutting trunnels

for fences, and the women were carrying rails from the swamp side to the division fence.

One of the most revealing journals on the condition of female slaves in the South is the diary of Frances (Fanny) Kemble, an English actress married briefly to Pierce Butler of Georgia. The following diary entries were written for one day's visitations, and present a firsthand account of the pitiful condition of female slaves.

> Fanny - has had six children all dead but one. She came to beg to have her work in the field lightened.
> Nanny - has had three children; two of them are dead. She came to implore that the rule of sending them into the field shortly after their confinement might be altered.
> Sophy - Lewis' wife came to beg for some old linen, she has had ten children and five of them are dead. The principal favor she asked was a piece of meat, which I gave her.
> Sally - Scipio's wife has had two miscarriages, three children born and one of whom is dead.
> Charlotte - Renty's wife has had two miscarriages and is with child again. She was almost crippled from rheumatism and showed me a pair of poor swollen knees that made my heart ache.
>
> Sarah - has had four miscarriages had brought seven children into the world, five of them are dead. She is again with child and complaining of pains in her back, and an internal tumor which swells from the exertion of working in the fields.
> Molly - has had nine children, six of them still alive.

Frances concluded from her observations of female slaves and their child birthing history that,

> The number they bear as compared with the number they rear is I think a fair gauge of the effect of the system on their own health and that of their offspring. There was hardly one of these women who might not have been a candidate for a bed in a hospital and they had come to me after working all day in the fields.

Ironically, although slaves in the South lived in a caste system based on race and class, they coexisted with whites closely and intimately. A poignant example of this was the slave mammies who often acted as *wet nurses* or surrogate mothers to these white children.[2] According to visitors in southern homes, white babies suckled by female slaves were quite commonplace. Mrs. Carter, of the famous Shirley plantation in Virginia, told Englishman Phillip Fithian that all eleven of her children had been nursed by slave women. The practice is also documented in newspapers, such as the advertisement which appeared in the *Georgia Gazette.*

Wanted by the Month

A Healthy Careful Negroe [sic] Wench for a Wet Nurse Preferable one without a child will be most agreeable, or with a child, not above six months old.

Georgia Gazette

Outside of southern culture, the practice was regarded as unseemly. The English Reverend Jonathan Boucher confided to a friend his concern for rearing a family in colonial Virginia,

> I cannot be reconciled to having my bairns [babies] nursed by a Negro wench. Seriously, that is a monstrous fault I find among the people here and surely it is the source of many disadvantages to their children

The practice of using slaves as wet nurses produced some strange attitudes and behavior. When Eliza Lucas Pinckney, of South Carolina, visited the English Royal family, the Princess Augusta was pleased that Eliza's daughter, Harriet, showed no alteration in her

2. *Wet nurse*, a woman who breast feeds another woman's child.

hair or complexion from having been suckled by a black woman. Englishman John Davis heard a southern lady say of her son that, "Richard always grieves when Quasheehaw is whipped, because she suckled him."

The slaves' quarters at the Hermitage Plantation. Slaves lived in one-room, dirt-floored shacks which bred infectious diseases such as typhus, dysentery and lockjaw. (Photo courtesy of the Library of Congress.)

Some slaves were assigned domestic work in the big house, i.e. the master's residence, and worked as cooks, mammies, or housekeepers. White women and slaves interacted daily in the comings and goings of tending a household and farm. Plantation mistresses trained their slaves in domestic crafts, as dairy or poultry maids, or textile weavers, or hired other women to teach them. With the exception of those who learned to spin and make cloth, female slaves were not compensated for their work. In contrast, male slaves skilled in trades such as carpentry, black smithy, or ironmongery could work for wages and save earnings toward the purchase of their freedom. Slave women who worked as domestics saw less of their families than those who worked in the fields. A personal servant had no privacy and remained on call twenty-four hours a day. Frances Kemble Butler observed that,

> Chambermaids and seamstresses often sleep in their mistresses apartments, but with no bedding at all. (Black chambermaids and valets slept on the floor.) I know of an instance of a woman, who has been married eleven years, and yet has never been allowed to sleep out of her mistress's chamber.

Slave women also worked longer hours than the men. After a day's work in the fields, which during harvest or a full moon could continue until 11:00 p.m., the chores of their own households and child care were waiting.

The Peculiar Institution of American Slavery

The contribution of slave labor to the colonial economy is inestimable. Many plantation owners became wealthy from the intensive work of slaves who received no pay for their labor. Slaves brought knowledge of yam and rice cultivation, and experience in cattle breeding to the colonies. They introduced foods and plants as yet unknown in the New World and many of the dishes regarded as southern cuisine or *Creole* were African and introduced by the female slaves who cooked for the entire plantation. The slave women created artistic quilts characterized by their African patterns and red-dyed fabrics. Slave labor was utilized throughout the English colonies, both north and south, but there were distinctive features. Typically, a northern household might own one or two slaves. But, after the Indian wars in New England, more Native Americans were captured and enslaved. Some were shipped to the West Indies slave market, but others were purchased for Puritan households. In the southern colonies planters who could afford slaves might own as many as one-hundred. (At the peak of his plantation's production, Thomas Jefferson had owned 200.) African-Americans made up a greater portion of the southern labor system and the population. In the colony of South Carolina, slaves predominated as the majority of the population.

Whether or not they were granted permission, slaves married. If sanctioned by their master, he might perform the ceremony himself, with his family as witnesses. In other instances, a black minister officiated. Some used the African custom of jumping the broom for festive wedding celebrations. When slave couples exchanged vows, they omitted the oath, "till death do us part" and substituted, "till separation do us part" or "till death or master do us part."

In the seventeenth century, slaves were generally housed in barracks or in barn lofts under the same roof with livestock. Later, by the eighteenth century slave owners erected individual slave cabins which consisted of one room with a fireplace. Their housing was always inferior consisting of a dirt floor which became a breeding ground for diseases such as typhus, dysentery and lockjaw. Slaves constructed their own furniture and obtained castoffs such as kettles, pots, pot racks, frying pans, and dishes from the master's house. They often maintained their own vegetable gardens and more fortunate slave families might own a few pigs.

Clio's Corner - What Have Historians Said about Female Slavery?

Historians have studied the effects of slavery from many different angles. In one focus, the slave family has been studied to see if their hardships had any effect on succeeding generations of African-American families. Revisionist historians emphasize that despite the break up of families through slave sale, obstacles to slave marriage and the lack of legal protection for slaves, many sustained two-parent families. Slaves also maintained complex though flexible kinship networks. Frederick Douglass, for instance, details how older female slaves cared for children as surrogate grannies. When he was separated from his mother as a young boy, an elderly female slave he thought was his grandmother, took care of him.

Another misconception has been to categorize the treatment of slaves geographically, i.e. that slaves on plantations in the Deep South received harsher treatment than those in the Upper South or North. Perhaps the labor intensive nature of agriculture in the Deep South, such as the cultivation of sugar, indigo, and rice led to this conclusion. The cruel treatment and work experience of slaves such as Harriet Tubman who lived in the Upper South belie this notion. Also mistaken is the view that female slaves did not perform heavy field labor but worked only as domestic servants.

Deborah White, in *Arn't I a Woman? Female Slaves in the Plantation South*, argued that females experienced slavery much differently than male slaves did. The stark realities of life for slave women included sexual exploitation by their master, the performance of heavy field labor, and the burdens of their own household. Professor White found slave families tended to be *matrifocal* and the very survival of the family depended upon the mother. Conversely, unencumbered by children, it was easier for male slaves to attempt escape.

Consider the stereotype of Mammy immortalized in *Gone with the Wind.* She is characterized as a ubiquitous domestic manager and surrogate mother of the white children, full of compassion and folksy wisdom, a majestic authority second only to the white plantation owners. In reality, black women were not revered and when they became old and infirm most were cast off, abandoned or left to die. Deborah White points out that by portraying Mammy as the eternal devotee to white children, we have overlooked the role the white mistress played in rearing slave children. If there was no elderly or disabled slave woman to supervise slave children during the day when their parents worked in the field, the responsibility fell to white mistresses. White women also played an important role in the health care of slave children.

Professor White demythologized the Jezebel stereotype of the sexually promiscuous female slave. When white male traders first beheld African women they regarded these women as sensual beings. Europeans interpreted the semi-nude slave women who were acclimated to the African heat, as lewd and promiscuous females.

Historian Catherine Clinton in *The Plantation Mistress: Women's World in the Old South,* looked at the relationship between the white mistress and the female slave to see if their common gender made white women more empathetic to slaves. But she found that mistresses valued slaves as property just as white masters did. Finding no compassion among female mistresses, Catherine Clinton emphasized how white women directed their personal hatred to slaves, not to the institution of slavery. White women were as racially biased and class conscious toward slaves as white men were.

Female slave working in a peanut field. (Photo courtesy of the Library of Congress.)

The Colonial Home and Housekeeping

> A man works from sun to sun but a woman's work is never done. Sometimes I knit and sometimes I spin sometimes I wash and at times do wring. There is never a day from morn to night but I with work am weary quite. For when the game with me is best I hardly take an hour's rest. A maid may merrily bask in the sun but a woman's work is never done.
>
> *Anonymous*

The colonial woman lived out her days and years in the domestic sphere. In seventeenth century Virginia, her home was assembled quickly, constructed poorly and usually intended for temporary use. These homes could barely withstand the storms and winds of winter and must have been impossible to keep clean, warm and comfortable. Over the century, as Virginians thrived on the tobacco economy, settlements stabilized and more permanent, fashionable houses were built.

In New England, the home of the goodwife was often built in the English tradition as a gabled two-story home with long timbers, and a central chimney, an early form of central heating which contained the heat within the walls. The first floor was laid out in two rooms, the hall or great room where most family activity took place, and a kitchen. The upstairs was partitioned off into bedrooms adjacent to the central fireplace. In this floor plan, family members had little or no bedroom privacy.

In the middle colonies, where fieldstone was available, homes were constructed more solidly of masonry and timber. Quaker families built substantial homes and furnished them handsomely, sparing no expense. Some of the most luxurious homes in America were built by prosperous Dutch colonists along the Hudson River Valley. Families of means might import silver candlesticks, fine china, clocks and furniture from England. Most middling families made do with a few wooden bowls, some pewter ware and handmade furniture. Functional and unadorned, large trunks were used for linen and clothing storage. By today's standards, colonial homes were very small with little space for each family member. Tourists now visiting the home and upholstery shop of famous Philadelphian Betsy Ross get some idea of the diminutive space of city houses, where just maneuvering a small winding staircase was a feat.

The colonial woman might live in a simple wooden hut with a dirt floor, or one more elegantly finished in masonry with wooden-planked floors. Carpets, for those who could afford them, were not used extensively in homes until the 1800s. Even with a roaring fire, the colonial dame's home was cold in winter, sweltering hot and swarming with flies in summer. The fireplace added odor and soot. Amid all of this unpleasantness, women labored to keep their houses tidy, and their families well fed and clothed. A housewife took pride in her achievements: fine needlework, creative quilts, or a jar of homemade jam.

The colonial home served many functions as the family residence, the training and work station, and a place of business. Most colonials engaged in farming and the family was an economic entity, composed of servants, perhaps slaves, and often apprentices or indentured servants all working together under one roof. Especially in New England, parents utilized a practical apprentice system whereby their adolescent children would live with another relative or in a neighbor's household to learn a trade. Puritans apparently feared spoiling their children and not giving them proper training.

Women's Work in the Colonial Economy

Because England controlled trade and currency, there was little money in circulation in the colonies. Money consisted of a strange conglomeration of English, Spanish, French and Dutch currency, IOUs, and Virginia tobacco notes. The economy of the colonial family relied on self-sufficiency. Housewives lived frugally, learned to innovate and utilized a system of barter. The research of women historians reveals a whole network among colonial women who traded eggs, butter, cheese, and garden produce in exchange for necessities for their families. Because many families lived in remote areas, faced long harsh winters in isolation, and had limited access to market day, colonial housekeepers had to plan ahead. They stocked food and fuel, and manufactured their own household articles such as soap, candles, textiles and clothing. To support themselves single mothers, particularly widows hired themselves out as dairy maids, weavers, or seamstresses.

Manufacturing household items from "scratch" was tedious. After the harvest was gathered and before the shortened days of winter set in, time had to be set aside for making candles. Because of the labor involved, candles were costly and used sparingly. Consequently, homes were very dark and people worked from the rising to the setting sun, in natural light as much as possible.

The assignment of work by gender meant men built houses and barns, made furniture and performed heavy farm labor. Besides caring for young children, the colonial wife produced food, prepared textiles and made clothing, tended a kitchen garden of vegetables and herbs, cared for the small livestock such as chickens or pigs, and slaughtered and prepared meat for consumption.

Of all her chores, food preparation, which involved more than cooking, was most labor intensive. She gathered firewood, maintained the fire, and prepared food for storage by smoking, pickling, cooking, drying and preserving, grinding and roasting. Processing of dairy foods was time consuming, from tending the dairy cows and milking, to churning butter and making cheese. Housewives performed much of their work in volume and set aside certain days for laundry, candle making, needlework, sausage stuffing, soap making and housecleaning.

A Typical Work Day

Diary of Elizabeth Fuller

August 1st: I wove ten yards, three-quarters and three inches, I picked blue wool, I broke blue wool, I carded blue wool and red. Ma spun.

Diary of Abigail Foote

Fix'd a gown, mended Mother's riding hood, spun short thread, fix'd two gowns for the Welsh's girls. Carded, tow'd and spun linen, worked on the cheese basket, Hannah and I hatchelled flax for linen, 51 lbs a piece. Pleated and ironed. Spooled thread. Spun fifty knots of linen. Milked cows. Set a red dye, scoured the pewter, made a broom of wheat straw, and carded two pounds of whole wool. Dyed the wool scarlet.

Colonial Ambiance – a Little Soap, and a Potpourri of Odors

Colonial housekeeping required constant effort to maintain any semblance of order or cleanliness. Americans' homes were surrounded by dirt, dust and mud. The surrounding filth of livestock and poultry was constantly tracked into the house. Insulation and sealing of windows and doors was nonexistent so homes were damp, insect-infested and thickly dust-covered. Standards of personal hygiene were also negligible. The number one affliction of Americans, bad teeth, led to other serious illnesses. Colonials thought bathing was unhealthy as one could catch pneumonia and they believed an accumulation of grime and body oil was actually beneficial. To prepare for winter, some colonials rubbed their bodies with goose fat, placed minced onions or garlic in their clothing, and sewed the under layers of garments together to be worn all winter! Colonials also regarded hair washing as unhealthy, because cold heads and wet hair brought on illness. So, to keep the hair and scalp healthy (which did not equate with clean) women would brush their hair the requisite one-hundred times daily for shine. The regimen for dandruff sufferers was to rub bran into their scalp. (Evidently, bran flakes on the lapel was more acceptable than dandruff flakes!) Some cures for colonial baldness included rubbing goose fat, onions, rosemary, castor oil, pig urine or wild honey onto the scalp.

Colonial She-Merchants

The escalating Indian Wars widowed many women, and fishing and maritime trades called men away from home for months at a time, leaving women to run the family farm or business. With bustling trade in cities such as Charleston, Baltimore, Philadelphia, New York and Boston, shopkeeping broadened women's economic opportunities. Stores or shops were on the first floor at street level and the family quarters occupied the upper floors. By the eighteenth century, trade and commercial enterprise were evident as women advertised their wares.

> Just imported from London, and to be sold at the Broad street shop of Lucy Weaver, china, cups and saucers, glass decanters for water or wine, as well as Bohea tea, refin'd sugar, fine laces, trims, and edgings, hoop-petticoats, women's and children's stays, children's toys and sundry European imports at reasonable rate.

In Nantucket, one woman started out with small transactions – selling pins and needles – as one visitor observed, but she eventually became quite prosperous.

> The richest person now on the island [Nantucket] owes all of his present prosperity to the ingenuity of his wife. While he was off performing his cruises, she traded with pins and needles, and kept a school. Afterward, she purchased more considerable articles, which she sold with so much judgment, that she laid the foundation of a system of business, that she has ever since prosecuted with equal dexterity and success.

Femme sole Margaret Brent, widow Eliza Lucas Pinckney, and deputy husband Abigail Adams had particular skills in farm management. Margaret Brent operated plantations in Maryland and later Virginia; Eliza Lucas Pinckney maintained both the Lucas and Pinckney estates. Abigail Adams managed the family estate at Braintree, Massachusetts, during John's frequent absence in public service. According to family accounts and John's reckoning, Abigail managed their farm so efficiently that the Adams' family fortune was free of the debts which plagued other founding fathers.[3] Abigail operated the Braintree farm with sound business management and kept John informed of progress and setbacks at home,

> We have had fine spring rains which make the husbandry promise fair but the great difficulty has been to procure laborers. A man will not talk with you who are worth hiring under 24 pounds per year. Isaac insisted upon my giving him 20 pounds or he would leave me. He is no more and I found very unfit to take the lead upon the Farm, having no forethought or any contrivance to plan his business, or in the faithful execution thereof. I ask advice of my friends and neighbors. They have all advised me to let Isaac go. I settled with him and we parted. Mr. Belcher is now with me and has undertaken to conduct the business which he has hitherto done with Spirit and activity. We are just now ready to

---

3. Thomas Jefferson, for example, considered a wealthy country squire, went bankrupt and it was only at the mercy of his bankers that he was allowed to remain in his home at Monticello in his last years.

> plant, the barley looks charmingly. By another year, I shall be quite a Farmeress.

Mothers of Invention: She-Merchants and Women's Work in the Colonies

By mid-eighteenth century, newspapers had gained popularity in the colonies and the busy printing trade attracted female printers. As early as 1694, the widow Dinah Nuthead, who had inherited a printing business from her husband, operated a print shop in Annapolis, Maryland, and served as the official printer for the Maryland Colonial Assembly. Elizabeth Timothy entered newspaper publishing in 1738, as proprietress of the *South Carolina Gazette.* Benjamin Franklin, a business associate of Elizabeth's husband Lewis, praised Elizabeth as far superior to Lewis in the trade. Another successful printer, Mary Katherine Goddard, co-founded the *Maryland Journal* in Baltimore with her brother William. When William organized an inter-colonial postal system, Mary became the city's official printer and took sole proprietorship of the paper. The city appointed her postmistress, perhaps the first one in the colonies, but officials dismissed her stating that only a man could supervise the postal system. After her dismissal as postmistress, Mary operated a book shop in Baltimore and remained a *femme sole* and independent business woman for the rest of her life. Also notable in early colonial publishing, Anne Catherine Green published the *Maryland Gazette,* and Clementina Rind of Virginia published the *Virginia Gazette.* Clementina printed government documents as well.

> 1685 - Elizabeth George upon certificate from the Selectmen of Dorchester had her licence renewed to keep a house of publique entertainment and to sell wine and beer and Sider by retail for the year ensuing. Who gave in bond with Sureties for her observance of the Laws respecting Innkeepers and that she should not sell Sider for more than two pence a quart.

Women converted household management into business opportunity and took up occupations keeping shops, inns or taverns. Taverns and inns provided food, drink, a meeting place, hospitality and overnight lodging for travelers. Although inn keeping was usually a business operated by husbands and wives together, widows frequently inherited and owned inns and taverns for self support. The business of running inns and taverns ran the whole gamut from the very posh to the slovenly. Colonial traveler Madam Sarah Kemble Knight attests to the variety of accommodations, inedible food, and modest comfort.

> Here having called for something to eat, the woman bro't in a twisted thing like a cable. But something whiter; and lay it on the board, tugg'd for life to bring it in to capacity to spread; which having great pains accomplished, shee served in a dish of Pork and cabbage, I suppose the remains of Dinner. The sause was of a deep purple, which I tho't was boil'd in her dye kettle; the bread was Indian, and everything on the Table service Agreeable to these. I being hungry got a little down. But my stomach was soon cloy'd and what cabbage I swallowed served me for a Cudd the whole day after.

Sometimes one spare room in a home served as an inn to receive guests,

> Being come to Mr. Havns', I was very civilly received, and courteously entertained, in a clean comfortable house. I then betook me to my apartment which was a little room parted from the kitchen by a single bord partition there. Whereafter I had noted the occurances of the last day. I went back to bed, tho' pretty hard, yet neet and handsome.

The inn keeping business afforded women the means not only to support but in some cases to better themselves. Elizabeth Marriott (really) operated a tavern, *The Sign of the Ship*, in Annapolis, which she willed to her daughter, Anne Howard. Annapolis offered a prime location for this business, and Anne Howard took full advantage. In 1757, she converted the tavern to an inn to accommodate assembly representatives, and advertised its amenities in the local newspaper.

> Whereas Anne Howard, living at the *Sign of the Ship*, where her mother formerly kept a tavern, in Annapolis, having a number of very good spare beds, bedding and a convenient house for entertainment, will take in Gentlemen of the Assembly, at the ensuing session, at a fee of three shillings per day. N.B.: Mistress Howard also keeps a House of entertainment for strangers as usual.

Business thrived for Anne, and her lodgings were noted for comfort and respectability. Her Inn, *the Sign of the Ship* could boast that George Washington really had slept there when he visited Annapolis.

Conclusion

In the period from the fifteenth to the nineteenth centuries, millions of Africans were packed onboard slave ships as human cargo, brought to America and sold at slave auctions in port cities such as Richmond, Charleston, and Boston. Female slaves were utilized as domestic or field hands, as nannies and for their procreative power. They were the backbone of the southern agrarian economy. Female slaves were not exempted from heavy field work such a plowing and experienced the double oppression of the institution—as African-American slaves and as women.

For all women, the care of a large family and agricultural cultivation filled their waking hours with the unending tedium of housework, gardening, butchering and food and clothing production. With the devastation of colonial wars and increased economic demands on the family, and out of dire necessity, women took on more responsibilities; in many cases, they acted as the family's sole provider and maintained a family farm or small business. With surplus commodities, they engaged in barter trade and used their skills with needle and thread and weaving to augment the family income.

In the English colonies, by the eighteenth century many more women engaged in business and served as tavern owners, innkeepers, or entered trades such as printing. Women living in communities in New York, New Spain or New France, who had always been able to engage in commerce and business, continued to do so.

Part II

Women in the War of Independence and the Early Republic

Women and the War of Independence

Women in the New Republic

Chapter 6
Women and the War of Independence
A Brave Defense against Invasion

Key topics

Rumblings of Revolution
Women's Role in the Revolutionary War
Notable Women of the Revolutionary Era

Chronology

1770 - Boston Massacre
1773 - Boston Tea Party
1775 - April, Battles of Lexington and Concord
May, Continental Congress Convenes
June, Battle Breed's Hill, Boston
1776 - July, Congressional Declaration of Independence
1781 - British Surrender at Yorktown
1783 - Treaty of Paris
1805 - Publication of Mercy Otis Warren's *History of the Rise, Progress and Termination of the American Revolution*

Introduction

In tracing the origins of the War of Independence, John Adams perhaps expressed it best saying that the Revolution was in "the hearts and minds of the people." That seemed apparent as early as 1733, when a group of widows wrote to a New York newspaper,

> *We are House Keepers, Pay our taxes, carry on Trade and most of us are she Merchants, and as we in some measure contribute to the support of Government, we ought to be entitled to some of the sweets of it; but we find ourselves entirely neglected, while the Husbands that live in our Neighborhood are daily invited to Dine at the English Governor's court; we have the vanity to think we can be full as entertaining and make as brave a defence in case of an invasion and perhaps not turn taile so soon as some of them.*

If the possibility of imminent invasion was anticipated forty-two years before the Revolution, then it seems likely that the immediate consequences of the last imperial war, the Seven Years or French-Indian War, merely added fuel to a slow burning fire. When the British won supremacy in the New World and claimed French territory, the Crown mandated that colonists bear a portion of America's defense through taxation, but colonists perceived this shift in imperial policy as an active imposition and sudden usurpation of their rights. From 1770 to 1775, colonists willingly resisted the armed strength of the British government in confrontations which escalated into war.

The War of Independence (1775-1783), the longest protracted war in American history, divided families, friends and communities as some supported the rebel cause of independence, (Patriots or Whigs) many remained loyal to England (Loyalists or Tories) and others supported neither side. During the war, John Adams estimated that at any given time, a third of the colonists were patriots, a third loyalists and a third simply indifferent. Women played a vital role in the war effort both on the battlefront and at home.

Rumblings of Revolution and Independence

An abolition movement to free slaves began in the northern colonies as early as the 1730s under the leadership of New Jersey Friend John Woolman. Quaker meetings strongly encouraged members to free their slaves immediately or in their estate wills. By 1774, meetings were coercing members to release their slaves or face expulsion from religious membership.

That same year, other Americans sensed an imminent conflict with the mother country:

> It seems we have troublesome times a coming for there is great Disturbance abroad in the earth and they say it is tea that caused it. So then if they will quarrel about such a trifling thing as that, what must we expect but war and I think or at least fear it will be so.
>
> Jemina Condict October 1774

When the colonies passed the Non-Importation Agreements and refused to purchase many British goods, women used their purchasing power to stage protests of trade. An obvious target was textiles and household goods. By the mid-eighteenth century, fabric was readily available in shops and many women no longer spun wool and cotton for clothing. But during the Pre-Revolutionary movement American homespun apparel became a symbol of protest, pride, and patriotism; spinning wheels once relegated to the attic were dusted off to spin thread into clothing. Because of the scarcity of certain products, women's protests became boisterous as noted in the following description,

> You must know that there is a great scarcity of sugar and coffee, articles which the female part of the state are very loth to give up, especially whilst they consider the scarcity occasioned by the merchants having secreted a large Quantity... It was rumour'd that an eminent, wealthy, stingy, merchant had a hogshead of coffee in his store which he refused to sell to the committee under six shillings per pound. A number of females, some say a hundred, some say more, assembled with a cart of trucks marched down to the Ware House and demanded the keys which he refused to deliver, upon which one of them seazed him by the Neck and tossed him into the cart. Upon his finding no quarter, he delivered the keys when they tipped up the cart and discharged him. Then opened the Warehouse, hoisted out the coffee themselves, put it in the carts and drove off. A large concourse of Men stood amazed as silent spectators during the whole transaction.
>
> Abigail Adams 1777,
> Braintree, Massachusetts

When colonists refused to buy certain British imports, the women created substitutes for tea, using sassafras, sage, currant, raspberry, and strawberry. The women of Edenton, North Carolina, who actively "renounced the pernicious drinking of tea," vowed not to wear any manufactured clothing from Britain. The Edenton women inspired other colonial women's groups to boycott British products and to empty their tea canisters of loathsome British tea. Women also organized groups for mob demonstrations against customs agents, and tax collectors. They engaged in a number of assaults on Loyalists - such as the Hillsborough treat. More insult than injury, the treat consisted of large amounts of horse manure smeared on a Loyalists front door. Mobs of men and women also tarred and feathered government agents. The image of tarring and feathering sounds comedic but it was violent and cruel. This involved apprehending a Loyalist, covering his body with hot melted tar and feathers and then setting the feathers aflame.

Victims often suffered a painful death or slow torture from toxic infection and the loss of skin.

Two notable colonial women, Abigail Adams and Mercy Otis Warren, actively participated as members of the revolutionary organizations, the Sons of Liberty and the Committees of Correspondence. Abigail's husband, John Adams, who would later serve as Ambassador to France and England, then as Vice President and finally as President of the United States, was at the center of the revolutionary storm as an activist in Massachusetts and inter-colonial politics. During John's years of public service, both during and after the war, Abigail, typical of many wives and mothers who kept the home fires burning cared for their five children and managed the family farm at Braintree, Massachusetts. While known for her frugality she wined and dined some of the famous people of her day and would maintain homes in France and London while John served as an American Emissary. Abigail dished out meals on a shoestring budget. Although she lived a life in the spotlight, nothing pleased her more than tending her own farm and household,

> Retiring to our own little farm feeding my poultry and improving my garden has more charms for my fancy, than residing at the court of Saint James where I seldom meet with characters so innofensive [sic] as my Hens and chickings, or minds so well improved as my garden.

In the spring of 1776, Abigail's letters to John admonished him, as a member of the Continental Congress, "to remember the ladies "when drafting the new government.

> I long to hear that you have declared an independency, and by the way in the new Code of Laws which I suppose it will be necessary for you to make I desire you would Remember the Ladies, and be more generous and favorable to them than your ancestors. Do not put such unlimited power into the hands of the Husbands. Remember all men would be tyrants if they could. If particular care and attention is not paid to the ladies we are determined to foment a Rebellion, and will not hold ourselves bound by any Laws in which we have no voice or Representation.

John Adams responded,

> As to your extraordinary Code of Laws, I cannot but laugh. We have been told that our struggle has loosened the bands of government everywhere. That children and apprentices were disobedient 'that schools and colleges were grown turbulent' that Indians slighted their guardians and Negroes grew insolent to their masters. But your letter was the first intimation that another tribe more numerous and powerful than all the rest were grown discontented.

Abigail Smith Adams, a congregational minister's daughter, was descended from a distinguished colonial family. Her marriage to John Adams was a union of mind and heart. She was a key figure in revolutionary politics, wife of the second President and mother of the sixth, John Quincy Adams. (Picture courtesy of the Library of Congress.)

Realizing John did not take the request seriously, Abigail asked Mercy Warren to join her in a petition campaign to the Continental Congress, on behalf of women's rights.

> He is very saucy to me in return for a list of female grievances which I transmitted to him. I think I will get you to join me in a petition to Congress. I thought it

> was very probable our wise Statesman would erect a New Government and form a new code of laws. I ventured to speak a word in behalf of our sex, which are rather hardly dealt with by the Laws of England which gives such unlimited power to the husband to use his wife.

Whether or not Mercy Otis Warren or other women joined Abigail in a petition to the Congress is unknown as no further record of debate has been found.

Abigail's friend, Mercy Otis Warren, was drawn into revolutionary politics by way of her brother James Otis, an attorney who had argued the principles of liberty and colonists' rights in the Massachusetts courts. Because of James' colonial sympathies, British Loyalists brutally attacked him in a Boston tavern. He suffered head injuries, and the consequent brain damage left him a deranged and permanent invalid. In his remaining years, Mercy cared for James and took up the patriot cause by waging a writing campaign. Her husband, James Warren, a representative in the Massachusetts Assembly, served during the war as paymaster for General Washington, and as a major general in the Massachusetts Militia. Mercy's brother-in-law, the famous patriot-martyr, Dr. Joseph Warren, was one of the first heroes to die at the Battle of Breed's Hill in 1775. Mercy, like Abigail and other women, was defined by the men in her life.

The Warren home became the gathering place for many of the celebrities of the revolution—John and Abigail Adams, Samuel Adams, John Hancock, James Otis, and Paul Revere. Mercy wrote for the underground committees but her most famous works were a series of satirical plays; *The Adulateur*, *The Defeat*, and *The Blockheads* were never performed but served as patriot propaganda.

Other notable women of the Revolutionary era performed men's work within the restrictive boundaries of the upper class. One such woman, Eliza Lucas Pinckney, a member of the South Carolina aristocracy, and ranked as a southern belle, bore no resemblance to that stereotype. Her father, George Lucas, had served as the royal governor in the British West Indies and a major general in the British Army. Eliza enjoyed a privilege not afforded many women of the era, to be sent to England for a classical education. In 1738, when she was fifteen, her father moved the family to Wappoo plantation in South Carolina. When military duty called her father away, Eliza cared for her invalid mother, her younger siblings and ran the family's three South Carolina plantations. Her classical training was of little use for business, so Eliza instructed herself in bookkeeping, animal husbandry, and agronomy and found time to teach her sister Polly and "two black girls" how to read and write. She also established a plantation school for slave children.

Eliza's desire to find plants which would yield higher production for the plantation, led to more diversified agricultural production for the entire South Carolina colony. Through bold crop experimentation, she introduced the cultivation of silkworms, and plants such as ginger, indigo, lucern, cassava, alfalfa and cotton. Most important was Eliza's development of the indigo plant. From cuttings her father sent from the West Indies, she developed a textile dye and it proved of potential for production in South Carolina. Despite attempts by competitors like Nicholas Cromwell to sabotage her experiments, Eliza's introduction of the indigo dye made it a chief South Carolina export. By 1747, when cultivation doubled, exports reached 100,000 pounds and indigo became the vital cash crop for South Carolina for the next 160 years.

Eliza Lucas had refused the prospective suitors her father chose and instead married Charles Pinckney of South Carolina, a widower twenty years her senior, who was a distinguished attorney and landholder. Charles designated Eliza to oversee his estate as he was frequently away on business, but her responsibility to the Lucas family continued. With a total of seven plantations to supervise, Eliza continued crop experimentation testing flax and hemp and set up a silk manufacturing plant.

Eliza and Charles had four children, the most notable being Charles Cotesworth Jr. and Thomas, who as adults entered military and public service. In 1758, Charles, Sr. contracted malaria and died. After her husband's death, Eliza Lucas Pinckney founded a hospital for the treatment of malaria and smallpox and continued to manage the Pinckney plantations until well after the Revolutionary War.

During the Revolutionary War, a new religious sect, the Shakers, offered haven to other pacifists at their colony in Niskeyuna, located near Albany, New York. This settlement and others like it at Poland Hill, Maine, and New Harmony, Massachusetts, had been founded by Mother Ann Lee who had emigrated with eight converts from Manchester, England, in 1774.

This sect which believed in sexual purity and practiced sexual abstinence and the abnegation of marriage, relied upon adult conversion as well as the adoption of orphans to build church membership. Away from the influences of the world, sheltered within a Shaker village, they lived in accordance with Ann Lee's testimony by abstaining from war, politics, alcohol, tobacco, marriage and sex.

Women's Roles in the Revolutionary War

Some 250,000 patriots went off to fight for independence, but the women who stayed home also experienced the war firsthand. On the home front, women were more frequently in harm's way than were the men in combat. On the frontier, distanced from community or government help, a common practice of women was to "make a show of hats," that is, to dress in men's clothes to give the enemy the impression that the settlement was full of men. Using this strategy, frontier settlements defended by females survived. On the Kentucky frontier, one mother defended her home against Indian attack, killing six natives in the onslaught.

Women in cities such as Boston, Philadelphia and New York were also under attack, as the civilian population was neither safe nor spared. These women contributed to the war effort in any capacity that would further the American cause. They raised money which the Continental Army desperately needed for supplies. Ester De Beret Reed, the wife of the Royal Governor of Pennsylvania, organized the largest aid society, The Association, to procure clothing, food and supplies for American soldiers. When she died in 1780, leadership shifted to Sarah Franklin Bache, the daughter of Benjamin Franklin. Dividing the city into thirteen districts, the women of The Association canvassed Philadelphians for money and raised over $7,000 in gold currency (equivalent to about $30,000 in paper money). Women also helped by making flags, drums, guns, ammunition, weapons, clothing, and printed pamphlets and documents. Baltimore printer, Mary Katherine Goddard, put out the first edition of the Declaration of Independence.

Philadelphia Quaker Betsy Ross lived with her husband John in a rented home, from where she operated an upholstery shop. It was here that she made flags for the Pennsylvania Regiments and the first flag of the United Colonies. (Picture courtesy of the Library of Congress.)

Philadelphia Quaker Betsy Ross ran an upholstery business in her modest home. Historical tradition credits Betsy with making the first American flag, and her grandson perpetuated her patriotic role as flag maker in the late nineteenth century. In May, 1776, General George Washington, Robert Morris and Colonel George Ross visited her shop to show her the design for an American flag and asked her to make it.

The Ross family typified many colonial families divided over the strife between Loyalists and Patriots. Her husband John Ross, an Anglican, fell out with his own family who were staunch Loyalists. He joined the Pennsylvania Militia and was killed in an ammunition explosion January 21, 1776. Betsy, widowed once more during the war, made ends meet as a seamstress, upholsterer and a flag maker. She is reputed to have made clothes for George Washington and flags for the Pennsylvania regiments. It is believed the government used Quaker/pacifist Betsy Ross as a patriotic figure to attract other non-participants into the war. She became a unifying symbol for Patriots in Philadelphia, the stronghold of Loyalists.

Colonists were expected to "give quarter," i.e. shelter, to soldiers, and women converted homes, barns, taverns or inns into makeshift barracks to house soldiers or prisoners. Thousands of other women anonymously performed heroic work for the war effort. Elizabeth Marshall Martin harbored injured Continental soldiers in her home and prevented their capture by the British.

Since women could come and go unsuspected, they served well as couriers and spies. During the South Carolina campaign, American General Nathaniel Greene enlisted young Emily Geiger to convey military information to General Sumter. The second day of her ride British Lord Rawdon's troops took her prisoner, but before a matron could search her, Emily swallowed documents she was about to deliver. When the British released her, Emily proceeded to General Sumter's camp to deliver the information she had memorized. Because of her efforts, Patriot forces were victorious. In another instance of espionage, Grace and Rachel Martin, the wives of two brothers serving with General Greene, disguised themselves, intercepted British documents and delivered them to the General.

When British General Howe occupied Philadelphia, he used the home of Quakers William and Lydia Darrah for his headquarters. Lydia overheard the British plans to attack Washington's army; she slipped through enemy lines to inform the General and her warning enabled the Continental forces to repel the British attack. Another Patriot, sixteen-year-old Sybil Ludington, the daughter of an American militia colonel, on the night of April 26, 1777, rode forty miles to rouse members of the militia of Danbury, Connecticut, to come to the city's defense. Although she completed the mission, Sybil's ride is not mentioned in history texts, perhaps because the militia did not respond in time to save Danbury, and Sybil's ride, unlike Paul Revere's, is associated with a defeat, not a victory.

Other women transformed their houses into hospitals to shelter the wounded and the dying. The military also hired women to serve as nurses. Women recruited for the hospitals at Williamsburg, Virginia, and at Yellow Springs, Pennsylvania, were offered a stipend twice the amount of a Continental Sergeant's monthly salary, but at seven dollars a month, only the most destitute served as nurses. They risked infection as disease and epidemic swept through the camps.

Women in the Camps

Historians speculate on how many women actually served in the military during the war. Estimates range from 10,000 or 20,000. Some women, referred to as ammunition wives like the legendary female patriot cannoneer, Molly Pitcher, volunteered in the artillery divisions and fought alongside their husbands. At least two women contend for the title of Molly Pitcher. The first candidate, a young soldier's wife named Mary Ludwig Hayes, entered the war record June 28, 1778, when she signed up with Captain Francis Proctor's Company in the Pennsylvania artillery. Described by the men in her company as a twenty-two-year-old illiterate pregnant woman who smoked, chewed tobacco and swore as well as any of the male soldiers, Mary endeared herself to the troops with unusual courage and hard work under fire. During the Battle of Monmouth, it has been said, she earned the nickname Molly Pitcher for performing the exhaustive work of supplying battle-fatigued and wounded men with drinking water in the heat of combat. When her husband collapsed from heat stroke (some sources say he was injured in battle), Mary took his place at the cannon performing skillfully and heroically. Tradition states that she, like other Patriots, received the personal thanks of General Washington. Her presence at Monmouth is validated by an eyewitness, Private Joseph Plumb Martin. In his engaging war diary, he described a humorous incident when a woman was firing cannon,

> A woman whose husband belonged to the artillery and who was then attached

> to a piece in the engagement, attended with her husband at the piece for the whole time. While in the act of reaching a cartridge and having one of her feet as far before the other as she could step, a cannon shot from the enemy passed directly between her legs without doing any other damage than carrying away all the lower part of her petticoat. Looking at it with apparent unconcern, she observed that it was lucky It did not pass a little higher, for in that case it might have carried away something else, and continued her occupation.

Patriot-Cannoneer Molly Pitcher firing a gun. At least two female veterans could have inspired the nickname "Molly Pitcher" — Margaret Corbin or Mary Ludwig Hays McCauley. Both women were artillery wives with Pennsylvania regiments and fought at the Battle of Monmouth. (Courtesy of the National Archives and Records Administration.)

Some forty-four years after the war, the State of Pennsylvania awarded her an annual pension of $40 for her heroism at Monmouth. She died January 22, 1833, and is buried at Old Graveyard, (the name of the town) in Pennsylvania near Carlisle. During the Centennial of the Revolution in 1876, the citizens of Cumberland county marked her grave as that of an honored soldier. The battlefield monuments at Monmouth and her grave site commemorate Mary Ludwig Hayes (McCauley) as "Molly Pitcher," for her heroism.

Another woman serving as a cannoneer, Margaret Corbin could also have been called Molly Pitcher. Margaret and her husband, John also served under Captain Francis Proctor in the First Company of the Pennsylvania Artillery. Margaret Corbin, the first woman pensioned by the Continental Congress, holds the unique honor of being the only soldier of the Revolutionary War buried at the Military Academy at West Point, New York. Patriotic literature commonly refers to Margaret as "Captain Molly." She wore a uniform but made no attempt to conceal her sex. At the Battle of Fort Washington when her husband, John Corbin, was killed, Margaret took his place immediately on the firing line and was wounded in the engagement with the British. Captured by the British, she was subsequently released and reassigned to the Invalids Corps at West Point to perform guard duty. Military officials regarded Margaret Corbin as a regular soldier. This perception is based upon her treatment as a prisoner of war, her reassignment to garrison duty as a member of the Invalid Corps and the pension stipulations granted by the Continental Congress, which gave her half pay because of her disability. Officers from her regiment petitioned for her to receive both state and Federal pensions, and on July 6, 1779, the Continental Congress listed her as a discharged soldier on the Invalid Regiment Rolls for April, 1783.

> Resolved, That Margaret Corbin, who was wounded and disabled in the attack on Fort Washington, whilst she heroically filled the post of her husband who was killed by her side serving a piece of artillery, do receive, during her natural life Or the continuance of the said disability, the one-half of the monthly pay drawn by a soldier in the service of these states; and that she now receive out of the public stores, one complete suits of cloaths, or the value thereof in money.

Some women disguised themselves as males in order to enlist. One of the most famous female Revolutionary soldiers Deborah Sampson, who masqueraded as a male, signed up with the Third Massachusetts Regiment under the name Robert Shurtleff. According to her testimony, she was promoted to sergeant and was seriously wounded in battle receiving a bullet in the thigh. In order to avoid having her sex detected, she removed the bullet herself. Records certify her superior officer was Colonel

Henry Jackson and that she received an honorable discharge.

The female Patriots demonstrated that they could and would fight for independence and to protect their families and homes. In a letter dated August 19, 1776, Abigail Grant reprimanded her husband for his cowardice and offered to fight in his place:

> I hear by Captain William Riley news that makes me very Sorry for he says you proved a Grand Coward when the fight was at Bunkers hill... If you are afraid pray own the truth and come home and take care of our children and I will be Glad to Come and take your place, and never will be Called a Coward, neither will I throw away one Cartridge but exert myself in so good a Cause. [sic]

Women also volunteered in the camps, serving alone or bringing their children. Their status ranged from full military personnel to paramilitary and volunteers. Initially, Washington disapproved of having women in the army because he believed they would slow down troop movement. These women, known as camp followers, served as nurses, cooks, laundresses, foragers, and as beasts of burden carrying all the equipment. After battles, they cleared fields and scavenged corpses for needed clothing and equipment before burying the bodies. Eventually even Washington realized that the services the women performed kept the army going.

Some of the women followed the troops and lived in the camp to be with their husbands or sweethearts; most needed the army's protection and daily rations to subsist. Some women gave birth in camp or on the march. Eyewitnesses who saw camp followers attested to their miserable condition and unkempt appearance. In a letter to close friend Mercy Otis Warren, Hannah Winthrop described one such march through Boston when camp followers came through with Burgoyne's Army.

> To be sure the sight was truly astonishing. I never had the least idea that the Creation produced such a sordid set of creatures in human Figure - poor dirty, emaciated men, great numbers of women, who seemed to be the beasts of burthen having bushel baskets on their back, by which they were bent double, the contents seemed to be Pots and kettles, various sorts of furniture, children Peeping thro' gridirons and other utensils, some very young infants who were Born on the road, the woman bare feet, cloathed in dirty rags, such effluvia filled the air while they were passing, had they not been smoaking all the time, I should have been apprehensive of being contaminated by them.

With American and British troops running rampant, women were constantly in danger. Loyalist women had property confiscated, and suffered social ostracism and exile after the war. Pacifist Quakers were persecuted for their lack of participation in the war. Frequently, when Quaker men refused to fight, they were taken into custody, and relocated to Virginia or Maryland. Quaker women attempted to locate their men and petitioned the government for their release. Both Loyalist and Patriot women were subject to abuse by soldiers. Some cases of rape were reported, but countless were not. British and American soldiers committed these crimes and were guilty of other atrocities as well. It is known that soldiers committed gang rapes, some reportedly on females as young as ten years old and on women still confined to bed recuperating from childbirth. Women were violated by either a retreating army or a victorious one, and horrible incidences were reported during the Revolution, such as the attack on Christiana Gatter. When British and Hessian troops raided Christiana's Connecticut home, they beat her husband and gang-raped her. In New Jersey soldiers raped Abigail Palmer, just thirteen years old, for four successive nights even though she was not alone or unattended. When her aunt and another woman tried to protect her and treat her injury they were also raped. Women knew of these kinds of atrocities and, if warned of the army's approach, they fled grabbing in haste whatever provisions they could.

The Saga of Jane McCrea

One woman's tragic death during the Revolutionary War became legendary—the romantic saga of Jane McCrea. Before war broke out, Jane became betrothed to British Lieutenant David Jones who served with General Burgoyne. When the British took the American forts along the Hudson River Valley, settlers were left unprotected as so many abandoned their homes. Because Jane had remained, Jones arranged for her safe escort to Fort Edwards. En route, on July 27, 1777, Jane and friend Sarah McNeil were captured by some of Burgoyne's Native American scouts. Sarah managed to escape and arrive at camp safely but Jane did not. Her body was discovered riddled with bullets and she had been scalped. The scouts claimed Jane had been shot by Patriot snipers. Since it is known that at the time General Burgoyne offered bounty for American scalps, it is plausible that if the scouts found her dead, they scalped her. When they brought Jane's hair to camp, Jones recognized it and reputedly was so grief stricken that he never recovered from the shock and died a few years later.

After the tragic death of Jane McCrea, the daughter of Reverend John McCrea, she was elevated to a patriotic heroic figure of the American Revolutionary War. (Picture Courtesy of the Library of Congress.)

When news of Jane McCrea's tragic death circulated throughout the colonies, more Patriots rallied to the American cause and Burgoyne's forces were defeated three months later. Details of her tragic demise also spread to England. In the English Parliament, distinguished member Edmund Burke delivered a rousing speech in the House of Commons about the tragedy and urged Parliament to forbid British troops from using Native Americans as scouts and auxiliaries. Consequently, General Gates, the British Commander, forbid the policy of bounties for American scalps and he reprimanded Burgoyne for Jane's death.

Clio's Corner - Was there a Golden Age for Women before the Revolution?

A leading interest among scholars has been what effect the war may have had on women. Was the war a turning point for them? Were women better off before or after the war and what advantages, if any, did they gain or lose as a result?

The often quoted research of Lois Green Carr and Lorena S. Walsh, in "The Planter's Wife: The Experience of White Women in Seventeenth-Century Maryland," suggests that anomalous circumstances in Maryland in the seventeenth century benefited colonial women. Their research supported the notion of a golden, albeit brief, age for women. Before the revolutionary era, the status of women in Colonial Maryland was heavily determined by four factors: (1) that the population of Maryland was predominantly immigrants, (2) males had a shorter life span, (3) women married later, after they had served out their term of indenture and (4) there were proportionally more men than women in the population. Given these conditions, Lois Green Carr and Lorena S. Walsh concluded that these women enjoyed greater freedom from social and sexual restraint than did women in England. Because of the sexual imbalance of the colonial population, they had greater freedom in choosing a husband, inherited property directly, and achieved the status of a planter's wife.

This led other scholars to inquire into the nature of women's status in the colonial era and in the post revolutionary period. Joan Hoff -

Wilson, in "The Illusion of Change: Women and the American Revolution" in Alfred F.Young, ed., *The American Revolution: Explorations in the History of American Radicalism*, argued that women experienced only an illusion of change as a result of the war. Joan Hoff-Wilson hinged her interpretation on a shift in America from a farming economy to an industrial one. This change was a step back because it offered women no opportunities to better themselves, since factory jobs offered little pay and long hours. Women in the New Republic remained in such constrained social roles that they were unable to enjoy or even experience independence.

Mary Beth Norton, in *Liberty's Daughters, The Revolutionary Experience of American Women, 1750-1800*, examined Loyalist women during and after the war. When thousands of these Loyalist widows relocated to England after the war and petitioned the British government for property losses in America, they had difficulty estimating their net worth. Mary Beth Norton argued that Loyalist women were unable to do so because they lacked knowledge of their husband's financial holdings. She concluded that the women had a limited role in the family's financial affairs before the war.

Linda Kerber, in *Women of the Republic, Intellect and Ideology in Revolutionary America*, also wanted to know how the Revolution affected women. Could a woman function as a Patriot during time of war? If so, how could she participate? If her husband remained loyal to the Crown was she also obligated to do so? Linda Kerber concluded that because many women had participated in the war, some of the old assumptions about them had been challenged, at least temporarily. Women had not benefited from the Revolution, but had only experienced changes in their lives. Although laws of *coverture* were still enforced, divorce became more accessible. Linda Kerber pinpointed Republican Motherhood, a postwar ideology developed by Dr. Benjamin Rush which paved the way for women to receive an education, if only to educate "future generations of sensible" male Republicans. Even with the status of Republican Mothers, women were still on the fringes of the body politic.

On the other hand, as Republican Motherhood won approval, female academies emerged in eastern cities. Eighteenth century writer and educator, Judith Sargeant Murray, took Republican philosophy one step further and proposed that female education could not only produce virtuous citizens and happier, more stable families, but also reap benefits for the women themselves. Murray wrote in 1798 that she envisioned the education of young women would form "a new era in female history." Female academies enrolled young ladies of privileged families and instructed them in the social graces. A typical program included etiquette, dancing, music, art, French, and sewing. Benjamin Franklin concurred with Judith Sargeant Murray that if schools added accounting, grammar, history, mathematics, and geography to the curriculum, they would prepare women more adequately to sustain themselves and manage an industrious household.

Joan Gundersen, in *To Be Useful to the World, Women in Revolutionary America, 1740-1790*, believes the Revolution cannot be measured as gain or loss for women. By 1790, women were part of a new generation, shaping a new world. Although women's roles and work looked the same, they had an entirely different meaning. Professor Gundersen sees the experience for women as a series of trade-offs. Republican Motherhood gave upper class women an air of moral respectability: but poor women, especially blacks and Native Americans became more economically repressed. Women had gained greater freedom in choosing a husband, but they also had to behave with greater restraint. Companionship in marriage brought husbands and wives closer, but childbirth was becoming more risky. When comparing the world of women in 1740 with that in 1790, Joan Gundersen concluded that life was neither better nor worse, just different. After the Revolution, women had gained some benefits, but they also faced a whole new set of challenges.

Mothers of Invention: Phillis Wheatley, an American Muse

On July 11, 1761, packed onboard the slave ship *Phillis* with other unfortunate Africans bound for the Boston slave market was a young, frail girl about eight-years-old. Since authorities kept few vital records of slaves, her birthrate is reckoned sometime in the year 1753, and her birthplace Senegal, Africa. She had miraculously survived the dreaded Atlantic passage on the slave ship, but remained frail and in poor health the rest of her life. Descriptions of her condition suggest she suffered from tuberculosis. Bostonians John and Susannah Wheatley purchased her, named her Phillis, for the slave ship that brought her from Africa and gave her their surname. Although the Wheatleys welcomed her into the family, which included their twins Mary and Nathaniel, and provided her with comforts extraordinary for a slave, they also maintained the boundaries of class and race. Phillis was required to take her meals at a separate table. A precocious child, Phillis was tutored by Mary Wheatley in English, Latin, religion, scripture study, history and geography. Phillis wrote poetry and in one poem she memorialized her transport to America as a slave,

> When I, young in life, by seeming cruel fate,
> Was snatch'd from Africa's fancy'd happy Seat
> What pangs excruciating must molest
> What sorrows labour in my Parent's breast!
> Steel'd was the soul and by no misery mov'd
> No more than stone ne'er soft compassion mov'd
> That from a Father seiz'd his babe belov'd.
> Ah, such my case, Thus I deplore the day
> And can I then but pray
> That others may never feel this tyrannic sway?

Susannah Wheatley arranged for Phillis's poems to be published in London. An engraving of Phillis survives today because her sponsor, the Countess of Huntington, arranged a portrait sitting from which a print was reproduced in her book of poems.

In compliance with the last wish of Susannah Wheatley after her death in 1774, Phillis was manumitted, i.e. granted her freedom. One of the brighter moments in her life occurred in October 1775, after Phillis sent a poem to George Washington entitled "Ode to General Washington." He received her in a personal visit while encamped with the Continental forces in Cambridge. Thomas Paine, editor of the Pennsylvania Magazine, printed her "Ode to General Washington" in April 1776, which included the by line, "written by the famous Phillis Wheatley, the African Poetess." The visit with General Washington and the publication of her poems granted her some celebrity, but the hardships of the war, family separation, and the death of John Wheatley in 1778, left Phillis desolate. Mary Wheatley advised Phillis to find a suitable freedman for a husband.

Phillis married John Peters, a manumitted African-American in 1778, and they had three children. Peters was imprisoned for debt frequently and Phillis struggled to keep her family together. She sold precious keepsakes from Mary and hired herself out as a domestic servant. Little is known of Phillis' children, two of whom died at an early age. In 1779, Phillis planned to publish more poetry and advertised in the Evening Post and General Advertiser for sponsorship. Twenty poems largely on the subject of death appeared that same year in her book, *Proposals*. In September of 1784, the last of her poems was published, on the subject of her own baby's death. In December of 1784, a Boston newspaper announced the death of Phillis Wheatley, "Last Lord's day died, Mrs. Phillis Peters aged thirty-one known to the literary world by her celebrated miscellaneous Poems." She and her last child had died of malnutrition and were buried in an unmarked grave. Information on the gravesite was lost over the years and the site is unknown today. John Peters sold many of her manuscripts along with her book collection to pay off his debts. Some of Phillis' books and letters were eventually purchased by Harvard University. Phillis Wheatley's education and extraordinary literary talent had failed to spare her from a tragic life and early death. After the deaths of John, Susannah and Mary Wheatley, Bostonian society provided no place for a free black woman.

Phillis Wheatley, captured by slave traders in Africa in 1761, and brought to America, was purchased by John Wheatley of Boston. Her poems were published in 1767; she died in poverty December 5, 1784. (Picture courtesy of the Library of Congress.)

Conclusion

The Revolutionary War had brought many changes to America. A republic and independent state governments were formed as well as our first Federal institutions, a confederation government, the Continental Congress and the Continental Army, but a significant portion of the population – women and slaves who had fought for independence – did not enjoy its fruits.

By 1794, the Quaker anti-slavery campaign had organized abolition societies in many northern cities to liberate the slave population there. Although Quaker activism created a climate for reform, and northern colonies had liberated slaves much sooner, severe prejudice toward African-Americans continued in the North.

For a brief period in the postwar years, the Shaker Community expanded. By the time of Mother Ann Lee's death in 1784, Shaker membership had increased to several thousand. In 1830, the Shaker Community reached its greatest numbers with twenty Shaker villages in eight states and 3,000 members. During this period they gave refuge to runaway slaves who were treated as equals in the Shaker communities. Although they offered converts and refugees a sense of order and stability, the practice of celibacy hastened their extinction and today many former villages remain as outdoor museums. The Shakers live on in the style which they developed, which became an American classic: a simple utilitarian design in architecture, machinery, furniture and crafts.

After the war, Mercy Otis Warren wrote a three-volume history of the American Revolutionary War, *the History of the Rise, Progress, and Termination of the American Revolution,* which was published in 1805. Her longtime friend, John Adams criticized the work stating, "ladies ought not to write history."

The Pinckney family stayed in the forefront of colonial politics. Charles, Jr. who had served as an Aide de Camp to General Washington, and fought at Brandywine, Germantown, and the defense of Charleston was detained by the British as a prisoner of war for two years. In 1787, he represented South Carolina as a delegate to the Constitutional Convention in Philadelphia. As a special envoy to Paris, Charles C. Pinckney, Jr. along with John Marshall, and Elbridge Gerry were embroiled in the famous XYZ affair. In 1800, Charles ran for vice president on the Federalist ticket with John Adams. He campaigned for the presidency as the Federalist candidate in 1804 and 1808. Eliza's younger son, Thomas who had served in the South Carolina militia during the Revolution was wounded and captured at the Battle of Camden. From 1787 to 1789, Thomas served as Governor of South Carolina.

When President Washington made his grand tour in 1791, Eliza Lucas Pinckney received him at her home. In 1792, she was diagnosed with cancer and sought treatment in Philadelphia and died there that same year at age seventy-one. At her funeral, George Washington served as a pallbearer and helped carry Eliza Lucas Pinckney to her resting place in St. Peter's churchyard, in Philadelphia.

Washington appointed Thomas Pinckney minister to England, and he served in that office from 1792-1796. As Envoy Extraordinary to Spain he negotiated the Treaty named for him. Thomas, also a Federalist was elected to the United States Congress from 1797-1801. During the War of 1812, he was promoted and served as a major general.

The Revolutionary War established an all too familiar pattern. During wartime when women's services were needed for the war effort, society allowed women to cross the boundary of gender and domesticity and perform duties normally reserved for men. After the war, society demanded that women return to their traditional place. Either way, in war or peacetime, society dictated the role women would play.

However, Eliza Wilkinson indicated that women were vocalizing their discontent. "The men say we have no business with the politics. But I won't have it thought that because we are the weaker sex as to bodily strength we are capable of nothing more than domestic concerns. They won't even allow us liberty of thought and that is all I want."It was only a matter of time before women would demand more than liberty of thought.

Chapter 7
Women in the New Republic
True Women and American Girls

Key Topics

Poverty in the New Republic
Women in the Domestic Sphere
Women in the Workplace

Chronology

1791 - Samuel Slater Builds the Spinning Frame and First Factory
Susanna Rowson Publishes *Charlotte Temple*
1812 - 1815 - War of 1812, American Victory, Age of Federalism
1818 - The Revolutionary War Pension Act
1822 - Lowell Mills, the Boston Manufacturing Company
1821 - 1858 - Publication of *Godey's Ladies Book*

Introduction

The generation of Americans who lived during the Revolutionary War and the New Republic witnessed a dramatic transformation as thirteen separate English colonies became one sovereign nation, and developed into a prosperous and independent country. But, women had gained neither citizenship, nor civil rights; the political domain continued to assert privileged white men. Women had assumed that the new democratic Republic would extend citizenship to all; however, the ideals of the Declaration of Independence that "all men are created equal" and are granted "inalienable rights" excluded poor men, all women, slaves, and Native Americans. For all intents, the Revolution had merely replaced the government of one group of propertied men for another

Nonetheless, in the New Republic, change was evident. More fathers provided for their daughters in wills, and permitted them more freedom in choosing a husband. By the mid nineteenth century, the increasing numbers of spinsters (i.e. single women) in the population indicated that some women did not seek nor favor the married state.

After the Revolution, modes of work also changed as the American economy gradually shifted to a factory system, with mills powered by water. The new manufacturing dramatically affected American families. The colonial home, which had been the primary workplace, became a private domestic sphere, devoted to household management and child rearing.

At a time when most people did not survive beyond the age of forty, the early nineteenth century marked a great growth spurt for a new and young Republic. The population increased from 2.5 million in the revolutionary years (1775- 1783), to 3.9 million by 1790. At the end of the eighteenth century, about 200,000 Americans lived on the new frontier west of the Allegheny and Appalachian mountains.

Thirty years later, in 1820, the national population had tripled to 9.6 million, and of that number two million Americans lived west of the Appalachians, distributed among nine new states and three territories of the New Republic.

Poverty in the New Republic

For many Americans, life in the New Republic was a hand-to-mouth existence. Evidence of the escalating poverty is found in the household inventory lists of the Revolutionary Veterans Pension rolls which contain 60,000 veterans of the American War of Independence. For instance, after the war, Margaret Corbin, (a.k.a. Molly Pitcher), an invalid, lived in straitened circumstances. She died on January 16, 1800, as a result of her war injuries at the age of forty-eight. Deborah Samson Gannett, who had masqueraded as a male soldier, lived on a meager pension. She was very likely the first American woman to appear on the theatrical stage. To augment her income, she performed in Boston and New York theaters charging seven dollars per appearance. In 1802, the Mercury and New England Palladium, a Boston newspaper, billed her as "Mrs. Gannett equipt in complete uniform will go through the Manual Exercise. The whole [sic] to conclude with the Song and Chorus of 'God Save the Sixteen States.'"

In 1818, when the Federal government passed the indigent pension legislation, the application procedure required that veterans prove poverty by submitting an inventory of their household goods. Some families, who were turned down, continued to petition for years. In rare instances, widows could petition to receive any unpaid benefits still due to their deceased husbands. Widows would not qualify to receive benefits directly until 1836, sixty years after the war.

To qualify for an indigent pension, the government reckoned $100.00 in personal inventory as the norm for defining pauperism. The American Revolutionary Pension Rolls reveal widespread poverty in the early Republic, and a large class of Americans living as paupers. Ninety percent of the Revolutionary veterans did not own property and eked out a living as day laborers, or tenant farmers. Data on veterans' households show a state of even more severe "decomposition" with 60 percent of them falling below fifty dollars in personal assets. Widows with young children had an especially hard go of it. The pension applications describe how poor families with only meager assets suffered from untreated illnesses. Of those veterans who had fought for independence the cases are rather stark. Veteran Allen Evens, for example, never received a pension. Allen had served for six years in the war, and at age sixty, he and wife Betsey claimed total assets of only $110.00, with outstanding debts of sixty dollars. After the war, Samuel Chase and his wife had traveled from place to place seeking work. In 1820, Chase's wife languished, weak and unable to work; two of their seven children were handicapped. In 1836, and again in 1853, the government repeatedly denied a pension to Rebecca Everett, a veteran's widow with twelve children. Some veterans, wholly destitute of any assets, suffered starvation. William and Marcy Hutchings and their fifteen children reported that when there was nothing to eat, they would dig up and eat roots to stave off hunger pains.

Women in the Domestic Sphere

In the New Republic, as schooling became available for women, an increase in female literacy was evident in the proliferation of ladies' magazines and readership. Feminine popular literature abounded with romantic novels, flowery poetic verse and moralistic stories. Historian Ann Douglas, in *The Feminization of American Culture,* suggests that women's literature created a new *mentalite* in the nineteenth century, a culture with feminine tastes and values. Barbara Welter, in "The Cult of True Womanhood: 1820-1860," also observed a trend in nineteenth century ladies magazines, which depicted middle class women living in an ideal cocoon. Ladies magazines, according to Barbara Welter, were an effective means to pressure women to conform and maintain the status quo during a time of dramatic change.

The rise of business and industrialization forced American Society to redesign itself and to adjust to changes; males and females defined their space more sharply, and operated in separate spheres. Men dominated the workplace and women became in Professor Welter's words, "hostages in their own homes."

Many essays composed by ministers appeared in ladies' magazines. They gave advice to American women and defined acceptable behavior. Society, they preached, expected women to be feminine, pleasing, virtuous, attractive, submissive and refined. Ladies magazines like the famous *Godey's Lady's Book* featured an ideal, the cult of domesticity or true womanhood. Writers instructed women and girls on proper behavior, dress, marriage, household management, child care, and ways of coping in various social situations. Magazines promoted exclusivity, catering to upper and middle class women, because only females of the middle or upper class were considered proper ladies. Those who did not work outside the home qualified as members of the cult of domesticity. Females acquired the status of true womanhood by exploiting the labor of poor women, whom they hired as domestic servants.

Advice literature prescribed that true women embodied four cardinal virtues - piety, purity, submissiveness and domesticity. Barbara Welter notes that by living up to these attributes, women lived with a "series of suppressed emotions." The editor of *Godey's Lady's Book*, Sara Josepha Hale, believed it was feminine for women to suffer in silence since, "To women God hath given moral insight and the patience that endures physical suffering." Not only was it a woman's fate to accept male domination, but it also ensured the survival of civilization. Domesticity protected females who stayed at home, living a life of composure, secure from the evils of the outside world. They preserved virtue, morality, religious devotion, and piety. A wife took on the responsibility to control her husband's unbridled passions, and as mothers, preserved family morals.

On the surface, the ideology of True Womanhood appeared stifling for women but it allowed them to seize opportunities in education and reform work. Given the duty to maintain values of home and family, women could justify taking on social problems as well. Ironically the Cult of Domesticity which was meant to keep women in their place, succeeded in doing the opposite. In the New Republic things were out of order. Crime, social deviancy, domestic violence, prostitution and alcoholism were taking their toll on American society. Men had made a mess of things, and it was up to the women to go public and to restore order. Taking the message of Republican Motherhood and True Womanhood to heart, women mobilized for reform.

A multitude of women spread the doctrine of domesticity but none did so more diligently than Sara Josepha Hale, the editor of *Godey's Lady's Book*, for more than forty years. Widowed in 1822, and in poor financial straits, Sara had turned to writing. In 1837, Louis Godey, publisher of *Godey's Lady's Book*, appointed her editor. Their collaboration made the periodical the most widely circulated magazine in the United States. In *Godey's,* Sara Josepha Hale created the prototype of the American woman's periodical. The colored images of ladies' dress styles became a distinguishing signature of *Godey's Lady's Book.* The magazine also featured food recipes, housekeeping hints, social etiquette, home decorating tips, advice on rearing children, and medicinal cure-alls. By 1860, the publication boasted a readership of 150,000.

Mothers of Invention - Elizabeth Bayley Seton, an American Saint

Elizabeth Ann Bayley, the daughter of Catherine Charlton and Dr. Richard Bayley, a prominent New York physician, attended Madame Pompelion's school where she applied herself to the piano, religious instruction, dancing and French lessons. At age fourteen, Elizabeth danced with George Washington at his Inaugural Ball in New York City. The Bayley family were devout Episcopalians and Elizabeth's father instilled rigid character training in his children. From an early age, Elizabeth displayed a deep spirituality and a compassion for those less fortunate.

In 1794, at age nineteen, Elizabeth married William Magee Seton, a young merchant with a thriving business. They had five children, born between 1795 and 1802. During this period of young motherhood, Elizabeth busied herself with social pleasures and, arduous works of charity, such as the Widows Society of New York, to help destitute widowed mothers, for which she earned the title Protestant Sister of Charity.

The new century ushered in a great deal of sadness and misfortune for the Bayley and Seton families. William Seton's business suffered adversely, forcing him to declare bankruptcy. In 1801, Dr. Bayley died, a victim of yellow fever which he had contracted while treating patients during the epidemic in New York City. In 1803, William was diagnosed with tuberculosis, and his health deteriorated rapidly. Adhering to medical beliefs of the time, Elizabeth and William set sail for Italy to recuperate in its warmer climate. Unfortunately, when they arrived in Italy, passengers were quarantined because they had left port during New York's Yellow Fever epidemic. Placed in a cold damp cell in the Lazaretto, a public hospital, William's grave condition worsened and he died thirty-eight days later.

Elizabeth Ann Bayley Seton, the first female Native-born Saint of the United States, pioneered women's education and founded the religious order the Sisters of Charity of Saint Joseph. (Picture courtesy of the Library of Congress.)

Adjusting to sudden widowhood, Elizabeth was consoled by William's Italian business associates, the Filicchi's, and an Irish Catholic priest. When she returned to New York in 1804, and expressed an interest in Catholicism, her family tried to dissuade her. Elizabeth became a Roman Catholic and as soon as she converted, her family disinherited her and friends ostracized her. From 1805-1808, Elizabeth tried a number of ventures to support her five children, including a school and a boardinghouse. When these failed, Elizabeth sought the friendlier Catholic environment of Baltimore City where she arranged to establish a school for girls. Her sisters-in-law Cecilia and Harriet, also recent converts to Catholicism joined her there.

Church officials like Maryland Archbishop Carroll recognized in Elizabeth Seton superior abilities as an educator and administrator. Elizabeth had contemplated the possibility of establishing a community of religious women dedicated to teaching and in 1809, she founded the Sisters of Charity of Saint Joseph. She took religious vows before Archbishop Carroll, who called her Mother Seton and appointed her director of the new community. That same year Elizabeth, her sisters-in-law, and newly recruited Sisters of Charity settled on a farm in western Maryland at Emmitsburg. In 1812, after several years of hardship, the community succeeded and Mother Seton built and administrated Saint Joseph's Academy for young women. She also trained teachers, wrote educational texts, translated French religious books into English, composed spiritual treatises, and maintained extensive correspondence with notable people of her time. Mother Seton and the Sisters of Charity visited the sick and the poor, and converted many of their African-American neighbors to Catholicism. In 1814, Elizabeth Seton established an orphanage in Philadelphia operated by her order, the Sisters of Charity. In 1817, she founded another orphanage in New York City. In 1818, she buried three of her five children and fell ill herself. She died from tuberculosis in 1821, at the age of forty-six, and is buried in the community's cemetery at Emmitsburg.

In 1882, Cardinal Gibbon proposed her sainthood. Canonization is the achievement of sainthood in the Roman Catholic Church and occurs in three stages. First, an individual must be recognized as heroic or *Venerable*; second as *Blessed;* and, finally sainthood is granted. In 1975, timed for the United States bicentennial celebration, Elizabeth Ann Bayley Seton was canonized and became the first Native-born North American to become a saint in the Roman Catholic Church.

Her achievement in education is significant. She created the first parochial school system in the United States and the first American-based Catholic order for nuns. Today in North and South America, Italy and in foreign missions, thousands of women in twenty-one communities belong to the Sisters of Charity of St. Joseph. Five other communities in New York, New Jersey and Halifax, Nova Scotia trace their development to the Sisters of Charity founded by Mother Seton. The institution she founded, St. Joseph's College, advanced higher education for women at a time when no other female colleges existed.

Women in the Workplace

> "While women's intellect is confined, her morals crushed, her health ruined, her weaknesses encouraged, and her strength punished, she is told that her lot is cast in the paradise of women."
>
> Harriet Martineau,
> English visitor To America, 1830

In the 1820s, the textile industry became a major factory system in the United States. Francis Cabot Lowell, who established textile mills in the New England town named for him, hired young females *en masse* as the first factory labor. Removing young girls so far from their homes was a bold departure for the apprenticeship system. Lowell had to reassure families their daughters would work in a safe place. He built company sponsored dormitories, where the girls were supervised by housemothers. Bringing so many young people under one roof to work called for a disciplined work environment. Lowell created an operative, known as the *Waltham System,* which regimented life for the girls with a twelve-to-fifteen-hour work day and a strict curfew. On their day off, church attendance was mandatory. The girls took all of their meals at the dormitory and were packed into small sleeping quarters. They earned about two dollars weekly and judging from their letters home, they were expected to send their earnings home to their families. In some instances, mill girls' earnings contributed to their brother's college tuition. Factory owners demanded that mill girls maintain their innocence even as management exploited their physical labor and robbed them of their youthful vigor. Within a decade, the girls who came to Lowell full of enthusiasm and ideas about improving their lives became quickly disillusioned.

One mill girl, Lucy Larcom, began working at the factory at age eleven, and later organized a literary magazine, *The Lowell Offering*. Initially, mill owners viewed the journal as a harmless venture, but as soon as the magazine acted as a sounding board for worker discontent, mill owners censored the paper. In 1837, the girls staged a walkout which completely shut down the Lowell Mill. One participant, Harriet Hanson Robinson, described the futility of the workers,

> When the day came when the girls were to turn out, those in the upper room started first, and so many of them left that our mill was at once shut down. The agent of the corporation took some small revenge on the supposed ring leaders. It is hardly necessary to say that so far as results were concerned this strike did no good. The dissatisfaction of the operatives subsided, or burned itself out, and though the authorities did not accede to their demands, the majority returned to their work, and the corporation went on cutting down wages.

The first textile factory workers were girls recruited from New England farm families. (Photo courtesy of the Library of Congress.)

Despite their frustration, girls like Harriet Hanson Robinson and Sarah Bagley created the first significant labor union in the country — The Lowell Female Labor Reform Association, the LFLRA. Bagley in particular fought for improved working conditions, collected signatures on petitions and organized workers in other towns. From 1840-1880, management gained more of an upper hand. As more mill girls organized and protested, the owners simply hired immigrant women and their children to replace them. In 1836, less than four percent of the 7,000 mill girls were immigrants but thirty years later, sixty percent of the mill employees were foreign born women. For the mill girls unionizing efforts, the only change evident in the workplace was the ethnic composition of the mill workers and the closing down of company boardinghouses. On their meager salary, the immigrant workers had to furnish their own housing and meals.

Sarah Bagley continued a campaign and through her efforts the LFLRA merged with the New England Workingmen's Association. This alliance petitioned the Massachusetts legislature for a ten-hour workday. Lawmakers responded by siding with moneyed interests and supported the position of the mill owners.

The mill girls exemplified the dramatic changes taking place in the New Republic and how they affected women. Stepping abruptly into the industrial age, these eager workers went off to work in the mills with high hopes. Lucy Larcom, chronicled the life of the mill girls in her autobiography, *A New England Girlhood,*

> The girls who toiled together at Lowell were clearing away a few weeds from the overgrown track of independent labor for other women. They practically said, by numbering themselves among the factory girls, that in our country no real odium could be attached to any honest toil that any self-respecting woman might undertake.

Lucy Larcom remembered how the excitement of factory work wore off quickly after girls put in a twelve-to-fifteen-hour workday and their health deteriorated from tedious work. The working conditions at Lowell were dismal. The factory rooms filled with the new large power looms were hot, noisy and damp. The air, moistened with steam and sizing to preserve fiber from splitting, created an environment healthier for thread than for humans. Many young factory workers contracted tuberculosis from inhaling lint and sizing and from living in overcrowded spaces where other highly contagious diseases spread. Some suffered from tinnitus and eventually became deaf from the deadening noise of the machines. It was not unusual for workers to lose fingers or mangle hands and limbs in the machinery. Yet, for any infraction of company rules, girls could be terminated from their job. These conditions stood as ironic testimony in a society which touted female virtue and true womanhood.

The Lowell Textile Mills revolutionized American Manufacturing, operating a large factory and housing workers in company-run dormitories. (Photo Courtesy of the Library of Congress.)

The Character of Charlotte Temple

As factory life drew young girls farther from home, society's concerns about the dangers and temptations of city life increased. Popular literature flooded the market with morality tales warning girls about the consequences of succumbing to male advances. Moralistic authors stressed that it was a woman's responsibility as the *weaker* sex to control man's lust and his possible assaults on her.

The most famous of these morality novels, *Charlotte Temple*, written by Susanna Rowson, remained on the best seller list in the United States for over a century. Published in 1791, and first read by the Revolutionary generation, it spoke directly to factory girls who faced homesickness, disillusionment and a loss of innocence. In the novel, *Charlotte Temple*, a young British female is seduced by a handsome young soldier, Montraville, who then brings her to America, still unmarried. When Charlotte becomes pregnant, Montraville abandons her. Although Charlotte, the suffering heroine, is perceived as a good woman, Rowson makes it clear that Charlotte's own poor judgment caused her demise.

> In affairs of love, a young heart is never in more danger than when attempted by a handsome young soldier, when beauty of person, elegance of manner, and an easy method of paying compliments are united to a scarlet coat, smart cockade, and military sash, ah! Well-a-day for the poor girl who gazes on him; she is in imminent danger; if she listens to him with pleasure, tis all over for her.

Charlotte Temple, written as moral advice literature for adolescent girls, became popular with readers of all ages and was printed in over 200 editions. Much of the formula for the plot was drawn from Rowson's own life, which was nearly as tragic as Charlotte's. As a young girl, Susanna had migrated to America a decade before the American Revolution. During the War, her Loyalist family had suffered relocation, loss of property, and imprisonment. Her husband William squandered their money in poor business deals. To support herself, Susanna found success in education. In 1797, she established the Young Ladies Academy of Boston and introduced one of the first feminist studies there. She developed a curriculum and wrote textbooks which were gender specific; her *Abridgment to Universal Geography,* for example, ranked how women fared in countries around the globe. In 1811, she published *A Present for Young Ladies,* a historical anthology of famous women.

Rowson never received one cent in royalties for the great success of *Charlotte Temple.* Her publisher pocketed the profits for the forty editions of *Charlotte Temple* published in her lifetime.

Women's Housekeeping in the New Republic

> I expect ain't much reason to have a woman if she ain't of no use. Every man ought to have a woman to do his cookin' and such like, since it is easier for them than it is for us. They take to it kindly and naturally. I reckon women are some like horses and oxen, the biggest can do the most work, and that's what I want one for.
>
> Newlywed Husband

Whether women worked outside the home or not, the demands of housekeeping never ceased. Food preparation was the most time consuming but women also maintained lighting for the home, and prepared textiles and clothing. Farm women cultivated flax for linen, wool and cotton, all of which required intensive labor. Housekeeping entailed waging a relentless and never ending war on dirt, dust, insects, rodents, and other critters. One of the most laborious chores for women was laundering, and this included making their own soap. Water had to be hauled into the house and heated. Clothes were soaked, scrubbed by hand on a washboard, hung outside to dry, then pressed with heavy flatirons. Housewives took great pride in their achievements and judged each other on domestic skills. A *slut* referred to a woman who shirked her duties and had little regard for the sanctity and hygiene of her home.

As Americans settled on the frontier and the prairie, living greater distances from their own family, self reliance was the key to survival. Faced with isolation, bonding with other women was a mainstay for their emotional well-being. To reduce the tedium of work, housewives invited other women for a working bee. Quilting bees and apple bees were the most popular, but women also showed up for wool-picking, spinning and weaving bees. The hostess provided food so the women could sew, and a working bee group could begin and finish a quilt all in one day. Visitors shared favorite recipes and medicinal remedies; they exchanged stimulating gossip and enjoyed much needed female companionship.

I've been a hard worker all my life, but 'most all my work has been the kind that perishes with use as the Bible says. That the discouragin' thing about a woman's work... if a woman was to see all the dishes that she had to wash before she died, piled up before her in one pile, she'd lie down and die right then and there. I've always had the name o'bein' a good housekeeper, but when I'm dead and gone there ain't anybody goin' to think o'the floors I've swept, and the tables I've scrubbed, and the stockin's I've darned. But when one of my grandchildren sees one o'these quilts they'll think about Aunt Jane, and wherever I am then, I'll know I ain't forgotten.

Aunt Jane, Kentucky

Needlework provided a great pastime for women of every social class, ethnic group and region of the country. More than anything else, the ability to sew a fine stitch defined female skill. By the nineteenth century, American quilt patterns had evolved into an art form and were a unique record of rites of passage in one's life: a birth, a marriage, a parting of friends, or a funeral. Special quilts were made for a new baby, as wedding gifts for a new bride, and an album or friendship quilt was given to a woman leaving home and moving west. Pioneers crossing the prairie used quilts to bury their dead.

Lydia Maria Child, an active social reformer, editor and author, kept a log for one year of all the tasks she had completed. It should be noted that her list of accomplishments (see page ninety-three) is a modest one, and atypical because Lydia and David had no children; it reflects work for a household of only two people. The average housewife's list would have been much longer.

The following figures from the United States Senate document the numbers of women employed in industry from 1850 to 1880. No accurate labor statistics are available before 1850.

These figures are limited since they do not include the following groups of female workers, women who worked for businesses which hired females exclusively such as commercial laundries, urban women who would have been employed in a cottage industry or as domestic servants, and women engaged in farming. However, these figures are useful to show how, as the industrial revolution progressed in the nineteenth century, the number of women workers increased significantly. Women were hired to work in factories because owners could pay them less, often half the salary of a male employee.

These figures show the woman in the work force, 1850-1880

Industry:	**Total female workers for 1850**	**Total female workers for 1880**
Clothing and Textiles	202,246	408,138
Printing and Paper	7,027	29,762
Tobacco and cigar making	1,975	20,480
Food production	919	23,276
Other manufactures (viz. Ceramic, glass, stone, chemicals, metal production [other than iron and steel]	9,538	38,390

Lydia Maria Child
"All in a Year's Work"

Wrote 235 letters
Wrote six articles for newspapers
Wrote 47 autograph articles
Wrote out my will
Corrected proofs for Sunset Book
Read aloud six pamphlets and 21 books
Made 25 needle books for the Freedwomen
Made 2 bivouac caps for soldiers
Knit two pair hospital socks
Grew, gathered and made bushel pickles
for the hospital
Knit pairs of socks for David
Made two pairs of suspenders for D.
Knitted six baby sweaters for friends
Knitted one large afghan
Made spectacle case for D.
Made one doormat
Made one woolen cape
Made 3 corsets
Made 2 shirts for D
Made 1 chemise
Made 2 flannel shirts for D
Cut out and made three gowns
Made a shirt with waist
Made a thick cotton petticoat
Made one quilted petticoat
Made a silk gown
Cut out and made a sac for myself
Cut and dried a peck of apples
Made one pair of carpet slippers for D
Made four towels
Made three large curtains and lined them
Sewed three small pairs curtains, lined
Sewed four new pillow cases
Made collars and wristbands for six shirts
Made one nightcap
Made one pair summer pantaloons
Made a starred crib quilt and quilted it
Spent four days collecting and sorting
Papers, pamphlets scattered by the fire
Mended five pairs of drawers
Mended 70 pairs of stockings
Cooked 362 dinners
Cooked 362 breakfasts
Cooked 365 midday meals
Swept, dusted, mopped sitting room and
Kitchen 362 times
Cleaned, filled oil lamps 362 times
Swept, dusted chamber and stairs 40 times
Preserved all the barberries
Innumerable small jobs
Made 5 visits to elderly women
Tended an invalid friend for two weeks
Went to Medford - one day's visit
Made three visits to Boston
Made seven calls upon neighbors
Made a woolen dressing gown for David

Conclusion

After the War of Independence, Americans experienced bold changes, but unfortunately many who had sacrificed so much to win independence did not enjoy the fruits of it after the war. In the New Republic, poverty was widespread. To fuel the emerging American Textile industry, females were recruited to work in factories, mills, and sweatshops. As young American girls became the first factory workers, literature warned of the danger for females living away from their families. The Waltham System seemed to address these concerns by setting up company-run dormitories and maternal supervision.

The women who worked outside their homes (usually out of necessity and not by choice) were compensated with very meager wages. Some performed the labor intensive duties as servants for more affluent families. Others ran their own households, cared for their children, operated a family business or maintained a family farm. Women continued to be poorly paid for their work or were not paid at all.

Dr. Benjamin Rush's ideology of Republican Motherhood—that women should be educated because of their critical role as primary educators of their sons, i.e of the future citizens of the Republic—did pave the way for women to get a formal education but few were able to do so right away. Female pioneers in education, such as Judith Sargent Murray and Elizabeth Seton, promoted women's education and established schools with an academic curricula. Within a short period of time, although few in number, educated women would make a significant social stir.

Part III

The Age of Reform

The Anti-Slavery Crusade and the Women's Movement

Women and the Antebellum Reform Movement

Women and the Pioneer Movement

The Role of Women in the West

Women in the American Civil War

Chapter 8
The Anti-Slavery Crusade and the Women's Movement
Turning our Thoughts from Stockings and Puddings

Key Topics

Women and the Anti-slavery Cause
Unlikely Abolitionists: The Grimke Sisters
Starting a Women's Movement

Chronology

1801 - The Cane Ridge, Kentucky, Revival
1820 - The Second Great Awakening
1830 - The Abolitionist Movement Established
1840 - The International Conference on the Anti-Slavery Crusade
1848 - The Seneca Falls Conference

Introduction

In the early 1800s, a religious revival, the Second Great Awakening, began stirring the country, and initiated from 1820-1850, a period known as the Antebellum Reform Era. Americans participated in a wide array of social crusades. Inspired by the Awakening preachers, converts believed that through their efforts America could be made a perfect society. Folks, especially women, boarded the reform bandwagon and played an active part in the movement.

An event which sparked this energy occurred in 1801, when 50,000 participants attended a camp revival meeting at Cane Ridge, Kentucky. It must have been quite a sight and sound to behold! As the faithful and newly converted began singing and praying, one observer noted that they raised a noise "like the roar of Niagara."

Beginning in the mid 1820s, a major player in this movement was Charles Finney, a former lawyer turned minister. He conducted a series of revival meetings in New York and Ohio and his message inspired audiences everywhere. Finney rejected the Calvinist theme that mankind was depraved. Instead he instilled hope and optimism by preaching that human perfectibility was attainable. When Finney appointed women to pray over souls and visit the homes of potential converts, the conservative clergy decried his use of women in the revival. The ministers felt that female activism in the churches was inappropriate and they worried because Finney delegated power and authority to women. Ultimately, Charles Finney's mantra on perfectibility became the clarion call in the decades preceding the American Civil War.

Women and the Anti-slavery Cause

Although women were barred from speaking in public to mixed audiences, that is, to groups where males and females assembled together, nonetheless, they dominated antebellum reform associations as organizers and volunteers. Women were particularly active in the anti-slavery cause, a movement in which various groups attempted different strategies. In 1817, a group of like-minded Americans, who believed that gradual reform was the means to wipe out slavery, formed the American Colonization Society, ACS. To that end, the ACS proposed that free blacks be sent to Africa. By 1821, their fundraising had secured a colonial society in Liberia and provided for the transport of several thousand African-Americans to Africa. They also raised funds to help emancipate slaves, but the impact of the colonization effort was limited. In some ways it simply reflected the prejudice which existed in America toward blacks that white people were more willing to remove African-Americans from the United States than to deal with the problem of slavery. The American Colonization Society did little to eradicate slavery, because by the nineteenth century most slaves had traced their ancestry back many generations in America, and they had cast their lot, for good or ill, with their country, the United States.

In 1831, reformers launched the Abolitionist movement, which was a more radical approach to the eradication of slavery. Because the Abolitionists rebuked gradual reform and demanded the immediate release of slaves from bondage with no compensation to slaveholders, Americans in both the North and the South regarded Abolitionists as dangerous extremists. William Lloyd Garrison, considered one of the most radical abolitionists, founded a newspaper *The Liberator* to promote the cause and in 1833, Garrison and his associates founded the American Anti-Slavery Society.

Before proceeding, it is well to remember that the anti-slavery movement was spearheaded early in 1740, by English and American Quakers. So it is not surprising that by the nineteenth century, Quaker women, nurtured on ideas of social equality, took an active role in the anti-slavery crusade. Worthy of mention are Quakers Prudence Crandall, Lucretia Mott, Lydia Maria Child, Maria Weston Chapman, Sarah and Angelina Grimke, and Susan B. Anthony. They were joined by non-Quaker women, notables such as Elizabeth Cady Stanton, Harriet Beecher Stowe, Julia Ward Howe and hundreds more.

In 1832, Prudence Crandall, founder of a girl's school in Canterbury, Connecticut, had admitted a "pious colored female" and town residents protested. When the community pressured Prudence to refuse the student admittance, she opted instead to shut down the school. One year later in 1833, Prudence Crandall reopened her school, as a private boarding school exclusively for black girls and admitted seventeen students. Facing legal injunctions against the school, she continued instruction despite her own arrest and incarceration. However, after numerous acts of vandalism and arson had occurred, fearing for the safety of the pupils, Prudence Crandall saw no alternative but to close the school.

Women's activism in the anti-slavery crusade gained momentum in 1833, when Garrison organized the abolitionists. Lucretia Mott founded the Philadelphia Female Anti-Slavery Society, and women such as Maria Weston Chapman co-founded the Boston Female Anti-Slavery Society and served as a supporter, ally and volunteer in Garrison's American Anti-Slavery Society. Lydia Maria Child, already an accomplished and published writer, authored a scholarly work, *An Appeal in Favor of that Class of American called African,* but she paid dearly for her outspokenness; the notoriety forced her to relinquish a promising writing career. Boston society shunned Lydia and publishing companies would not accept her work. At the time, the hostility directed at abolitionists came from the North as well as the South, underscoring the fact that racial hatred had no geographic boundary.

Nevertheless, women responded to the overwhelming task of organizing an anti-slavery crusade by gathering petitions; writing, publishing and distributing literature, fundraising, organizing meetings and speaking to women's groups. Although thousands of female volunteers shall remain anonymous, their efforts brought them valuable experience, and while some women openly joined the anti-slavery cause, others aided slaves fleeing the South.

Les Gens de Couleur Libres[1]

In 1790, there were more than 59,000 free Blacks in the United States. By 1810, that number had risen to 186,446. Most of these were in the North, but Revolutionary sentiments had motivated a few Southern slaveholders to free their slaves by manumission or in their wills. However, lest we leave an overly optimistic impression, bear in mind, that of the entire antebellum black population throughout the United States, 95 percent were still enslaved.

By the early nineteenth century, in the City of New Orleans, changes in the African American population were evident. *Les gens de couleur libres,* or free people of color owned $2.5 million in property. They operated their own schools, usually private ones in the educators' homes and some students (male as well as female) were sent to France or to schools in the northern states to be educated.[2] Historian John Blassingame describes the cultural and social life of the free Negroes [sic] as quite varied with attendance at the theater, opera, the races, cock fights, and circuses. At the New Orleans French Opera and Theater free people of color had box seats in the second tier; on Sundays they attended mass at the St. Louis Cathedral, and during the week they kept a busy social schedule of balls and parties. In the antebellum era, free blacks participated in social and benevolent societies and established an orphan asylum in the city. Their population rose sharply as shown in the changes from the 1769 census where ninety-nine free people of color were recorded as residents in New Orleans to 1830 when their numbers had increased to 12,000. Generally they enjoyed a healthy relationship with the city's white citizens but this would change with the heightened fears and polarization in the decades preceding the Civil War.

From its inception, Louisiana and especially New Orleans had faced a shortage of females. The *Code Noir* or Black Code strictly forbade marriage between the races so French and Spanish men became habituated to choosing native women. European patterns of marriage dictated the age of thirty plus years favorable for men to marry. Bachelors were expected to confine their sexual activity to lower class women or take on a mistress. With the continued scarcity of white women a system known as *plaçag*e also developed.[3] P*laçag*e became a recognized extralegal system in which French, Spanish and later Creole men entered into the equivalent of common-law marriages with women of mixed racial descent.[4] It was acceptable for a man to take a mistress as young as twelve years of age.

The women were never legally recognized as wives, but referred to as *placées*. Their relationships were regarded among the free people of color as a *mariage de la main gauche* or a left-handed marriage. *Placées,* often women known as quadroons were renowned for their beauty and light skin.[5] Quadroon*s* were the offspring of white males and native or slave women who had produced a population of *métis* and in the succeeding generations, their children were of lighter skin (*mulatt*os). Not all free women of color became *placées* and not all *placées* were Quadroon*s* but a great many were. In much of the historical ephemera the term *placée* and quadroon are used interchangeably.

---

1. *Free people of color* here the term denotes those people in the City of New Orleans who were African-American, or *métis* (French for *mestizo*) who had achieved free status. This material is reprinted here with the permission of the author who holds the copyright.
2. These children were educated in France, because there were no schools available to educate mixed-race children, and it was illegal in the South to teach Blacks to read and write.
3. P*laçag*e from the French, *placer* meaning 'to place with.' P*laçag*e was a social arrangement whereby a white man took a woman of color for a concubine or mistress. The female was referred to as a *placée.*
4. Here we are using the term creole to denote men of European decent living in Louisiana.
5. Quadroon, literally one-quarter, is a racial category of hypodescent used to describe a person of mixed-race with a quarter African and three-quarters Caucasian ancestry.

Quadroon women of New Orleans posing for a group picture. Many quadroon women known for their beauty and light skin became placées to white men under a contractual arrangement known as plaçage. (Photo courtesy of the Library of Congress.)

We do know that by 1788, some 1,500 women of color were being maintained by white men in a certain lifestyle. The man was wealthy, lived outside of New Orleans on a plantation with his white family, and maintained a second address in the city for purposes of entertaining and socializing among the white elite. His *placée* and their children would live primarily in the house he provided for her in New Orleans. The man took part in and arranged for the upbringing and education of their children. Naturally, the ideal *plaçag*e arrangement could cost thousands of dollars per year.

Most men did not choose to maintain a *plaçag*e relationship exclusively as men of means had to legally marry to produce a rightful heir but within society there were variations. Eugène de Macarty, for instance, content for many years to maintain a relationship only with his *placée*, did not care to legally marry a white woman and produce suitable heirs. Eugène's brother, Augustin de Macarty, although married, reputedly had numerous, complex affairs with women of color; at his death, there were six Augustin de Macarty heirs from several different mothers making claims against his will. On his deathbed in 1845, Eugène de Macarty married Eulalie de Mandeville a former *placée* and then willed to her all of his property valued at $12,000; his will was contested by his white relatives but the courts upheld Eulalie's inheritance claim. After she died, her surviving children faced yet another claim and won. By that time the value of Eugéne de Macarty's estate had ballooned to over $150,000.

Most men were content to keep the relationship with their *placées* after marriage. Thus, a wealthy white man could possess not just one, but two (or more) families. One family with a white woman to whom he was legally married and the other with a light-skinned woman of color, a *placée,* who was faithful to him until death. So *plaçag*e was for all intents, an extralegal form of bigamy for males. Their mixed-race children became the nucleus of the class of free people of color l*es gens de couleur* in Louisiana. This would explain in part the increase in this group by the nineteenth century.

Marie Thérèse Coincoin was for twenty years, the *placée* of a French colonial planter, Claude Thomas Pierre Métoyer. At the onset of their *plaçage*, she was already the mother of five children and would bear Métoyer ten more! In 1778, he freed her after the parish priest filed charges against Coincoin as a "public concubine" and threatened to have her sold in New Orleans if Métoyer did not end the relationship. As a free woman, she remained with Métoyer until 1788, when his growing fortune persuaded him to take a wife who could provide legal heirs.

Upon the death of her protector and lover, the *placée* and her family could, on legal challenge, expect up to a third of the man's property. There were cases of white lovers who attempted—and succeeded—in making their mixed-race children primary heirs over other white descendants or relatives. *Placées* inherited plantations as well. Some *placées* owned slaves themselves, many at least one. But these were exceptionally generous cases and customarily the outcome was less favorable. If a white lover abandoned the *placée* or died without making provision for her which many did, the former *placée* had to find another source of income. Necessity and adversity for these women motivated entrepreneurship. Some acquired property, rented rooms or operated a boardinghouse. Others became tradeswomen working as hairdressers, seamstresses, shopkeepers or vendors. It was possible for a former *placée* to become a *placée* to yet another man or bring up her daughter to become one and an ex-*placée* could legally marry or cohabit with a man of color. Marie Thérèse Coincoin's daughter, Marie Susanne became a *placée* also. As a young woman, apparently with the blessing of both parents, she entered into a relationship with a New Orleans physician, Joseph Conant. When he left after the birth of their son, she formed a second and lifelong *plaçage* with the planter, Jean Baptiste Anty. As a second-generation *placée,* Susanne became far more successful than her mother had been. When Marie Susanne died in 1838 her estate was worth $61,600 (the equivalent of $1,500,000 in today's U.S. currency).

In New Orleans, p*laçag*e continued for more than a century. Promoters of the system developed a kind of 'coming out' ball for young women of color who hoped to make a *plaçag*e contract. Known as the Quadroon Balls these elegant and elaborate social events were designed to market and display these women. The quadroon's mother usually negotiated a *plaçag*e contract with a male admirer. Typical contractual terms included some financial payment to the parent, financial and housing arrangements for the quadroon herself, and paternal recognition and support of any children the union might produce. Males and females who entered these contracts regarded them with the same exclusivity as marriage. (At least the females were expected to do so.) Quadroon mistresses could parlay their beauty and had the power to destabilize white marriages and families, something white wives and their families much resented.

Contrary to popular misconceptions, *placées* were not and did not become prostitutes. But men of color seemed to be of two minds about them. They deplored *plaçag*e as denigrating to the virtue of women of color, while at the same time many of them were children of *placées.* Although many in society condemned women of color for seeking these contracts with white men, in reality, the women had few options available. They outnumbered free black men and could not legally marry white men. If a free woman of color married a slave, she and her children easily slipped into bondage. So they found an innovative means within the bounds of decency to secure a life for themselves and their children. As historian Joan Martin maintains, a mulatto mother and her quadroon daughter sought within the rigid confines of a black and white world some semblance of economic independence and social distinction from slaves. While they did not deliberately wish to live as concubines, they did choose to survive.[6]

Mothers of Invention: Black Women in the Abolitionist Cause

Former slaves and free blacks joined the abolitionist cause as devoted volunteers. Maria Stewart, a free black abolitionist purported to be the first African-American woman to speak publicly, lived in Boston and published many of her speeches in Garrison's *Liberator.* Maria argued that free blacks were no better off than slaves. She was convinced that only education and solidarity within the black community would enable all African-Americans to achieve freedom and a better life in the United States. A free black teacher in Baltimore, Frances Watkins Harper, served the movement as an accomplished, well-published poet. One of her poems, "The Slave Auction," expressed the tragedy of a slave family's separation,

> And mothers stood with streaming eyes,
> And saw their dearest children sold,
> Unheeded rose their bitter cries,
> While tyrants bartered them for gold.
> And woman, with her love and truth-
> For these in sable forms may dwell-
> Gaz'd on the husband of her youth,
> With anguish none may paint nor tell.

Frances, a volunteer on the Underground Railroad and an abolitionist lecturer, donated her publication earnings to aid fugitive slaves. By the 1840s, a small community of wealthy, educated free blacks also championed abolitionism. Among them were outstanding

6. Paraphrased here, see Joan M. Martin, "Plaçage and the Louisiana Gens de Couleur Libre," in *Creole,* edited by Sybil Kein, Louisiana State University Press, Baton Rouge, 2000.

women such as Sarah Mapps Douglass, Mary Ann Shadd Cary, Sarah Redmond and Charlotte Forten. These women gave of their financial resources and worked for abolitionism by speaking, writing and teaching.

After the State of New York abolished slavery, a slave known as Isabella was granted her freedom in 1828. Unfortunately, New York laws came too late to prevent two of Isabella's children from being sold away. Upon manumission, Isabella devoted her new life by choosing a new name, Sojourner Truth. She became an itinerant preacher, and despite illiteracy, had an articulate style, with excellent recall of Biblical passages and other literary works. Sojourner Truth developed into a charismatic speaker and in 1840, the Abolitionists recruited her. She often spoke on the podium with Frederick Douglass, a runaway slave who had also joined the Abolitionist cause.

Unlikely Abolitionists: The Grimke Sisters

Two remarkable converts to abolitionism, Sarah and Angelina Grimke, served as credible witnesses to the evils of slavery. Sarah and Angelina had grown up in South Carolina, daughters of John Faucheraud Grimke, a prominent judge and wealthy slaveholder. At the age of twelve, Sarah learned about the punitive world slaves inhabited. In her diary, Sarah noted a ritual which occurred almost nightly until she was caught,

> ...I took an almost malicious satisfaction in teaching my little waiting-maid at night, when she was supposed to be occupied in combing and brushing my long locks. The light was put out, the keyhole screened and flat on our stomachs, before the fire, with spelling book under our eyes, we defied the laws of South Carolina.

When Sarah's father discovered the nocturnal tutoring, her little waiting maid was threatened with a beating and Sarah was severely reprimanded for trying to teach the slave to read. Later, in 1821, while visiting Philadelphia, Sarah made acquaintances among the local Quaker friends and decided to become a Quaker, live in Philadelphia and join the Philadelphia Friends Meeting. A few years later, when reunited with her younger sister Angelina, they took up the abolitionist cause together. Under the guidance of Abolitionist Theodore Dwight Weld, the Grimke sisters joined Garrison's group and trained as abolitionist speakers. Angelina published an anti-slavery tract in 1836, *An Appeal to the Christian Women of the South,* and where society permitted, she began a round of parlor talks for women's groups in New York City.

The Grimke Sisters, Sarah and Angelina were raised on a South Carolina plantation, relocated to Philadelphia, joined the Quaker meeting and became the first females to publicly speak out for the anti-slavery cause and women's rights. (Photos Courtesy of the Library of Congress.)

Because these two southern women described vividly and convincingly the evils of slavery, they were in popular demand. As their celebrity spread, men and women flocked to their meetings defying social convention by allowing women to speak. Criticism of their participation came from an unlikely source, Catherine Beecher, a member of a prominent New England family who championed abolitionism. Catherine published a pamphlet attacking the Grimke's, *An Essay on Slavery and Abolitionism with Reference to the Duty of American Females,* stating she had no objection to abolitionism in principle, only to female abolitionists. Beecher asserted that God intended for women to subordinate themselves to men. Catherine Beecher believed that the Grimke sisters could make a more substantial contribution by staying home rather than by appearing in public.

Catherine Beecher held contradictory ideas on women's rights. In one sense, she defied social convention with her innovative ideas for female physical education. At a time when many physicians opposed any strenuous physical training for females, she advocated exercise, sports and physical education to improve women's health. Although Catherine Beecher's vision for female health and education seemed tailor-made for the women's crusade, she rigidly opposed feminism and frequently spoke out against the movement:

> So much has been said of the higher sphere of woman and so much has been done to find some better work for her that, insensibly almost everybody begins to feel that it is rather degrading for a woman in good society to be much tied down to family affairs; especially since in these Woman's Rights Conventions there is so much dissatisfaction expressed at those who would confine her ideas to the kitchen and the nursery.

Catherine Beecher disassociated herself from female reformers because as she said, "There has been a great deal of crude disagreeable talk in these conventions, and too great a tendency of the age to make the education of woman anti-domestic." However, she believed every woman had rights as a human being, rights that ought to be freely conceded to them, but she fell short of explaining just how women could attain them. While she adamantly believed that women should keep traditional roles, and be submissive to men, she promoted sex education for women, including information on contraception. She also talked of equality of the sexes and believed women would not be on an equal par with men until they received an equivalent education and could support themselves, but at the same time she disapproved of women working in factories.

In *Letters to Catherine Beecher*, Angelina Grimke defended her right to shoulder the burden of the anti-slavery cause. Angelina believed women had the right to lobby for laws and to petition the National Congress. She said "the right of petition is the only political right that women have," and they have just as much right to "sit in solemn counsel in conventions, conferences, associations and general assemblies" as men do. By defending women's rights to participate in the anti-slavery crusade, the Grimkes formulated a *justification for feminism*, and Angelina became the first woman to speak before a legislative body when she addressed the Massachusetts legislature,

> I stand before you as a southerner, exiled from the land of my birth by the sound of the lash and the piteous cry of the slave. I stand before you as a repentant slaveholder. I stand before you as a moral being I feel that I owe it to the suffering slave and to the deluded master, to my country and to the world to do all that I can to overturn a system of complicated crimes, built upon the broken hearts and prostrate bodies of my countrymen in chains and cemented by the blood sweat and tears of my sisters in bonds.

The Grimke Sisters' testimony of the grim life of slaves sparked Catherine's sister, Harriet Beecher Stowe, to write *Uncle Tom's Cabin,* a riveting novel about southern slavery, and the Grimkes attracted other women to the anti-slavery cause and feminism including, Lucy Stone, Abby Kelley Foster, Susan B. Anthony and Elizabeth Cady Stanton.

Sarah Grimke also addressed women's status in her *Letters on the Equality of the Sexes and the Condition of Woman*,

> I ask no favors for my sex. I surrender not our claim to equality. All I ask of our brethren is that they take their feet off of

> our necks and permit us to stand upright in the ground which God has designed for us to occupy.

Their notion that women could sit in counsels would be tested soon enough. The Grimkes' response to Catherine Beecher in 1837, expressing women's rights to political equality, forecasted the women's movement still a decade away.

Starting a Women's Rights Movement

In 1840, a number of distinguished Americans attended the World Anti-Slavery Conference in London, including Henry Stanton accompanied by his new bride Elizabeth Cady. When women in the American delegation were denied a place on the convention floor and ordered to sit in a curtained gallery off to the side, reserved specifically for them, William Lloyd Garrison and Wendell Phillips, leaders of the group, protested by refusing to participate in the conference. For her remaining days in London, newcomer Elizabeth Cady Stanton spent hours discussing issues with Lucretia Mott, the Quaker activist whose insightful views on the inequalities of women enlivened Elizabeth's awareness.

Elizabeth Cady Stanton later described her impression of Mott and how the quiet Quaker lady had set her mind on ideas which would change her life,

> Mrs. Mott was to me an entire new revelation of womanhood. I sought every opportunity to be at her side, and continually plied her with questions. I had never heard a woman talk what, as a Scotch Presbyterian, I had scarcely dared to think....When I first heard from her lips that I had the same right to think for myself that Luther, Calvin and John Knox had, and the same right to be guided by my own convictions, I felt at once a new born sense of dignity and freedom.

This discrimination of female abolitionists at the London Conference, became the catalyst for further reform. At the conclusion of the conference, Lucretia and Elizabeth pledged to address the wrongs suffered by women, and to hold a women's convention as soon as they returned to the States, and to "form a society to advocate the rights of women." But it would be another eight years before Stanton and Mott could implement their plan for a women's convention.

Early Women's Rights' Activists Starting at top and clockwise, Lucretia Mott, Elizabeth Cady Stanton. Anna Elizabeth Dickinson, Mary Ashton Livermore, Susan B. Anthony, Lydia Maria Child, and center, Grace Greenwood. (Picture Courtesy of the Library of Congress.)

The quiet composure of Lucretia Mott, a seasoned abolitionist, belied her intensity and dedication to reform. She had actively served as a teacher, a Quaker minister, and as mentioned, the founder of the first female anti-slavery society, in Philadelphia. Lucretia had also somehow found time to care for five children and manage a busy household. Elizabeth Cady Stanton, a graduate of the Troy Female seminary, received a practical education while working at her father's law office where male clerks regaled her with stories of what happened to women under New York property and custody laws. When Elizabeth married Henry Stanton she omitted the word *obey* from their marriage vows.

After returning from the London conference, both Mott and Stanton were preoccupied the next few years with family obligations. Henry Stanton, an attorney and abolitionist introduced Elizabeth to the leading reformers and literary figures of the day. At their reunion in

1848, Lucretia and Elizabeth again discussed women's issues, and made hasty plans for a women's conference that July which Elizabeth would chair. The conference, the first women's convention in history, held at Seneca Falls, New York, in July 1848, included 300 women and forty men including the famous Frederick Douglass. Henry Stanton, fearing that women's demand for suffrage would doom the movement, opposed the conference and refused to attend.

Delegates of the Seneca Falls Conference discussed and passed a number of resolutions on issues such as property and custody laws and women's suffrage. Oddly enough the most unpopular idea was the women's vote. Lucretia Mott believed that pushing for women's right to vote was too controversial. Nevertheless, a determined Elizabeth drafted *The Declaration of Sentiments,* which paraphrased the Declaration of Independence, and focused on women's rights. Delegates spoke against her ninth resolution, that "the duty of the women in this country is to secure to themselves their sacred right to the elective franchise" and adopt a suffrage objective. But Frederick Douglass spoke up and urged the women to fight for their right to vote, because without it, he argued, men could continue to enact laws restricting women's rights. A few days later, Douglass published the speech in his abolitionist journal, *The North Star.* The following is an excerpt.

> All that distinguishes man as an intelligent and accountable being is equally true of woman; and if that government only is just which governs by that free consent of the governed, there can be no reason in the world for denying to woman the exercise of the elective franchise, or a hand in making and administering the laws of the land. Our doctrine is that "right is of no sex."

Frederick Douglass convinced delegates to vote in favor of women's suffrage. One hundred delegates including Douglass signed the Declaration.

Absent from the Seneca Falls Conference were two women who would later become synonymous with the movement—Susan B. Anthony and Lucy Stone. After a decade of teaching, Susan had left the profession when she discovered female teachers were paid much less than male teachers. She became interested in abolitionism and began working in the Temperance Movement. Temperance dramatized for her the plight of women and children who were the victims of alcoholism, and all its attendant miseries—abandonment, domestic violence, and economic hardship. Susan realized the necessity for women to have "power over their own purse" when she saw how men, the chief consumers, spent family income or inheritance on alcohol.

Lucy Stone had worked diligently as a school teacher from age sixteen to twenty-five to save money for a college education. In 1847, Lucy graduated from Oberlin College with honors and went to work for the American Anti-Slavery Society as a full-time writer and lecturer. Lucy, who was particularly adept at working hostile crowds, angered Abolitionist officials when she advocated the women's rights issues.

When she married Henry Blackwell, who championed women's rights, they wrote their own wedding vows.

> While acknowledging our mutual affection by publicly assuming the relationship of husband and wife, yet in justice to ourselves and a great principle, we deem it a duty to declare that this act on our part implies no sanction of, nor promise of voluntary obedience to such present laws of marriage, as refuse to recognize the wife as an independent, rational being, while they confer upon the husband an injurious and unnatural superiority, investing him with legal powers which no honorable man would exercise, and which no man should possess.

Lucy Stone kept her own name after marriage and was always addressed as Mrs. Lucy Stone.

Sojourner Truth also became a spokeswoman for the women's movement. At the Akron, Ohio, Women's Rights Convention in 1851, Sojourner addressed the crowd in what became a famous speech, entitled "Ain't I a Woman?" Here is an excerpt of that speech.

> Dat man ober dar say dat womin needs to be helped into carriages, and lifted

> ober ditches, and to hab de best place everywhar. Nobody eber helps me into carriages, or ober mud puddles, or gibs me any best place! An ain't I a woman? Look at me! Look at my arm! I have ploughed and planted and gathered into barns, and no man could head me! And ain't a woman? I have born thirteen children and seen em mos all sold off to slavery and when I cried in my mother's grief, none but Jesus heard me! And ain't I a woman?

The movement forged Elizabeth Cady Stanton and Susan B. Anthony into a lifelong, dynamic friendship. Despite the fact that they would not see results of their efforts for women in their lifetime, their political partnership laid the important groundwork for the cause. Their abilities complemented collaboration; Stanton, a gifted writer and speaker, was also a mother with seven children. Unmarried and independent, Anthony became the legs of the movement, a tireless campaigner and a skillful organizer.

An issue of concern was the fact that married women in the nineteenth century continued to live under laws of *coverture.* A notable southern lady, Mary Chestnut, expressed the degradation women felt with this status:

> 24 January 1862
>
> ...why do I feel like a beggar, utterly humiliated and degraded when I am forced to say I need money? I cannot tell, but I do; and the worst of it, this thing grows worse as one grows older. Money ought not to be asked for, or given to a man's wife as a gift. Something must be due her, and that she should have, and no growling and grumbling nor warnings against waste and extravagance, not hints as to the need of economy, nor amazement that the last supply has given out already. What a proud woman suffers under all this, who can tell?

One unsung heroine of the women's movement, Ernestine Rose, a Jewish immigrant from Poland had petitioned the New York legislature in 1836, to grant married women rights to property. Although her petitions were turned down at least twelve times, Rose persevered and in 1848, *The Married Women's Property Bill,* which safeguarded women's real and moveable property became law. Although Ernestine had promoted *the Married Women's Property Bill* specifically for poor women to protect their earnings, the law favored rich women instead. Ironically, upper class men who intended to preserve the wealth, inheritance and property of their wives and daughters supported the measure.

Susan B. Anthony also lobbied for women's rights and in 1855, submitted petitions to the New York State Legislature on behalf of working women. Anthony believed that women should be able to retain their own wages, and in the case of divorce, should have custody rights of their children. In this petition, Anthony also requested that women be given the right to vote. In 1860, after Anthony and Rose's hard campaigning in New York, the State Legislature passed *The Married Women's Property Act,* granting women the right to own property, to retain their own wages, to inherit their husband's estate and to bring a suit before the court.

Even though the Seneca Falls conference had drawn mostly local women, it initiated a decade of women's conventions held annually from 1850 through 1861. In 1850, Lucy Stone addressed the first Women's Rights *National* Convention in Worcester, Massachusetts, and in 1856, she presided over the Annual Women's Convention. The women who attended the annual conventions committed to the feminist cause and pledged to promote the social, economic and political equality of the sexes. This agenda became the defining mission of the movement to further the cause of sexual equality.

Conclusion

In the Antebellum era, society experienced one of its busiest periods of reform in American history. Establishing a free and independent republic with a divided population, some free and some slave, had produced an ideological, political and social contradiction. The paradox of

American Democracy existing alongside the peculiar institution of slavery could not continue and needed to be addressed.

By getting involved in the cause of abolition, crusading women gained a more heightened awareness of their own inferior social status and that discontent led to the formation of a women's movement. In 1848, Elizabeth Cady Stanton and Lucretia Mott gathered 300 delegates for the Women's Rights Conference at Seneca Falls and set an agenda for their cause in the *Declaration of Sentiments*.[7] The Seneca Falls Conference signified the beginning of a women's rights movement, the first of its kind in the United States or anywhere for that matter. As a spin-off of the anti-slavery cause, the women's rights movement emerged, moved front and center and would dominate women's political activism in the nineteenth century.

The feminist crusade would take many twists and turns over the next decades. In succeeding chapters, the progress of the women's movement and how women eventually got to vote will be developed further.

---

7. *Declaration of Sentiments,* See the appendix for the full text of the Declaration.

Chapter 9
Women and the Antebellum Reform Movement
Like Bees in a Hive

Key topics

Women and Moral Reform
Slaves and the Underground Railroad
Health and Dress Reform in the Antebellum Period
Educational and Professional Advances for Women

Chronology

1834 - The New York Female Moral Reform Society Formed
1836 - Mount Holyoke Female Seminary Founded by Mary Mason Lyon
1844 - Margaret Fuller Publishes *Woman in the Nineteenth Century*
1847 - Elizabeth Blackwell Graduates from Geneva Medical College
1852 - Harriet Beecher Stowe Publishes *Uncle Tom's Cabin*

Introduction

As people moved with greater ease along canals, turnpikes, rivers and rails and the population of the New Republic grew, towns and cities multiplied. Young people, both men and women, migrated to cities, seeking employment and a new life. Accompanying these changes, poverty, crime, social deviance, alcoholism and domestic violence also increased.

Officials in emerging factory towns also attempted to maintain order, but how much protection could they give to single women, poor women, and orphaned or abandoned girls who sought work, experienced exploitation, and lived a marginal existence?

Contrasted with working class females were the women of privilege whose days were spent in the domestic cocoon, taking care of a husband and children. Many of these middle and upper class women filled the ranks of volunteers in charity and church organizations. In this capacity, women were perceived as extending a matronly and virtuous influence on their community. Thousands of women in cities all over America formed charitable organizations into what reformers called the Benevolent Empire. The ladies mobilized for dress and health reform, temperance and moral crusades. A few brave women founded schools and others fought for women's right to enter the staid male professions of medicine and law.

Women and Moral Reform

In the nineteenth century, as America industrialized, more women were lured to cities where they might be hired as clerks, bookkeepers, factory operatives, seamstresses, or domestic servants. Many people saw a direct connection between rapid industrialization, demographic changes and the breakdown of civility in society. Reflecting social concern, nineteenth century etiquette books addressed these changes by prescribing specific rules and guidelines of behavior. Women were advised to conduct themselves appropriately in public to avoid scandal, the slightest smudge on their reputation or the advances of strangers.

> *It is understood, that very young girls are never seen anywhere without some older person as an escort. Too great freedom engenders a coarse loud manner which is distasteful. There is no place where one's manners are more plainly discernible, or where the natural selfishness inherent in all will exhibit itself more conspicuously than on the street or in crowded places. And one is apt to be judged very harshly sometimes by their deportment on the public promenade. A young lady should never permit one of the opposite sex to address her in a slangy fashion, touch her on the shoulder, call her by her first name before strangers. All such little familiarities, although intended innocently enough, will give others the impression that she is not held in the highest esteem.*

Journalists and authors related the tragic circumstances of runaway girls who had left home in search of something more exciting in the city. Out of desperation or poor judgment, some women who fled to cities became prostitutes. In April of 1836, a sensational scandal rocked New York City when a young prostitute named Helen Jewett was found murdered in her bed. Her client, a young clerk named Frank Robinson, was charged with the homicide, sent to trial and acquitted. Just five years later, in the summer of 1841, the brutally beaten body of Mary Rogers was pulled out of the Hudson River. Mary had plied her trade on the streets of New York under the ruse of selling cigars. Her homicide was never solved.

The real names, identities and family backgrounds of Helen and Mary are covered in uncertainty since both women changed their names when they left home. Perhaps there were hundreds more victims like Helen and Mary, never identified and whose murders were never solved. But these crimes roused respectable middle class women to rescue other girls from the grips of prostitution through moral reform societies which they established throughout the country.

The widow Isabella Graham had founded the Society for the Relief of Poor Widows and Small Children in New York in the late eighteenth century and by 1820, that organization had aided hundreds of widows and children. Evidently benevolence ran in the family, as Isabella's daughter Joanna Bethune established the Society for the Promotion of Industry which provided work for women as seamstresses and textile spinners. She also founded the Orphan Asylum Society to care for the growing number of homeless and orphaned children.

In 1834, middle class ladies in New York City organized the New York Female Moral Reform Society and elected Lydia Finney, wife of evangelist Charles Finney, to serve as their first president. The Moral reform crusade took on so swiftly that four years later, the Society boasted 250 chapters throughout the state with a total of 16,000 members. By 1840, it had grown into a national organization, the American Female Moral Reform Society, with 560 chapters in northern states.

The Female Moral Reform Society called for nothing short of ending prostitution in cities such as New York and rescuing their "fallen sisters" from the brothels. They also pledged to protect single women from the predatory appetites of sexually aggressive men, and targeted houses of ill repute which they entered on the premise of looking for runaway girls. While conducting their search, the women would note the names and faces of male clients frequenting the house. Since these men were often of social standing, the threat of disclosure could be quite intimidating. While assembled at the brothel, moral reform women also delivered sermons on the evils of carnal sin, offered prayers, and sang hymns to win converts. Groups such as the New York Female Moral Reform Society also established shelters for destitute homeless women, prostitutes fleeing the trade, or women escaping an abusive home. Their efforts paid off in some small measure and by 1848, in Massachusetts and the State of New York, laws were enacted making seduction (rape) a crime. But legislating was one thing, enforcement and prosecution another.

Women Reformers and Women in Prison

Female reformers centered much of their efforts on women in prisons. With the introduction of the penitentiary system in the nineteenth century, the women who were sentenced to prison, were most frequently charged with prostitution. Respectable society regarded them as outcasts, and little attention was paid to them until Quakers in Philadelphia began prison visitations in the 1820s, and because Great Awakening ministers preached that all individuals were capable of perfection, prisoners were deemed worthy of attention too.

Quaker prison reformers introduced the concept of the rehabilitation of convicts. They believed that in a controlled prison environment, inmates could work and receive religious instruction and would experience deep remorse for their crimes. Seeing the error of their ways, some prisoners begged forgiveness and sought a new life. Once this conversion occurred, officials declared a prisoner reformed and eligible for release.

Against this backdrop, Quaker women in Philadelphia and Moral Reform Women in New York City, formed the Female Auxiliary of the Prison Association, and joined the crusade to aid women in prison. They visited female inmates, gave them religious instruction, taught them to sew, read and write. Reformers also set up halfway houses where female parolees could find shelter and help in their transition from prison to civic life. One success story, a New York halfway home established in 1845, was expanded in 1865, and provided shelter for 3,000 women. Margaret Fuller, the feminist/intellectual, staunchly advocated helping female prisoners. While writing for the *New York Tribune*, she reported the deplorable conditions for females in penal institutions. She also supported the Awakening doctrine that prisoners were redeemable, and in need of "only good influences and steady aid to raise them from the pit of infamy into which they have fallen."

Female prisoners faced severe problems such as sexual exploitation by prison guards. One of the longest battles waged in prison reform, was to provide separate prison facilities for women. In 1874, the first all-female institution opened in Indianapolis. Unfortunately, the only training that female prisoners received was as domestic servants and this only exacerbated their condition. Once released, and working as servants in private homes, they were easy prey for sexual exploitation by their male employers. Meager salaries and stressful working conditions kept them in poverty.

Health Reform in the Antebellum Period

In the nineteenth century people did not enjoy good health because of the lack of standards for sanitation, drinking water, nutrition and medical care. But health reformers, both doctors and patients, tried new cure-alls and fads, and flocked to health resorts, such as those in the Catskills and Adirondacks, which were very popular from 1840 to 1880. Clients enjoyed the latest innovation from Germany—the water cure treatment. Although it was not the panacea it was touted to be, it did offer patients, particularly women, relief from common afflictions such as cystitis. At these resorts, women, freed of the burden of childcare, housework, and the sexual demands of husbands, enjoyed each other's company. Women receiving the water cure spent time reading, partaking of simple meals, and wearing comfortable clothing. Having shed their restrictive clothes and corsets, they indulged themselves with frequent hot baths and leisurely walks. Two health reformers, Doctors Sylvester Graham and John Harvey Kellogg, prescribed special diets for women. Graham advised his patients to avoid meat and eat fresh fruits, vegetables, and whole grains. Kellogg advocated a comprehensive regimen of good diet, sexual abstinence, cleanliness and exercise.

In the most sustained nineteenth century health reform—the Temperance Movement—reformers aimed to eradicate alcoholism in America. Temperance was initially organized and led by businessmen's associations who came together to address the problems of employees' drinking. Alcoholism affected business profits with work related injuries, absenteeism and an overall slackness in job performance. Temperance reformers targeted the working poor and immigrant population and saw temperance as a moral crusade. The movement caught on quickly. The American Temperance Society, formed in 1825, and members had organized five thousand local chapters by 1840. These associations boasted membership of a million, most of whom were females. Working through church affiliations, Temperance gave women a noble cause—to protect women and children from alcoholism's by- products—domestic violence, poverty, neglect and abuse. But as thousands of women joined the temperance and women's movements, liquor manufacturers and factory owners feared female alignments. If granted the right to vote, women would first move to pass laws banning the manufacture and sale of alcohol and then work toward more equitable wages for women and children. Businessmen's concerns were well founded since women such as Susan B. Anthony worked tirelessly for temperance, women's rights and women's trade unions.

One reform cause launched in 1838, demonstrated the difference one person could make. Through the remarkable efforts of Dorothea Dix, the public was informed of horrible conditions in prisons, asylums, orphanages and workhouses. She visited the women's quarter of the Cambridge Massachusetts Jail on a frigid Sunday morning in March, 1841, and found inmates in shocking condition, wearing filthy rags and housed in unheated cells. When she complained to the jailer, he responded that "Mad folks don't know hot from cold."

Dorothea Dix not only addressed the dilemma of the insane, but also challenged social beliefs about mental illness and single-handedly did more to bring about change for those confined to asylums than any other American in the nineteenth century. She presented her findings in memorials (formal petitions) to state legislatures on behalf of the mentally ill who were housed in all manner of places ranging from caves to cages.

> I proceed, Gentlemen, briefly to call your attention to the present state of Insane persons, confined within this Commonwealth (Massachusetts), in cages, closets, cellars, stalls, and pens! Chained, naked, beaten with rods, and lashed into obedience.

Dorothea Dix single-handedly changed the care of the insane in the nineteenth century. She addressed state legislators on the plight of the mentally ill and worked tirelessly to build hospitals for their care. (Picture courtesy of the Library of Congress.)

Dorothea kept a journal in which she noted the conditions of prisoners and inmates most of whom were insane,

> At Lincoln: found a woman in a cage. Medford: One idiotic subject chained, and one in a close stall for seventeen years. Williamsburg: the almshouse has several insane, not under suitable treatment Granville: One often closely con-

fined; now losing the use of his limbs for want of exercise.

Ironically, the cases of individual suffering such as this which warranted confinement, supervision and treatment were those who were actually abandoned or sorely neglected. Such was the case of a woman Dorothea found living in filth, subject to fits and self mutilation. Through her work, Dorothea Dix saw to the establishment of thirty hospitals for the treatment of the mentally ill. Because she had spent years as an unpaid volunteer, providing adequate shelter for the insane, she was never financially solvent herself. In her later years, Dorothea Dix lived at the Mental Asylum in Trenton, New Jersey, one of the many hospitals she had founded. She died there in 1887.

Women's Attempts at Dress Reform

Feminists saw in dress reform a way to alleviate the suffering, poor health and restrictive movement caused by nineteenth century fashion. The bloomer style which they introduced was named for Amelia Bloomer, the post mistress of Seneca Falls and editor of the newsletter, *The Lily*, and one of the first to model the new clothing. But it was actually designed by Elizabeth Smith Miller, the daughter of famed abolitionist Gerit Smith. Elizabeth, inspired by the Turkish soldiers' uniform, made a comfortable, attractive and practical outfit consisting of pantaloons (which came to the ankle, and were similar in appearance to harem pants), a long sleeved blouse, a waist length jacket and an overskirt. Elizabeth Cady Stanton, Susan B. Anthony and Lucy Stone also wore the new outfit.

Stanton was particularly grateful for the bloomer attire. Now it was possible to do the simplest tasks with ease and safety. While holding a kerosene lamp, she could ascend stairs carrying an infant, and assisting other small children underfoot without endangering herself. Although the outfit was modest and less revealing than other fashions, women got a negative reaction when they wore the bloomer ensemble. Newspapers ridiculed them; they were jeered publicly and often had things thrown at them. Clergymen labeled the garments unfeminine and immoral and argued that women who wore bloomers violated the commandment that, "woman shall not wear that which pertaineth unto a man." Not all women however, were fond of the bloomer style. Anne Royall, a popular writer, disapproved of the bloomer costume and defended the current fashion mode,

> We think bloomers indelicate, unbecoming and highly inconvenient. Do our sisters intend to part with their last and best treasure modesty; that grace of symmetry in motion, the sweet rounding waist, the unspeakable charm of a swelling bosom.

Surprisingly, Stanton was the first to yield to public criticism and give up the bloomer style, not because of intimidation but because she believed the bloomer controversy detracted from more serious issues of the women's crusade. Within a short time, other women followed suit and returned to their former socially acceptable, uncomfortable, restrictive costume.

The Bloomer Costume – a nineteenth century dress reform introduced by Elizabeth Gerit Smith and adopted by Amelia Bloomer and other female reform activists. It consisted of harem style pants, a shorter overskirt and waist-length jacket. (Picture Courtesy of the Library of Congress.)

Margaret Fuller, an Intellectual Voice for the Women's Movement

As educational opportunities opened up for women, many contributed to the arts, letters, philosophy and literature of the nineteenth century and excelled in scholarship and education, particularly women's education. Among the outstanding American female scholars none left a more lasting imprint than Margaret Fuller. She was acknowledged in her lifetime by Elizabeth Cady Stanton and Susan B. Anthony as a woman who "possessed more influence upon the thought of America than any woman previous to her time." Margaret touched many lives through her writing, her ideas, her vision and her charisma. What was the essence of her great genius? She achieved international fame as an intellectual who could articulate in her writing well reasoned insights about women's issues and needs.

Margaret Fuller was born in 1810, in Cambridgeport, Massachusetts, and grew up during a prodigious period of philosophical activity in New England. She was a precocious child, whose father lavished her with a comprehensive classical education, authoritarian dominance and rigorous discipline. She became the only female member of the Concord Circle of the American Transcendentalists, which included Ralph Waldo Emerson, Bronson Alcott, Henry David Thoreau, and George Ripley.

At the Peabody Bookshop in Boston, Margaret engaged participants in a series of subjects ranging from literature, education, women's rights, art, mythology and philosophy. She also edited the quarterly Transcendentalist journal, *The Dial*. In 1840, seeing the need to explore new roles and places, she visited the Midwest and chronicled the trip in *Summer on the Lakes in 1843.* In this work, Margaret expressed empathy for the plight of Native Americans, a sentiment uncharacteristic at the time. Horace Greeley employed Margaret as the first female journalist for the *New York Tribune.* As a newspaper writer "on the beat," she came in touch with poignant social issues. For one assignment, she visited Sing Sing Prison, then a new landmark penitentiary to report on conditions for the female inmates there. In 1845, she published her signature work *Woman in the Nineteenth Century.* In this book Margaret vented ideas about women in American Society. Women, she argued, needed meaningful work to reach their full potential just as men did, and she believed there was no limit to the occupations women could fill. Margaret proposed that women should have an equal determination in legislating laws and controlling their property. Her ideas gave a substantive voice to the newly emerging women's rights movement and *Woman in the Nineteenth Century* became a feminist classic.

Margaret Fuller, a literary and intellectual figure of the mid-nineteenth century whose ideas inspired activists such as Elizabeth Cady Stanton and Susan B.Anthony. (Picture Courtesy of the Library of Congress.)

In 1846, Margaret went to Europe, where she met famous literary figures such as George Sand and discovered to her amazement that she was internationally known. She arrived in Italy in time to report the history making Italian Revolution of 1848, for the *New York Tribune.* In her vivid newspaper accounts, she called for American aid in the revolutionary struggle. With romantic fervor, Margaret met and married Italian-nobleman-turned-revolutionary, Giovanni Ossoli, and became caught up in the revolutionary struggle herself. Margaret ran a hospital and supplied her husband's garrison. In 1849, when the revolutionary republican government was overthrown, the Ossolis fled Italy, with their infant son, to return to America. As they sailed into New York harbor, their ship sank just off the coast of Fire Island. The bodies of Margaret, Giovanni and their young son were never recovered. Although she did not live long enough to participate in the emerging women's movement, Margaret Fuller's ideas influenced feminists of her and succeeding generations.

Poet Laureate Emily Dickinson

Like Margaret Fuller, Emily Dickinson, New England's poet laureate, left a lasting mark in American literature. From a distinguished family in Amherst, Massachusetts, Emily's father had served in Congress. Emily left Mount Holyoke school to be with her family and without the Christian conversion which Director Mary Lyons required of her students. Emily began writing poetry and this became her lifelong vocation. Although she was outgoing as a young woman, over the years she became progressively more shy and reclusive.

In her lifetime, Emily Dickinson never achieved national or international fame, and only a few of her poems were published. Her poetry describes the inward struggle for self realization, and deals mostly with themes of love, death, fame and immortality. Her poetic style appears deceptively simple, but in form is filled with off-beat rhythms and quite innovative, as in the following,

> This is my letter to the world, that never wrote to Me—
> The simple News that Nature told—with tender Majesty
> Her Message is committed to hands I cannot see—
> For love of Her Sweet-countrymen
> Judge tenderly of Me

Emily Dickinson produced volumes of poetry. In 1878, a schoolmate and friend, the famous writer Helen Hunt Jackson, submitted some of Emily's poems for publication in *The Republican*. At her death in 1886, her sister Lavinia discovered a remarkable legacy: 1,775 poems still unpublished. Lavinia submitted three volumes of Emily's for publication. But it was not until 1945, that the remainder of her poetry and correspondence was published and secured her international fame as one of America's foremost poets.

Those Damned Scribbling Women

Nathaniel Hawthorne observed that American Society by mid century was "wholly given over to a damned mob of scribbling women." He regarded their writing as "trash" and characteristic of the general slump in popular taste. Indeed, a whole generation of women writing popular novels filled with sentimentality and melodrama earned them more money than some great literary figures. Leading the pack of scribbling women was Harriet Beecher Stowe, daughter of the famous minister Lyman Beecher. Harriet turned to writing after marrying Calvin Stowe, an educator and Biblical scholar. With seven children to feed, Harriet's writing supplemented the family's income and became her creative escape from the demands of motherhood and housekeeping.

Harriet Beecher Stowe, a member of the famous Beecher family, sister to Catherine Beecher and author of Uncle Tom's Cabin. (Photo courtesy of the Library of Congress.)

Her stories centered on the domestic sphere—maternity, children and death, the kind of sentimental topics into which scribbling women delved. However, her focus shifted abruptly when the Fugitive Slave Laws were reinvigorated within the Compromise of 1850. Caught in the whirlwind of the slave controversy, her abolitionist friends urged her to write a story about runaway slaves. The result, one of the most famous American novels, *Uncle Tom's Cabin,* became an instant best-seller, and was eventually translated into other languages for worldwide circulation. The book was a success, but the reviews characterized the division in the country over the slave question. Abolitionists claimed Harriet Beecher Stowe's treatment of Southern slavery was too soft, and southerners thought the novel was highly exaggerated. Nevertheless, Harriet intended to emphasize the tragedy of slavery, the separation of slave parents and children and the consequent devastating effects on family life. A decade before the Civil War, *Uncle Tom's Cabin* did just that. The book raised public sensitivity to the harshness of slavery. The novel had such an impact that it is reputed, when Harriet met President Lincoln at a White House reception some years later, he remarked, "So this is the lady who started the war."

Another successful book, *Ruth Hall*, an autobiographical novel written by Sara Payson Parton, under the *nom de plume* of Fanny Fern, challenged women's domestic role and attacked men strongly. In the story, the heroine Ruth is a widow who receives criticism but no help from relatives and is forced to support herself and her children through her writing. Praise for the book's authenticity came from none other than Nathaniel Hawthorne, the critic of women's writing.

Educational and Professional Advances for Women

Progress in women's education in the New Republic continued as women established schools with more demanding curricula for females. Ignoring popular notions that girls' brains were more fragile and could not support rigorous studies, educators such as Emma Hart Willard and Mary Lyon integrated mathematics and sciences into women's education.

Emma Hart, sibling number sixteen in a family of seventeen children, showed such an adeptness for geometry and philosophy that her father encouraged her education. In 1802, at the age of fifteen, Emma was enrolled at the Berlin Academy and within two years, she was teaching there. In 1809, at age twenty-two, she was appointed head mistress of a female academy in Middlebury, Vermont, where she met and married Dr. John Willard, a local physician twenty-eight years her senior. With his support, she started the Middlebury Female Seminary in their home in 1814, and offered girls what she called "non-ornamental studies," namely mathematics and science. In 1819, Emma promoted the curriculum in a treatise, *An Address to the Public: Particularly to the Legislators of New York, Proposing a Plan for Improving Female Education.* She hoped the New York State Legislature would fund an entire school system for girls but legislators decried her proposal as "Contrary to God's Will." They believed females should learn ornamental subjects such as dancing, needlepoint, art and music. However she did win an influential backer in New York Governor De Witt Clinton. He endorsed her academic vision and invited her to open a school in New York. In 1821, she moved to Troy, New York, where the Common Council of the town raised $4,000 and donated public land. Her school, the Troy Female Seminary, became the most influential school for women in America. By 1831, 300 young women were enrolled there. Emma instituted a number of programs which aided the school's success and its influence on education, including a teacher training program which allowed the graduates of Troy to take their place in the growing numbers of female school teachers. Willard financed the school with much needed income by writing her own textbooks. A short list of her publications includes: *A Treatise on the Motive Powers which Produce the Circulation of the Blood* (1846); *A Guide to the Temple of Time, Universal History for Schools, Last Leaves of American History* (1849); *Astronography: Astronomical Geography* (1854); and *Morals for the Young* (1857). She died in 1870, at the age of eighty-three, and in 1895, the Troy Female Seminary was renamed the Emma Willard School.

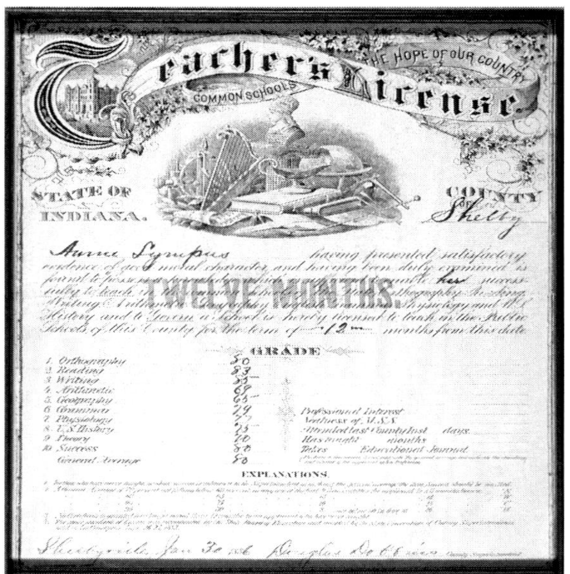
Teacher's License
The Hope of Our Country
Common Schools
State of Indiana.
County
Twelve Months.
Grade
Explanations.

This nineteenth century Teaching License was valid for twelve months, and included the grades the instructor had earned while training as well as a place for the evaluation of her teaching.

As much as she was for progressive women's education, Emma Willard insisted that the primary function of females in society was to be wives and mothers. Although she stayed out of political debate, stating it was not a woman's place, many alumnae entered professions such as education, or fought for reform. Among them was one of Troy's most famous alumna, Elizabeth Cady Stanton.

In order to pay for her schooling, seventeen-year-old Mary Mason Lyon taught in a New England country school. She attended a number of female academies including Sanderson, Amherst, and Byfield. In 1836, Lyon established the Mount Holyoke Female Seminary at South Hadley, Massachusetts. Lyons offered higher education to young women from lower income families. She persuaded school patrons that low income students could be accommodated if the school provided custodial, housekeeping and cooking jobs for them. By implementing this plan, the school became an instant success. Within one year with boosted enrollment, space was at a premium and in 1838, some 400 applicants were denied admission. At her death in 1849, the school became Mount Holyoke Seminary and College. It retains its excellent academic standards today and is ranked as a leading institution of higher learning.

Mothers of Invention: Harriet Tubman, Freedom Conductor

Harriet Tubman born in 1822 Araminta Ross, a slave achieved greatness in her lifetime and yet is one of the most underrated heroines in American history. As a child she was cruelly mistreated and on one occasion so severely beaten on her head with a lead pipe that the wound dented her skull. She was left to die, untreated and bleeding for several days and eventually recovered on her own but suffered for the rest of her life from disabling seizures, blackout spells, narcoleptic attacks, and headaches. In 1849, Harriet and her brothers Ben and Henry managed to escape to Philadelphia but she immediately returned to Maryland to rescue her family. Harriet had heard that her family had been legally manumitted, and she hired an attorney to investigate their legal status. She in fact discovered that her father's former owner had freed him and his family (including all of his children) but that the legal stipulation had been ignored as another white slaveholder took possession of them. It was then that she decided to steal her family from slavery. As she explained later, "there was one of two things I had a right to, liberty or death; if I could not have one, I would have the other."

She became a conductor on the Underground Railroad which was a network of anti-slavery activists, safe houses, trails and routes to help slaves escape from the South. Slowly, one group at a time, she brought relatives out of Maryland and eventually guided dozens of other slaves to freedom. Traveling by night, Tubman never lost a passenger. Her success became so widespread that large rewards were offered for her capture, one group of southern slaveholders reputedly posting a bounty of $40,000. It is unknown how many more trips she made into the South to help more runaways; some sources report as many as twenty more missions. Harriet was named "Moses" by the abolitionist leader William Lloyd Garrison, an allusion to Moses the prophet in the Bible who led the Hebrews out of Egypt to freedom in the Promised Land. Harriet would crusade for the antislavery cause and also for the women's suffrage movement.

As a runaway slave, once escaped the first time, it would have been safer and wiser for Harriet to stay put and slip into obscurity but she risked her own life returning to the South, and serving as a conductor on the Underground Railroad. We will revisit Harriet Tubman in Chapter 12 and discuss her exploits during the Civil War when she courageously ventured into enemy territory once again.

Harriet Tubman a runaway slave who helped other slaves escape to freedom also crusaded for women's rights. (Picture courtesy of the Library of Congress.)

The Slave Population and the Underground Railroad

From 1830 to 1860, the black population in the United States numbered approximately three million people, among whom about 500,000 were free. Surprisingly, half of those free African-Americans lived in the South where life was precarious at best. Work for wages was scarce, and southern free blacks could expect no legal protection. In that society, the presence of free black men and women threatened the status quo, and in the North and the South, neither free blacks nor slaves could be employed by the government, join the militia or be issued a passport. Considering the restrictions on *free* blacks in the South, one wonders how their freedom could have made any difference. They were forbidden to assemble or meet for any purpose, and were required to carry freedom papers at all times, as documented proof of their status. Living in this caste system, they were barred from many occupations. Massachusetts was the only state in the union which allowed blacks to testify in court. In 1850, the new California State Legislature adopted the no-testimony ruling for blacks.

The Underground Railroad was neither underground nor a railroad, but a network of people who helped slaves escape from the South, hide out and eventually get to the North and freedom. (Picture courtesy of the Library of Congress.)

In the decades just before the Civil War, several factors exacerbated slaves' marginal status; namely, slave insurrections and the acceleration of runaways heading North with the aid of the Underground Railroad. Members of the Underground Railroad had all types of devices in their homes: secret passageways, concealed doorways and hidden rooms. In Newport, Indiana, the home of abolitionists Catherine and Levi Coffin, which offered sanctuary for runaways, featured a large indoor well which eliminated the problem of detection as individuals did not have to go outside for water. For escapees, a particularly welcome sight was a red slave quilt hanging over a clothesline which signaled that the home would offer refuge. The escape route of the Underground Railroad extended from the southern states all the way to Canada, a destination many preferred in order to avoid recapture in the United States under the jurisdiction of the Fugitive Slave Laws. Using the fixed compass point of the Polestar, runaways made their way north to freedom.

Conclusion

Between 1820 and 1860, women took the upper hand as moral reformers addressing the plight of prostitutes and prisoners and also became leading educators. School teaching as a feminine profession received its blessing from education pioneer Horace Mann, who proposed that teaching was an extension of women's domestic role. The truth of the matter was that female teachers could be paid a lot less. Their salaries ranged from 30 to 50 percent less than male teachers' wages. In contrast, female factory workers, who were grossly overworked and underpaid, earned *six to seven times* more than female schoolteachers. Consequently, many women left teaching for factory work because the pay was better. Despite these disparities and inequities, by the 1890s, the majority of America's school teachers were women—overall about 65 percent of the teachers in rural areas—and an overwhelming 90 percent in the cities.

Women in the nineteenth century broke down the male bastion of medicine and some succeeded in becoming doctors. Among those pioneers was Harriot Hunt who founded the Ladies Physiological Society, and conducted a lecture series on female hygiene and physiology. In her hometown of Boston, she contributed greatly to poor working class women's health by teaching them basics about health and hygiene. Harriot Hunt had not practiced with a formal medical credential or license, but in 1853, the Female Medical College of Philadelphia awarded her an honorary medical degree. The Blackwell sisters, Elizabeth and Emily, not only became the first bonafide female physicians but also created an institution dedicated specifically to women's health, the training of nurses as well as a medical school for women.

Chapter 10
Women and the Pioneer Movement
The Great Principle of Progress

Key Topics

Sacagawea and the Lewis & Clark Corps of Discovery
The Trail of Tears
Women on the Trail
Settling on the Frontier
The California Gold Rush
Lady Pioneers in Professions

Chronology

1803 - President Jefferson Purchases Louisiana Territory from France
1804 - Congress Authorizes- the Lewis and Clark Expedition
1830 - Western Migration -the Oregon Trail
1838 - The Cherokee Trail of Tears
1849 - The Gold Rush in California, Migration of the 49ers
1850 - California Enters the Union as a Free State
1881 - Helen Hunt Jackson Publishes *ACentury of Dishonor*
1887 - Congress Passes the Dawes Act

Introduction

In 1803, the United States made a major land acquisition when President Thomas Jefferson purchased the Louisiana Territory from France for $15 million. The American ambassadors were prepared to offer Napoleon as much as $10 million just for the port city of New Orleans, so the French counteroffer was quite a windfall. In one stroke, the purchase had extended the United States from the Mississippi River west to the Rocky Mountains and more than doubled the size of the entire country. In a mood of generosity, Congress allocated the President an additional $2500 to finance Meriwether Lewis and William Clark to conduct a Corps of Discovery; that is, a trip west, to ascertain the topography, flora and fauna and grid out in as much detail as possible maps of the area. When Lewis and Clark started out, they discovered like so many explorers before them that the territory was already occupied. On their expedition they encountered over 150 Native American Tribes who called the Louisiana Purchase Territory "home." Their people had inhabited the area for thousands of years.

Much of the success of the Lewis and Clark Expedition must be credited to Sacagawea, the young wife of the French Trapper Toussaint Charbonneau, who accompanied them. Following closely after the Lewis and Clark expedition were thousands of American men, women and children who journeyed across America and endured hardships all along the way. Native American women played a unique role in the western migration and were critically affected by it. White women who endured the journey found their lives greatly altered. Once they arrived in the West their lives would never be the same.

Sacagawea and the Lewis and Clark Corps of Discovery

In the autumn of 1804, Meriwether Lewis and William Clark, with a staff of fifty men arrived at the Mandan tribal camp, near present-day Bismarck, North Dakota, to wait out the severe winter. They contracted French Canadian trapper Toussaint Charbonneau to be their guide for the rest of their journey and hired one of Toussaint's wives, an eighteen-year-old Shoshone girl named Sacagawea (Bird Woman), to act as their interpreter. Because of Sacagawea's language skills (she spoke numerous Native American dialects) and her familial connections to several tribes, she was an indispensable aide to Lewis and Clark. She obtained provisions, horses and safe passage further west, particularly through the Bozeman Pass, an area regarded by Native Americans as sacred land. On one occasion, when a canoe capsized, she salvaged much of the valuable scientific instruments and supplies.

Native America women were vital to the success of explorers and pioneers of the American West. (Photo courtesy of the Library of Congress.)

In April of 1805, as the expedition proceeded on the trail, Sacagawea gave birth to a son, whom she named Jean Baptiste (Lewis and Clark called him Pompey). In August of 1805, while in Shosone country, she had a joyous reunion with an elder brother, Cameahwait, a chieftain. In 1809, she and her husband parted company with the expedition and entrusted William Clark to foster their son in order to see to his education. Historical tradition maintains that Sacagawea died of putrid fever at Fort Manuel (Omaha, Nebraska) in 1812, at the age of twenty-six, but in 1875 an eighty-five-year-old woman living among the Shoshones in Wyoming claimed to be Sacagawea.

The Trail of Tears

There were Americans who migrated west against their will. A tragic chapter in the history of Native Americans occurred in 1838, when the Cherokees and other native tribes were forced to leave their ancestral land. The Cherokee community in northeastern Georgia had tried to avoid conflict by emulating white American culture. They had established schools, a newspaper, and formed a constitutional government. In settled communities, they adopted the English form of inheritance, primogenitor (from father to son), and relinquished their own matrilineal custom from mother to daughter. They converted to Christianity, and hoped they could live a peaceful coexistence. But when word got out that gold had been discovered on Cherokee land, authorities in Georgia used every legal and illegal means they could to take the Cherokee domain. In 1832, President Andrew Jackson ordered that the Cherokee be forcibly removed from Georgia under military escort and relocated to Oklahoma. The 1,200 mile trek to Oklahoma, the *Trail of Tears,* became a death march for many Cherokee. In 1838, the Cherokee numbering 14,000 began the long trek, but along the way 3,000 died from starvation, disease and exposure.

Women on the Trail

The first major trip west was the movement to Oregon which started in the 1830s and crested in the 1850s. In 1848, with the discovery of gold in California at Sutter's Mill near Sacramento, thousands more migrated west.

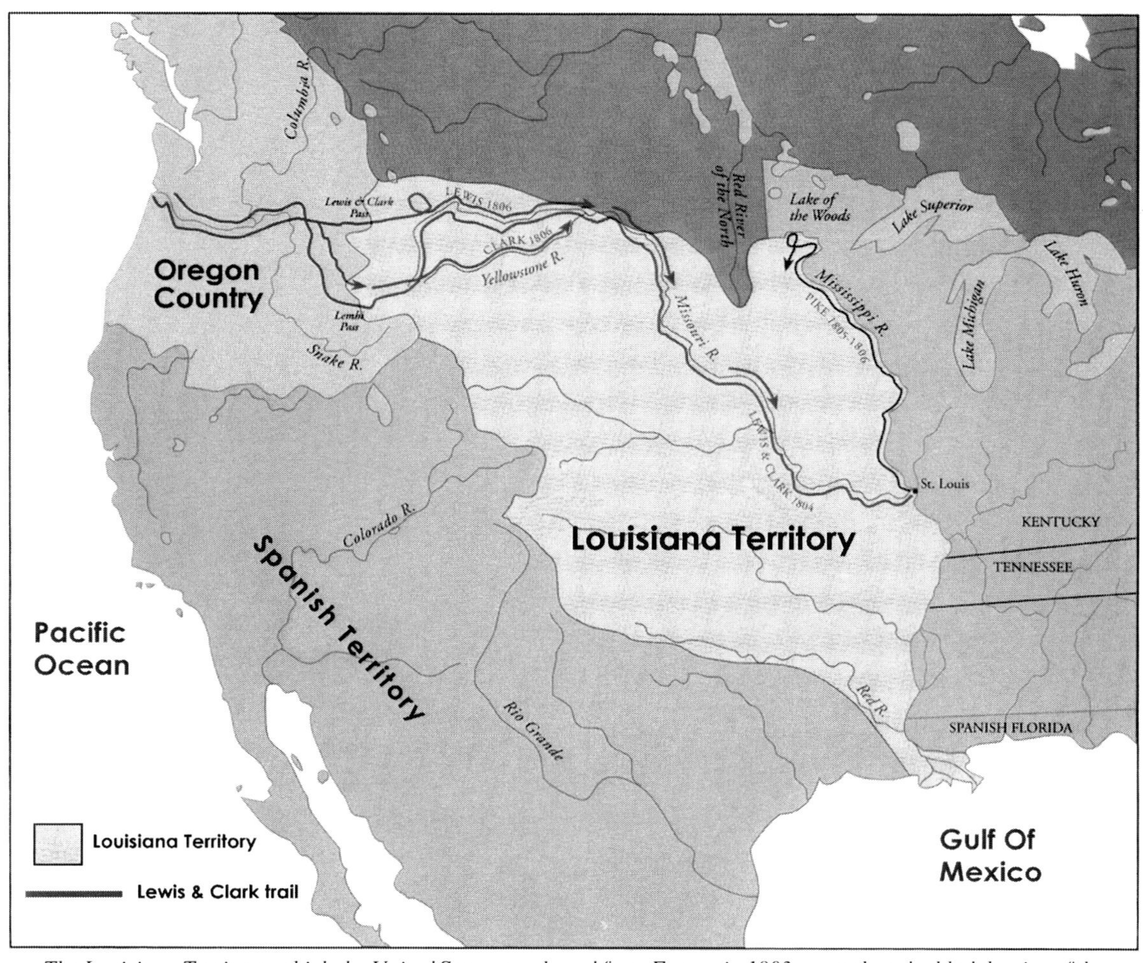

The Louisiana Territory, which the United States purchased from France in 1803, more than doubled the size of the United States. Congress allocated the funds and President Jefferson appointed Meriwether Lewis and William Clark to organize an expedition to map and investigate the new land America had acquired.

The rush to California is understandable, as thousands were struck with gold fever, but why did Americans want to go to Oregon in 1830?

By the 1830s, only 400 white settlers lived in Oregon, but they wrote to relatives back home that they had discovered paradise. Although Oregon was not part of the United States at this time, the government encouraged settlement there in the hope that a greater American population in Oregon might legitimize the United States' claims to the territory.

By 1837, when the United States experienced a severe economic depression, moving west for better opportunity enticed more poor people to migrate across the continent. The new fashion of beaver hats, which were all the rage in Europe, drove American trappers to hunt the rivers and streams for the prized pelts. This was advantageous for pioneers, because trading posts and forts formed an economic link and served as supply and relief stations.

Land, opportunity, adventure and a sense of curiosity were some of the incentives for the *overlanders* to venture west. But once they arrived in Oregon, many emigrants did not put down roots in any one place for very long. In Oregon and California, two out of every three families who reached their western destination moved again, some regularly every two or three years. Evidently, the "itch to move on" was characteristic of many American pioneers. But what motivated them to migrate and risk the dangers and hardships?

Newspaperman Horace Greeley encouraged young men to go west, but he also believed those who did so were crazy. Their daring cannot be written off as ignorance, since many knew about the hardships they would endure. Most overlanders, as they were called, purchased guidebooks which detailed the trip and what they might expect.

Pioneer Wedding Stack Cake

1 cup butter
1 teaspoon baking soda
1 teaspoon salt
1 cup milk
Applesauce
2 tablespoons spiced whipped cream
chopped nuts
1 cup sugar
1 cup molasses
3 eggs
4 cups flour

The frontier stack cake, a traditional wedding cake, was put together for the bride and groom during the wedding celebration. Each guest baked and brought one layer of the cake, composed of different flavors and colors. Layers were stacked and applesauce was spread on each layer to bind the cake together. The top of the cake was covered with whipped cream and nuts. Depending upon how many guests were invited, a Pioneer Wedding Stack Cake could be quite tall.

From: *Better Home and Gardens Heritage Cookbook*

In some of the most popular guides, such as Lansford Hastings' *The Emigrants Guide to Oregon and California*, and Joseph Ware's *The Emigrant's Guide to California,* travelers were warned that after the first month out, they would encounter problems.

Female pioneers recorded the actual perils of the westward migration along the Oregon Trail and related the real story more accurately than the guidebooks. After making the journey, Lucia Williams vowed she would "never camp out again."

> There's not a log to make a seat
> Along the River Platte,
> So when you eat you've got to stand
> or sit down square and flat.
>
> It's fun to cook with buffalo chips,
> Take one that's newly born.
> If I knew once what I know now,
> I would have gone round the Horn.

Much ado has been made about the hard trip traveling from Missouri to Oregon and rightly so; it is a wonder that any arrived in Oregon at all. Often overlooked in the story was the difficulty of getting from home to Missouri, the jumping-off point for the trip. Most emigrants were poor folks, who sold everything they had to raise the money needed to finance the trip. Women were chiefly responsible for preparing and packing provisions for the journey.

> Now, I will begin to work and plan to make everything with an eye to starting out on a six month trip. The first thing is to lay plans and then work up to the program so the first thing is to make a piece of linen for a wagon cover and some sacks; I will spin mostly in the evenings while my husband reads to me.
>
> Keturah (Kit) Belknap 1847

Preparations, made months in advance, began with assembling supplies, sewing warm clothes and packing. Kit Belknap crossed the Oregon Trail in 1848, with what was left of her small family (she had lost two children the year before). Kit kept a diary of the preparation, and the journey to Oregon.

> There was nothing done or talked of but what had Oregon in it and the loom was banging and the wheel buzzing and trades being made from daylight til bedtime... We have one little baby boy left. So now I will spend what little strength I have left getting ready to cross the Rockies. Have cut out four muslin shirts for George and two suits for the little boy, Jessie. Added to what he already has that will last him (if he lives).

The overlanders' lack of foresight seems incredible to us. Many women assumed that they would ride in the wagon and the men would walk so they made warm clothing for their husbands and packed inadequate clothing for themselves and their children. Consequently, women and children were unbearably cold and unprotected from brush, thorns and insect bites. In 1853, Agnes Stewart described an ordeal: "Yesterday was a windy cold day. I had to walk to keep myself warm and going about with a blanket round me it was hard to tell me from an Indian." And Amelia Knight observed that same year, "The children and myself are shivering round and in the wagons, nothing for fires in these parts and the weather is very disagreeable."

The Pioneer Sod House or soddie was a common dwelling on the prairie frontier. The houses were made entirely from prairie sod and topped with a timber roof. (Photo courtesy of the Library of Congress.)

Overlanders did know the journey to Oregon covered 2,000 miles. Families purchased only one pair of boots per person, and these generally wore out after the first 400 miles. Emigrants described walking the rest of the way in crudely made moccasins, in stockings stuffed with grass or just barefoot for great distances.

Unfortunately, guidebooks had been compiled by writers unfamiliar with the trails. They often recommended untried shortcuts. Following their advice, many overlanders lost their way, became stranded and some died. Lansford Hastings' Guide suggested uncharted cutoffs. The ill-fated Donner Party followed his advice and wound up stranded in the High Sierras in a severe snowstorm. But the Donner Party is a testament to the endurance of women on the trail. Of the ten men in the group only two made it to settlement in California but all five of the women survived.

The largest investment for the trip was procuring a wagon or wagons. Ideally a family had two wagons, and oxen, generally teams of eight per wagon, plus their supplies. The purchase of one wagon, a team of oxen and supplies cost $2,000. Oxen were slower and cheaper and were preferred over horses or mules because they could pull the weight and bear the work much better. In addition, the Native Americans were less tempted to steal oxen than the more highly prized horses.

Women's accounts of the journey refer affectionately to the oxen. Families often treated these great beasts like family pets and gave them names. They appreciated their ability to perform stoically under the worst conditions, and knew that with strong oxen to get them there, they would arrive safely. Diarists also wrote emotionally of the loss of a dependable team of oxen. When oxen died in accidents along the way, from disease or starvation, emigrants were doomed and they knew it. Once overlanders reached the desert of Utah and Oregon, lacking grass or fodder to feed the oxen, families shared food and women often fed the oxen loaves of bread in a desperate attempt to keep them alive.

The wagon had to serve as the family's moving van and home on wheels for at least four months. Wagons were constructed and sold at the "jumping off places" such as Council Bluffs, Iowa; and St. Joseph's or Independence, Missouri. The ideal size for a wagon was 22- or 24-feet-long by 11-feet-wide. Since a Conestoga or farm wagon was too long and could not make the steep climbs, special wagons were built which were lighter, shorter and stronger.

The weight on a wagon mounted as pioneers packed bedding and mattresses, tents, cooking utensils, clothing, and personal items such as medicines, Bibles, pictures or sewing machines. The guidebooks recommended that for each adult the following would be necessary: 200 lbs. flour, 75 lbs. bacon, 10 lbs. rice, 5 lbs.

coffee, 2 bushels dried beans, 1 bushel dried fruit (to prevent scurvy), 2 lbs. tea, 10 lbs. salt, 25 lbs. sugar and 10 lbs. corn meal. Women did much of the preparation and packing. Every inch of space was critical. They made sacks to hold and store sugar, flour, salt, rice, coffee and tea, put the eggs in the flour and rice; packed the bacon in the cornmeal to keep it fresh; layered the wagon with flat goods, and the men placed four large wooden barrels at each end of the wagon to hold water, and to act as ballast. The women utilized every inch of space and sewed large pockets into the canvas wagon tops for storage. The men built long, narrow boxes to hold tools, chains, and spare parts. A fully packed wagon weighed over 12 tons and a team of oxen could haul it adequately until water deprivation, hunger, and the altitude of the western slopes slowed them down. Then all manner of personal items and necessities were thrown away to lighten the load.

The wagons used on the Oregon Trail, the Old Santa Fe Trail and for the trip to California were commonly referred to as Prairie Schooners. Thick canvas or linen covers which resembled sails were added to withstand rain, hail and dust. As the wagons traveled through the tall grasses of the Platte River in Nebraska, with only canvas covers visible, from a distance they appeared to be ships floating across the plains. More than one woman observed the similarity of their experience crossing the American Great Plains in their canvas-sailed wagons to that of their ancestors who had crossed the Atlantic in ships not much larger than Prairie Schooners.

Once the wagons were piled high with provisions, overlanders waited for an opportune departure. Timing was everything. By leaving too soon, one might face deep mud and spring floods from the prairie storms. Leaving too late, travelers could encounter snowstorms by the time they reached the High Sierras. Wagon masters commandeering wagon trains usually gauged their departure by the growth of the prairie grasses just after the spring rains. When the grass had reached four inches high, it was time to move.

The trip to Oregon could take from four to six months. The first month passed by pleasantly. Women wondered at the beautiful sights, stopped to pick wildflowers and got acquainted with other women in the group. They described evenings around the campfire, the anticipation they felt, the pride with which they maintained their wagons and cooked meals on the trail. Women were up before daylight packing, cleaning, and preparing breakfast as most wagon party's preferred to break camp and be on the trail by 7:00 a.m. Getting an early start while it was cool would spare the oxen the heat as much as possible, and help ration the water supply. When they stopped at noontime, women prepared a large meal while everyone else rested for a few hours to wait out the hottest part of the day. The party resumed travel by late afternoon, and stopped at about six or seven in the evening. During the evening meal, families would socialize and someone might provide musical accompaniment for group singing and dancing which helped relieve the stress of the day. Following this routine, if the wagon train did not have major problems, they averaged about 20 miles per day. On the trail, everyone walked except infants, toddlers, the very elderly and the infirm.

Women who were pregnant when they left Missouri, had grave concerns about giving birth on the trail so it was important to seek the help of other women. Even so, wagon trains rarely stayed intact for the entire journey. Looking for a shorter route, most split up at some point, and women might find themselves stranded when they went into labor. Thirteen-year-old Martha Gay Masterson recalled the birth of her sister on the trail,

> Early on the morning of June 14, I was awakened from a nervous sleep by the wailing of an infant. I asked my mother whose baby was crying so. She said it was hers. I said not a word for some time, fearing I might have to welcome another brother. I already had nine brothers. I was so anxious to know I asked, "Is it a little brother?" Imagine my joy when she said it was a little sister. Then I hastily dressed and wanted to see it. I thought it surely was the cutest and sweetest little sister in the wide world.

By the time overlanders had crossed the Rockies and Sierras, they had endured the heat, the cold, wagons breaking down, rattlesnakes, and accidental deaths. Young children frequently fell from wagons and some were crushed by the oxen or the wheels. People were wounded or killed when guns misfired, or died in prairie fires, storms, or stampedes of livestock or buffalo.

The stock image in Hollywood Westerns of wagon trains traveling single file is inaccurate. The amount of trail dust kicked up would have blinded or choked those who followed the lead wagon. Wagon trains formed side by side, abreast, and moved forward like a massed army. Even in that formation, dust blinded and choked travelers so badly that many became blind. Emigrants were stricken with diseases of all kinds: typhoid, malaria, and tuberculosis. They contracted bacterial infections, mostly from drinking polluted water. They were riddled with insect bites, sick from spoiled food, and suffered from many unidentified viral infections. Cholera, the most dreaded disease, claimed the most victims on the trek west and it spread so quickly that victims could die within 24 hours. Signs of cholera infection included severe stomach pain, dehydration and skin that was so dry it hardened and turned blue. It is estimated as many as 30,000 emigrants died on the trail and most from cholera. Those who completed the trek said they found the way to Oregon by using the graves of victims as trail markers, which were spaced about every 80 yards.

Many overlanders who arrived at their destination agreed that it was the women who had sustained them. Women on the trail had cooked, nursed, sewn, mended, given birth, cared for their loved ones and found time to write about it. Improvisation often meant survival. They astonished themselves at what they accomplished on the journey. Women milked cows, churned butter, baked, butchered and prepared wild game, and all this while constantly on the move! When firewood was no longer available, women learned to bake bread, pies and other edibles using buffalo chips for fuel. For some women, survival meant maintaining the simple civilities of housekeeping. They not only washed clothes but ironed them too, and often set an attractive table with linens and a bouquet of wildflowers.

In the face of deprivation unimaginable today, women kept themselves and their families going. Some women finished the journey without husbands, fathers or sweethearts. Many early Oregonian homesteaders were widows whose husbands had died on the trail. Pioneer Ellen Smith had continued the trek after her husband's death in 1846, with eight children. In order to survive, Ellen and the children set fires in small brush or logs to scare out the burrowing critters such as field mice which they roasted and ate.

Indian attacks, which motion picture and television westerns hype as the most dangerous force, rarely occurred. From 1820 to 1870, Native Americans posed little threat to the wagon trains, as natives were nothing more than curiosity seekers. At their worst, natives pestered the overlanders for food. More often, at their best, they rendered assistance to wagon trains which had run amuck. But, years later, when white hunters had reduced the buffalo herds, and the Plains Indians' way of life was threatened with extinction, some tribes fought back. Overlanders knew to avoid the southern route over the Old Santa Fe Trail where hostile Apache and Comanche roamed. In some cases, the risk of encounter was more threatening for Native Americans than overlanders.

The migration of the overlanders took its toll on the native population. In 1800, the western Native American population totaled one million but by 1860, it was reduced to 200,000. The total overlander losses due to Indian attack amounted to 300. Before railroads modernized travel west, Indian raids on wagon trains were also rare. Only after 1869, with the completion of the Trans-Continental railroad and the depletion of buffalo herds, did Indian attacks increase.

Nonetheless, there were isolated incidents of wagon trains attacked by natives, and these stories got lots of attention in the press and stereotyped Native Americans as savages. The Oatman Massacre is one such tragedy. When a wagon train of seven families, including the Oatman and Thompson families, reached Yuma, Arizona, against everyone's advice, Royce Oatman split up from the main group and proceeded with only his family. They stopped on the Gila

River when Mrs. Oatman went into labor and it was there that they were attacked by a band from the Yavapais or Tolkepayas tribe. Fifteen-year-old Lorenzo Oatman, partially scalped and left for dead, walked for three days back to the original wagon party to seek help. But by the time the wagon party found them, Mr. and Mrs. Oatman, the newborn, two daughters and a son had been killed. Two girls, twelve-year-old Olive and Mary Ann, aged seven, were taken as captives. A year later, Olive was traded to the Mojaves (her sister Mary Ann had died some months before.) Her brother Lorenzo spent the next five years searching for her, and after arranging her release from the Mojaves, they were reunited at Fort Yuma, Arizona.

Olive Oatman a victim of the Oatman Massacre in which six family members were killed was taken captive at age thirteen but later released and reunited with the only other member of her family to survive, her brother Lorenzo. Olive became somewhat of a celebrity during her lifetime with books, plays and poems written about her. The town of Oatman, Arizona is named in her honor. (Photo courtesy of the Arizona Historical Society.)

Olive became somewhat of a celebrity and went on to give public lectures. She explained that the Mohave tattooed their captives to ensure they would be recognized if they escaped. "You perceive I have the mark indelibly placed upon my chin." Her tattoos were blue like those of most Mohave women who wore chin tattoos. In 1857, Rev. Royal B. Stratton wrote a book about Olive and Mary Ann's captivity experience which sold 30,000 copies, (best-seller status for that era.) Olive Oatman firmly denied allegations that she had been raped by the Yavapai and was quoted by Stratton as having declared that "to the honor of these savages let it be said, they never offered the least unchaste abuse to me". In November, 1865, Olive married a wealthy rancher John B. Fairchild and went to live in Sherman, Texas, where they adopted a baby girl, they named Mamie. Although she always spoke of the Mohave with great affection, she did continue to have adverse reactions from the captivity experience. In her forties, Olive battled debilitating headaches and depression. In 1881, she spent nearly three months bedridden at a medical spa in Canada and displayed symptoms of some chronic form of post-traumatic stress disorder for the rest of her life.

Another victim of Indian attack was Fanny Kelly, along with her husband and an adopted daughter. When they joined a wagon train at Fort Laramie, Kansas, in 1864, and were attacked by Oglala Sioux, the white men were killed but the women and children were captured. Fanny survived the five month ordeal and wrote a best seller, *Narrative of My Captivity among the Sioux Indians*, in which she described narrowly escaping death a number of times. On one occasion, she discarded a sacred peace pipe which the chief had given her. This was considered a sacrilegious act. Fanny boasted that before she was released, the Oglala Sioux and the Blackfoot Sioux vied for her as a valuable hostage. Supposedly her captors had named her "Real Woman" for her bravery.

Settling on the Frontier

Native and settler women were instrumental to the success and survival of the early pioneers who settled in the Midwest and the West. Although pioneer wives often reluctantly accompanied their husbands west, it was women's efforts to make a home in the wilderness that were critical to the outcome. Frontier women faced extreme hardships, living in remote and desolate areas including harsh weather, shortages of food and water, and more intense work demands than their mothers or grandmothers had ever experienced. Historian John Mack Faragher goes so far as to say that Midwestern women were *more* essential to the family's survival than the men. As Faragher explains,

> By no means were men the "breadwinners" of this economy both women and men actively participated in the production of family subsistence. Indeed women were engaged in from one-third to one-half of all the food production of the farm, the proportions varying with regional and individual differences....To be sure, men and women alike worked hard to make their farms produce. But one cannot avoid being struck by the enormousness of women's work load.

Contrary to notions that men's work was more strenuous than women's, Professor Faragher points out that it was the females who performed the backbreaking chores. Their responsibilities included cooking, butchering, spinning, weaving, and sewing. They gathered whatever firewood might be available for cooking fuel. Women tended the henhouse, collecting eggs, feeding and caring for the poultry, and performed the unpleasant task of cleaning out manure. The care of dairy animals—both feeding and milking twice a day—was often women's work.

At a time when women living in the East could purchase calico and other fabrics, off the bolt, frontier women made everything from "scratch;" linen from flax, wool from sheep, and long wearing linsey-woolsey, from linen and wool. If it was available, women also spun cotton. Faragher estimated that to clothe a family of four for a year required a minimum of 40 yards of cloth. Preparing this much cloth required many hours.

In the 1800s, the average Midwest frontier family consisted of five or six children. Children performed chores at an early age, usually by six or seven years, but most families trying to eke out a living on a modest 50 acre farm succeeded only by hiring help, usually for harvest.

Pioneer family portrait–a woman's greatest concern in making the overland trek was that she might face childbirth alone, unattended by either a physician or another woman who could serve as a midwife.

Although having large families was desirable, few assessed the toll it took on frontier women. Faragher's study found that more than half of the Midwestern farm women gave birth in the first year of marriage, and 98 percent by the third year. In their childbearing years, women had a pregnancy about every 2.5 years. When not expecting a child, women were nursing and caring for a baby. Infant mortality was still very high, with one child in five not surviving to its fifth birthday. Prenatal loss resulted in one out of every five pregnancies miscarried or stillborn. Facing dogged work and the rigorous round of pregnancies, frontier women, who needed the support of other females during childbirth, were less likely to have other women nearby and faced childbirth without the support of a midwife or family.

Arriving in Oregon

For those women who arrived safely in Oregon, the hardships were just beginning. Women had left families they would never see again, and when they arrived in Oregon Country they settled in remote areas devoid of neighbors or the companionship of other women. Some went mad; others suffered from chronic depression for the rest of their lives. Writing, scripture reading, and sewing offered some consolation, for as one woman stated, "I must keep on writing to remember who I am." In solitude, women relied on the sustaining comfort of their faith; if literate they could find spiritual consolation in scripture reading. The isolation bit sharply into their lives as women faced lying in, childbirth, and the post partum recovery period alone.

> This week Rhoda was born I cooked for fifteen men who had come to help stack the hay. In intervals of serving then I would collapse onto my bed - I was so tired. Through the bedroom window I could see the mare and the cow turned out to pasture for weeks because they were going to have their young.

Many women who could not read relied on work of a contemplative nature—quilting, embroidery, knitting or crocheting—to provide a certain measure of artistic expression. Some of the personal literature such as women's diaries and letters alludes to insanity as the high cost of isolation and hard work. One woman confided, "I would have gone crazy were it not for the occupation of my time quilting." (Perhaps the crazy quilt denotes more than just a random design.)

The Whitmans' Mission

One family of overlanders, for whom missionary work was a strong calling, was the Whitmans. Narcissa Whitman was one of the first of two missionary women to emigrate to the West. In 1836, Narcissa accompanied her husband Marcus, a missionary-doctor, and they established a Christian mission near present-day Walla Walla, Washington. The only woman with whom Narcissa had close contact was another missionary, Eliza Spalding. The two had come over the Oregon Trail together but upon arrival lived miles apart. In the absence of close companionship, Narcissa and Eliza agreed to pause every morning at 9:00 a.m. to pray for each other. When Marcus left to recruit more settlers in the east, Narcissa lived in solitude, like so many western women. She found comfort in her baby Alice, as she explained in a letter to her sister, "O, how many melancholy hours she has saved me, while living here alone so long, especially when her father is gone for so many days together." At the age of two, Alice Whitman drowned, and a grief stricken Narcissa held her for four days. Her behavior showed to what depths of despondency women could fall when left alone in the wilderness and faced with the loss of a child. In a letter to her parents, Narcissa explained her need to cling to the corpse, "She [Alice] did not begin to change in her appearance much for the first three days. This proved to be a great comfort to me for so long as she looked natural and was so sweet and I could caress her, I could not bear to have her out of my sight."

At the onset of their mission, the Whitmans were warmly welcomed by local natives, the Cayuse Indians, and this success encouraged other missionaries to come to the Oregon Territory. When Marcus returned in 1843, bringing 900 more settlers, they unfortunately also brought disease. Hostilities arose when a measles epidemic killed many Native Americans but spared most of the white settlers. Perceived by the Cayuse Indians as "agents of the pestilence," the Whitmans were killed by them.

Whether a family remained in one settlement or moved about, the women displayed the same stoicism they had on the trail and often with a dash of entrepreneurial spirit. Tabitha Brown was sixty-six years old when she completed the trip to Oregon. The story is told that Tabitha found a coin in a glove which served as upstart capital for her Glover's business. Tabitha's business success led to other ventures like the establishment of the Forest Grove orphanage, which was eventually transformed into Pacific University. Harriet Bailey grew flax and from it knitted socks which she sold for $0.50 a pair. Sarah Owens manufactured twine and also processed fine linen, to make men's shirts which she sold. After settlement, Abigail Scott Duniway went on to fight for female suffrage relentlessly for forty-two years.

Women in all the western settlements faced hardship and isolation. Wyoming shepherdess Sedda Henry, who had moved to the West from Ohio, tended her herds alone. Pitching a tent near her covered wagon, Sedda made her "home on the range" for six months at a stretch. As more western states passed legislation conducive to female land ownership, women often inherited farms and ranches. The

1850 Oregon Land Donation Act granted a married man 640 acres of free land, but *only half as much if he were single.* Legislators had intended the law as an incentive for men to marry and settle down. This law and the fact that males far outnumbered females put much social pressure on women to marry and enticed single women to move to the West to find a husband.

Women having settled in Oregon could not assume that this was necessarily the end of the trail, as many husbands quickly "got a hankering for some place else." Upon arrival in Oregon, the Stewart and Love families moved seven more times. Elizabeth Gay tells how, by her fourteenth wedding anniversary, she had moved to twenty-one different locations. Elizabeth added dryly, "My husband was considered a visionary by his friends." This constant restlessness, lifelong discontent and hankering for someplace else, characterized like nothing else, the men who migrated west, and two out of every three men who settled in Oregon left shortly afterwards to search for gold in California.

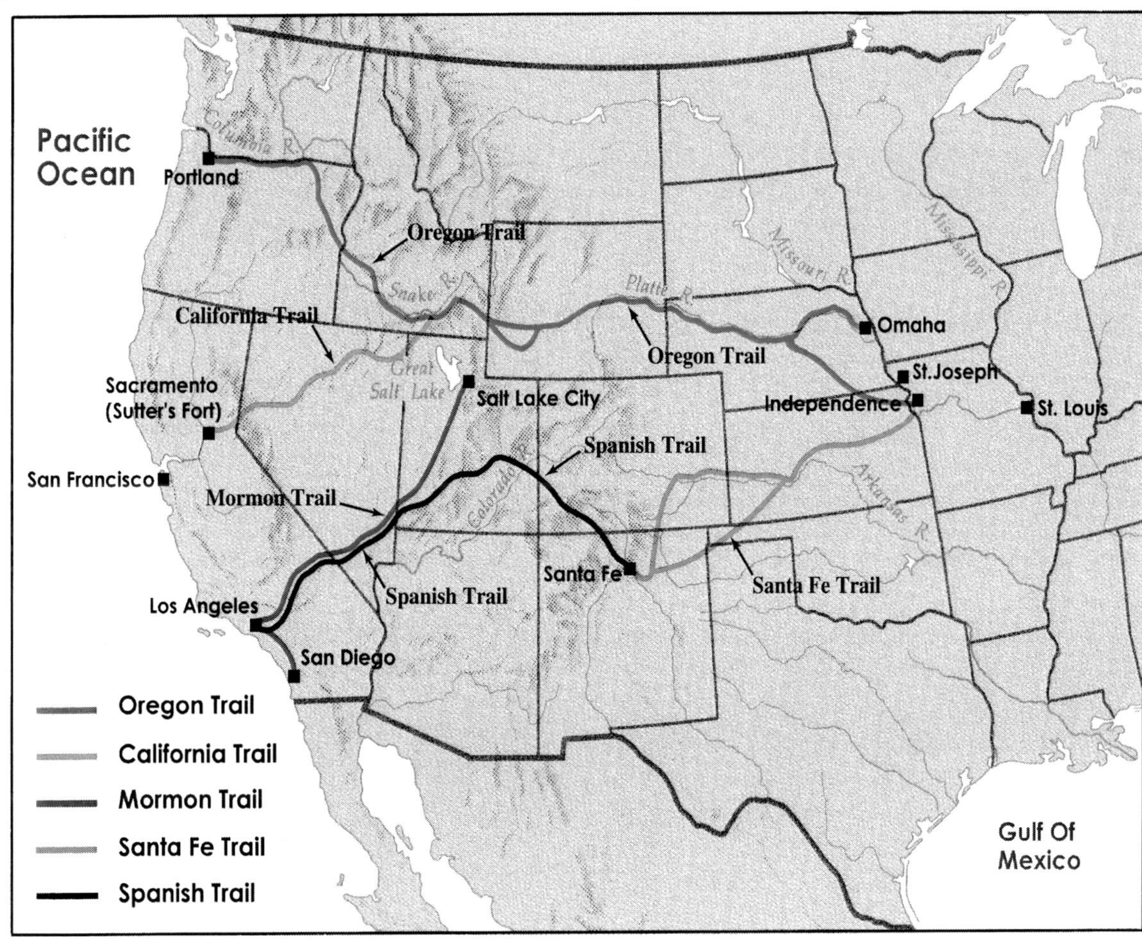

In the 1830s, thousands of pioneers known as the Overlanders followed the Oregon Trail to the Pacific Northwest. Additional routes and trails developed as pioneers ventured West to other regions such as California, Utah and the Southwest.

The California Gold Rush

> All the talk and excitement is the Calafornie [sic] mines any able bodyed men are off to the mines. The families will double up and leave one old feable man to look after some families. But indeed who will care for everyone until they return? It is we women folks.

The Gold Rush in California incited international migration. Stores, restaurants, saloons, banks and brothels were hastily built to outfit, supply and entertain the male fortune hunters who poured into the area. In California, women were in short supply. The San Francisco census of 1847, lists 138 women living in that area. As a longstanding colony of Spain and later Mexico, Californians made up a vibrant mix of people including those of Spanish ancestry, white settlers from the United States, a *mestizo* population, Native Americans, and immigrants from China, Central and South America and Europe.

Women sought lucrative work in the mining camps and adventure in panning for gold. Elizabeth Bays Wimmer, or Jennie, played a crucial role in the discovery of gold in California. In 1846, she had migrated to California with her husband Peter and seven children. When Peter took employment at Sutter's Mill, in 1848, Jennie took on the job of cooking and laundering for the entire work camp. It was John Marshall, the mill's carpenter, who found the first gold nuggets, and he needed to determine their authenticity without calling any attention to the discovery. Jennie, who was making soap at the time, suggested adding the nuggets to the caustic lye solution. After the soap solidified, Jennie cut it into squares. She reached into the residue of potash and pulled out gold "as bright as it could be." A few women bitten by the gold bug went prospecting and panning for gold. Lucena Parsons worked the diggings and got a little gold, but most were women like Jennie Wimmer who accompanied miner husbands and provided housekeeping, feeding and laundering for the men in the camps.

Many women lived independently. Widow Eliza Farnham came to California in 1850 with her two children and settled on land her late husband had purchased. In 1852, Eliza married William Fitzpatrick, but she continued to augment the family's failing farm, by teaching school. After four years of severe abuse, and the deaths of two of her children, Eliza sued Fitzpatrick for divorce. In 1856, she became one of the first women to obtain a divorce under the new law. For all her misfortunes, Eliza expressed an unusually positive and prophetic outlook on women's future in the new state when she wrote later in a book about homesteading in California,

> "...California will ultimately be connected by railroad, with the east and in a few years she will be the garden of the Union. There is no prosperity to which she cannot attain, with true manhood to control, and true womanhood to preserve her."

Mothers of Invention: Speaking for Our People - Suzette La Flesche and Sarah Winnemucca

The western migration brought tragedy to the Ponca tribe who experienced disastrous treatment from white people when the government relocated them from their homes in the Dakotas to Oklahoma, a march of 500 miles. When approximately one-third of the tribe died from a malaria epidemic in Oklahoma, Ponca Chief Standing Bear made a death bed promise to his son, a malaria victim, that he would bury him on their ancestral ground in Dakota. In 1879, attended by thirty of his braves, Standing Bear began the funeral march. On the way, he stopped at the eastern Nebraska reservation of the Omahas and accepted the hospitality of Chief Joseph La Flesche. But there, Standing Bear and his retinue were intercepted by the United States Army who entered the reservation, took them into custody and confiscated the remains of Chief Standing Bear's son. Officials then ordered them to return to Oklahoma or face charges as runaways.

When *Omaha Herald* journalist Thomas Tibbles, got word of the melee and printed the story in the newspaper, it caught the attention of Suzette La Flesche, daughter of the Chief La Flesche of the Omahas. Suzette La Flesche, both articulate and eastern educated, wrote to Tibbles about the plight of the Poncas. Thomas Tibbles filed a suit of habeas corpus and won freedom for Chief Standing Bear and his retinue. Standing Bear's suit became a landmark court case because for the first time, a United States Court had defined a Native American as a person with rights. Not stopping there, Tibbles realized that publicity could bring public support for the Poncas and he arranged for Standing Bear to make a tour of eastern cities to promote his cause. With Suzette La Flesche as his spokesperson, Thomas Tibbles accompanied the Chief.

On tour, Suzette La Flesche reported that those curious but not particularly sympathetic to the Indian cause became instant converts. Two spectators in particular, author Helen Hunt Jackson and United States Senator Henry Dawes, were deeply moved. Helen Hunt Jackson related how previously she had held Native Americans in contempt but after hearing Suzette speak she became a passionate advocate for them. In her first book, *A Century of Dishonor,* Helen Hunt Jackson documented the long history of broken treaties and the shameful treatment of Native Americans. Helen Hunt Jackson's next book, *Ramona,* which became a classic, so affected Senator Dawes that he took up the Indian cause and initiated the Dawes Act, which Congress passed in 1887. With good intention, the Dawes Act granted homesteading land to Indians, but it failed to recognize their tribal affinity and communal lifestyle. The Dawes Act required that in order to farm homestead land, natives must renounce their tribal status. To enforce the law, the government sent Helen Clark, the daughter of a white trader and Blackfoot mother, to transfer the land allotments to the Ponca tribesmen. Although the Dawes Act failed, it did advance more humane treatment for Native Americans.

The resolution of the Ponca tragedy was bittersweet: Suzette La Flesche and Thomas Tibbles were married, and continued to petition, write and lecture on behalf of all Native Americans. They used Congressional hearings in particular as an effective venue. Standing Bear was allowed to bury his son's bones, but the government never allowed the Poncas to return to their homeland in the Dakotas.

In 1844, an Indian prophesy had foretold the coming of white people as a benevolent omen. Paiutes in Nevada territory welcomed white settlers. Paiute Chief Truckee, overwhelmed at the knowledge and technology of white people, arranged for some Paiute children to live with white settlers. Young Sarah Winemucca, who was one of those children, became fluent in English and an ardent champion for her people.

When the Comstock Silver Lode was discovered in 1859, and fortune seekers flooded into the arid-alkaline basin of Nevada, troubles began for the Paiutes in the form of confrontation with whites. In 1865, soldiers killed a small fishing party of men, women and children including Sarah Winnemucca's brother. When Chief Truckee died, Sarah's father became chief and appointed her chief negotiator/ interpreter to the whites. Over the next decade the territorial government continuously relocated Paiutes until 1875, when the tribe found a resting place in Oregon.

Sarah Winnemucca's troubles were just beginning when her father was taken prisoner by the hostile Bannock tribe in 1881. She joined a United States army patrol as a scout and tracked the Bannocks to Oregon, and rescued her father and several hundred Paiutes. For her part in the so-called Bannock wars, General Oliver Howard granted her a $500 reward, but he also marched the Paiutes off to an Army detention camp in Yakima, Washington. Adding insult to injury, the Paiutes branded Sarah a traitor. When she pleaded for fair treatment for the Paiutes, San Francisco newspapers circulated the story, and officials invited her to Washington to plead her case. Sarah had a brief audience with President Hayes. In her meeting with Secretary of the Interior Carl Schurz, he authorized the liberation of the Paiutes, their safe passage to Oregon, and a compensation of 160 acres of land for each male tribal member. But on her return to Yakima, disappointment set in when local government agents refused to carry out the federal directive, stating that it might incite a riot among the white population.

In 1883, Sarah Winnemucca authored *Life Among the Paiutes* and with the backing of Boston reformers started a lecture tour in the East. Sarah petitioned the government once again, but despite persistent efforts, Secretary Schurz's directive was never carried out. When she returned to her tribe, they honored her with the title of "Mother," but Sarah believed that her mission for the Paiutes was a failure. She died, some say of a broken heart, in 1891.

Conclusion

For those who had survived the trek across North America to Oregon or to California it was said that they "had seen the elephant." This summed up an entire, unique and never to be forgotten experience. Graffitti along the Oregon Trail painted on canvas wagon covers or carved on rocks read: "Have you saw the elephant?" This popular expression seen along the trail, even before the California Gold Rush, can be traced to a tale of a farmer who went to town to see the circus. Desiring to see a real elephant, he hitched up his wagon to take his produce for market day. Before he could get to town, a circus troupe led by an elephant making its procession alongside him, terrified his horses who upset his entire wagon of produce. With nothing to sell, and unable to stay for the circus, he returned home penniless. On the way, passersby jeered at the farmer who had lost his wagon load. To which the farmer replied, "It does not matter for I have seen the elephant."

This became an analogy for the trek to the West. It was not for the fainthearted, and one risked everything for the adventure. Having seen the elephant, survivors were members of a special band who had endured misfortune, hardship and tragedy.

As white settlers encroached on western land, native residents were driven off or confined on reservations. In 1838, Cherokee and other tribes were forced off of their land by Federal order and "escorted" by the United States Army to land in Oklahoma.

The western migration was an endeavor by families who risked everything and invested all they had to go west and start a new life. Thousands never made it. Disease and deprivation claimed many who were buried along the way. Those who succeeded in overcoming hardship, used tremendous personal effort and adjustment to reestablish themselves and build communities and towns. The women who experienced the great western migration were less inclined to tolerate abuse and inferior status. In their new digs, women took on ventures, enterprises, and professions which had been less accessible to them in the Midwest and the East. It is no surprise to us then that these assertive women in the western territories would be the first to gain the right to vote.

Chapter 11
The Role of Women in the West
No Virtuous Woman is Safe near a Cowboy

Key Topics

Femmes Fatales and Heroic Women
Women of a Civilizing Influence
Western War of Expansion
Slaves or Free People in California
Professional Women in the West
Mormon Women in the West

Chronology

1820 - American Settlers Homestead Northern Mexican Territory
1820 - 1840 - Removal of Native Americans from their Ancestral Lands
1846 - 1848 - War with Mexico
1848 - The Treaty of Guadalupe Hidalgo

Introduction

In 1848, after the Mexican War, the United States advanced migration and economic expansion for white settlers. But the terms of peace, the Treaty of Guadalupe Hidalgo, made those Mexican Nationals who lived on their ancestral land second-class citizens of the United States.

An unbelievable stroke of good luck occurred as soon as the United States took California under the Treaty. Gold was discovered there and thousands more white settlers came west. The gold-mining camps became an international convergence with fortune seekers from Asia, Europe, Central and South America and other parts of North America. The pioneers who took up residence in the new settlements of Oregon, California, Nevada, Utah, Arizona, New Mexico, Colorado, Wyoming and Montana experienced life on a new scale.

The West attracted adventurous men and determined women. Only the strongest people could survive in the challenging environment. Women from all walks of life and every ethnic group played a vital role in the development of California and the West. The women who migrated west performed every kind of work imaginable: as entertainers, outlaws, sharpshooters, cattle ranchers, freelance artists, suffragists and prospectors, and in doing so defined new roles for American females. The formation of western communities and eventually states was largely determined by the female missionaries, teachers, homesteaders, nurses, midwives, laundresses, cooks and laborers who brought a civilizing influence and stability to the new frontier.

Femme Fatales and Heroic Women

Female entertainers in the West ranged from the mediocre to the gifted. Keeping company with the latter, performer Lotta Crabtree had charmed audiences singing and dancing as a child prodigy and shocked them in her teens by smoking cigarettes in public, and baring legs and arms on stage. Making several world tours as an entertainer, she gained wealth and fame so that at her death, Lotta Crabtree's net worth was valued at four million dollars. Another actress, political émigré Helen Modjeska, had fled Poland during the Russian oppression and arrived in California in 1876. Modeled after the philosopher-inspired Brook Farm, Helen founded a Utopian Farm in Anaheim, where she hoped to assemble like-minded European idealists. When it failed she worked as a diction coach and later billed, as Madame Modjeska, resumed a successful acting career appearing on the stage in San Francisco, New York, London and Poland.

Miss Annie Oakley posed with the rifle which was a gift from Buffalo Bill and proudly displaying the medals awarded to her for her marksmanship. (Photo courtesy of the Library of Congress.)

In a class by herself, expert riflewoman Annie Oakley became a world famous entertainer. Born Phoebe Ann Moses, she had hunted game on the family farm in Ohio to support her widowed mother and save the family farm from foreclosure. Annie Oakley went on to become a famous sharpshooter and toured with Buffalo Bill's Wild West Show. In 1876, she married Frank Butler, a marksman, vaudevillian and fellow member of Buffalo Bill's troupe. After their marriage, Butler forfeited his career and became her lifelong manager. When the Buffalo Bill show went on tour in Europe, Annie Oakley got top billing. Performing before the crown heads of Europe, she shot cigarettes from her husband's mouth. During the Berlin command performance, Prussian Crown Prince Wilhelm held the cigarette in his mouth while Annie aimed. Her marksmanship (markswomanship?) was incredible; at 30 paces, she could aim, shoot and split a deck of playing cards held on edge, or hit tossed dimes. Annie could also shoot a hole into a single playing card tossed into the air. Because of this skill, punched-out, used theater tickets are still referred to as "Annie Oakley's."

Martha Jane Canary, a.k.a. Calamity Jane, gained her reputation in the 1870s gold rush days in the Dakota Territory. Even in rough and ready Dakota, Calamity scandalized society when she worked as a bartender and a prostitute. Examining Calamity's life, it is hard to weed fact from fiction, as she was often her best promoter and exaggerated her derring-do. By her account, she served as an army scout, wagon driver on the Deadwood stage, Indian fighter and claimed to be the wife of Wild Bill Hickok. In reality, she was a stunt rider and sharpshooter briefly in Buffalo Bill's Wild West Show, where she shot holes in her Stetson while tossing it in the air (targetwise, no competition for Annie Oakley). At her death in 1903, she was buried alongside of "Wild Bill" in a Deadwood cemetery.

Mary Fields, one of the most colorful western women and known affectionately as "Stagecoach Mary," was born a slave in Tennessee. At age thirty-three, when the Civil War ended, Mary moved west to Cascade County, Montana, with an order of Ursuline nuns and helped them build a mission school there. But the nuns turned Mary out of the mission because her hard-drinking, gun-slinging lifestyle was unsuitable for the convent. One source states that the nuns helped set her up in business operating her own cafe. Evidently Mary's generosity in feeding the "down and out" ate up all the profits. Finally in 1895, at age sixty-three, she found her niche when she got a government job driving a stagecoach to deliver the mail. Stagecoach Mary died in 1914, and is buried in Cascade, Montana.

Martha Jane Canary, remembered as Calamity Jane, was one of the colorful females of the American West who tended bar, drove a stagecoach and was a stunt rider in Buffalo Bill's Wild West Show. (Photo courtesy of the Library of Congress.)

Western legend portrayed Myra Belle Shirley (a.k.a. Belle Starr) as an outlaw and cattle rustler who ran a thriving rustling trade as head of a gang in the Oklahoma Territory. Belle's brother was a member of the famous Quantrill's Raiders, a group of former confederates turned outlaws after the Civil War. Belle, who had associated with the notorious from an early age, had a child by Cole Younger, a member of the Younger Brothers gang, and became Jim Reed's common-law wife. She operated a livery stable briefly in Dallas and in 1880, moved to Oklahoma and married a Cherokee named Sam Starr. Their home became a hideout for other outlaws, including Jesse James. In 1883, the Starrs were indicted for horse theft and sent to a Federal prison in Detroit, where she served nine months. She was charged in at least three more crimes but never convicted. Sam Starr was shot in the back in 1887, and Belle came to the same end February 3, 1889, in an ambush at her cabin. At her grave, Belle's daughter erected an impressive tombstone with a carved bell and star in her mother's honor. The legend of Belle Starr was romanticized by Richard Fox whose stories about her were published in the National Police Gazette. Fox portrayed Belle as a beautiful, blonde southern belle who had turned to crime to avenge her brother's death. According to Fox, Belle's brother had been a heroic Confederate officer.

There were other femme fatales of the West. Pearl Hart, considered the last stagecoach bandit in the West, served five years in an Arizona prison for robbery. Denver madam Georgianna Shorthouse was sentenced to three years in prison for performing abortions. Outlaw Jessie Wyatt and transvestite Nina Patchen were both acquitted of murder. Two young girls known as Cattle Annie and Little Britches served as scouts and lookouts for the famous Doolin Gang, but after Annie and Britches were apprehended and served brief prison terms, they went straight.

Gold Diggers, Prostitutes and Exploited Women

The Gold Rush attracted a great cross section of nineteenth century adventurers to the West. No sooner had someone shouted "Eureka" than women arrived to work the bars, saloons, dance halls, brothels and fandango houses in boomtowns such as San Francisco, Sacramento and the small mining towns. In Nevada, Montana and Colorado, dance halls known as hurdy-gurdy houses sprang up. Dance-hall girls might hold down a number of jobs as entertainers, card dealers, and mixers; i.e. women paid to ply the liquor trade.

Prostitution became a lucrative trade in San Francisco, particularly along the infamous Barbary Coast. The treatment of prostitutes reflected the racial bigotry of society at large and women were ranked by ethnicity and skin color. Although they were still regarded as chattel, French women were the most highly prized. In the trade, a single French woman was equivalent to twenty other women. Latin American, Asian and Afro-American women, less welcome in western towns, were debased and often mistreated. As ships rounded the Horn bringing passengers headed for California, women from South America came to California. Some ships' captains denied women of questionable morality onboard their ships. Others offered them free passage; then once onboard held them as hostages. Upon arrival in port, the women were sold to the brothels and kept in debt bondage. Their new owners took the lion's share of their earnings and deducted the remainder for room, board, and clothing.

Tragic cases of female exploitation in California involved the trafficking of young Chinese girls for the prostitution trade in San Francisco. In 1852, the 20,026 Chinese male emigrants in the city comprised the population at the founding of Chinatown. That same year, shiploads of Chinese girls, "*daughters of joy*" were delivered to San Francisco from the faraway ports of Canton and Hong Kong. Daughters, a liability in poor Chinese families, were often sold into slavery and wound up as prostitutes. The stereotype of Asian female exoticism promoted the sale and price of these young girls. Jo Ann Levy, in *They Saw the Elephant, Women of the California Gold Rush,* notes "depending upon their age, beauty and the prevailing market" the girls might bring from 300 to 3,000 dollars when sold by Chinese organizations. Agents operated from *barracoons,* i.e. basements, in San Francisco where the girls were processed for sale. Chinese prostitutes had a very short life span. Taken from China usually when they were under the age of twenty, they died young. Chinese prostitute Lee Lan, just twenty years old, attracted curiosity seekers to her elaborate funeral. Evidently, Lee Lan's birth into a high caste in China had not earned her a decent life but had merited an expensive funeral. Rarely did Chinese prostitutes survive to maturity but one enterprising woman, Madame Ah Toy, did; her fortunes rose and fell with the times. Toy availed herself of the courts and police protection but eventually left San Francisco when anti-prostitution laws were initiated.

Early street scene in Chinatown, San Francisco, with highly dense residences, shops, and traffic. Young girls were shipped into Chinatown and held hostage as prostitutes. (Photo courtesy of the Library of Congress.)

Prostitutes lived meanly and on borrowed time. The work took its toll on the women in terms of venereal disease, abortion, alcoholism, addiction to opiates, or physical abuse. The so-called *soiled doves*, i.e. women under the age of twenty, could expect to work only until their mid-twenties. Some entered the *profession* to abandon husbands or forsake an unhappy marriage but others did so to find a husband. About the only hope of survival for a soiled dove was to marry out of the profession. Ironically, those who became madames were gold diggers and exploiters themselves who in turn sold the sex of young prostitutes.

Most of the brothels, or sporting houses, maintained prostitutes' quarters known as cribs, which were nothing more than filthy shacks. Exceptional brothels, such as Lillian Power's house, were high-end establishments. Located in Cripple Creek, Colorado, the legendary Miss Lil' advertised a well-managed house of cribs, furnished attractively with lace curtains and clean linens; in other words, with all the comforts of home.

For prostitutes arriving in a western town, timing was critical and many experienced mixed social receptions. In 1850, women were a rarity; the California census showed a female population of eight percent. In the early phase of a town's settlement, prostitutes were the only women who offered companionship, and brothels and saloons became the gathering place. A more civilizing influence occurred in the second phase when respectable women arrived, married and established schools and churches. As the community stabilized, efforts were made to clean up the town. Then the status of prostitutes declined sharply. Wives and mothers quickly organized to remove the more unseemly element from their communities. By 1854, leading cities had passed anti-prostitution laws, and officials enforced ordinances to drive prostitutes out of town. One man lauded the arrival of respectable women as the "sweet gentle, and saving influence of woman." A California journalist acknowledged the civilizing influence of respectable ladies as, "A woman in society is like cement to the building of stone. Society here has no such cement; bring a woman here and at once the process of crystallization will set in place."

Women of a Civilizing Influence

In San Francisco, as early as 1853, Mrs A.B. Eaton established the *Ladies Protection and Relief Society.* Churchwomen all over town joined her in this endeavor to protect and assist sick and dependent women and children. The Society also built an orphanage and a temporary shelter for destitute women. Women also introduced culture and the arts to the West. Ina Coolbrith, for instance, a poet laureate and the first public librarian in California, devoted her life to literacy, culture and education for women.

Missionary work was considered a noble, if not dangerous, endeavor for women. Christian Women's Societies visited Native American settlements to convert them. They also established schools, like The Cherokee National Female Seminary in Park Hill, Oklahoma, to provide education for Native American girls. Although missionary work among the Native Americans preoccupied white women, helping natives remained controversial. The ongoing military campaign to exterminate Native Americans had split the American public into two camps those who sympathized with natives and those who supported the military credo that "the only good Indian was a dead Indian." Coloradan Rose Meeker supported the latter. When her family was attacked by the Ute Indians, Rose's father, mother and sister were captured. Rose spoke out in public lectures against Native Americans and condemned them as savages.

Women in religious orders made a major contribution to western settlements by establishing schools and hospitals. It is hard to imagine today but the nuns who came to missionize America in the nineteenth century had to travel in disguise because of the hostile anti-catholic sentiment. The Ursuline Order, already well established in New Orleans by the 1800s, briefed other groups such as the Sisters of St. Joseph of Carondelet, who emigrated from France and established their first schools and hospitals in St. Joseph, Missouri. In 1870, the Sisters of Charity sent twenty-two-year-old Sister Blandina to Trinidad, Colorado, a town two blocks long and two streets wide. Sister Blandina's phenomenal success as an educator branched out to criminal justice in Trinidad. She took on the harsh justice system and saved lynched men from execution. Sister Blandina also worked tirelessly helping the sick and the poor. Mother Joseph of the Sisters of Providence built St. Mary's Hospital in Astoria, Oregon, in 1885. She built the first school in the Pacific Northwest and raised money to establish some thirty additional schools and hospitals in Oregon and Washington.

By 1890, there were one thousand female artists in the west! Among them was Evelyn Cameron who had emigrated with her husband from England. Evelyn photographed the pristine beauty of the Montana territory and homesteaded there. The western landscape served as an inspirational backdrop for artists like Grace Carpenter Hudson, whose classic renderings of the California Pomo Indians, such as *The Empty Basket,* featured the funeral procession for a Native American infant. *Little Mendocino,* a realistic painting of a crying papoose, marked her as a great artist with a lifelong passion for Native Americans. The famous landscape artist, Eliza Barchus, known as "The

Oregon Artist," was a widow with children who found time to paint and teach school. Portrait artist Helen Tanner Brodt overlanded from New York to California in 1863, and painted there until her passing in 1908. Helen Brodt's painting of Lily Langtry immortalized the beauty of that famous actress.

The War of Western Expansion

The Mexican-American War began in 1846, but the stage for the war was set when Americans from the South who had settled in Texas introduced a slave economy. Bringing slaves was a direct violation of the Mexican Government's directives. The American press made the annexation of Texas into the United States a front page issue. One reporter, John L. Sullivan, coined annexation our *manifest destiny*. President Polk ordered troops be placed along the border near the Nueces and Rio Grande Rivers, and before long, shots were fired and war erupted. The war was a swift victory for the United States, and a bitter defeat for Mexico which lost almost fifty percent of its landmass in territorial concessions.

The Mexican-American War was, for Mexican Nationals living in the upper borderland of Mexico, a civil war in which families were torn apart. Territory acquired by the United States included what would become the states of California, Texas, Arizona and New Mexico. Under the terms of peace, the Treaty of Guadalupe Hidalgo, Mexican Nationals who lived in these regions lost their Mexican citizenship and in many cases their homes and land. Mexican Nationals had two choices. They could either abandon their homes and resettle farther south in Mexico or remain in the United States and become second-class citizens. Many, like Luisa Garfas, lost everything in the Mexican- American War. Luisa was so harshly treated that she chose emigration and left her home in California to live in Mexico. Those who stayed faced persecution, discrimination and a reduced financial status. As the territorial governments introduced English as the official language of the Southwest region, those families who had lived for generations under Spain and then the Republic of Mexico, faced cultural loss as well. Today those families are treated as unwanted immigrants. As Professor Deena Gonzalez explains in *Refusing the Favor,* in the case of her own family, who are fourteenth generation New Mexicans, they became United States citizens through a "geographical slight." After the treaty settlement, she explains, they had not come to the United States, rather, "it had come to us."

For its part, the United States depicted the victory over Mexico as a progressive step forward. The United States had not only won the territory but many believed deserved it, and would use its superior technology and capitalist venture to improve the acquired region. Indeed, the United States gained land two and a half times the size of France, territory rich in mineral deposits, precious metals, and the oil producing regions of California and Texas.

Looking at the impact of the Mexican-American War, Professor Gonzalez found in her research of Spanish-Mexicans, [her term] that the United States acquisition did not bring prosperity but poverty to many families. In areas such as Santa Fe, individuals were duped out of their property or lost against the rising tide of competition of a *new white* merchant class. Men and women were forced to work for meager wages and live a hand-to-mouth existence. Women in Santa Fe from 1850 to 1880 did not assimilate with Euro Americans but held on to their own language and culture. Hence, "By 1880, many were financially impoverished but culturally rich."

Over several generations, members of the Latino community have brought cases of property loss before American courts. In 1960, Reyes Lopez Tijerina founded the Alliance of Land Grants to present before U.S. District courts the question of ownership under the Spanish and Mexican Land Grants, but these cases have had no tangible results for claimants.

Slaves or Free People in California?

After the War with Mexico and as part of the Compromise of 1850, Texas entered the union as a slave state and California was admitted as a free state. Although California's State Constitutional Convention in compliance with the 1850 Compromise, declared that former slaves would be free, the illegal trafficking in slaves continued. Slaveholders continued to bring slaves into California. When slaves learned of their legal status in California, many fled from their owners. Other concessions in the 1850 Compromise bill, such as enforcement of the Fugitive Slave Laws made matters more complex. Under this proviso, escaped slaves in the North and the West were to be returned to their owners. In defense of runaways, abolitionists secured the freedom of many African-Americans. Former slaves were advised to carry documentation in the form of Freedom Papers. Without these papers, they could be taken as runaways and returned to former owners. California slaveholders defied state law, going so far as to advertise rewards for the return of runaway slaves. In addition, newspapers in this free state disregarded the law and advertised slave auctions.

To make matters worse, officials would not protect free blacks. In 1852, the court heard the case of a mulatto woman who had been brought from Missouri to California. The slave owner protested that in coming to California, he had not intended to take up permanent residence; he was merely on his way to another state. He succeeded in using this ploy, and the court ruled that the woman was his property. But in a similar case Biddy Mason, a Mississippi slave, came to California in an entourage including another female, their respective children and their owner Robert Smith. Biddy's owner had planned to take his slaves from there to Texas. Receiving a tip about Smith, Los Angeles County Sheriff Frank De Witt prevented the transport of Smith's slaves. In Biddy Mason's case, the court ruled in 1856, that persons of color were entitled to their freedom and could not be held as slaves in the State of California. The strength of that decision by Judge Benjamin Hayes granted Biddy freedom and the chance to fulfill her life's dream of helping others. Working as a nurse, she amassed a fortune. Biddy Mason established the first African Methodist church in Los Angeles, and the first grade school for black children. She assisted the needy and engaged in numerous charitable works for her community.

Mary Ellen Pleasant, also a former slave, came to San Francisco in 1849, via Boston. In San Francisco, Mary operated a boardinghouse and became a financial adviser and moneylender to city officials. Mary Ellen used her financial gain to help others, particularly the slaves who had been brought into California. With nebulous status, their attempts to gain freedom had been thwarted by another state law which stated that, "No black or mulatto person, or Indian, shall be permitted to give evidence in any action to which a white person is a party, in any court of this state." Since 99 percent of these cases involved slaves seeking freedom from white masters who testified against them, their attempts were futile. In 1852, Mary Ellen Pleasant formed the Franchise League in San Francisco to secure civil rights for African-Americans, especially the right to testify on their own behalf. But the "no testimony rule" remained in force until 1863, when the California legislature rescinded it. In the intervening years, crimes against African-Americans, such as theft, rape, and assault were committed with impunity. Ironically, African-Americans had no legal recourse in California, a state whose constitution declared them to be free.

Before 1863, African-Americans lived anxiously in California, a state which only half-heartedly acknowledged their status. Despite this precarious position, women like Elizabeth Thorn, a free black woman from New Bedford, Massachusetts, went to California in 1851, and established the first elementary school for black children in Sacramento. Elizabeth, along with Biddy Mason, Mary Ellen Pleasant and countless other African-American women rejected the status quo and engaged in civic and philanthropic work to strengthen their community.

Lady Pioneers – Professional Western Women

A few years after settlement, western women made dramatic inroads into the male dominated professions of medicine, law and education. In 1873, Dr. Mary Sawtelle ranked as the first female awarded a medical degree from Willamette University in Oregon. Dr. Sarah Hall established her medical practice at Fort Scott, Kansas, in 1870, specifically for the treatment of children's and women's diseases. Dr. Bethenia Owens-Adair had supported her family with a millenary business and made house calls as a nurse in her community of Roseburg, Oregon. She borrowed medical texts such as *Gray's Anatomy,* and studied at the Philadelphia School of Hydropathy[1]. She received an M.D. degree at the University of Michigan and later completed postgraduate study in Europe. In 1881, at the age of forty-one, Bethenia set up her practice for the treatment of ear and eye diseases in Portland, Oregon.

When Frances Treadwell's application to dental school was denied, she learned all about extracting teeth on site while working in a dental school. She set up her own practice in San Francisco in the 1890s with an office sign that read, "The Lady Dentist, Dr. Frances Treadwell."

The Federal Census of 1870, listed the predominant occupations for western women as housekeeping, laundering, nursing and teaching. As communities were established, local associations began fund raising and organizing for the establishment of schools, churches and libraries. School mistresses from the East made a significant contribution in western communities. Many women who came to the West to set up schools and teach, did so at the urging of Catherine Beecher. By the mid-nineteenth century, schoolmasters were leaving the field in great numbers because of the poor wages. In her popular book, *The Duty of American Women to their Country,* Catherine Beecher stated that women were best suited to teach. In fact it was cheaper to hire women. Single women were contracted to teach for $25 a month; the town was supposed to keep the schoolhouse in good repair and provide fuel. Because female teachers were usually young and single (often not much older than the students themselves), communities controlled a teacher's license by requiring they show good moral character. Looking back on her early efforts to establish educational institutions in the West, Lucia Darling, a schoolmistress in Montana, stated that "Pioneer women had a more lasting influence than was realized at the time." Lucia had packed all of her books for the trip out West in testimony to her belief that "a higher civilization has always followed closely in the footsteps of the women pioneers."

Indeed, communities in the Midwest and West were so hungry for culture that teachers were welcomed, respected, held to high standards, but underpaid and grossly overworked. In 1880, Miss Nannie Blaine was hired to teach in Grand Junction, Colorado, and all businesses (including the bars) closed every Sunday afternoon at 2:00 p.m. so that the townsfolk could gather to hear Miss Blaine read from the Bible. Teachers held classes in lean-tos, arbors, abandoned buildings and churches. When women were not teaching in schools, they were raising funds to build them.

Clara Foltz discovered that women could not enter law practice; and even though she had passed law exams, with honors, she could not retain clients because California law restricted legal practice to *white male citizens.* This law was based upon the same fallacious arguments which barred women from medical practice. Namely, that women belonged at home sheltered from the indelicacies of life. Clara Foltz single handedly took on the system and authored the Woman Lawyer's Bill. After lobbying the Governor's office, to make sure he would sign it, she got the bill passed, and became the first woman admitted to the California Bar. Clara introduced legislation which created the public defender system and she took on *pro bono* cases. Because of Clara Foltz's crusade for women lawyers, Aura Gordon, a young Hastings graduate, and others would eventually argue cases before the United States Supreme Court.

Mormon Women in the West

The rest of the country was quite stunned when, in 1870, Mormon women were granted the right to vote in Utah, by the Territorial Legislature. Since most people did not equate polygamy,

1. *Hydropathy* was a nineteenth century medical practice which involved the use of water baths or high pressure hoses for pain-relief and treating illness. The term hydrotherapy itself is synonymous with the term water cure as it was originally marketed by practitioners and promoters in the nineteenth century who established health spas where patients (predominantly women) could seek treatment.

commonly practiced among Mormons, with women's suffrage, there was more surprise when voting Mormon women did not move to outlaw polygamy entirely. But Brigham Young, the Mormon Patriarch, had predicted women would remain faithful and vote in support of the church and male members on any issue. Since non-Mormon emigrants were coming to the territory, granting Mormon women the vote ensured that Mormons would control Utah politically. One journalist reported, "When Mormon women vote it is simply duplicating the male vote over and over again, they simply all vote the same ticket, the one given to them." Mormon polygamy remained a controversial issue. Although non-Mormons viewed polygamy as contemptible, it appeared that Mormon women did not; that is, until some women began to speak out.

The experience of Ann Eliza Webb, a young Mormon woman, made national news when she shared how Mormon women felt about polygamy. When her father took on three more wives, Ann recalled her mother had accepted this condition with quiet resentment. Although the church preached that polygamous marriages were the means to achieve eternal happiness, as Ann stated, "They [women] did not like a polygamous life, and only endured it because they thought they must." Sixteen-year-old Ann caught the attention of Brigham Young, and he set about courting her despite the forty-three-year difference in their ages. To elude him she married actor James Dee, but when that marriage failed, Young intervened and procured a civil divorce for her. Ann married Brigham Young and, depending upon which account one consults, she was either wife number nineteen, or twenty-seven. Ann Eliza Webb later published an exposé of married life with Young in her book, *Wife No. 19, or the Story of Life in Bondage.* She claimed Young had coerced her into marriage by threatening to ruin her brother financially. From the onset of the marriage, Ann rebelled by refusing to cohabit with Young and his other wives in the Lion House, as his residence was called. Eventually when she filed for divorce, suing him for $200,000, the case made all the newspapers. The divorce helped publicize her book and promoted a round of speaking engagements. Ann never received a financial settlement from Young, but her public appearances, the book, and the wide press coverage of the divorce, sensationalized Mormon polygamy, and brought it to the forefront of national controversy. In 1882, the United States Congress passed a law forbidding polygamous marriages in the territories and in 1890, the Utah Territorial Legislature, in an effort to ease entry of statehood, also abolished polygamy. In 1896, Utah became a state.

Mothers of Invention: Laura Ingalls Wilder, Pioneer Author

For most of us our first introduction to learning about pioneers was in reading the Little House books by Laura Ingalls Wilder. The Ingalls family, especially Laura's father, characterize the pioneer movement. Laura Ingalls sharp memory and descriptive writing captured it all. Her stories of life in the wilderness and the untamed prairie were etched from her own childhood. Laura Elizabeth Ingalls (Wilder) was born in 1867, in the "Big Woods" of Wisconsin, to Charles and Caroline Ingalls. She was the second of five children and her siblings give testimony to the slim chance for the survival of children on the frontier. Her sister, Mary Amelia, went blind and a brother Charles Frederick, died in infancy. Her childhood in Wisconsin was retold in her classic children's book *Little House in the Big Woods*. Although Laura's family was recent immigrants to Wisconsin they were not newcomers to America; her ancestry went all the way back to the Puritan fathers. She was a descendant of a much earlier American, Edmund Rice, a 1638 English immigrant to Massachusetts Bay Colony.

In Laura's early childhood, her father had settled on land not yet open for homesteading in what was then Indian Territory (Kansas) and that formed the basis of Ingalls' novel *Little House on the Prairie*. Within a few years, Charles Ingalls restless spirit packed the family off to Minnesota. In 1879 he accepted a railroad job which led him to eastern Dakota Territory, where he was joined by his family that same year.

In 1879-1880 Laura witnessed the town of De Smet, South Dakota rise up from the prairie and she endured the following winter, 1880-1881, one of the most severe on record in the Dakotas. That winter she later described in her book, *The Long Winter.* Once the family took root in De Smet, Laura Ingalls was able to attend school, make friends, and met bachelor homesteader Almanzo Wilder whom she later married. This time in her life as a young woman is well documented in the book, *The First Four Years*.

At age sixteen Laura accepted her first teaching position, in a one-room schoolhouse in De Smet. To help her family financially she also worked as a dressmaker. Laura married at age eighteen and enjoyed prosperity on Almanzo Wilder's homestead claim, owing to favorable weather in the early 1880s, and the couple's prospects seemed bright but the next few years brought trials. Complications from a life-threatening bout of diphtheria left Almanzo partially paralyzed. Like so many homesteaders they endured a whole series of misfortunes including the death of a newborn, the destruction of their home and barn by fire, and several years of severe drought that left them in debt, physically ill, and unable to earn a living. Faced with so many hardships the Wilders reversed the prairie migration pattern of her family and sought Florida's climate to improve Almanzo's health.

The Wilders moved a final time to Mansfield, Missouri, and bought undeveloped property they named Rocky Ridge Farm. What began as 40 acres of thickly wooded, stone-covered hillside with a windowless log cabin, over the next 20 years evolved into a 200-acre relatively prosperous poultry, dairy, and fruit farm. The ramshackle log cabin was eventually replaced with an impressive 10-room farmhouse and outbuildings. The couple's climb to financial security was a slow process. Initially, the only income the farm produced was from wagon loads of firewood that Almanzo sold for 50 cents in town. It was backbreaking work along with clearing trees and stones from land that only gradually evolved into fertile fields and pastures.

Laura Ingalls Wilder's books were a collaborative effort with her daughter Rose Wilder Lane and their success allowed her to retire from farming. Wilder once said the reason she wrote her books in the first place was to preserve the stories of her childhood for today's children, to help them to understand how much America had changed during her lifetime. They help us understand and imagine in some small way the persistence, struggle and fortitude of those who ventured west.

Clio's Corner - How Do Historians View the Experience of Women in the West?

Jo Ann Levy, in *They Saw the Elephant, Women in the California Gold Rush*, describes how women who homesteaded faced unspeakable deprivation. Living in isolation, frontier women were often the victims of domestic violence and were at great risk for sexual crimes. Rape was often described in veiled language such as that used by one newspaper which reported the apprehension of a suspect for "the commission of an act too infamous to record."

More frequently, women of color were victims of rape even though the literature painted them as loose women. In stories and ballads, the legendary passion of the senoritas characterized them as women who were easy. The system did not favor or even feign to protect these women as in the case of a Josefina, a resident of Downieville, California, during the Gold Rush heyday. Josefina was arrested, tried, sentenced and hanged *all on the same day* for killing a man in self defense. At her quick trial, Josefina testified that, "I had been told that some of the men wanted to get into my room and sleep with me; it frightened me so, that I used to fasten the door and take a knife with me to bed." On July 4, 1851, a man named Cannan had entered her house and created a riot and a disturbance. The next morning when he attempted to enter her house again, she stabbed him with a large Bowie knife. When Josefina was executed on July 5, at 4 o'clock in the afternoon, about 500 spectators witnessed the hanging. Onlookers noted that she was calm and composed, and placed the noose around her own neck. When asked if she had any last words, Josefina had this to say: "Nothing; but I would do the same again if I was so provoked."

Although western women had a tougher life to some degree, they were less tolerant of abuse. Susan Butruille, *Women's Voices From the Oregon Trail*, found that western women were more inclined to leave and/or divorce abusive husbands than eastern women in the same situation. Jo Ann Levy explains that California women worked hard at housekeeping and independent enterprises to support their families. Having endured the rigors of trail life and the hardships of homesteading, western women would not suffer any further abuse. They had proved to themselves they could survive. The most desperate circumstances gave them confidence and a sense of autonomy. Their strength and endurance could measure that of any man. Jo Ann Levy found that as a result "they divorced at an astonishing rate." Consequently, the State of California complied by passing more liberal divorce laws than other states. Courts could dissolve a marriage on grounds of "natural impotence, minority, adultery, extreme cruelty, habitual intemperance, desertion, willful neglect, consent obtained by force or fraud and conviction for a felony." Consequently, California courts, which ruled marriage a civil contract, granted divorces willingly. For women of financial means, serial marriages became commonplace. Legislative delegates such as Henry Hallack voiced support for women's rights when he said, "I do not think we can offer a greater inducement for women of fortune to come to California. It is the very best provision to get us wives."

Historian Sandra Myres, *Westering Women and the Frontier Experience, 1800-1915*, believes that the first and second generations of American women transformed the role of females in the West. While establishing their families on the frontier, they were among the first women to enter professions, or become ranchers and entrepreneurs. Seeing their contribution in a positive light, Myres argues that *westering* women's activism made the frontier much different than it would have been without them. On the other hand, John Mack Faragher, *Women and Men on the Overland Trail*, saw women in the West as disadvantaged. Pioneering reluctantly at the behest of their authoritarian husbands, women lacked basic rights, could not vote, and the law recognized their husbands as head of the household.

Conclusion

The remarkable changes and challenges faced by those who settled in the West cannot be underestimated. Many women lived in dire circumstances such as the Chinese women brought to California to be exploited as prostitutes. For these young women, coming to America was a bitter and tragic experience. When white immigration increased, Native Americans were uprooted from their ancestral lands and from their way of life; Native American women championed the cause of their people.

The War with Mexico left deep grooves in American society. Mexican Nationals living in the West became second-class citizens and in many cases lost their homes and property when the United States acquired the western and southwestern territory of Mexico by agreement under the Treaty of Guadalupe Hidalgo. Although California entered the Union as a free state, African- Americans were not protected by that mandate or by the state's courts. Despite the difficulties that free African-Americans encountered, many who migrated to California not only made a new start for themselves but also a life of purpose and service to their community. Extraordinary females like Annie Oakley, Abigail Scott Duniway, Tabitha Brown and Biddy Mason, to name a few, exemplified the daring and entrepreneurial spirit of American women.

Chapter 12
Women in the American Civil War
Shaking Away the Bonds of Slavery

Key Topics

Northern Women in the War Effort
Southern Women in the Confederate Cause
After the War - Southern Reconstruction

Chronology

1860 - Abraham Lincoln Elected President
1861 - April 14, Confederates Fire on Fort Sumter
Civil War begins.
1862 - Anthem *Battle Hymn of the Republic* Published
1863 - The Emancipation Proclamation
Women's National Loyal League Founded
1865 - April 9, Lee Surrenders to Grant at Appomattox
April 14, President Lincoln Assassinated
1865 - 1876 – Period of Southern Reconstruction

Introduction

Because the South had threatened to leave the Union should Lincoln be elected, in November of 1860, when Presidential election results revealed Lincoln's victory, southern secession seemed a foregone conclusion. One southern newspaper did not mince words but stated southern intention, "Let the consequences be what they will, whether the Potomac be crimsoned with human gore or Pennsylvania Avenue paved with mangled bodies ten fathoms in depth, we of the South will never submit to such humiliation and degradation as the inauguration of Abraham Lincoln." Since retiring President James Buchanan had taken no action to incite or prevent secession, Americans realized that war was imminent. From November 1860 to January 1861, as states abandoned the Union, southern towns solemnly marked the secession by ringing church bells, tolling once for each state which had left the Union.

The Civil War that began in April, 1861, and ended in April of 1865, engaged Americans in a horrible conflict that separated families, friends, business associates, political parties, former schoolmates, and church congregations into northern and southern camps. Over 600,000 American military personnel died in the Civil War. Many soldiers who survived returned home maimed, handicapped and emotionally shattered. Whether men were fighting for the Union or defending the Confederacy, their families experienced tremendous losses.

Women in the North and the South rallied to support their troops on site. They served as nurses, cooks, provisioners of supplies, military auxiliaries, and some served as soldiers. On the home front women worked in volunteer organizations to support the armies and became the mainstay of their families, running farms, schools and businesses and some took on government jobs.

Northern Women in the War Effort

Julia Ward Howe, an active social reformer, poet, writer, abolitionist, and feminist, in collaboration with her husband, Samuel Gridley Howe, published an abolitionist newspaper, *The Commonwealth.* Over Samuel's protests, (he believed that men should have the upper hand) she had been elected the first president of the New England Suffrage Association, and served in the American Woman Suffrage Association.

On a visit to Washington, D.C. in 1861, Julia Ward Howe was especially moved while watching regiment after regiment of McClellan's troops marching in review outside her window at the Willard Hotel. She spent a restless night and at sunrise the next day, began composing the lyrics to *The Battle Hymn of the Republic,* which became the Union's war anthem and inspired both Union and Confederate troops, who sang it on the march and around the camps. In 1862, *The Atlantic Monthly* published the lyrics and paid her four dollars for the poem. Union troops were taken by the stirring apocalyptic and crusading moral message it conveyed,

> Mine eyes have seen the glory of the coming of the Lord
> He is trampling out the vintage where the grapes of wrath are stored;
> He hath loosed the fateful lightning of his terrible swift sword: His truth is marching on
>
> I have read a fiery gospel writ in burnish'd rows of steel
> As ye deal with my contemners so with you My Grace shall deal
> Let the Hero born of woman crush the serpent with His heel
> Our God is marching on

Mothers and sons posed for photographs before soldiers left for duty. Boys as young as eight were recruited. The youngest soldier reported killed in the Civil War was nine years old.

During the war, women frequently went to the train station to bid farewell to loved ones who had enlisted, and on happier occasions to welcome them home. On June 17, 1861, Lucinda Richards, of Chambersburg, Pennsylvania, properly chaperoned by her brother Thomas, went to the station and greeted soldiers returning from the first battle at Fort Sumter. She wrote to a friend to share the excitement of meeting a dashing Union officer.

> Yesterday afternoon Thomas and Mrs. Nixon came hurrying to get me. A short distance a train was lying containing Capt. Doubleday and his men from Fort Sumter and Young Governor Sprague of Rhode Island. Mrs. Nixon has a son an officer in the regular army at Fort Leavenworth. We went to the train and were introduced to the officers. On shaking hands with Captain Doubleday I said: 'I feel highly honored by shaking the hand of so noble a defender of our country.' He very politely and modestly replied, 'I think the honor is conferred upon me.' What a noble fellow Gov. Sprague is. He was dressed exactly like the common soldiers. Capt. Doubleday thinks the war

will end in a month, but who can know? Time will tell.

After the attack on Fort Sumter, northern women's response to the outbreak of war was immediate. Using institutions already in place, they organized for the war effort quickly. Julia Ward Howe, Lucinda Richards, Elizabeth Cady Stanton, Susan B. Anthony, and countless others, each in their own way supported the Union cause. For their part, Stanton and Anthony founded the Women's National Loyal League in 1863. They organized the Loyal League for the express purpose of collecting signatures to petition the Congress to pass a Constitutional amendment to free the slaves. In one year, Stanton and Anthony gathered over 400,000 signatures which Senator Charles Sumner presented to the United States Senate. Josephine Griffing, an effective speaker for the Loyal League, campaigned to get aid for fugitive slaves who were being treated as contraband of war, and conscripted as labor for the Union Army. Josephine Griffing got the financial support of Congress for the growing number of destitute freedmen and women. Sixteen-year-old Anna Dickinson delivered rousing speeches for abolition, emancipation, a union victory and women's rights. She was such an effective speaker that political candidates hired her to campaign for them and she may have been the first female to work as a campaign publicist.

Leading the northern effort, Drs. Elizabeth and Emily Blackwell converted their New York dispensary into a training facility for army nurses. Elizabeth Blackwell conceived and organized the Women's Central Relief Association, WCRA, the first of its kind which became the model and inspiration for the Sanitary Commissions, which evolved into a massive network of volunteers throughout the country. Men served as administrators of the Commissions but the majority of volunteers were women. Volunteer women in the Sanitary Commission held fairs and auctions which raised over $50 million to supply the Union forces with food, clothing, bedding, and medical supplies. They also established and maintained field hospitals, relief camps and hospital ships. In the Midwest alone there were 3,000 local sanitary commission aid societies raising funds and sending supplies. In 1863, Jane Hoge and Mary Livermore staged one Sanitary Fair that raised $450,000. By cleaning up the military camps, volunteers reduced disease and mortality by as much as sixty percent.

Not only did the commissions' work affect the health of the Union soldiers but in some instances the outcome of a battle as well. When Grant laid the siege of Vicksburg, Mississippi in 1863, volunteer Mary Livermore worked out the logistics for delivering to the General 60,000 pounds of dried fruit, 3,000 cans of fruit, and some 18,000 bushels of fresh vegetables. Surrounding the town, Grant's army was eating well while the people of Vicksburg faced food shortages and starvation.

Mothers of Invention: Mary Bickerdyke, the Calico Colonel

Mary Ann Ball Bickerdyke, a forty-four-year-old Ohio widow, followed Grant's army during the western campaign and supplied Sherman's troops during the march to the sea at the close of the war. She was called Mother Bickerdyke by the soldiers who appreciated her efforts to keep them fed, clothed, and alive. Mary was also known as the calico colonel and the cyclone in petticoats. She served the duration of the war in nineteen battles during some of the bloodiest campaigns including Shiloh, Lookout Mountain, Chattanooga, Missionary Ridge, and the siege of Vicksburg. In late November, 1863, at the Battle of Lookout Mountain, in bitter cold weather, Mary Bickerdyke tended 2,000 wounded men. While the Union camp and field hospital were pelted with freezing rains, and some soldiers drowned in the torrential floods, she threw together a field hospital on the Tennessee River five miles outside the city of Chattanooga, using old storehouses and tents and built cooking stoves from piles of bricks. She defied army regulation by tearing down defensive breastworks, to burn for firewood to keep patients in the hospital warm. On Christmas Day, she served up fresh baked bread, several hundred peach pies, and cookies, and to boost morale, built a roaring campfire where soldiers gathered for group singing and a taffy pulling contest.

Because of her battlefront experiences Mary Bickerdyke was well known but she avoided public acclamation. On one occasion, Mary Livermore urged her to speak to the Milwaukee Chamber of Commerce because they had pledged $1,200 *monthly* for the duration of the war. Mary Bickerdyke clarified for the audience what *donation* meant,

> Suppose, gentlemen you had got to give tonight one thousand dollars or your right leg, would it take long to decide which to surrender? Two thousand dollars or your right arm; five thousand dollars or both your eyes; all that you are worth or your life? But I have got eighteen hundred boys in my hospital...who have given one arm and one leg, and some have given both, and yet they don't seem to think they have done a great deal for their country....Oh, gentlemen of Milwaukee, don't let us be telling of what *we* have given, and what *we* have done! *We* have done nothing, and given nothing in comparison with them! And it's our duty to keep on giving and doing just as long as there's a soldier down south fighting or suffering for us.

An incident often told about Mary Bickerdyke involved her dismissal of a drunken, disorderly army surgeon whose neglect had cost the lives of many Union soldiers in Tennessee. When the doctor was removed from duty, he complained to his commanding officer who replied, "If it was Mother Bickerdyke, I can do nothing for you. She ranks me." Renditions differ whether the commanding officer was General Grant or Sherman since Mary Bickerdyke served with both.

At the close of the war, she rode with the Union army in the victory parade on May 23, 1865, in Washington, D.C. After the war Mary Bickerdyke ran a veterans' home in Salina, Kansas, and raised funds for the Illinois Soldier's Orphans Home. Later she performed social welfare work in New York and Chicago. After friends lobbied the government, Congress granted her a special pension in 1886, for extraordinary service to the Union Army.

Sanitary Commission work changed the lives of female volunteers who had their first work experience away from home. Those women who stayed home when their husbands and fathers went to war had taken on more family responsibilities. As the war dragged on, some women took government jobs vacated by men, and others took on hazardous work in munitions factories making cartridges and shells.

Nurses in the Union Army

Volunteer nurses performed heroically on the battlefront and placed themselves in harm's way. Dorothea Dix, the champion of the mentally ill, had already learned how to surmount government red tape to get things done. During the war, she expedited a system of supply distribution to military hospitals. She remained an unpaid volunteer throughout the war but held sway over the doctors and staff who pleaded for supplies. Her chief duty was to recruit, train and supervise army nurses. Dorothea could be autocratic and demanding, but her methods raised medical standards, saved lives and elevated nursing to a respectable profession. She screened recruits carefully. It is said she once rejected a nun, believing the young woman was seeking amorous adventure as an army nurse. Her regulations for nursing candidates were explicit,

> No woman under thirty need apply to serve in government hospitals. All nurses are required to be plain looking women. Their dresses must be brown or black, with no bows, no curls, no jewelry and no hoop skirts.

Louisa May Alcott served as a volunteer nurse from 1862 to 1863. Her family saved her letters, which were later compiled into her first book, *Hospital Sketches.* Alcott's account is a grim description of the men brought to her for care,

> I spent my shining hours washing faces, serving rations, giving medicine, and sitting in a very hard chair, with pneumonia on one side, diphtheria on the other, five typhoid on the opposite, and a

dozen dilapidated patriots. In they came, some on stretchers, some in men's arms, some staggering on crude crutches and one lay stark and still with covered face as a comrade gave his name to be recorded before they carried him away to the dead house.

Louisa May Alcott had never bargained for what she experienced as a military nurse, assisting at amputations and dressing ghastly wounds. She contracted typhoid fever, was given the usual treatment of the day, mercury, and sent home to recover. She never regained her health but in the post war years wrote when she could and graced American literature with classics such as her autobiographical novel *Little Women*.

Author Louisa May Alcott worked as a nurse for the Union army during the Civil War. Although her volunteer service was cut short by a bout with typhoid fever, she used her wartime experiences in her novel, Little Women *and memoirs,* Hospital Sketches. *(Photo courtesy of the Library of Congress.)*

Before the war, Clara Barton had worked in the United States Government Patent Office, one of the first women to hold a civil service job. Clara volunteered to serve with the army when a group of soldiers were attacked during riots in Baltimore. She came to their aid with food, supplies, and medical care. Then, as Union soldiers retreated hastily to Washington, D.C., from the first Battle of Bull Run, she acted quickly to care for the wounded. What disturbed her most was the lack of provisions for soldiers' care despite the abundant Union resources. Clara Barton realized most men died in the hospitals from lack of immediate care on the battlefront. If wounds were not treated immediately, infection or death resulted. More often, gangrene set in necessitating amputation.

Clara Barton, on her own initiative, organized medical care for the Union soldiers wounded at the First Battle of Bull Run. She established the first organization to find men missing in action, and later founded the American Red Cross. (Photo courtesy of the Library of Congress.)

Clara Barton had served briefly under Dorothea Dix but preferred to work independently, caring for soldiers on the battlefield. She managed to circumvent Dorothea's authority and plead directly to the War Department for supplies. At the battle of Culpepper, she took matters into her own hands and rushed a supply wagon to Cedar Mountain where she set up a triage on the battle line.

> When our armies fought on Cedar Mountain, I broke the shackles and went into the field. Five days and nights with three hours sleep a narrow escape from capture and some days of getting the wounded into hospitals at Washington brought in Saturday August 30. And if you chance to feel that the positions I occupied were rough and unseemly for a

> woman, I can only reply that they were rough and unseemly for men. But under all, lay the life of the nation. I had inherited the rich blessing of health and strength of constitution such as are seldom given to woman and I felt that some return was due from me and that I ought to be there.

At Bull Run, Chantilly, Sharpsburg, and Fredericksburg, Clara Barton was continuously in harm's way. She described one such incident at Antietam.

> A man lying upon the ground asked for a drink; I stopped to give it and having raised him with my right hand, I was holding him. Just at that moment a bullet sped between us tearing a hole in my sleeve and found its way into his body. He fell back dead.

At Fredericksburg, she single-handedly cared for 1,200 wounded Union soldiers for days after the battle. Clara Barton wrote of the grim walk through the hundreds of bleeding men, "When I arose from the side of the couch where I had knelt for hours I had to wring the blood from the bottom of my clothing before I could step."

Based on names listed on military payrolls, as many as 10,000 women may have served as nurses for the Union during the Civil War. There were about 800 Catholic nuns who volunteered as nurses in both armies. The hardest population to estimate would be black nurses; many were fugitive slaves and brought their children to the camps for shelter and protection and worked for no pay or so much as a meager subsistence. When Congress passed the Nurses Pension Act in 1892, at least 3,000 women applied and received a pension, but the numbers who served unofficially as volunteers can never be reckoned. No matter how many served, there were never enough nurses; many divisions never saw a nurse, doctor, or a field hospital. Women like Clara Barton and Mary Bickerdyke worked alone caring for several thousand men. Women camp followers of all classes and ethnic groups also augmented the work of sanitary commission volunteers and nurses. Officers' wives accompanied their husbands, but there is little indication they contributed to the general welfare of the troops as the volunteer women did. Immigrant women accompanied their husbands, lived in tents and tried to keep their families together.

The Confederate Prison Camp at Andersonville, Georgia, where Clara Barton and her volunteers identified and buried Union soldiers interred there. (Photo courtesy of the Library of Congress.)

Female Soldiers in the Union Army

Volunteer work was not enough for some women who wished to participate in the war more directly. Some enlisted as soldiers; perhaps 400 women in the north masqueraded as men and served with the Union forces. Researcher Lauren Cook Burgess has identified 127 female Union soldiers. Sarah Edmonds (a.k.a. Frank Thompson), who served with Flint, Michigan, Company F, fought at the First Battle of Bull Run and at Fredericksburg. Sarah Edmonds was so convincing cross-dressing as a male that her commander ordered her to go behind enemy lines *disguised as a woman* to gather information. In the spring of 1863, Edmonds contracted malaria, and deserted briefly to seek treatment elsewhere in order to avoid detection by army medics. As she explained,

> Had I been what I represented myself to be, I should have gone to the hospital and had the surgeon make an examination of my injuries, and placed myself in his hands for medical treatment – and saved years of suffering. But being a woman I felt compelled to suffer in silence and endure it the best I could, in order to escape detection of my sex. I

> would rather have been shot dead than to have been known to be a woman and sent away from the Army under guard as a criminal.

Eventually when her sex was discovered, Sarah Edmonds shifted to nursing in the camps. In 1885, she secured testimonies from former comrades of her service and received a monthly pension of $12.00. Sarah Edmonds was distinguished as the only female mustered into the Grand Army of the Republic, a Civil War Veterans Organization, which lobbied Congress for pensions.

Volunteers divulged in their memoirs that some of the soldiers they treated were females. Clara Barton treated a soldier named Mary Galloway at the Battle of Antietam. Mary Livermore, a sanitary commission volunteer, also intimates the presence of women.

> Someone has stated the number of women soldiers known to the service as little less than four hundred. I cannot vouch for the correctness of this estimate but I am convinced that a larger number of women disguised themselves and enlisted in the service, for one cause or other, than was dreamed of. Entrenched in secrecy, and regarded as men, they were sometimes revealed as women, by accident or casualty. Some startling histories of military women were current in the gossip of army life.

Sarah Rosetta Wakeman who enlisted as Lyons Wakeman described how male comrades helped protect the identity of female soldiers by not reporting them. She was so bold as to purchase a soldier's identification ring and have it engraved, "Rosetta Wakeman." She enlisted in 1862, and saw action April of 1864, at the Red River Campaign. Just two months later, she contracted dysentery from drinking polluted water and died in a military hospital in New Orleans. She was buried at the Monument Cemetery in New Orleans, and her tombstone was inscribed "Lyons Wakeman, New York." For nearly a century, Sarah's service went unacknowledged by her family and her Civil War letters were all but forgotten. In 1940, her great nephew Jackson Doane found the letters and discovered that Sarah Wakeman was never spoken of in the family because she had posed as a man to fight in the war.

The most evasive masquerade was that of Jennie Hodgers who enlisted as Albert D.J. Cashier. Jennie Hodgers not only made it through the war undetected but retained her male persona until 1911, when at age seventy she was treated at a hospital after an auto accident and her sex was discovered. Interviewed during recovery, she confessed, "Lots of *boys* enlisted under the wrong name. So did I. The country needed men, and I wanted excitement." Kady C. Brownell who served with a Rhode Island regiment as a regular soldier did not bother to disguise her sex, but wore a uniform. She received an honorable discharge from the service. Years later her husband Robert told how eighteen-year-old Kady Brownell had followed him into the service. Wearing a makeshift uniform, she cut off her hair and most soldiers thought she was a boy, even though she answered roll call as "Kady." She carried the company colors into battle, and was wounded at the First Battle of Bull Run.

Doctor Mary Edwards Walker, a graduate of Syracuse Medical College, had been a cross-dresser before entering the military. Despite hindrances and discrimination, she was determined to do her part for the Union. When the war broke out, she volunteered to serve in the Medical Corps. Even though the army desperately needed doctors, she was turned down. Mary Walker then volunteered as a nurse and served in military hospitals in Washington, D.C., until 1863. That year, she was contracted as an assistant surgeon with the Army of the Cumberland, and later as a civilian contract doctor with the 52nd Ohio Regiment in Tennessee. Mary Walker adapted a standard officer's uniform which included wearing trousers and she frequently rode out to the front Union lines to treat soldiers or to deliver mail dispatches. On one such an errand, on April 10, 1863, she was captured by Confederates. Because she was carrying military dispatches, she was arrested for espionage and imprisoned at Richmond's Castle Thunder Prison. Detained there from April to August of 1864, Mary Walker was constantly harassed because of her appearance, as noted in a letter written by her captor, Confederate Captain B.J. Semmes, in April, 1864.

> This morning we were all amused and disgusted too at the sight of a thing, that nothing but the debased and depraved Yankee nation could produce, a "female doctor." She was taken prisoner yesterday and brought in by the pickets this morning. She was dressed in the full uniform of a Federal Surgeon, boots, hat and all and wore a cloak. She was about twenty-five or twenty-eight years old, fair, but not good looking and of course had a tongue enough for a regiment of men. I was in hopes the General would have her dressed in a homespun frock and bonnet and sent back to the Yankee lines or put in a lunatic asylum.

While imprisoned, Mary suffered an eye infection which left her blind in one eye. After release, she was reassigned to a women's prison hospital, but the inmates refused her services and petitioned to have her removed. As a post script to her Civil War service, in 1865, the Union awarded Mary Walker a Congressional Medal of Honor for her military service.

Southern Women in the Confederate Cause

The diaries of southern women inform firsthand their experiences during the tempestuous war years. One diarist, Mary Chestnut, described what women endured and she seems to have been everywhere reporting everything. In 1865, from her father-in-law's Mississippi estate, Mulberry, she witnessed the path of Sherman's destruction: "On one side of the house every window had been broken, every bell torn down, every piece of furniture destroyed, every door smashed in." She believed only the intervention of General Sherman saved the family's estate at Mulberry from total destruction, but other friends were not as fortunate,

> Poor Mrs. Middleton has paralysis. Has she not had trouble enough? How much she has had to bear, their plantation and home on Edisto destroyed, their house in Charleston burned, her children scattered, starvation in Lincolnton, and all as nothing to the one dreadful blow her only son was killed in Virginia.

Confederate women were in a bind to make ends meet during the war. The South, predominantly agricultural, had few factories, a smaller population than the north and little capital. Most planters operated on credit and depended upon northern or European markets for manufactured goods. Fighting the industrialized North, the South lacked essential goods and was short on manpower and female volunteers.

Southern women, who maintained the home front and tried to aid the army, had none of the resources that were readily available to northern women. The blocks to their efforts were exacerbated because when Union Armies occupied their territory, they looted what little goods southern households had on hand. With wartime inflation, the cost of a barrel of flour, sugar or coffee escalated to several hundred dollars. Sometimes as many as 300 women engaged in bread riots. Confederate newspapers downplayed the problem to avoid dampening southern spirit and to prevent more riots. Facing dire shortages, women recycled and found innovative substitutes, such as using berries and plants to make drinks when coffee and tea were unavailable. Women preserved herbs and roots for medicine and made hats and shoes out of palmetto fronds. Even the well-to-do learned how to *make-do*, as noted in this song.

> My homespun dress is plain 'tis true
> My hat's palmetto too
> It only proves what southern girls
> For southern rights will do.

The South had fewer highly populated cities. (New Orleans was the only southern city with a population over 50,000.) Because most of the southern population lived on small farms, organizing a central, urban volunteer effort was difficult. Southern women mobilized as they could on a small scale, working through churches and charitable associations, to supply the Confederate army with blankets and clothing. They also rolled bandages and prepared food for the army. They harvested Spanish moss from the trees to make rope, and thorns from certain plants to be used as hypodermic needles.

Southern women, caught in the paths of the two armies, used their homes as makeshift hospitals to care for the Confederate wounded and the dying. As one woman put it, "In the South every home was a hospital." They also formed Home Guard units to prepare for the inevitable invasion. Some drilled in military formation and conducted target practice. A Georgia home guard named their unit after Nancy Hart, a local heroine of the American Revolutionary War. The state of medical care in the Confederate Army was grim with few field hospitals and medical staff, and provisions in short supply. To add to the problem, southern society, more traditional than northern society, discouraged female volunteers; considering the Confederacy's desperation, how could officials refuse female help?

Hampered by discrimination, social ostracism, harassment, and little compensation, southern women, like their northern counterparts, fought the war on two levels. Asserting *their right* to help the cause and then doing *their part* in the war effort. When twenty-eight-year-old Sally Tompkins volunteered, she converted a Richmond home into the best hospital around. Caring for 1333 patients, Sally had only 73 casualties, a record not matched by any other hospital, Union or Confederate during the war, and her success is credited to high hygienic standards. When the Government shut down other hospitals, a questionable act in itself, Sally Tompkins was commissioned a Captain and her hospital designated a government dispensary.

Chimborazo Confederate Hospital in Richmond, the largest hospital in the North or the South, housed 8,000 beds, a dairy, brewery, and bakery which produced 12,000 loaves of bread daily. When Miss Phoebe Pember, the daughter of an upstanding Savannah family, came to Richmond to seek an appointment at Chimborazo as the hospital's matron/supervisor, she encountered the usual discrimination,

> About the time Chimborazo was to be opened, the wife of George W. Randolph, the Secretary of War, offered me the superintendence, a rather startling proposition to a woman used to all the comforts of luxurious life....A preliminary interview with the surgeon-in-chief gave necessary confidence. He was energetic, capable, skillful. A man with a ready oil to pour upon troubled waters. The day after my decision was made found me at "headquarters." The chief surgeon had not made his appearance that morning, and while awaiting him, many of his corps, who had expected in horror the advent of female supervision, walked in and out, evidently inspecting me. There was at the time a general ignorance on all sides, except among hospital officials, and the decided objection to a *petticoat* government. There was no mistaking the whispers from the open door of the office that morning, when the contract surgeon passed by and informed a friend he encountered in a voice of ill-concealed disgust that, "*one of them had come*."

Phoebe Pember contended with all sorts of nuisances, from the acrimony of the male staff to fending off drunken soldiers with a pistol to protect the hospital's store of whiskey.

Confederate camp followers known as *vivandieres,* (literally, women who followed an army camp to sell food and liquor*)* took care of the men and lived in the camps at great risk. Not only were vivandieres exposed to disease and danger but also to scandal. It was unthinkable for a woman to live among strange men and camp-following could bring dishonor to one's family. Risky as it was, these women defied convention and responded to the desperate need for help. Vivandiere Mary Ann Webster Loughborough, an officer's wife, traveled from camp to camp. Most vivandieres in the Confederate Army were nurses, cooks, and laundresses as well.

Confederate officials denied that women served in the military. When one female Union soldier was captured at the Battle of Chickamauga, Confederates returned the prisoner to her unit with a message which read, "As the Confederates do not use women in war, this woman, wounded in battle is returned to you." But Confederate women did serve by masquerading as males. Following the course of true love, Loretta

J. Velasquez had defied her parents and eloped with the man of her choice. When her husband enlisted and left home without her, she assumed the alias Harry Buford, donned a false moustache, and disguised as a man, enlisted in the Confederate Army. When her husband was killed, she organized her own regiment. Confederate General Jubal Early regarded her memoirs, *The Woman in Battle,* as fictitious but General James Longstreet believed it was an accurate account.

According to Linda Grant De Pauw, in *Battle Cries and Lullabies*, some female soldiers disguised as males were able to conceal a pregnancy to full term and remain on duty. However, substantiating more female soldiers is another matter, as De Pauw explains,

> The first stage for recent students of women's military history during the Civil War has been simply to prove that women soldiers existed. Several researchers are now pooling their efforts to piece together the documentary evidence. So much material survives from the Civil War era, much of it still in private collections that combing it thoroughly for reports of women soldiers is a task that can continue indefinitely. The data are so slight for some soldiers that tracing down the official military record of an individual will be impossible.

Scouts, Spies and Smugglers

Because Union generals lacked maps of the South, scouts were of vital necessity. One scout, Harriet Tubman, a runaway slave and experienced conductor on the Underground Railroad, proved to be valuable since she knew southern roads like the back of her hand. During the war, she traveled with Union forces as far as South Carolina and was able to obtain vital information from slaves behind Confederate lines. In one daring mission, Harriet Tubman led an all-black regiment into enemy territory, destroyed bridges on the Combahee River, relayed intelligence of Confederate movement, and delivered 750 slaves to freedom. She also assisted in the camps as a nurse and laundress.

After the war, she founded the Harriet Tubman Home for Orphans and Aged Negroes, at her modest farm in Auburn, New York. In 1890, after many years of petitioning the government, Congress awarded her a pension of $20 per month for her heroism and sacrifice. She died in Auburn, New York in 1913 at age ninety-three.

Isabelle Boyd, La Belle Rebel, a confederate spy, went on to act in the theater after the war. (Photo courtesy of the Library of Congress.)

Spies were everywhere during the Civil War, and there were reports of Confederate spies apprehended as far north as New England and Canada. Slave Mary Elizabeth Bowser served in a prime location at President Jefferson Davis' Richmond headquarters. There she was privy to the vital secret plans of the confederacy. Isabelle Boyd, only seventeen years old when the war broke out, had just finished school at the Mount Washington Female College in Baltimore. Back in her hometown of Martinsburg, Virginia, Isabelle Boyd, bored with the round of women's fundraisers, found excitement when northern troops occupied Martinsburg. She mingled with the Union officers to gather information for

Confederates. Isabelle was appointed a courier for Generals P.G.T. Beauregard and Thomas J. Stonewall Jackson. Nicknamed LaBelle Rebelle, she earned notoriety in the North, celebrity in the South, stints in Union prisons and aided in several confederate victories. During one imprisonment, Federals took an extraordinary measure to detain her: they transported her to Canada. She escaped and returned to the South via London after she acquired a British officer for a husband and procured necessary supplies. After the war, she earned a living with her memoirs, *Belle Boyd in Camp and Prison,* public lectures on her war exploits, and an acting career on the New York stage.

Before the war, Rose O'Neal Greenhowe had served as a prominent Washington hostess and confidante to men in the Federal government. When the war broke out, Rose stayed in Washington, D.C., and declared she was a Union loyalist. By 1861, Rose Greenhowe was a widow pursued by several suitors who worked for the Union, so Confederate officials recruited her to spy and gather information from these higher-ups in the Federal government. She relayed specific details of Union battle plans to General Beauregard and was partly responsible for the Confederate victory at the First Battle of Bull Run. Once her activities were discovered, Alan Pinkerton, Chief of Union Army Intelligence, placed her under house arrest, but Rose continued to spy for the Confederacy. She was once detained at the Old Capitol Prison, and was brought in just as Isabelle Boyd was being released. In June, 1862, the Union exiled Rose Greenhowe to the South, where President Jefferson Davis gave her a jubilant welcome. He then sent her on a secret mission to Europe to procure foreign aid. While in England, Rose was feted as a celebrity, and courted by British Lord Granville. On return to America, October 1, 1864, Rose Greenhowe drowned when Federal gunboats attacked and sank the ship just off the Virginia coast.

Another female Confederate spy, Antonia Ford, aided Confederate Cavalry officers Major John Mosby and General James Ewell Brown Stuart, (JEB Stuart). When *Union* Major Joseph Willard arrested Antonia Ford, he fell in love with her, secured her pardon, and married her. After their marriage, Antonia continued to gather intelligence for Mosby and other southern commanders. Somehow their marriage survived their divided loyalties and after the war they settled down in Fairfax, Virginia.

Isabelle Boyd paired spying and smuggling. Mary Chestnut indicates that southern women engaged in so much smuggling that officials disregarded the standards of feminine modesty and conducted body searches, in some cases requiring women to strip completely,

> "False hair is searched for papers... Pistols are sought for with crinoline, reversed bustles are suspect. All manner of things, they say come over the border under the huge hoops now worn. Arms, not legs are looked for under the hoops and sad to say, found."

Practically unstoppable, Confederate nurse Mary Roberts, made frequent trips to Canada to procure medical supplies. To avoid northern checkpoints altogether, she would haul great quantities of supplies by dogsleds to the St. Lawrence River for transport by sea to the Atlantic Ocean, destined for the Gulf of Mexico.

In the twilight hours of the Confederacy, with a short-staffed government in tatters, many women, particularly war widows, worked for public agencies in Richmond. The family of Mrs. Bartow, a government clerk in Richmond, pleaded with her to quit her job and end their social embarrassment. Mrs. Bartow refused, stating "she would not give up her independence or her job for anything." By 1865, Mrs. Bartow was working in the government mint cutting money into bills and earning an annual salary of $500.00, but paid in inflated Confederate money.

Life for women in both the North and the South changed dramatically because of the war. Women's public work tested the social norms of "true womanhood."

Clio's Corner - Historians Speak about the Perils Southern Women Faced during Civil War and Reconstruction

In the South, the home front was the battlefront and southern women were always vulnerable, and often left completely unprotected. Their condition is of interest to scholars who hope to gain a better understanding of the nature of crimes against women. In *Against Our Will: Men, Women and Rape*, Susan Brownmiller argues that rape in wartime is the ultimate weapon, intended to demoralize the enemy by destroying his property, i.e. mothers, wives, daughters, and sisters. Professor Brownmiller concludes that the American Civil War was a *low-rape war*, meaning rape was infrequent. She defends this thesis with the explanation that this war, which divided families, some choosing Union and others Confederate, was a conflict of a *fraternal nature*. As such, American men fighting fellow Americans upheld the sacred code of male honor. Men did not often violate females because collectively the women were their sisters or their buddies' sisters. But we need to ask, does Susan Brownmiller's conclusion consider the dynamics of American society, specifically interracial relations?

Historian Reid Mitchell, in *The Vacant Chair: The Northern Soldier Leaves Home*, agrees that it was a low-rape war, but only for *white women*, not for African-American women. Black women were still as they had been in the past, victims of white male aggression. In South Carolina, for example, General Nathan Banks reported that Union soldiers raped black women in the presence of white women and children. Unionists believed that white secessionists were more effectively punished by forcing white southern women to *witness* the rapes of their slaves, than if they were raped themselves. The rationale was that it was more shocking to watch such a savage act than to be a victim of it. Reid Mitchell believes soldiers maintained nineteenth century standards of morality, which dictated upholding the honor of white women and sparing them, but the men relieved their sexual impulses by raping black women. This would explain why Yankee soldiers chose to rape black women rather white women. In such a racist society, the rape of a white woman was a grave violation, whereas a man could rape a black woman with impunity. The documentary evidence shows that brutality and sexual violence toward black women was widespread and commonplace. The diary of Civil War physician, Dr. Esther Hill Hawks, dispels any doubt.

> During the first year of our soldiers coming the blacks probably suffered more from their tyranny and insults, than ever in their lives before. It is a sad comment on humanity, but I believe in this case, a true one! No colored woman or girl was safe from the brutal lusts of the soldiers and by soldier I mean both officers and men. The 55th Penn Reg would, no doubt bear off the palm in these affairs, if they could have their just dues. The colonel for a long time, kept colored women for his especial needs, and officers and men were not backward in illustrations of his example. Mothers were brutally treated for trying to protect their daughters, and there are now several women in our little hospital who have been shot by soldiers for resisting their vile demands. One poor woman but a few months since, was caught by the hair as she still struggled, shot through the shoulder. She is still in the Hospital. No one is punished for these offences for the officers are as bad as the men.

During General William T. Sherman's infamous March to the Sea, his officers indulged in attacks on women. Hundreds of eyewitness testimonies confirm that violence to black women was committed in other Union regiments also. Taking the investigation a step further, Military Historian Charles Royster, in *The Destructive War,* estimates most civilian murders in the South during the Civil War were committed on black women who were summarily stripped, raped and killed because it was easy to do. Black women who had been victimized by their masters in the pre-war South could expect no mercy at the hands of the enemy. Between social racist attitudes and military complicity, there was no protection for the women and no punishment for these brutal war crimes.

Can we assume that southern white women were spared simply because there is little documentary evidence? Although the word *rape* and phrases suggesting sexual violation seldom appear in women's letters, diaries and memoirs, the absence of these descriptions does not necessarily mean that white women were not raped. It may suggest that white women were violated but could not bring themselves to talk about it. For example, there are references to rape in some of the southern white women's diaries. An entry in Anna Maria Green's diary states "November 23, 1864, the worst of the acts was committed to poor Mrs. N. violence done, an atrocity committed that ought to make her husband an enemy unto death." The diarist insinuated rape, but she omitted the victim's name. The victim was a married woman, and Anna states that atrocity "ought to make her husband an enemy unto death." Anna's remark implies that an incidence of rape would cause a serious breach in the marriage of Mr. and Mrs. N.

Historian Jane Schultz, in "Mute Fury: Southern Women's Diaries of Sherman's March to the Sea, 1864-1865," in *Arms and the Woman: War, Gender, and Literary Representation*, analyzed the text of thirty-seven southern white women's diaries. She discovered that when Union soldiers invaded their homes, women described feelings of helplessness, and some were so terrified that they were immobilized. Some diarists made no further entries, and those who resumed writing expressed feelings of guilt and melancholy. Their reaction is typical for rape victims who are unable to or have difficulty talking about the experience. Professor Schultz blamed Confederate women's sense of futility for their silence. Confederate Mary Row, for instance, stated that "what we experienced that night is indescribable....I have not yet found words to express half of the suffering we witnessed and my feeling during the reign of Satan Sherman and his imps." One diarist who hinted at sexual violation left a blank space in her diary. Several weeks later she cryptically noted that "my life will never be the same."

Since southern men were not there to protect their women, Jane Schultz concludes that, "without the social structure that assured them protection, and without the forms in language that had sustained them early on in their struggles with the enemy, southern women for the first time during the war acknowledged defeat in silence." Although this silence prevents us from knowing whether or to what extent it was a low-rape war for white women, there can be no doubt, it was *not a low-rape war* for black women, who experienced firsthand excessive brutality from the enemy.

After the War–Soldiers Missing in Action

It was not until the American Civil War that any concern for missing or unidentified soldiers was ever raised. After the war, Clara Barton, the heroic Union nurse, cared for soldiers who had been imprisoned, and tried to identify those missing or dead. Clara Barton became the first female to head a Federal agency when in 1865, within her own rooms at a boardinghouse in Washington, D.C., she established the Office of Correspondence with the Friends of the Missing Men of the United States Army. It received no government funding, so Barton spent her inheritance and savings to do the work, processing hundreds of letters per day.

In July, 1865, she traveled to the prison camp at Andersonville, Georgia, to care for Union survivors, supervise burials, and search for missing Union soldiers. Despite efforts at record keeping, at the close of the war, about half of the 360,000 Union dead were still unidentified. Invaluable to her search was Dorence Atwater, a former Union prisoner, who had surreptitiously recorded names of 13,000 prisoners who had died at Andersonville. Clara Barton took to the lecture circuit to raise money and the public amassed to hear about her war exploits. In 1868, after some 200 speeches, she had raised funds to staff her office and continue work for the Friends of the Missing Men. Her one-woman operation, which answered 44,000 inquiries about soldiers missing in action and located 22,000 of them, would change the way the government handled such matters. She initiated her search for men missing in action by printing and distributing 100,000 circulars. Her technique for listing personal information on each soldier resulted in the military's practice of issuing dog tags for servicemen by the turn of the twentieth century.

Southern Reconstruction

When General Robert E. Lee surrendered to General Ullysses S. Grant at Appomattox Courthouse in Virginia on April 9, 1865, the American Civil War ended and a new era began. The war had claimed the lives of 620,000 men; a mortality rate divided equally between the North and the South. An additional 600,000 soldiers were seriously wounded and/or maimed. It was the bloodiest war Americans had ever fought, with casualties totaling more than those of all previous wars combined.

When the war, which had dragged on for four agonizing years, ended, events moved rather swiftly. On April 14, five days after the Confederate surrender, President Lincoln was shot and the country mourned the death of its leader, the first president ever assassinated. Lincoln had made plans for recovery, with a ten percent plan, i.e. when ten percent of the voting population in each rebellious state signed a loyalty oath to the Union, that state would be reinstated into the Federal system. Lincoln's untimely death made postwar recovery a political joust between the new President, Andrew Johnson, and the Congress. In the midst of this political wrangling, four and a half million former slaves found themselves unemployed, homeless, and starving. A "destitute, demoralized and devastated South" needed relief.

Reconstruction, the period from 1865 to 1876, denotes the years after the war when the President and the Congress attempted to rebuild, reform and renew the South. During this postwar period, the old guard of the southern aristocracy reclaimed power and the Civil War Amendments XIII, XIV, and XV, which were intended to free slaves and grant freedmen citizenship and the vote, bestowed them nothing but freedom, as little else was done for the former slaves.

The Port Royal Experiment

An early blueprint for Reconstruction, known as the Port Royal Experiment, occurred when Union forces secured the Sea Islands in November 1861, and set up headquarters at the town of Port Royal, South Carolina. There a topsy-turvy situation existed as ten thousand slaves remained on the island plantations while their white masters escaped to the mainland. At Port Royal, the Union Army organized a school for slaves, and the War Department called for volunteer teachers from the North to come to the Sea Islands and instruct them. In March of 1862, teachers arrived and formed the Port Royal Experiment. The staff, comprised mostly of New England abolitionists, taught, raised money and distributed clothing, food, medical supplies, books and other essentials to the slaves who inhabited these islands. The Port Royal teachers acted as missionaries to the South, and operated schools in makeshift, ill-equipped buildings, living on meager army rations. The significance of the Port Royal Experiment was threefold: (1) it attracted talented, dedicated teachers; (2) it gave many female teachers their first job, and (3) it became a prototype of the later Reconstruction schools which Congress would establish under the Freedmen's Bureau.

Dr. Laura Towne came to Port Royal in 1862, sponsored by the Philadelphia Port Royal Relief Committee. Dr. Towne eventually established the Penn School, a permanent institution on the Sea Islands, which included classes from elementary through high school levels. Towne also adopted an ambitious program of reading, writing, arithmetic, geography, Greek and Latin. For many years the Penn School provided the only secondary education for blacks in this region. She also served as the chief medical officer and legal advisor for the Port Royal residents. In 1865, she advised former slaves who were ordered by President Johnson via Union General Howard to move off of land they had occupied since 1861. The property was to be returned to white landholders. Black farmers protested but were defeated when they petitioned the President directly for justice.

> We the freedmen of this Island, and the State of South Carolina, Do hereby petition you as the President of these United States, that some provisions be made by which every colored man can purchase land, and hold His own. We wish to have a home if it be but a few acres. Without some provision is made our future is sad to look upon. With the support of the Federal government and the Union, former slave masters prevailed but Dr. Towne's efforts enabled some black residents to stay there and to purchase farmland.

One teacher, Charlotte Forten, an African-American, was the granddaughter of James Forten, head of the Philadelphia Forten merchant dynasty. The Fortens were antislavery crusaders who moved in the highest intellectual circles of the day and corresponded with William Lloyd Garrison, John Greenleaf Whittier, Maria Weston Chapman, Ralph Waldo Emerson and Walt Whitman. When the war began, Charlotte looked for an opportunity to serve the Union. When the Sea Islands were secured, she went there in 1862, to teach at Dr. Laura Towne's school on St. Helena Island, where she noted, "that the whole race was trying to go to school." Charlotte Forten's teaching career at Port Royal launched a lifelong dedication to social activism and writing.

One of Port Royal's first alumna, slave Susie King Taylor, a native of the Sea Islands, had married Edward King, a Volunteer in the black Union Regiment at Port Royal, and accompanied him into combat. Susie Taylor served as a laundress and nurse. In camp, she taught soldiers of the United States 33rd Colored Regiment to read and write. In her Civil War memoirs, *Reminiscences of My Life in Camp,* she explained why she became a nurse and teacher,

> I taught a great many of the comrades in Company E to read and write, when they were off duty. Nearly all were anxious to learn. My husband taught some also when it was convenient for him. I was very happy to know my efforts were successful in camp, and also felt grateful for the appreciation of my services. I gave my services willingly for four years and three months without receiving a dollar. I was glad, however, to be allowed to go with the regiment, to care for the sick and afflicted comrades.

After the war, Susie King Taylor tried to support herself and family as a teacher by setting up her own school in Savannah, Georgia. When the Freedmen's Aid school edged out smaller, independent schools, in desperation Susie King Taylor went to work as a domestic servant.

The Freedmen's Bureau Schools

In 1865, Congress created the Freedmen's Bureau, a government agency to rehabilitate the South. Federally supported, the Bureau was the brainchild of Josephine Guffing, a volunteer of the Women's National Loyal League. The Freedmen's Bureau extended credit to black farmers, and offered medical care, farming tools, some minor land redistribution and an education. Like the Port Royal experiment, the Freedmen's Bureau hired Yankee women to teach former slaves. Their distinguished graduates included Booker T. Washington, who studied further at the Hampton Institute and Lucy Laney, who at age fifteen entered the University of Atlanta. In 1886, Lucy Laney founded the Haines Normal and Industrial Institute in Augusta, Georgia, which included a kindergarten and nurses' training program.

Martha Scofield gained her first teaching experience at Laura Towne's school in the Sea Islands, and later taught for the Freedmen's Bureau Schools in Aiken, South Carolina. When Reconstruction terminated in 1876, and the Freedmen's schools closed, Scofield solicited northern philanthropists to build schools for black students. The Scofield School combined a traditional academic curriculum with vocational courses including carpentry, blacksmithing, printing, nursing, sewing and cooking.

Freedwomen in the Postwar South

Nothing expressed the dashed hopes of former slaves during Reconstruction better than the slogan "Forty Acres and a Mule," which referred to the Congressional proposal to give each freedman 40 acres and a mule for a new start in life. Although the plan never materialized, rumors of government aid lingered and continued to stir the hopes of freedmen who wandered from place to place in search of the elusive "forty acres."

Slaves picking cotton, a labor intensive task, shown with their white overseer. After the war many female slaves were held on plantations against their will to do heavy field work such as plowing, hoeing and planting, as well as clearing land. (Photo courtesy of the Library of Congress.)

In her study, *Labor of Love, Labor of Sorrow: Black Women, Work, and the Family from Slavery to the Present*, and *"Freed Women? The Civil War and Reconstruction," Women, Families and Communities,* historian Jacqueline Jones pays particular attention to the plight of southern black women and the government's feeble attempts to bring former slaves into the agricultural system during Reconstruction.

Professor Jones found that at the end of the war, there was no universal jubilation for slaves, because many were still in bondage, unaware that they had been emancipated. For example, on one Kentucky plantation, Hannah Davidson remained in bondage until the mid 1880s. Even freed persons who worked as paid labor were treated as slaves. Their owners curtailed their movement, inflicted harsh whipping and torture, and terrorized many who demanded their wages. Professor Jones' research revealed that black women remained slaves longer and were treated more harshly than their male counterparts. Surprisingly, she saw little difference between conditions for blacks in the *North and in the South*. In both regions, former female slaves were expected to perform heavy labor and field work. Southern farmers maintained the semblance of the former slave system because, "the female field hand who plowed, hoed and picked cotton under the ever-watchful eye of an overseer came to symbolize the old order." Those freedwomen who preferred to care for their families, or tried to act like ladies, were accused of being lazy, or of putting on airs.

After the war, change did not come easily. Professor Jones notes that "the humiliations of slavery remained fresh in the minds of black women who continued to suffer physical abuse at the hands of white employers." Black women had a vital family role and garnered more authority and respect, yet they walked a fine line between newfound respect within the family, and recrimination from whites. "Black women paid dearly, for their own assertiveness and for that of their sisters who dressed, spoke up, shouted and acted like free women." To keep them in their place, black women were terrorized. Margaret Martin was beaten and choked by her employer for "freely" visiting a relative without permission. Lucretia Adams was whipped by eight white men who told her, "we were sent for to come here and beat you and to make the other damned niggers work." Shaking away the old bonds of slavery, freedmen tried to distance their wives and daughters from white employers in order to protect them from physical abuse. The degree to which a freedman could prevent harm to his family was the measure of his success and new status. It indicated whether he could act independently and control his own destiny.

Using data from the 1870 Federal census, state censuses and Farm Bureau records, Jacqueline Jones' analysis dispels former notions which had characterized the postwar black family, such as the idea that fathers abandoned their families or that many migrated from the South. She found that:

* Ninety percent of the freedwomen remained in rural areas

* Fertility rates did not decline sharply after the war; in 1870, the average southern black mother had six children

* Black fathers and husbands *were* a visible presence in the family, and eighty percent of the southern black families had a male as head of household. This compared equally with the number of white male heads of households, which was also eighty percent.

Conclusion

Women in the North were critical to the Union's victory. In the South's staggering defeat, women sustained their families and communities. Undoubtedly, the hardships of war were felt most severely in the South where the war was fought in plowed fields and blossoming orchards, in towns, near churches and in the vast areas of wilderness that stretched from Virginia to Texas and beyond. The Union Army burned homes, looted granaries and storehouses, destroyed farms, bridges and railroads. They slaughtered livestock and draft animals essential to southern agriculture. One estimate of the devastation to the southern infrastructure calculates losses at five billion dollars.

The personal tragedy and the economic effects of the Civil War left the South a depressed economy for many decades. In the postwar South, freedwomen struggled in poverty in the hope that somehow their children might have a better future. To that end, they valued education, but trying to improve their situation or that of their children was an uphill climb. Even though various programs modeled after the Port Royal experiment and the Freedmen's Bureau set up private and federally funded schools in 1870, eighty percent of the southern black population could not read or write.

In 1876, the termination of Congressional Reconstruction reeked havoc on the southern black population. In the southern postwar economy, parents fought to keep black schools open. With the end of the Reconstruction program, the Union Troops withdrew. Their evacuation from the South left black communities unprotected and an easy target for the radical fringe groups that emerged. White terrorist groups, such as the Ku Klux Klan and the Knights of the White Camellias, lynched black people, burned Freedmen's schools, black churches and homes and intimidated or raped white Yankee schoolmarms for teaching the children of former slaves. Today, the continued misery of southern sharecropping families is a grim reminder of the South's slow recovery from the war, the government's short-sighted attempt to rebuild the South, and its failure to implement an effective Reconstruction program.

Part IV:

Women in the Gilded Age

The Women's Movement in the Postwar Period

Women and the Postwar Reform Movement

Women's Culture in the Victorian Age

Women's Health in the Nineteenth Century

Chapter 13
The Women's Movement in the Postwar Period
Let None Stand Idle Spectators Now

Key Topics

The Women's Suffrage Movement
The Western State Movement

Chronology

1866 - First Postwar Women's Rights Convention, New York City
1865 - 1870- Amendments XIII, XIV, XV Ratified
1867 - Elizabeth Cady Stanton and Susan B. Anthony's Kansas Campaign
1868 - Schism in the National Women's Movement
1872 - Victoria Claflin Woodhull Runs for President
Susan B. Anthony Arrested for Voting in Presidential Election
1875 - *Minor v Happersett*

Introduction

Although women performed extraordinary service for the war effort, with the Union victory secured, society expected them to return to domestic life and the pre-war status quo. Attempts to pick up where the war had left off were futile. By 1865, women had been politically active for nearly four decades, crusading for health, temperance, anti-slavery and the feminist movement. Just because women had temporarily turned to war work from 1861-1865, did not mean they had totally abandoned their own cause.

Elizabeth Cady Stanton had assumed, perhaps naively, that if women showed loyal support for the Union, they would be rewarded with citizenship and the vote. Strategist Susan B. Anthony remained skeptical, and expected that history would repeat itself. Women, she believed, would be returned to "their place" after the war. Events confirmed her suspicions sooner than expected, when the New York State legislature rescinded the Married Woman's Property Act, voiding women's rights of property and guardianship of their children. By 1862, Susan B. Anthony feared that not only would women be forced to return to the status quo, but that serious backsliding might result. She and some of her cohorts, determined to preserve women's gains and move forward, made a bold move to vote in the 1872 presidential election. Victoria Woodhull assumed that not only could women vote but that they could also hold political office. In the 1872 election, Victoria nominated herself and ran for President of the United States.

The crusade for women's rights and suffrage showed progress in the West. As early as 1869, the Wyoming Territory granted women the vote. Soon other states and territories in the West would follow suit.

The Women's Suffrage Movement

When President Lincoln issued the Emancipation Proclamation in 1863, Massachusetts Senator Charles Sumner had already proposed a constitutional amendment to shore up the presidential decree, but congressional support looked dubious. Henry Stanton saw a ray of hope and believed women could be of some influence and he encouraged his wife, Elizabeth, and her ally, Susan B. Anthony, to gather signatures in support of an amendment for emancipation. During the Civil War years, Elizabeth Cady Stanton, Susan B. Anthony and Lucy Stone had engaged in a unified effort for women's rights. Elizabeth Cady Stanton, Susan B. Anthony, and others organized the Women's National Loyal League and together they gathered 400,000 signatures for a petition to emancipate women, i.e. grant them citizenship and the voting franchise in the proposed constitutional amendment.

> The undersigned women of the United States, above the age of eighteen years, earnestly pray that your honorable body will pass at the earliest predictable day an act emancipating all persons of African descent held to involuntary service of labor in the United States.

One year later, when the Women's National Loyal League submitted their document to Senator Sumner, it comprised the largest collection of petition signatures ever gathered in the United States. The accolades the petition received in Congress portended a victory for the seventeen-year-old women's crusade, but in May of 1865, when the work seemed near completion, events took a sudden turn. Wendell Phillips, President-Elect of the Anti-Slavery Society, cautioned that adding the women's right to vote to the constitutional amendment would impede the enfranchisement of two million freedmen and the amendment would fail. To avoid failure, women's rights would have to be postponed. As Phillips explained, "This hour belongs to the Negro just as Abraham Lincoln had said, 'one war at a time'; so I say, one question at a time this is the Negro's hour." His statement shocked Elizabeth Cady Stanton and Susan B. Anthony who felt betrayed and Phillips left little doubt that *Negro* meant *male Negro.*

The feminist response was immediate. In a letter to Phillips, Elizabeth inquired "May I ask just one question based on the apparent opposition in which you place the Negro and the woman? My question is this: do you believe the African race is composed entirely of males?" Elizabeth Stanton saw clearly the political implications—Congressional Republicans hoped to secure the freedmen's franchise, and in turn his vote—and that would give northern Republicans a power base in the postwar South. Feminists realized they must do everything to seize the opportunity of this historic moment. If radical Republicans in Congress (most of them Elizabeth and Susan's abolitionist allies) would not support them, then who would? Elizabeth knew they must act while a "constitutional door was open;" women must do everything possible to walk through that door escorted as she said by "the strong arm and blue uniform of the black soldier." If women did not step into civic life with the Freedmen, the opportunity would be lost indefinitely.

Threatened with exclusion, Susan B. Anthony and Elizabeth Cady Stanton wrote another petition pressuring Congress to rewrite the Fourteenth Amendment and include women in it. They collected 10,000 signatures, but Senator Sumner, who criticized their efforts as ill-timed, refused to submit them to Congress, and the amendment text remained "male citizens." During the ratification process in the summer of 1866, violent mobs who opposed the amendment demonstrated in southern cities. These demonstrations alerted Congress of the necessity to pass the Fifteenth Amendment ensuring that "the rights of citizens of the United States to vote shall neither be denied nor abridged by the United States or by any state, on account of race, color, or previous condition of servitude." In the Fifteenth Amendment text, women were excluded once again.

In May of 1866, the annual meeting of the Women's Rights Convention which had been canceled during the war resumed in Boston. Angered over the Fourteenth Amendment, feminist leaders invited the Anti-Slavery Association to attend in order to form a coalition. This might, according to Elizabeth, strengthen the newly hatched American Equal Rights Association, and "bury the black man and the woman in the citizen, and our two organizations into a broader network of reconstruction."

The Kansas Campaign

In 1866 Lucy Stone founded the American Equal Rights Association and in 1867 she became President of the New Jersey Woman Suffrage Association. Elections also looked promising. In 1867, a referendum on the Kansas ballot allowed voters to decide if women and blacks could vote in that state. In June of that year, a Constitutional Convention in New York placed women's right to vote on the agenda. It was decided that Lucy Stone would campaign for the women in Kansas and Elizabeth Cady Stanton and Susan B. Anthony would head the New York campaign. Elizabeth and Susan conducted a massive petition drive and presented 28,000 petitions to the New York Constitutional Committee, pleading for women's right to vote. Once again *friends, not foes* opposed them. Horace Greeley, newspaper editor and chair of the New York Constitutional Committee, and a longtime supporter of women's rights struck the first blow. Greeley argued that, "however defensible in theory, we are satisfied that public sentiment does not demand and would not sustain an innovation so revolutionary and so sweeping." Adding insult to injury, Wendell Phillips denied Elizabeth and Susan any of the anti-slavery funds which had been allocated for women's suffrage.

Undaunted, Stanton and Anthony arrived in Kansas, late in September 1867, to help Lucy Stone in the women's and black suffrage crusade. With little money, and dogged by living in rough-and-ready Kansas, Elizabeth and Susan found a benefactor in George Frances Train, an unscrupulous politician and white supremacist, who offered financial help to their sagging campaign. Train had designs to become President of the United States and saw the female vote as the means to achieve it. Although his candidacy never materialized, his money made it possible for Elizabeth and Susan to complete the Kansas Campaign and establish a weekly newspaper, *The Revolution*. In their paper they proclaimed a mission of "principle not policy, justice, not favors, men their rights and nothing more, women their rights and nothing less."

Although Stanton and Anthony's hard campaigning in Kansas failed, they claimed a victory: "without organization, without money, without political rewards to offer, we gained one-third of all the votes." But the Republican Party would not support the Kansas Referendum for women's suffrage and it lost by a sixty percent margin. Elizabeth and Susan had risked even more by joining with Train. Lucy Stone led the opposition; she believed their association with Train degraded the women's movement. The unholy alliance with Train split up friendships and revealed ideological differences with Anthony and Stanton on one side and Stone and her followers on the other.

Upon their return from Kansas, Stanton and Anthony discovered that Lucy Stone, Julia Ward Howe, Antoinette Brown Blackwell (Stone's sister-in-law), Frederick Douglass, and Stephen and Abby Kelly Foster had severed ties with them and the National Suffrage Association. The opposition, led by Lucy Stone and Julia Ward Howe, reorganized in Boston as the American Woman Suffrage Association, (AWSA) which included prominent male members such as Henry Blackwell (Lucy's husband) and the Reverend Henry Ward Beecher. Under Stone's guidance, the AWSA set women's suffrage as their only agenda and published their own paper, *The Women's Journal*, which remained the authoritative voice of the movement until 1917.

The New York based National Woman Suffrage Association (NWSA), led by Elizabeth Cady Stanton and Susan B. Anthony, continued. The NWSA excluded men from membership and addressed women's social problems related to marriage, divorce, property laws, child custody, labor and the inferior role of women in the churches.

Women Vote in the 1872 Presidential Election

Women tried to intercede in the voting process in the 1872 Presidential Elections. Two leading participants were Virginia Minor and Susan B. Anthony. Plans for election germinated when Virginia's husband, Attorney Francis Minor, argued the Fourteenth and Fifteenth Amendments already extended citizenship and suffrage to women. Since the government could not prevent them from doing so, women would go to the polls to vote.

On November 1, 1872, Susan B. Anthony went to the local barbershop in Rochester, New York, and registered to vote. Anthony and at least fifteen other women did so on Election Day. There were no incidents and it appeared officials would comply with women voting or ignore them and do nothing. Three weeks later, a United States Marshal issued a warrant for Susan B. Anthony's arrest. She was charged with voting,

> without having a lawful right to vote in the said election district, the said Susan B. Anthony, being then and there a person of the female sex, as she, the said Susan B. Anthony, then and there well known contrary to the statute of the United States of America...did knowingly, wrongfully, and unlawfully, vote.

Susan B. Anthony, the other 15 women who had voted, and the registrars who had accepted their ballots were all arrested and fined $500.00, a penalty Susan refused to pay. Because Henry Selden, Susan B. Anthony's attorney, paid the fine, her right to an appeal to the Supreme Court was disallowed. On June 17, 1873, Justice Ward Hunt heard Susan B. Anthony's case and he had predisposed the outcome. She could not testify, because Hunt said women were incompetent to do so. Hunt barred any evidence, read a prepared decision, and instructed an all-male jury *not to deliberate* but *to find her guilty.* Susan B. Anthony found the judge "punctilious in manner, scrupulous in attire, conscientious in trivialities and obtuse on great principles." Hunt did make one mistake however, when he asked Anthony if she wished to make a comment before he pronounced sentence. Susan B. Anthony took the opportunity to express her outrage.

> Yes your honor, I have many things to say; for in your ordered verdict of guilty you have trampled under foot every vital principle of our government. My natural rights, my civil rights, my political rights, my judicial rights are all alike ignored. Robbed of the fundamental privilege of citizenship, I am degraded from the status of citizen to that of a subject and not only myself individually but all of my sex are, by your honor's verdict, doomed to political subjection under this so called republican form of government.

In addition to the fifteen women who voted with Susan B. Anthony, 200 other women had attempted to vote in the 1872 election. Recent scholarship suggests that women may have disguised as men in order to vote. In St. Louis, Missouri, Virginia Minor tried to register to vote but was refused. Her husband, Francis Minor filed a legal suit against the voting registrar Reese Happersett, and in 1875, the case reached the Supreme Court on appeal. On *Minor v Happersett*, the court ruled out any possibility that women would win the vote through the judicial process. In a unanimous majority decision, justices ruled against Virginia Minor. Moreover, they defined citizenship as, "membership in a nation and nothing more" and stated that suffrage was granted by each state in the union. Therefore, it was up to the individual states to determine who might vote.

The *Minor v Happersett* case had tremendous fallout as it backfired for the gains of freedmen. When the court interpreted the franchise as each state's right, southern states used the *Minor v Happersett* decision as the means to restrict voting for newly enfranchised freedmen. Seeing the broader implications of the decision in the long term, Susan B. Anthony lamented the *Minor v Happersett* decision. She believed that with the sanction of the Supreme Court, once the right to vote depended on the whim of state lawmakers, any group, or individual might be targeted for exclusion.

> If we once establish the false principle that United States citizenship does not carry with it the right to vote in every state in this union, there is no end to the petty freaks and cunning devices that may be resorted to in order to exclude one or another class of citizens from the right of suffrage.

Nineteenth Century Milestones in the Women's Rights Movement

1848 - First Women's Rights Conference, Seneca Falls, New York

1850 - First Meeting of Annual National Women's Rights Convention, Worcester, Massachusetts

1854 - Elizabeth Cady Stanton addresses New York Legislature regarding married women's rights, and child custody

1860 - New York Legislature passes *Married Women's Property Act*

1869 - Elizabeth Cady Stanton and Susan B. Anthony establish the National Woman Suffrage Association. November: Lucy Stone forms the American Woman Suffrage Association

1872 - Susan B. Anthony votes in the presidential election; she is arrested, tried and fined $500, which she refuses to pay.

1875 - Supreme Court decision states that since suffrage is granted by the states they have the prerogative to withhold voting privileges for women

1878 - Elizabeth Cady Stanton and Susan B. Anthony introduce the Women's suffrage Amendment to the United States Congress

1890 - Reunification of the National Woman Suffrage Association (Elizabeth and Susan) with the American Woman Suffrage Association (Lucy Stone) becoming The National American Woman Suffrage Association

The Western Suffrage Movement

Women on the western frontier had challenged traditional roles for men and women. In the western territories, women's skills, economic production, and stamina had made it possible for their families to survive. Men tried to maintain their dominance over them, but political realities influenced change. In order for a territory to become a state, a quota of 60,000 citizens was required, and in the sparsely populated West, women were needed to meet that quota, and western regions became the first to grant women full participation in civic life. An early women's rights activist in the West, Esther Morris, influenced Wyoming territorial elections in 1869. She held a reception for legislative candidates from both parties and secured their guarantee that a women's suffrage bill would be introduced in the legislature. That same year, a bill was promptly passed by the territorial legislators which secured the following: women's property rights, equal pay for female schoolteachers and the right of women to serve on jury panels. When the Wyoming law gained attention in the East, Esther Morris was featured in political cartoons; suffrage leaders were inspired by what she had accomplished in a short time, especially in a predominantly male territory. Esther also secured an appointment as Justice of the Peace, and served in that office with an enviable judicial record. Of the forty cases Esther heard, none of the decisions were reversed.

In 1889, when Wyoming Territory applied for statehood, a political battle ensued in Congress because of Wyoming's equal franchise. But Wyoming representatives defended their women's right to vote, and informed the Congress that they were prepared to "stay out of the Union a hundred years, but we will come in with our women." Congress just barely voted the admission of Wyoming as a state.

Seventeen-year-old Abigail Scott (Duniway) ventured out West from Illinois to Oregon in 1852; she was orphaned when her mother died of cholera. She succeeded as a business woman and established the Portland *New Northwest*, a newspaper dedicated to the women's rights crusade. With subscribers throughout the Northwest, Abigail spread the suffrage message far and wide. She also traveled the lecture circuit speaking for women's rights, co-founded the Oregon Equal Suffrage Association and in 1912, from her wheelchair, she authored the bill which granted Oregon women the vote.

Utah's move for women's suffrage became entangled in a political crossfire with the Mormon Church. In February 1870, Utah became the second territorial government to grant women the vote, but the church's practice of polygamy came under review by the United States Congress. National officials worried that if Mormon women gained the vote, Mormon males would coerce them to support polygamy if it came to a political battle with Congress. Mormon Patriarch Brigham Young predicted that if polygamy came to a plebiscite in Utah, Mormon women would support the church's position on plural marriage. To eliminate this possibility, in 1887, Congress banned both polygamy and women's suffrage in Utah. However, after Congress granted statehood to Utah in 1896, the state legislature restored women's right to vote. Looking westward to the early success in Wyoming and eventual suffrage in Utah, feminists could see that a state-by-state campaign might be more effective than a national referendum for women's suffrage. However, by the late nineteenth century, the women's movement had languished, and seemed threatened with extinction; however, in 1890, Lucy Stone, representing the AWSA, and Elizabeth Cady Stanton and Susan B. Anthony of the NWSA, healed a twenty-two-year rift in the movement and reunited as the National American Woman Suffrage Association, (NAWSA). With a heavy endorsement from Susan B. Anthony, Elizabeth Cady Stanton won election as president of the NAWSA. Susan B. Anthony became Vice President at large and Lucy Stone served as chair of the executive committee.

Clio's Corner - What Have Historians said about the Suffrage Movement?

In *Sex and Citizenship in Antebellum America*, author Nancy Isenberg focuses on the Women's

Rights Movement before the Civil War, and within the political context of the antebellum era, when anti-slavery, temperance, labor reform, the war with Mexico, and the passing of married women's property laws challenged social notions of citizenship based upon the common man, the party man and the citizen soldier. Nancy Isenberg asks how feminists framed their understanding of rights within the antebellum concept of citizenship, and how the struggle over rights incorporated several distinct but overlapping legal and political debates. The issues of prostitution, seduction, and the death penalty, she argues, "underscored the sexual double standard in the law, reinforced by women's exclusion from juries." Women, according to Isenberg, were able to circumvent the double standard by promoting the politics of family. Devotees of labor, temperance and health reform also addressed the dangers of exploited female workers, domestic violence and sexual abuse. Professor Isenberg concludes that the women's rights movement drew on the language of the times to link the equal rights argument to the evolution of democratic ideals within the larger framework of the antebellum republic. She discounts the entrenched view of distinct and separate spheres for men and women and that the women's rights movement emerged from anti-slavery reform, noting that feminists were actively involved in a much wider array of political activity.

In hindsight, women's attempts to win the vote and secure equal rights seemed to elude the thousands of women who worked tirelessly for the movement over seventy-two years. But in the longer historical perspective, it can be argued, the success of the American women's movement came swiftly. Nineteenth century feminists made great advances by the close of the century and the movement did not lag. According to Aileen S. Kraditor, in *The Ideas of the Woman Suffrage Movement, 1890-1920,* "the suffrage movement did not sleep" and their accomplishments from 1848-1890 marked significant advancements for women. Legislative gains in New York State gave married women ownership of pre-marital property. Kentucky in 1838, Kansas in 1861, and Michigan and Minnesota in 1875 granted women school suffrage - the right to vote in school board elections. Aileen Kraditor notes that in an odd twist, feminists measured progress even in failure.

> Defeat after defeat rewarded their efforts. After the first state referendum in Kansas in 1867, which failed, fifty-five more such popular votes on state woman suffrage amendments took place over the next fifty years. Altogether there were 480 campaigns to induce state legislatures to submit amendments to their electorates; 277 campaigns to persuade state party conventions to include woman suffrage planks in their platforms; nineteen campaigns with nineteen successive congresses; and the ratification campaign of 1919 and 1920. Between 1869 and 1916 there were forty-one state amendment campaigns, with nine victories and thirty-two defeats.

Aileen Kraditor estimates that in 1893, there were about 13,350 members of the National American Woman Suffrage Association. Fourteen years later, membership had more than tripled. In just seventy-two years, American women had overturned the long history of no access to civic life and gained the status of citizenship, the vote, the right to own property, to divorce, and to sue for custody of their children. Elizabeth Cady Stanton, Susan B. Anthony, Lucy Stone and the hundreds of other feminists had in such a short time changed one of the oldest traditions in the human experience — the inferior status of women.

Victoria Claflin Woodhull

It would be a serious omission to discuss the women's movement in the post-Civil War period without introducing Victoria Claflin Woodhull, and quite another matter to place her into any particular niche, as she lived life on her own terms. After opening an investment firm on Wall Street with the financial backing of Cornelius Vanderbilt, she also published a newspaper, *The Weekly,* which promoted everything for women, from free love and short hemlines to legalized prostitution.

Victoria Woodhull presenting a petition to the Congressional Committee, in which she argued that women already had the right to vote. (Picture courtesy of the Library of Congress.)

In 1871, Victoria Woodhull took on the government and presented to a Congressional Committee a memorial petition which stated that, according to the Fourteenth and Fifteenth Amendments, women had the right to vote. All Congress need do, according to Victoria, was to pass a Declaratory Act. Members of NWSA, in Washington for their conference, attended the Congressional Committee hearings and were impressed with Victoria's presentation. Susan B. Anthony invited her to speak at the NWSA convention, but Victoria then overwhelmed feminist leaders with her aggressive style. By the next NWSA convention in New York City, she had moved to take control of the entire organization and publicized the meeting as the Weethalle Convention. There at the NWSA New York convention, Victoria delivered her famous secession speech,

> It is my conviction, arrived at after the most serious and careful consideration, that it will be equally suicidal for the Women Suffragists to attach themselves to either of these parties... If Congress refuses to listen to and grant what women ask, there is but one course left them to pursue... We will have our rights. We say no longer by your leave. We have besought, argued, and convinced, but we have failed; and we will not fail. We will try you just once more. If the very next Congress refuse women all the legitimate results of citizenship; if they [refuse to pass] a proper declaratory act...then we give here and now, deliberate notification of what we will do next...one year...from this day...we shall proceed to call another convention and to erect a new government... We mean treason; we mean secession... We will overslaught [sic] this bogus republic and plant a government [that] derives its power from the consent of the governed.

A Thomas Nast cartoon which vilified Victoria Woodhull as Mrs. Satan. Her attack on Henry Ward Beecher alienated her from other women's rights activists. (Picture courtesy of the Library of Congress.)

Victoria Woodhull formed the People's Party, and declared herself that party's candidate for the presidency, and much to his surprise, named Frederick Douglass her vice presidential running mate. Her campaign failed and that same year, when she publicized an illicit affair between the Reverend Henry Ward Beecher and one of his parishioners, Victoria was attacked by the Beecher family, vilified by the press, and abandoned by liberal feminists. Even longtime benefactor Commodore Vanderbilt withdrew his financial support.

Anthony Comstock, a New York Postmaster, had Victoria Woodhull arrested for posting obscene literature in the mail. In court, Victoria's attorney defended her right to free speech, but by the time the trial ended, her prominence in public life was destroyed. The press turned on her and advertised details of Victoria's own flamboyant private life. Evidently one transgression was bigamy. Apparently she had two husbands residing at her Murray Hill home: Colonel Blood, a Mississippi gambler and former Confederate, and Dr. Canning Woodhull, a physician.

Mothers of Invention: Maria Mitchell, an Astronomer Sweeping the Skies

Maria Mitchell became an astronomer at a time when most girls in the United States neither attended school nor studied mathematics and science. Maria did not receive much schooling either and left school at age sixteen. She taught school and served as librarian at the Nantucket Atheneum. This job gave her the leisure to study and to "sweep the skies" as she called it. Looking at the stars became second nature to Maria, as she explained,

> It was in the first place, a love of mathematics, seconded by my sympathy with my father's love for astronomical observation. But the spirit of the place had also much to do with the early bent of my mind in this direction. In Nantucket people quite generally are in the habit of observing the heavens, and a sextant will be found in almost every house.

As a young child, Maria had helped her father plot the stars to make nautical charts to aid the whaling fleets which came into the Nantucket Port. This early training helped her use keen logic and simple observation. Using a small telescope set up on the rooftop of her house, Maria Mitchell won worldwide fame as an astronomer on October 1, 1847, when she discovered a comet, subsequently named for her — Mitchell's Comet. For this discovery she received a gold medal from the King of Denmark. To celebrate her success, a group of friends bought her a larger telescope.

She worked for the United States Nautical Almanac Office sighting satellites, nebulae and sunspots and became the first woman elected to the American Academy of Arts and Sciences. In 1865, when Vassar College opened, Maria Mitchell became director of the Vassar Observatory and accepted the Professorship of Astronomy, becoming the first female Professor of Astronomy in the United States. Professor Mitchell taught many of the leading women scientists of the next generation who studied at Vassar College.

Rather than disclaim women's domestic role Maria encouraged her students to see in domestic tasks their natural aptitude for the sciences:

> Observations of this kind are peculiarly adapted to women. Indeed, all astronomical observing seems to be so fitted. The training of a girl fits her for delicate work. The touch of her fingers upon the delicate screws of an astronomical instrument might become wonderfully accurate in results; a woman's eyes are trained to nicety of color. The eye that directs a needle in the delicate meshes of embroidery, will equally well bisect a star with the spider-web of the micrometer. Routine observations, too, dull as they are, are less dull than the endless repetition of the same pattern in crochet work.

Conclusion

After the Civil War, leaders of the Women's Rights movement faced disappointment after disappointment. Despite the efforts of the Women's National Loyal League to petition Congressional support for a constitutional amendment which would recognize women (along with freedmen) as citizens and voters, their petitions were denied. Elizabeth Cady Stanton and Susan B. Anthony's Kansas campaign to pass women's suffrage on the ballot in that state also failed. Ideological and tactical differences among the leaders created a major split in the women's rights crusade which divided into two camps. On one side, the National Women's Suffrage Association was led by Elizabeth Cady Stanton and Susan B. Anthony, and on the other, the American Women's Suffrage Association had Lucy Stone, Julia Ward Howe, Antoinette Brown Blackwell, and Abby Kelly Foster at the helm.

More extremist measures and leaders also emerged. Susan B. Anthony, Virginia Minor and others defied the law and voting practices and went to the polls to vote in the 1872 Presidential election, without the desired effect however. While Susan B. Anthony was arrested and hoped to appeal her case in court, when her lawyer paid her fines this negated any further appeal. Although Virginia Minor's case went before the highest court on appeal, the Supreme Court's decision deferred to the states for voting rights. Victoria Claflin Woodhull insisted before a Congressional hearing that women already had voting rights, formed her own political party, and ran for president.

The only hope for women's suffrage came from the West when in 1869, the territory of Wyoming gave women equal franchise, followed by the territory of Utah in 1870, and the state of Oregon in 1912. In Wyoming and Oregon, it was the efforts of women who championed the equal franchise that secured women's suffrage.

But by 1869, ideological differences split the movement into two opposing camps, with Lucy Stone and members of the New England Suffrage Association forming the American Woman Suffrage Association, and Elizabeth Cady Stanton and Susan B. Anthony heading the National Woman's Suffrage Association. The women's quest for suffrage remained controversial both within the movement and without. In 1876, as the country prepared for the Centennial Anniversary of American Independence, Stanton grieved over the lack of progress for women's independence,

> Looking over these twenty eight years, I feel that what we have achieved, as yet, bears no proportion to what we have suffered in the daily humiliation of spirit from the cruel distinctions based on sex. The undercurrent of popular thought, as seen in our social habits, theological dogmas, and political theories still reflects the same customs, creeds and codes that degrade women in the effete civilizations of the old world.

In 1890, although the National Women's Suffrage Association (NWSA) and the American Women's Suffrage Association (AWSA) had reunited and merged as the National American Women's Suffrage Association (NAWSA) the women's movement would split again over ideological differences.

Chapter 14
Women and the Postwar Reform Movement
Measuring Our Progress One Step at a Time

Key Topics

Women and the Populist Movement
The Women's Temperance Movement
African-American Women and Social Reform
Female Immigrant Labor in the New World
Women in Medicine and Law

Chronology

1874 - Emergence of the Women's Christian Temperance Union
1883 - The Statue of Liberty Placed on Bedlow's (Liberty) Island
1890 - Populists Emerge as a Third Political Party
1892 - Populist Party Nominates a Candidate for President

Introduction

By the 1870s and 1880s, it was not unusual for middle- and upper-class women to take on a number of social causes; in fact, it was quite commonplace for them to be politically active. Women extended their nurturing concern as wives and mothers to social outreach and helping their communities.

Postwar women's reform activity also aimed specifically at improving life for women. They formed social networks which gave them a sense of solidarity and resolve. Middle- and upper-class women remained active in social reform but also joined clubs and literary groups. The greatest momentum for reform came in the Temperance Crusade which women organized throughout the country. Black women, barred from participation in the white women's movements, organized their own crusades to protest discrimination and lynching.

In the late nineteenth century an agrarian movement emerged which eventually amalgamated numerous farming unions or Farmer's Alliance throughout the United States. Eventually this widespread grassroots movement would lead to the formation of a new political organization, the Populist Party. Like the Farmer's Alliance, the new party sought to protect farmers from the capitalistic and industrial powers of monopolies (such as railroads and banks) and unsympathetic public officials. They hoped to enact a more equitable tax system, a graduated personal income tax, the free coinage of silver and issuance of paper money. Some women, novices to politics participated in the Alliance movement as well as the Populist Party and they gained valuable experience in the process.

The massive immigration from 1840 to 1920 increased the number of working poor in American cities. Immigrant women, with their children working alongside them, took jobs for the most meager pay and took up the cause of labor. Others cleared the way for women to cross the bar and join the legal profession.

Western Women and Populism

In the postwar era, the movement known as populism grew from local farmers' social groups, like the Patrons of Husbandry or the Grange, to regional associations of the Farmers' Alliance. These organizations educated farmers in the newest agricultural methods, economic trends and the inner workings of politics. Threatened by the controlling forces of capitalism, farmers saw in the Alliance a way to mobilize against railroads, the banking establishment and corporate control. The Farmers' Alliance quickly escalated into a national third party system, the Populist Party.

Women in these organizations gained firsthand political experience. Populist Mary Elizabeth Clyens Lease had moved to Kansas to take a teaching position but got involved in local politics. Her first taste of politics involved work as a stump speaker for the Union Labor Party, the Knights of Labor, and the Farmers' Alliance. Mary Lease is remembered for her effective oratory which motivated the masses to join the Populist crusade. In 1892, she supported the nomination of James Weaver as the Populist presidential candidate. Mary completed no less than 160 speaking engagements and urged farmers to "raise less corn and more hell." She ran for the United States Senate, but lost the election and withdrew from the Populist Party when it endorsed Democratic presidential candidate William Jennings Bryan in 1896. After that election, Mary Lease shifted gears. She moved to New York and wrote for the *New York World,* and expanded her political involvement as a speaker-reformist for women's suffrage, birth control, progressivism and prohibition. In 1895, still promoting Populist reform, she wrote *The Problem of Civilization Solved* which called for an end to big business monopoly, poverty, militarism, the nationalization of utilities and railroads and free trade agreements.

Annie La Porte Diggs was first drawn to reform activism in the Temperance crusade when she moved to Kansas in 1873. She published the *Kansas Liberal* with her husband Alvin S. Diggs. Annie's *forte* was organization, and she almost single-handedly made the Kansas Farmers' Alliance a success, transforming it into the Populist Party. She was a keynote speaker at all of the regional Populist campaigns. In 1897, when currency became a political issue, (whether to remain on the gold standard, bimetal – both silver and gold, or to print more paper money) the Kansas Women's Free Silver League elected Diggs its president. In 1899, the Kansas Equal Suffrage Association also elected Annie Diggs president. Annie campaigned but was unable to secure a state amendment for woman's suffrage in Kansas. Although Annie Diggs and Mary Elizabeth Lease rubbed elbows in a common cause, they never collaborated. Annie not only disliked Mary but distrusted her as well. Nevertheless, their lives ran parallel and Annie Diggs, like Mary Lease, retired to New York State in later life and authored books on the Populist movement.

As a third party, the Populist was short lived and never won a presidential election, but its reform agenda had a lasting effect. Within the next seventy years, Populist objectives like those of Mary Elizabeth Lease would be implemented, including municipal control of utilities, government acquisition of railroad passenger service, Federal loan programs to farmers, agricultural cooperatives, a graduated income tax, constitutional amendments for prohibition and women's suffrage, lifting the ban on birth control, and much more.

Women in the Temperance Crusade

By the nineteenth century, drinking in the United States had reached epidemic proportions. In his landmark study, *The Alcoholic Republic, An American Tradition*, William Rohrabaugh notes that between 1800 and 1830, alcoholic consumption in America increased dramatically. At an annual rate of five gallons per capita, it was triple the amount Americans consume today. Nineteenth century society viewed drinking alcoholic beverages as an exclusively male prerogative. Women were not permitted to drink in public houses, taverns or inns. Even though standards of feminine behavior frowned upon women drinking publicly, in an unregulated pharmaceuticals market, women purchased medicines with high alcoholic content. In the privacy of their homes, women consumed alcoholic or narcotic nostrums as *medicinal remedies*.

Alarmed at the severity of America's drinking, businessmen had spearheaded the temperance movement in the 1820s. Temperance appealed especially to women and they spread the temperance message with religious zeal. With alcoholism so widespread, everyone had a relative, friend or neighbor whose life had deteriorated through alcoholic addiction. Women were more likely to suffer the effects of alcoholism, especially through that of a husband, and endured physical abuse, abandonment and poverty.

When women organized their own temperance movement reform, this seemed at cross-purposes with the campaign for women's rights. Opposition to the Women's Rights Movement came from industrialists and the whiskey lobby. These groups feared that if women got the vote, they would bring drastic social reforms. Women might promote laws to ban alcoholic drink, and lobby for better working conditions for women and children. Undoubtedly, if women could have voted and campaigned for political office, they would have prioritized sweeping changes in industry, including laws to eliminate child labor, and to institute an eight hour workday. However, reforms of this kind could dip deeply into the pockets and high profits of big business. Industrial barons and the whiskey manufacturers saw women's suffrage as a direct attack on their dominion. Their concerns were well-founded since feminists definitely intended to upset the status quo. Temperance women were engaged in an all-out war against alcohol. Reformer Susan B. Anthony, for example, championed both temperance reform and the women's union movement.

By 1873, an evangelical-missionary movement affiliated with the temperance crusade, and more women got involved. That year, women's Christian groups gathered in Ohio to sing and pray and initiated an anti-saloon campaign. As the idea gained momentum throughout the Midwest, it gathered more support. In 1874, the anti-saloon campaign coalesced into the Women's Christian Temperance Union, the WCTU. Frances Willard served as its president, and drew thousands of women into the organization. She combined temperance, women's rights, labor unions, social purity and women's health all into one national campaign. She served as president of the WCTU for twenty years and inspired women to "Do Everything." Among her many talents, Frances Willard's genius for organization materialized with well orchestrated conventions complete with stirring pageantry. Through the use of music, banners, flowers and uplifting speeches, her guiding hand moved the WCTU forward and she massed membership by crossing social and regional lines.

Frances Willard was the master organizer of the WCTU. In 1880 she had already identified the problem of alcohol addiction as an international problem. (Photo courtesy of the Library of Congress.)

The women least likely to get involved, upper-class conservatives and southern women, succumbed to Frances Willard's persuasion and joined the Temperance Crusade. In one petition drive, she secured 100,000 signatures for a Home Protection Plan which she submitted to Illinois lawmakers. This petition stated that women ought to be allowed to vote on alcohol-related issues. The Illinois legislators tabled the petition but her plan inspired women in other states to push similar petition campaigns.

At the National Convention of the WCTU in 1880, Frances Willard endorsed the women's suffrage movement, and in 1881, she invited Susan B. Anthony as keynote speaker. For her 1883 campaign, Frances went to every state in the Union. That year she also joined forces with Mary C. Leavitt to take the Temperance Crusade to the international level. Her message, known as the *Polyglot Petition,* was intended to ban the international drug trade, already a serious problem in the nineteenth century. As a result, the WCTU called an international meeting in Boston with delegates from twenty-one nations. This delegation elected Frances Willard president of the international WCTU. Always seeing the potential for consolidation and merger, Frances Willard continued organizing. In 1889, she established the Universal Peace Union, and the General Federation of Women's Clubs.

Carrie Amelia Moore Nation, a women's temperance crusader known for her hatchet-wielding destruction of bars and saloons. (Photo courtesy of the Library of Congress.)

From 1889 to 1892, Frances Willard collaborated with Dr. Anna Howard Shaw, an activist for women and temperance, to join the objective of the WCTU with that of the Women's Suffrage Movement. With the rise of populism in the 1892 presidential election, Frances also tried to merge temperance with populism but the coalition failed to materialize because of the conflict of interest: namely, that farmers sold grain to breweries and whiskey distillers.

Undoubtedly, the icon of the Women's Temperance movement was Carrie A. Nation who stormed the saloons with her hatchet. Carrie Nation had experienced the abuses of alcoholism firsthand. The widow of an alcoholic, she had struggled to support her family. When she married David Nation, a minister, newspaper journalist and lawyer, they moved to Medicine Lodge, Kansas, in 1889, and there she found her life's vocation. She joined the Women's Temperance Movement. Kansas was a dry state, i.e. one which prohibited drinking, but pro-alcohol people were working vigorously to have the state's prohibition laws repealed. Since drinking was illegal in Kansas, Carrie Nation reasoned that any establishment which sold liquor was also illegal and therefore did not merit legal protection. In 1899, accompanied by other temperance women she launched a hatchet-smashing campaign, invading bars, saloons and gin mills. The women entered saloons singing hymns and proceeded to chastise the drinking clientele. Then the hatchetting would begin as Carrie Nation's brigade smashed bottles of liquor, the bar, the furniture, and generally laid waste the property. Frequently arrested for vandalism and disturbing the peace, Carrie Nation always managed to pay the fines or make bail and the arrests only served to broadcast her notoriety and publicize temperance. She met legal expenses and supported herself with public speaking, contributions, and the sale of miniature souvenir hatchets.

No saloons were spared from Carrie Nation's hatchet wielding. In 1901, she smashed up the bar in the Hotel Carey in Wichita, Kansas, an establishment owned by a Kansas State Senator. Once when Carrie led a demonstration in the United States Senate chambers, she was physically ejected from the gallery. In her later years, she wrote a newsletter, published several books and appeared in vaudeville and a theatrical adaptation of *Ten Nights in a Barroom* which was billed as *Hatchetnation.*

Carrie Nation's unconventional methods did bring attention to the temperance cause, but her boisterous fight for temperance took a personal toll on her life. By 1909, failing health left her unable to continue her lecture tours. Some claimed her health deteriorated because of the physical assaults she had suffered while campaigning, and that those attacks had hastened her death in 1911.

Ladies' Clubs and Professionalism

Because of the feverish pitch of reform causes before and after the Civil War, it is difficult to pinpoint exactly when the women's club movement started since many of the reform organizations served dual purposes of reform activism and socialization with no clear distinction between the two. By the late 1860s, women's clubs had evolved to having a singular club activity. As was so often the case, it was discrimination which spurred the formation of women's clubs. When female journalists were not allowed to attend a reception for Charles Dickens at the New York Press Club, (an all-male association), one of them, Jennie Croly, established a women's club known as The Sorosis (sisterhood). Simultaneously in Boston, Julia Ward Howe, a longtime activist for women's rights, founded the New England Women's Club. The clubs provided literary, artistic, and educational enrichment for women. The organizing of women's clubs was concurrent with a larger movement toward professional organizations in law, medicine and education which all barred females. Joining a women's club gave individual women a sense of belonging and recreation.

In 1890, Julia Ward Howe furthered the women's club movement when she organized a new national organization, the General Federation of Women's Clubs. Susan B. Anthony approved the blossoming "club engrossment by women." Feminist author Charlotte Perkins Gilman believed that the women's club movement marked an important historical development for women, who learned to take the first timid steps toward social organization. Women established such diverse groups as the Ladies of the Grand Army of the Republic, an auxiliary of the Civil War Veterans' Association, the Women's Conference of the Unitarian Association, the Universal Peace Union, the Daughters of the American Revolution, the Women's Division of the Knights of Labor and the Parent Teacher Association. Whether joining professional societies, attending club meetings or working for social reform, women were demanding recognition and designing an agenda for change in America.

African-American Women and Social Reform

African-American women organized themselves into associations but not necessarily for socializing. Unlike white women's clubs, which attracted members from the middle- and upper-class, the black women's club drew women from all walks of life. This new class of professional black women had their work cut out for them. One leader, Fannie Barrier Williams sought solutions to the urgent problems within black communities such as lynching, poverty, unemployment, discrimination and the lack of educational opportunities for young people. In 1893, she delivered the "Intellectual Progress of the Colored Women of the United States since the Emancipation Proclamation" address to black club women, stressing the critical role that black women could play,

> Benevolence is the essence of most of the colored women's organizations. The humane side of their natures has been cultivated to recognize the duties they owe to the sick, the indigent and the ill-fortuned. No church, school or charitable institution for the special use of colored people has been allowed to languish or fail when the associated efforts of the women could save it.

Activist Ida Wells Barnett organized the first anti-lynching campaign, carrying it from the South to the North and Midwest and eventually to England. One can appreciate the challenge for Barnett and her followers. Bringing the crime of lynching to public attention was risky business.

In the process, she confronted entrenched attitudes of hatred and bigotry, such as that of James Jacks, a southern white man who attacked the work of the anti-lynching society and defended lynching in the South on the premise that "all Negroes were immoral." James Jacks' racial slurs stirred Josephine St. Pierre Ruffin to convene a gathering of black women's clubs in Boston in 1895. At the Boston Convention, Josephine Ruffin addressed James Jacks',

> Too long have we been silent under unjust and unholy charges.... Year after year southern women have protested against the admission of colored women into any national organization on the ground of the immorality of these women, and because all refutation has only been tried by individual work, the charge has never been crushed, as it could and should have been at first... It is to break this silence, not by the noisy protestations of what we are not, but by a dignified showing of what we are and hope to become, that we are impelled to take this step, to make of this gathering an object lesson to the world.

The Boston Convention worked as a catalyst for the black women's social crusade. Attendees formed the National Federation of Afro-American Women, under the leadership of Margaret Murray Washington (the wife of Booker T. Washington). The National Federation included some thirty women's clubs. When the National Federation merged with the Colored Women's League of Washington, it became The National Association of Colored Women and elected Mary Church Terrell its first president.

Mary Church Terrell, the daughter of former slaves and a graduate of Oberlin College, along with her associate Frederick Douglass, had appealed to President Benjamin Harrison after the lynching death of a friend, Thomas Moss. They asked the president to address the racial violence of lynching which claimed hundreds of African-Americans every year. When the President offered no support, Mary Church Terrell organized a number of women's groups, including the Colored Women's League and the National Association of Colored Women, to speak out against injustice and discrimination.

In her study, *The Red Record*, Ida Wells-Barnett argued that a flimsy justification for lynching was the concern over interracial marriages and relationships. White communities classified these liaisons as rape, but Ida Wells-Barnett defended the rights of individuals to enter freely into interracial sexual relationships and unions. Contrary to old southern arguments against miscegenation, southerners chose to overlook centuries when black slave women were raped by white men. Ida Wells-Barnett wrote the following editorial which was printed in her paper, *Free Speech,* May 21, 1892. In retaliation for her writing the article, Ida Wells-Barnett's property was destroyed.

> Eight Negroes lynched last Saturday morning. Citizens broke into the penitentiary and got their man; three near Anniston, Ala., one near New Orleans; and three at Clarksville, Georgia. The last three for killing a white man, and five on the same old racket the new alarm about raping white women. The same program of hanging, then shooting bullets into the lifeless bodies was carried out to the letter. Nobody in this section of the country believes in the old threadbare lie that Negro men rape white women. If southern white men are not careful, they will overreach themselves and public sentiment will have a reaction; a conclusion will then be reached which will be very damaging to the moral reputation of their women. But threats cannot suppress the truth. Virtue knows no color line, and the chivalry which depends on complexion of skin and texture of hair can command no honest respect.

To address discrimination, Mary Church Terrell helped establish the National Association for the Advancement of Colored People, (the NAACP). In her book, *A Colored Woman in a White World,* Mary Church Terrell described firsthand the restrictive life for colored women in the late nineteenth and early twentieth centuries.

> For fifteen years I have resided in Washington. As a colored woman I might enter Washington any night, a stranger in a strange land, and walk miles without finding a place to lay my head. Unless I happened to know colored people who live here, or ran across a chance acquaintance who could recommend a colored boardinghouse to me, I should be obliged to spend the entire night wandering about. As a colored woman, I may walk from the Capitol to the White House, ravenously hungry and abundantly supplied with money with which to purchase a meal, without finding a single restaurant in which I would be permitted to take a morsel of food, if it was patronized by white people, unless I were willing to sit behind a screen.

African-American women such as Ida B. Wells-Barnett and Mary Church Terrell campaigned so that African-American women would be included in campaigns granting *all women* the right to vote. Countering their efforts, Susan B. Anthony excluded black women from the National Suffrage Movement, arguing that their inclusion might lose votes with politicians and southern white women. This was an unusual rationale since the South, as a region, did not support women's rights anyway. Nonetheless, Ida B. Wells-Barnett and Mary Church Terrell sought membership in NAWSA, and challenged the exclusionary policy, but Stanton and Anthony would not budge. In response, Ida Wells-Barnett summed up the sentiments of African-American women stating that "although she [Susan B. Anthony] may have made gains for suffrage, she had also confirmed white women in their attitude of segregation." It was clear to Ida Wells-Barnett that the women's suffrage movement was exclusively a white women's suffrage movement. This would leave a mark on the Women's Suffrage crusade, and it would be another sixty years before black women were welcomed into the movement.

NAWSA's discrimination moved Ida Wells-Barnett to form her own organization and work for social change. Ever the optimist, Ida Wells-Barnett did not pursue a separatist policy but worked for an integrated and unified women's suffrage movement. After her appeals to NAWSA for a black women's chapter were denied, she organized a black women's organization, the Alpha Suffrage Club of Chicago. African-American women not only persisted in their own suffrage crusade, but women such as Mary Church Terrell and Ida Wells-Barnett worked to raise the public's awareness of lynching. They campaigned for over sixty years to eradicate the racial violence and lawlessness of lynching from the South.

Immigration to America

Since early settlement, America had been settled in a steady flow of immigration from Europe, Africa and Asia, but increased immigration between 1840-1920 marked a phenomenal growth. Estimates range to as many as twenty-five million new immigrants within that fifty-year span. To appreciate this increase some comparisons before and after the Civil War are instructive. In the pre-war period less than eight percent of the population lived in cities, but by 1890, over twenty-five million Americans resided in urban areas. When New York City became the major port of entry for postwar immigration, the size of the city exploded. In 1850, New York had a population of 1.2 million people; by 1900, it had risen to three million, and in 1910, it had reached five million. Chicago's growth was even more startling. In 1831, the outpost of Chicago boasted only twelve families; in 1860, residents totaled 100,000. In 1900, with a population of two million people, the city of Chicago was second only to New York.

The adjustments and problems which accompanied this massive growth were staggering, with poverty, homelessness, vagrancy, crime, overcrowded housing, disease, traffic congestion and pollution topping the list. Demographic changes took other forms. The population of cities also grew from internal migration. The number of Americans abandoning farm life increased from 1880 to 1890, as Bonanza Farms (corporate owned and operated) pushed traditional family farm operators out of business. In 1900, as new factories offered employment, cities lured rural residents. Of the forty-two million

Americans who lived in cities, eleven million were former farmers who had migrated there.

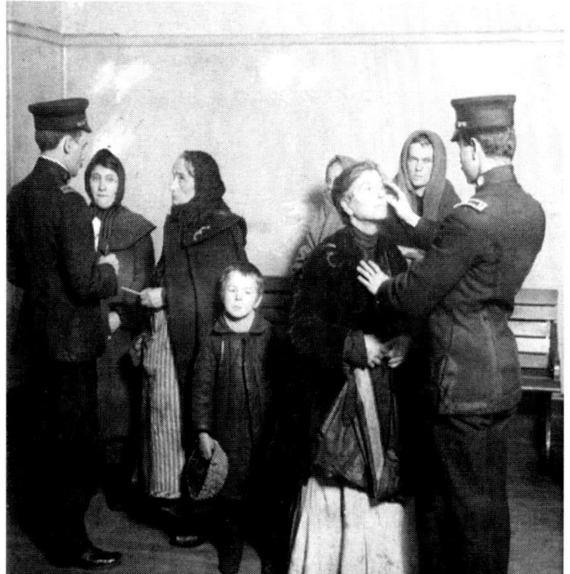

The massive immigration to the United States in the late nineteenth century supplied the cheap labor for industrialization. Here women are being examined during induction at Ellis Island. (Photo Courtesy of the Library of Congress.)

Industry's demand for labor tripled from 1870 to 1890, and industrialists preferred to hire white immigrants over African-American migrants. The mass exodus from the South known as the Great Migration, brought African-Americans north looking for work and for a safer place for their families to live. By 1910, some 500,000 African-Americans from the South had migrated north; and by 1920, over two million had done so. Of that number, only six percent were hired as factory labor; the rest held menial jobs as janitors, waiters, domestic servants or railroad employees.

Some European peasants who immigrated arrived in the United States penniless, and unable to buy land. They were forced to acclimate not only to a new country, culture and government but also to a new work environment in the city. Immigrants flocked to urban centers to find employment in factories. In large cities such as New York, Russian peasants converted sewing skills into the needle trades in the garment sweatshops, and in their cold water tenement flats, they set up a crude cottage industry in which women and children worked for pennies.

Immigrants took the lowest paying jobs. Employers could tap from an abundant labor pool and employees who made the slightest demands were easily replaced. Despite their efforts to unionize, in the late nineteenth and early twentieth centuries, much of the labor force continued to work long hours with no compensation for overtime, work-related injuries, or healthcare. Living at best a marginal existence in good times, the poor felt the crunch most severely when economic crises struck.

With the lure of the Gold Rush in 1849, California attracted thousands of immigrants and people from faraway places came to the American West to strike it rich. Chinese immigrants referred to the journey to California, or the United States, as coming to *gold mountain*. Immigrants from Asia came to the American Pacific Coast; initially the Chinese arrived in the 1860s, as little more than conscripted labor to build the transcontinental railroad linking the West to the East. Asian immigrants were predominantly male laborers. However, from 1870-1890, the Asian immigration pattern shifted as women came to join their husbands or settle permanently with their family.

After the western link of the transcontinental railroad was completed in 1869, and investors had no further need for the Chinese laborers, Congress passed the first law restricting further Chinese immigration to the United States. The Chinese Exclusionary Act of 1882 stopped legal Chinese immigration for ten years. When that law lapsed, the Immigration Act of 1902 made the exclusion of Chinese immigrants a more permanent policy. In addition, the State of California mandated legislation in 1905, excluding Japanese immigrants from the United States, and followed up in 1913, with the Alien Land Law Act which rendered the Japanese ineligible for citizenship and barred them from acquiring property in the state. The 1882 and the 1902 immigration laws coincided with the influx of female Chinese immigrants who came to America to settle or reunite with their families. The legislation left no doubt that United States policy was clearly biased as the majority of immigrants allowed into the country were white Europeans. The Exclusion and Immigration Acts curtailed Asian immigration, but legislation to control European immigration never banned them entirely, and not until the Immigration Acts of 1921 and 1924 set quotas for the numbers of Europeans who could come to America.

Female Immigrant Laborers in the New World

Although very poorly paid, immigrant women and girls worked to contribute to the family's income. From 1870 to 1890, the number of women earning wages rose by almost 66 percent. By 1900, women made up 25 percent of the entire labor force. Thirty percent of all African-American women worked outside the home as compared to only five percent of the women in the middle class. Among recently arrived female immigrants, the numbers were probably much higher. Those figures are harder to determine since immigrant women were not counted as industrial workers on wages. Since working class families could not sustain their households on just one salary, children were not spared from doing harsh labor. Daughters went to work in factories and young boys known as breakers worked in the coal mines by the age of ten. In the cotton mills of North Carolina, young girls worked long hours at the mechanical looms.

In the 1890s some northern states boasted laws *prohibiting* child labor but these laws were ineffective and did nothing more than *regulate the hours* a teenager could work. State labor laws were ignored or flagrantly violated, not only by factory owners but also by the parents of young workers. State child labor laws required children under age fourteen to attend school a requisite number of weeks per year. At the same time, compulsory public education remained a luxury most working families could not afford since they needed their children's labor to survive. In 1900, despite state child labor legislation, one out of every five children under the age of sixteen worked for wages. When legislation was passed cutting back the number of hours children could work, more mothers went to work to supplement their families' incomes. Employers paid meagerly and wages were scaled by class, gender and age. At the turn of the twentieth century, the average male factory worker earned about nine dollars weekly, females about seven, and children even less.

Many African-American and Irish women found employment as domestic servants. For other jobs, it was common to see signs posted which read "Help Wanted, Irish Need Not Apply." Domestic servants were paid almost nothing. Families hiring them justified the cheap wages contending that room and board were an additional expense and had to be deducted from a servant's salary. In practice, the live-in status of domestic servants was just another form of exploitation. Living-in meant that servants were on call around the clock to take care of children and the household. They had little time off and no privacy. The pool of female immigrants needing work made it possible for middle class families to afford live-in servants and to pay them meager wages. In 1900, being an upper-middle-class family meant being able to employ at least four live-in servants. While paying domestic help inadequate wages in return for service 24/7, middle-class families could live comfortably.

Many young immigrant women worked in garment factories, in the printing trade, as clerks in department stores, small shops and businesses. At first, Western Union and Bell Telephone Company hired young boys as operators and clerks, but by 1900, store clerk and telephone operator were regarded as "strictly female" jobs. Rose Schneiderman, a Jewish immigrant from Poland who went to work in the garment district of New York, became a labor advocate, and related her own family's struggle in *A Capmaker's Story.*

> My name is Rose Schneiderman, and I was born in some small city of Russian Poland. When I was about five years of age my parents brought me to this country and we settled in New York. My father got work as a tailor and we lived in two rooms on Eldridge Street. I went to school until I was nine years old, enjoying it thoroughly and making great progress, but then my father died of brain fever and mother was left with three children and another one coming. So I had to stay at home to help her and she went out and got work in a fur

> house, earning about $6 a week, and afterward $8 a week for she was clever and steady. I was the house worker, preparing the meals and looking after the other children the baby, a little girl of six years and a boy of nine. I managed very well though the meals were not very elaborate....I was a serious child, and cared little for children's play, and I knew nothing about the country, so it was not so bad for me as it might have been for another...

Despite the "rags to riches" stories of immigrant success promulgated in popular novels, coming to America was not a positive experience for many immigrants who became disillusioned, destitute and homesick for the old country. Some immigrants returned to their countries of origin. Most of the returnees, the so-called *birds of passage* were men whose departure from the old country had created a hardship on the family left there. Unfortunately, returning often signaled the abandonment of a wife and child in America. Those immigrants who stayed in the United States struggled to survive. They endured poverty and the exploitation of their labor.

Mothers of Invention: Mary Baker Eddy and Christian Science

Mary Baker Eddy was born in 1821, and grew up in New Hampshire. She received no formal education but her brother, a student at Dartmouth College, tutored her. Mary suffered poor health from early childhood and intermittently for the rest of her life. One source describes her symptoms as frequent seizures and nervous collapse. In 1842, she married George Glover and when he died the following year her childhood bouts with seizures resumed. For the next decade, she lived as a semi-invalid. It was her constant struggle with illness that motivated her to seek alternative healing and she eventually founded the Health Religious Movement. Mary married Doctor Daniel Patterson, a dentist and homeopathic practitioner, but his frequent absences and reckless business dealings left her in dire poverty. She went to Portland, Maine, to seek the help of noted physician Dr. Phineas Parkhurst Quimby, and she claimed he cured her. When Dr. Quimby died in 1866, Mary suffered a relapse, divorced her husband and went into confinement again.

Mary Baker Eddy spent the next few years reading the Bible and developing a new system of healing. She proposed that since the mind is the sole reality, the body could be cured by one's mental effort. She attracted a group of followers including Asa G. Eddy, whom she married in 1877. Incorporating her new ideas about healing, in 1879, Mary Baker Eddy established the Church of Christ Scientist and a charter school. In 1886, she began publishing the *Christian Science Journal* and *Science and Health.*

At the Mother Church in Boston, she exerted tremendous influence on her followers, enforcing a rigid authoritarian structure under laws and edicts. Her church grew rapidly, promulgated largely through publications which were made readily available through reading rooms established in every major city in the United States. In 1908, Mary Baker Eddy returned to seclusion but continued to administrate her Church until her death in 1910. The Society publishes *The Christian Science Monitor*, one of the premiere newspapers in the United States.

Women in Medicine and Law

Despite the obstacles to getting ahead in America, a few women entered professions such as medicine and law. A great passion for science attracted Mary Putnam to a career in medicine. In 1866, after her extensive education in the United States, the *Ecole de Medecine* in Paris admitted Mary Putnam as its first female student. Upon return to the United States, she founded a pediatric service, published medical works, instructed female medical students and organized the Association for the Advancement of Women in Medicine. In her publications, she attacked the popular medical theory that intellectual development weakened female reproductive organs and made them invalids. Doctor Mary Putnam-Jacobi was among the first scientists who suspected environmental conditions as a leading cause of disease. As a physician and feminist, she worked actively for women's suffrage.

In 1871, at age twenty-four, Anna Howard Shaw became a licensed Methodist preacher and served in the ministry while attending Albion College. In 1876, after completing Divinity School at Boston University, the New England Conference of Methodist churches had licensed her to preach, but would not allow her to administer the sacraments. Anna Howard Shaw then pursued becoming a doctor. She entered Boston University in 1883, and received a medical degree in record time in 1886.

In the meantime, Anna Howard Shaw took to the lecture circuit, dividing her speaking engagements equally between the causes of women's suffrage and temperance. When she met Susan B. Anthony in 1888, Anna joined the National American Woman Suffrage Association, and served as the vice president from 1892-1904, and president from 1904 -1915.

Although it was easier for women to obtain a law degree in the nineteenth century than a medical degree, the actual practice of law was another matter. There was less formal training involved, and therefore it was easier to access a law education. Most aspiring lawyers unable to attend law school or to purchase expensive law books apprenticed themselves to an established attorney and worked as law clerks. Female clerks encountered little opposition as apprentices, until they applied for a license to practice. Change was evident by 1870, as state legislatures became less tradition bound than the courts on the licensing of female lawyers, and by 1890, states were admitting women to the bar. The loosening of restrictions opened the door to two female legal pioneers, Myra Bradwell and Belva Lockwood. Once arrived in the profession, they worked to remove other legal obstacles which women still encountered.

Myra Bradwell had served as a volunteer in the Sanitary Commission during the Civil War and afterwards studied law with the support of her husband, a judge in Cook County, Illinois. In 1868, she began publishing *The Chicago Legal News,* which became a leading legal journal in the Midwest. Myra Bradwell's application to the bar of the Illinois Supreme Court was rejected. She challenged that decision, citing the legal precedent of an Iowa court which had already admitted a woman in 1868. Myra Bradwell lost the case and appealed to the Supreme Court which upheld the Illinois decision, i.e. that licensing lawyers fell under the purview of states. Justice for Myra and other female attorneys came four years later, when the state legislature of Illinois passed a bill which gave women the right to petition the state bar for a license.

The Illinois Bar admitted Myra Bradwell in 1890, and in 1892, she pleaded a case before the United States Supreme Court. Myra Bradwell's access to present a case before the Supreme Court is credited to Belva Lockwood, who with similar determination had pursued a legal education in Washington, D.C. Belva Lockwood's first application to Columbia College School of Law had been denied because school officials believed that a woman would "distract the attention of the young men." When she completed law studies at the newly formed National University Law School, the administration would not grant her a diploma. It took a formal petition of protest to President Grant to force National University to issue Belva Lockwood's diploma.

When Belva Lockwood argued her first case before the Federal Court of Claims, that court ruled she could not bring any future cases there because of her sex. An exasperated Belva Lockwood wrote "For the first time in my life, I began to realize that it was a crime to be a woman." Like Myra Bradwell, she resorted to changing rather than fighting the laws which barred women from the high courts. She urged Congress to create legislation to allow qualified female attorneys admission to the United States Supreme Court, and her lobbying efforts paid off when such a law was passed in 1879.

Belva Lockwood also secured the legal guarantees of women's property rights in Washington, D.C., and successfully lobbied for female government employees to receive equal pay for equal work. Throughout 1884, Lockwood spoke at women's suffrage conventions to promote herself as a presidential candidate on the National Equal Rights Party ticket. Like her predecessor, Victoria Woodhull, twelve years before, she received no support from national suffrage leaders such as Susan B. Anthony.

Conclusion

In the last decades of the nineteenth century the United States had undergone rapid industrialization which affected every sector of American life including employment, industry, transportation, communication and agriculture. More mechanized machinery increased farm production but the average farm family could not afford to upgrade the harvesting and processing of crops with this more expensive technology. As corporations bought up land and utilized mechanized farming, the small independent farmer simply could not compete. In response, farmers in every region of the country had organized a grassroots movement known as the Farmers' Revolt. Out of that movement a third party, the Populists, emerged. Women took on leadership roles in the Populist Party, which afforded them useful political experience.

Women also organized their own campaign for temperance reform throughout the country. President of the Women's Christian Temperance Union, Frances Willard, extended the crusade to the international level but failed in her attempts to merge temperance and populism.

African-American women organized an anti-lynching campaign, the Colored Women's League and the National Association of Colored Women to fight injustice, violence and discrimination. Excluded from the national crusade for women's rights, African-American women such as Ida B. Wells-Barnett and Mary Church Terrell established local clubs like the Alpha Suffrage Club of Chicago. They and other black women dedicated themselves to a long campaign to rid America of the lawlessness of lynching, and to advocate the voting franchise for all women.

By the close of the nineteenth century, prominent people like Doctors Elizabeth and Emily Blackwell had paved the way for women to enter professions. Teaching, which became the most accessible profession for women, had less to do with liberation than money. The feminization of the teaching profession in America at the end of the nineteenth century is linked to the general decline in wages for teachers in grammar school (at that time, grades one through twelve). As men left teaching for more lucrative jobs, it was much cheaper to pay a female teacher.

Chapter 15
Women's Culture in the Victorian Age
Society is Held Together with Dignity and Civility

Key Topics

Housekeeping in the Victorian Home
The Rites of Courtship and the Institution of Marriage
Victorian Death and Mourning

Chronology

1837 -1901 - Reign of Queen Victoria, the Victorian Era in the United States
1861 - President Lincoln Decrees Thanksgiving a National Day of Prayer and Remembrance
1869 - Catherine Beecher Publishes *The American Woman's Home*

Introduction

Romantic or repressed, prudish or hedonistic, descriptions of Victorians read like a string of incompatible opposites. Indeed, the Victorian era, from 1837 to 1901, is a study in contrast. It epitomized prudery, conservatism and restraint, and at the same time brought bold change in business, transportation and communication in the industrial age. The Victorian age, both eclectic and exciting, is named for Queen Victoria, the icon of propriety.

Upon the death of her uncle in 1837, Victoria, the inspiration for this age, became the Queen of Great Britain and ruled for sixty-four years, longer than any other British monarch. She was crowned at the age of seventeen, celebrated a golden jubilee in 1887, a diamond jubilee in 1897, and died in 1901, at the age of eighty-two. During her reign, Great Britain reached its zenith of territorial dominance as an empire with colonies strewn all over the globe. The period has been stereotyped as conservative, tradition-bound and devotedly Christian.

Queen Victoria not only influenced Great Britain but also the United States, and American society adopted Victorian tastes and sentiments in toto. The Victorian Era in the United States ran parallel to Victoria's reign and featured an emerging middle class acutely aware of its moral responsibility. With more opportunities for social mobility than ever before, the middle class scrambled to take their place, and to make their presence known by living ostentatiously, preserving tradition, adhering to strict social norms and engaging in social reform. They played a critical role in defining the tastes and values of Americans. We note here the focus of this chapter, the culture of Victorian women in the United States refers with little exception only to the life style of middle and upper- class women.

Housekeeping in the Victorian Home

> The perfection of womanhood is the wife and mother, the center of the family, the magnet that draws man to the domestic altar that makes him a civilized being, a social Christian. The wife is truly the light of the home.
>
> *Godey's Lady's Book*

At this time, the Industrial Revolution in America was in high gear and brought great prosperity to the upper classes. The rise in immigration to the United States made available to Victorian women a cheap and steady supply of domestic labor. Middle- and upper-class women, relieved of the drudgery of housework, had more time to entertain at home and to engage in social activities, charity and volunteer causes. Victorian matrons had a busier social life but retained responsibility for the supervision of their children and the overall management of their households.

The Cult of Domesticity and True Womanhood gained nearly religious stature in the nineteenth century. Home, hearth and motherhood were enshrined in Victorian culture. The woman's touch in the home was evident in Victorian tastes and an interest in things domestic. Unlike her predecessor, the Victorian housewife had more conveniences and housekeeping information at her fingertips. This did not make things easier, however, because Victorians set high standards and housework followed a regimented routine.

Most women spent time in the kitchen. They baked the family's bread, cakes and pies at least once a week. At mid-century only ten percent of all bread consumed in the United States was commercially baked. Fifty years later, that figure had only risen to 25 percent. Baking and cooking remained tedious chores even with the conveniences of new stoves like the Sterling Range, which had separate baking and roasting ovens, but it required some ingenuity to maintain wood or coal stoves burning at a steady rate.

The introduction of home appliances and kitchen gadgets such as mills, grinders, egg beaters and mass-produced standardized bowls, colanders, bakeware, and cookware were welcomed conveniences. The Lovell hand-cranked rubber wringer for clothes offered the latest high tech solutions to the tedium of wringing the clothes and large bed linens by hand, and alleviated the "weekly affliction" of wash day for the housewife and servants. Some appliances were not necessarily convenient. In 1888, Sears & Roebuck manufactured a washing machine with a paddle agitator for clothes that operated by means of a fly wheel. It sold for $3.50, but consumers did not rush to buy one. This washing machine operated with a limited capacity, and the early models tore up the clothes, leaked, and left rust stains on clothing. Ironing clothes was another tedious chore. Garments were heavily starched, and flatirons made of heavy cast iron were awkward to use and had to be reheated continuously. Clothing required the use of several different flatirons for different parts of a garment.

Victorians covered their floors with heavy carpets or rugs which were cleaned by sweeping, or they were hung on a clothesline and beaten. Sears and Bissell made an early version of the vacuum cleaner which required hand cranking to activate pistons. It was inadequate, very expensive, blew dust everywhere and spread the dirt back on the floor. In 1873, the Bissell Carpet Sweeper Company introduced a push-type carpet sweeper on wheels which, until electric vacuum cleaners were invented, was the only effective means to clean carpet. Rugs and carpets could be sent out for commercial steam cleaning for about two dollars each. Some housewives splurged and had rugs done commercially for the ritual spring cleaning. After a serious illness in the family, all bedding, curtains and rugs were cleaned thoroughly and in some cases burned and replaced.

Furnishing a Victorian Home

The style of the Victorian home reflected the woman who lived there and defined her as well. In the nineteenth century, the shift to the mass production of furniture allowed the middle class to decorate on a grand scale. Sears and Roebuck's catalogues of the era offered whole suites of sturdy oak furniture at prices ranging from $50 to $100.

Furniture became more gender defined, especially chairs, which were designed differently for men and women. Chairs for men, built larger in scale, allowed them to relax. They featured high backs for comfort and sturdy arms to support men's bodies. The lady's chair was not intended for comfort but for the conformation of the woman's body. A lady's chair was smaller in scale, lower in height and armless to accommodate sitting down with multiple layers of clothing, a bustle, or a hoop skirt. A lady was expected to sit erect in the chair with hands folded in her lap, and clothes modestly draped over the furniture. Women were not supposed to lean, slouch, lounge or get comfortable while seated even in the privacy of their own home. Other gender specific furniture pieces included men's and women's dressers, men's smoking chairs, men's desks' and ladies' writing tables and the ladies fainting couch which was similar to a chaise. The fainting couch accommodated women whose corsets were so tight and their breathing so restricted that they suffered weakness from lack of oxygen. It was assumed that if they fainted, a fainting couch nearby would hold them as they collapsed.

By the nineteenth century, women decorated their homes with curtains, draperies, lace doilies, slipcovers, carpets, tapestries, pictures, ceramics, china, glassware, and other collectibles. They busied themselves with intricate needlework, quilt making, lace tatting, appliqué, embroidery, knitting and crocheting, and all in an effort to beautify their space. Victorians, fascinated by exoticism, filled their homes with mementoes and souvenirs from their travels to faraway places. Victorian women regarded their homes as conservatories and cultivated plants, especially exotic ones such as palms and ferns. If space permitted, they dedicated an entire room as a solarium (sun room) to contain an indoor garden and unusual plants. They were especially fond of floral motifs and embellished them on clothing, fabric and china.

The most public area of the home was the front hall, or vestibule, where guests were received. In the entry stood a hall tree, an accessory with special compartments to hold guests' coats, hats, gloves, walking canes, and umbrellas, and an attractive silver tray where visitors left their calling cards. Adjoining the entry hall was the parlor, or sitting room, which was used for formal occasions and usually housed musical instruments

The Sewing Machine

Since tailor-made clothing was expensive, making the family's clothes helped stretch the budget. During this era, the ladies magazines added more incentive for home sewing by reproducing fashion color plates, and *Godey's Ladies' Book*, was one of the first to feature mail order dress patterns. Companies such as Butterick sold commercial ready-made patterns.

Elias Howe's invention of the sewing machine made sewing much easier. By mid-century, the chief manufacturer of sewing machines, the I.W. Singer Company, sold over 200,000 per year. At a cost of $75, a sewing machine was an expensive purchase for the average family. I.W. Singer, in a clever marketing ploy, offered installment buying and organized sewing clubs for housewives. In sewing clubs, women pooled their money to purchase one sewing machine which club members shared. The sewing machine not only revolutionized women's work, but in a short time a Singer paid for itself and became the most cost-effective equipment in the home.

Women skilled at dressmaking hired themselves out to make clothing for other women and earned extra income. Major sewing projects were undertaken in the spring and winter seasons. A housewife would hire a dressmaker to spend a few weeks with her, and together they would make clothing for the entire family.

The public responded enthusiastically to the sewing machine. Many believed it would prove a blessing to womankind, clothe the poor, and be useful for churches and other associations in their charitable efforts and missionary work. Ladies' magazines also extolled it, but once the sewing machine became the means to mass produce clothing, it quickly became the tool of a sweatshop industry. Factory owners hired young men, women and children, usually immigrants, to make garments, hats, purses and shoes. Bent over sewing machines in dimly lit rooms, garment workers would labor under abysmal working conditions and were paid a pittance.

Holidays, Celebrations and Entertaining

Victorians enjoyed entertaining and invited family and friends to their homes on many special occasions. Children were encouraged in music lessons and women were expected to entertain guests by playing the piano or organ. Victorians instituted many of the holidays and customs we celebrate today such as sending cards for Valentines Day, Christmas and birthdays.[1] They also instituted special holidays such as Mother's Day, Father's Day, and Children's Day, but well into the nineteenth century, most Americans did not observe Thanksgiving or Christmas. Up to this time, Thanksgiving had only been commemorated in New England, its place of origin. During the Civil War, President Abraham Lincoln made Thanksgiving a national holiday, a day of prayer and feasting, but it was Sara Josepha Hale who had endorsed the last Thursday in November from "this time forth as long as our Banner of stars floats on the breeze," to be the day when American families "enjoy a national union and feast of gladness rendering thanks to Almighty God for the blessings of the year."

The long-standing Dutch tradition of Christmas celebration did not catch on quickly and this holiday observance in America varied from region to region. Christmas was celebrated in the South, but New England churches denounced it as a pagan holiday. The popularity of Christmas spread after the introduction of steel construction in the nineteenth century. This made possible the multi-storied American Department Stores which were built as temples of commerce. Merchants looked for ways to attract customers to the new stores and pitched products to Victorian housewives who took to shopping with almost religious zeal. Then Christmas became a national holiday celebrated throughout the country. To promote Christmas as a children's holiday, catalogues displayed clothing designed for children, children's books and a wider variety of toys than ever before.

Christmas stories such as Charles Dickens' *A Christmas Carol*, O. Henry's *The Gift of the Magi*, and Clark Clement Moore's *A Visit from Saint Nicholas* promoted gift-giving and conveyed a sense of miraculous and magical events on Christmas Eve. These stories promoted the Christmas season and helped create the modern commercial Christmas, a genuine Victorian holiday. Author Penne Restad points out in *Christmas in America* that the Christmas holiday was not gradually subverted into a commercial enterprise; it was created *specifically* for that purpose. The success of Christmas, the most celebrated family holiday of the year, can also be credited to Victorian mothers who added all the trimmings — baked goods, gifts, decorations, a tree, caroling and music, entertaining, crafts and sewing projects all in an effort to make the holiday special for their children.

Whether celebrating or entertaining, Victorian society made clear how men and women should conduct themselves down to the last detail. The formal dinner party, for example, distinguished what men versus women ate and drank. When Victorians sat down to a formal dinner the usual bill of fare consisted of twelve to eighteen courses. Since it was never appropriate to be fashionably late, guests were expected to arrive fifteen minutes early. Each gentleman present offered a female guest his arm and escorted her in formal procession into the dining room where all took their places at a magnificent table. The individual place settings of silver flatware could number as many as fifteen separate utensils and an individual china place setting could exceed thirty pieces. No pre-dinner drinks were served, as Victorians started feasting promptly.

Dinner lasted at least three hours. During the meal, each of the courses was accompanied by a different wine. Although a lady might be served as many as twelve glasses of wine, she sipped daintily, while the men drank gustily. After dinner, ladies regrouped to a smaller drawing room for tea, coffee and little finger cakes. Gentlemen retired to a men's drawing room to

1. Before the nineteenth century, birthdays were not widely celebrated. Poor working-class people, and of course slaves, were usually unaware of their date of birth.

enjoy a fine cigar and heavier drinks. To stage a formal dinner required a full staff of servants and butlers, but a middle-class lady could *make do* with four or five live-in servants to help with serving.

The Rites of Courtship

By the nineteenth century, society marked the age of sixteen as the time when a young lady progressed from girlhood to womanhood. Before age sixteen, young girls behaved in a carefree manner wearing dresses just above the ankle, and their long hair loose and flowing. Although boys were given much wider berth, girls could also engage in games and outdoor activities such as cycling, sleigh riding, ice-skating and stick-ball. Opinions on female participation in sports were mixed. Some doctors thought exercise was beneficial for girls and others believed it was harmful, but everyone did agree that when a girl reached puberty, sometime between fourteen and sixteen years old (by the onset of menses), the time for frivolous games ended and her new status as a young woman began. Her clothes signified a change in her appearance. Frances Willard expressed her dismay over coming of age, writing in her journal that,

> Mother insists that at last I must have my hair done-up woman-fashion. My back hair is twisted like a corkscrew; I wear eighteen hairpins; my head aches miserably; my feet are tangled in the skirt of my hateful new gown. I can never jump over a fence again as long as I live.

A young woman's coming out in society marked the time for her to participate in the courtship ritual by putting her hair in an "up do," and wearing a floor length dress which covered her ankles. Not all families believed that *young girls* should wear a dress reformer or corset, but for *young ladies* it was a mandatory detail of refinement. In her new attire, a young woman advertised her eligibility for marriage, and could receive gentleman callers. A young man's visit was limited to fifteen minutes, but if he seemed like a good prospect, the length of the next visit might be extended to thirty minutes. In return, a young lady could pay a call at a suitor's home to show him that she was interested.

Young ladies of the Victorian era would mark the time of coming out. To announce their availability to be courted, they no longer wore their hair down. An upsweep was the proper hairdo when a young woman came of age. (Photo courtesy of the Archives of the Fullerton College Library.)

Etiquette books came into wider use in the nineteenth century. The books informed middle-class Victorians and guided them through the processes of courtship, marriage, birth, death and mourning and various other social situations. *Godey's Lady's Book,* for instance, offered advice on courting to young women. It was acceptable for ladies to flirt in order to show off their charms and social graces.

> Flirting is to marriage what free trade is to commerce. By it the value of a woman is exhibited, tested, her capacities known, her temper displayed, and the opportunity offered of judging what sort of wife she may become.

While condoning this kind of behavior seems manipulative, Victorians did not see it that way. Author Harvey Green explains in *Light of the Home, An Intimate View of the Lives of Women in Victorian America,*

> Although this suggests that a woman was passively marketing herself to men, much as a horse trader could a race horse, flirting offered a woman some control over her situation. Since she could not properly propose marriage, her only real choice was among the men who expressed an interest in her. Flirtatious behavior gave her the opportunity to broaden that network of eligible and interesting men, enabling her to make a wiser choice about which man she would allow to court her and which proposal she would accept.

Victorians structured social visitation into an absurd formality. For one thing, the social call was not for the obvious intention of seeing or visiting with someone. In the days before the telephones, cell phones, faxes and E-mail, no rapid form of communication existed other than telegraph which was generally used only by businesses. Since the person being called upon had no forewarning of the visit, they often were not at home, so the visitor left a calling card with a servant. Even if the residents were at home, unless visitors were coming for a specific social event, servants were often instructed to tell callers that the residents were not at home or were indisposed. As Green explains, "this formal procedure allowed people to communicate their social intentions without face-to-face interaction." If the person called upon, wished to socialize with the caller, they responded by calling on the caller, following the same formality, and leaving their card. This seemingly endless round of visitation became highly ritualized.

With the exception of the gentleman's courting calls, women of the middle class made most home visitations. Victorians followed a protocol for calling cards which noted specific circumstances. When leaving a calling card, one folded it to encode a specific message. A fold on the upper right corner denoted that the caller had delivered the card herself. Folding the upper left corner indicated that the caller wished to extend congratulations of some sort. When making a call to say good-bye, one folded the lower right corner; folding the lower left corner expressed sympathy and condolences. If the card was folded in half, the caller stated she had visited to call upon all the ladies of the house, not one person in particular.

While the Victorian custom of calling seems rigidly formalized, it made rituals like courtship less intimidating. A gentleman showed his interest by leaving his card but if the lady did not reciprocate, he was spared a face-to-face rejection. During courtship, young people engaged in many of the same activities which had occupied couples in previous centuries such as skating, canoeing, sleigh riding, choral fests, picnics and church activities. By the nineteenth century badminton and croquet were added. Bicycling allowed courting couples more freedom and privacy to get away to an isolated spot. Young people also attended parties, concerts, balls, luncheons and teas where they socialized under the watchful eyes of adults. By the 1890s, it was permissible for courting couples to go away for a weekend together as long as they were chaperoned by a married couple.

Music and dancing remained popular forms of socializing, but were more formalized in the nineteenth century. Dance cards and dance programs, and a complete protocol, guided a young lady on every aspect of the event. Etiquette specialist, Annie R. White in her book, *Polite Society at Home and Abroad*, recommended the following procedure when ladies arrived at the dance,

> The ladies' room must be provided with several glasses, brushes, combs, hair pins, and all the accessories of the toilet. A maid must be ready to assist the ladies. After the ladies have adjusted their toilets, they rejoin their escorts, proceed to the ballroom, advance toward the hostess and pay their respects in a few well- chosen words.

If a lady was escorted to the ball, she was expected to dance the first dance with her escort. One could avoid dancing with a less desirable person by filling up the dance card with names of more desirable partners, but etiquette demanded that one never dance with a likeable partner for more than two dances as this would encourage gossip. Refusing to dance with someone when there was space on your card was considered impolite, but in some situations, a lady could refuse to dance with a man if he behaved rudely, or had danced with another woman too much during the evening. In Mrs. Annie R White's etiquette guide, ten pages are devoted to the protocol of dancing and attending balls, including everything from sending invitations and receiving them to the procedure of the dance itself. Mrs. White covered every possible situation to help readers avoid embarrassment or a difficult situation,

> Young men sometimes commit the error of fancying that it is impolite to leave a young lady's side until some other gentleman engages her in conversation. Such an idea places both parties under restraint. It is good manners to excuse yourself and to seek the society of another, after having shown some attention to a lady.

Victorian Floral Language

The Flower	***The sentiment*:**
Acacia	friendship
Azalea	temperance
Barberry	sharp temper
Sweet Basil	good wishes
Bluebells	constancy
Buttercup	prosperity
Clover, 4 leafed	be mine
White Clover	think of me
White Carnation	innocence
Yellow Carnation	disdain
Rose buds	confession of love
Red rose	love
Yellow rose	jealous lover

Families discouraged courting couples from exchanging expensive gifts. For a lady, a gift of flowers or candy was acceptable. For a gentleman, a handmade gift such as a watercolor, a scrapbook or an album was appropriate. Once couples announced their engagement, usually at a formal family dinner, gifts began to pour in. The Reverend Henry Ward Beecher constantly warned against buying extravagant engagement or wedding gifts. But among the middle class the competition to "outdo the Joneses" lead to more lavish gift buying with each succeeding decade. Sending flowers as gifts was a highly specialized practice and choosing exactly the right flowers was important. Victorians obeyed a subtle language of flowers, and etiquette books described over 500 different flowers, including what they symbolized and their sentiment. The wise suitor consulted the flower glossary before making his selection for someone special.

A Victorian couple pose for their engagement photo. The young lady's clothing would have been suitable as a wedding outfit as well.

The suitor chose an engagement ring of a diamond, pearl, ruby, sapphire, or amethyst in a solitaire setting. If he could not afford an expensive engagement ring, he purchased a gold wedding band, which the prospective bride wore on her left third finger until the wedding. Before the Victorian era, a white wedding gown was not customary. Out of practical necessity, a bride wore dark colors such as brown, blue or gold satin so she could wear the dress of a fashionable color after the wedding. It was over the course of the nineteenth century that the wedding ceremony became an extravagant event. The Victorian bride was expected to wear her wedding dress on formal occasions during the first year of marriage and on her first anniversary. A home wedding held in a garden setting was the favorite of the era. Victorians also instituted the custom of doing the couples' wedding portrait and sending guests home with handmade mementoes or souvenirs of the nuptials.

The Wedding Ceremony

Queen Victoria introduced the current wedding fashion by wearing an opulent white gown for her winter wedding in February of 1840, to Prince Albert of Saxe-Coburg-Gotha. This practice caught on almost immediately with brides in England and America, who chose plain white gowns for their wedding as well. By the end of the nineteenth century, Victoria's white wedding gown came to symbolize a bride's purity, virginity, piety, and innocence. Another custom derived from Victoria's wedding was having many attendants, especially bridesmaids who represented the world the bride was leaving. Wedding etiquette required that bridesmaids be maidens, that is virgins and younger than the bride.

This wedding photo features a bride in a white gown. The custom of brides wearing white was introduced by Queen Victoria.

Victorians also obsessed on staging the "perfect wedding," and instituted the honeymoon vacation with trips to Niagra Falls, the Adirondacks, or other getaways. Etiquette manuals advised honeymooners to avoid embarrassment by not advertising their newlywed status while staying at hotels and resorts. One manual recommended that the couple remove any telltale signs of their newlywed status by spreading newspapers on the floor to catch any grains of rice that fell from their clothing. Honeymooners, and for that matter all couples, refrained from any displays of affection in public. Victorian advice manuals censured kissing in public or in private except under the most ideal conditions.

Victorian custom dictated that engaged couples be chaperoned when traveling. (Photo courtesy of the Archives of the Fullerton College Library.)

During the first year of marriage, an endless round of dinner parties to honor the newlyweds were hosted by the couple's family, wedding party attendants and close friends. Social rules dictated that the bride also hold several teas, luncheons, and receptions to receive guests in her new home. Annie R. White offered advice on the adjustment period after marriage. She suggested that the couple should live alone without interference from relatives, and a bride must overlook her husband's faults, keep no secrets from him and maintain a neat home. She should keep herself attractive for her husband, not conceal any bills, or confide in anyone but him. Whether in the public eye, or in the privacy of her own home, a wife must first and foremost maintain ladylike behavior. The wife must be gentle, frank, honest and courteous to her husband, and "perfect in all things."

Mothers of Invention: Catherine Beecher and the Domestic Economy

Catherine Beecher, the daughter of the Reverend Lyman Beecher, a celebrated New England minister, took on maternal responsibilities for her siblings when her mother died in 1816. Catherine, the eldest daughter at age sixteen, also taught school and at age twenty-three organized the Hartford Female Seminary in Hartford, Connecticut, which became a prestigious private academy for girls.

Catherine developed domestic science as part of the college curriculum but drew a sharp line between the advancement of a woman's work and the advancement of a woman's rights, as she explained in her *Treatise on the Domestic Economy*:

> Women have an equal interest in all social and civil concerns and that no domestic, civil or political institution, is right, that sacrifices her interest to promote that of the other sex. But in order to secure her the more firmly in all these privileges, it is decided, that in the domestic relation, she take a subordinate station, and that in the civil and political concern, her interest be entrusted to the other sex, without her taking any part in voting, or in making and administering the laws.

Her book, *The American Woman's Home,* established Catherine Beecher as an authority on all things domestic. This popular manual was consulted by women of succeeding generations. At a time when young women were leaving home and settling great distances from family, Catherine's book was a handy source for advice on housekeeping. In 1869, the expanded edition of her book, *The American Woman's Home*, was a pioneering study of interior design which pre-empted by sixty years, time-motion engineering studies, environmental standards in the home, and modern trends in home construction. Because she felt a woman's place was in the home, Catherine believed no one else was better qualified to design it. Her designs featured light, airy, unadorned, clean, and all around wholesome dwellings. She prioritized topics such as the comfort and health of the occupants and the ease of maintaining the home. On blueprints, she plotted the number of steps a housewife would tread in completing chores and designed the spaces accordingly to maximize efficiency. She took into account proper sanitation and ventilation of the home, and discussed organic gardening, housekeeping, cooking and nutrition, personal hygiene, medicinal cures and health care. She described in some detail how to efficiently utilize a then state-of-the-art cook stove complete with rotisserie, a boiler compartment for hot water and a convection oven. The book also detailed the proper care of livestock.

The effect and response to Catherine Beecher's designs for the American home were positive and immediate. The Massachusetts Institute of Technology, which was established as one of the first schools of architecture in the United States in 1857, began admitting women in 1880. Louise Blanchard Bethune became the first female architectural graduate and the first woman admitted to the American Institute of Architects. Others such as Sophia Hayden and Minerva Parker Nichols would follow. Although construction and architecture had long been male domains, women took on these careers more easily than those women who aspired to enter the medical or legal professions. Catherine Beecher had carved a niche for women to design living spaces, and female architects gained easier access to the profession.

Clio's Corner - What Have Historians Said about Victorian Female Relationships?

Dramatic social changes in the nineteenth century resulted in very different living arrangements and lifestyles for women. More women lived the single life or developed more intimate relationships with other females and spinsterhood became more commonplace. Friendships in which women shared the same household were termed a "Boston marriage." The letters and diaries of these women indicate that some of the friendships were sexual in nature, based on romantic notions of love, and were part of the liberating experience for women.

For her study of female relationships in eighteenth and nineteenth-century America, Carroll Smith-Rosenberg, in "The Female World of Love and Ritual," gleaned women's correspondence of that bygone era. She points out that prior to the twentieth century, society had viewed sexual behavior differently. From a contemporary vantage point, we perceive our ancestors as prudish and narrow-minded, but Professor Smith-Rosenberg's research shows that their cultural norms allowed for greater freedom because many women had a different regard for same-sex relationships. Women had bonded with each other emotionally and intimately in relationships which society regarded as natural. Young girls formed close same-sex friendships which continued after marriage.

The criteria in pre-Freudian society for sexual relationships, friendship, courting and heterosexual marriage were based on different assumptions and experiences. Girls and boys socialized with their own gender and had little contact with each other. Because men and women grew up in "relatively homogenous and segregated sexual groups," marriage posed a major adjustment for members of the opposite sex. After marriage, the close ties between female friends did not diminish, and in fact may have facilitated the difficult transition to married life. This adjustment period might involve a female friend or friends accompanying the bride on her honeymoon or making frequent home visitations to the newlyweds.

Friendships among women were emotionally as well as physically intense. Among married women, the visit of female relatives or close female friends was anticipated with great excitement. The female guest and hostess often occupied the same bed and in such instances the *master* of the house was directed to sleep elsewhere. Other changes which occurred in the nineteenth century also promoted female partnering.

Until the nineteenth century, with the exception of women in religious orders (where communal living had existed for centuries), it was rare for women to live together as partners or for women to move away from home other than in marriage. For the first time, with the advent of female academies, women's colleges, and mill town factory boarding houses, all-female dormitory living arrangements were provided. Women were living together, separately from men, and becoming economically self-sufficient. Under these conditions, young women formed bonds of friendship and committed to long lasting female relationships.

Lillian Faderman, in *Odd Girls and Twilight Lovers: A History of Lesbian Life in the Twentieth Century*, indicates that these new living arrangements made a difference in women's life choices. Between 1880 and 1900, some ten percent of American women did not marry, but among those young women who went off to college, 50 percent remained single.

Victorian Death and Mourning

> I am now a Widow, I have no bosom friend to go to in seasons of perplexity for advice, no one with whom I can unreservedly share all my griefs and Sorrows, [sic] all my Joys and pleasures. I did love him, alas but too tenderly. We lived together on such terms as man and wife ought to live, placing perfect confidence in each other, hearing one another's burdens and making due allowances for human imperfection.
>
> From the Diary of
> Sarah Ripley Stearns, 1818

Americans in the nineteenth century experienced death at every turn and on a wide scale. Severe epidemics of cholera broke out in 1832, 1849 and 1866, and there were also intermittent outbreaks of typhoid, typhus, diphtheria, and poliomyelitis. Smallpox, the only communicable disease for which there was an inoculation, still claimed victims, and devastating epidemics returned in 1872 and 1873. In the era before immunization and antibiotic drugs, childhood diseases such as scarlet fever, measles and mumps were so virulent that many children did not survive to the age of six. Between 1861-1865, when the North and South made war on each other and over 600,000 men died in the Civil War, death and grief became a national observance.

Women played a significant role in these life passages. Mothers nursed family members back to health and helped each other when members of the community were stricken with severe illness. Women who assisted other females in childbirth were familiar with the dangers it imposed on the mother and the newborn. Before the twentieth century people were medically treated, convalesced and died in their homes. Children were accustomed to seeing family members die and corpses were laid out for viewing in the home. In all these situations, visitations to the sick and the dying were the women's responsibility. Before morticians and funeral parlors institutionalized death and grieving, it was the midwife's job to prepare the corpse for burial.

In order to cope with the losses of loved ones, Victorians devised an intricate ritual of mourning. By the 1870s, mourning had become chiefly the domain of women; mourning and grieving were, by definition, expressions of sentiment and emotion, aspects of human nature which the nineteenth century society relegated to the preserve of women. Moreover death was a religious issue and by the 1870s religion itself had become the domain and responsibility of women.

One clergyman promoted this role for women because he believed that women were more pious, more sympathetic, and more gentle than men. Indeed, Victorians had worked out a simple syllogism— mourning was emotional, and since females were emotional creatures they should be the official mourners.

Although funeral parlors (an extension of the Victorian parlor), funeral directors, and new burial practices were introduced in the Victorian era, many families preferred to hold the viewing of the corpse at home; but as practices changed, feminine influences were seen in Victorian funerary arrangements. Caskets, both the name and the shape were adopted from women's jewelry boxes known as jewelry caskets. Funeral caskets, which were much more ornate, replaced the former simple wooden coffins. Attention to details like embalming to preserve the body, dressing the body in clothing rather than a shroud, and using makeup for a more lifelike appearance on the corpse, were all meant to give the impression that the deceased was simply sleeping in their Sunday-go-to-meeting clothes, awaiting departure for the journey. With the invention of photography, Victorians memorialized their departed loved ones by taking pictures of them on their deathbeds or in open caskets. Postmortem photography also became a means to document a death. Victorians were particularly fond of taking pictures of deceased children. Mothers would make a memorial picture of the deceased, embellished with a needlework border, to hang in the parlor, near a vase of fresh flowers, creating an altar or shrine.

These elaborate preparations and memorials all emphasized the Victorian way of death, a perception that in the afterlife the deceased went to reside in heaven, an idyllic place. Like most facets of Victorian life, mourning rites were formalized, both public and private. An evergreen funerary wreath with a purple ribbon placed on the front door signified a death in the household. Inside the curtains were drawn and the windows festooned with black crepe. Clocks were stopped at the hour of the departed's death and remained at that time for the entire mourning period. Mirrors were covered up so the dead person's spirit might not be trapped in the looking glass. Candles were left burning during the first twenty-four hours after a death as a vigil. All those in mourning wore black. Family members kept the daytime vigil, and servants, also wearing black mourning clothes, took the night shift.

The rules for mourning widows were quite rigid and marked by three stages of grieving during which social activities and clothing were carefully prescribed. The widow's first stage of mourning, considered *deep mourning,* was the most intense. For three months after the death of her husband, she observed complete seclusion, going out only to attend church services. The only visitor she could receive was her minister. During the first stage, the widow did not participate in any activities outside the home. She dressed completely in black, could wear no jewelry, and when attending church masked her face with a black veil. One etiquette manual suggested a widow's undergarments should also be black.

> If a lady lifted her skirt ascending her carriage to avoid a puddle, she must show by her black petticoat, and black stockings that her mourning had penetrated her innermost sanctuary.

A widow was expected to mourn for a period ranging from eighteen months to two and a half years (it varied from region to region). When changing clothes, one never left mourning clothes out, as this was considered bad luck. During the Civil War, because women were expected to do war work and communities were in constant mourning, some of the rules for first-stage widows were slightly relaxed.

Immediately following the death of a loved one, the grieving family sent out mourning notices. Victorians were so intent on not making any *faux pas* regarding mourning rites that they consulted special mourning etiquette books sold in mourning shops.[2] As the widow proceeded through the next two stages, family and friends were alerted to her progress by her clothing, activities and type of stationery she used. It was a serious error to use mourning objects inappropriately; for example while one would receive a letter from a widow on mourning stationery, no one would send a letter *to a mourner* on mourning stationery.

The second stage, known as *public or non-joyous mourning*, lasted about one year. During this period, the widow wore a lighter veil, her clothing might be embellished with some lace and black jewelry, but she could not wear anything shiny such as gold or silver jewelry. Victorian widows also introduced a new craft for mourning, called hair jewelry. Some of the deceased person's hair was woven or braided into a necklace, bracelet, ring or watch fob. The braided and woven hair of the deceased was used to frame a memorial picture of the dead person which was then placed on display in the home.

The third stage, *half-mourning,* began the second year when the widow cast off black clothing and wore grey, lavender, deep purple, or mauve garments. At half-mourning, the widow could attend social events, but had to behave somberly. Finally, when mourning was complete, the widow marked the end of her seclusion by coming out into society again. Chaperoned by a female friend, she visited friends and neighbors, or left her calling card.

By comparison, the mourning process for a widower was much easier. His mourning period lasted one year. Since a widower had to conduct business as usual, he went back to work immediately after the funeral. A widower's mourning clothes consisted of a black suit, black gloves, black necktie and a hat with a deep black band. He, like his children, was expected to refrain from social activities. If a widower remarried within the first year of his wife's death, (and many did), his new bride was expected to wear black and mourn his deceased wife along with him. Children wore black clothing for one year when mourning for a parent. Women also mourned and went into seclusion when an in-law died. Society prescribed that parents mourn the death of a child for one year, the death of a grandparent for six months, and the death of an aunt, uncle, or cousin for three months.

Although these mourning practices appear extreme and maudlin to us today, Victorian rites served a useful purpose. Ritualized grief gave people a means to express their loss. Guidelines in etiquette books took the guesswork out of how to deal with grieving families. By following the rules one avoided offending people when they were most vulnerable. Those in mourning wore black to alert others of their loss and offered them an opportunity to express empathy and support. As Mrs. Annie R. White stated,

> Much can be said in favor of the custom. A mourning dress is a protection against the thoughtless or cruel inquiries. It is also in consonance with the feelings of the one bereaved, to whom brightness and merriment seem almost a mockery

2. Mourning shops were stores devoted entirely to funerary objects which were needed for the grieving period, articles such as clothes and stationery.

> of the woe into which they have been plunged. With such, garments of mourning are 'An outward sign of inward sorrow,' and they cling to them as the last token of respect and affection which they can pay the dead.

In its entirety the ritual of mourning brought Victorians comfort and the compassionate support of their community. Some aspects of the Victorian custom are surprising. After a widow succeeded through the mourning stages, she actually had more freedom than a married or single woman. Although the death of her husband meant that she was burdened with more responsibilities, she was also freer to attend to her own affairs. Considering what we have described here, it is surprising also that a widow could be courted. Indeed, when a suitor paid a call it was considered bad taste for a widow to wear her mourning clothes. While it would be hard for us to gauge what was too much by Victorian standards, when individuals grieved excessively or mourning practices were prolonged or extreme, the family minister might chastise the mourners. The clergy insisted that death was simply God's call to come home, nothing more. The Reverend Henry Ward Beecher, speaking on the Victorian practice of grieving, admonished his congregants to: "Draw not over yourselves the black tokens of pollution. Do not blaspheme by naming that despair, which is triumph and eternal life." The Reverend Beecher went so far as to encourage mourners to abandon wearing black altogether, but his parishioners refused and clung to the custom. Vesting in black remained the practice. Nevertheless, Reverend Beecher's advice was not completely ignored. His suggestion to send flowers to the family or to the funeral parlor, as a token of remembrance and a symbol of life, was adopted wholeheartedly.

Conclusion

The Cult of True Womanhood and Domesticity reached its full development in the Victorian period. The upper and middle class in the United States embraced and adhered to the values, rules and rituals of Victorian culture. Victorian society left no doubt about how people were to interact and they prescribed every facet of human interaction from courtship, marriage and funerary practices to architecture, interior décor, fashion design, entertaining and holiday traditions. Striving to better themselves, middle-class Americans were assured that by following Victorian norms they too were people of refined tastes and sensibility.

Social roles for women held them to a rigid standard of perfection. Victorian housekeepers were expected to manage large households efficiently and decorously. However, conveniences such as cheap domestic labor and new home appliances made life for the middle and upper classes much easier and gave Victorian matrons leisure time for entertaining, shopping, making social calls, and doing charity and reform work in their community.

Victorians instituted many of the traditions we celebrate today such as sending gifts, cards and flowers on special holidays, as well as commemorating Thanksgiving as a national holiday. The Victorians initiated the modern celebration of Christmas.

Lifestyles and living arrangements for Victorian women offered them more choices. As more girls lived together in factory boardinghouses or in college dormitories, lifelong friendships and intimate committed relationships were forged with one another. Spinsterhood became more commonplace as more women preferred and freely chose the single life.

Victorians created and institutionalized modern funerary practices. The rites of mourning were highly ritualized and a greater responsibility for the grieving process was placed on women.

Chapter 16
Women's Health in the Nineteenth Century
What Ails Our American Women?

Key Topics

Women's Fashion of the Victorian Era
Childbirth and Motherhood
Medical Theory and Practice
Changes in Women's Medical Treatment

Chronology

1800 - 1890 - The Demographic Transition
1809 - Dr. Mc Dowell Performs Abdominal Surgery
1847 - Founding of the American Medical Association, Philadelphia
1868 - 1880 - Epidemic of Child Bed Fever in American Hospitals

Introduction

The nineteenth century marked a transition in the history of medicine. At this time physicians adhered to old theories and therapies, but also incorporated untested new procedures and techniques. Allopathic physicians organized professional societies in the nineteenth century and initiated regulations of medical standards, hospital staffing, medical training and licensing. Surgery, hospitalization and specializations such as obstetrics and gynecology promised to advance medical treatment for women and improve their health. As more women preferred a physician's assistance in childbirth to the customary midwife, this was perceived as a move in the right direction for better health care for women.

American women, recipients of these new ideas, would experience medical treatment differently than their mothers or grandmothers had. Medical approaches to female health and disease reflected not only new medical concepts but also nineteenth century perceptions of woman's role and place in American society at a time when women were demanding their political rights and making deliberate choices to limit family size.

Physicians expressed concern over the general state of American women's health; they addressed specifically the condition of women of the middle and upper classes who could afford their services. Many factors contributed to women's poor health; a few practitioners observed that women's fashion and diet were leading problems. To treat female illnesses, some physicians resorted to radical surgery or new therapies. All in all, the state of women's health turned a crucial corner in the nineteenth century.

Women's Fashion of the Victorian Era

The Victorian concept of feminine beauty, an extreme hourglass figure, consisted of a petite waist of 20 inches or less, a voluptuous bosom, and a prominent derriere. Ideally, a man would be able to encompass his lady's waist within his handspan. According to nineteenth century economist Thorstein Veblen, who coined apt phrases like "conspicuous consumption," Victorian female fashion was meant to display a wife as an adornment of her husband's wealth and success. For single women, Victorian fashion emphasized (with some help from supporting undergarments) the breasts, waist and full hips, and advertised her reproductive capacity in order to attract a prospective husband.

Contradiction was evident; while fashion promoted the voluptuous body of the female, society feigned prudish attitudes. Victorians went so far as to rename the breast of the turkey "white meat" in order to avoid saying breast. A woman's legs and arms were called limbs. And, fearing that the legs of a piano might remind a man of a woman's limbs, Victorians painstakingly covered piano legs with velvet leggings in order to subdue male arousal.

Women's clothing in the nineteenth century was cumbersome and uncomfortable. An outfit could comprise at least fifteen layers of undergarments and weigh as much as 20 pounds (winter woolen clothes as much as 30 pounds). Women wore a steel framed hoop under their dress to produce an exaggerated bell shape to the lower torso. A bustle, which was worn hanging from the posterior waist, added inches and roundness to the derriere. Sleeves were set tightly into dresses, blouses and jackets to prevent a woman from raising her arms, a gesture Victorians regarded as unladylike. In this getup, and walking in high heels, a Victorian woman was literally enslaved to fashion, encumbered in layers of starched, heavy clothing and appurtenances, and restricted in bodily movements.

Some doctors disapproved of the Victorian style for women. Commenting on the extreme discomfort of women's clothing, Dr. John Harvey Kellogg, a reformer in the health crusade, described a woman's walk as a "stiff, unnatural mincing gait of the fashionable which is not so much an affectation as a necessity with her." The effect of these extreme fashions on a woman's health was devastating. The exaggerated hourglass figure was achieved by wearing a restrictive corset which displaced organs and caused broken ribs, shallow breathing and an overall deterioration of the body from lack of oxygen. Women would often feel weak or faint, a condition known as "suffering from the vapors," which necessitated carrying a fan to cool oneself. Wearing a tightly-laced corset restricted the circulation as well. Without an adequate blood supply, wearing a tight corset increased incidence of inflammation, infection, varicose veins, phlebitis or *edema*.[1] Over time, dependence upon a corset for support weakened the abdominal musculature and made labor and childbirth prolonged and more difficult. This loss of muscle tone from wearing a tight corset, coupled with the additional strain of multiple pregnancies, also led to prolapsed uterus, a serious condition which resulted when the uterus inverted and dropped through the vagina, and often out of the body. To treat this condition, physicians invented devices known as *pessaries* which were worn in the vagina to support and maintain the position of the uterus inside the abdominal cavity.[2] The pessary prescription, which resulted in internal injury or introduced infection, caused more harm than therapeutic benefit.

The heavy clothing of the nineteenth century lady was also unsanitary and impractical wear for any kind of work. The floor-length dresses and skirts hung like heavy mops and accumulated all the dirt and debris from floors and streets. Fancy ball gowns made of non-washable fabrics were seldom cleaned and certain textile dyes used in women's clothing were injurious to health. Victorians adored the color green for their home décor and fashion. This color was produced in textiles with an arsenic-

1. *Edema,* the retention of fluid resulting in swelling of the legs and ankles.
2. *Pessary,* an instrument or substance placed in the vagina to support the uterus or rectum or to serve as a contraceptive device.

based dye. Women who wore green -dyed clothing suffered from slow poisoning and general malaise as the arsenic dye was gradually absorbed into their skin.

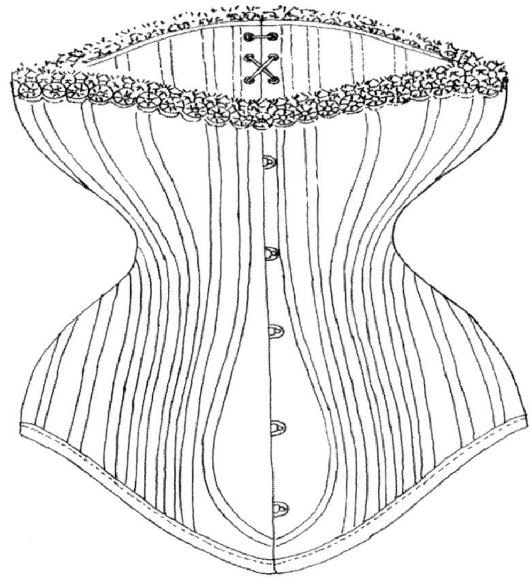

The nineteenth century corset—to achieve an hourglass figure women in the nineteenth century wore the tightly laced corset reinforced with bone or steel stays. Tight corsets restricted women's breathing and often displaced internal organs.

Childbirth and Motherhood

In the past, pregnancy was a time of preparation and reflection, when an expectant mother lived with the real possibility that in bringing a life into the world she might die. As medicine made dubious progress in the nineteenth century, the lot of women in childbirth did not improve. Statistics on female mortality show increased risks of death in childbirth; hence, a woman's life expectancy did not extend to menopause. One figure suggests that thirty percent of the women born in Massachusetts in 1850, died before their twentieth birthday. Twenty-six percent of all females born in the United States in 1890 were dead by 1910. The rate of infant and child mortality in the not-so-distant past was equally alarming, as many died in infancy, or before the age of six. In the New York City population of 1853, forty-nine percent of those who died were children.

Changes in family planning, childbirth and medical practice in the United States affected women's health and treatment. When women took more control of their health and their bodies by limiting the size of their families, officials became alarmed. In the declining decades of the nineteenth century, a marked decrease in the birthrate showed a forty percent reduction in the size of the middle- and upper-class family, a sudden drop which had occurred in less than a century. In 1800, middle- and upper-class families had at least seven children who survived and there were approximately 280 live births per 1,000 women. By 1900, family size had dwindled to 3.42 children. By 1910, only 140 live births were recorded per 1,000 women. This decrease in the birthrate, known as the *Demographic transition,* was more distressing among xenophobic officials who considered other factors. The working poor, especially immigrants recently arrived from Europe, continued to have large families. The survival of settled Americans appeared threatened. Authorities feared that if the current trends held, the immigrant population would exceed the birthrate of the middle and upper class. Coupled with resentment and discrimination toward recently arrived immigrants, officials believed that it was only a matter of time before the new immigrants dominated America.

Fearful of dramatic population changes, officials looked for causes and solutions. The first step was to find out what contraceptive methods women used and how they were terminating pregnancy. Eighteenth and nineteenth century sources, such as advertising, medical advice, and diaries reveal that women had long used herbal folk remedies to abort pregnancy. By the early nineteenth century, specialists in pharmacopoeia had developed more effective medical concoctions for inducing an abortion known as *abortifacients.*[3] Catherine Beecher observed firsthand the tribulations of her sister Harriet who had six children. In her essay, *An Appeal to American Women*, she expressed concern for the health of American females.

3. *Abortifacient*, any medication, drug, or herbal preparation, such as pennyroyal, which might induce an abortion.

> Let us now look at the dangers which are impending. And first, in regard to the welfare of the family state, the decay of the female constitution and health has involved such terrific sufferings, in addition to former cares and pains of maternity, that multitudes of both sexes so dread the risks of marriage, as either to avoid it, or meet them by methods always injurious and often criminal.

But Catherine Beecher's greater concern was the growing tendency for women to self induce an abortion, and she warned of the penalties for violating nature as children were "a heritage of the Lord."

Despite Victorian society's promotion of childbirth as woman's "highest and most harmonious development," abortions were easy to come by. The going rate for the procedure was about ten dollars. One estimate published by the Michigan Board of Health in 1898, states that as much as thirty percent of all pregnancies were terminated by an artificial abortion.[4] In addition, by 1800, the development of the French syringe had enabled women to use more potent douches for contraception or to induce abortions. And by the mid nineteenth century these effective contraceptive devices could be purchased through discreet mail-order companies. Herbal compounds such as pennyroyal proved an effective abortifacient. Dr. A. M. Mauriceau's *The Married Woman's Private Medical Companion* encouraged "the use of abortifacient in an age when promiscuity, prostitution, venereal disease, Caesarean butchery and the increased propagation of lesser intellects of the species was rampant."

The more recent study of Anthony Wohl, *Women and Victorian Public Health*, points to poor diet as a leading cause of many failed pregnancies and to infant mortality. Wohl shows that of the women who were deficient in the main staples of the diet, such as dairy foods, green vegetables and fruit, *seventy percent* were either suffering from pernicious anemia or from a contracted pelvis due to bone *atrophy.*[5] Taken with other statistical data, this suggests that the average female of childbearing age was much smaller in the Victorian Age, and the risk of fetal mortality doubled for a woman measuring five-feet-four-inches in height or less. Nutritional deficiency was prevalent not only among poor working class women, but also among affluent young women who ate like birds in order to maintain their hourglass figures.

At the beginning of the nineteenth century, women of childbearing age averaged a pregnancy about every two years. Personal diaries indicate that some women abstained from sexual intercourse in order to limit the number of children or to space them further apart. In *the Light of the Home, an Intimate View of the Lives of Women in Victorian America*, author Harvey Green suggests that what seemed like Victorian prudery was actually women's fear of pregnancy and the dangerous risk of childbirth. Scholars believe that the rise of invalidism among Victorian women indicates they feigned illness in order to abstain from intercourse as a means to prevent pregnancy. Although doctors doled out advice on the optimum period during which to abstain, the function of ovulation was unknown until the twentieth century.[6] So what physicians advised as the safest time for intercourse — mid cycle — was actually the most fertile period. Given this kind of medical advice, it is somewhat of a wonder that the Demographic transition ever occurred.

Society responded to women's attempts at family limitation in a number of ways. Leading ladies' magazines extolled the virtues of motherhood. Pregnancy, they claimed, did everything from increasing a woman's beauty, to postponing old age and "fulfilling woman's physiological and moral destiny." Concerned

4. Physicians differentiate a *spontaneous abortion* as an event occurring naturally from an *artificial abortion* which is induced and brought on intentionally.
5. *Atrophy,* a wasting away or shrinking in size of some part or organ of the body, usually caused by injury, disease, or lack of use such as in muscle atrophy.
6. This practice and medical advice were not yet referred to as contraception or birth control; these terms were introduced later by Margaret Sanger, a birth control advocate.

about the drastic reduction in the birthrate, doctors, ministers, and public officials joined league with ladies' magazines and ardently promoted childbearing. For the well-being of the mother and the developing fetus, doctors advised that during pregnancy women abstain from intercourse, avoid alcoholic drink and inhaling tobacco fumes, and refrain from wearing tightly-laced corsets. Most medical advice on pregnancy was at best ambiguous and often contradictory. Some doctors advised pregnant women that exercise was healthy and that they should not be embarrassed about their appearance, while others warned that exercise was harmful and that they should not *advertise* their condition. The word *pregnant* was considered harsh, blunt, and not used. Instead, euphemistic terms for pregnancy such as "her sacred secret" and "being in the family way" were preferred.

The Theory and Practice of Medicine in the Nineteenth Century

In the nineteenth century, physicians known as regular, or allopathic (iliopathic) doctors, organized professionally as the American Medical Association, the AMA. In 1847, at their first meeting in Philadelphia, they adopted a Code of Ethics and standards for medical education and for the doctoral degree in medicine. In 1848, the AMA proposed that the use of anesthesia for surgical and obstetrical procedures be evaluated. Members of the AMA began to define medicine under the aegis of allopathy, a practice of medicine with strong reliance on diagnosis through clinical observation and therapy dependent upon drugs and surgery. At this time, allopathic physicians began to focus on specific organic systems of the body. Physicians developed specialized areas such as cardiology, gynecology, geriatrics, pediatrics and oncology, just to name a few.

The Victorian Age has often been referred to as the *poisoning century*. Physicians prescribed heavy doses of toxic harmful drugs, such as mercury for the treatment of infections from typhus, typhoid, scarlet fever or venereal disease. Doctors ignorant of the effects of drugs dispensed toxic medicine — often habit-forming narcotics — which were more harmful than restorative. Paregoric for example, a camphorated form of opium was commonly given to toddlers for relief from teething. Some tonics and elixirs contained as much as thirty-eight percent alcohol. The sale of drugs went unregulated and the public could readily obtain potent medications from a pharmacy, general store, mail-order company, traveling salesman or touring medicine show. Individuals could easily self-prescribe and self-medicate themselves. One practitioner, Dr. Mary Wood-Allen, believed female complaints of pain and illness were indications of narcotic or alcohol addiction by "that portion of the female sex who have ample time and leisure to indulge in any luxury which is agreeable to their tastes." In Dr. Wood-Allen's estimation, women had become addicted to these drugs and would complain of maladies in order to be allowed to continue taking them.

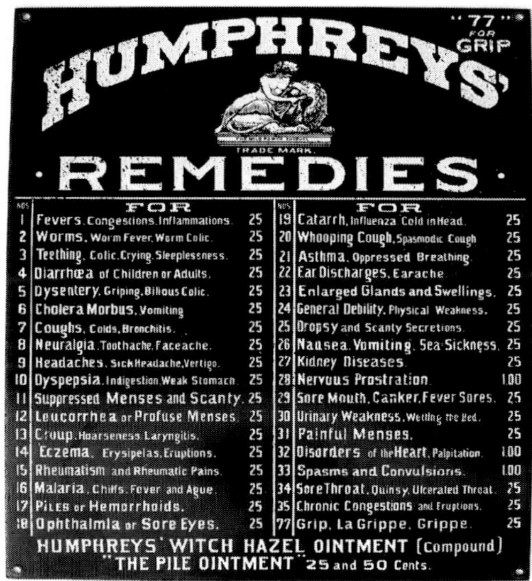

Before the regulation of drugs, the widespread use of medicine promoted healing for all sorts of illnesses. A medicinal such as Humphrey's Remedies could be bought over the counter and was advertised as a cure-all.

Western medicine was based heavily on the medieval European concept that the body was composed of four humors, or fluids: blood, phlegm, black bile and yellow bile. Doctors believed disease occurred when either an excessive or decreased amount of any humor caused an imbalance in the body. Physicians resorted to harsh measures to restore the body's balance, with purging, blistering, vomiting, cupping or bleeding. They believed the use of laxatives could purge the body of undesirable fluid and that the deliberate blistering by chemical irritants burned into the skin would release toxic fluid produced under the blister. Harsh compounds such as alum and calomel taken orally acted as emetics, causing the patient to vomit, or overstimulated the salivary glands to draw out saliva. Doctors also used the cupping method; they burned the skin and applied a glass cup in order to form a vacuum, then used suction which drew out impurities through the skin. The most futile technique of all was bloodletting, which is, using leeches or sharp lancets to open a vein and bleed the patient. This procedure only robbed the patient of the life sustaining, healing properties of blood. One Ohio family's journal disclosed such a treatment: "The doctor came everyday. He purged, bled, blistered, puked and salivated his patient, but he never cured him." Some lucky patients recovered in spite of the physician's efforts, through the body's natural healing processes.

Changes in the Medical Health Treatment of Women

In the annals of American History, medicine entered the modern age on Christmas day in 1809, when Dr. Ephraim Mc Dowell operated on forty-seven-year-old Jane Todd Crawford at his home in Danville, Kentucky. The patient had a severely swollen abdomen and appeared to be well over term in her pregnancy. Upon examination, Dr. McDowell diagnosed Jane's condition as an enlarged ovarian cyst and related how he "gave to the unhappy woman information of her dangerous situation. She appeared willing to undergo an experiment." During the twenty-five minute surgical procedure, Dr. McDowell removed a 15 pound ovarian cyst from Mrs. Crawford. At a time when most surgeries were performed on the battlefield in the form of amputations to prevent gangrene, Dr. McDowell's surgery was quite an undertaking. McDowell's operation, like amputation procedures, was accomplished in the pre-anesthesia, pre-antiseptic era. During battlefield surgeries, wounded soldiers were given whiskey if available, and a leather belt or a bullet to bite down on in order to endure the pain. Dr. McDowell's patient took none of these. It was reported that Mrs. Crawford was awake during the entire operation and sang hymns to divert her "mind from the agony." The operation was a success and the patient, who suffered no post-operative infection or stress, was up and about in five days. Jane Crawford lived for thirty-one more years, leading an active life until she died at the age of seventy-eight.

Allopathic physicians assumed their approach was the most enlightened and effective. As they extended their control over medicine in the nineteenth century, women endured traumatic changes in medical treatment, particularly in the birthing experience. Applying the theory of the four humors, physicians who assisted with childbirth used bloodletting techniques and other harsh procedures. It was not unusual for a doctor to bleed an expectant mother of several pints of blood during labor. Formerly, midwives had let nature take its course and merely *assisted* women in childbirth. Gradually, as doctors organized professionally, they regulated the practice of midwifery more stringently. Midwives were required to work under the supervision of the local physician. Maine midwife Martha Ballard expressed her frustration with inexperienced and inadequate doctors who insisted on delivering babies, despite their lack of training and expertise.

By the end of the nineteenth century, midwives were no longer exclusively delivering babies or making sick calls on families. In the name of progress, medical doctors had driven many of them out of practice. This takeover by male doctors came at an unusual juncture of women's history, marked by the Demographic transition, the formation of obstetrics and gynecology, technical advances in surgery and the rise of the suffragist movement.

The Age of the Womb

The Victorian era is also referred to as the *age of the womb* as officials were obsessed with women's procreative qualities and formed obstetrics and gynecology, two of the earliest medical specializations. One physician, reflecting on the female anatomy, stated that "it is as if the Almighty, in creating the female sex had taken a uterus and built up a woman around it." Writers poured out all kinds of advice literature and speculated on the nature of female health complaints. Doctors began to ask what was ailing American women. Dr. John Harvey Kellogg, an eccentric health reformer, zeroed in specifically on women's habits which he saw as a threat to their declining health. Kellogg saw his female patients as much weaker than the Revolutionary generation of women.

> The declining health and strength of American women has come to be a very common observation. Very few young ladies of the present day can compare with their grandmothers of the last generation in powers and physical endurance.

Dr. Kellogg attributed all sorts of things to the general malaise of females: poor diet, restrictive fashionable clothing, harmful drugs, sexual sins, and laziness. He noted how medical practices were thriving, with seventy-five percent of a doctor's caseload devoted to treating women. Other doctors eager to find the source of feminine weakness picked up on Kellogg's theory and many came to the astonishing conclusion that female health problems originated in women's reproductive organs. In conjunction with this idea, some doctors saw stark differences between the vitality of men and women. They believed that boys grew physically stronger as they reached maturity but that with the onset of menstruation, a girl's strength was severely taxed. They overlooked their own inconsistent view of females. Women were expected to bear many children and do strenuous work but were considered, after all, the weaker sex.

Physicians promoted femininity and motherhood but viewed menstruation as an illness rather than a normal female function. Doctors advised that housework and childcare were the panacea for menstrual pain and that certain forms of relaxation were not. Since female energy was finite, and essential to development of reproductive organs, it could be further sapped by reading or other intellectual pursuits. Doctors advised young women to refrain from too much brainwork, particularly during menses. In works such as *American Nervousness: Its Causes and Consequences,* and *Eating and Drinking: A Popular Manual of Food and Diet on Health and Disease*, the author George Beard argued that women should not engage their minds on substantive issues, but on mere trifles, because the female brain capacity was only 90 percent that of a male. In *Sex in Education*, Dr. Edward Clarke warned that a formal education for a young lady might cause such a strain that she would become sterile or suffer a physical or mental breakdown.

Doctors went so far as to state that the general state of a woman's health was dysfunctional at best. They diagnosed most female ailments, which included extreme fatigue, chronic depression, cystitis, infections of the reproductive system, and depression after childbirth as nervous disorders with catchall terms like neurasthenia, chlorosis or *hysteria*. Descriptions of hysteria, considered an entirely female disease, included paranoia, suicidal tendencies, insanity and manic depression. An article by Dr. Charles P. Uhle, in *Godey's Lady's Book* in 1870, described it this way:

> A hysterical woman is a pitiful and unfortunate object-full of aches and pains, and imaginary ills, capricious in character, whimsical in conduct, excitable, impatient, obstinate, and frivolous-a regular Gordian knot for friends, family and physician to unravel. She possesses a most variable and imaginative disposition, which, in spite of all that can be done, keeps her in a continued whirl of excitement from morning until night.

Physicians concluded that female reproductive organs were the principle source of their illnesses; Women got sick because they were unfeminine. All sorts of behavior ranked as unfeminine, including sexual aggression, an excessive appetite, *dysmenorrhea*, a cussed personality, or male-like ambition, (the latter defined as a desire to read books).[7] Physicians

7. *Dysmenorrhea*, dysfunctional menstruation

tried extreme therapies on women. One introduced by famous surgeon Dr. Robert Battey in 1876, was the ovariotomy, i.e. removal of the ovaries. Dr. Battey surmised that even if the ovaries appeared normal, they might be viciously or abnormally performing their function. Doctors saw great potential in the Battey procedure for curing all sorts of illnesses for which they could find no other cure. Robert Battey's attitude toward women and his description of the surgical procedure in a nineteenth century medical text speaks for itself:

> The surgeon should not hesitate to take out the ovaries and the tubes [fallopian tubes] for which he can find no other cure. After the surgeon has laid violent hands on the ovaries, it matters not what becomes of the uterus.

Physicians were anxious to practice these newly acquired surgical skills via the Battey procedure on patients whom they diagnosed as insane, hysterical, unfaithful to their husbands, or suffering from depression. Dr. William Goddell, a colleague of Dr. Battey, defended the hysterectomy and ovariotomy operations as *progressive therapy,* because surgeons were preventing women from transmitting "the taint of their insanity onto their descendants."

This outlook was part of a craze in medicine beginning in 1869, inspired by Francis Galton's work, *Hereditary Genius,* which promoted the treatment of certain illnesses through surgical Eugenics. Doctors of Eugenics hoped to stem the tide of immigration and the breeding of people they labeled as "inferior types." At the height of the Eugenics craze, numerous surgeries were performed, such as the *pan hysterectomy* and the ovariotomy, for sterilization.[8] Females diagnosed with nervous disorders might be sexually mutilated by the surgical procedure of a clitorectomy. What is diagnosed today as dysmenorrhea as well as many of the symptoms of menopause would qualify a Victorian woman for confinement in a mental asylum and women in asylums were often forcibly sterilized.

By the 1890s, the use of anesthesia and new surgical tools emboldened more doctors to perform hysterectomies, and this surgical procedure became common for the treatment of female hysteria. In spite of the risk — a 40 percent mortality rate and prohibitive cost of $1,000 per procedure — a surgeon might perform a hysterectomy to cure any illness a physician could not cure. Paradoxically, a society, which placed much importance on motherhood and was alarmed about women limiting the number of children, would allow surgeons to remove normal, healthy female reproductive organs. Medical historians estimate that in the later Victorian Era, as many as sixty percent of all the hysterectomies performed were unnecessary. Ironically, physicians neither explored nor offered any effective treatment for the suffering of women diagnosed with terminal illnesses such as breast, uterine and ovarian cancer beyond administering narcotics for the pain.

The Rest Cure

Radical surgery was not the only means used to treat female complaints. Dr. S. Weir Mitchell offered what seemed to be a more humane treatment for women's problems; it was known as the rest cure. Mitchell's treatment was memorialized in the novel *The Yellow Wallpaper*. The author, his famous patient, Charlotte Perkins Gilman, had complained of fatigue after the birth of her daughter. She was very likely suffering from postpartum depression. Her condition became intolerable as chronic depression set in. Mitchell ordered her to stay home, give up writing and all intellectual pursuits and forbid her to receive any visitors. She was "never to touch a pencil, pen or brush, as long as [she] shall live." She was to devote herself completely to household chores and the care of her daughter. Mitchell's rest cure, a kind of aversion therapy, forced complete bed rest as a "bitter medicine." What is striking about Charlotte Gilman's experience is the almost godlike control Mitchell exerted over her and the devastating effects the rest cure had on her health.

Under this regimen, Charlotte Perkins Gilman said, "I came perilously close to losing my mind." She saved herself from plunging into

8. *Pan hysterectomy,* the surgical removal of the uterus, cervix, fallopian tubes and ovaries.

madness only by canceling the therapy. Literally sicker from the treatment than she was from the illness, she dropped Mitchell as her attending physician, divorced her husband and resumed her writing. She intended that her exposé of the rest cure, in *The Yellow Wallpaper*, help other women with similar complaints.

In the story, the main character, Charlotte, is under the care of her physician husband and confined to an attic nursery. Her books and writing materials are confiscated and she is heavily medicated to sleep. With only the disturbing yellow wallpaper to look at, Charlotte becomes fixated on it and her imagination runs wild. On a small notepad, which she secretly keeps, she describes her chilling "descent into madness." Charlotte's experience in *The Yellow Wallpaper* became an important discourse in feminist literature and was intended to educate women on the importance of controlling their own lives and bodies for the sake of their mental and physical well-being.

Childbed Fever

Despite the monopoly of allopathic medicine, with its emphasis on formal training and licensing, the medical treatment of women's illnesses in the nineteenth century was regressive and became more risky. Particularly as doctors intervened more frequently in childbirth, the number of women dying of childbed, or puerperal fever, increased[9]. The celebrated American physician, Oliver Wendell Holmes, dismayed at this trend published *The Contagiousness of Puerperal Fever* in 1843, in which he raised questions about medical procedures. In 1847, Austrian physician Dr. Anton Semmelweis, whose own wife had died of childbed fever was convinced that the source of the fever stemmed from medical treatment. He set out to prove that the delivery methods of the doctors were the problem. Dr. Semmelweis conducted his research at the Vienna Lying-In Hospital in Austria, where he set up two control groups. On ward number one, he assigned only mothers delivered by physicians. Ward number two housed only mothers whose babies had been delivered by midwives. All of the mothers received the same post-delivery treatment. On the first ward, there was an alarming thirty percent mortality rate of mothers who died of childbed fever. On ward number two, among mothers whose babies were delivered by midwives, less than two percent mortality occurred.

What could account for the dramatic difference in mortality and survival between the two groups? As Dr. Semmelweis investigated further, he discovered that many of the surgeons who had delivered babies had just come from treating people with contagious diseases or performing postmortems on diseased and putrid cadavers. This research indicated that these were not isolated outbreaks of childbed fever; the high incidence of mortality from infectious childbed fever at the Vienna Lying-In Hospital was typical of many hospitals in Europe and the United States. As more women went to hospitals for physician-assisted deliveries, the incidents of childbed fever reached epidemic proportions.

In 1868, at New York's Bellevue Hospital, cases of childbed fever were increasing at an alarming rate. From 1870 to 1880, fifty percent of all maternal deaths at the hospital were caused by childbed fever. In 1874, in one month alone, an epidemic raged at Bellevue, and of the 166 physician-assisted deliveries, thirty-one of the mothers died of puerperal fever, a mortality rate of nearly nineteen percent. Because doctors did not take the precaution of scrubbing before or after surgery, they endangered all of their patients. Moreover, after Louis Pasteur and Robert Koch introduced germ theory in 1880, most doctors remained skeptical of the cause of childbed fever and refused to practice cleanliness in the birthing room. When pioneering surgeon William Dewees demanded that his interns wash their hands before *any* medical procedure, he and like-minded physicians were openly ridiculed by their peers for their belief in invisible

9. Puerperal or childbed fever, indicates or can develop into an infection; it is contracted by a woman during or shortly after childbirth, miscarriage or abortion. If untreated, it is life-threatening. The infection can originate in genital, urinary or respiratory tract or from an inflammation of breast tissue, i.e. mastitis.

bugs and for practicing what the profession called *spook medicine*.

Phasing Out Midwives

Two sharply defined approaches to pregnancy, labor and childbirth existed in the medical community. Some physicians believed like the midwives before them, that having babies was a natural process. During delivery, the physician merely waited and assisted. By the late 1800s, however, other doctors transformed what had been a natural process into a surgical procedure. As physicians intervened more actively in delivery, the midwife's perception of *obstetrik* as an art disappeared and physicians' practice of obstetrics as a science and specialized field of medicine prevailed.

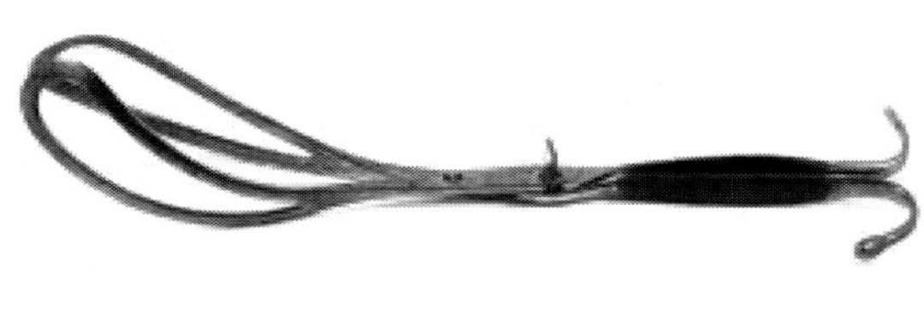

Nineteenth century physicians introduced the use of the long- handled forceps in order to facilitate the birthing process; this procedure often caused internal lacerations to the mother and serious or fatal injury to the fetus

At first women welcomed delivery by a physician and assumed that their intervention would ease the trauma and pain of childbirth. Indeed, surgical tools such as the forceps, in the hands of a skilled physician, could save lives. But in the hands of a novice, forceps increased the risk of injury to mother and child. Regina Morantz and Sue Zschoche, in "Professionalism, Feminism and Gender Roles: A Comparative Study of Nineteenth Century Medical Therapeutics," found that forcep-deliveries and the use of drugs during delivery increased alarmingly in the nineteenth century. Some doctors justified using surgical procedures, arguing that women's health had deteriorated from the effects of urban life. But in 1912, Dr. Whitridge Williams, of the Johns Hopkins Medical School, lamented the phasing out of midwifery and criticized the obstetric practice for not training physicians adequately. Dr. Williams stated that "the average practitioner through his lack of preparation does more harm to his patients than the much-maligned midwife."

The Founding Father of Gynecology

In contrast to the poorly trained surgeons and ill prescribed surgeries, Dr. James Marion Sims practiced his surgical skills with acumen. From 1835-1845, Sims performed experimental surgeries on five slave women to test the effectiveness of various suture materials such as silk and silver wire. He created a makeshift surgical theater in a stable at his Alabama estate. Sims operated on them without anesthesia, although it was available at the time. On one slave, Anarcha, he performed over thirty vaginal surgeries and the patient was required to assist him. If Sims was interested at all in his patient's recovery, he never indicated it. His well documented journals do not include a postoperative diagnosis, prognosis or whether or not his patients ever recovered. Nonetheless, Sims did describe his experiments as overwhelming successes. In his autobiography, he characterized the research as the most important discovery of the age for the relief of human suffering. Sadly, the record is silent on the opinion Sims' patients had of his experiments in gynecology.

In 1850, Dr. Sims left the South and moved to New York. There his treatment of upper-class women brought him professional fame and more patients. He continued conducting his experimental surgeries in New York, operating on poor working-class women, most of whom were Irish immigrants. Sims co-established the New York Women's Hospital, and served as chief surgeon there. For his surgical experimentation and role in establishing the New York Women's Hospital, Sims is revered in the History of American Medicine as the founder of American Gynecology, the new field of the study of women's diseases. Dr. A. Marion Sims regarded his work as divinely appointed, or as he said, as "a mission to the altar of science." The presence of his statue, which stands in front of the Women's Hospital as a monument to his pioneering research in the cause of women's health, has been contested by feminists for decades.

Mothers of Invention: the Blackwell Sisters Become Lady Physicians

In 1847, Elizabeth Blackwell broke down the barriers for women in medicine when she gained admittance to the Geneva Medical College. Geneva officials believed her application was a male prank and going along with the joke, they wrote her a letter of acceptance. To their surprise, Elizabeth Blackwell turned up at Geneva prepared to enter medical school. As the first female medical student, Elizabeth endured extreme harassment and was taunted by both male students and townspeople alike. Frequently barred from attending lectures or demonstrations, particularly dissections and surgeries, Elizabeth wrote in her journal: "November 15th, today, a second operation at which I was not allowed to be present. This annoys me. I was quite saddened and discouraged by Dr. Webster requesting me to be absent from some of the demonstrations."

Despite these prejudices, Elizabeth graduated first in her class of 1849, and was the first female Doctor of Medicine in the United States. But no hospital would admit her onto its medical staff and New York officials prevented her from renting space for a private practice. In 1853, she opened a dispensary in the slum district of New York City, and brought her younger sister Emily Blackwell, who had received her medical degree from Western Reserve University, as her physician associate.

In 1857, the doctors Blackwell expanded their practice and established the New York Infirmary for Women and Children. In 1868, Elizabeth founded the Women's Medical College at her New York Infirmary, consisting of a four year medical training program, a system which set the standard for other medical schools in the United States. By 1899, the college boasted 364 female graduates. Dr. Elizabeth Blackwell worked closely with notables such as Florence Nightingale and established the National Health Society in Great Britain.

Clio's Corner - What Have Historians Said about the Dilemma of Women's Health in the Victorian Age?

While allopathic doctors purportedly advanced healthcare for women in the nineteenth century, evidence suggests that women's conditions under physicians' treatment worsened. Deborah Kuhn McGregor's *From Midwives to Medicine: the Birth of American Gynecology* emphasizes that the development of gynecology for the specific treatment of women's diseases was laden with gender and class discrimination. Detailed study of surgical case histories shows Dr. Sims' callous attitude toward his patients. A patient identified as "L," a mulatto, at the New York Women's Hospital died of an infection caused by Sims' procedure used in an ovariotomy. Sims tried a new draining tube procedure on her and she died several days after the operation. Dr. Sims' noted that "in her death, she would give *greater service* than she had in life by *saving more valuable lives* [emphasis by author]." In many similar cases Sims' was never held accountable by the medical community and he never acknowledged the severity of his bungling. Dr. Sims' ghastly practice of surgical experimentation on female slaves and poor immigrant women is just one example of the blatant discrimination toward African-American and working-class women and the callous treatment of them.

Historian Sarah Stage, in *Female Complaints: Lydia Pinkham and the Business of Medicine*, theorizes that physicians' tendency to treat women's illnesses with surgery as a cure was not progress for science. Sarah Stage notes the revival of an old theme in a new mantle,

> The bifurcation of human attributes that became evident in the nineteenth century, in which manhood became synonymous with strength and womanhood with weakness did not mark a new departure so much as it exaggerated an

ancient perception common in Judaeo-Christian thought. Early arguments about women's inferiority drew support from the Bible, but by the middle of the nineteenth century the Bible began to lose its hold as a source of social wisdom. Science, the new faith of the century provided the framework within which the social questions of the day were examined.

The social question for women focused on the right to vote, property rights and control of their own destiny. For men the social question concerned what steps might be effective to ensure the survival of the species, maintain a white male dominated society, and how to keep a woman in her place. This was summed up as the *woman problem*, and gynecologists used new approaches to address men's concerns. As Professor Stage explains,

> As a guardian and counselor, the physician became something of a moral arbiter whose pronouncements, colored as they were by the cultural and class biases of the time, worked to buttress the status quo. Few physicians could resist the temptation to enlist biology in the fight against women's rights.

Because the new medicine, surgery in particular, was well suited for the fight against feminism, it gave gynecologists an effective means to wage ultimate control over women. Professor Stage analyzes the manipulation of female sexuality through surgical procedures.

> Doctors also denounced women's attempts to control their reproductive lives. Those who did offer contraceptive advice only increased the chance of pregnancy for their patients. As the woman's rights movement gained momentum in the second half of the nineteenth century, many doctors became increasingly shrill. They dismissed feminism, whether social or political as unnatural, unhealthy and undesirable. A host of physicians used spurious arguments to relegate advocates of woman suffrage to the ranks of hermaphrodites.

Surgeons violated their own code of ethics by performing unnecessary surgeries and removing healthy organs. Gynecologists not only used surgical techniques to sterilize women and render them asexual creatures but they also violated the Hippocratic oath by denying women treatment that would have alleviated their pain and suffering.

Dr Elizabeth Blackwell the first woman in the United States to receive a medical degree. She spoke out against male physicians who performed unwarranted surgeries on women such as hysterectomies and ovariotomies. (Photo courtesy of the Library of Congress)

By the mid-nineteenth century, two changes were evident: Physicians had replaced the religious ministry as the guardians of social morality and they used surgery to sterilize and sexually mutilate women — a violation of social mores and medical ethics. The medical community contradicted the very social values they promoted, the Victorian ideals of true womanhood, the vitality of the family and the sanctity of motherhood. They blamed the women's movement for the increase of *defeminized women*, when in fact it was the physicians themselves who had robbed women of their femininity. Female castration was the result of surgeons' misogyny. Dr. Elizabeth Blackwell, who struggled as a female physician in patriarchal medicine spoke out against the surgical and sexual mutilation of women. She stated the case best. Negative attitudes toward women were most evident in what she called *prurigo secandi*, "the surgeon's itch to cut."

Conclusion

Nineteenth century changes in the specialization, training, and licensing of physicians presented a potential for improved standards in healthcare and the practice of medicine. Those changes directly affected the female population because the first fields of specialization were gynecology and obstetrics. Although science and medicine made advances, the quality of women's health did not improve. The decline in their health was due to several factors: fashion, lifestyle, medical theory and medical care.

Women's fashions, which included restrictive corsets, high heels, hooped-frames and other cumbersome clothing were particularly detrimental to their health. Tight corsets and multiple pregnancies often produced the severe condition of prolapsed uterus as well as circulatory and respiratory problems.

Americans were notorious for self medicating themselves at a time when harmful drugs were easy to purchase and went unregulated by the government or the medical community. Doctors as well as their patients misused and abused strong medication.

With the use of more effective anesthesia, physicians advanced experimental surgery but strongly refuted germ theory. This had devastating effects on women. Doctors who discouraged the use of midwife-assistance at childbirth introduced surgical procedures in the birthing room. But their own lack of cleanliness during delivery led to an outbreak of childbed fever of epidemic proportion.

Women attempted to reduce their risks of death in childbirth by limiting the size of their family through *voluntary motherhood.* Using means of family limitation such as abortifacients, douches, pessaries and abstinence, women significantly reduced the number of pregnancies and live births. Using these methods, the size of the middle-class and upper-class American families were dramatically reduced by forty percent. This resulted in a dramatic shift in the population known as the *Demographic transition.*

Part V:

Women in the Early Twentieth Century

Women and Progressive Reform

Winning the War and Winning the Vote

Chapter 17
Women and Progressive Reform
Shirtwaist Progressives and Radical Reformers

Key Topics

The Settlement House Movement
Social Feminists and Muckrakers
Margaret Sanger and the Birth Control Movement
Women Union Organizers
The Triangle Shirtwaist Factory Fire

Chronology

1889 - Jane Addams Establishes Hull House in Chicago
1890 - 1920 - The Progressive Era
1895 - Lillian Wald opens Henry Street Nurses' Settlement
1902 - Death of Elizabeth Cady Stanton
1906 - Death of Susan B. Anthony
1911 - The Triangle Shirtwaist Factory Fire
1912 - Presidential Elections- Jane Addams Nominates Theodore Roosevelt

Introduction

The Industrial Revolution created an even wider gap between the rich and the poor than had existed before 1860. A few men like Andrew Carnegie, the steel magnate, earned a yearly income of $23 million in the era before personal income tax. His wealth contrasted sharply with that of the average American worker who brought home a meager $500 in annual wages. While industrial barons lived like the crown heads of Europe in palatial homes, their workers, mostly poor immigrant men, women, and children, lived in crowded disease-ridden tenements without heat or water.

These families sought relief in the only means available, through the political machine which had gained control in the larger cities. But crime, vagrancy, prostitution, child labor, and communicable diseases degraded cities into unseemly places. It was evident that something needed to be done and someone needed to do it. Progressivism, a new reform movement led by members of the middle class, was created in the late nineteenth century to address these problems. Seeing the great disparity between the haves and the have-nots, they blended personal enthusiasm with the Victorian sense of moral responsibility in order to work for social change.

Female Progressive reformers were, in some cases, the first in their families to go to college or rebel against the prescribed social role for the middle-class lady. Female Progressives, or Social Feminists were especially concerned about the working class, particularly immigrant women and children and they founded institutions to improve conditions of the poor.

As Social Feminists, they believed that suffrage presented an opportunity to achieve progressive goals. It was plain and simple. If women could vote, women could use the vote to initiate reform.

In contrast, the more radical female reformers, such as Emma Goldman, Mary Harris (Mother) Jones and Elizabeth Gurley Flynn, embraced the philosophies of socialism and anarchism. They were willing to go to prison, endure hunger strikes, social ostracism, and poverty in order to bring about social change.

The Settlement House Movement

By 1895, settlement houses operated independently as unique organizations and staging areas for reform activities. Located in American cities, each had a specific mission. In Hampton, Virginia, for instance, Janie Porter Barrett, the daughter of former slaves, established a settlement program in her own home to address the needs of the black community. At Janie Barett's institution, the Locust Street Social Settlement, students from the Hampton Institute (a prestigious school for African-Americans) served on the staff. Janie Barrett, a Hampton graduate herself, utilized Locust House to provide care and hot meals for children, and as a recreational and educational base for the community. Locust Street received generous funding from northern philanthropists. Janie Barrett was joined by Ida B. Wells-Barnett, the famous journalist and social activist.

Two settlement house founders in particular, Jane Addams in Chicago, and Lillian Wald in New York, characterized Progressive reform. In 1889, Jane Adams and her friend Ellen Gates Starr found a house to rent, the Hull Mansion on the corner of Polk and Halstead streets, located right in the middle of Chicago's Nineteenth Ward. Although Hull House mansion had once stood in the fashionable suburbs, a new population had grown up around it. The neighborhood, comprised of about 50,000 people of twenty different nationalities, included Russians, Germans, Italians, and Greeks, all crowded into makeshift tenement houses. Jane Addams described her new neighborhood as one where the streets were inexpressibly dirty, the number of school's inadequate and the paving miserable or altogether lacking. In the alleys and smaller streets, the foul smells from the nearby stables was beyond description. These were the places where people lived and children played.

Before coming to Chicago, Jane Addams' staff of volunteers, composed largely of college graduates from well-to-do families, had been sheltered from scenes of urban poverty. Because most volunteers were single females, (some divorced, some widowed), Hull House gained a reputation for harboring old maids. Jane Addams, surrounded by women at Hull-House, dedicated her life to helping women, particularly poor immigrant and working-class women.

Jane Addams, founder of the Chicago Settlement, Hull House. Jane Addams established many social institutions there and joined the International Peace Movement as well. (Photo courtesy of the Library of Congress.)

In keeping with Jane Addams' philosophy that the arts were not the preserve of the wealthy, the Hull House staff created a cultural center for their neighbors by starting modestly with reading parties, music recitals and art exhibitions. As public interest in Hull House grew, contributions came pouring in from wealthy patrons who financed an art gallery, theater, music school, gymnasium, free library, and additional funds to construct new buildings.

At its completion, the Hull House Settlement occupied thirteen buildings. By 1893, Hull

House with its' thriving community center had clubs for people of all ages, a kindergarten and day nursery, classes in prenatal and postnatal care, intramural sports and a residence for working women. Initially, Jane Addams' goal was to fill the working women's need for childcare but education quickly gained center stage. Eventually, the staff added classes for Americanization, and domestic management training for housewives and new mothers. This innovative program was a prototype of what would become the adult education movement.

Facing the grim realities of life in their new neighborhood, it was not uncommon for the Hull House staff to admit a battered wife seeking refuge, or to welcome a midwife there to deliver an unwed mother's baby. It was not long before life in this working-class neighborhood gave the staff a keener awareness of horrible factory conditions, inadequate sanitation, and the host of other problems that their neighbors endured. Hull House became the springboard of much social reform.

Living in the Nineteenth Ward drew Jane Addams and her staff inevitably into municipal politics. In *Twenty Years at Hull House,* she described scenes of young children playing near the carcass of a dead horse or cow which had been left to rot in the gutter. Convinced that the high death rate in their district was exacerbated by heaps of garbage piling up in the alleys, Jane Addams ran for and was elected Sanitary Inspector. During her tenure in office, she managed to get streets cleaned up and garbage collected regularly.

Children, when arrested, were locked up with adult criminals. Jane Addams campaigned successfully for a juvenile court system and she initiated the Hull House Police Boys' Club. This athletic program provided intramural sports for youth as a positive means to crime prevention. She believed that if the economic outlook of the poor was improved, the incentive for committing crime would be reduced. She tried to reshape social perceptions of prostitutes and female criminals, from sinful, fallen women to people in need of social service; but Progressive programs fell short and kept these women in perpetual poverty by training them in labor intensive jobs such as farming, sewing, and laundering.

The influence of Hull House went well beyond its west side neighborhood. In 1912, Jane Addams endorsed Theodore Roosevelt's candidacy for president and was allowed to second his nomination at the Progressive Party Convention. Her support of Roosevelt came under criticism as critics thought partisan politics was no place for a woman. Jane Addams used the Progressive Party platform to campaign for children, the elderly and overworked girls and workers. Women, she believed, could bring moral energy to politics and had an important role to play as "social housekeepers." As matron of Hull House, Jane operated within the traditional confines of domesticity which enabled her to support reform causes such as the legal system for juveniles and women's suffrage. (Her role in the women's suffrage movement is detailed in the next chapter.) Jane Addams' work in the Hull Settlement House contributed to a string of positive changes in American life, and was in operation for forty-six years, surviving well beyond the Progressive era.

In 1889, Lillian Wald, a Rochester socialite, came to New York City and entered nurses' training at the New York Hospital. Upon graduation, she worked at the New York Juvenile Asylum, an orphanage, where she witnessed abusive treatment of children. This motivated her to find work that would help the disadvantaged. She started home nursing care classes for immigrant women on New York City's Lower East Side. This experience made her realize that tenement residents were too sick, too poor, and too afraid to come to a hospital for treatment. With her friend Mary Brewster, Lillian Wald opened a Lower East Side clinic, but the two young nurses were quickly overwhelmed by the caseload.

Lillian Wald believed health care was a public responsibility and that medical care should be free. She used her close ties to the wealthy, and solicited contributions from Wall Street philanthropists to purchase buildings on Henry Street for a Nurses' Settlement House. With a staff of eleven, she instituted a new concept in medicine: public health care and a visiting public health nurse system. With trained personnel and an affiliation with the New York City Board of Health, she established the first public school of nursing in the country. It was an idea whose time had come; the visiting health nurse program spread quickly throughout the United States.

Patients and reformers flocked to the Henry Street Settlement, which became like Hull House, a hub of community activity. Remembering the plight of orphans, Lillian paid special attention to the needs of children. She built parks and playgrounds and, with the help of reformer Florence Kelley, lobbied to abolish child labor. She also cofounded the Federal Children's Bureau under the Department of Labor. From 1893 until 1933, Lillian Wald administered the health care system and numerous organizations, including the National Women's Trade Union League, the Children's Bureau, the Council of National Defense, the National Child Labor Committee, the National Organization for Public Health Nursing, and the Town and Country Nursing Service.

Helen Keller and Juliette Low

After contracting scarlet fever at the age of nineteen months, Helen Keller lost her sight, hearing and ability to speak. Her well-to-do southern family refused to accept Helen's handicap and believed that she could be as normal as other children. By age six, Helen's frequent outbursts and tantrums moved her parents to seek help from the famous inventor Alexander Graham Bell, and he recommended the teacher who would change her life — Anne Sullivan Macy.

Legally blind herself, Anne Sullivan Macy taught at the Perkins School for the Blind. Working with Helen, she made a remarkable breakthrough one day at the water pump. She ran water through Helen's fingers, pausing to write the letters *w-a-t-e-r* in Helen's palm. When Helen suddenly connected what Anne was trying to do, her silent universe opened and everything clicked. In the following weeks and months, Sullivan spent hours with Helen, teaching her the names of many things: trees, leaves, animals, household objects and countless others.

After learning to read by braille, Helen Keller began the even more frustrating challenge of learning to speak. She spent two years at the Perkins School and later studied under Sarah Fuller at the Horace Mann School for the Deaf in Boston. At the age of fourteen, she attended the Wright-Humason School for the Deaf in New York City, and at age sixteen enrolled at the Cambridge School for Young Ladies in Massachusetts. Helen applied to Radcliffe College in 1900, and graduated *cum laude* in 1904.

Helen Keller, who was blind, deaf and dumb, graduated from Radcliffe College cum laude and became a leading advocate for the blind. (Photo courtesy of the Library of Congress.)

In the succeeding years, Helen Keller became America's advocate for the disabled. She wrote on taboo topics such as the leading cause of blindness in children — venereal disease. Helen Keller reported on the seriousness of industrial accidents, which left many men, women and children not only blind but also uncompensated. In 1913, she became the spokeswoman and fund- raiser for the American Foundation for the Blind, and established a two-million-dollar endowment fund. She believed blind people should receive equitable treatment and adopted the socialist philosophy. Helen, who often resided at Hull House, wrote and published over fifteen books.

Juliette Magill Gordon Low was born to an upstanding Savannah, Georgia, family firmly rooted in southern tradition. Juliette became deaf in one ear as a child and would eventually lose her hearing completely. This handicap contributed to her learning difficulties.

After her marriage to William Low at age twenty-six, she relocated to England where she made the acquaintance of Lord Robert Baden-Powell, the founder of the British Scouting movement. On return to the United States, she formed the Girl Guides. Membership was open to girls of all races and religions. In 1915, Juliette renamed the Girl Guides the Girl Scouts, established her national scouting headquarters in Washington, D.C. and added a Campfire Girls program. Service to the scouts, whom she regarded as extended family, became her life's work. Juliette Low believed that the Girl Scouts program could educate girls between the ages of five and seventeen and enable them to develop into happy, resourceful women.

Muckrakers and Social Feminists

Elizabeth Cochrane Seaman, known by her *nom de plume*, "Nellie Bly," pioneered a place for women in investigative journalism. In 1885, while working for the *Pittsburgh Dispatch*, she introduced a form of journalism, known as muckraking, which investigated and exposed social problems. On assignment from the *Pittsburgh Dispatch*, she reported on working conditions and tenement life for Pittsburgh's factory girls. In 1886, Nellie Bly went to Mexico to report on the exploitation of Mexican labor. For writing the exposé, *Six Months in Mexico*, Mexican authorities expelled her from that country.

Nellie Bly produced a wild plan to get hired at Joseph Pulitzer's, *New York World.* She faked her own insanity and got herself committed to the New York Mental Asylum at Blackwell's Island. From inside, she reported firsthand on the treatment of inmates. Nellie endured being locked up in a flat restraining bed, known as the crib, and being slapped and beaten. She recounted that ordeal in *Ten Days in a Mad House*, and her news story led to a grand jury investigation of the hospital and eventually improvement in patient care. In another scheme, Nellie shoplifted in a store so she would be arrested and booked into city jail. Nellie also conducted *sub rosa* investigations of New York lobbyist corruption and conditions in sweatshops and factories. Nellie Bly was one of the first reporters to interview activist Emma Goldman in 1893.

Jules Verne's popular novel, *Around the World in Eighty Days*, inspired one of Nellie's publicity stunts. She proposed to her editor that she could beat Phineas Fogg's fictional around-the-globe-in-eighty-days trip. Since Verne's hero was sheer fantasy and officials were confident that it was an impossible feat for a female, they accepted her challenge. This kind of hype sold *New York World* newspapers and Nellie started packing. She took one suitcase containing two changes of clothing and a jar of cold cream. Beginning and ending the trip in Jersey City, New Jersey, Nellie Bly traveled by steamship, train, carriage and rickshaw. People sighted her all along the way in her signature tattersall deer stalker's cap, overcoat, and cape, *a la Sherlock Holmes*. On the journey, she stopped in France to visit Jules Verne at his estate. Bly finished her trip in seventy-two days, six hours and eleven minutes to be exact. It marked the high point of her career. In 1890, she capitalized on her venture by publishing *Around the World in Seventy-Two Days*.

Muckraking journalist Ida M. Tarbell wrote for American publications such as *Scribner's* and *McClure's.* Having grown up in Titusville, Pennsylvania, where her father owned a small oil refining company, she had working knowledge of the oil refining process. The *McClure's* editor accepted her series of articles on the Standard Oil Trust, a company which had squeezed out smaller oil producers like her father. Ida Tarbell's research led to the publication of *The History of the Standard Oil Company,* a sensational book in which she sharply criticized the methods of Standard Oil and its controlling stockholder, John D. Rockefeller. She described how Rockefeller had used unfair advantage to eliminate all competition.

> John D. Rockefeller was willing to strain every nerve to obtain for himself special and illegal privileges from the railroad which were bound to ruin every man in the oil business not sharing them with him.

The book received wide acclaim and in 1906, she teamed up with Lincoln Steffens, Ray

Stannard Baker, Finley Peter Dunne and William Allen White to publish *American Magazine.* President Woodrow Wilson praised her work *The Tariff in Our Times,* stating "She has written more good plain common sense, about the tariff than any man I know of." Ida Tarbell did not support the women's suffrage movement because she believed it would negate the gains women had made in the Progressive era; she believed women would "lose their independent power and capacity for innovation."

Florence Kelley, a Progressive activist, lived and managed reform activities between two settlement houses, Hull House in Chicago and the Henry Street settlement in New York, and she frequently appeared before the United States Congress as a lobbyist for various causes. Co-workers described her as "an impatient crusader, no gentle saint," who placed objectives above personal feelings.

When Florence, a Cornell graduate, was refused admission to law school in 1882, she attended the University in Zurich, Switzerland, where the study of socialism heightened her concern for workers. She returned to the United States a single mother with three children in need of work and shelter, and Hull House provided her with both.

In 1892, the Illinois Bureau of Labor Statistics hired Florence Kelley to investigate conditions in garment industry sweatshops as a fact-finding investigation which would aid state officials in enacting legislation like the Factory Act. This law prohibited child labor, curtailed working hours of women and developed standards for garment workers. Her work came to the attention of Illinois Governor Altgeld, who appointed Florence chief factory inspector. Her detailed reports on factory inspection were not only useful at that time but have become an invaluable historical source on working conditions for children in the 1890s. In one report, she described the tasks of young boys who worked in the Chicago Stockyards,

> Some of the children are boys who cut up the animals as soon as the hide is removed, little butchers working directly in the slaughterhouse, at the most revolting part of the labor performed in the stockyards. These children stand, ankle deep, in water used for flooding the floor for the purpose of carrying off blood and refuse into the drains; they breathe air so sickening that a man not accustomed to it can stay in the place but a few minutes; and their work is the most brutalizing that can be devised.

Chicago, the nation's clearinghouse for livestock, was the prime location for Florence Kelley to investigate conditions of child labor in the slaughterhouses. When she enlisted muckraking journalist Upton Sinclair, he exposed these problems in his book *The Jungle.* Florence Kelley's testimony before the Congress on the abhorrent conditions in the slaughterhouses resulted in the landmark legislations, the *Pure Food and Drug Act* and the *Meat Inspection Act,* both of 1906. This legislation regulated food, medicine and the meat packing industry which would be subjected not only to Federal inspection but also packing and labeling standards, hygienic regulation and quality control.

Florence Kelley, a socialist, had opted for the Progressive method in order to bring about reform by using the investigative-legislative process. In 1899, when the National Consumer's League appointed her the general secretary, she promoted workers' issues. Florence and the League were a good fit. The organization enabled her to address the hours, wages, and working conditions of women and children. The League called attention to manufacturers who produced goods under inhumane conditions, using child labor. Women from the League investigated working conditions in retail stores, noting wages, hours and sanitary facilities for the workers. The League also investigated companies hiring children. If stores met League standards, they were *White Listed* and the public was encouraged to buy from them. *Blacklisted* businesses, those using child labor, faced boycott by female shoppers, and their substandard practices were publicized.

In 1908, Florence Kelley gained protection for female employees in the landmark Supreme Court case, *Muller v Oregon.* This case involved Curt Muller, an Oregon commercial laundry owner, and his violation of an Oregon State Law which forbid women employed in commercial laundries from working more than ten hours a day. Muller had lost his case in the Oregon Court, and when he appealed to the Supreme Court, Florence enlisted Josephine Goldmark, a social researcher with good family connections, to help. Josephine and her brother-in-law, attorney Louis Brandeis, set to work on the Muller case. Josephine collected a large amount of data on the physical and mental effects of fatigue on women and also on the conditions at Muller's laundry which had affected employee health. When Louis Brandeis presented this case in court, it made legal history as a new approach to legal argument, known as the *Brandeis Brief*; it was the first brief in the U.S. that relied on analysis of factual data rather than pure legal theory to argue a case. This brief, filled with Josephine's statistics, gave overwhelming evidence which convinced the Supreme Court to uphold the Oregon Court's decision. Florence Kelley celebrated another triumph in 1912, when Congress created the Children's Bureau, and appointed Julia Lathrop, a protégée from Hull House as its director. Florence Kelly and Lillian Wald also promoted the work of the Bureau. Their effort to ban child labor which had culminated in the Owens-Keating Act of 1916 was short-lived. In 1922, the Supreme Court ruled the Owens-Keating Act unconstitutional.

Margaret Sanger, the Birth Control Movement and the Comstock Law

In the swell of moral reform, the Purity Crusades, sought to cleanse America of prostitution, obscenity, and other sexual vices. In 1873, the United States Congress passed the Comstock Law, a Federal statute which called for the suppression of trade in and circulation of obscene literature or any articles intended for immoral use. The law banned any mail distribution or importation of materials regarded as obscene, and this included literature about birth control, advertising about abortifacients, birth control devices, or information about abortions. The law's namesake, Anthony Comstock, was Postmaster General of the State of New York and a leader in the moral reform crusade. Individuals convicted of violating the Comstock Law faced charges of five years in prison with hard labor, and up to $2,000 in fines.

As a visiting nurse from Lillian Wald's Henry Street Settlement, Margaret Higgins Sanger witnessed firsthand the hardships and dangers working class women faced for lack of birth control information. (Photo courtesy of the Library of Congress.)

Margaret Higgins Sanger worked as a public health nurse out of Lillian Wald's Henry Street Settlement Clinic and made visits to Hell's Kitchen, one of the toughest neighborhoods on the Lower East Side. While making maternity calls on poor women in the area, she witnessed the staggering toll of infant mortality, and maternal deaths from self-induced abortions. Seeing the suffering of these women hit close to home. Margaret's own mother had given birth to eleven children and died from the debilitating effects of so many pregnancies. Her frustration with nursing increased because of the restraints placed on doctors and nurses by the Comstock Law. Since the law defined contraceptive information as obscene material, medical authorities were forbidden to advise women on birth control.

In 1912, Margaret Sanger left nursing after serving twelve years in the profession in order to devote herself completely to distributing information about *birth control*, (a concept and phrase she originated). In 1914, when she established the National Birth Control League, and began publishing *The Woman Rebel,* a newspaper which addressed the serious consequences of unplanned and unwanted children, Anthony Comstock secured a warrant for her arrest for distributing "obscene literature." Margaret Sanger, with the help of close friends, escaped to England where she stayed for a year. Upon her return in 1915, she set up America's first birth control clinic, in Brooklyn. Law enforcement officials, setting a trap for her, sent a female informant to her clinic to seek her advice and obtain contraceptive literature. The court determined she had flouted the Comstock Law charged her with creating a public nuisance and sentenced her to a public workhouse for thirty days. Margaret Sanger, with mounting public support, appealed the charge, and the New York State Court of Appeals dismissed the case against her. Under that court's decision, doctors could distribute birth control information but Margaret could not dispense birth control devices. Over the next decade she smuggled thousands of diaphragms, a then new contraceptive aid from Europe, into the United States. She also organized conferences to educate women on birth control.

While married to William Sanger, an up-and-coming architect, their home had become the gathering place for socialists and intellectuals like Emma Goldman, Mabel Dodge Luhan, and William Schlesinger. The Sangers claimed allegiance to socialism and Margaret stirred controversy at a time when Americans were just awakening to notions of modern sexuality. Her conviction that women should be sexually fulfilled was revolutionary and shocking. When she wrote articles on women's health for the Socialist newsletter, *The Call,* polite society was aghast at her openness about topics such as sexual intercourse, pregnancy and birth control. Margaret Sanger also challenged social convention by asserting that every woman's right to control her body was a human right. She believed that every child should be wanted and cared for and that the decision to have a child was personal.

Mothers of Invention: Emma Goldman and Mary Harris "Mother" Jones

Emma Goldman and Mary Harris "Mother" Jones were immigrants who got involved in the early union movement. Emma Goldman, a Lithuanian-Jewish immigrant, worked in a garment factory at age sixteen and experienced firsthand the harsh conditions for workers. She had come to the United States during a volatile period for immigrant labor, when trade unions were largely ineffectual to negotiate with factory owners for better working conditions. Radicals spoke on street corners, in meeting halls, and in taverns to unionize workers or to recruit them for the socialist or anarchist cause. At age eighteen, Emma Goldman had become an anarchist herself after six anarchists accused in the bombing deaths of policemen in the Chicago Haymarket riots were executed. She met and befriended radical Alexander Berkman. They conspired to assassinate Industrialist Henry Clay Frick, who had enraged labor when he hired Pinkerton guards to fight strikers on the picket lines during the steelworkers strike in Homestead, Pennsylvania. In the assassination attempt, Frick was wounded and Berkman was arrested and sentenced to fourteen years in prison. Her association with this attack brought Emma notoriety and labeled her as a violent revolutionary.

During the economic downturn of 1893, Goldman delivered the impassioned "Bread and Roses" speech to a gathering of unemployed workers in New York's Union Square. Shortly after making this speech she was arrested, found guilty of inciting to riot, and sentenced to serve a year at the New York Blackwell Island Prison. In 1901, when President McKinley was assassinated, his assassin, Leon Czolgosz boasted that Emma Goldman had inspired him. She insisted that Czolgosz, should have a fair trial and although no evidence ever linked her to the assassination, she came under constant government surveillance. She was marked a public enemy and immigration officials resolved to use any pretext to deport her. In 1906, she published the periodical *Mother Earth* and was in and out of prison because of the opinions she stated in print. In 1908, officials took away her citizenship and in 1917, publication of *Mother Earth* was banned.

In 1885, sixteen-year old Emma Goldman immigrated to the United States from Lithuania, a province of Russia. She endorsed birth control for women, free speech, and worker's rights, and opposed America's involvement in World War I. She was imprisoned and eventually deported for her beliefs. (Photo courtesy of the Library of Congress.)

Dubbed by the American press as "Red Emma," this image of a wild-eyed radical became the icon of American radicalism. Her dogged fight for free speech marked an era in United States history when the Bill of Rights had been all but forgotten. Her crusade eventually shifted the free speech controversy from the fringes of immigrant radicalism to the center of American debate. She was willing to go to prison, if need be, to revitalize the American tradition of dissent.

Labor leader Mary Harris emigrated from Ireland to the United States as a young girl and grew up in the Midwest, where she became a school teacher. When a yellow fever epidemic tragically took her husband, James Jones, and their four children in 1867, she relocated to Chicago to set up a modest dressmaking business. When her shop was destroyed in the Great Chicago Fire, she turned to the Knights of Labor for help. It was at this point that her life took a very dramatic turn.

Mary Harris "Mother" Jones, a labor activist, targeted especially the suffering of children put to work in mines and factories. (Photo courtesy of the Library of Congress.)

The Knights of Labor, one of the first unions to organize in the United States in the 1860s, reached out to all workers regardless of sex, ethnicity, or work experience. They welcomed both skilled and unskilled workers into the organization. Mary Harris Jones' affiliation with the Knights filled her with a sense of purpose and she would spend the rest of her life fighting for the working class. Her work took her all over the country, into mill towns and mining camps. She could be easily spotted wearing her signature widow's black silk dress and bonnet; everyone called her Mother Jones.

As a labor agitator, Mother Jones supported the Pittsburgh railroad strike in 1877, and in the 1880s, she allied with the coal miners and became a paid organizer for the United Mine Workers. During the miners' strike in Arnot, Pennsylvania, she led a band of miners' wives, armed with mops, brooms, dishpans, and pots and pans, with these instructions,

> You lead the army up to the Drip Mouth. Take that tin dishpan you have with you and your hammer, and then, when the scabs and the mules come up, begin to hammer and howl and be ready to chase

> the scabs with your mops and brooms, and don't be afraid of anyone.

In 1900, the fact that one-fifth of the nation's children worked under abysmal conditions for meager wages moved Mother Jones to crusade for them. Children worked mercilessly long hours in dangerous and unhealthy environments in textile mills, mines, factories, and the garment industry. Mother Jones described the accident of an eleven-year-old girl whose scalp had been torn off when her hair was caught in mill machinery. Intent on researching child labor conditions, she went from one cotton mill to another, posing as a worker, and recording what she saw.

> Little girls and boys, barefooted, walked up and down between the endless rows of spindles, reaching thin little hands into the machinery to repair snapped threads. They crawled under machinery to oil it. They replaced spindles all day long. Tiny babies of six years old with faces of sixty did an eight hour shift for ten cents a day. If they fell asleep, cold water was dashed in their faces and the voice of the manager yelled above the ceaseless racket and whir of machines.

In 1903, Mother Jones gathered children from Philadelphia and marched them to President Roosevelt's home at Oyster Bay, New York. Many children were too weak to finish the march, known as the Children's Crusade, and some were transported the rest of the way by train. Although Roosevelt posed himself as a Progressive and humanitarian, he refused to meet with the marchers. Nonetheless, that year the State of Pennsylvania passed a law barring children under the age of fourteen from working.

Mother Jones had frequent run-ins with law enforcement. In 1912, when a factory guard was killed during a strike in West Virginia, authorities arrested, convicted and sentenced her to serve twenty years in prison for conspiracy to commit murder. She was pardoned by the West Virginia Governor when the United States Senate threatened to investigate the affair.

The renowned labor photographer, Lewis Hine, whose camera recorded the bleak faces and blank stares of workers, publicized what factory work did to children. Like Mother Jones, labor activist Marie Van Vorst often posed as a factory worker to observe firsthand what happened in the mills and to gather documentary evidence. She saw children uncompensated and untreated when they lost fingers and limbs in dangerous machinery. She noted that sixty percent of the employees in one South Carolina textile mill were women and children. Marie Van Vorst also lobbied for protective legislation for children, and laws restricting child labor.

Neither Emma Goldman nor Mother Jones supported Progressivism or the women's movement. Emma Goldman who never compromised or moved toward a moderate position reflected on the Progressives shortcomings noting that, "teaching the poor to eat with a fork is all very well but what good does it do if they have not food?" Once, when asked about women's suffrage, Mother Jones retorted "You don't need a vote to raise hell! You need convictions and a voice." She believed the women's movement was a step backward, and a deliberate ploy by men to divert middle-class women into futile projects. She explained "The plutocrats organize their women, they keep them busy with suffrage and prohibition and charity."

Women's Organizers, Labor Unions and Strikes

The attempts to consolidate the skilled and unskilled workers into a world union culminated in the organization of the International Workers of the World, the IWW, also called the Wobblies. The IWW, which existed for about twelve years, was intended to fill the gap left by the American Federation of Labor (AFL). Under Samuel Gomphers' leadership, the AFL had paid only lip service to women and unskilled labor, but the IWW welcomed them with open membership. Mother Jones, who had fought for industrial unionism, joined the IWW at the founding convention on June 27, 1905, along with Emma Goldman and socialist Elizabeth Gurley Flynn. They believed that only extreme measures would reconcile the gross injustices and cruel repression of the American working class. Outraged at the callous treatment of the poor, Goldman and Flynn saw as their first priority to ensure that they would be heard. Obtaining the right to speak freely was the first step.

Elizabeth Gurley Flynn, the child of Irish immigrants, had been weaned on socialist ideas. As a young girl, she accompanied her father to socialist rallies and by 1906, at age sixteen Elizabeth worked full-time for the Socialist Party. She gave street corner speeches opposing women's unpaid domestic labor. She was hired by the IWW to speak and organize for the union. Because of her beauty, fiery delivery, and charismatic personality, people turned out to hear her. She organized the Lawrence, Kansas, Bread and Roses Strike, the Paterson and Passaic Strikes, and led the Free Speech Campaign of 1909, throughout the Northwest, and was arrested in Spokane, Washington, and in Missoula, Montana. She observed the extreme poverty of the workers on the picket line.

> I saw them all go to the Paterson strike, without shoes, in the middle of winter with rags on their feet. I went into one family to have a picture taken with a mother with eight children who didn't have a crust of bread or a bowl of milk in the house, But the father was out on the picket line... Hunger was gnawing at their vitals; hunger wearing them down; and still they had the courage to fight it out for six months.

Leonara Kearney Barry, of County Cork, Ireland, came to the United States in 1852. For twenty years, Leonara a widow with ten children worked as a school teacher to support her family. Because factory jobs paid better than teaching, she went to work in a New York garment factory, for $0.65 in weekly wages. She joined the Knights of Labor in 1884, and achieved leadership status quickly by organizing two cooperative shirt factories. Her reports for the Knights of Labor contributed to the enactment of extensive factory inspection laws in Pennsylvania in 1889. After her marriage, Leonara, then Mrs. Barry Lake, had the leisure to take up women's causes such as suffrage and temperance. Addressed as Mother Lake, she became a popular speaker on the Chataqua and Redpath lecture circuits, drumming up support for prohibition throughout the Midwest.

Mary Kenney, who started working in a bindery at age fourteen, became highly skilled at her trade and moved on to organize workers. In 1880, at age twenty-four, she was a full-time union organizer and formed the Woman's Bookbinding Union in Chicago. One of the first activists at Hull House, she later moved onto New York to work for the American Federation of Labor and organized women laborers in the printing, binding and garment factories. In 1894, Mary Kenney married Jack O' Sullivan, a labor editor, and they collaborated for the labor cause. She enlisted Jane Addams' support in founding the National Women's Trade Union League, the NWTUL.

The League's objective was the eight hour day and a living wage for everyone. The NWTUL founded local Leagues in Boston, Chicago, and New York. Membership was open to men, women and non-working middle-class women. Society women, known as the "Mink Brigade," joined the WTUL. After the WTUL supported the Capmakers' Strike, Rose Schneiderman, a member of the Capmaker's union, also joined the League. In the WTUL, Rose Schneiderman worked with socialites like Mary and Margaret Dreier. The Dreier sisters donated money to train women in union work. The WTUL also offered working class women an opportunity for better paying administrative jobs in the union. Some went from this experience into the government and business sectors. The WTUL also choreographed effective strikes and supervised picket lines. Bail money for members arrested during strikes constantly tapped the union's treasury. Although fundraising for the League was time consuming, it was necessary in order to maintain the legal assistance fund.

At the turn of the twentieth century, the first American cover girl, the Gibson Girl, created by magazine illustrator Charles Dana Gibson, set a new style for young women's fashion. Her image, displayed everywhere, in magazines, greeting cards, advertising, paintings and sketches epitomized feminine grace, charm, and elegance. The Gibson Girl look was all the rage among working girls who adopted the style. It was inexpensive for them to copy and comprised the namesake shirtwaist blouse, an ankle-length tailored skirt and hair swept in an updo.

This photo of a young woman shows the more relaxed, tailored style of the Gibson Girl fashion.

By 1909, in order to meet the demand for the popular shirtwaist blouses, there were 500 shirtwaist factories employing over 35,000 working girls in New York City.

The period from 1909-1911 was a particularly volatile period for the female garment workers and the WTUL. Within a short period of time, the union recruited 20,000 members from workers in the shirtwaist companies, eighty percent of whom were female. In November 1909, these women staged strikes in New York and Philadelphia, each known as "the uprising of the 20,000," the largest strikes by women workers in American history. The momentum continued to build and the WTUL recruited new members at the rate of 1,000 per day. In order to pay Union dues, members walked to work and saved streetcar fare. Unfortunately, the strike yielded no gains. Since many factories refused to recognize the union, the strike ended in February 1910. But the 20,000 women who had been willing to strike together had laid the groundwork for an expanded union: the International Ladies' Garment Workers' Union, the ILGWU.

The Triangle Shirtwaist Factory Fire

> This is our funeral, these our graves, Our children, the beautiful, beautiful flowers destroyed, Our lovely ones burned, their ashes buried under a mountain of caskets.
>
> Morris Rosenfield,
> The Jewish Daily Forward

During the ILGWU formation and protest, one shop, the Triangle Shirtwaist Factory in New York City, fired a number of girls who had joined the union. There were hundreds of factories like the Triangle Shirtwaist Company. They were nothing more than sweatshops, makeshift facilities occupying a few rooms or floors of a high-rise building. During the three month strike, employees at Triangle and other shirtwaist companies complained of dismal working conditions. After the strike, owners refused to negotiate with the union and employees returned to work without any changes.

At the Triangle Factory, female employees were closely supervised in the bathrooms, exit doors were locked, clocks were covered and employees' handbags were searched. On a weekly salary of three dollars, the girls were required to supply their own needle and thread and pay for the shop's electricity. Employees had frequently complained about electrical wiring, how it gave off visible sparks and how the electrical current arched in the poorly lit workrooms.

The Triangle Shirtwaist Factory was located in the Asch Building at Greene and Washington Place and 500 workers were packed onto the eighth, ninth and tenth floors. On March 25, 1911, a Saturday as well as a payday, at 4:30 p.m., thirty minutes before closing time, an explosion and flash fire erupted on the eighth floor and spread rapidly to the top floors. Panic-stricken workers rushed the doors to get out and many, overcome with smoke, burned to death in the shop rooms. Some were unable to exit via the stairs and elevator because exits were already jammed with hundreds of workers. By the time passersby noticed the fire, it looked as though employees were throwing large bolts of flaming cloth out of the windows. On second glance, onlookers realized they were witnessing a devastating tragedy. Girls with flames in their hair and clothing were jumping out of the windows, to their certain deaths on the pavement below. Facing only fatal options, the girls chose to quickly die from the jump rather than slowly from the flames. Some of those who fell were impaled on the spiked railings of iron fences below. Eyewitness Mary Heaton Vorse described the tragedy,

> I hurried over to the Square, drawn by the contagion of disaster...People ahead of me were crying "Another's jumped! Another's jumped, all on fire!" Like burning torches, girls jumped into the street. One hundred twenty-nine were burned to death that day. Two little painted girls were standing near me. One said to the other, "Now, Eva, ain't you glad you left the factory?"

The fire, which burned for about an hour, took its toll within thirty minutes. When the smoke cleared, officials counted 146 fatalities, including 126 women and 20 men, 99 of whom had burned to death inside and 47, who had plunged to their death.

Officials trying to identify the victims of the Triangle Fire who had jumped from the upper floors. Because of the impact of their fall, some went through the sidewalk. (Photo courtesy of the Library of Congress.)

The Triangle Fire was a disaster waiting to happen in any number of sweatshops in the city. The Fire Department speculated that a lit cigarette may have started the fire, but the ensuing investigation revealed that the lack of maintaining safety standards was the cause. Poorly wired workrooms, which were cleaned about once a year, were filled with baskets of textiles, oily rags, and other debris. There were fire escapes but only on the top four floors and they had buckled under due to the intense heat. The factory owners kept workroom doors locked to prevent employees from leaving early, and to discourage workers from sitting on the landings to eat lunch. The 500 people packed onto three floors had never had a fire drill and no fire extinguishers had been installed.

Firefighters arrived within ten minutes after the fire started, but their efforts were futile. Ladders only reached to the sixth floor and the water hoses only to the seventh. Safety nets used to catch the jumpers split as three or four bodies hurtled down and hit all at one time. One thirteen-year-old female worker managed to hold onto a ledge for several minutes until the flames burned her hands so badly that she let go. Eyewitnesses were moved by seeing a young man assisting the girls out of the windows. When the fourth girl came to the ledge, he embraced and kissed her and suspended her momentarily before dropping her. After she fell, he quickly followed.

The bodies were sent to several makeshift morgues where relatives and friends could make positive identification. A feeling of gloom and anger fell over New York City in the aftermath of the fire. Most of the victims had been Italian and Jewish immigrants and ethnic newspapers such as the *Yiddish Language Press* ran stories about the girls. Workers massed for memorials and repeated demands for safety protection, worker's compensation and factory inspection laws.

The WTUL staged a mass memorial for the victims on April 2nd in the Metropolitan Opera House. It quickly became a protest of the abuses at Triangle and other shirtwaist factories. WTUL representative, Rose Schneiderman, delivered an impassioned speech,

> I would be a traitor to these poor burned bodies if I came here to talk good fellowship. We have tried you good people of the public and we have found you wanting. This is not the first time girls have been burned alive in this city. Every week I must learn of the untimely death of one of my sister workers. Every year thousands of us are maimed.

A mass funeral for the victims was held on a rainy April 5th. The procession of 120,000 people paid tribute to the girls who had died at the Triangle Shirtwaist Factory.

Funeral procession for the victims of the Triangle Factory Fire. Trade unions and garment workers turned out by the thousands to honor their fellow workers. (Photo courtesy of the Library of Congress.)

Although the city was stunned by this terrible tragedy, it still took thousands of letters from WTUL members and public outcry before New York officials acted. In the criminal trial, Triangle owners Max Blanck and Isaac Harris, who had escaped the fire by climbing onto the roof and reaching an adjoining building were acquitted of manslaughter. Justice did not prevail in the civil case either; Blanck and Harris were fined a mere $75 per victim for violations of safety regulations. They relocated the factory and, with the $65,000 in insurance money they collected for damage to their property, resumed business as usual.

The Triangle Fire illustrated the all too familiar practice of precaution *following* tragedy. The State of New York appointed Robert F. Wagner as Chairman and Alfred E. Smith as Vice Chairman of the fire investigation. The Wagner Commission's four-year study presented recommendations and produced protective legislation, the first of its kind in the country. With no less that fifty-six laws regulating fire hazards and unsafe machinery, the state required factories to install safety equipment such as fire escapes, fire doors and exits. They were subjected to stringent inspections and regulations for proper electrical wiring, sanitation, and safe machinery; but passing safety legislation was one thing, and enforcing it was another.

Pauline Newman, a union organizer who had worked at Triangle as a child, described how the abuses continued after the fire. Workers were promised improved wages and shorter hours, a reduction of weekly work from fifty-six to fifty-two hours, but a typical workday remained from 7:30 a.m. to 9:30 p.m. for adults and children. Even with state regulations, those factories which employed children found ways to hoodwink or bribe labor inspectors, as Newman explains.

> Well of course there were [child labor] laws on the books, but no one bothered to enforce them. The employers were always tipped off if there was going to be an inspection. "Quick" they'd say "into the boxes!" And we children would climb into the big boxes the finished shirts were stored in. Then some shirts were piled on top of us, and when the inspector came- no children. The factory always got an okay from the inspector, and I suppose someone at City Hall got a little something too.

The New Feminism of Charlotte Perkins Gilman

> Woman should stand beside man as the comrade of his soul not the servant of his body.
>
> -Charlotte Perkins Gilman-

Charlotte Perkins Gilman, an advocate for domestic reform, was a fourth generation member of the Beecher family and the niece of Harriet Beecher Stowe and Catherine Beecher. Charlotte joined Progressive friend Jane Addams at Hull House in 1895, to participate in the settlement house experiment. As a Socialist, Charlotte Perkins Gilman espoused a "social revolution" for women, but unlike Emma Goldman and Elizabeth Gurley Flynn, Charlotte supported both feminist and Progressive attempts to change society and to elevate women's status. She admired suffragists Elizabeth Cady Stanton and Susan B. Anthony whom she believed displayed, "a splendid bit of heroism."

As a writer and lecturer, Charlotte Perkins Gilman articulated feminist thought. She put forth her ideas in *Women and Economics*, published in 1898, a book which made her famous in the United States and Europe. Using the socialist framework, she analyzed the relationship between the sexes from an economic standpoint, and concluded that getting the vote *would not solve* the inequities women faced daily. Without equal opportunities in education and employment the vote would only rank women second-class citizens. Women, she believed, were subordinate because of their economic dependence on their husbands and as long as women accepted a restricted domestic role, they would remain perpetually and negatively bound to men.

Charlotte Perkins Gilman believed that heredity and evolution were powerful determinants in human destiny and concluded that social roles for the sexes were not permanently fixed, but evolving. In the past, women had developed alluring traits such as sexuality, physical attractiveness, domesticity and subservience as a means to acquire a husband, to ensure their security and to propagate children. But, by focusing on these traits, she thought that women had neglected the development of their own intelligence and physical strength. She believed that women would never find marriage fulfilling until they could stand equal to men.

In her self-styled socialism, Charlotte Perkins Gilman believed that class differences were not the only problem. The entire domestic arrangement was poorly executed and a wasteful means of feeding, clothing and cleaning humanity. In *Women and Economics*, she suggested that the domestic economy needed a complete restructuring:

> It would be a home where the cleaning was done by efficient workers. Not hired separately by the families, but engaged by the manager of the establishment; and a roof garden, day nursery and Kindergarten, under well-trained professional nurses and teachers would insure proper care of the children.

Charlotte Perkins Gilman attacked what she called, "the beloved dogma of the maternal instinct," the belief that by virtue of being a mother, a woman inherited the sole responsibility for her children. She also challenged the idea that a mother would automatically know what was right for her children. She believed parents needed to exercise reason, not instinct alone, in order to effectively train children. But parents alone did not shape and educate them. She advocated communal living arrangements to take care of households, augmented by teachers, doctors, and nurses, who all shared in the family enterprise. Such a plan would allow mothers time to develop interests outside the home and that, she believed would contribute more toward a child's development than if mothers stayed at home. She disputed the concept of a female mind. Thinking was neither male nor female, it was an acquired cultural trait. As Gilman argued "the brain was not an organ of sex, for if it was one might as well speak of a female liver."

Charlotte Perkins Gilman realized that her ideas were radical and that reform would require major changes in the ways in which men and women interacted. Her ideas were quite popular at the turn of the century, and if her attack on the restrictive domestic role for women and the inequality of the sexes sounds contemporary, it is because her ideas played a key role in articulating modern feminism.

Conclusion

Progressives came in all shapes and sizes, but were generally white, urban, middle-class, Christian, and college educated. Progressives, whom a more cynical society might have called do-gooders, launched an ambitious program spanning several decades from about 1890 to 1925. They left an indelible stamp on American life as they established social and political reform, and gave help directly to working-class people. Their efforts made a difference. Whether administering first aid to an ailing society or lobbying for legislative reform, they showed a common concern for the decline of American democracy, the plight of labor, the condition of cities, the difficulty of assimilating immigrants and the excesses of industrialization. Reaching its zenith from 1900-1917, Progressivism brought not only social reform but also created a third political party which challenged the bipartisan system.

The Progressive movement, like most historical trends, represented both continuity and change. Reformers came from all walks of life. Under the nonthreatening guise of social housekeeping, women such as Jane Addams and Lillian Wald established settlement houses and new social institutions such as day care, free clinics, adult education, and park and recreation programs.

Juliette Low served as the national president of the Girl Scouts until 1920 and lived to see Girl Scout troops and organizations in every state in the Union and her birthday, October 31, 1860 officially declared Founder's Day. When Juliette Low died in 1927, the city's entire population of Girl Scouts attended her funeral in Christ's Church, Savannah, Georgia. Since the founding of the Girl Scouts more than eighty-five years ago forty million girls have become members of the Girl Scouts.

Radical Emma Goldman championed the rights of free speech and a fair deal for American workers. Mary Harris "Mother" Jones organized strikes and demonstrations for labor and called particular attention to the plight of children who worked in mills and mines. Reformer Margaret Sanger, a public health nurse, worked to ease the burden of women whose only options were unwanted pregnancies or harmful abortions. In order to create more efficiency and harmony in the domestic economy and marriage, Charlotte Perkins Gilman sought a dramatic departure from society's restrictive roles for men and women. Although their strategies and philosophies of reform differed, whether Progressive or Socialist, these women all shared a common vision that the world *could* and *would* be healed by women.

Chapter 18
Winning the War and Winning the Vote
Munitionettes and Suffragettes

Key Topics

Women in the Great War
American Nurses at the Front
Women Gain the Right to Vote

Chronology

1912 - Woodrow Wilson Becomes President
National Suffrage Parade Staged in Washington, D.C.
1914 - World War I, the Great War, Begins
1916 - Woodrow Wilson Re-elected
1917 - America Declares War on Germany
Suffragists Picket the White House
1918 - World War I Ends with Armistice, German Surrender
1920 - Nineteenth Amendment, the Susan B. Anthony Amendment, Ratified for Women's Suffrage

Introduction

The United States entered World War I, the Great War, in 1917, and because America's engagement ended with the Armistice in November of 1918, women's participation in the war effort was short-lived. While most Americans on the home front supported the country's involvement, some were opposed to the war and the draft. Suffragists walked a fine line, pushing their political agenda while showing their patriotism and support for the war effort. Suffragist Carrie Chapman Catt thought women's involvement might improve their chances for a women's equal suffrage amendment. She pledged NAWSA's support for the war and urged women to get involved in war work. Carrie Chapman Catt insisted that whether women volunteered to go overseas, sold war bonds, or conserved food in their kitchens, they helped America win the war, and a victorious country should reward them.

When American soldiers shipped out for France, women on the home front filled positions traditionally held by men; they worked as mail carriers, police officers, machinists, taxi and truck drivers, and farm laborers. Because women filled these vacancies patriotically and temporarily, the public accepted them wearing men's attire and working as streetcar and train conductors, railroad engineers, dispatch riders for courier services, chauffeurs and defense plant workers. Eight million women were already working for wages, and an additional one million were hired as defense workers. Wartime employment presented opportunities to leave lower paying for higher paying jobs; nonetheless, women were paid less than men for the same jobs, and they knew that after the war, they would be forced to return to the lower paying occupations.

Women in the Great War

> In these days, the outstanding marvel is the way mothers and wives have gone through sorrow not callously but with an extraordinary sense of hopefulness. One thing the war has done is to knock on the head all such shallow optimism as telling people to look on the bright side of things or that every cloud has a silver lining. There are some clouds that are black all through.
>
> Oswald Chamber, Army Chaplain

Although the United States did not enter the war until 1917, American women responded quickly to help in the defense effort. A Women's Committee of the United States Council for National Defense was organized with suffragist Dr. Anna Howard Shaw as chairman. She toured as a spokeswoman for President Woodrow Wilson to promote his peace plan for the postwar world. Muckraking journalist Ida Tarbell served on the Women's Committee of the United States Council for National Defense along with suffragist Carrie Chapman Catt to encourage America's involvement in the war. The National American Woman Suffrage Association (NAWSA) maintained a hospital in France for the care of American soldiers.

In 1917, fifty-year-old reporter Elizabeth Cochrane (alias Nellie Bly) continued to scoop the news. During the war, she went to Europe as one of three war journalists to report the fighting at the front. Nellie Bly served in uniform as the only female war correspondent for a United States newspaper.

The women who worked in armament and ammunition factories in Europe and America were known as the *munitionettes*. They donned their overalls and went to work for the war effort, making bombs, bullets and torpedoes. This was dangerous work and some munitionettes suffered the ill effects of working near the explosives. TNT poisoning, a silent killer, was unknown to workers at the time but could be easily diagnosed by doctors. Women whose hands were yellow and waxy were already dying of the toxicity. Another symptom was the hair turning a ginger color from absorbing TNT chemicals. In Great Britain, 200 deaths of munitionettes from TNT poisoning were documented. In the United States, where no documentation is available, anecdotal evidence such as letters, memoirs, and newspapers suggests that neither industry nor the government took precautions to protect these women. Deaths of munitionettes from accidents and explosions in the armaments factories also went unreported by the government and industry.

The female images of Joan of Arc, the Statute of Liberty, and a girl in a sailor's uniform exclaiming "Gee, if I were a man I'd sign up and fight," were used on recruitment posters. Young women, particularly nurses who worked in teams, entered beer or music halls, and theaters, to give their pitch for the war and enlistment.

The American Red Cross called for nurse volunteers to serve in Europe, and nurses were used to recruit soldiers. (Picture courtesy of the Library of Congress.)

British diplomat James Balfour noted that "behind every man in the trenches there are ten persons making it possible for him to stay there. In 1917, seven of the ten are women." The French General Joseph Joffre observed firsthand that "We have two armies, one in the trenches and one behind the trenches. The one behind the trenches is composed mostly of women."

Women had served officially in the military for the first time during the Spanish-American War in 1898, but in World War I, Federal Records indicate that up to 30,000 women served in uniform. Because of statistical discrepancies in government records, it is likely that many more women must have served. For these women, World War I was a unique experience in that Congress had created the Army Nurses'

Corps in 1901, and the Navy Nurses' Corps in 1908, which allowed women to serve legally and officially in the armed forces for the first time in American history. With the combined efforts of the Navy, Marine Corps and Coast Guard, some 13,000 women were recruited. Coast Guard servicewomen were known as yeomanettes, such as twin sisters Gene Viere and Lucille Baker. Women worked in the Signal Corps as radio and telephone operators, and at military installations as translators. Female military personnel served in office jobs, processing troops for transport, recruiting, doing intelligence work, and creating military camouflage designs and logos.

American Nurses at the Front

> ......what with the steam, the ether, and the filthy clothes of the men... the odor in the operating room was so terrible that it was all any of them could do to keep from being sick...no mere handling of instruments and sponges, but sewing and tying up and putting in drains while the doctor takes the next piece of shell out of another place. Then after fourteen hours of this with freezing feet, to a meal of tea and bread and jam, then off to rest if you can, in a wet bell tent in a damp bed without sheets, after a wash with a cupful of water one need never tell me that women can't do as much, stand as much, and be as brave as men.
>
> Nurse Julia Stimson

Most women who enlisted served as nurses and were desperately needed at the front in France, Belgium, Italy and England. They tended the wounded on the battlefield, at casualty clearing stations, in field hospitals, on troop trains and onboard ships. In the line of enemy fire, some American nurses were wounded and some died in Europe and are buried there. Congress awarded the Distinguished Service Cross to several Army nurses, and France bestowed its highest award, *Le Croix de Guerre*, the War Cross, to twenty American nurses.

In addition to caring for the wounded and assisting in surgery, nurses drove ambulances, set up makeshift first-aid stations, prepared supplies, washed linens and clothes, maintained hospital equipment and cooked. Volunteer Red Cross nurses performed the same duties as the military nurses but were not paid. Auxiliary to the nursing corps were a cadre of military women who served as physical and occupational therapists, known as reconstructionists. They had the task of trying to rehabilitate amputees, soldiers blinded by gas, and victims whose lungs and organs were deteriorating from the effects of poisonous mustard gas.

Women volunteered and served in World War I as machinists, chauffeurs, police officers, nurses, ambulance drivers, and recruiters. (Photo courtesy of the Archives of the Fullerton College Library.)

Nurse Helen Fairchild

On April 5, 1917, Helen Fairchild, R.N., a graduate of the Pennsylvania Hospital in Philadelphia, who had volunteered to serve in the Army Nursing Corps, shipped out to France with sixty-seven other nurses. Helen was assigned to Casualty Clearing Station #4, in Flanders, where some of the heaviest fighting occurred during the Battle of Passchendaele. Casualty clearing stations were crude, rugged medical facilities for soldiers which often consisted of underground shelters. Nurses lived in rude huts, but during heavy shelling they slept in trenches just as the soldiers did. These trenches, which measured about three feet by six feet and two feet deep, often caved in from the shelling and filled with mud and water.

The industrial technology available in World War I introduced ghastly weapons which caused unprecedented devastation. The new technology allowed armies to fight 24 hours a day: shelling, shooting, bombing, and gassing the enemy. During an attack, as hundreds of casualties, usually victims of mustard gas poisoning, poured into the makeshift hospitals, nurses like Helen Fairchild were required to work a 48-hour shift. During her tour of duty, nurse Fairchild wrote many letters home telling of the war, the medical work, and her expectations for homecoming. Three months after her arrival in Europe, Helen was already tired of wearing the regulation army uniforms.

Casualty Clearing Station #4
August 1917

Dear Mother,

I am with an operating team about 100 miles from our own Base Hospital, closer to the fighting lines. I'll sure have a lot to tell about this experience when I get home. I have been here three weeks and see no signs of going back yet, Just as soon as I get home I am going to get dresses all colors of the rainbow, but never again blue serge or a blue felt hat. Gee, now I know how the kids in orphan asylums must feel when they all have to wear the same kind of clothes. Another of our operating team left for a place further up the lines this am. They went to relieve Dr. Mitchell, Dr. Packard and Miss McClelland, who has been up there since July 21st, and who are tired out. This team will take their place so they can come home. Rained some last night and is frightfully windy and cold. I put on some woolen clothing for we do not have any fires in the hut yet, but in spite of two pairs of stockings my feet are cold. Right now I stopped writing and got two hot water bottles and have my feet on one and the other in my lap. Please write letters often, they mean more to me than a package, for I get a little homesick sometimes. Heaps and heaps of love and a big kiss to every one, your very own,
Helen.

Helen served at the front from the summer through December of 1917. On January 13, 1918, she underwent surgery for an enlarged gastric ulcer. In her last letter to her mother, Helen indicated she had been hospitalized.

Base Hospital No. 10, December 28, 1917

Dear Mother,

Had a letter from the States this week and was glad, for being sick this far from home is no fun, but everyone has been fine to me. My room is filled with flowers they bring me, and fruit galore. Dr. Norris was just in to see me and told me I could stop some of my medicine. He said my throat looked much better but I still can't go on duty "till I eat and get some color, so I see my finish, for as usual, I look like the wrath of Kingdom come, but I'll make them let me go back soon, for its too lonesome here to be off duty. Gee but I'll be glad to see you all by the time this war is over, but at the same time I am glad to be here to help take care of these poor men, and I'll be doubly glad when our own U.S. boys will be [in this part of France] with us, for they will be so far from home, and they will have no one but us American nurses to really take any genuine interest in them, for their own friends will not be able to reach them. What the Red Cross and the YMCAs are doing for us here means so much to us. Really, it would be awful to get along without the things they send us. Most of the pleasure that the troops get are the ones provided by the YMCA. If you could only see what the boys here have to go through sometimes, you would see they need all the comfort possible. Without the supplies sent to us by the Red Cross Society, we could not do half as much for them as we are. Please tell me what it was that everyone seems to have heard concerning me at home. Of course whatever it was, as you know, is not correct, for as I [sic] have told you often, anytime, anything should happen, you would be notified. Heaps of Love, your very own,
Helen

Helen died three days after her surgery. It is very likely that exposure to mustard gas exacerbated her condition. In January of 1918, Helen's father received the letter informing him of his daughter's death.

War Department
Office of the Surgeon-General
Washington, D.C.
January 24, 1918

Mr. Ambrose Fairchild
Allenwood, Union County,
Pennsylvania

Dear Mr. Fairchild,

It is with regret that I have to inform you of the death of your daughter, Miss Helen Fairchild, RN, on January 18, 1918, while on duty with Base Hospital #10, American Expeditionary Forces, France.

D.E. Thompson, Superintendent
Army Nurses Corps

Opposition to the War

The government passed the *Espionage Act of 1917*, which defined as undesirable anyone who voiced criticism of the government. The law imposed a fine of $10,000 and a prison sentence of up to twenty years to anyone conveying information with intent to interfere with the success of the U. S. and its armed forces, including interfering with the draft, or to promote its enemies. The Sedition Act set the same penalties to anyone who denounced enlistment, or discouraged the sale of war bonds. Radicals Emma Goldman, Kate Richards O'Hare and Elizabeth Gurley Flynn all opposed both the war and the draft. Emma Goldman, who had publicly denounced the war, was arrested and imprisoned from 1917 to 1919, as an undesirable alien. When socialist Kate Richards O'Hare opposed America's involvement in World War I, she was sent to prison in 1919, under the Espionage and Sedition Acts. There she met Emma Goldman and after their release, they worked for the pardon of other political prisoners.

Jane Addams enjoyed national celebrity until World War I, but all that would change after her visit to American troops in France. On return to the United States, Jane incensed officials by reporting that soldiers were neither brave nor patriotic, just terrified. She said that faced with the constant barrage of shelling, the deadly effects of mustard gas, and living in muddy trenches, troops were in a constant state of alcoholic stupor. When Jane Addams spoke out against the war, the American press labeled her unpatriotic, and she quickly fell out of the public's favor. Undaunted, she took on humanitarian war work, continued the programs at Hull House and never compromised her pacifist principles. She joined prominent Americans, such as Andrew Carnegie, and organized the International Peace Movement to voice her discontent.

World War I

Country	Mortality
United States	106,900
Russia	1,700,000
Germany	1,800,000
France	1,385,000
England	947,000
Austria-Hungary	1,200,000

The Aftermath of World War I

In terms of the human cost of World War I, the United States had the lowest mortality. Although losses were tragic, the statistics show that the United States' war losses did not compare with that of European countries.

It appeared that the war had taken its toll by 1918, but Europeans continued to experience hunger, a freezing winter and the devastating mortality of an influenza epidemic which claimed more victims than the war did. This was considered the worst epidemic in recorded history, and Public Health facilities in every country were strained to the breaking point. The United States government extended the tour of duty for American military nurses, to care for both military and civilian victims of the influenza outbreak.

Mortality Figures for the Influenza Epidemic, 1918- 1920

Europeans and Turks	8,000,000
United States	48,000
Americans Overseas	27,000
Other Countries	11,925,000
Worldwide Population	20,000,000

Postwar Europe was dramatically altered, particularly in Russia, where a revolution and regime change transformed Imperial Russia into the socialist government of the Union of Soviet Socialist Republics. American officials were alarmed that the Russian (Socialist) Revolution of 1917 might infiltrate other countries and threaten capitalism. This fear affected American policy and led to the arrest and imprisonment of hundreds of people in the Palmer raids, initiated by Attorney General A. Mitchell Palmer. Under this directive, in December of 1919, Emma Goldman and 247 other aliens were arrested and deported from the United States. Goldman, a Lithuanian-Jewish immigrant, was sent to the Soviet Union.

Achieving Women's Suffrage with a Constitutional Amendment

During World War I, suffragists continued to wage their own battle for women's rights. By the early twentieth century, activists had come to realize the benefit of a state-by-state campaign for women's suffrage, but they did not abandon their objective to gain suffrage through an amendment to the Federal Constitution. Under the amending process, two options were possible. Each required a two-step process. (See the table, How do we make an Amendment to the Constitution?)

Suffragists Work to Gain the Vote

The Progressive argument that the women's vote would end political corruption, sanctify the cause and help recruit thousands more to the crusade, countered an earlier feminist idea, the *argument from justice*. This stated that women should get the vote as their *natural right* as guaranteed in the Declaration of Independence and the Constitution. In the final stages of the women's suffrage crusade, Progressivism breathed fresh air into the feminist movement in a number of ways. Progressive female reformers had shown what women could do. Jane Addams and other reformers had pushed for legislative reform and created programs that dignified immigrants, but suffragists had represented the prejudices of the white middle-class. African-American feminists who were not welcomed in the National movement, faced going it alone and waged a separate battle. In this climate of hypocrisy and schism, securing woman's suffrage was going to be a tough job. From 1896 to 1910, the suffrage campaign languished and suffered from lack of leadership.

By 1906, both Susan B. Anthony and Elizabeth Cady Stanton had died and their successor, competent organizer Carrie Chapman Catt, had resigned. Her successor, Dr. Anna Howard Shaw, a medical doctor, minister, and charismatic speaker, served as NAWSA president from 1902 to 1915, but she proved more effective at speech making than organizing. By this time, the movement had become so stagnant that NAWSA ceased to hold annual conventions. Women's suffrage lacked a visionary leader and a strategy to bring everyone back together again.

In the second decade of the twentieth century, a new generation of suffragists was ready to take on the fight. Their enthusiasm and call for action aroused the NAWSA out of the doldrums.

The Open-Air Tactics

Harriet Stanton Blatch, the daughter of Elizabeth Cady Stanton, had spent several years in England learning the tactics of the British suffragettes. In England, the women's suffrage movement, led by Emmeline Pankhurst, held open-air meetings and staged parades to broadcast women's rights as front-page news. They also harassed politicians and deliberately provoked officials to arrest them.

Taking a purposeful direction, Harriet Stanton Blatch revived the American Suffrage Movement. In 1907, to eliminate elitism and to promote unity, she formed the Equality League of Self-Supporting Women, in New York, which brought working-class and professional women together. Bringing the aggressive methods of British suffragettes to America, she adapted open-air tactics, held dramatic outdoor meetings, and staged festive parades. Harriet campaigned against anti-suffrage legislators in Albany, and acted as a poll watcher on election days. At first, a startled public regarded her methods as unladylike and dangerous for women, but these strategies soon became a regular feature of suffrage activity. Harriet recruited to the suffragist cause women from the labor movement who in turn informed the middle class members of the needs of working class women.

Harriet Stanton Blatch's efforts paid off and the new solidarity was visible at suffrage gatherings. One reporter covering a suffrage parade in New York, in 1912, observed that,

> Women who usually see Fifth Avenue through the polished window of their limousines...strode steadily side by side with pale-faced, thin-bodied girls from the sweltering sweat shops of the East Side. Mrs. O.H.P. Belmont walked but a few steps ahead of Rebecca Goldstein, who runs a sewing machine in a shirtwaist shop.

As Harriet Stanton Blatch had hoped, suffrage clubs became trendy throughout New York and other cities. The clubs were organized by election districts so that members could meet voters personally at the precinct level in order to build up support. These efforts to establish a base in eastern cities would bear fruit some years later.

Union activist Rose Schneiderman attacked the old political argument that if women were granted the franchise, they would lose their femininity.

> We have women working in the foundries, stripped to the waist, if you please, because of the heat... Surely these women won't lose any more of their beauty and charm by putting a ballot in a ballot box once a year than they are likely to lose standing in foundries or laundries all year round. There is no harder contest than the contest for bread, let me tell you that.

The Western Campaign

In 1910, it had been fourteen years since any state had initiated women's suffrage, but suffragists chalked up a victory in 1911, when the state of Washington gave women the vote and California soon followed. The California women's suffrage referendum had actually succeeded through the efforts and donations of women outside of California. In 1912, the states of Arizona, Kansas and Oregon, gave women the vote and in 1913, Illinois followed suit becoming the first state *east* of the Mississippi to do so. Much of the Illinois victory can be credited to the groundwork of Progressives such as Jane Addams. In 1914, Montana and Nevada adopted equal suffrage, but in Wisconsin, Ohio and Michigan, voters defeated the equal suffrage referendum. Despite the setback in these three states, it was clear that a state-by-state campaign could achieve results. More importantly, as the number of female voters increased, political candidates and officeholders could not afford to ignore women's strength at the polls. But eventually as the momentum of the first eight states' victories for women's suffrage slowed down, feminists saw the necessity to renew the campaign. They felt that an effort to campaign again for a Federal constitutional amendment might push women's suffrage across the victory line.

How Do We Make an Amendment to the Constitution?

Proposal	Initiated in the Congress passes when a majority by 2/3 vote, in both houses of the Congress approves	**OR**	Initiated by State legislatures 3/4 of which request Congress to convene a Constitutional Convention
Ratification	By a vote of 3/4 of the State legislatures (38) vote to ratify amendment	**OR**	Constitutional conventions In 3/4 of states (38) vote to ratify amendment

Alice Paul's Strategy

In 1913, Alice Paul, a young Quaker who had gained suffrage experience in England, invigorated the movement and the push for a constitutional amendment. She had been imprisoned with the British suffragettes for participating in demonstrations. Like Harriet Stanton Blatch, Alice Paul was convinced that only direct methods would gain the vote for women. In January of 1913, she set to work with her friend, Lucy Burns, to be appointed to the NAWSA Congressional Committee and to attend the Washington, D.C., conference which had been organized to petition the government for a constitutional amendment. Alice and Lucy were counting on a large gathering of visitors in Washington, D.C., for Woodrow Wilson's inauguration. So they deliberately scheduled a massive parade on March 13, 1913 the day before the presidential inaugural events. Inez Milholland, an articulate suffragist and lawyer, led the parade of 5,000 women. That same day, when President Wilson arrived at Union Station in anticipation of his inauguration, he expected cheering crowds to greet him. There were none. Aides informed the President that nearly everyone in Washington, D.C., was watching the suffragist parade.

Parade organizers had taken the precaution to obtain permits, and to ensure that the event was dignified, but as the ladies passed in review, the crowd grew more and more hostile. When women were attacked, beaten, and dragged, the police made no attempt to protect them. What onlookers described as an initially beautiful pageant quickly turned into a chaotic fiasco. Newspapers gave front-page coverage to the parade and the violent demonstrations.

Ida B. Wells-Barnett's group was barred from participating with the Illinois delegation in the parade. White leadership feared that participation by black women would alienate southern white women marching in the parade. In a flimsy concession, leaders informed Ida Wells- Barnett that her delegation, the Alpha Suffrage Club of Chicago, could walk at the end of the parade. Seeing this as a greater insult, Ida slipped into the ranks of the Illinois women, and marched with them down Pennsylvania Avenue.

In the following month, Alice Paul and Lucy Burns formed the Congressional Union, as an ad hoc committee within NAWSA. The committee's objective was the pursuit of a Federal amendment, but when differences arose over ways to achieve the amendment, Alice Paul and Lucy Burns left NAWSA to refashion the Congressional Union as a separate, more cohesive organization of militants. Alice Paul organized the members of the Congressional Union as well-disciplined troops, and assigned women military rank such as lieutenant, captain, etc. She also devised a two-pronged strategy. *First*, to stage events such as pageants, parades, pickets and vigils in order to raise the public's awareness, and *second,* to attack the party in power, Wilson and the Democrats, and to hold them responsible for women's suffrage. As part of this strategy, Alice Paul called on western women voters to drive Democrats out of office. In 1914, and again in 1916, major Congressional election years, Alice's group, renamed the Woman's Party, waged war on western Democratic candidates. This tactic not only angered Democrats but also further alienated Alice Paul's organization from the NAWSA. Since the anti-suffrage position cut across party lines, NAWSA officials believed Alice Paul's strategy to target the Democrats was unfair and unwarranted.

The 1913 Suffrage Parade was staged in Washington, D.C., to take advantage of the gathering crowds and media attention on Woodrow Wilson's inauguration day. (Photo courtesy of the Library of Congress.)

Although Woodrow Wilson won reelection in 1916, Alice Paul regarded the western campaign as a major defeat for the Democrats. Congressional elections showed only slim victories in her western campaign, and the results were difficult to interpret as votes by gender were not differentiated. Because Alice Paul had garnered press publicity and more women had joined the suffrage crusade, she ultimately scored a success in the western campaign. In 1916, during the western campaign, Inez Milholland, the suffragist leader who had led parades in New York and Washington, D.C., just three years earlier, collapsed from exhaustion in Los Angeles. She died a few weeks later. In her last speech, Inez Milholland had asked Woodrow Wilson, "Mr. President, how long must women wait for liberty?" That question became the slogan for the Woman's Party campaign, emblazoned on banners and carried in parades. At memorial services for Milholland, which were held in major cities, women dressed in white carried banners imprinted with her poignant question.

Alice Paul, one of the first American women to earn a Ph.D. in political science, brought new tactics and organization to the suffrage movement. (Photo courtesy of the Library of Congress.)

White House Pickets

On January 10, 1917, Alice Paul revved up the campaign by placing "silent sentinels" in front of the White House. Women stood vigil in shifts, wore white, and carried purple and gold banners asking, "How Long Must Women Wait for Liberty?" The women were instructed to remain silent, look straight ahead, and not confront any onlookers. Using the president's residence to draw attention, the silent sentinels prevailed in all kinds of weather. Initially through the cold winter months, the women were treated kindly; in fact, the president ordered hot tea be served to the women picketing the White House. But in March, as international events closed in on Wilson, the mood of the government changed. On April 2nd, the president appealed to a special joint session of Congress for a declaration of war against Germany and four days later Congress made that formal declaration.

Once the United States entered the war, public opinion of the White House picketers changed abruptly and many regarded Alice Paul's brigade as unpatriotic. Suffragist leader Carrie Chapman Catt deemed the protest inappropriate and called upon Alice Paul to call off the White House vigil. When Alice persisted, Carrie Chapman Catt openly criticized the demonstrations as disrespectful of the president. The silent sentinels responded with new banner slogans, such as "Democracy Should Begin at Home." These sentiments were not appreciated by onlookers and the hostility which mounted among the spectators set off a near riot on June 17th. As some angry men and soldiers began to storm the picket lines, police stood by passively as they attacked the women. When Alice Paul received word that officials intended to arrest the suffragists, she insisted the sentinels were breaking no law. Police arrested the women anyway and charged them with obstructing traffic. White House picketing continued throughout the summer and autumn of 1917. Their banner quotes became more strident, and horrified the public. One compared the president to the German Kaiser and labeled him Kaiser Wilson.

During the first round of arrests, most suffragists were charged but summarily dismissed. By the end of summer, as arrests increased, authorities detained about 200 women, including suffragist-journalist Dorothy Day. Some women were sent to the Occoquan workhouse in Virginia, and others were held at the District of Columbia Jail. When those facilities became overcrowded, protesters were incarcerated in kennels at the city's dog pound. Before long, the press reported on the cruel treatment of the women and the harsh conditions of their detention. Incarcerated with prisoners suffering from contagious diseases, suffragists were fed worm-infested food, left handcuffed to metal bars, or placed in solitary confinement.

At this point, Alice Paul and Lucy Burns decided to escalate the protest. Alice had witnessed the British suffragettes' hunger strikes and knew the dramatic effect this could have. When the women began to starve themselves, dehydration and fevers set in. Some were so weak that prison officials began force-feeding them. At Occoquan, Lucy Burns documented the tortuous experience surreptitiously written on small bits of paper which were smuggled out of the prison. The force-feeding she described was administered by placing a rubber hose through the victim's nose,

> I was held down by five people at legs, arms, and head. I refused to open mouth. Dr. Gannon pushed tube up left nostril. I turned and twisted my head all I could, but he managed to push it up. It hurts nose and throat very much and makes nose bleed freely. Tube drawn out covered with blood. Operation leaves one very sick. Food dumped directly into stomach feels like a ball of lead. [sic]

When newspapers publicized Lucy's account of the force-feedings, the public's outrage against the government became so intense that in November of 1917, officials released all the suffragist prisoners.

Carrie Chapman Catt's "Winning Plan"

When Congress placed the vote for the suffrage amendment proposal on the agenda in mid-December of 1917, the Women's Party claimed a victory, but they had not single-handedly worked to secure an amendment. Other women also had worked tirelessly to secure equal suffrage.

When Carrie Chapman Catt returned to NAWSA as the president in 1915, she reorganized the association into a more disciplined group. After working on the western state referendum campaigns, Catt directed her energies toward winning equal suffrage with a state-by-state campaign. In 1916, she implemented what she coined, the "winning plan," to obtain a Federal constitutional amendment within six years. In 1917, the states of North Dakota, Ohio, Indiana, Rhode Island, Nebraska, and Michigan granted women suffrage.

A breakthrough came when Arkansas, the first state of the conservative South, granted women the vote. But the most significant victory occurred in New York, where from 1915 to 1917, Carrie Chapman Catt had conducted a well orchestrated strategy. Dividing New York into districts, volunteers canvassed from door to door reaching almost sixty-six percent of all the state's registered voters.

Suffragist Carrie Chapman Catt had a winning plan for women's voting rights - to take the campaign state-by-state. (Photo courtesy of the Library of Congress.)

The canvassers drummed up support for a state referendum, and recruited about 80,000 more women for the Women's Suffrage Party. Carrie Chapman Catt's team also translated voting pamphlets for the immigrant populations and staged concerts in the parks, where they served ethnic foods and entertained with multicultural music. Her workers also obtained the signatures of one million women on a petition to the state government. In 1915, Carrie Chapman Catt's team lost the vote in New York but tried again in 1917, and secured a victory with a margin of 102,000 votes. Suffragists were elated because New York's decisive number of electoral votes meant that presidential hopefuls, (Woodrow Wilson for example, who hoped to be reelected) needed to carry New York and would have to court the women's vote. With New York State onboard, the national referendum for equal suffrage could finally move forward.

Opposition to women's suffrage did not fall neatly along party lines or regions of the country. There were congressman on both sides of the aisle, both democrats and republicans and representatives from the North, South and the West who were against adoption of the amendment.

The House of Representatives scheduled the vote for the Susan B. Anthony Amendment (the name suggested by Alice Paul) in January 1918. The amendment passed in the House with the necessary two-thirds majority, 304 for to 89 against.

The Senate vote on the amendment was set for October 1918. President Wilson worked diligently and urged by letter and personal interview that every Southern Congressional delegate give way and vote for women's suffrage. On September 30, he delivered in person his memorable speech to the Senate calling for political unity and a favorable vote.

> I had assumed that the Senate would concur in the amendment because no disputable principle is involved, but only a question of the methods by which the suffrage is to be extended to women. There is and can be no party issue involved in it. Both of our great national parties are pledged to equality of suffrage for the women of the country.

President Wilson stated that equal suffrage was necessary for the successful prosecution of the war, and that the people of Europe were watching America to see if our great democracy could lead the way to a new world where both men and women played their part on equal footing.

Alice Paul and the Woman's Party stepped up the tempo, with White House protesters dramatically burning copies of Wilson's speeches. Meanwhile, Carrie Chapman Catt directed the NAWSA campaign to win over more states. On October 1, 1918, the Senate's Equal Suffrage proposal came up two votes short of passing. By February, 1919, things looked bleak after the Senate defeated the amendment again, but another breakthrough offered hope. While attending the Paris Peace Talks, President Wilson called for a Joint Session of the Congress to pass the Anthony Amendment. The Senate debate continued and included a proposal by Senator Underwood of Alabama, to submit the amendment to state constitutional conventions, instead of state legislatures for ratification. Senator Wadsworth of New York, an uncompromising opponent who insisted that states should decide on women's suffrage, also put forth a proposal. After several more agonizing days of debate, the Senate passed the measure on June 4, 1919. Thirty-six republicans and twenty democrats voted for adoption. Eight republicans and seventeen democrats voted against adoption.

The Nineteenth Amendment to the Constitution

The Susan B. Anthony Amendment

Article, Section 1 - The right of citizens of the United States to vote shall not be denied or abridged by the United States or by any State on account of sex.

Section 2 - Congress shall have the power, by appropriate legislation, to enforce the provisions of this article.

After a struggle of seventy-two years, the sweet victory deserved a grand celebration, but there was no rest for the weary. Congressional consent was only an initial step in an uphill climb. The next phase, ratification of the amendment, required approval of a 3/4 majority of the states, or thirty-six states. The state ratification process to be conducted by sessions of state legislatures would take another year to complete. Alice Paul responded to the Congressional vote, "There is no doubt of ratification by the States. We enter upon the campaign for special sessions of Legislatures to accomplish ratification before 1920 and in the full assurance that we shall win." Equally confident, Carrie Chapman Catt stated,

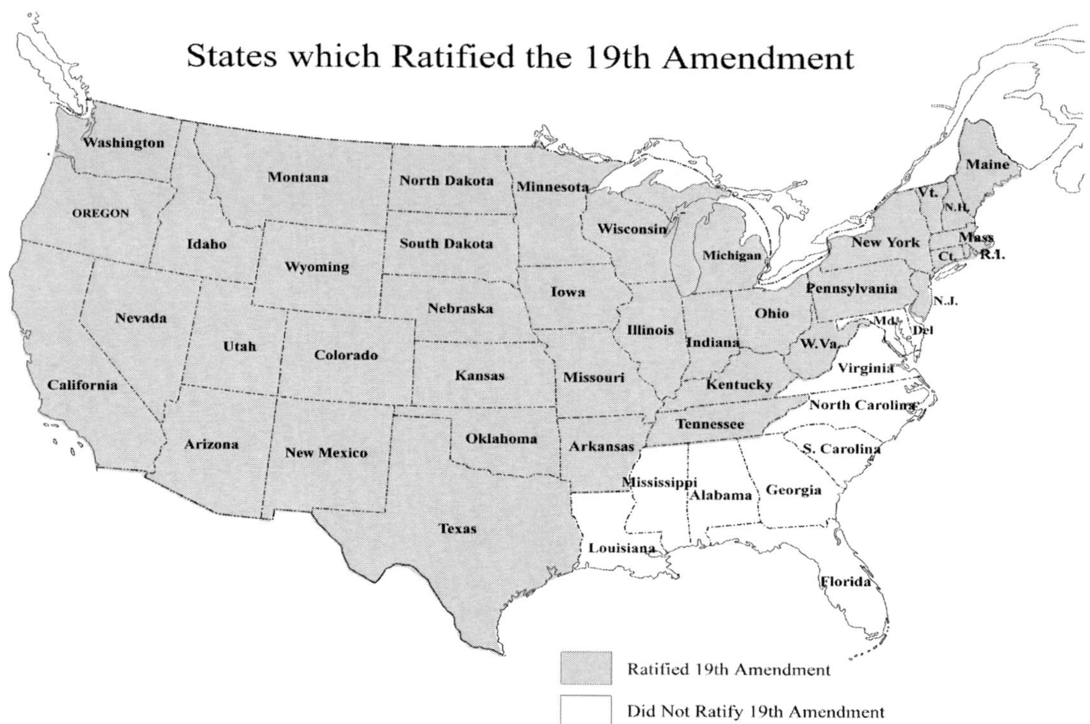

> The last stage of the fight is to obtain ratification of the amendment so women may vote in the Presidential Election of 1920. This we are confident will be achieved. The friends of woman suffrage in both parties have carried out their word. Eyes front is the watchword as we turn upon the struggle for ratification by the States.

Carrie Chapman Catt's earlier work in the western states proved valuable experience and the NAWSA machinery went to work to get ratification votes.

Help came from various groups in every corner of the United States. In New Mexico, for example, support emerged from old, landed gentry Republican Adelina Otero Warren, a sixth generation *Hispana,* whose family had longstanding service in New Mexico politics. Adelina Warren worked hand-in-hand with Alice Paul, the Women's Party, and Carrie Chapman Catt to secure ratification in the State of New Mexico.

Ratification of the Anthony Amendment

The fight for state ratification was not just a matter of convincing legislators to endorse the amendment; suffragists also had to square off against the anti-suffrage forces. The opposition engaged every ploy imaginable, from political threats and bribery, to free booze. Before Congress had approved the Nineteenth Amendment, twenty-seven states had already granted women full or presidential suffrage including Wyoming, Colorado, Utah, Idaho, Washington, California, Kansas, Arizona, Oregon, Montana, New York, Oklahoma, South Dakota, Michigan, Illinois, Nebraska, Rhode Island, North Dakota, Iowa, Wisconsin, Indiana, Maine, Minnesota, Missouri, Arkansas, Nevada and Texas. The ratification campaign schedule depended upon when state legislatures might adjourn for the summer, which might call extra sessions and, in the case of Wisconsin and Florida, whether an election might take place before submission of the amendment for ratification.

Suffragists studied and lobbied every state legislature and pressured state governors whose delegates had not yet ratified the amendment, such as Governor Hart of Washington. By February 1920, thirty-one states had approved the suffrage amendment including Washington, Nevada and Arizona, followed in June by Indiana and Illinois.

By June 1920, less than a year after Congressional approval, thirty-five states had ratified the amendment, but most southern states, ensconced in tradition, were opposed to ratifying the women's suffrage amendment. With only one more state needed, it came down to the vote in Tennessee. Considered a border state, it appeared to be the only southern state that might pass the amendment and became the final battleground for ratification. Knowing that every vote counted, Carrie Chapman Catt took her army of suffragists to Nashville to lobby all the Tennessee state legislators.

Tennessee women and legislators either wore yellow roses indicating their support of women voting, or red roses declaring their anti-suffrage feelings. This became known as the War of the Roses. Every delegate having been accurately polled, it appeared that Tennessee's ratification would deadlock in a tie or lose by one vote. However, when the final roll call vote was taken, the tie was broken by the youngest legislator, twenty-six year old, Republican Harry Burn. In a surprise move, Burn, wearing a red rose, changed his *nay* to an *aye*, after receiving this letter from Febb King Ensminger Burn, his mother:

> Dear Son:
> Hurrah and vote for suffrage! Don't keep them in doubt. I noticed some of the speeches against. They were bitter. I have been watching to see how you stood, but have not noticed anything yet. Don't forget to be a good boy and help Mrs. Catt put the rat in ratification.
> Signed, Your Mother

Changing his vote to a *yes*, Harry Burn made Tennessee's vote the final one needed to ratify the Susan B. Anthony Amendment. On August 26, 1920, the Nineteenth Amendment to the Constitution granted twenty-six million women the right to vote.[1] Three months later, American women in all forty-eight states of the Union, could vote for the first time in a presidential election.

Carrie Chapman Catt assessed the efforts of the suffragists.

> It is doubtful if any group—men or women—who ever kept ward and watch over legislation at Washington ever came to know the true inwardness of the Congress of the United States as suffragists came to know it. For one thing, the suffrage vigil was so long maintained. For another, it engaged the energies of so many different women with so many different points of view from so many different parts of the country, all flashing in their reflections of the Congressional body like so many mirrors held up to nature, man's nature, at every conceivable angle.

Carrie Chapman Catt explained how in the process of campaigning, suffragists had received invaluable experience and a political education,

> They learned Congress through and through, those women, its way of work, its machinery; its tricks; the men in it, their pet foibles, their fundamental weaknesses, their finer abilities, their human quality. Quietly sitting in the galleries of House or Senate, listening to floor speeches, or watching floor tactics, they learned. They learned talking across desks, in animated discussion with those same men in private Senatorial and House offices. Pleading at public hearings, before committees of House or Senate, they learned. They learned the cheap bi-partisanship that dominates the Congress; its insensate capacity to block justice for party advantage. They learned that the State's rights cry of the Southern Congressman voiced a great principle—to be used as expediency dictated... They learned that Massachusetts Republicans could find it in their hearts to be stern State's righters when it came to the point of defeating

1. See Appendix A: the *Constitution of the United States, Amendment XIX*, "Proposal and ratification of the amendment," for the complete chronology of ratification by states.

suffrage, though determined federalists on all other scores... And, finally, they learned that here and there in the Congress were men who stood up like mountain peaks, as unswerving in their devotion to the principle of self government as they were intelligent in their understanding of it. It was on these men that suffragists banked their hopes as they went forward with their final program to secure the submission of the Federal Suffrage Amendment...

The women who campaigned for and achieved suffrage displayed a new confidence as displayed in this humorous photo depicting female assertiveness.

In historical hindsight, gaining the vote seemed inevitable but it was not. The seventy-two-year crusade had been marred by many disappointments, setbacks, physical suffering and dogged work. There was a brief moment of elation but as southern black men could attest, passing a constitutional amendment was one thing, enforcing it was an entirely different matter. After the 1870 passage of the Fifteenth Amendment, which prohibited the states or Federal government from using race, color, or previous status as a slave as a voting qualification, southern states had resorted to poll taxes, literacy tests, the grandfather clause, and blatant intimidation to prohibit freedmen from voting. Black women would face similar obstacles in trying to vote after passage of the Nineteenth Amendment; these included intimidation from the Klan, discrimination, and literacy requirements to be met in order to register to vote.

A Suffrage Time Line

1869 - Wyoming Territory grants women the vote
1870 - Utah Territory grants women the vote
1893 - Colorado grants women the vote
1896 - Idaho grants women the vote
1910 - Washington grants women the vote
1911 - California grants women the vote
Anti-suffrage organizes and forms the National Association Opposed to Woman Suffrage
1912 - Kansas, Oregon, and Arizona grant women the vote
1913 - Alice Paul forms the National Woman's Party
1914 - Montana and Nevada grant women the vote
1916 - Jeanette Rankin, from Montana, is elected the first Congresswoman
1917 - New York grants women the vote
1918 - House of Representatives passes Anthony Amendment
1919 - Senate passes Anthony Amendment
State ratification process begins
1920 - Susan B. Anthony Amendment, the 19th Amendment, ratified

The Next Step

The women's rights movement had focused on getting the vote, but once that was achieved, the movement lost its drive and momentum. Feminists disagreed on what the next step was. What form should equality take, and using the power of the ballot, what other rights should women seek? Alice Paul reasoned that the next step should take the form of an Equal Rights Amendment, (ERA). She believed the movement would not succeed unless and until women received full and equal protection under the law. In 1923, the National Woman's Party held a celebration at Seneca Falls, New York, to observe the seventy-fifth anniversary of the first Women's Convention there in 1848. Alice Paul delivered her proposal for the *Lucretia Mott Amendment, (the Equal Rights Amendment)* which read "Men and women shall have equal rights throughout the United States and every place subject to its jurisdiction." The Equal Rights Amendment was introduced to the Congress in 1923, but it was defeated. Although the National Woman's Party continued to support the ERA, other women's rights activists prioritized differently the rights of females. They concentrated on female laborers' rights because they felt it was more important to campaign for *specific, protective* laws for women in the workplace than for an Equal Rights Amendment. They also believed that an Equal Rights Amendment would subvert the efforts they had already made for working women. Once again the movement seemed to be splitting into two different camps; nevertheless, the issues suffragists had raised would become the basis of continued activism and discourse in the cause of women's rights.

Mothers of Invention: Madame C. J. Walker and Maggie Walker, Lady Entrepreneurs

Sarah Breedlove McWilliams Walker, born in 1867 to former slaves Owen and Minerva Breedlove, grew up in the Mississippi Delta country of Louisiana where her family struggled as sharecroppers. Sarah was orphaned at six years old, and when she was widowed at age twenty after a lynch mob killed her husband, she moved with her daughter, Lelia, to St. Louis, Missouri, and worked there as a laundress. The work paid little and took a terrible toll on her health; Sarah began to lose her hair. In her efforts to find a remedy for her hair loss, she developed a hair restorer and hair care method for African-American women. These products launched a successful business which grew into a financial empire.

By 1910, she had set up a corporate office in Pittsburgh, Pennsylvania, and a manufacturing plant in Indianapolis, Indiana. As an innovator, she was one of the best. In Indianapolis she founded a vocational training school, one of the first of its kind, with about 2,000 Walker agents selling door to door, a catalogue merchandising department and commission-incentives for sales representatives. By 1919, about 25,000 African-American women had moved from low paying jobs to become Walker Agents. But as she drove her company to multimillion dollar profit, Walker encountered criticism, mainly from the black ministers who accused her of trying to make black women look like white women. Ministers railed from the pulpit that if God had wanted women of African heritage to have straight hair he would have created them that way. Madame C. J. defended her products and argued that black women felt inferior because of their hair and appearance, and women of color should be able to make themselves attractive.

Madame C.J. Walker made her fortune and created an industry in beauty treatments and hair care products for African American women. (Photo courtesy of the Library of Congress.)

Madame C. J. Walker's crowning achievement was her stature as the first American woman to become a self-made millionaire in business. With newfound wealth, she purchased land on the Hudson River and built a neoclassical mansion, *Villa Lewaro,* near Irvington, New York. After building her multimillion dollar business enterprise, Madame C. J. Walker plunged into philanthropy and educational programs. The charities and benefits she endowed are too numerous to list but include the NAACP, the restoration of Frederick Douglass' home, Mary McLeod Bethune's School for Negro Girls, the Bethune-Cookman College, the Lucy Laney Haines Institute, the National Rights League, and the National Association of Colored Women's Clubs. Because of her own climb out of poverty, Madame C. J. Walker believed that through self-help black women could succeed and she urged them to aspire to something better,

> The girls and women of our race must not be afraid to take hold of business endeavors. I started in business eight years ago with one dollar and fifty cents. [Now I am) giving employment to more than a thousand women...I have made it possible for many colored women to abandon the washtub for a more pleasant and profitable occupation

Financier and banker, Maggie Lena Draper Walker shared a lot in common with Madame C. J. Walker. Both were southerners, daughters of former slaves, born into poverty, "firsts" in their fields, and successful black female entrepreneurs and philanthropists. At age nineteen, Maggie Walker had taken a job at the Order of St. Luke, a banking society devoted to helping African-Americans become financially sound. At that time, the society had 3,408 members but was in serious financial straits. In 1903, Maggie established the St. Luke's Penny Savings Bank, in Richmond, Virginia, to instill thrift habits among African-American adults and children, and instituted her slogan "turning pennies into dollars." Penny by penny, she built the St. Luke Penny Savings Bank into a solid financial institution. By 1924, the St. Luke Penny Savings Bank had blossomed into a financial house with fifty employees and assets of $400,000; and under her guiding hand, the society of St. Luke would eventually expand to 50,000 members organized into 1500 local chapters. Maggie Walker consolidated her gains by buying up smaller banks in Richmond and in 1929, the Penny Savings Bank became the Consolidated Trust Company. Maggie Walker also worked as a full-time philanthropist with numerous associations and served as the President of the Richmond Council of Colored Women. She raised funds for Janie Porter Barrett's institutions—the Locust Street Settlement and the Virginia Industrial School for Colored Girls.

Maggie Lena Draper Walker - an entrepreneur and philanthropist established the St. Luke's Penny Savings Bank in Richmond Virginia. (Photo courtesy of the Library of Congress.)

Conclusion

When the United States entered the Great War in Europe in 1917, women answered the call to serve as nurses, munitions factory workers, ambulance drivers, chauffeurs and volunteers. At the same time, the American women's suffrage movement made the final push for a constitutional amendment.

Alice Paul and her followers organized the National Woman's Party and a Suffrage Parade in Washington, D.C., and aggressively picketed the White House. Perceived as unpatriotic, Alice Paul's suffragists faced arrest and imprisonment. NAWSA, under Carrie Chapman Catt's leadership, had disassociated from any affiliation with Alice Paul and the NWP. Carrie Chapman Catt had devised a winning plan to obtain a Federal amendment staging a state-by-state campaign. It took many attempts to push the amendment through the Congress and only through the efforts of both strategists and thousands of suffragists, did women finally gain the vote in 1920, just in time to participate nationally in their first presidential election. Carrie Chapman Catt noted the significance of the suffragist crusade as the "largest lobby ever maintained at the national capital." Toward the end of the campaign women were scurrying to "the National American Woman Suffrage Association in Washington from every state in the union, in relays of dozens, fifties and hundreds."

The crusade for equal rights had scored its first victory. Alice Paul would take the campaign to the next level, to work for an Equal Rights Amendment.

Part VI:

Women from the Post-Suffrage Period through World War II

Women in the Twenties

Women and the Great Depression

Women and World War II

Chapter 19
Women in the Twenties
Bernice Bobs Her Hair

Key Topics

Women in Politics
Black Women in Leadership Roles
Prohibition and the New Prosperity
Women of Letters and the Arts

Chronology

1920 - The Eighteenth and Nineteenth Amendments Ratified
Republican Warren G. Harding Elected President
1921 - Margaret Sanger Founded the American Birth Control League
1924 - The Immigration Act
1927 - The Jazz Singer, First Sound Motion Picture

Introduction

What made the Roaring Twenties roar? Events and trends which lent excitement to this decade were Prohibition, the celebrity of great heroes and heroines and motion pictures. The Roaring Twenties also signaled a decade of recklessness, described by an iconic writer of the era, F. Scott Fitzgerald who reflected nostalgically on the twenties some years later during the hard times of the thirties:

> *Sometimes, though there is a ghostly rumble among the drums, an asthmatic whisper in the trombones that swings me back into the early twenties when we drank wood alcohol and every day in every way grew better and better... it all seems rosy and romantic to us who were young then, because we will never feel quite so intensely about our surroundings any more.*

The twenties boom economy which allowed Americans to spend lavishly had been made possible by America's advantageous position in World War I. Compared with European Nations which were ravaged by a four-year war, the United States had entered the conflict late, fought on foreign soil and suffered fewer casualties. In the aftermath, America emerged as a creditor nation. With the sound U.S. dollar, American housewives could purchase all the new convenience appliances — toasters, mixers, washers, and vacuum cleaners — on credit or through installment buying. This booming consumerism which followed the war, promised to be one long spending spree. In the midst of prosperity, euphoric Americans believed the good times would last forever. The American woman's role as a consumer took on more importance in a growing economy. Women also displayed social change in their clothing and demeanor as women's fashion and mores made a radical departure from the past.

Women in Politics

After voting nationwide in the first presidential election in 1920, women activists regrouped to consider new goals. Florence Kelley, of the National Consumer's League, prioritized protective legislation for women and children in the workforce. African-American women reminded the National Women's Party that despite the Susan B. Anthony Amendment, they still could not register and vote in the South, where lynching remained a deterrent to male and female suffrage. Alice Paul downplayed these concerns and wanted instead to work for the removal of all laws which restricted women's freedom and equality. The suffrage victory had not eradicated divisiveness from the movement or addressed the plight of African-American women.

Women seeking political office used the "widow's gain," i.e. approximately two-thirds of the women who served in the Congress were appointed, not elected, to office by fulfilling their husbands' unfinished terms. In 1920, the League of Women Voter's and the Women's Joint Congressional Committee, the WJCC, provided a glimmer of hope when they organized a voting bloc to pressure the political parties. The WJCC was especially effective, with a coalition of ten national women's organizations. They became influential lobbyists in Washington. In 1921, they succeeded with the passage of the Sheppard-Towner Federal Maternity and Infancy Act, which became the country's first nationally funded health-care program. Congress allocated 1.25 million dollars for well baby clinics, health education and a visiting nurse program. The Sheppard-Towner Bill was not an indicator of Congressional concern for mothers and infants; as one politician stated, it was motivated by the fear that if congressmen did not pass the legislation, women might vote them out of office. The success of this landmark legislation, however, was short-lived. After analyzing voting patterns, in the 1920 election, politicians noted that women did not vote as a bloc, but as their husbands voted. After pressure from the American Medical Association, Congress reconsidered and rescinded funding for the Sheppard-Towner Act in 1929. This was a clear indication that although women could vote, they could not bring about political change. It was still a man's game.

Post-Suffrage Feminism

After achieving suffrage, there was also a shift in feminist perspectives. In the post-suffrage decade of the 1920s, Ruth Pickering, a progressive feminist journalist who had aided the cause of labor from 1900 to 1920, expressed how suffragists felt about the woman's cause:

> I have traded in my sense of exhilarating defiance (shall we call it feminism?) for an assurance of free unimpeded self-expression (or shall we call that feminism?). In other words, I have grown up.

Leading journals and ladies' magazines also reacted and were quick to set feminist activism in a bad light. Young women of the twenties already viewed suffragists as boring, unattractive, too assertive and masculine. But feminism was not forgotten entirely and those dedicated activists who had campaigned for women's suffrage kept at it. They worked in volunteer associations such as the WCTU, to help enforce and implement prohibition: the American Association of University Women, the National Federation of Business and Professional Women's Clubs, the National Parent-Teacher Association, and the National Council of Jewish Women, to promote professionalism; the Women's Trade Union League, and the National Consumer's League to lobby for labor; and the Women's International League for Peace and Freedom, to promote world peace.

Although the Progressive Movement was in decline, the doors of settlement houses remained open throughout the twenties, and Jane Addams, Lillian Wald and Mary McDowell continued their work among the poor. Mary McDowell, an associate of Jane Addams, branched out and founded the University of Chicago Settlement House which included playgrounds for children, a public bathhouse and citizenship classes for immigrants. She ran for public office in 1923, and was elected Chicago's Commissioner of Public Health. Mary Margaret Bartelme, a settlement house worker who had worked in the progressive juvenile court system, was appointed the first female judge in the State of Illinois in 1923, and in 1924, the city of Seattle, Washington, got its first female mayor, Bertha Knight Landes, also a settlement house rookie, who had taken a stand as a staunch prohibitionist.

In the twenties, the League of Women Voters, an organization founded six months prior to the ratification of the Nineteenth Amendment, initiated a mission to educate women voters to the political process and to provide pamphlets for primary and general elections which contained information on candidates and issues.

Black Women in Leadership

Black women were active in a number of organizations. Their chief cause, the anti-lynching crusade, was fielded by Jessie Daniel Ames and Mary Talbert, who moved the campaign via the Federation of Colored Women's Clubs, beginning in 1922. Black leader Marcus Garvey's United Negro Improvement Association (UNIA), offered an auxiliary role for black women in the "New Negro Women's Crusade" led by his wife, Amy Jacques Garvey. She ran a weekly column in Garvey's paper, *The Negro World*, entitled "Our Women and What They Think." The UNIA believed African-Americans should retain a separate black identity, and unify all black people in the Pan African Movement. This, according to Marcus Garvey, was more desirable than integrating into white society. He promoted positive models for black Americans and tried to reduce discrimination and racial stereotyping. Accenting black pride, Marcus and Amy Garvey preempted the "Black is Beautiful" movement by nearly fifty years.

Southern black leadership was traditionally centered in churches; in 1922, new visionary groups emerged such as the Women's Council of the African Methodist Episcopal (AME) Church. The Commission on Inter-Racial Co-Operation, an inner committee of the AME Church initiated a dialogue between black and white women in the South. Parents in the black community instilled in their children a mission to serve and improve conditions for all African-Americans. Clara Jones, the daughter of former slaves, explained how her grandfather's directive set her straight on the *true* purpose of her education, "You're going to get your education and it's not yours. You are doing it for your people." In 1970, she became the first African-American to direct a major U.S. public library, the Detroit Public Library. Clara Jones joined the accomplished poet-librarian Anne Spencer, who contributed profoundly to African-American literature, and together they labored for black education, and raised white consciousness about the racial injustices endured by the black population.

The YWCA Young Women's Christian Association), founded in 1858, began as a boarding house for women. But as the YWCA took on more programs and became increasingly involved in women's issues, branches sprang up all over the country. They were devoted to job training, physical education, and sponsorship of female athletes; the YWCA also served as a haven for women seeking financial security and independence, or as asylum from homelessness and mistreatment. In 1922, the YWCA set up a committee composed of black and white women to study racial problems.

Prohibition and the New Prosperity

Prohibition, the Eighteenth Amendment to the Constitution, was the culmination of nearly a century of temperance reform efforts. The amendment became effective January 20, 1920. Anticipating it would become law, Congress had passed the Volstead Act (the National Prohibition Act) in October 1919, as the means to enforce it. The Volstead Act prohibited the manufacture, sale and transportation of intoxicating liquors within the United States and the importation and exportation of alcohol for beverage purposes.[1] The Eighteenth Amendment and the Volstead Act ushered in the Prohibition Era which lasted from 1920 to 1933. During these years, neighborhood saloons were shut down and quickly replaced by illegal bars known as

1. Liquor was legally defined as an intoxicating beverage if it contained one-half of one percent alcohol.

speakeasies. The organized crime syndicates amassed great wealth from their underground operations of bootleg liquor, and crime and violence escalated.

Prohibition affected the manner in which Americans socialized. Until the twenties, social convention frowned upon nice women drinking in public. The neighborhood tavern had been a place where predominantly men congregated. Speakeasies became widely accepted social gathering places during prohibition, because drinking was illegal and alcohol was not available elsewhere.[2] A doorman or lookout controlled entry and patrons gained admittance with the right password, or a proof of social connection. Many of the speakeasies if not owned by gangsters were controlled by them and extorting protection money from proprietors became very lucrative for organized crime.

Historians interested in Prohibition have examined the effects of this legal reform. Their inquiries include questions such as: was it a dismal failure, a naive attempt at reform or somewhat successful? Some studies show that on one hand, many Americans actually ceased or reduced alcohol consumption because bootleg was so expensive. Money previously spent on booze by the head of the household might be diverted or redirected to consumer items such as household appliances. In some cases, because a family's spending power had increased, there was capital available for a start-up small family business. However, motion pictures, advertising and consumerism presented an unrealistic view of the American economy. Many Americans never experienced postwar prosperity. Coal miners, textile workers and farmers continued to struggle at the poverty level.

Mass Production and a Mass Market

One of the most significant changes in American life in the twenties was the escalation of technology, especially the production of automobiles. Consequently, as more Americans drove cars, the new transportation brought economic and social transformation. The wide popularity of the automobile in the twenties created the American drive-in phenomenon, with movies, restaurants, churches, and motor hotels (motels). Cars gave young people more freedom and privacy. When young people were not in cars, they talked on the telephone — much less private than being in a Ford, since telephone operators or someone on the party line could eavesdrop on a conversation.

Automobile production increased industrial success and prosperity in the twenties. It also gave more Americans the means to travel and young people more freedom and dating intimacy. (Photo courtesy of the Archives of the Fullerton College Library.)

The sales of phonographs, phonograph records, magazines and the growth of radio broadcasting molded a mass American popular culture. Phonograph recordings preserved the voices and artistry of Mamie Smith, Ma Rainey, Bessie Smith, Ida Cox, Ethel Waters and Clara Smith. Radio broadcasting broadened by 1929, with over 800 radio stations across the nation, and forty percent of all American families radio owners. Journalism's mass readership of 2.5 million Americans included ladies' shelter (home design and related) magazines such as *Ladies Home Journal*, and *Good Housekeeping,* which ranked in the top ten.

The Female Image and Motion Pictures

The film industry projected a veil of glamour, and Hollywood boosted the sale of hair care products and cosmetics. The beauty parlor industry (so-called because owners converted their home parlors into beauty shops) offered women the means to self-employment and finan-

2. A speakeasy was a clandestine, illegal bar often tucked away in a Brownstone apartment, behind a reputable business establishment, a walk up private flat, or a step down to a basement apartment.

cial independence; with little capital a woman could start up her own beauty parlor business.

Hollywood pictures presented beautiful women who gained box office appeal. Lillian Gish, who enjoyed a long career, premiered in 1915, in *The Birth of a Nation*, and appeared in her last film in 1987, at age ninety. Gloria Swanson and Joan Crawford began in silent films. Mary Pickford, billed as America's sweetheart, played innocent roles such as *Rebecca of Sunnybrook Farm* and co-founded United Artists Studio, becoming one of Hollywood's wealthiest producers.

Lois Weber was one of the first female movie directors in Hollywood beginning in the silent film era. (Courtesy of the Academy of Motion Picture Arts and Sciences.)

No doubt about it, in Hollywood sex sold. The image of wild women enjoyed popularity, touted in films such as *The Joy Girl, Women Who Give, Sinners in Silk*, and *Ladies of Pleasure*. Clara Bow went to Hollywood after winning a beauty contest. She arrived in 1921, at the age of sixteen, and was cast as the new woman – the Flapper, the consummate party girl. With unbundled energy, flirty eyes, and flaming red hair, Clara Bow became the signature flapper or, Jazz Baby. American writer, F. Scott Fitzgerald, defined a flapper as a young woman between the ages of sixteen and twenty-five of the middle- or upper-class who indulged in "flirting, kissing, dancing, viewing life lightly, saying *damn* without a blush; a sort of mental baby vamp." The flapper set a new fashion style and body image — corsetless, with rolled down stockings, bobbed hair, and dressed in tight-fitting clothing with short hemlines. Her behavior was even more daring. She partied all night long, smoked cigarettes, drank bootleg hooch and danced the Charleston. Ideally, in motion pictures, the flapper appeared thin and sensual, but not promiscuous. In the plot, she married the leading man in the final scene and popularized the Hollywood happy ending.

In reality, the flapper represented a small fraction of American women, but Hollywood mass marketed the look to promote feminine products, fashions and movies. The flapper style reached girls of other ethnic groups as well. To the horror of traditional families within the Latino and Asian communities, the new fads led many daughters to bob their hair and affect flapper styles.

In 1921, capitalizing on the commodity of the female sexual image, Atlantic City businessmen also got into the act. In order to extend the vacation season at the famous seaside resort, they staged a beauty pageant in late summer, crowning one winning female contestant "Miss America" after the requisite bathing suit review.

Studies of the sexual habits of females in the twenties, specifically college coeds, reveal a new sexual license that was considered scandalous by the older generation. Surveys of college women revealed that 92 percent of them engaged in petting, and 33 percent in sexual intercourse. Coeds confided that sexual intimacy was permissible with a prospective husband or fiancé. However, the new promiscuity superceded accurate information about ovulation, which scientists did not validate until 1929. Sexual freedom for women was problematic. In real life, women were still denied access to birth control, and those who imitated the wild women on the screen were at risk for unwanted pregnancy or sexually transmitted disease.

Working-Class Women

In the post-suffrage glow of the twenties, ethnic minority women were more exploited than liberated. Black women, the lowest paid workers in the country, encountered racial hatred and discrimination on a daily basis. This often came from white women's groups who excluded them from union labor. To alleviate this discrimination, African-American Nannie Burroughs founded the National Association of Wage Earners in 1920, and campaigned for better wages for those women who worked as domestic servants. The discriminatory practices of trade unions also prevented Mexican-American women from joining. They worked in the lowest paying jobs in the garment business, factories, commercial laundries, bakeries, and as domestic servants. The labor movement effected in the same way the Asian-American women who worked in commercial laundries, food packing plants, and as domestic servants. In an age of prosperity, ethnic minority women were barely living on the fringe and would have to address their own labor grievances.

Socialist Elizabeth Gurley Flynn co-founded the American Civil Liberties Union and engaged in the legal defense of individuals arrested during the Palmer Raids of 1918-1921.[3] In the late twenties, Gurley Flynn organized and chaired the International Labor Defense movement. Her experience as a labor activist illustrates the futility of the union/labor movement for *all groups* at this time. In her essay, "A Woman Who Died for Labor in 1919," Elizabeth Gurley Flynn relates the death of Fanny Sellins, a forty-nine-year-old, Irish-American widow who had become a labor organizer. During the 1919 nationwide steel strike, Sellins went to Natrona, Pennsylvania, to help organize the Allegheny Steel Company strike. Elizabeth Gurley Flynn describes what happened to her,

> The miners had gone out on strike and were picketing a sultry August afternoon. Suddenly a group of drunken sheriff's deputies on guard duty began shooting at the pickets. One Polish miner fell to the ground, mortally wounded. Mrs. Sellins rushed in to push some children nearby through a fence and out of danger. Then she came back to try to stop the deputies who were clubbing the prostrate pickets. A mine[3] official struck her with a club and she fell to the ground. As she arose and dragged herself toward the fence, three shots were fired each mortally wounding her. As she lay unconscious on the ground a deputy emptied his gun into her body. Another deputy then crushed in her skull with a club, before the helpless little group of miners their wives and children. One deputy grabbed her hat, put it on and danced around her body and said, "I'm Mrs. Sellins now."

Sister Aimee's Evangelism

Evangelicalism drew dubious attention in the Twenties with Aimee Semple McPherson, or "Sister Aimee," who built a crusading empire in Los Angeles. Construction of Sister Aimee's $1.5 million Angelus Temple began in 1921. Sister Aimee founded the Church of the Foursquare Gospel in 1923, and instituted one of the first media ministries, with live broadcasts over the radio. Part con artist and part entertainer, her sense of dazzle and showmanship made Angelus Temple as theatrical as vaudeville or motion pictures. Sister Aimee staged pageants, preached seven nights a week, and appeared in various costumes. Her preaching focused on faith healing, adult baptism by immersion, and in step with the times, unlimited optimism. She published both weekly and monthly newspapers and books including *This is That*, 1923; *In the Service of the King*, 1927; and *Give Me My Own God*, 1936. The number of Aimee's Foursquare Gospel Churches grew to 400 in the United States and 200 in Canada.

Eugenics, Birth Control, Nativism and Immigration

Although the twenties did not hold exclusive rights to radicalism and extremist views, the era did leave a unique mark. The science of Eugen-

3. The Palmer Raids, a series of controversial raids by the U.S. Justice and Immigration departments on the radical left, were named for U. S. Attorney General Alexander Mitchell Palmer.

ics, which deals with improvement of hereditary qualities in race and breed, had become popular when Darwin's theories emerged in the nineteenth century. The Eugenics Movement, which continued to be popular in the 1920s, ascribed physical traits and health and fitness to certain racial types. As the work of pseudo scientists, it became a thinly disguised means to promote racist attitudes.

Margaret Sanger, founder of the birth control movement has often been associated with the Eugenics Movement, but she did not support Eugenics' racial stereotyping. Appealing to logic, she argued that intelligence and other traits varied by individual and not by group. In *The Birth Control Review* in 1919, she discussed her views on Eugenics.

> Eugenicists insist that a woman's first duty is to the state; we contend that her duty is to herself. We maintain that a woman possessing an adequate knowledge of her reproductive functions is the best judge of the time and conditions under which her child should be brought into the world. We further maintain that it is her right, regardless of all other considerations, to determine whether she shall bear children or not, and how many children she shall bear if she chooses to become a mother.

Margaret Sanger did continue her crusade. Illustrating the gravity of the infant death rate in the United States in 1920, she reported that infant mortality increased by birth order, with significant increases for the sixth-born (twenty-nine percent mortality) to the twelfth-born child, whose probable mortality was sixty percent. She hosted the Birth Control Conference in New York in 1921 and again in 1925. Margaret Sanger founded the American Birth Control League in 1921. In 1927 she organized the International Contraceptive Conference in Zurich, and in 1931, the National Committee on Federal Legislation for Birth Control.

The Eugenics question, however, reached the hallowed halls of the U. S. Supreme Court in 1927, in the case of *Buck v Bell.* A majority decision supported by Justices Oliver Wendell Holmes, Louis Brandeis, and six other justices, ruled that it was *constitutional to involuntarily sterilize* the developmentally disabled, the insane, and those with uncontrollable epilepsy. But where did Margaret Sanger stand on this issue? When treatments for many hereditary and disabling conditions were still unknown, she maintained that reproductive decisions should be made by an individual, free of social or cultural pressure. She did support the Progressive philosophy of her day which favored:

> incentives for the *voluntary hospitalization* and/or sterilization of people with non treatable, disabling, hereditary conditions; adoption and enforcement of stringent regulations to prevent the immigration of diseased and 'feeble-minded' people into the United States; placing illiterates, paupers, unemployables, [sic] criminals, prostitutes, [and] dope fiends on farms or open spaces as long as necessary for the strengthening and development of moral conduct.

The Eugenics Movement added more fuel to the Nativist Movement.[4] As nativism resurged in the twenties, Ku Klux Klan rallies in major cities expanded the Klan's base of operation from the South to the North and into the Midwest and West. Waving the banner of social purity and protection of southern white women, Klan membership attracted 500,000 women who formed their own KKK branch, and proudly posed for group photographs wearing their hoods and robes. In many areas like the rural Midwest, the Klan became so integrated into the culture that many women assumed that their Klan activities were part of being a white Protestant American. Women were initiated by secret rites in which they were blindfolded and recited the creed: "One God, one country, one flag, the supremacy of the white race, chivalry toward women [white of course] purity and cleanliness among men." The Klan's motto, "America First" promoted White Anglo-Saxon Protestants,

4. Nativism was the fear and exclusion of immigrants by certain Americans who organized and politicized their views.

WASPS. By 1924, the Klan had recruited 4.5 million members and spread a message of hate and fear of Catholics, Jews, blacks and foreign immigrants. During the twenties, the Ku Klux Klan boldly marched down Pennsylvania Avenue, in Washington, D.C., disguised in hoods and robes, past monuments of liberty and democracy.

Japanese Immigration increased from 1891-1900, when some 25,492 Japanese came to America. But in 1906 the Japanese Exclusion Act had halted Japanese immigration. Naturally, as more Asian men remained in America, they sought prospective wives from their respective native countries. Some Japanese men circumvented the immigration law by arranging a proxy marriage to a prospective bride who was still in Japan. Then the groom could show documentation and the wife could enter the United States. From 1900 to 1920, many Japanese and Chinese women came to America as picture brides, who had responded to proposals by letter and exchanged photos by mail with Japanese and Chinese males who were living and working in the United States.

Nativist attitudes culminated with the Immigration Act of 1924, which climaxed a period of extreme *xenophobia* in America.[5] This law set a quota on the number of people who could immigrate to the United States, at two percent of the total of any given nation's residents in the United States as reported in the 1890 census. Some immigrants such as college students, professors and ministers, were exempted from the quota. Initially, immigration from Latin America was allowed, but measures were quickly developed to deny legal entry to Mexican laborers. The clear aim of this law was to restrict the entry of immigrants from Southern and Eastern Europe, but to continue to welcome large numbers of newcomers from Britain, Ireland and Northern Europe. This legislation reflected earlier discriminatory sentiments that had surfaced during the Red Scare of 1919-20 and the Palmer Raids. One provision of the 1924 law, which barred entry to those ineligible for citizenship, was aimed at effectively ending the immigration of all Asians into the United States and undermined the earlier "Gentlemen's Agreement" with Japan. When the Japanese government protested, a Japanese citizen committed *seppuku* (suicide) outside the American embassy in Tokyo. The government of Japan declared May 26, 1924, the effective date of the legislation, as a day of national humiliation in Japan. The Immigration Law of 1924 added another in a growing list of Japanese grievances against the United States.

American Heroines

The Twenties' sports world bedazzled Americans with impressive personalities and showcased female athletes. But American society disapproved of women in competitive sports. In spite of the social stigma of unladylike conduct, women continued to participate in sports and break athletic records. At the 1924 Olympics, seventeen-year-old Gertrude Ederle won gold and bronze medals in swimming competitions. In 1926, she swam the English Channel in fourteen hours and thirty-one minutes, breaking all former records of male swimmers. On her return to America, she was greeted in New York City with a tickertape parade. Glenna Collett broke par at eighty in eighteen holes of golf, the first woman to do so, and Floretta McCutcheon took the national bowling title from Jimmy Smith and Hazel Wightman won the U.S. tennis title.

Officials who opposed female athleticism voiced concern that sports would de-feminize women who tried to compete on the athletic field with men. But a leading spokeswoman, Lou Hoover, wife of Herbert Hoover, championed female athletes. She ignored the opposition and created a separate athletics organization for women, The National Amateur and Athletic Federation. Nonetheless, stereotypes of female athletes lingered.

After Gertrude Ederle retired from competitive swimming, she worked to make the female athlete's image more feminine. She was hired as a fashion consultant to design attire for female athletes. Tennis celebrity Helen Wills revolutionized women's tennis attire, changing it

5. *Xenophobia,* the fear or hatred of stranger or foreigners, or of anything that is strange and foreign.

from long dresses to the practical sleeveless, short tennis dress. When Helen Wills won tennis titles in 1926, the press described her "wonderful womanhood that uses sports to enhance its womanly charms instead of to affect an artificial masculinity." Helen Wills captured seven straight national singles titles in tennis from 1923 to 1931, as well as eight Wimbledon titles from 1927 to 1938.

In 1928, opposition groups organized to ban female athletes from Olympic competition for track and field, and managed to have women excluded from the 800-meter race. Despite these rulings, Elizabeth Robinson won a gold medal for the United States in 1928 in the 100-meter race.

Mothers of Invention: Julia Morgan, Castle Architect

During her lifetime, architect Julia Morgan designed and supervised the building of more than 700 buildings, the most famous of which was Hearst Castle. A graduate of University of California at Berkeley in 1894, she was the first female to graduate from the prestigious *Ecole des Beaux-Arts*, in Paris. In 1906, after passing State Boards and with architectural license in hand, Julia Morgan became the first practicing female architect in California. That same year her architectural office was completely destroyed in the San Francisco earthquake that hit the sleeping city on April 18, at 5:12 a.m. The temblor, the worst in California's recorded history, killed 700 people, and left 300,000 people without shelter. Over 28,000 buildings were in shambles but one structure sustained no damage — the Campanile at Mills College, designed by Julia Morgan. She built churches, colleges and YWCA buildings from Utah to Hawaii, including the YWCA camp in Monterey at Pacific Grove which she named Asilomar, "refuge by the sea."

Julia Morgan, the California Architect on site with William Randolph Hearst looking over the plans for Hearst Castle. (Photo courtesy of the Library of Congress.)

In 1919, William Randolph Hearst visited her to propose a building to house his vast art collection. For decades, Hearst had been gathering art and architecture from Europe's castles, monasteries, cathedrals, and galleries. The castle compound eventually included the main house, *La Casa Grande, La Cuesta Encantada* with 144 rooms, a theater, two swimming pools, a 28-foot refectory and three guest cottages. Julia planned and constructed a harbor to accommodate sea shipments, a five-mile road, retaining walls and several bridges on the property. In addition, she executed landscaping the desolate windswept site by planting orchards, hauling trees (some weighing 600 tons), and filling in with endless wagon loads of topsoil to the hilltop. She designed and built cottages to house artisans and laborers on the job. During the building process, the diminutive Miss Morgan could be seen scaling steep scaffolding and climbing all over to inspect every inch of the project. Almost as remarkable as Julia Morgan's commitment to undertake the mammoth construction of the castle was her collaboration with Hearst, a partnership that would continue for thirty years.

In all her architectural designs, Julia Morgan set high standards for aesthetics and durability. In 1929, the University of California at Berkeley awarded her an honorary doctorate for the "building of stately homes and great buildings nobly planned."

Women of Letters and the Arts in the Early Twentieth Century

More women were graduating from college and there was an appreciable 50 percent increase in the number holding jobs in ladies' professions such as librarians, social workers, and teachers, but the more elite professions in law, medicine, science, business, professorships, and journalism remained the male domain.

Women writers of the era made a significant contribution to American Literature. In the Twenties, one of the great wits, the writer and literary critic Dorothy Parker, wrote for upscale magazines such as *The New Yorker* and *Vanity Fair.* She joined writer Robert Benchley, playwright Robert Sherwood, journalists Frank Adams and Alexander Wollcott and editor Harold Ross in a literary group, the Round Table, which met at the Algonquin Hotel in New York City. She won the O. Henry Prize for her story, *The Big Blonde,* about a woman locked in the clutches of alcoholism who attempts suicide. Much of her work focused on alcoholism and suicide, like her screenplay for the film *A Star is Born*. In Dorothy's case, art imitated life as she struggled with alcoholism and attempted suicide several times herself.

By the early twentieth century, a cadre of female writers known as regionalists or local colorists, published works which celebrated particular regions of the United States. Two of them, Edith (Jones) Wharton and Willa Cather received the Pulitzer Prize; Edith Wharton for *The Age of Innocence* in 1921, and Willa Cather for *One of Ours* in 1923. Edith, of blue-blooded pedigree, wrote about the New York aristocracy. While she outwardly conformed to the rigors of upper-class rituals, or what her character Madame Olenska in *The Age of Innocence* called "the blind conformity to tradition, someone else's tradition," Edith Wharton personally waged her own rebellion by becoming a writer. At age twenty-three, she married Theodore Wharton, a wealthy banker but soon divorced him to live the life of a well-heeled bohemian in Europe. With a home in Paris, and one on the Riviera, Edith entertained artists and writers such as Henry James. In her novels, she depicted marriage as a trap for both men and women. But true to her class, her books were sympathetic to the old aristocracy who were slowly giving way to the new industrial barons whom she regarded as ill-mannered and ill-bred. In later novels, such as *The Custom of the Country*, her own class consciousness shows even more. Edith Wharton was openly scornful of the *nouveau riche*, and the country bumpkins from the Midwest who were trying to climb the social ladder.

Like Edith Wharton, Willa Cather disdained new social upstarts and championed old-fashioned values, but here the similarity ends. Willa Cather grew up on the Nebraska frontier among European immigrants of diverse backgrounds: Germans, Swedes, Russians, and Poles who were struggling to homestead farms in America. Willa developed her skills writing for magazines like *McClure's*. The greatest influence on her writing came from writer Sarah Orne Jewett who urged her to find "the quiet center of her life." Heeding Sarah Jewett's advice, Willa based most of her novels on the prairie experience like *O Pioneers!* and *My Antonia.* Some of her later works like *Death Comes for the Archbishop*, set in Santa Fe New Mexico; and *Shadows on the Rock,* set in Quebec, reached further back into history to a simpler time when tradition, spirituality and heroism had prevailed.

Sarah Orne Jewett wrote about her native New England, where as a young girl she had accompanied her father, a country doctor, as he made calls. Sarah's vivid recollections made her work a written canvas with lush landscapes. Regarded as her best work, *The Country of the Pointed Firs* is set on the Maine coast, with rugged, intelligent heroines.

Writer Kate O'Flaherty Chopin developed strong female characters in novels set in the French Creole culture of New Orleans. In 1899 her novel *The Awakening*, a study of a young woman's sexual and artistic desires, presented a bold step forward for women's literature. However, her vivid descriptions of mixed marriages and female sexuality were much too candid for the times. The controversy which surrounded *The Awakening* contributed to her decision to give up writing. Kate O'Flaherty Chopin died five years later in 1904. Today, *The Awakening,* considered one of her best works, is required reading in most college Feminist Studies courses.

Women also braved the odds in the arts, both visual and performing. Mary Stevenson Cassatt attended the Pennsylvania Academy of Fine Arts, in Philadelphia before traveling to Europe in 1866. After six years in Europe, Mary settled in Paris, an artists' Mecca, and opened her first Paris show. Making a permanent home in Paris, Mary Cassatt counted among her close friends impressionists Edgar Degas and Gustave Courbet. Distinguished as the only female American Impressionist in Paris, Mary focused on subjects in women's art and painted intimate glimpses of mothers and daughters. What has often been overlooked is her contribution to American galleries and museums. An American in Paris with the best connections, Mary oversaw the purchases of Impressionist masterpieces for the American market, for both private and public collections. It is no wonder then, that Philadelphia has a Rodin Museum with the largest collection of his sculpture outside of France, and the Pennsylvania Academy of Fine Arts holds some of the most cherished masterpieces from France. Mary Cassatt, like Edith Wharton, was from a wealthy family, had education, and the means to take on this lifestyle. But her decision to become an artist was not welcomed by her father who responded, "I'd rather see you dead."

Other outstanding artists of the period were Maria Oakey Dewing, known for prize still life exhibitions; Lilla Cabot Perry, who developed her own unique style of landscape and portraiture, and Cecilia Beaux who painted Mrs. Theodore Roosevelt and blended the old masters style with Impressionism.

Advances in photographic technology made the medium more accessible at the end of the nineteenth century. Several female photographers are notable such as Gertrude Kasebier whose life began as a child/pioneer in Colorado. After she attended art schools in New York and Paris, photography became her life's work. In partnership with Alfred Stieglitz, she founded the Photo-Secession group which was dedicated to promoting photography as a creative art. Her portrait photography was published in *McClure's* and *Scribner's*. Her photographs of Buffalo Bill and famous Native Americans of the Plains serve as a lasting memorial to them. Frances Johnston's pictures of Theodore Roosevelt are some of the best publicized. In her Native West Virginia, a region known for strip mining, Frances Johnston produced important photo-journal essays of mining, as well as studies of life in the Pennsylvania coal fields. She also covered the news beat, with historic photos of Admiral Dewey's return from Manila after the Spanish American War. Frances, probably the most eclectic female photographer of the period, staged a hit with her works at the Paris Universal Exhibition of 1900. Her photographs also recorded unique architectural studies with pictures of American buildings.

The work of photographers Alice Austen and Chansonetta Emmons went unnoticed by their generation. Alice Austen the earliest of the female photographers, took up the hobby at age ten when her seafaring uncle presented her with a box camera. She learned to develop her own film and took thousands of photo studies of people, particularly women, and left a wonderful visual legacy of the period. Austen photographed the hustle and bustle of the Lower East Side of New York and contrasting upscale Manhattan. Chansonetta Emmons considered her photography a hobby and roamed from Maine to California snapping pictures of America. Her pictures of black communities in the South preserved the stark reality of poverty there from 1895-1920. Were it not for the recent discoveries of the important works of Austen and Emmons, their photographs might have been lost, destroyed or forgotten.

In traditional American society, young women studied music as a mark of refinement and to provide musical accompaniment for family entertainment, but that training was not intended to lead to a musical or theatrical career. From 1890 to 1920, several women became notable in the performing arts. The era, remembered as The Golden Age of Opera, witnessed great divas such as Lillian Nordica, Mary Garden, and Olive Fremstad. The achievement of one woman, Amy Cheney Beach, the symphonic musician and composer stands out. Her marriage to physician H. A. Beach, twenty-five years her senior, allowed her the time to devote to composing musical scores. Working in various forms, she wrote chamber music, concertos for piano and oratorios. She is remembered for major works such as the *Mass in E Flat, Festival Jubilate for Chorus and Orchestra*, and the *Gaelic Symphony.*

Isadora Duncan, the pioneer of modern dance, had an atypical childhood for the period. Her mother scrimped together money for Isadora's music and dance lessons. Isadora danced with numerous theater companies as a teenager, but rejected traditional ballet and developed a free- spirited style. On tour, her new dance style was well received by European audiences, but modern dance never caught on in American theater during her lifetime. Isadora Duncan established modern dance schools in Europe including Russia and, despite financial setbacks, she trained a generation of students who made her modern dance a classic form in the performing arts.

The Harlem Renaissance

In the Twenties, white Americans searching out exciting nightlife discovered the theaters and clubs in Harlem, New York, which had become a trendy black enclave by the 1900s. Black entertainment at the Apollo Theater and the Cotton Club showcased some of the most talented performers east of Broadway. Black performers, artists, musicians and writers who migrated there were well received and Harlem became their personal and artistic haven. Writer Langston Hughes described Harlem as the place where "young Negro artists [could] express their individual dark-skinned selves without fear or shame." The shows, artists and black cultural awareness were all part of a blossoming movement known as the Black or Harlem Renaissance. Two unique female artists of the Harlem Renaissance were Zora Neale Hurston, a writer of simple eloquence, and Josephine Baker, a dancer who became an international entertainer. Zora Neale Hurston had worked as a domestic servant in Baltimore, Maryland in order to attend Morgan State Teacher's College, and went on to New York's Barnard College and Columbia University on scholarships to major in Anthropology. In her writing, which celebrated common folk, she used the rhythms and idioms of black speech. She had an extensive and productive writing career, with short stories, novels, and screenplays for Warner Brothers. She also taught for a number of years at the North Carolina College for Negroes. Among her published novels were *Jonah's Gourd Vine, Mules and Men, Tell My Horse, Moses: Man of the Mountain, Dust Tracks on the Road* and, one of her best, *Their Eyes were Watching God.*

Josephine Baker, a singer and exotic dancer dazzled, audiences at the Plantation Club in Harlem with her famous banana dance, for which she wore a costume consisting of a G-string strung with bananas. She also appeared on Broadway in *Shuffle Along* and *Chocolate Dandies*. Josephine started life somewhat compromised – fatherless and in poverty. At the age of eight, she dropped out of school to help her mother, and at sixteen left home to join a dance troupe in Philadelphia. By 1925, she was a sensation on Broadway and in Harlem, and was offered top billing in a Paris show, *La Revue Negre*. Josephine was "the highest-paid chorus girl in vaudeville."

Josephine Baker performed at nightclubs in Harlem during the district's renaissance. She became an international celebrity and a citizen of France. (Photo courtesy of the Library of Congress.)

On October 2, 1925, she opened in Paris at the Théâtre des Champs-Élysées. Her instant success was partly due to her erotic dancing and also for appearing practically nude on stage.

Baker's success coincided with the 1925, Exposition des Arts Décoratifs, which gave birth to the term "Art Deco", and also with a renewal of interest in ethnic forms of art, including African, and Baker served as the icon of this fashion. In later shows in Paris she was often accompanied on stage by her pet cheetah, Chiquita, who was adorned with a diamond collar. The cheetah frequently escaped into the orchestra pit, where it terrorized the musicians, adding more excitement to the show.

She became a permanent resident in Paris and a French citizen. When Josephine appeared in Paris clubs, she captured adoring fans with her signature ballad, *Two Loves Have I*, which expressed her deep love of her adopted country, France, and her country of origin, America. Her flamboyant lifestyle wowed the French and she became the darling of the Parisian cabaret crowd. Josephine Baker could often be seen walking her pet cheetah or her swan on a leash (but never together) up the fashionable Champs-Élysees.

Conclusion

In the twenties, Americans enjoyed a spending spree brought on by the postwar prosperity. Automobile production increased and the new installment buying made it possible for many American housewives to own household-convenient appliances. The boom economy gave families an unprecedented purchasing power.

The passage of the Eighteenth Amendment to the Constitution, the Volstead Act which prohibited the manufacture and sale of alcoholic beverages, culminated nearly a century of temperance reform efforts. During the Prohibition era from 1920 to 1932, bootleg liquor made some Americans, particularly those in organized crime, wealthy and this resulted in the escalation of crime and violence. With the emergence of the speakeasies, the new generation of women, whose mothers and grandmothers would never have frequented a tavern or saloon, imbibed the new nightlife with gusto.

Nowhere was the euphoria of the twenties more evident than in motion pictures. Hollywood created female characters for the screen such as vamps, virgins and flappers. The new female movie stars stimulated a new industry in cosmetics and hair salons, and a revolution in women's fashion. A cadre of female writers and artists celebrated America's diverse regions and black writers and entertainers gifted the 1920s with the Harlem Renaissance.

Margaret Sanger founded the American Birth Control League, held international conferences and continued her efforts to distribute birth control information to American women. The extremist views of nativists and racists reemerged stronger than ever and in the Immigration Act of 1924, the Congress set quotas and restrictions for immigration.

After the ratification of the Nineteenth, or Susan B. Anthony, Amendment, women voted for the first time in the presidential election of 1920, in which Republican Warren G. Harding became President. Within the Federation of Colored Women, Jessie Daniel Ames formed the anti-lynching campaign targeted at southern states where attackers lynched black men with impunity. Despite great personal risk and no public support, Jessie Daniel Ames and her followers would continue that campaign over the next four decades.

Chapter 20

Women and the Great Depression

Harder Times

Key Topics

Women and New Deal Reform
First Lady Eleanor Roosevelt
Minority Women in Politics
Working Women in the Great Depression
Labor Union Organizers

Chronology

1929 - October 29, Stock Market Crashes
1932 - Franklin Delano Roosevelt Becomes President
1933 - Roosevelt Administration Initiates the New Deal
Repeal of 18th Amendment Ends Prohibition
1936 - FDR Re-elected
1937 - Disappearance of Amelia Earhart
1937 - Federal Government Legalizes Birth Control

Introduction

Mellon pulled the whistle
Hoover rang the bell
Wall Street gave the signal
And the country went to Hell

The New York Stock Market crash of October 29, 1929, signaled the beginning of the longest economic downturn the United States has ever experienced. When it hit, Herbert Hoover, just ten months into his presidency, faced three more agonizing years and seemed helpless to deal with the problem. He assumed like others that in due time, the economy would recover.

In 1932, Franklin Delano Roosevelt, FDR, the aristocratic governor of New York, opposed Hoover in the presidential election and offered Americans hope. After his victory, FDR dealt with the crisis by setting up a program for relief, recovery and reform called the New Deal. In his first one-hundred days, FDR pushed a record breaking amount of legislation through Congress. The group of agencies created under the New Deal: such as the National Relief Administration, the NRA, the Civilian Conservation Corps, the CCC, the Tennessee Valley Authority, the TVA, and the Works Progress Administration, the WPA, were known as the alphabet soup agencies and gave the Federal government a more visible role in the economy. In spite of all those innovations, the Great Depression lingered for twelve bitter years, until 1941, when wartime production bailed out the sinking economy.

As America's First Lady, Eleanor Roosevelt broke precedent in that role as an activist and champion of the underdog. Mrs. Roosevelt became the standard by which to measure all the first ladies who followed her.

The Depression affected every socio-economic group but none with as much devastation as the poor. Working class women struggled to keep their families together. Women from many trades and ethnic groups organized labor unions and worked tirelessly for change.

The entertainment industry formed around radio programs and motion pictures. Housewives could tune into daily soap opera dramas and enjoy movie stars on the silver screen. Motion pictures provided a brief escape from the bread lines, unemployment and general misery of the world outside.

Women and New Deal Reform

Florence Kelley's groundbreaking initiatives for labor inspired young Progressive Frances Perkins who had worked at Hull House. Later, Frances Perkins commented on Florence Kelley's impact on her life, stating she "had opened my mind to the necessity for and the possibility of the work which became my vocation." Frances Perkins had worked under Florence Kelley's guidance in the National Consumers' League, and became an expert factory inspector. With that résumé, Frances Perkins gained an appointment as industrial commissioner for New York, in the administrations of Governors Al Smith and Franklin D. Roosevelt. Under Governor Roosevelt she had served as the State Commissioner of the Department of Labor. Based on her experience as a labor advocate, Frances Perkins was the natural choice for a Washington cabinet post. Florence Kelley, her mentor, lived to see her become the first woman to hold a presidential cabinet position, as Franklin D. Roosevelt's Secretary of Labor.

In 1938, the United States Congress passed the Fair Labor Standards Act which banned child labor and established the forty-hour week. It became effective October in 1940, and the Supreme Court upheld its constitutionality in March 1941. To the credit of Labor Secretary Frances Perkins and the efforts of labor activists such as Emma Goldman and Mary Harris "Mother" Jones, the ban on child labor in the United States had finally materialized.

On the whole, New Deal legislation was not beneficial to working-class women. The Social Security and Fair Labor Standards Acts barred the majority of women in domestic service from receiving protective benefits, and young women were prohibited from working in the Civilian Conservation Corps. Although it seemed like a beneficial program for women, the Women's and Professional Projects Division, the WPPD, an agency of the Works Progress Administration, administered by Ellen Sullivan Woodward, a former Mississippi social worker, provided women with only menial domestic work or sewing projects, and the WPPD's work hiring practices discriminated against African-American and Mexican-American women. Despite the optimism for FDR's administration's reform initiative, the New Deal legislation set codes for women's earnings at 25 percent below those for men in jobs in which they performed the same work.

However, under Frances Perkins' guiding hand, landmark legislation such as Social Security and the eradication of Child Labor brought alleviation and reform. She created many work programs like the Civilian Conservation Corps which gave young men work, room and board. Frances Perkins, distinguished as the only cabinet member who stayed on during the entire Roosevelt years from 1933-1945, served longer than any other cabinet member in American history. Despite sexual harassment, accusations of being a communist, constant public scrutiny as the only female cabinet member, and criticism for trying to do a man's job, Frances Perkins carried out her duties in a professional, competent manner, and made a lasting contribution to the government setting high standards for the Department of Labor.

In the midst of the economic downturn and busy political reform, the truly forgotten people in the Thirties were those in prison. Socialist Kate Richards O'Hare, arrested during the Palmer Raids, had been befriended by Emma Goldman, a fellow prison inmate. Upon release, Kate put aside her Socialist agenda to focus on prison reform. She succeeded to some degree.

Kate Richards O'Hare produced a scathing documentary on the conditions in the Missouri Prison at Jefferson City. During the Thirties, she targeted the more progressive State of California for penal reform and her lobbying efforts helped transform the California Prison System into one of the most advanced at that time.

Eleanor Roosevelt, first lady during the unprecedented four presidential terms of her husband, Franklin Delano Roosevelt. Her proactive role in the White House became the prototype for succeeding first ladies. (Photo courtesy of the Library of Congress.)

First Lady Eleanor Roosevelt

> You have to accept whatever comes and the only important thing is that you meet it with the best you have to give.
>
> Eleanor Roosevelt

Florence Kelley's progressivism and early settlement house work inspired many visitors to Hull House, among them, the young Eleanor Roosevelt. Later, First Lady Eleanor Roosevelt advocated the rights of labor and brought the plight of American workers to the front page.

Eleanor Roosevelt (ER), the wife of Franklin D. Roosevelt, was a very active first lady. During the Roosevelt years, she served as an unofficial vice president, logging in 40,000 air miles per year, visiting work sites and foreign dignitaries, as well as making fact-finding tours for her husband. ER literally did the legwork for her husband, a polio victim, crippled and confined to a wheelchair. Eleanor's mobility, energy and vision were a great asset to her husband and the New Deal Administration, and Mrs. Roosevelt seemed to be everywhere, doing everything. One never knew where she might turn up next, a tendency caricatured in a New Yorker cartoon in 1933, which showed a coal miner deep in the earth's pit, remarking to fellow miners, "For gosh sakes, here comes Mrs. Roosevelt."

Fifteen years previous, in 1918, her life appeared irretrievably shattered when she discovered, after thirteen years of marriage, her husband was having an affair with her social secretary, Lucy Mercer. Eleanor consented to divorce but FDR's mother urged her to "maintain a semblance of propriety." The Roosevelts salvaged their marriage for the sake of his political career. He had already served as Assistant Secretary of the Department of the Navy, and in 1920, had campaigned as the Democratic Vice Presidential candidate, but the democrats lost the election to Warren G. Harding. In 1921, FDR was suddenly stricken with polio and became an invalid. Franklin's political aide, Louis Howe urged him to stay in the political game and run for Governor of New York. Howe befriended Eleanor and tutored her on the finer points of being a politician's wife. In 1928, Eleanor conducted a whistle-stop campaign through the State of New York to help her husband win the governorship. From there the next stop was the White House.

Eleanor Roosevelt's work as first lady and the uniqueness of the Roosevelt presidency, have been described as "the Roosevelt magic." Their partnership is summed up by historian James Henretta.

> He was the pragmatic politician, always aware of what could be done; she was the idealist, always pushing him—and the New Deal to do more. Indeed, Eleanor Roosevelt served as the conscience of the New Deal.

Despite tragedy and infidelity, FDR and ER became one of the most successful long lasting political partnerships in American history, maintaining a national public image for nearly seventeen years. While in the political spotlight,

ER also raised six children, became a doting grandmother and served as the nation's hostess to domestic and foreign dignitaries for twelve years. During the Depression Mrs. Roosevelt built a furniture factory on the family estate, Val-kill, in Hyde Park, New York. In this way, she provided jobs for people in her community.

The Roosevelts were the first presidential couple to use the media to their advantage. In 1933, Mrs. Roosevelt premiered a First Lady's press conference at the White House. Concerned about sexual discrimination in the hiring and firing of female reporters, she insisted that all reporters at her press conferences be women, and she used the press time to promote women's work across the country. In concert with FDR's weekly radio program, *The Fireside Chats,* Eleanor also delivered a weekly fifteen-minute radio broadcast and found time to write a daily syndicated newspaper column, "My Day," on every topic under the sun. The following eulogy, written about her mother-in-law, Mrs. Delano Roosevelt, characterizes both her candor and magnanimity.

"My Day"

Hyde Park, Sunday - An anxious twenty-four hours culminated a little before noon today in the death of my husband's mother. Had she lived she would have celebrated her eighty-seventh birthday...

Her life was rich and full. She had seen her only son inaugurated President of the United States, three times, and she still felt that her husband was the most wonderful man she had ever known.

She had no hesitancy about telling her near and dear ones their faults, or criticizing their behavior, but if anyone else in the world were to attack a member of her family, she would rise in their defense like a tigress. Whatever the family did, in the end she accepted and condoned before the world, no matter what her private feelings might be... She would give away large sums of money and save small ones. The President's mother always attributed her little economies, like undoing string and folding wrapping paper for future use, to her New England upbringing. She was not just sweetness and light for there was a streak of jealousy and possessiveness in her where her own were concerned...

She wanted her son to live up to high standards of character and conduct and never believed that he failed in this. She spoiled her grandchildren perhaps a little but they had great affection and respect for her. I think even some of her great-grandchildren will remember her when they grow up as a very beautiful stately old lady who loved them and made them feel that Hyde Park would be their home as long as it was hers. E.R.

Mrs. Roosevelt's influence on FDR and the New Deal is incalculable. A 1939 Gallup Poll revealed that she had a sixty-seven percent approval rating (higher than the president's), and *Life* magazine praised her as the greatest American woman alive. Much of her popularity can be credited to her championing the disadvantaged, the poor, black Americans, children, labor, women, and the handicapped. She also took on liberal causes such as Civil Rights. Her recommendations helped an unprecedented number of women obtain high-level government positions. Women such as Molly Dewson who was appointed to head the National Democratic Party's Women's Division. Molly Dewson, like Secretary of Labor Frances Perkins, was a Progressive reformer who promoted the New Deal agenda and recommended women for top jobs in the Works Progress Administration (the WPA), the Federal Mint and for vacancies on the circuit court of appeals. National Democratic Leader James Farley credited Mrs. Roosevelt with at least 4,000 appointments of women in Federal jobs, most of which were in the postal system.

Minority Women in Politics

When Concha Ortiz y Pino won the election in 1936, she became the first Spanish-speaking woman to serve in the New Mexico State legislature. Her political victory was not so much about a woman taking political office as it was about the supremacy of the Hispanic aristocracy in New Mexico. Concha Ortiz y Pino was a member of one of the old land owning Hispanic families which had power and influence. In New Mexico people cherished and respected Spanish/Indian heritage and her family had served in politics since the eighteenth century. When *Anglos* had settled in and seized land in New Mexico, her ancestors had vowed to remain politically active; and in every election since then, keeping the promise made by her great grandfather, either a Pino or an Ortiz had run for a seat in the New Mexico State Assembly.

Concha Ortiz y Pino brought change and reform to politics. She also brought aid to families in her hometown of Galisteo who were hit hard by the Depression, and she organized a vocational program to market artisanal crafts of New Mexico and to give people work.

In 1936, although she switched her party affiliation from Republican to Democrat and campaigned to get FDR re-elected, her politics did not always resound with New Deal policy. She was opposed to banning child labor or limiting the hours women could work, but she did introduce the first bill to make women eligible to serve on juries; proposed a civil service merit system to protect female employees; and sponsored a bill which required the teaching of Spanish in grammar schools. Her proposal for bilingual education, one of the first in the country, marked New Mexico's bilingual education program as one that worked. Today, the official first language of the State of New Mexico remains Spanish. Mindful of the rights of the disabled, Concha Ortiz y Pino also pushed legislation to make all public buildings wheelchair accessible.

In FDR's second term in the White House, Mrs. Roosevelt collaborated with black educator Mary McCleod Bethune and brought her into Washington politics. Before joining the Black Cabinet, educator Mary McCleod Bethune, a success story in her own right, had promoted a program of self-help for African-Americans. In 1904, with only $1.50 and a prayer, she established Bethune-Cookman College in a rented house in Daytona Beach, Florida. By 1923, the school had grown to a twenty-three-acre campus, with eight buildings and 300 students. Mary Bethune became an inspirational force in many black causes including the National Association of Colored Women, the Council of Interracial Cooperation, and the Association of Southern Women for the Prevention of Lynching.

In 1935, the FDR administration named Mary McCleod Bethune to the National Youth Administration, a New Deal Program, to find jobs for young adults from ages sixteen to twenty-four. When other African-Americans joined Mary Bethune in Federal jobs, they formed an unofficial group known as the Black Braintrust, or the Black Cabinet. This included men such as Robert Weaver, Frank Horne and William Hastie who joined the New Deal government in executive posts or as heads of advisory councils. As insiders, this black leadership held an advantageous position to develop strategies and objectives for a civil rights cause. In 1937 and 1939, the Black Cabinet hosted two National Negro Conferences in Washington, D.C., for that purpose. In 1938, sixty-seven African-American female leaders convened at the White House, to open, "a door that has been sealed for 200 years." With Mrs. Roosevelt's endorsement and support, Mary McCleod Bethune hoped to gain blacks positions in the Federal system, and to use the new power base to get equitable treatment for all African-Americans.

The Depression Family

During the Depression, families struggled to provide the basic needs for their children. Between 1929 and 1935, deflation reduced the cost of living by 20 percent so families had to adjust their budgets accordingly. Prices on consumer goods were not significantly reduced and widespread unemployment made it very difficult to maintain a household. The use of telephones decreased sharply, but gasoline sales remained steady. New car sales were almost non-existent as families who relied on an automobile had to keep the old car running. People simply learned to make do. More women learned to sew, reused fabric over and over again, and even recycled flour sacks to make clothing. Disregarding gender, brothers and sisters wore hand-me-downs. Families planted vegetable gardens and preserved fruits and vegetables. When unemployment reached the middle class, housewives let domestic servants go and did their own cleaning.

The Depression hit the poorest people the hardest; working-class Americans were driven to desperation. Jessie Lopez de la Cruz, a future farm worker's union organizer remembered the Depression years, when her mother died of cancer and her grandmother raised the family in a labor camp. Jessie picked mustard greens and mushrooms and her little brother hunted wild rabbits to keep the family fed. She remembered a schoolteacher who gave her leftover food from her own lunch to take home to the family.

One of the most dramatic changes appeared in the birthrate, which dropped 14 percent as women made a conscious decision to limit the size of their family. A baby born in the thirties carried the stigma, Depression Baby, meaning a child unplanned, or unwanted. In 1929, support emerged for birth control advocate Margaret Sanger under unlikely circumstances. When New York City police raided her clinic, ransacking and confiscating patient's medical records, New York physicians viewed the police impounding of confidential medical files as a gross violation of confidentiality and a breach of privacy. As a result, the medical community rallied behind Margaret Sanger's cause, which encouraged continuance of her organization's mission to educate Americans on birth control and family planning.

In 1936, the United States Supreme Court reinterpreted the Comstock Law, and struck down all Federal restrictions on the distribution of birth control information and contraceptive materials. This meant that physicians could legally dispense birth control information and contraceptive devices, such as the diaphragm. After the ruling, condoms were sold in pharmacies and were placed in vending machines in men's public bathrooms in some states. By 1937, the American Medical Association endorsed birth control. The Gallup Poll taken that same year, revealed the public's changing attitudes toward birth control with sixty-three percent in favor of making it readily available. In 1939, Sanger joined the American Birth Control League and the Birth Control Research Bureau to form the Birth Federation of America. Margaret Sanger's long fought crusade for a woman's right to choose between maternity and contraception had scored a victory but it had taken a devastating and severe economic depression to bring change.

Because of the bleak job market, more young people stayed in school; in the early thirties, less than 50 percent of American youth finished high school. In the closing years of the Depression, 75 percent of the nation's youngsters were awarded a high school diploma. New Deal Programs enabled more young people to attend college and about two million took advantage of government funding and pursued higher education.

Many women took in boarders, set up makeshift restaurants, bakeries or beauty parlors in their homes, hired themselves out as domestics or worked extra jobs, if they could find them. It was commonplace for people to go door to door seeking work, and offering to do odd jobs to earn a few cents. Letters from destitute mothers came pouring into First Lady Eleanor Roosevelt's White House office. One woman who wrote asked Mrs. Roosevelt for a government loan and enclosed her wedding ring in the letter as collateral. Another writer, identified as Mrs. H. C., requested that Mrs. Roosevelt send some baby diapers and clothing.

The Depression brought increased tensions and unbearable stress to families. In their despondency, many husbands deserted their wives and fathers abandoned their families. Victims of the "poor man's divorce," wives and mothers were left with the burden of being sole providers for their families. For some of the men who stayed, the Depression merely intensified problems which already existed. Writer Studs Terkel described his own experience in *Hard Times:* "My father led a rough life; He drank. During the Depression he drank more. There was more conflict in the home... Everything was sharpened and hurt more by the Depression." (That must have made life tougher for Studs' mother.)

By the twenties, hospitals and medical schools certificated nurse's training, and state boards licensed nurses. The nurse featured in the photo, Mildred May DeVilbiss, graduated in 1929 from Franklin Square Hospital, Baltimore, Maryland, and entered her profession in the Depression economy. Millions of Americans faced unemployment but qualified nurses found work. Typically, a nurse worked a continuous twenty-five- day schedule, consisting of a twelve-hour day for a monthly salary of $29.

Social Scientists who have studied the effects of the Great Depression on the American family report that women were better suited to cope with the crisis than men. Wives and mothers had multiple tasks to perform at home but unemployed men tended to become lethargic and depressed. An explanation offered suggests that ever since the advent of the industrial revolution, male identity and worth had been associated with productivity outside the home. If men were not productive, they had no value. Even so, under these extraordinary circumstances of the Depression, sociologists conclude that more families worked together, and stayed together, than fell apart.

Working Women in the Great Depression

> My heart it is breaking,
> it's Christmas Eve night
> I'm in the slums on the east side
> without any light I've no gas and
> electric to make myself a cup of tea
> Oh tell me fellow workers, how can
> this be?

Homeless, jobless women of the Depression, known as the *invisible unemployed,* were especially vulnerable on the streets, so they sought shelter in the most unobtrusive places possible, such as the bathrooms of subway or railroad stations, or in large industrial heating ducts. By 1932, throughout the country an estimated two million women were the *invisible unemployed* and the homeless. In New York City alone there were at least 75,000. The most tragic victims of the Depression were the children, cast-offs, such as the thousands of young girls who resorted to prostitution for their livelihood and became victims of crime and exploitation.

Despite the vigorous activism of women in the labor movement, women remained underemployed, underpaid, and underrepresented in unions. Newspaper editor Norman Cousins actually blamed working females for the unemployment problem.

> There are ten million people unemployed in the country, and ten million women who are still holding down jobs. Simply fire the women, who should not be working anyway, and hire the men. Presto! No unemployment. No relief rolls. No Depression."

Cousins failed to recognize that women supported themselves and their families. If men had worked in those deadbeat jobs, they would have had union representation.

The female workforce was changing. About 96 percent of the stenographer, secretarial and telephone operators' positions had become a strictly female domain, known as "pink collar employment." These jobs were typically low salaried. If female telephone operators married, they were terminated from their jobs. Other low paying jobs reserved for women were nursing, teaching, domestic service and industrial labor.

Women's demands for equal pay for equal work had less punch during the Depression, as anyone who had work was not about to quibble and was grateful for the wages. But women had played a critical role in labor union organizing since the nineteenth century. For example, the ubiquitous Mother Jones had campaigned for labor for fifty years. In later years, she received belated recognition for her contribution. On May 1, 1930, for her one-hundredth birthday, Mother Jones received, among the thousands of good wishes, a congratulatory telegram from former opponent, John D. Rockefeller, Jr. When she died at her home in Silver Spring, Maryland, on November 30, 1930, thousands of workers mourned her death. A song composed in her honor became the chant in mining towns during the desperate Depression years "The Death of Mother Jones,"

> Mother Jones was ready to help them;
> She never let them down.
> In front with the striking miners
> She always could be found;
> She fought for right and justice;
> She took a noble stand.

With the increased hiring of women as secretaries and typists, Pink Collar employment necessitated schools offering typing classes. (Photo courtesy of the Archives of the Fullerton College Library.)

Latina Labor Union Organizers

Throughout the Southwest, from Texas to California, *Latinas* had been fighting for better working conditions and organizing unions since the early 1900s. In the early days, women had assumed responsibility for the conditions in their own neighborhoods and villages and formed *mutualistas* (mutual aid societies) to help those in need. The *mutualistas* raised funds to establish life and health insurance, legal assistance and to stage festive celebrations for the community. Some *mutualistas* offered classes to teach recent arrivals English and prepare them for citizenship. The *mutualistas* were more than volunteer associations. They often served as the command center for any action taken in a community. The Latinas who galvanized the trade union movements had witnessed the daily activity of their mothers, aunts and grandmothers busy in church work, charity, and aid to the needy, all in the spirit of the *mutualistas*. Later they became the staging areas for unionization and political protest. Other associations like the *Club Mexicano Independencia*, CMI, catered to the working classes, but the more elitist *Club Femenino Orquidia*, organized in San Antonio, Texas, was founded as a women's group.

By 1929, the League of United Latin American Citizens, LULAC, composed of middle-class Mexican-Americans, had recruited thousands of members. LULAC captured the spirit of the times and developed into an activist civil rights group for Latinos. LULAC was in many ways a *mutualistas* with a broader base of support. Women in LULAC cooked, baked, fed, and distributed food baskets for the needy, raised money to purchase toys, clothing and milk for children and were otherwise available as needs arose in their communities. Many of the Latinas who later went into politics or a profession had taken their first steps toward activism in LULAC. It's first female Vice President, Alicia Montemayor, published one of the first Latina feminist tracts in 1937 in the *LULAC Newsletter*, entitled "*Son Muy Hombres*," which attacked the whole Latino structure of male superiority. For Alicia Montemayor, participating in community associations was one way to work for change; for others it was organizing union picket lines.

By the thirties, the Latino population in the Southwest comprised 25 percent of the factory workforce. In California, attempts to unionize the field workers met with strong resistance and little success. All the workers were up against the growers. In October 1933, when 18,000 workers went on strike and camped out on empty land, the women in the camps cared for strikers and families by distributing food and clothing. These women also took an active part in the strike by confronting the strikebreakers.

Most of the Latina field labor in California worked either in the San Joaquin Valley, picking cotton, or throughout the state as cannery workers. About 70 percent were single women, either unmarried, widowed or divorced, who provided the sole support of their families. The canneries in California were some of the most hazardous places for women to work. Machinery was dangerous to operate, women were frequently injured, and their wounds became easily infected. Workers could barely walk on the slippery floors in buildings which were poorly ventilated and dark.

Among the most desperate during the Depression were the working poor migrant workers whose hardships are characterized in this classic photo of this thirty-two-year-old mother of seven children who labored as a pea-picker. (Photo courtesy of the Library of Congress.)

Latina union workers campaigned for all *Latinos* who were underrepresented in labor unions or not represented at all. Two key labor organizers, Luisa Moreno and Emma Tenayuca, formed the United Cannery, Agricultural, Packing and Allied Workers of America (UCAPAWA). Luisa Moreno had good credentials having worked as a labor organizer for the American Federation of Labor (the AFL). Luisa had also unionized the garment workers in Spanish Harlem, New York City and the Cigar Factory workers in Florida.

In 1935, Emma Tenayuca formed two locals for the International Ladies Garment Workers Union, (the ILGWU) and in 1938, she organized the pecan shellers throughout Texas and New Mexico and staged a series of strikes. When thousands of female pecan shellers who went on strike and picketed were arrested and beaten, Emma enlisted the help of the Congress of Industrial Organizations, (the CIO) which eventually won a salary increase for them. When Emma Tenayuca and Luisa Moreno joined forces in UCAPAWA, they represented a wide range of field workers, from black sharecroppers in Mississippi to Filipino lettuce packers in California, as well as Mexican field hands working throughout Texas, California and other Southwestern agricultural regions.

In August of 1939, UCAPAWA Local Chapter 75, staged a strike against the California Sanitary Canning Company in Los Angeles. Dorothy Healey, a young union activist who organized the strike, raised a boycott against stores that sold California Sanitary Canning Company products. After the shutdown, which lasted several months, brought no results, Dorothy Healey marched strikers to the homes of the cannery owners to demonstrate there. That move motivated owners to negotiate with union organizers, but workers were only given a small pay increase.

Historian Vickie Ruiz estimates that as many as 65 percent of the labor organizers in UCAPAWA were women. Although the union-secured minimal benefits for field hands this only lasted a few years, but the effort served as valuable experience for women organizers.

Discrimination, Immigration, and Repatriation

Signs of desperation were everywhere during the Depression. Minority women stood economically on the bottom step, and often had to take on several jobs just to keep the family together. In Chicago, in 1931, when black women staged food and rent riots which escalated into a mass demonstration, they were beaten by police.

Chinese women who came to the United States faced their own obstacles. Chinese entering the United States were processed at Angel Island in San Francisco, California. They were detained there for interrogation, physical examination and, in the case of illness, were placed in quarantine and returned to China. The first generation of Chinese women who had immigrated to America lived in the Chinatowns of San Francisco, Riverside or Los Angeles, where they struggled to succeed. Some worked in retail stores (mostly grocery), commercial laundries, as domestic servants or in agriculture. Chinese women worked in garment sweatshops or at home doing piecework for the garment industry. The first generation labored intensely to provide a formal education for their children. Traditionally Chinese-American families invested in higher education for their sons rather than their daughters but despite this tendency some women entered professions. In 1930, Sau Ung Loo Chan graduated from Yale University Law School and Bessie Jeong became a physician. Overcoming many cultural barriers at this time, Anna May Wong became a Hollywood film star.

Under the injunction of Confucian Philosophy, Chinese women were expected to observe the "Three Obediences" to father, husband and son. But a rare instance of assertiveness occurred in 1938, when for three months Chinese-American women in San Francisco directed a labor strike at garment factories. They demanded higher wages and improved working conditions. In San Francisco's Chinatown, the women organized social, charity and civic associations. When Japanese troops staged a full-scale invasion of China in 1937, Chinese-American women in the City of San Francisco raised funds and organized war relief for China.

One of the most ignoble acts of the Depression passed by FDR's New Deal government was the Federal Repatriation Act which linked with similar laws passed by the State of California. The Repatriation Act made it possible for the State of California and the Federal government to expel 300,000 people from the United States and send them to Mexico without due process of law. Repatriation was a misnomer. At least 55 percent of the emigrants were American citizens denied access to the courts to fight forced emigration. Because evacuees were moved on such short notice and transported on trains, they had little time to dispose of property and could not take many possessions with them. With no prior consultation, the United States informed Mexican officials that émigrés were being sent back to Mexico. The United States offered no justification for repatriating Mexican-Americans or Mexican Nationals but most assumed that the economic downturn and lack of jobs in the United States was the reason.

Mothers of Invention: Dorothy Day and the Catholic Worker

Dorothy Day, who had taken up journalism in the Twenties writing for socialist newspapers such as *The Call, The Liberator* and *The Masses,* covered a wide range of issues affecting women such as rent strikes, birth control and the peace movement. Her conversion to Roman Catholicism in 1927 presaged her life's mission. During the Thirties, she struggled to find a way to reconcile her new faith with her radical social values. Her focus sharpened in the winter of 1932, when a reporting assignment for *Commonweal Magazine* took her Washington, D.C., to cover the Hunger March. Dorothy Day observed protesters parading down Pennsylvania Avenue carrying signs calling for jobs, unemployment insurance, old age pensions, relief for mothers and children, health care and housing. The march had been organized by Communists, a party at war not only with capitalism but also with religion.

Dorothy Day made her mark as a journalist and social worker. Her newspaper the Catholic Worker and her Catholic Worker houses brought hope and relief to the poor. (Photo courtesy of the Library of Congress.)

Dorothy found the means to forge her radical socialism with Catholicism after she met Peter Maurin, a French émigré, who had adopted the Franciscan attitude of poverty as a vocation. He urged Dorothy to create a newspaper to publicize Catholic social teaching and to promote the peaceful transformation of society. Dorothy Day quickly embraced the idea and got a press to print 2,500 copies of an eight-page newspaper for $57. Her kitchen became the editorial office and she priced the paper at a penny a copy, "so cheap that anyone could afford to buy it."

As soon as the first copies of *The Catholic Worker* were handed out on Union Square on May 1st, 1933, her publishing venture met with immediate success. By December, 100,000 copies were being printed each month. *The Catholic Worker* expressed dissatisfaction with the social order and took the side of labor unions, but its vision of the ideal future challenged both urbanization and industrialism. It was radical and religious. Dorothy and Peter's editorials did not merely complain but called on their readers to make personal responses. For the next six months the message of *The Catholic Worker* spread and offered hope to the poor.

As the winter of 1934 approached, homeless people began to knock on her door. Dorothy Day adopted Franciscan belief which included a renewal of that religious order's practice of hospitality to those who were homeless. In 1936, she established the St. Joseph Houses of Hospitality and moved into two buildings in Chinatown, but expansion could not accommodate all those in need.

Catholic Worker Houses spread across the country. In contrast with most religious charitable centers, no one at the Catholic Worker set about converting those they helped. The Catholic Worker also experimented with farming communes on Staten Island and Mary Farm in Easton, Pennsylvania

The Catholic Worker's pacifism did not trouble readers until the Spanish Civil War in 1936, when the fascists led by Franco presented themselves as defenders of the Catholic faith. Nearly every Catholic bishop and Catholic publication supported Franco. Because *The Catholic Worker* refused to rally to either side in the war, they lost two-thirds of their readers. To those backing Franco, Day warned that they ought to "take another look at recent events in [Nazi] Germany." She expressed anxiety for the Jews and later was among the founders of the Committee of Catholics to Fight Anti-Semitism.

Female Athletes in the News

The Thirties featured outstanding women in sports such as Mildred "Babe" Didrikson, who took the 1932 Olympic Gold Medal for the javelin and hurdles events. During the Thirties Babe toured with women's basketball and baseball teams.

Physicians in the nineteenth century had disagreed on the healthiness of Physical Education for women, but by the twenties more women participated in sports and took physical education in school. (Photo Courtesy of the Archives of the Fullerton College Library.)

For young Helen Stephens, a farm girl from Fulton, Missouri, there were no girls' sports programs in high school. In 1935, Helen entered her first national track and field meet with the Amateur Athletic Association and won in track competition. In 1936, at the Olympics in Berlin, she took two Gold Medals, in the 100 meter and 400 meter races. Her 100 meter race set a world record that would not be broken for twenty-four years. In 1938, Helen toured with a women's basketball team which she had organized, the Helen Stephens Olympic CO-EDS. Alice Marble won the United States Open Tennis Singles Championship four times from 1936-1940, and took top honors at Wimbledon in 1940. Although women were not allowed to play professional basketball, football, or baseball, in

1931, during an exhibition between the New York Yankees and a minor team, the Chatanooga Lookouts, seventeen-year-old Virne "Jackie" Mitchell struck out both Babe Ruth and Lou Gehrig.

Popular Culture

During the Depression, for only five cents, Americans long on hope and short on cash could see a movie. At least 60 percent of the American public managed to see a movie at least once a week. For the homeless, movie houses were shelter from the cold and a place to sleep. For those few hours while watching a movie, one could forget the harsh realities of the Depression and enjoy the smooth dancing of Fred Astaire and Ginger Rogers tap-dancing their way through life as young wealthy sophisticates. Talented African-American actresses such as Hattie McDaniels and Butterfly McQueen in *Gone with the Wind*, and Ethel Waters in *Cabin in the Sky,* starred typecast in roles as slaves or domestic servants. Movies of the Thirties often portrayed the dark side of life with *film noir*, portraying evildoers and gangsters as anti-heroes.

A disturbing undercurrent of Depression films condoned violence towards women. In the film *Public Enemy Number One*, James Cagney punched Mae Clark in the face with a grapefruit. Film star Carole Lombard, in *Love before Breakfast*, sported a black eye. Carole Lombard once remarked that unless "you have been slugged, kicked, shoved down a flight of stairs, or hit over the head with a frying pan, you haven't played a role as a leading lady." Was Hollywood's treatment of leading ladies and the violence toward women in the movies a matter of art imitating life? Domestic violence and child abuse were on the rise. The films of the Thirties presented the battering of women as acceptable, justifiable and often as sexual and erotic. Moreover, audiences did not regard the physical and verbal abuse of women as unusual or abnormal.

In the misery of the Depression decade one little girl, movie star Shirley Temple, lifted America's spirits. She became an American icon marketed in dolls, clothes, books, and recordings. In stark comparison to Shirley Temple were the new female sirens: blonds like Jean Harlow, Carole Lombard, Marlene Dietrich, Greta Garbo and Mae West. When they appeared in Depression era movies, drug stores could not stock enough bottles of peroxide. It seemed that every woman in America wanted to be a blond. When comic strip artist Chic Young introduced "Blondie" to readers, he featured her as a gold digger, setting a snare for Dagwood Bumstead, a wealthy playboy.

Radio also provided some relief for Depression misery. By the Thirties, the radio had become the media to reach the masses, and radio programs began to mold a national popular culture. In 1930, about thirteen million homes had a radio and by 1938, households with radios had increased to 27.5 million. News broadcasts kept Americans better informed. Radio programs, also an inexpensive form of entertainment, brought laughter with the comedy of Jack Benny, Burns and Allen, and Edgar Bergen and Charlie McCarthy. Daytime programming lightened the housewife's work with the serial dramas or soap operas, such as Ma Perkins, Stella Dallas, and the Young Widow Brown. A new parlor game also provided a diversion, when Parker Brothers introduced Monopoly, a board game which provided the pretense of wealth. The family could play for hours spending phony money to purchase bogus real estate.

Amelia Earhart, Pioneer Aviator

America celebrated the Age of Aviation when Charles Lindbergh flew solo and nonstop across the Atlantic in 1927. Looking at vintage airplanes today, it is hard to imagine anyone having the courage to pilot them. Famed aviatrix Amelia Mary Earhart, convinced that everyone should learn to fly a plane, took lessons in 1921, at age twenty-four. Because Amelia resembled aviator Charles Lindbergh (they could have passed for siblings), the press often called her Lady Lindy.

In her short life of forty years, Amelia Earhart served as a nurse with the Canadian Army in World War I; worked at the Denison Settlement House in Boston; taught at Columbia University and University of Massachusetts; and served at Purdue University as a career counselor for female students. She joined the staff of

Cosmopolitan Magazine as Aviation Editor; co-founded and served as President of the Ninety-Nines, a women's pilot club; and as Vice-President of Luddington Airlines, one of the first commercial passenger airline services. Her celebrity was chiefly the work of her publisher husband, George Palmer Putnam, who financed her flying missions as publicity for his newspapers and magazines. Her fame also boosted sales of her books, *20 Hrs. 40 Min.*, about her transatlantic flight, and *The Fun of it,* published in 1932.

Although Amelia broke more aviation records than Lindbergh, her fame as an aviator became legendary because of her mysterious disappearance in 1937. On her last flight, in a twin engine Lockheed Electra, she flew with navigator Frederick Noonan. They were attempting a circumnavigation of the world but ran into all sorts of problems, beginning with a takeoff accident in Honolulu, Hawaii. One month later, on July 2, while flying over the air space from New Guinea to Howland Island, Amelia and Frederick experienced mechanical problems and radio contact was lost. Her plane was never found, and new theories about her disappearance, are raised periodically.

Amelia Earhart, pioneer aviatrix, set more flying records than Charles Lindbergh. Her publicist husband and her disappearance made her an aviation legend. (Photo courtesy of the Library of Congress.)

Amelia Earhart's Aviation Records and Awards

1922: Set women's altitude record, 14,000 feet.

1928: First woman to fly Atlantic (as passenger and standby pilot)

1929: Flight from Santa Monica, California, to Cleveland, Ohio, Women's Air Derby

1932: First woman to solo transatlantic flight, fastest non-stop record

1932: Received Harmon trophy, Distinguished Flying Cross

1934-1935: Set top speed and altitude records in planes and autogiros

1935: First person to solo flight from Hawaii to United States (a longer distance than transatlantic)
First non-stop Mexico City to New York
First non-stop from California to Mexico
Only person to solo flight transatlantic twice
Took First Lady Eleanor Roosevelt on a flight

1937: Attempted first world circumnavigation, completed Florida to New Guinea, approximately 22,000 miles.

In the shadow of Amelia Earhart, other female pilots such as Harriet Quimby have been forgotten. Harriet, the first woman to receive a pilot's license in the United States, began flying in 1911, and crowded a lot of excitement into what would be her last year. She combined journalism with aviation, and wrote for aviation publications. Harriet flew with the Aero Club of America, performed demonstration flying with Moisant International Aviators, and participated in aviation exercises at the Mexican Presidential inauguration in 1911. On April 16, 1912, Harriet flew across the English Channel, the first aviatrix to do so. She died July 1, 1912, in a crash over Dorchester Bay, Massachusetts.

Conclusion

The presidency of Franklin Delano Roosevelt was unprecedented; elected to office four times, he served for twelve years. His political partner and wife, Eleanor Roosevelt, left an indelible mark and became a hard act to follow as a proactive first lady who took on the causes of many forgotten Americans during the desperate years of the Great Depression. ER championed the rights of women, black African-Americans, the handicapped and the poor. During the Roosevelt Administration, the Congress passed record breaking legislation which instituted social security, various agencies and programs for relief, recovery and reform as well as enacting a ban on child labor.

By 1927, the American Medical Association had endorsed birth control, but it took the extreme conditions of the Great Depression to finally give women some measure of reproductive rights. In 1938, Margaret Sanger's long fought crusade came to fruition when the Supreme Court's interpretation of the Comstock Law lifted restrictions on the practice of birth control. Women remained the mainstay of the family as abandonment of wives and children, euphemistically called the "poor man's divorce" escalated during the Depression years.

Women union leaders organized female labor in canneries, migrant workers on farms and women in factories. Latina union organizers built the United Cannery Agricultural Packing and Allied Workers of America, or UCAPAWA.

Despite being barred from professional leagues and lack of public support, female athletes excelled in sports competition. Radio broadcasting formed a national popular culture and radio programs as well as motion pictures gave the American public a brief respite from their suffering and hardship during the longest economic downturn in American history.

Chapter 21
Women and World War II
Since You Went Away

Key Topics

Women in Military Service
Women's Work on the Domestic Front
Manzanar Relocation Camp

Chronology

1939 - Germany Invades Poland, World War II Begins
1940 - FDR Re-elected
1941 - Japanese Attack Pearl Harbor, Hawaii, United States Enters the War
1942 - Executive Order 9022, Relocates Japanese-Americans
Congress Creates Women's Military Divisions
1944 - FDR Re-elected
1945 - April 12 - Death of FDR
May - Germany Surrenders
September - Japan Surrenders

Introduction

When Japanese planes attacked American military bases at Pearl Harbor, Hawaii, on Sunday morning, December 7, 1941, the United States was pulled into the war it had managed to avoid since 1939. Japan, a member of the Axis Powers along with Germany and Italy, had entered that defensive alliance with the agreement that if war was declared on one them, all of them would declare war on the aggressor. The day after the attack on Pearl Harbor, President Roosevelt addressed the United States Congress and requested a declaration of war against Japan. With only the dissenting vote of Congresswoman Jeanette Rankin of Montana (who had also voted against American entry into World War I), Congress declared war on Japan, and the United States joined Great Britain and the U.S.S.R. in the Grand Alliance. In response, Germany and Italy declared war on the United States. From 1942 to 1945, United States Armed Forces were engaged in four theaters of war in Europe, Africa, Asia and the Pacific.

In 1941, the United States had a standing army of 1.6 million men, and every male between the ages of eighteen and forty-five became eligible for the draft. Of the thirty-one million men drafted, fifteen million men were qualified to serve. Military women did their part for the war effort, serving in all branches of the Armed Forces. American women also made a significant contribution working in defense plants and other industries. On the home-front, women served as volunteers and adapted their households to war shortages and rationing. War work and military service uprooted many Americans. The immediacy of war displaced the population, separated families, altered relationships and brought dramatic change to American society.

Women in Military Service

> These Government Issue shoes don't fit,
> My girdle bunches when I sit,
> "Come on rookie, you can't quit"
> Just heave a sigh, and be GI!

In the spring of 1941, anticipating America's imminent involvement in World War II, Congresswoman Edith Nourse Rogers initiated a bill for the creation of a Women's Army Auxiliary Corps. The bill designated permanent women's divisions but Rogers faced serious opposition. It would be another year and, at the insistence of General George Marshall, the Army's Chief of Staff, with support from First Lady Mrs. Eleanor Roosevelt that the bill to establish a women's army corps would be passed.

During World War II about 400,000 women were inducted into the military, and permanent women's divisions of the United States Armed Forces were created. When women joined the Army and the Navy, women's director Oveta Culp Hobby urged them to give up their silk dresses and stockings for khaki and be done with it. But in the Women Appointed for Volunteer Emergency Service, or WAVES, members of the United States Navy wore uniforms styled by a New York Couturier.

The United States Army established a remote operation at Camp Hale at an elevation of 10,000 feet, in the Rocky Mountains near Leadville, Colorado, to train elite troops for mountain warfare. Along with the 16,000 men who trained there, 200 women were among the first volunteers to serve in World War II as part of the Women's Army Corps Detachment. These female soldiers worked in the motor pool, communications, and as medical and clerical personnel.

Technically speaking, women did not serve in combat, but over 200 service women died in World War II. By far, the largest number of military women served as nurses. About 78 percent of the civilian nursing population signed up to serve as volunteers. Among those decorated after the war, 1,619 nurses received medals and commendations. Sixteen medals were posthumously awarded for nurses who had died by enemy fire and thirteen for flight nurses who had died in crashes while on active duty.

Marguerite Noutary had completed studies at Fullerton College and nurses' training by 1937. When the United States entered the war in 1941, she volunteered to serve in the Army Nurses' Corps, but her unit was not sent overseas until 1944. Marguerite, who would later retire from the Army with the rank of lieutenant colonel, was assigned to the China-Burma-India Theater of the war. Traveling by troop ship, her company arrived in Calcutta just in time for the monsoon season. During the intense rains, nurses worked four hour shifts round the clock, four hours on and four hours off.

Marguerite recalled that nurses worked in mud up to their knees while treating the plane loads of wounded soldiers being shipped in. They set up a triage of critically wounded, severely wounded, moderately wounded, and

Women's Divisions	Number of recruits	Director
WAC, Women's Army Corps	140,000	Lt.Com. Mildred McAfee
WAVES, Women Appointed for Volunteer Emergency Service, (Comprised the Women's Naval reserve and Marines Corps Women's Reserve)	23,000	Maj. Ruth Streeter
SPARS, Semper Paratus Women's Coast Guard	13,000	Lt. Com. Dorothy Stratton
WASPS, Women's Army Unofficial but formed by Service Pilots	1,000	Jacqueline Cochran and Nancy Harkness Love

were also responsible for identifying and tagging the dead and preparing them for shipment home. With the magnitude of suffering, nurses often performed physician's duties such as sewing up ghastly wounds. Nurses also cared for retrieved American prisoners of war in the Asian campaign who were, according to Marguerite, treated medically and "fattened up" before their return to the states.

Nurses, continually in harm's way, worked close to the front. In 1942, they were among the first women shipped to the South Pacific, and assigned to Guadalcanal, New Guinea, Guam, Tinian and Saipan. When Americans were forced to surrender to the Japanese in the Philippines, sixty-seven army nurses were taken as prisoners of war to Santo Tomas Internment Camp, and held there for three years.

Over 2,000 members of the Women's Army Corps, or WACs, stationed in North Africa served with the 5th Army Division and were sent to Italy in 1944, for the long-fought Peninsula campaign. There, at the Battle of Anzio, six army nurses died as a result of the German bombing raids which hit hospital tents, and four nurses who survived were commended the Army's Silver Star for "extraordinary courage under fire." Mary Roberts Wilson, an Army nurse known as the Angel of Anzio, was the first woman ever to receive the Silver Star. German bombs and artillery struck the surgical tent as she worked and shrapnel flew all around her. Mary Wilson remembered that the shelling went on continuously for thirty minutes in one instance. When the nurses were offered evacuation, they refused and continued to treat the wounded and run the surgical units.

By January 1944, WACs were being shipped out to the Pacific Theater, and in June, WACs and military nurses landed on the beaches of Normandy for the D-Day invasion. WACs were stationed in England, France, Germany, Australia, on numerous Pacific Islands, and in the Philippines. Sixteen women, injured by enemy fire, were Purple Heart recipients. Another 565 service women received the Bronze Star, and some 700 WACs received other medals and citations as well.

Among the war's unsung heroines, the Women's Army Service Pilots, or WASPS, flew countless miles, suffered losses and were never granted full military status. WASPS died in crashes while testing new planes and flying long missions to deliver supplies. The WASPS were neither awarded nor recognized for their service and bravery. Even though WASPS lost thirty-eight pilots in the line of duty, the government denied these women military burials.

During the War, women also served in espionage and intelligence gathering; who they were has yet to be determined and how many may never be known. But one known was Alice Marble, the famous tennis star of the Thirties, who served the United States by taking on espionage missions to survey the business dealings of Swiss bankers and Nazi agents.

Hedy La Marr the Austrian-born Actress was also a Mathematician whose research contributed to the American War effort. (Photo courtesy of the Library of Congress.)

One celebrated not as a spy but as an international film star was Hedy Lamarr an Austrian who had starred in German films in the 1930's and headlined as the most beautiful woman in all of Europe. She escaped from Nazi Germany and managed several careers in the United States during the war years. Lamarr worked for American military intelligence and was also an inventor and mathematician who co-invented — with composer George Antheil — an early technique for spread spectrum communications and frequency hopping, which was used by the United States military for torpedo guidance systems[1].

Also augmenting the overseas forces, women's nursing groups who volunteered included: Salvation Army nurses, Red Cross nurses, the Cadet Nurses Corps, and American Legion Women's Auxiliary nurses. In addition, volunteers from the YWCA served the men and women of the Armed Forces by providing lodging, transportation, and communication services to military families. The United Service Organization (USO) sent thousands of actors, actresses, musicians, and dancers overseas to entertain the troops.

Discrimination in the Military

Even though the crisis of war called for every able-bodied volunteer, women were neither welcomed nor wanted in the services. Gender discrimination in terms of rank, promotion, salary, pension and commendation showed gross injustice toward women. In order to prevent scandal, the Army, Marine Corps and Navy segregated men and women. Sexist attitudes toward women were commonplace and are well documented in the old newsreels and training films which referred to the women as girls, melons, and peaches. Oveta Culp Hobby, a corporate executive and wife of the former Governor of Texas, was appointed director of the Women's Armed Forces and she endured denigrating names such as sparkplugs and hot lips. Male military personnel did not consider women's service helpful or patriotic. One Marine officer, when informed that WAVE personnel were being sent to his Division, replied "They'll be sending us dogs next."

But it is well to remember that the government's discrimination was not limited to women. Society regarded homosexuality as taboo and when gays joined the military they were labeled as immoral and undesirable. Homosexuality was punishable with dismissal from the service. General Eisenhower wished to rid his battalions of personnel who were lesbians but changed his tune when his aide, Sergeant Johanna Phelps informed him that if his orders were carried out, he would lose her and most females under his command. Sgt. Phelps pointed out that a number of gay women in the Army had received commendations for their service and had no incidents of venereal disease or disorderly conduct. Spurred by patriotism and the war effort, straight and gay women worked side by side in military service and wartime industry. The immediacy of war lent only a brief hiatus from the social ostracism of homosexuals; the veil of tolerance was only temporary.

During World War II, America sent a segregated army to fight on foreign soil with 700,000 African-American servicemen in segregated units performing the most menial work. The hypocrisy was not lost on the NAACP, who rebuked the government for "trying to fight a war for a free world with a Jim Crow Army." The military's segregation policy reeked not only of injustice but also of gross inefficiency. It is incredible to ponder the planning, logistics and wasteful expense that must have gone into separating military personnel by color while attempting to fight a war on a global scale. About 4,000 African-American women who served in the Armed Forces in military units were separated from white service women. They lived in segregated barracks and used separate recreational facilities.

Apparently, maintaining a segregationist policy was more important than life itself. Initially, only fifty-six black nurses were assigned to take care of black patients. One instance illustrates the tragic circumstances of segregation. When white American pilots were shot down in Europe and rushed to English military hospitals, their medical care was delayed because only African-American nurses were available. It was not until 1944, at the close of the war that black women were allowed to serve with the WAVES.

But women and minorities were chipping away at the old order. Women of Asian heritage volunteered in the war effort for their newly adopted country. With the demand for workers in industrial war jobs, Chinese-American women worked as nurses, secretaries and clericals, and many pursued a career in the military. Emily Lee Shek, the first Chinese-Ameri-

---

1. The Lamarr-Antheil research for frequency hopping also made possible wireless communication during World War II and up to the present day including the technology for cellular phones.

can officer served with the WACs, followed by Helen Pon Onyett, who achieved the rank of colonel in her thirty-five years of service as an Army nurse, and Maggie Gee, a WASP, flew military craft.

When the war broke out in 1941, just as abruptly as they had been expelled from the United States, the government invited back émigrés who had been exiled to Mexico during the Depression under the Federal Repatriation Act. They were asked to come back to work in defense plants and serve *their country* in the military. Not only did young men and women return to serve the United States during World War II, but repatriated Mexican-American citizens were among the most highly decorated servicemen and women in the Armed Forces.

Notable Patriotic Women

First Lady Eleanor Roosevelt worked and traveled constantly for the war effort. Logging 40,000 air miles annually, she went to the front, visited wounded soldiers in hospitals, and officiated at awards ceremonies to honor the military heroism of servicemen and women. In her spare time, and based on the success of her syndicated column, "My Day," she added another in 1941, "If You Ask Me," which ran in the *Ladies Home Journal*.

Support for the war came from all political persuasions. Socialist Elizabeth Gurley Flynn had joined the Communist party in 1937, but was a staunch advocate of America's involvement in the war. She also fought for American women's right to equal pay for equal work. She analyzed conditions for women working in wartime industry and prioritized the following needs:

1. Equal opportunity to work for all women (Negro and white) at all occupations
2. Adequate training for jobs, under government and union supervision
3. Equal pay for equal work
4. Safe and sanitary shop conditions
5. Equal membership, protection and participation in labor unions
6. Federally funded and well supervised child care centers
7. Adequate modern housing

The daughter of American Presbyterian missionaries, Nobel Prize winner Pearl S. Buck had been raised in China. During World War II, she founded the Pearl S. Buck Foundation, an adoption agency to aid thousands of homeless war orphans. Many were Eurasian children born to American GIs and Asian mothers. Pearl and husband John Buck handled the adoptions of thousands of these refugee children and adopted eight Chinese orphans themselves. Pearl Buck continued this work for many years after the war.

Entertainer and expatriate Josephine Baker served as a Red Cross volunteer in Paris. When Germany invaded France and established the Vichy government, Josephine joined the French Underground Resistance Movement. After the war, France rewarded her valor with the *Croix de Guerre, Legion de Honor*, and the *Rosette de la Resistance*. She, too, worked to place war orphans in new homes and adopted many of the children herself, calling them her Rainbow Family. Hollywood stars Loretta Young, Carole Lombard and many others toured the country, selling war bonds and boosting citizen morale for the war. Carole Lombard died in a plane crash en route from a war bond rally.

Women's War Effort on the Domestic Front

Although critics scoffed at FDR's call for production of 50,000 new airplanes per year, nonetheless in 1942, wartime industry produced 47,000 planes per year, and by 1944, annual production increased to 96,000 planes. This required every able-bodied person who could work and resulted in 100 percent wartime employment which ended the economic slump of the Great Depression. Even so, these production quotas were dogged by severe labor shortages which necessitated the call for seven million more workers. Factories increased capacity by operating twenty-four hours a day, on swing shifts: 5:00 a.m. to 5:00 p.m., 3:00 p.m. to 11:00 p.m., and graveyard from 11:00 p.m. to 7:00 a.m. Labor unions cooperated with the war effort by signing a no-strike pledge.

Workers were handsomely compensated for overtime and salaries were nearly double the wages that had been paid during the Depression.

With fifteen million American men serving in the military, women worked on the homefront in every sector of the economy — industry, business, agriculture, health care and wartime production. By 1943, women comprised seventeen million or 33 percent of the entire workforce. Government posters, employers' ads, and classifieds used interesting ploys to convince women that they could do men's work with appeals such as, "If you can sew on buttons, you can do spot welding," or "Women who know how to operate kitchen appliances, can run a drill-press," and "If you are precise in reading cooking recipes, you can learn to make ammunition and shells." The campaign succeeded by appealing to women's patriotism and by appealing to traditional gender roles, such as sewing, in order to promote *atypical* gender occupations, such as welding.

But did the demand for women's labor boost the value of women's work or the demand for pay equity? The National War Labor Board directed companies to give women equal pay for equal work, but pay equity was never implemented. In 1943, an affiliation of women's organizations—the General Federation of Women's Clubs, the National Association of Women Lawyers, the National Federation of Business and the Professional Women's Clubs—took the next step. They published for Congressional review a revised text of the Equal Rights Amendment that stated, "Equality of rights under the law shall not be denied or abridged by the United States or any state on account of sex." Somewhat encouraging was the broader base of support among women's groups; the Equal Rights Amendment no longer squeezed support only from Alice Paul's National Women's Party. Artist Georgia O'Keefe, a prominent advocate of the ERA, painted a canvas where "girls would grow up in a real democracy and stand equal under a blue sky." Georgia sent a personal plea to Mrs. Roosevelt asking for her endorsement. "I wish you could be with us in this fight you could be a real help to this change that must come." But the country, the Congress and the First Lady had been distracted with the serious crisis of war, and the ERA did not seem important or urgent to them.

Both the government and the public were amazed at women's competency in wartime industry. President Roosevelt was impressed with women's work in defense plants. In 1942, he had predicted that as the war lengthened and more men were shipped overseas, the number of women doing war work would have to increase. FDR's favorable impression of female workers was short-sighted; women had worked in industry from its inception, unnoticed, and under compensated. The difference between earlier female factory workers and women defense workers was that in World War II, for the sake of propaganda, women's employment was getting positive publicity. One female defense worker recalled, "We were very good at what we did. We had shown that there were not any differences between what women could do and the work that men performed." Female union leaders seized the opportunity to raise gender equity issues. The United Electrical Workers' Union spokesperson, Ruth Young, asserted that every man and woman who wished to work had a right to do so.

But the transformation of women's work during the war, particularly shift work, presented particular problems. Women working outside the home could not expect someone else to pick up the slack at home. One male politician complained, "Who will do the cooking, the washing, the mending, and the *humble homely tasks* to which every woman has devoted herself? Think of the humiliation! What has become of American manhood?" Counselors, psychologists, psychiatrists, and sociologists decried what might happen if children were not properly supervised while their mothers worked. Families with working mothers needed child care, a necessity the government did not consider until 1943, when the Lanham Act was passed to allocate Federal Funds for that service. But funding and child care centers were in short supply and never enough. An exceptional child care program operated at the Henry J. Kaiser Defense plants; unfortunately it only provided child care for about ten percent of the mothers working there.

American housewives were called upon to make greater rationing sacrifices during

World War II than they had in the Great War. Gasoline, meat, dairy products, sugar, cigarettes and automobile tires all were rationed and some products simply were not available. In 1942, Ford Motor Company of Detroit stopped making cars in order to build military vehicles. Americans backyard victory gardens supplied 40 percent of the fresh fruits and vegetables families needed during the war. Housewives recycled everything from tin cans, scrap metal, newspapers, and string, to glass bottles. Cooking grease was saved, cooked down and rendered pure to make soap. Coming out of an austere economic depression, Americans, already acclimated to shortages, dealt handily with wartime hardships which seemed minimal and besides, Americans were working again.

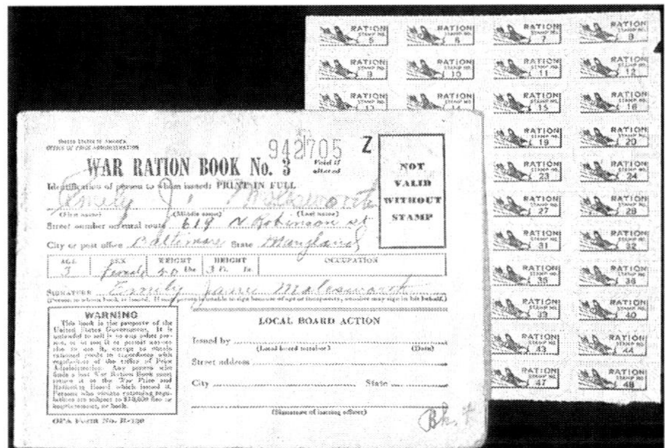
942705 Z
WAR RATION BOOK No. 3
NOT VALID WITHOUT STAMP
Identification of person to whom issued: PRINT IN FULL
Street number or rural route
City or post office ... State
AGE | SEX | WEIGHT | HEIGHT | OCCUPATION
SIGNATURE
WARNING
LOCAL BOARD ACTION
Issued by
Street address
City ... State
RATION

During World War II, the government issued war rations books to each family member for the purchase of meat and dairy products. Housewives planned meals based on what the government ration stamps would allow them to purchase and on what the family could afford.

Women made adaptations in clothing styles. Japanese occupation of certain regions had cut off the silk supply, and the silk that was available was needed to make parachutes. Business and industry tried to enforce one bit of folly in the female dress code. Women working in clerical jobs were required to maintain an aura of office glamour wearing dresses, heels and stockings. Scientists at the Du Pont de Nemours Company developed a synthetic textile, nylon, to use in making parachutes and ladies' sheer stockings. However, the military soon realized that the nylon used to make thirty-six pairs of stockings could make one parachute. Women soon dealt with the shortage of hosiery by wearing slacks to work. As overalls and pants became requisite attire in defense plants, they became fashionable for standard wear. It was acceptable for women to wear pants because it was considered patriotic. Beauty contests were held during lunch hours at the shipyards and defense plants, and women paraded in review for male workers. World War II poster campaigns portrayed very feminine workers. Famous illustrator/artist Norman Rockwell created "Rosie the Riveter" and a song about Rosie honored women in the defense industry. Female riveters and welders had their hair and nails done and wore makeup to work. Famous milliner Lilly Dashé designed glamorous work hats and headgear for women on the job. America's comic strip couple Blondie and Dagwood settled down to family life in the war years, and despite rationing Blondie indulged an occasional expensive new hat.

Women's fashions during World War II took on a more masculine line and featured large shoulder pads, tailored dresses, and suits and slacks which emphasized their role in wartime industry and the military. (Photo courtesy of the Archives of the Fullerton College Library.)

Wartime housing was always in short supply. Single women, including the thousands of southern black women who had gone north for war jobs had difficulty finding housing. Landlords preferred renting to single men.

The government and industry campaigned and advertised to recruit women as factory workers for wartime production. (Picture Courtesy of the Library of Congress.)

The Return to Domesticity

In April 1945, the United Auto Workers Conference and the Women's Bureau proposed that workers be evaluated for their skills and experience, not their gender. But by the time discussion of workers' issues had reached that level, the war was over and it was too late to raise *comparable worth* issues. Government and industry were already campaigning for women to return home. By 1944, advertising had moved from "Women, you can do the same work as a man," to, "Quit your war job and make a nice home and family for some GI." Madison Avenue co-opted the return to domesticity by pushing new home appliances. In 1945, Eureka and Westinghouse promoted housekeeping as essential to the "American Way of Life." Advertising appealed to *Mrs. America* to phase out of industry, and promised *Mrs. Stay at Home* an automatic washing machine to take the drudgery out of wash day.

With the war winding down, the media promoted domesticity. They characterized women's patriotic response to work in defense plants as a temporary interruption from their traditional role before the war. With victory secured, women should happily return to the domestic cocoon. Movies, magazines, radio and advertising stereotyped American women in a purely domestic mode, but the Bureau of Labor statistics revealed quite a different situation. Seventy-eight percent of the women who worked during the war had worked before the war as family providers. Based on government statistics, the chart Women in the Workforce shows a steady increase in female employment after the war, not a decrease.

Comparing women's wartime employment rates with postwar rates also belies common conceptions about the female workforce. In wartime, women comprised about 30 percent of the total labor force. Afterward, that population remained constant and women comprised 29 percent of the working population.

Women in the Workforce, 1938-1978

Year	Total percent working outside the home:
1938	26.5
1940	25.3
1945	30
1950	29
1960	34.5
1970	40
1978	50

Adapted from the Bureau of Labor and Statistics.

The statistics indicate neither a mass entry of women into the workforce at the onset of World War II, nor a mass exodus out of industry at war's end. From 1938 to 1978, there was a steady and gradual increase in the number of women working outside the home. What had changed in wartime production was the *type of work* women performed. This was an important distinction, since women had tackled men's jobs, and broken the barriers between men's and women's roles. Women could operate heavy machinery, (they always had in industry and farming) and served in the armed forces in military uniform. The bottom line was that women had always worked, and continued to work, because they needed to.

The Relocation of Japanese Americans

On March 21, 1942, by Executive Order 9022, the United States Government issued the Civilian Exclusion Orders throughout the western states and relocated 115,000 Japanese-Americans. These orders authorized the government to detain Japanese-Americans at camp centers for the duration of the war. Japanese-American families were given six days to dispose of their property, shut down businesses, and tend to investments and savings. None of these individuals had broken any law, but their civil rights were violated when their property and their liberty were taken from them. One internee explained, "We took whatever we could carry. So much we left behind, but the most valuable thing I lost was my freedom." In a slap of bitter irony, wartime housing became available to women and other ethnic minorities when Japanese-American families were forced out of their homes and relocated to government internment camps.

They were shipped to desolated areas such as Manzanar in California, and the Hood River Camp in Oregon. In a printed booklet, *Questions and Answers for Evacuees*, the government defended its action stating that Japanese-Americans had been relocated there for their own protection. A curious statement, as one prisoner queried, "If it was for our protection, why did the guns point inward, rather than outward?"

The Manzanar Relocation Camp was located on the flat, dry plain beneath the Eastern Sierra Mountains in Inyo County, California. Manzanar was an uninviting environment for the internees who were forced to live there. In the summer, temperatures soared to 120 degrees, and in winter, the weather dipped to freezing. When the wind blew through the barren valley, residents choked on the dust; as one recalled, "The main thing you remembered was the dust, always the dust."

As many as 10,000 internees were crowded into 504 barracks. The internees, a cross section of the Japanese-American population, comprised about 50 percent women, 25 percent children and the remaining 25 percent included men and the elderly. Yet somehow, on this barren land, camp residents managed to eke out a life and planted gardens where they raised fruits and vegetables. A family of four, allotted a living space measuring 20 by 25 feet, shared bathroom and laundry facilities with other families and everyone ate together in common mess halls.

In 1945, the government allowed the young men and women to leave Manzanar before the camp's shutdown, if they would enlist in the Armed Forces of the United States. Their divisions, such as the 442nd Regimental Combat Team of the United States Army which fought in Italy and France, were among the most highly decorated for military service in World War II. More than one-hundred *Nisei* women left the camps to enlist in the armed forces or serve as American Red Cross volunteer nurses, including Private First Class Margaret Fukuoka who joined the Women's Army Corps[2]. Kay Fukada served as a United States Cadet Nurse, and Aiko Hamaguchi, and Catherine Natsuko Yamaguchi volunteered as American Red Cross nurses. Among those women who remained in internment, some served in the relocation camps as teachers, nurses, seamstresses, laundresses, cooks, Sunday school teachers, or as workers in the commissary store and warehouses. Families meanwhile were burdened with more separation and grief when some youngsters and teenagers were turned out of the camps to find work while officials kept the parents in detention.

Although an assessment of the losses during the Japanese-American Relocation has been estimated at two billion dollars, the tragedy cannot be measured solely by monetary loss. Individuals were denied the opportunity to develop in a chosen profession, or suffered permanent scars to physical health and emotional stability. After many years of delay and debate, one lawsuit, *Yamamoto v the United States*, finally reached the Supreme Court and *Nisei,* who were still alive, or *Sansei* (their children), were granted reparations. For most, the remuneration was too little and too late. In 1981, as the Congress conducted the Commission on Wartime Internment, many former inmates came forward to testify. Mrs. Tetsu Saito was one of them. By then Mrs. Saito was eighty-one years old, a widow struggling to survive on a low

2. Nisei is a person born to parents (Insei) who emigrated from Japan. Sansei are children born of Nisei parents, so order of family lineage is Insei, Nisei, Sansei.

income in inner city Los Angeles. Her condition then contrasted sharply with her status in 1942. That year, her family had just paid off the mortgage to their business, the Ruth Hotel. The assessed value of their thirty-room hotel was $6,000. When they received word of the hasty evacuation and relocation to Manzanar, the Saitos accepted the best offer on the building, $300 in cash. They left behind sixty-four crates of possessions and a fleet of six trucks. At war's end, when they returned to Los Angeles, their possessions and vehicles had disappeared.

Yoshio Ekimoto had owned forty acres of farm land in Los Angeles County, and because he was one of the few internees who managed to hold onto personal records during internment, he was able to file a claim after the war. In 1942, when the government ordered evacuation, his property losses amounted to $23,824. During internment, his wife's health deteriorated, and she had suffered a miscarriage. In 1948, Mr. Ekimoto filed for losses with the government, and under the Evacuation Claims Act, he received $692.00 for his losses.

For other evacuees the stories were practically the same. Property had been confiscated or practically given away, possessions left for safe-keeping in storage had later disappeared or were stolen. The internees developed a kind of stoicism they called *Shikata-ganai* meaning "It is beyond control; it cannot be helped so accept it as it is." Or as one survivor said, "That we have not complained is not an indication that we have not suffered."

Clio's Corner - What Have Historians Said about Women's Work in World War II?

Historian James Henretta asserts that despite the come-ons for women to do war work, female workers were discriminated against and underpaid, largely because there was no equal pay for equal work policy. This drove many women to become union activists. Historian Sara Evans, in *Born for Liberty, a History of Women in America*, found that since women's employment shifted to men's occupations like welders, drill pressers, pipe fitters, sheet metal workers and riveters, the change in work was reflected in union membership and union leadership. Professor Vickie Ruiz concurs that women's unionization and the commingling of women in the workforce was a significant result of war work. The United Cannery Agricultural Packing and Allied Workers of America, (UCAPAWA) built a stronger organization by bringing together Mexican-American, African-American and Anglo-American women into a unified union which represented a more diverse workforce. Women were beginning to see the strength in solidarity.

Furthermore, Luisa Moreno's persistence had paid off. She had worked to build solidarity in the union from 1940 to 1946. Consequently, over sixty-six percent of the work contracts with UCAPAWA included equal pay for equal work. About seventy-five percent of the contracts included maternity and sick leaves for workers without any loss of seniority. In *Community of Suffering and Struggle: Women, Men and The Labor Movement in Minneapolis, 1915-1945*, Elizabeth Faue observed that the shift to women workers during the war gave them access to membership in the Congress of Industrial Organizations, (CIO) the United Electrical Workers Union, (UEWU) and other trade unions. Elizabeth Faue found a dramatic shift in trade union consciousness among women which she calls *gender realignment.* This gender realignment sharpened the awareness of defense workers such as Juanita Loveless who saw the escalation of factory production as well as distinct pay inequity among workers. One could not ignore the fact that some people were becoming quite wealthy through war production while others were not. Women and minorities were underpaid and black women were frequently underemployed. When black women were hired, management separated black and white female workers to discourage the two groups from fraternizing.

In his documentary *America Goes to War: a String of Pearls,* Patrick Trese makes the case that defense work gave women the confidence to work for change after the war. Trese argues that the Women's Liberation Movement really begins in World War II. He shows how corporate campaigns, government propaganda and trade union cants had mobilized women quickly for war production, and then at the close of the war, they tried to push women back into domesticity. In 1945, two million women were laid off from defense jobs and those who kept working had to shift to lower paying jobs. Patrick Trese asserts that whether women continued working for wages or became housekeepers, a major shift had taken place. Women had gained new strength, "They had learned about their abilities, and the seeds of discontent and permanent change had been sown."

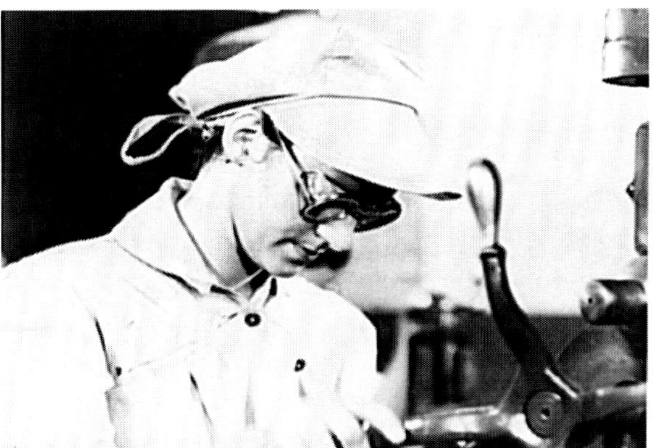

During World War II, women worked as welders, machinists and riveters building planes, tanks and ships for the war effort. (Photo courtesy of the Library of Congress.)

Historian Ann Firor Scott had kept a journal during the war years. She noted that as young men were drafted and enrollment in colleges dropped significantly, women gained easier access to scholarships and graduate school. Ann Firor Scott, one of those women who took advantage of the opportunity, felt a lingering sense of guilt for having sought a degree under those circumstances. Philip Wylie, in his book *A Generation of Vipers* published in 1942, criticized women who "used the war" to carve out a lucrative career for themselves. Wylie ignored the fact that women had always been paid less than men and faced limited opportunities. Despite Ann Firor Scott's guilt and Philip Wylie's furor, women pursued careers in law, education, medicine and engineering, proved their competency, and served their communities long after defense plants had shut down. The window of opportunity for women in higher education lasted briefly from 1941 to 1945, and women who entered professions in the 1940's and 1950's were not compensated on an equal par with men.

The Female Image and Changing Sexual Mores

Like all wars, World War II uprooted people and brought changes more quickly than people could assimilate them. Sexual practices, which had changed dramatically during the Twenties, underwent more change during and after the war. Marjorie Hillis' book *Live Alone and like it, a Guide for the Extra Woman,* had foreshadowed a changed perspective for the single woman in the 1940s. She explained that since the turn of the twentieth century, there was a growing tendency for women *to live alone, to enjoy living alone, and to look forward* to the single life. Marjorie Hillis laid the ground rules for the modern single woman.

With the use of birth control legalized just prior to the war, notions about using contraception and women's roles mainly as wives and mothers were changing. But Hollywood movie plots maintained prescribed social roles and guaranteed marriage and domestic bliss by the end of the film. In *Wedding Present* with Cary Grant and Joan Bennett, the message clearly was that getting married and having sex was a top priority for women; and Ginger Rogers as the *Lady in the Dark* gave up everything to marry hero Ray Milland. Rosalind Russell, in *Take a Letter Darling*, quit a lucrative job as the manager of a glitzy New York advertising agency in order to follow Fred MacMurray to the ends of the earth in a U-haul trailer. Nonetheless, there were subtle hints of change. The independent career woman popularized by Katherine Hepburn sparred with Spencer Tracy in a number of movie plots which featured them competing in the workplace.

Wartime artists created a new female sexual icon—the pinup girl—with exquisite pastels by Vargas. Photographs of movie stars such as Betty Grable, Rita Hayworth, and Lena Horne decorated the bunks and lockers of American GIs. Curvaceous female bodies were painted on battleships and airplanes. Comic book illustrators augmented super male heroes with strong heroines such as Sheena the Jungle Girl. Harvard-educated psychologist Dr. William Moulton Marston created the character of Wonder Woman to introduce as he said, "a feminine superhero for young girls to look up to." Cartoonist Tarpe Mills created Miss Black Fury, an avenging heroine who used lashes, whips and branding irons to defend democracy.

Because GIs were shipping out for overseas duty, the immediacy of the war and separation of partners chipped away at the old moral standards. Army training films presented sex more openly and used graphic images to warn *male GIs* [emphasis mine] about the dangers of venereal diseases. Despite evidence that service women were as promiscuous as the men, Director Oveta Culp Hobby resisted the idea that WAC's should be given contraceptive advice. Military women were expected to maintain old standards and to take responsibility for restraining male lust. In 1943, however, the military did an about-face and servicewomen were given sex advice on a par with that given to male personnel.

Social mores were changing for adolescents, and advice manuals responded by questioning the practice of going steady. Young women were advised to "limit the supply of yourself. Make yourself scarce and watch your value go up," or, "save yourself for the man of your dreams." The older generation worried more about the sexual habits of young females and with good reason. Teenage girls exhibited a disturbing increase in sexual promiscuity. *Victory Girls*, as they were called, hung around USO clubs and military bases, to get picked up and have casual sex with GIs. One popular tune, *Yes, My Darling Daughter*, sung by Dinah Shore, expressed social anxiety over the new sexual freedom.

Mothers of Invention: Maria Montoya Martinez, American Artist

The Pueblo potter Maria Montoya Martinez is a mother of invention synonymous with superb craftsmanship and artistic excellence who achieved in her lifetime international recognition for her work. She was born at the San Ildefonso Pueblo in northern New Mexico in 1887 (the exact month and day of her birth is not known). Maria learned pottery making at an early age from her aunt at a time when pottery skills had all but died out among the pueblo tribes. Fortunately, Maria's family had continued to experiment with different techniques and preserved the skill as well as the cultural art of the pueblo pottery style.

The story of her development of the signature black-on-black San Ildefonso style of pottery really began in 1908 during an archaeological excavation led by Professor Edgar Lee Hewett. At the Tyuonyi and Frijoles Canyon, near San Ildefonso, he discovered ancient examples of the monochrome black-on-black pottery. Because Hewett hoped to preserve the ancient art form and re-create pots of this type to put on display in the Santa Fe museum, he needed a skilled pueblo potter who could make this ancient type of pottery. Maria Martinez was the best known potter in the Tewa tribe (pueblo) at San Ildefonso. Her pots were the thinnest (a mark of quality) and the circular openings so accurate that they appeared to be machine made. Maria took on the work for Hewett and after some trial and error she and her husband, Julian successfully reproduced the black-on-black pottery style. Julian Martinez who became an accomplished artist himself, painted the native motifs on the pottery and mastered a unique burnishing technique which yielded the satin matte finish. Nonetheless, producing black ware pottery to replicate the ancient type was a long exacting process requiring patience and skill and entailed about eight steps to completion.

Her black on black pottery ware became famous and was displayed at world fairs, museums, and in galleries. Anyone fortunate enough to own a piece of Maria's pottery has something of museum quality. Her pieces today are much sought after by high end galleries and serious collectors. Some of her early work (from the 1920's) was not signed but for later pieces she used several different signature types such as: *Marie, Maria and Marie+Julian.* For her achievement, Maria received gifts, recognition, praise, medals, awards, and special invitations to the White House from a number of Presidents as well as Mrs. Eleanor Roosevelt. She received visitors at San Ildefonso Pueblo including other famous artists from all over the world. As Maria began losing her sight, she passed on her knowledge and skill to other members of her family, women in the pueblo, and students. Maria did not teach by hands on instruction but believed students learned best through observation, because she did not believe one could 'teach' someone how to craft pottery. One had to observe and then practice and apply the skill themselves.

Maria Montoya Martinez, the Native American Artist who created the black on black Pottery which became her trademark and an internationally acclaimed style of American art. (Photo courtesy of the Library of Congress.)

For nearly one hundred years, until her death in 1980, Maria's life at San Ildefonso centered on family, pottery making, and Tewa tradition. In her lifetime, Maria was a highly respected matriarch of her tribe who carried on the pueblo ceremonies and traditions, especially the rites, customs, and dances observed throughout the cycle of the four seasons at San Ildefonso. Growing up in the pueblo, nurtured on tribal custom, Maria learned to love her community and to respect the God-given gifts of the earth. She expressed this core belief when she said, "We all come from the clay of the earth, and we will return to the clay of the earth, so it is up to us to be happy and continue the harmony of mind and heart." Maria molded that belief into her own life and expressed it fully in her art.

Conclusion

During World War II, women responded to the call for military enlistment and served in non-combatant roles as service pilots, nurses, motor pool drivers, office clerks, and in communications. Military nurses serving in all theatres of war: Europe, Africa, the Pacific and Asia, were decorated for bravery and nurses captured in the Philippines were detained as prisoners of war along with male military personnel.

American women faced drastic changes during the war. On the homefront, women worked in defense plants, government jobs, clerical posts and hundreds of other jobs which were critical to the Allied victory. American housewives cultivated victory gardens, carpooled and rationed household supplies and food. Many women performed volunteer work for agencies such as the American Red Cross and the United Service Organization. Separated from their partners and spouses they supported their families and kept the home fires burning.

American women in the 1940s co-opted a fashion revolution. To accommodate work in defense plants and the shortage of silk and nylon hosiery, female attire took on a more relaxed and practical style and women's clothing had a more masculine and military look. Dresses and jackets had heavy shoulder pads, double breast pockets and epaulets, and a popular design for ladies' and little girls' hats was inspired by the military overseas caps. Nineteenth century women's rights activists had attempted a dress reform, wearing the bloomer-style harem pants but were unsuccessful. When women in the 1940s put on long pants such as overalls, blue denim dungarees and slacks, society accepted the change as part of the patriotic effort.

The war separated husbands, fathers and brothers from their families. The Federal government relocated Japanese-Americans into detention camps. Women, men and children in both Europe and Asia, displaced by the ravages of war, would seek refuge in America.

Part VII:

The Women's Experience - Mid-to-Late Twentieth Century

Women in Postwar America

The Civil Rights Movements

Closing of the Second Wave

Chapter 22
Women in Postwar America
Father Knows Best

Key Topics

Postwar Immigration
McCarthyism, Repression and Discrimination
Preview of the Civil Rights Movement

Chronology

1945 - World War II Ends, Postwar Immigration Begins
1945 - 1960 - Postwar Baby Boom
1950 - 1955 - Era of McCarthyism and the Red Scare
1954 - *Brown v Kansas* - Supreme Court Orders Integration of Public Schools
1955 - Rosa Parks Arrested, Montgomery Boycott Begins

Introduction

After World War II, the United States experienced a dramatic demographic transformation through immigration and an accelerated birthrate when American soldiers returned from the war and started their families. The quality and longevity of life for this generation of Americans improved dramatically with the introduction of antibiotic wonder drugs and widespread immunization of the Salk vaccine to end polio and infantile paralysis.

To ensure stability in the transition from the wartime to a peacetime economy, the Federal government funded the GI Bill (the Patman Act). This acted as a buffer against massive unemployment by diverting many returning soldiers from the job market into college to pursue a degree paid for by the government, and the GI Bill funded the mortgage on a veteran's first home. The GI Bill enabled many World War II veterans to move up to the middle class and economic stability.

In the conservative 1950s, Americans were settling down to family life in the suburbs. But beneath the conservatism of suburban America a storm was brewing. In 1954, the Supreme Court, under Chief Justice Earl Warren in Brown v Kansas, ordered that public schools integrate "with deliberate speed."

In postwar America, the United States victory signaled a return to domesticity. The government and the media promoted domesticity for women and radio, television and motion pictures portrayed the ideal family and women living in domestic bliss.

Postwar Immigration

World War II dislocated people globally, and women and children were especially affected. In 1945, millions of people sought asylum in America, and President Truman's directives eased the restrictions on immigration quotas. Some 42,000 displaced persons (those dislocated by war), were admitted into the United States. In 1948, by Act of Congress, 205,000 Europeans, including 3,000 orphans also came. In June of 1950, another 341,000 people and 54,744 war orphans were granted visas to come to America. In 1953, the Refugee Relief Act provided entry to America, specifically for those persons who were escaping persecution from Communist regimes; by 1959 another 500,000 Europeans were admitted into the country. Most of the German, French, and British women who came to the United States did so immediately after World War II, as displaced persons and war brides of American soldiers.

The following table highlights significant immigration legislation in the United States and shows that government policy predominantly discriminated against the Asian population.

United States Immigration Legislation

Chinese Exclusion Act of 1868-1880: Under this act in conjunction with the Burlingame Treaty, the United States would regulate, limit or suspend, but not prohibit Chinese immigration.[1]

Chinese Exclusion Act of 1882: Excluded and restricted Chinese immigration, particularly of laborers. Teachers, students, merchants and travelers were exempt. This Act also prohibited the naturalization of Chinese as citizens in the United States.

Geary Act of 1892: Extended by another decade the provisions of the Chinese Exclusion Act.

Immigration Act of 1904: Extended the Chinese Exclusion Act indefinitely.

Immigration Law of 1906-1924: Japanese Exclusion Act: The so-called Gentlemen's Agreement; Japan agreed to limit the number of emigrants leaving for America. The State of California also passed exclusionary laws regarding Japanese aliens and established separate schools for Asian children.

Immigration Act of 1924- 1925: Forbid Chinese-American males to bring wives to the United States from China; however, certain individuals were exempted from the law. This also included a New Quota Law which allowed for limited immigration from Europe, based on the number from each ethnic group in the 1890 census. In 1924, no more than two percent of the total number which had been admitted to the country in 1890, were allowed to enter. The quota system was an attempt to cut down the flow of immigrants coming to America, particularly those from Asia.

Repeal of the Chinese Exclusion Acts 1943: Established an annual quota of 105 Chinese Immigrants to enter the United States. Lifted the ban on naturalization of Chinese-born residents of U.S. Chinese aliens could apply for citizenship. The Act repealed all previous laws which had excluded or deported Chinese aliens.

The War Brides Act of 1945: President Truman's legislation allowed foreign-born war brides of United States servicemen to be admitted to the United States.

1. Previously in the nineteenth century, an estimated 75,000 Chinese males had been accepted into the United States as cheap contract labor to build the railroads in the West. However, as riots and hate crimes toward the Chinese escalated, the government limited immigration.

Persons displaced by the war in Asia, immigrated to the United States but the numbers of these immigrants contrasted sharply with those of European nationalities. Between 1931 and 1950, some 31,000 people came from Asia. (The U.S. Bureau of Statistics figures include Turkey.) During this time, thirty-four million people had immigrated to America from Europe and 950,000 from Asia.

Women from China were part of the influx of displaced persons who immigrated to the United States, entering as refugees or war brides. Like the earlier immigrants from Asia, they had difficulty adjusting to life in America, finding jobs, and learning English. But in the postwar assimilation, more Chinese-American women of the *second and third* generation were able to enter the mainstream, working as accountants, business executives, nurses, or technologists and some accessed the professions of teaching, law and medicine. In the 1950s, even though many Chinese-American families were no longer arranging marriages for their children, there was still pressure for a woman to marry a Chinese or Chinese-American man.

Displacement of people during World War II increased immigration to the United States. Many young foreign women, brides of American soldiers, came to America. (Photo courtesy of the Archives of the Fullerton College Library.)

Many Japanese war brides who married United States servicemen found limited employment in the United States, working as waitresses or as domestic servants. Japanese war brides stayed within the close confines of the family with little chance for an education, a career or the opportunity to learn English.

Postwar Repression and McCarthyism

When World War II ended so did the thinly veiled tolerance for gays in the military and a reactionary repression of homosexuality began. From 1947 to 1950, President Truman's policies sent out mixed messages. He had integrated the armed forces and ended a segregation policy in the military but on the question of gays in the military, he took a step back and ordered the discharge of 5,000 military personnel because they were homosexuals. In 1953, President Eisenhower ordered that gays and lesbians be barred from Federal jobs. State and local law enforcement officials aggressively policed and intimidated patrons of gay and lesbian bars.

The end of World War II marked the onset of the Cold War, a conflict between the United States and the United Soviet Socialist Republic, the USSR. In America, members of the Communist Party were regarded as enemies of the state. From 1950-1954, citizens suspected of being communists or communist sympathizers were brought before the Senate Investigating Committee headed by Senator Joseph McCarthy, who was convinced that conspiratorial forces were at work in the government:

> We have been losing to international communism at the rate of one-hundred million people a year. Perhaps we should examine the background of the men who have done the planning, and let the American people decide whether we've lost because of stumbling, fumbling idiocy, or because they planned it that way.

When the McCarthy hearings began, television was in its infancy and the Senate hearings provided what little drama there was on daytime TV; day after day, the public watched with curious concern.

The McCarthy Committee blacklisted anyone with left wing ideas, particularly union leaders and people in the arts and entertainment business. Among those blacklisted was Socialist Elizabeth Gurley Flynn. After the hearings and a lengthy trial, she was imprisoned from 1955-1957, for "conspiring to advocate the violent overthrow of the government. Elizabeth Gurley Flynn was not charged with *conspiring,* but *conspiring to advocate.* Union activist Dorothy Healey, branded by the press as the *Red Queen of L.A.,* had fought for women laborers. Because of her views on workers' rights, Dorothy Healey was sentenced to five years in prison and fined $10,000.

The McCarthy hearings created an atmosphere of fear in which many accused others in order to save themselves from being blacklisted, and many people lost their jobs, their reputations and their social standing. Guilt by association implicated many innocent people such as Actress Rosaura Revueltas, who was deported in 1953, for subversive activities. Rosaura Revueltas' crime had been acting in the film *The Salt of the Earth*, about a miners' strike in New Mexico. The film was directed and produced by blacklisted studio heads in Hollywood. Molly Castles, a writer at *McCall's,* was taken into custody by the FBI, and deported when she refused to testify against her former husband, the editor of *The National Guardian.* Senate conservatives urged McCarthy to subpoena the former First Lady, but the Senator was unwilling to take on someone as formidable as Mrs. Roosevelt.

In the House of Representatives, Congressman Richard M. Nixon, a California Republican conducted similar hearings for the House Un-American Activities Commission, (HUAC). California Democratic Congresswoman Helen Gahagan Douglas had held key posts in the State of California and the Federal government, serving the State and National Democratic Party in FDR's New Deal administration, in the Works Progress Administration and the National Youth Administration. In 1944, she had also won a Congressional seat and represented California for three terms. In 1950, when Helen Douglas opposed Richard Nixon for the U.S. Senate seat, he waged a smear campaign of *red-baiting* against her.[1] Although she lost the election, the following year, President Truman appointed her to serve as the United States Ambassador to the United Nations.

Luisa Moreno, the dynamic union organizer for the United Cannery, Agricultural Packing and Allied Workers of America, UCAPAWA, had been the first Latina to move up to the post of Vice President of a labor union. Luisa Moreno was brought before HUAC, accused of being a member of the communist party, and deported to Guatemala, or as the official order read: "voluntary departure under warrant of deportation." The government offered her a deal—repatriation back to the United States with her American citizenship intact—if she would testify against fellow labor organizers. Luisa refused and accepted *voluntary deportation* to Guatemala because as she explained, "I could not be a free woman with a mortgaged soul."

Senator Margaret Chase Smith, a Declaration of Conscience

Just as support for Joseph McCarthy soared in 1950, Senator Margaret Chase Smith, a Republican from Maine, also stood up to the red-baiting, and accused the Senator of running an investigation on "calumny, fear, ignorance and smear." Senator Smith had served a "widow's seat" in the House when her husband died in 1940, but succeeded that term with her own election victory. Regarded by her colleagues as a quiet woman, she called on her party to denounce Senator McCarthy for his violations of free speech and his procedures in the hearings. "I think that it is high time that we remembered that we have sworn to uphold and defend the Constitution... as amended; [it] speaks not only of the freedom of speech but also of trial by jury instead of trial by accusation." In her formal statement, "the Declaration of Conscience," which was later published in a book *The Declaration of Conscience, I and II*, she defended the basic principles of Americanism:

> The right to criticize
> The right to hold unpopular beliefs

---

1. *Red-baiting* - Red baiting- to accuse, denounce, intimidate or attack someone as a Communist, member of the Communist party or as a Communist sympathizer.

The right to protest and
The right of independent thought

Her Declaration received mixed reviews. President Truman quipped, "I wouldn't want to say anything that bad about the Republican Party." The financier-philanthropist Bernard Baruch stated, "If a man had made the Declaration of Conscience, he would [have become] the next President of the United States

Nonetheless, from 1950-1953, Senator McCarthy wielded power and anyone who challenged him faced imprisonment and blacklisting. Considering the risk involved, Senator Chase Smith later confided to Margaret Truman, the President's daughter, "To be honest with you, I was a little doubtful if I would be able to carry through on it. That's how nervous I was about it."

Margaret Chase Smith, the Republican Senator from Maine, challenged Senator Joseph McCarthy at the acme of his power and articulated a philosophy of public service in the Declaration of Conscience. (Photo courtesy of the Library of Congress.)

A Preview of the Civil Rights Movement

In 1954, the United States Supreme Court under Chief Justice Earl Warren handed down a decision in the *Brown v Kansas* case which mandated the integration of public schools. This landmark case reversed the Court's longstanding 1890 ruling in *Plessy v Ferguson,* which had decided that separate but equal facilities (in this case train transportation) for blacks was acceptable and fair. But implementation and enforcement of the Supreme Court Brown decision relied on the executive branch of the government. President Eisenhower directed Federal troops to southern locations such as Central High School in Little Rock, Arkansas; the University of Mississippi, the University of Georgia and other campuses in order to carry our the integration decision and to provide armed escort for black students trying to enter public schools. Although the Brown decision pertained only to the public school system, it was a big step forward. It raised expectations and mobilized forces within southern black communities for a civil rights movement.

The landmark *Brown v Kansas* decision had been accomplished through the legal efforts of Thurgood Marshall and renowned attorney Pauli Murray, an African-American woman who utilized the format of the Brandeis Brief to win the case. Drawing on statistics, she showed how the segregated school system had a negative effect on students, such as the plaintiff, Linda Brown. Pauli Murray argued before the court the hypocrisy of a segregated school system within a country based on democracy, freedom and equality. As she emphasized, the so-called separate but equal system of separate school facilities for blacks had never been equal.

In 1955 after the court-ordered public school desegregation, the struggle to eradicate *Jim Crow laws* in public transportation began in Montgomery, Alabama.[2] According to southern custom, if any white passengers were standing on a bus, blacks were expected to give up their seats. That practice came to the nation's attention when Rosa Parks, a member of the NAACP, boarded a bus on December 1, 1955. When Miss Parks refused to give up her seat, she was arrested, fingerprinted and fined. Rosa Parks'

2. *Jim Crow laws* - state and local laws enacted and enforced in the southern and border states between 1876 and 1965. These laws were aimed at treating and accommodating African-Americans as inferior, sustaining segregation of the white and black population, and maintaining separate facilities for each.

quiet, dignified defiance galvanized the Southern Civil Rights Movement in 1955, and triggered the black community's 382 day bus boycott, which practically shut down public transportation in Montgomery. At the onset of the boycott, twenty-six year old Baptist preacher Dr. Martin Luther King, Jr. was asked to speak at the Dexter Avenue Baptist Church to a gathering of 10,000 people from the community. His charismatic leadership molded the southern civil rights crusade into a nonviolent movement. Black women organized the boycott by distributing information and providing carpools, and babysitting. To make the bus boycott work, many black Montgomery residents in the community accepted the hardship of walking to work daily for over a year.

American Women, the Media, and Real Life

Writers Pearl Buck, Dorothy Thompson, Dorothy Sayers, anthropologist Margaret Mead, and artist Georgia O'Keefe spoke out for women's rights and would serve as excellent role models for the younger generation. But the 50s media portrayed women quite differently. Television, radio, ladies' shelter magazines, literature, motion pictures and marketing promoted a return to domesticity, urging women to devote themselves entirely to their husbands and family. What was deceptive about the media image was the characterization that the only possible *normal* role for females was motherhood and that most women were living the domestic life.

With the return to domesticity movement, fashions of the 1950s emphasized and exaggerated the female body. Christian Dior reinstated the extremely impractical, uncomfortable, women's clothing to define an hourglass figure. Dior revived the tight waist, full crinoline skirt, large hats and gloves, and stiletto heels (some women even had the fifth toe amputated to accommodate the pointed shoes). This was all supported by formfitting underwear which resembled a corset. American capitalism defined femininity. By 1955, American women were spending $1.3 billion on cosmetics, toiletries, beauty treatments, and medications to lose weight. Selling femininity and domesticity in the 1950s reestablished the American housewife as the key consumer. Television commercials portrayed her as a person obsessed with baking the highest layer cake and hanging out the whitest laundry in the neighborhood. Television programs which encouraged postwar domesticity focused on either a family-domestic theme or portrayed *macho* characters such as western gunslingers or private detectives. Domestic sitcoms featured an ideal American family and included *The Donna Reed Show, Ozzie and Harriet, Leave it to Beaver*, and *Father Knows Best*. One program, *I Love Lucy*, suggested that women were discontent with this arrangement. The plot, which never changed, featured Lucy using devious means to get in her husband's nightclub act. But Lucy's attempts to assert herself resulted in bizarre, wacky, and comedic escapades which always backfired with calamitous results. The Fifties television sitcoms portrayed incompetent women in a man's world, a world in which women stayed home and had babies. Reinforcing this idea, Lucille Ball became the first leading lady shown pregnant on television. The belief that men were superior, powerful, and authoritarian was reinforced by heroes armed with phallic weapons in westerns such as *Gun Smoke, Paladin*, and the *Riflemen,* or in the exploits of private detectives such as *Peter Gunn.*

Similar attempts to reinstate the cult of domesticity occurred in motion pictures. Scores of films were produced in which women fulfilled their destiny by finding the perfect husband. In the holiday classic, *A Miracle on 34th Street*, Maureen O'Hara plays Doris, a cold-hearted divorcée, working as a department store executive. She insists her daughter have no illusions about fairytales or Santa Claus. Hero John Paine is appalled at how daughter Suzy (Natalie Wood) is being reared by her mother. In order to raise Suzy properly, his mission is to transform Doris into a real woman and together find a house and get married. In the film *Christmas in Connecticut*, Barbara Stanwyck plays a successful food editor who acquired her job through deception. She wrote about cooking and homemaking and gave her readers the impression that she had children and lived on a fashionably appointed farm in Connecticut.

The Class of '58

On Sunday, September 20, 1998, a 40-year class reunion was held for alumnae of an all-female school in Baltimore, Maryland. Of the 600 students in the class, 120 attended the reunion, and biographical and statistical information was published for 350 of the graduates. Ranked socially, the all-female population ranged from middle- to upper-middle class; a profile of their status as of 1998, characterizes the conservatism and stability of the 50s generation as indicated by the following:

90 percent of the graduates had married
75 percent of the women remained in a first marriage
80 percent of the graduates had raised families
50 percent had grandchildren
60 percent had completed college
40 percent had a job outside the home
35 percent regarded their job as a career
18 percent had divorced and remarried
8 percent were cancer survivors
48 percent were Republicans
30 percent were Democrats
22 percent undeclared political affiliation
40 percent had married men with jobs in government, aerospace, or the military
32 percent indicated they had traveled internationally and/or lived abroad
Less than 2percent had pursued a career in the military
Less than 2percent had established their own business

When her publisher decides to "drop in" to spend Christmas, Stanwyck's fiancé quickly arranges a wedding and provides a baby to keep up appearances and save her job. From there the plot thickens, and a happy ending is secured when a decorated war hero rescues, marries and domesticates her.

Although the media placed a lot of emphasis on domesticity, the stereotype of the Fifties housewife had very little basis in real life. Women continued to challenge prescribed social roles and work outside the home.

In the 1930s, Olympic star, Mildred "Babe" Didrikson had been vilified in the media as a female athlete whose features and accomplishments were too masculine. But when she "settled down" and married George Zaharias, a professional wrestler, she became acceptable to the public as a domestic wife. Mildred Didrikson Zaharias continued her career in professional sports and served as a role model of female athleticism. She founded the Ladies Professional Golf Association in 1948. For over 40 years, she earned more medals, set more records, and won more tournaments in sports than any other athlete, *male or female*, in the twentieth century. In 1950, the Associated Press named her "Woman Athlete at Half-Century."

Differences between men and women in the workplace were distinguished by pay scale. After the war, women returned to the service sector and resumed low paying jobs. About 80 percent of the women working in the 1950s and 1960s worked as salesclerks, health care workers, stewardesses, receptionists, telephone operators, waitresses or secretaries. In terms of professional positions, women were still on the bottom rung. in the lower paying professions, 97 percent of all nurses and 85 percent of all librarians were females; but in higher paying professions, only six percent of all physicians and three percent of all attorneys were women. The teaching profession was still gender-segregated with the majority of elementary and middle school instructors being female, and college and university faculty predominantly male. Only high school faculty had a more balanced ratio of male to female teachers. Despite media stereotypes, women were still working in the 1950s as they had always worked, to support their families, but there was little change and no policy of equal pay was in effect; women in all jobs and professions continued to earn 60 percent of a man's salary for the same work, equivalent experience, training and seniority.

In the Fifties, the standard of beauty remained the young white female, and preferably a blonde. Hollywood offered two versions: Marilyn Monroe, who oozed easy eroticism, and Doris Day, the wholesome, freckle-faced girl next door. Even though sexual advice literature espoused that young women should be virgins when they married, Dr. Alfred Kinsey's study, *Sexual Behavior in the Human Female*, revealed a wide discrepancy between mores and behavior. Dr. Kinsey's 1953 research reported that 50 percent of all females were not virgins when they married.

After World War II, with the return to domesticity, high schools continued to promote Home Economic or Domestic Science Courses. The curriculum included classes in sewing, cooking, household management and child care.

Mothers of Invention: Clare Boothe Luce, American Ambassador

Clare Boothe Luce was a twentieth century renaissance woman who achieved fame as a playwright, publisher, editor, writer, Congresswoman and Ambassador. She was born into a working class family in 1903, and although her father had abandoned the family when she was eight years old, Clare's mother, a former chorus girl, struggled to provide her children with an exceptional upbringing. Clare attended private schools off and on and traveled to Europe with her mother.

In 1923, Clare married a prominent society millionaire, George Brokaw, but six years later they divorced. She received custody of her daughter and a substantial divorce settlement. In 1929, she went to work for the Conde Nast Publishing Company in New York, and later became managing editor of *Vanity Fair Magazine*. In 1935, Clare Boothe married Henry Luce, the cofounder of *Time Magazine* and the Luce's collaborated to establish *Life Magazine*. About this same time, Clare tried her skills at playwriting and enjoyed remarkable success with *The Women*, a biting satire about the powerlessness of upper-class women. It featured all female characters sharply stereotyped as shallow and materialistic. *The Women* ran on Broadway from 1936-1938, and was produced as a motion picture with an all-star cast.

Before she married Henry Luce, Clare had been a Democrat, but by 1940 she avidly supported Republican Wendell Wilkie for President. During World War II, she served as Life correspondent in Europe and published her observations of the war in *Europe in the Spring*. In 1942, Clare Boothe Luce won a Congressional seat and was reelected in 1944. She criticized President Roosevelt's "soft" war policy and at the same time vilified him for lying us into war. During her two terms in Congress, Clare Boothe Luce proposed racial equality in the armed services, the establishment of a postwar military agreement with Great Britain and France, independence for India, an end to restriction of emigration from China, and affordable housing for veterans.

She worked for the Republican Party as a lecturer and writer and campaigned for Dwight D. Eisenhower's presidential race in 1952. In 1953, President Eisenhower rewarded her with the Ambassadorship to Italy and nominated her, in 1959, for an Ambassador post in Brazil which she declined. Clare Boothe Luce's appointment to an American Ambassadorship was path breaking as she was the first woman to serve in the male domain of the Foreign Service, as an ambassador.

Conclusion

The decade of the Fifties often characterized as ultra conservative was in fact, a period of dramatic change. Immigration brought many people to America and the birth rate shot from an average rate of 2.8 million annual births in the war years to 3.4 million in 1946 and this birth rate would steadily increase until 1967.

The media endorsed the postwar prosperity and the expansion of suburbia by encouraging American women to return to domesticity. Advertising marketed domestic products and television portrayed the ideal family with a stay-at-home mom. However, the number of women employed outside the home actually increased after war defense plants closed and wartime production ceased. The reality was that many female wage earners needed to work and many women aspired to pursue a career or profession.

The 1954 Supreme Court decision, *Brown v Kansas, Board of Education*, called for the immediate desegregation of American public schools. This landmark case raised the hopes of the black community, and was the first step in overturning the old Jim Crow laws and segregation as a way of life in the South. The Brown decision foreshadowed the Civil Rights Movement of the 1960s.

Chapter 23
The Civil Rights Movements
In the Eye of the Storm

Key Topics

Women and the Civil Rights Movement
A Women's Liberation Movement
Expansion of Civil Rights Activism—Latinos and Native Americans
Women Ecologists

Chronology

1964 - Freedom Summer - Mississippi Voter Registration
Enactment of the Civil Rights Act
1965 - Enactment of the Voting Rights Act
Assassination of Malcolm X
1966 - Formation of National Organization of Women
1967 - Chicano Movement Organized
1968 - Assassinations of Dr. Martin Luther King, Jr., and Senator Robert F. Kennedy
1970 - Nixon Administration creates Environmental Protection Agency, EPA

Introduction

Civil Rights, a leading social movement in the 1960s, stirred various groups of disenfranchised Americans. The Civil Rights Movement began as a nonviolent crusade by blacks in the South, with boycotts of facilities such as public transportation and lunch counters. This initial campaign spun off into and encouraged other causes such as the War on Poverty, and the American Indian Movement (AIM), which attempted to bring public awareness to the plight of tribes in the United States. In the Latino community, the solidarity of the United Farm Workers Union, led by its charismatic President, Cesar Chavez, and Vice President Dolores Huerta, inspired young Latinos to organize the Chicano Movement, a grassroots campaign intended to preserve their heritage, and to enable the community to participate in politics.

Women's involvement in the Civil Rights Movement sharpened their awareness of their own status. The establishment of the Federal Commission on the Status of Women and consequent State Commissions renewed interest in women's issues. Feminist leaders formed a new organization to campaign for Women's Rights, the National Organization of Women, NOW. In the sixties and seventies, women who worked for a healthier, cleaner environment championed the ecological crusade.

The Civil Rights Movement

From 1955 to 1965, southern communities tried to subvert the Brown decision by privatizing their public school districts or flagrantly ignoring the Supreme Court's decision to integrate the public schools. Not only had President John F. Kennedy and his brother, Attorney General Robert Kennedy, failed in their attempts to move the Civil Rights agenda forward, but in addition, the Kennedy administration's policies had alienated Southern Democrats. In November of 1963, John Kennedy launched a strategic tour of southern states in an attempt to reunify the Democratic Party in preparation for his bid for reelection in 1964, but the President's plan to bring the party together was tragically and suddenly sidelined. On November 22, 1963, an assassin(s?) killed the President as his motorcade passed through downtown Dallas. His successor, Vice President Lyndon B. Johnson, a southern Democrat and experienced legislator pushed the Civil Rights Act of 1964 through the Congress in order to shore up the Brown decision which had only addressed segregation in the schools. The Civil Rights legislation banned discrimination of any person based upon race, color, religion, or national origin, and forbid discrimination in public accommodations. To give force to the Civil Rights Act, under Title VII, the United States Attorney General could request withholding Federal funding from entitlement programs, in cases where those funded practiced discrimination. Consequently, institutions which did not integrate could lose Federal funding. Money talked. Compliance with the Civil Rights Act was critical because without Federal funding many states were threatened with serious deficits. Congress created the Equal Employment Opportunity Commission, the EEOC, to arbitrate any grievances of discrimination.

Resistance continued after Congress enacted the Civil Rights Act. Obstacles to registration and voting for southern blacks took the form of intimidation and violence escalated. On September 15, 1963, as four black girls donned their choir robes and prepared for Sunday services at the 16th Street Baptist Church in Birmingham, Alabama, a bomb exploded inside the church killing all four. In the summer of 1964, college students known as Freedom Riders boarded buses bound for the Deep South to conduct voter registration for black Mississippians. When three young volunteers of the Congress of Racial Equality, or CORE—James Chaney, a black Mississippian and two white volunteers, Andrew Goodman and Michael Schwerner—disappeared during the voter registration campaign, the public outcry moved the FBI to conduct an investigation. Michael's wife, Rita Schwerner, pointed out in a press interview that if Cheney had been the only volunteer missing, nothing would have been done, but because two of the volunteers were white, the manhunt took on national importance. Six weeks later the FBI, found the bodies of the young men. The two white volunteers had been shot once in the head but Cheney had been beaten with a chain and shot several times. In 1964, during the Freedom Summer, 63,000 blacks were registered to vote in Mississippi, but the price was dear. Voter registration had cost the lives of fifteen civil rights volunteers, not to mention the countless black Mississippians who had been lynched over the years. The tragedy of the Mississippi murders dramatized the necessity for the Voting Rights Act which was passed in 1965, to bolster the Civil Rights Legislation package of the previous year.

Women in the Civil Rights Movement

Strong female leadership in the Civil Rights Movement was evident everywhere in the South. Black women played a central role organizing marches, leading protests, distributing leaflets, and expanding the voter registration drive. In 1957, Ella Baker had pioneered the work of the Southern Christian Leadership Conference, the SCLC, and mobilized democratic coalitions in grassroots community associations. In their "Don't buy where you can't work" campaign, Ella Baker and Daisy Bates led the black women's resistance in the South to end racial discrimination with an effective boycott against stores practicing discriminatory hiring.

In 1962, Ruby Doris Smith joined the Student Nonviolent Coordinating Committee, or SNCC, (pronounced SNICK). Ruby Smith, a

Freedom Rider, had acquired political expertise the hard way. As a demonstrator, she had been arrested and frequently beaten. Mississippi sharecropper Fannie Lou Hamer risked her life the summer of 1962, when she registered to vote. Fannie said she put "her hand as high as it would go" in order to register to vote and sign up as a volunteer with SNCC. In 1964, she became Co-chair of the Mississippi Democratic Party, the MDP, and took her delegation to the Democratic National Convention in Atlantic City, New Jersey. When attempts were made from the floor of the convention to bar her group from participation, Fannie Lou Hamer, on national television, addressed the Credentials Committee and explained the price the MDP delegates had paid to get there. She described the terror, violence and injustices blacks had suffered in Mississippi, including her own ordeal. The beating she received while in jail had left one hand crippled. When the National Democratic Committee conceded seats to only two of the MDP delegates, it was clear to black Mississippians that they faced the struggle all by themselves. Fannie Lou Hamer continued her work for the Democratic National Committee for Mississippi, the National Women's Political Caucus, the Delta Ministry, the Freedom Farms Corporation and Young World Developers.

Expanding the Civil Rights Movement

Once momentum built for this grassroots movement, many other disenfranchised groups would demand their civil rights. The Civil Rights Movement inspired poor working-class people, Native Americans, and women to organize for liberation and equal protection under the law.

As part of the President's Civil Rights agenda, Lyndon Johnson had introduced social legislation packaged as the War on Poverty, which gave brief political attention to the plight of the nation's poor. Bringing relief was another matter. One implementation of the program, operated by Johnnie Tillmon, a mother in the Los Angeles neighborhood of Watts, was organized as the Aid to Families with Dependent Children, the AFDC, which became the largest public assistance program in the country. Contrary to stereotypes about minorities on assistance, the program revealed that white women received help from the AFDC more frequently than black women did. In 1967, Dr. Martin Luther King, Jr., met with social welfare activists Johnnie Tillmon, Etta Horn, and Beulah Saunders to spearhead a Poor People's Campaign. They envisioned a mass alliance of all of the groups which had been denied access to opportunity in America. But on April 4, 1968, an assassin's bullet stopped that collective dream for poor people from materializing. Dr. King's death set off a series of violent race riots in a number of American cities, and other groups had started to take other action as well.

The American Indian Movement

The American Indian Movement, or AIM, began as a protest against Federal control and occupation of Native American ancestral land. On November 20, 1969, Grace Thorpe, a Native American who had served as an adjutant under General Douglas MacArthur in World War II, led a protest on Alcatraz Island with seventy-eight other Native Americans. Their occupation of the island and the Federal Prison in a twenty-month standoff produced nothing substantial, but did publicize their demands: to cleanse San Francisco Bay of pollution and to convert Alcatraz Island into a center for Native American Environmental Studies. AIM staged other protests at national shrines and sites important to Native American history. One was the seventy-one-day standoff at Wounded Knee, South Dakota, in 1973, at the site where United States soldiers had slaughtered 200 men, women and children of the Sioux Nation in 1893. At the Wounded Knee Memorial, Native Americans demonstrated to protest the lenient sentences given to white men who had killed a Sioux male in 1972.

Bearing out the tragic history of indigenous peoples, the AIM movement and Native American protests garnered little sympathy or public support, but their persistence did move the government to alter its policies. Since their contact with white society, Native Americans had endured shifts from one governmental policy or presidential administration to another. More recently, in 1953, Congress had passed the

Termination Resolution meant to discontinue Federal controls, funding and benefits to indigenous peoples. Stripped of all its legalese, termination stated that Native Americans would lose ownership and control of any land they still owned. From 1954-1960, the government removed sixty-one tribes from Federal supervision, and Federal trusteeship. In response, a number of associations, such as the National Congress of American Indians, organized to oppose the Federal policy of termination.

Native American Lucy Covington single-handedly lobbied the Federal government. She was a member of the Colville Tribes and Reservation, a collective in the Pacific Northwest which was threatened with termination. Lucy Covington stepped into leadership naturally; both her father and grandfather had served as chiefs and elders to their people. Throughout the 1960s, Lucy organized the Colville into an advisory council, scraped up funds to build a Reservation Council Center, made trips to Washington. D.C., and campaigned for self-determination and the cancellation of the termination policy. In July, 1970, Congress canceled its own Termination Policy and in 1974, passed the Indian Self-Determination Law. This law articulated what Lucy Covington had fought for, the right of all Indian people [her term], to self governance and sovereignty. Under the Indian Self-Determination Law, tribes assumed control of the Federal programs and the right to own and manage reservation land which in most cases had been declared Federal domain. Because of Lucy Covington's efforts, the Colville Tribes continue to own their land and govern through self-determination. As she had said in so many of her petitions, "Indian identifies himself with the land, if Indian owns no land; Indian is nothing" [sic].

Other Native American activists, Margaret Carlson, a Yurok, and Joyce Crow, a member of the Hoopa Tribe, organized a protest over the commercial fishing rights in the Puget Sound, mainly the Salmon Industry which had intruded into the livelihood of the Pacific Northwest Native American fishermen and polluted the rivers with cannery runoff. Their efforts would bring some government regulation, but the pollution continued since commercial fisheries had more money with which to lobby Washington than the Pacific tribes had.

The Stirrings of a Women's Movement

When John F. Kennedy became president in 1961, he had not received the blessing of a distinguished Democrat, Mrs. Eleanor Roosevelt. In fact, the former First Lady took the President to task for appointing so few women to his administration. Of the 240 Federal appointments, a grand total of ten were women. Mrs. Roosevelt maintained influence in the party and the President conceded to her suggestion to create a Federal Commission on the Status of Women, for the purpose of research and to identify the concerns of the nation's female population. President Kennedy appointed Mrs. Roosevelt to serve as Chair of the new agency. She served briefly before she died in 1962, one year before the president was assassinated.

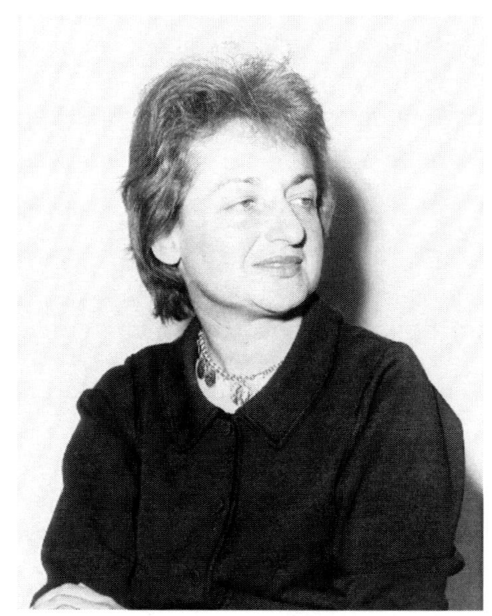

Betty Friedan, an author and activist in the second wave of the women's movement, initiated a new discussion on feminism with her book "The Feminine Mystique." (Photo courtesy of the Library of Congress.)

In 1963, while gathering material for her book, writer Betty Friedan interviewed a group of middle-class, college-educated, married women. Based upon those findings she wrote *The Feminine Mystique.* This book initiated a flood of feminist literature and inspired the second wave of feminism for the women's liberation movement of the Sixties and Seventies.

Lifting the veil of perfection from suburban life, Betty Friedan presented another side of domesticity. Housewives stagnated from boredom, reverted "to alcohol, tranquilizers, and in their more sober moments signed up for bowling leagues." In the chapter entitled "The Problem that Has No Name," Betty Friedan described the sense of futility which American middle-class housewives could not express. In the era of unprecedented prosperity, the suburban woman was supposed to live happily ever after, "freed by science and labor-saving appliances from the drudgery of housework, the danger of childbirth, and the illnesses of her grandmother." In reality, the suburban housewife spent her years unsatisfied and unfulfilled, as Friedan explained.

> If I am right, the problem that has no name stirring in the minds of American women today is not a matter of loss of femininity or too much education or the demands of domesticity. It is far more important than anyone recognizes. It is the key to these other new and old problems that have been torturing women and their husbands and children, and puzzling their doctors and education for years. It may well be the key to our future as a nation and a culture. We can no longer ignore that voice within women that says: "I want something more than my husband and my children and my home."

Although Betty Friedan's complaint seems trivial today, in the past years the housewife's discontent was perceived of as ingratitude, even as unpatriotic. After all, the prosperity that American housewives enjoyed in the Fifties and Sixties had been gained by America's advantageous position as a victor in World War II. Thousands of G.I.s had given their lives to keep America free, prosperous and, as one advertising jingle touted, "The land of opportunity for *every* girl and boy."

From Betty Friedan's vantage point, many suburban women spent time on the analyst's couch dealing with mommy guilt. One working mother described her frustration. "When I am at work, I feel that I should be at home, and when I am at home I feel that I should be at work." Betty Friedan believed that beyond the lack of fulfillment was disillusionment. After spending a lifetime of caring for others, most women wound up at age forty, fifty or sixty with *no identity* and no life of their own. As one woman said, "I feel as if I don't exist." For the American woman, outside of marriage and motherhood, "no other dream was possible."

> The ones in their forties and fifties who once had other dreams gave them up... For the youngest wives and mothers, this was the only dream. They are the ones who quit high school and college to marry, or marked time in some job in which they had no real interest until they married.

Betty Friedan surmised that women were living lives of quiet desperation. But not all of them were; some middle-class women worked for wages and for social change. Others, such as poor, working-class women, particularly minorities, could not indulge in a suburban lifestyle or engage in social reform. They struggled to make ends meet. By the Sixties, working-class women had switched from the *invisible unemployed* of the Depression to the *invisible employed* of the postwar era. Their work was taken for granted and remained undervalued and unacknowledged.

Creating a National Organization

Betty Friedan became an ardent activist for women and recruited a protégé from the Civil Rights camp, Aileen Clarke Hernandez. Aileen had served as one of the early appointees to the Equal Employment Opportunity Commission (EEOC). The daughter of immigrants from Jamaica, Aileen first got involved in the Civil Rights Movement through the National Association for the Advancement of Colored People, the NAACP, while a student at Howard University in Washington, D.C. Upon graduation, she went to work for the International Ladies Garment Worker's Union, the ILGWU, and stayed there as a director for eleven years. Aileen Hernandez' experience trained her for what lay ahead in the Women's Movement.

In 1964, seventy-nine-year-old Alice Paul was still active in the National Woman's Party and had not lost her keen sense of political opportunity. In a deviously simple maneuver, she objected to the Civil Rights Bill, stating it was discriminatory and did not protect "white Christian Women." That remark gained (as she had intended), the attention of the Congressional conservative opponents of civil rights by playing on their concern for white domination. In a great political turnabout, Alice Paul's demand to help white Christians (some of whom happened to be women) captured the Conservative vote. Congresswoman Martha Griffiths, a Democrat from Michigan, succeeded in getting her colleagues to add just three letters, S-E-X to the Civil Rights Act of 1964, and that legislation banned sexual discrimination along with race, religion, color, and national origin. The inclusion of the so-called Sex Amendment (Section 703) was as close as feminists would come to realizing an Equal Rights Amendment in the twentieth century.[1]

Congresswoman Martha Griffiths of Michigan, who in collaboration with Alice Paul, introduced the Equal Rights Amendment in Congress. (Photo courtesy of the Library of Congress.)

By 1966, States formed their own version of the Federal Commission on the Status of Women. That same year, Aileen Hernandez attended the third annual National Conference of State Women's Commissions in Washington, D.C., along with Betty Friedan, attorney Pauli Murray, and union activist Dorothy Haener. In a later interview, Aileen Hernandez described the sense of the conference. Attendees were angry, grumbling and anxious to get on with the women's cause. Betty Friedan addressed conference attendees on the urgency to form a women's movement. As discussions moved from hotel rooms and lunch tables, Betty Friedan, Aileen Hernandez and their colleagues formed the National Organization for Women, NOW. It started with twenty-eight members who elected Betty Friedan president, and Aileen Hernandez vice president.

NOW leaders envisioned a new era which would bring equality and opportunity for American women. They advocated a full and equal partnership with men, which included sharing child care and household tasks. Five years later, when Betty Friedan stepped down as head of NOW, Aileen Hernandez was elected president. It was an historic moment. In the past, African-American women had been excluded from participation in the women's movement and had formed their own groups. Aileen Hernandez became the first woman of color to hold a national post in the women's movement. Her serving as vice president and president, moved NOW forward as an integrated national organization. Because of her own ethnicity and work experience in labor and the EEOC, Aileen Hernandez embraced women from all backgrounds. She saw the movement as a civil rights crusade for *all* women. As she stated,

> Until women, black as well as others, gain a sense of their own identity and feel that they have a chance, a real choice in society nothing is going to happen in civil rights. It's not going to happen for blacks; Its not going to happen for Mexican-Americans; It's not going to happen for women.

---

1. See Appendix C documents for the full text of Section 703 of the Civil Rights Act.

Much of the early membership consisted of union activists, writers, students, women from the entertainment industry and road warriors from the 1964 Freedom Summer. Those early reformers made it clear that they were not only fighting for rights to full equality in a competitive world of business, they were also reaching higher to *change the world*, to transform it into a peaceable kingdom. Feminists did not focus narrowly on a campaign against men. For, as one woman asked, "Why should I have to compete with a man? I have already proven what I can do."

Esther Peterson, who had served as Assistant Secretary of Labor in the Kennedy Administration and Chief of the Women's Bureau in the Department of Labor in 1961, assumed leadership of the Commission. The Women's Commission became sharply divided between feminists on one side and Esther Peterson and her pro-labor followers on the other. Esther Peterson opposed an Equal Rights Amendment because she believed it would negate the protective legislation women had already secured. She advocated instead that women work for "specific bills for specific ills." The Commission on the Status of Women demanded equal pay for equal work, equal benefits for widows from Social Security, paid maternity leave, minimum wage legislation, and an end to sexual discrimination and discriminatory practices in jury selection.[2] Esther Peterson's strategy produced the Equal Pay Bill which was passed in June 1963. Although the Equal Pay Bill meant equal work, it did not apply to the issue of comparable worth. In the wider spectrum, advocates of comparable worth would argue that a secretarial position, (predominantly female) required skills, background, and training comparable to a forklift operator, (predominantly male). Comparable worth remains a highly controversial and contested issue in labor.

The Equal Employment Opportunity Act, the EEOA, was also passed and indicated a positive climate for women's issues. Under the EEOA legislation, a legal suit could be brought to the Federal Courts under Title VII of the 1964 Civil Rights Act. Congresswoman Edith Green proposed the Education Amendments, as addenda to the Civil Rights laws, which allowed class action suits by individuals in higher education (namely women and minorities). The Education Amendments banned sexual discrimination in schools which affected academic faculty positions, admission to colleges (particularly those formerly all male or all female) as well as sports programs. The effects of the Education Amendments were widespread, especially for female athletes and women's athletic programs which could demand more equitable funding and scholarships.

African-American women ran for political office and stepped into national view. Shirley Chisholm had moved up the political ranks in the 1950s, as a representative in the New York State Legislature and, in 1968, succeeded as the first black woman to serve in the United States Congress. Her political mission—to seek better conditions and wages for the poor, particularly domestic workers, and to create educational and hiring programs—reached a broader majority of working people.

Shirley Chisholm, the first African-American woman to serve in the United States Congress. She was reelected six times. In 1972, she entered the primaries as a presidential candidate. (Photo courtesy of the Library of Congress.)

2. In the State of New Mexico, for example until 1969, a woman could not serve on a jury

By 1967, Civil Rights organizations such as the Students for a Democratic Society (SDS); the Student Non-Violent Coordinating Committee (SNCC); and the Congress of Racial Equality (CORE), had recruited female volunteers.[3] But white women in these groups found themselves increasingly compromised. Casey Hayden and Mary King, two young white volunteers in SNCC, wrote about their experiences in the often quoted "Sex and Caste: A Kind of Memo." They complained that white female volunteers in the Civil Rights Movement were in a bind. If they spurned the sexual advances of black male civil rights workers, the women were accused of being racists. But if the women acquiesced, they were not treated as political equals. Only esteemed black female leaders such as Ruby Doris Smith were treated as political peers by the men. Casey Hayden and Mary King concluded that women in the movement were experiencing the same old cultural assumption—that men were superior. In their position paper, they held that the pervasiveness of male superiority was as "deep-rooted and every much as crippling" to all women as the assumption of white superiority was to the Negro.

When the media interviewed SNCC's black leader, Stokely Carmichael, and asked him if women were being treated as underlings in the movement and exactly what position women held in SNCC, he responded, "The only position for women in SNCC is prone." That response validated Casey Hayden and Mary King's observations. As historian Sara Evan explains, in *Personal Politics, the Roots of Women's Liberation on the Civil Rights Movement and the New Left,* Casey and Hayden had witnessed a turning point in the Civil Rights Movement,

> This "kind of memo" represented a flowering of women's consciousness that articulated contradictions felt most acutely by middle-class women. While black women had been gaining strength and power within the movement [the Civil Rights Movement], the white women's position at the nexus of sexual and racial conflicts had become increasingly precarious. Their feminist response, then was precipitated by loss in the immediate situation; but it was a sense of loss heightened against the background of the new strength and self-worth the movement had allowed them to develop.

Sara Evans' thesis, "That the fullest expression of conscious feminism within the Civil Rights Movement ricocheted off the fury of the black power and then landed with explosive force in the northern white new left," described the new feminism which had moved across the full spectrum from southern civil rights to the white northern left. To flesh out this theory, Professor Evans drew a parallel between the first feminist movement of 1848, which had evolved from the Anti-Slavery Crusade, and the Second Feminist Movement which evolved from women's participation in the Civil Rights Movement. Sara Evans likened the experiences of volunteers such as Casey Hayden and Mary King to those of Southern abolitionists Sarah and Angelina Grimke who had come to appreciate their own vulnerable condition as females when they were powerless to help the slaves within their own household. Like their predecessors in the nineteenth century, feminists used the tools the movement had given them: a language to name and describe oppression, and a deep belief in freedom, equality and community, which was translated into sisterhood.

Amid the intensity of the Civil Rights Movement, Casey Hayden and Mary King doubted there was enough interest in a women's movement but there were other people listening, reading and writing. As Sara Evans notes, events escalated after the Hayden and King publication. "One month later, women who had read the memo staged an angry walkout from a national SDS Conference at Urbana-Champaign, Illinois." Ironically, the only individual who defended their action was a black man from the SNCC.

In 1968, feminists assaulted patriarchal capitalism by protesting the Miss America Pageant on the boardwalk at Atlantic City. The pro-

3. CORE, the Congress of Racial Equality, was formed by James Farmer in 1942.

testers crowned a sheep, and piled what they labeled "all of the instruments of torture," bras, girdles, and high heels into a garbage can labeled freedom, and burned the contents. After that demonstration, the public trivialized their protest and *feminist* became synonymous with *bra burner.*

Scholars such as Oxford Professor Germaine Greer were also attracted to the cause, and feminist literature increased substantially. Women's Studies curricula were established at Westbury College, Cornell University and San Diego State University.

The Latino Movement

A Civil Rights Movement was inspired in the Southwest Latino Community, by United Farm Workers Labor Leader Cesar Chavez, the president of the UFW. In 1966, Cesar Chavez had strengthened the farm workers' union by affiliating with the largest trade union operative in the United States—the AFL-CIO. Chavez worked on behalf of the grape pickers, and the National Farm Workers, which amalgamated into the United Farm Workers, the UFW. Their successful boycott against the growers in Delano, California, from May, 1969 to July, 1970, had finally ended a five-year-strike. When it took the media spotlight, Chavez became a folk hero. But few people knew of Dolores Huerta's efforts as the backbone of the UFW, and how she had organized boycotts, strikes, meetings, publicity and membership. Dolores Huerta, a school teacher from Stockton, California and mother of eleven children, had gained experience as a union activist and community leader in the early fifties. Teaching in Stockton, in the agricultural belt of California, Dolores saw the dire poverty of farm working families, visible in their children who came to school ill-clad and hungry. It was Dolores who negotiated and secured a contract with the Delano Grape Growers in 1970. Her tireless efforts for UFW were finally recognized in 1973, when she was elected its vice president. Dolores Huerta also orchestrated the lettuce boycott in 1970, campaigned for civil rights for migrant workers, and supported the Poor People's Movement.

Latino student movements such as El Movimiento Estudiantil Chicano de Aztlan, or MECHA, drew from the tradition of the mutualistas and engaged in social service to their community. (Photo courtesy of the Archives of the Fullerton College Library.)

By 1967, sparked by the Civil Rights Movement and the courage of Cesar Chavez, the political awareness of college students of Latino heritage at Southern California schools emerged. They organized the Chicano movement at the Los Angeles campus of Loyola University, and at the California State University campuses at Los Angeles and Northridge. The Chicano movement had roots in intellectualism, a feature least noted in its historical analysis. At Loyola, students formed the United Mexican-American Students (UMAS) and dedicated their organization to studying their own ethnic heritage and performing community outreach in the spirit of *mutualistas.* UMAS put on fund-raisers to support the UFW and carried on a dialogue with other activist groups such as the Black Student Union and Students for a Democratic Society (SDS). By 1968, Chicanos had produced positive results with a Chicano Studies pilot program introduced at California State University, Los Angeles. Eventually, Chicano and Ethnic Studies formed an integral core curriculum and served as a venue for a disciplined major throughout the California University System. The intellectual curiosity and quest for knowledge relevant to their heritage was typical of the sixties' activists who used *relevancy* as the watchword for all their pursuits.

In 1968, Chicano awareness trickled down rapidly from college campuses into high schools as well. In Los Angeles, 12,000 students staged an impressive demonstration. Students emphasized that this was a serious matter, not an excuse to skip classes. They presented a comprehensive petition to school officials. Students asked for revisions of curricula in order to embrace Latino culture, the hiring of more Latino faculty, an enforced policy against racism, smaller classes, and counseling in order to encourage Latinos to pursue a college education. The Chicano movement engendered pride and restored hope and dignity for the Latino community. As the movement reached the campus of the University of California at Santa Barbara in 1969, students organized a conference which gave birth to *El Movimiento Estudiantil Chicano de Aztlan*, or MECHA. The protest had developed as a quest for their historical heritage, and out of the *mutualistas* concept of nurturing others. At the heart of MECHA's vision was *La Raza*, the people, and students pledged that their education was not solely for themselves but must benefit the community.[4]

Mothers of Invention: Preserving Mother Earth, Women in the Environmental Movement

In 1970, President Nixon signed legislation which created the Environmental Protection Agency, the EPA, to coordinate Federal government programs into responsible action to protect the environment. This culminated an environmental movement which had been integrated into the educational curricula and in the marketplace with biodegradable products as environmentally safe alternatives. Six years later, President Jimmy Carter, a nuclear engineer sensitive to environmental concerns, warned Americans of the immediacy of the energy crisis.

Although the public assumed that environmental and ecological concerns were unique to the seventies, the field had been pioneered in the nineteenth century by Ellen Swallow Richards, the first scientist to develop ecology as a science. While a student at Vassar College, Ellen Swallow Richards had studied under Maria Mitchell, the famous astronomer. She became the first woman admitted to the Massachusetts Institute of Technology, MIT. There she established the Women's Laboratory so that women could major in the sciences. Her research in chemistry extended to sea life, mineralogy and industrial development, and to something new—Sanitation Chemistry. At the Woman's Laboratory, she conducted experiments which she published in *The Chemistry of Cooking and Cleaning*, and *Food Materials and Their Adulterations.* To create a healthy environment, she promoted a Domestic Science curriculum in the Boston Public School System, but unlike our modern notions of Domestic Science (or Home Economics), Ellen Swallow Richards' curriculum did not include cooking, cleaning, and sewing classes. Professor Richards designed studies in conservation, chemistry, biology and hygiene. Her research on water and air pollution led to the full blown specialization of human ecology—or what she termed Euthenics—and was published in 1912, *Euthenics: the Science of a Controllable Environment.*

Environmental science or ecology would never be the same after biologist Rachel Carson, a graduate of Pennsylvania College and Johns Hopkins University, published her landmark studies. She began her research at the Marine Biological Laboratory at Woods Hole, Massachusetts, joined the faculty of the University of Maryland in 1931, and worked at the U.S. Fish and Wildlife Services from 1936 to 1952. Rachel Carson sharpened the public's awareness of the perils to the environment through her writ-

4. *El Movimiento Estudantil Chicano de Aztlan*, i.e. the Student Chicano Movement of Aztlan. The traditional name for the Aztec country was Atzlan but it is used in the title to denote that territory of the American Southwest taken from Mexico. *Viva La Raza!* The slogan of the movement, translated as long live the people, long live the race, or power to the people.

ing, namely, *The Sea Around Us*, and *The Edge of the Sea.* But in 1962, her greatest work, *Silent Spring*, became the *tour de force* for the environmental movement. Industry and the public regarded insecticides and pesticides as necessary in the fight against disease-infested insects like the mosquito; but Rachel Carson warned that the continued indiscriminate use of pesticides and herbicides would permanently destroy nature's delicate balance. Her revelatory study documented the deadly effects of DDT on the ecosystem, which led to a heated public controversy and a government inquiry which banned its use. The wheels of change turn slowly; when Rachel Carson died in 1964, no substantive enforcement of the ban on pesticides had been taken and harmful pesticides are still used today.

Women environmentalists also focused on the problems of pollution and the energy crisis. Karen Silkwood an employee, at the Kerr-McGee plutonium processing plant in Oklahoma, saw threats to health and safety at the plant where employees were being exposed to radioactive hazards. Karen Silkwood herself contracted cancer from exposure to radioactive materials. A member of the Oil, Chemical and Atomic Workers' Union, she conducted investigations of the company until she was killed in a mysterious automobile accident. Just prior to her death, she had been threatened and harassed by Kerr-McGee management. An investigation of her case was undertaken by the National Organization of Women (NOW), which brought charges of liability for the plutonium contamination of the deceased Karen Silkwood. The court awarded her family a settlement of $10.5 million.

Other female activists, members of the All Red Nations, an affiliate of AIM in South Dakota, were also concerned about pollution. These women began an investigation when an increased number of miscarriages and birth defects occurred on their reservation. Their inquiry revealed the cause—radioactive waste in the drinking water from sewage runoff and pesticide spraying. In another incident, Lois Gibbs, an organizer of the Love Canal Homeowner's Association, in Niagara Falls, New York, found high levels of toxins in the environment. Their homes and the local 99th Street Elementary School had been built on the site of Hooker Chemical Company. Hooker Chemical had dumped over forty-two million pounds of toxic chemicals into the ground. Lois Gibbs' son died of cancer traced to those toxins. At first, officials ignored the Love Canal incident, but on August 7, 1978, President Jimmy Carter declared Love Canal a Federal Emergency Zone. This acknowledgment provided Federal funds to relocate 239 families who lived in the streets closest to the dump. Not included in the government's settlement were the remaining ten blocks of residential homes, including that of Lois Gibbs. Her son had attended kindergarten at 99th Street School, which had been built directly over the toxic waste site.

Despite the political activism of the sixties and the seventies, the ideal woman remained the kitchen wife. (Photo courtesy of the Archives of the Fullerton College Library.)

Changing Images in the Media - The Liberated Polyester Woman?

Despite women's political activism in the sixties and seventies, the media's representation of the new woman was a subtle manipulation. Family sitcoms were still popular on television, and new programs seemed at first glance to promote the new liberated woman. One example featured Mary Tyler Moore, who in the sixties had played a dutiful wife on *The Dick Van Dyke Show.* A decade later on the *Mary Tyler Moore Show,* she played a single career woman. Her character, overprotected and somewhat intimidated by the boss, Mr. Grant, got entangled in plots involving dysfunctional people. If she tried to assert herself, Mary was often reduced to tears, particularly in Mr. Grant's office. Another dubious heroic character, Teresa Graves, in *Get Christie Love,* played a female cop who wavered between female erotica and tough woman. The comic book character *Wonder Woman* came to life on television in the body of Lynda Carter. As *Wonder Woman* Lynda Carter wore practically nothing and served as a male sexual fantasy, not as an icon of the liberated female. *Charlie's Angels* did nothing for feminist liberation either but it did boost sales of balsam shampoo. The plot involved three seemingly independent, tough and courageous young women. Each week the Angels, played by Farrah Fawcett, Jaclyn Smith and Kate Jackson, were challenged to take on a daring mission delivered to them by a middleman who represented their elusive commander-in-chief, Charlie. The mysterious, invisible, but audible Charlie maintained full control of the girls like a kind of big brother or voyeur. Under his constant surveillance, *Charlie's Angels* were neither liberated nor free.

Conclusion

The Civil Rights Movement generated hope for groups such as Native Americans, Latinos and Latinas who all crusaded for equality and recognition of their heritage. In the sixties and seventies, Americans became acutely aware of pollution in the environment and leading female scientists and community activists worked for a cleaner, safer America.

Women's involvement in the Civil Rights Movement was a resounding reminder to them that having had the vote for forty years had not eliminated discrimination of their gender. The establishment of the Federal Commission on the Status of Women and subsequent State Commissions renewed interest in women's issues, and new groups such as the National Organization of Women reinvigorated the women's rights cause. In the sixties and the seventies, feminists inspired by the Civil Rights Movement mobilized a Women's Liberation Movement and addressed among other things: inequities in the workplace, sexual harassment, domestic violence, rape crimes, discrimination in health care and medical research, pornography and the exploitation of women in the media.

Chapter 24
Closing of the Second Wave
We'll Remember in November

Key Topics

The Status of Women's Health
Women in National Politics
The Awakening of Latina Feminism
Working for an Equal Rights Amendment

Chronology

1960 - FDA Approves Birth Control Pill
1965 - *Griswold v Connecticut*
1966 - National Organization of Women Founded
1969 - Raid of the Stonewall Club, Greenwich Village
1970 - Congress Passes the Equal Rights Amendment
1972 - 1973 - Watergate Scandal - President Nixon Resigns
1973 - *Roe v Wade* Decision
1982 - ERA Fails Ratification

Introduction

A key concern of feminist activists, women's bodies and women's reproductive rights, gained ground with the introduction of the birth control pill in 1960, and the 1973 Supreme Court ruling in Roe v Wade, *but the quality of women's health care had not advanced significantly since the nineteenth century. Preventive medicine was practically nonexistent and an increasingly alarming number of unwarranted gynecological surgeries were being performed.*

Since the 1920s, repeated attempts of the National Women's Party had been unsuccessful in attaining the Equal Rights Amendment, ERA. Congress had repeatedly flat out rejected it. In 1953, the national leadership was divided on the issue and the Women's Rights Movement seemed barely alive. But a revival was in the making as female volunteers experiencing discrimination within the Civil Rights Movement became acutely aware of their own status.

Between 1966 and 1982, the Women's Liberation Movement crested in the Second Wave of Feminism, and a Latina Feminist Movement (Un Movimiento Feminista Latina), spurred by the Chicano Movement, was gaining momentum. Because the Latino community viewed feminista solidarity as disloyalty to La Raza, Latinas were torn between the civil rights issues of the greater Latino community or acting solely for themselves.

Defining Feminism and the Feminine

During the social and political discourse of the sixties and the seventies, differing views and definitions of feminism emerged which created confusion and discord. The women's movement fragmented into splinter groups with opposing views. Media reporting molded public opinion and showcased the more extremist feminist views. Radical feminist Shulamith Firestone, for instance, who described pregnancy as oppressive made sensational copy. When feminists described the suffering and danger of illegal abortions, the media reported feminists as advocates for indiscriminate abortions on demand.

In a speech before the American Academy of Arts and Sciences, Alice Rossi defined sexual equality as, "a socially androgynous conception of the roles of men and women." But words like *androgyny* seemed sci-fi scary in the sixties and the shock of the new soon followed with new trends in androgynous fashion, haircuts, and hair salons which catered to both men and women. These bold innovations alienated both conservative and moderate women, who did not embrace an androgynous world or wish to conform to a feminist norm. As one housewife argued, "Dictating what women should not want, how they should look, or what they should reject, was just as dictatorial as what women have put up with in the past."

In defining the movement, feminist Gloria Steinem directed most of her work toward helping women develop their self-esteem and she advocated the ERA. President Jimmy Carter appointed her to serve as a Commissioner for the Observance of the International Women's Year. Gloria Steinem typified the activism of feminist leadership. She founded *Ms. Magazine*, the Coalition of Labor Union Women, Voters for Choice, Women Against Pornography, and co-founded the National Women's Political Caucus. Gloria Steinem articulated an acceptable definition of feminism as "the belief in the equality and full humanity of men and women."

Issues of gender and equality escalated with attacks on homosexuals. In 1969, the police raided the Stonewall Inn, a gay club in Greenwich Village, New York City. The violence directed toward homosexuals unleashed a war over sexuality. Hate crimes, and gay bashing took the lives of hundreds of innocent people. What was unusual about the "coming out" of gays and lesbians in American society was the reaction of the heterosexual community. Until the twentieth century, homosexuality was a lifestyle practiced without much ado, but in a post-Freudian world homosexuality was labeled deviant and immoral.

Gloria Steinem, founder of "Ms. Magazine," articulated Women's Liberation in her writing and exemplified the activism of women in the Second Wave of the movement. (Photo courtesy of the Library of Congress.)

Feminists disagreed about how much importance to give to Gay Rights. In feminist organizations such as NOW and the Women's Commissions, there was dissension in the ranks. Women's issues were a definite priority but just how much concern should be given to lesbian rights was another matter. After Stonewall, which was a turning point for gay liberation, gay activists realized they would have to go it on their own and mobilize the gay community. Beginning with the 1972 Presidential Election, Gay Rights were put forward as a serious issue in each political campaign. The movement did not see any appreciable progress until 1976, when Jean O'Leary, a lesbian delegate and the coordinator of the National Gay Task Force, was duly elected to attend the Democratic National Convention. Jean O'Leary's election was proof positive that the gay community had politicized, organized and as she stated was, "not going to be kicked around anymore."

Change was evident elsewhere. The gathering strength of Women's Liberation reached the quiet enclaves of Chinatowns in the 1970s, as Mrs. Chang Jok Lee formed the Ping Yuen Resident's Improvement Association, and women in Chinatowns in San Francisco and Boston staged rent strikes and led resistance against evictions of residents in their communities. In Los Angeles' Chinatown, women campaigned for the community's right to control their school district, and in New York's Chinatown district, Chinese-American women fought for better housing. By 1970, some 30 percent of all Chinese-American women were marrying outside of their cultural sphere to non-Chinese-American men.

The Status of Women's Health

Birth control advocates Margaret Sanger and Katherine McCormick, and research scientist Gregory Pincus, persevered in developing an anti-ovulant birth control pill. With approximately three million dollars to conduct the costly hormonal research, the first clinical tests of Enovid were undertaken in Puerto Rico. In 1960, the FDA formally approved Enovid, as the first birth control pill. Physician John Rock, a Roman Catholic, was an early spokesman for Enovid. Easily identified as just *"the pill,"* it revolutionized modern society in the era of the *happy homemaker* and *nice girls don't*. For the first time, women could take control of their own bodies, and awareness for women's health became a leading issue of the liberation movement. In response to the introduction of the pill, members of the Catholic Church, which disapproved the use of any contraception other than the rhythm method (sexual abstinence during the female's fertile period), formed the Right to Life League. Realizing the pill was the most effective form of birth control and that females would become more sexually active, school districts introduced sex education in middle schools and high schools and colleges added human sexuality courses to their curriculum.

Although the pill offered women more control over reproduction, health care for women did not improve appreciably. The use of experimental drugs, such as Diethylstilbestrol DES and Thalidomide to treat women for morning sickness, brought serious consequences. Those women had a higher incidence of miscarriage and stillbirth, or gave birth to babies with serious defects and abnormalities. Legal suits by victims of these experimental drugs continue in the courts today.

Unwarranted surgeries remained the focus of gynecology. The statistics of hospital bioethics committees, which monitored surgical procedures, revealed no improvement since the nineteenth century. In the twentieth century, more than 60 percent of all hysterectomies performed in the United States were medically unnecessary. The treatment for breast cancer, the Halsted radical mastectomy, involved the removal of the breast, lymph nodes, upper pectoral muscles and tissue, or as one surgeon described the procedure, to cut, "right down to the bone."

In 1965, the Supreme Court ruled in *Griswold v State of Connecticut*, that the Connecticut law which banned contraceptives was unconstitutional because it violated an individual's right to privacy. That interpretation paved the way for the court to intervene in birth control matters. In 1972, the United States District Court of Pennsylvania rendered a landmark decision, stating that a fetus is not a person, and therefore not entitled to protection under the Fourteenth Amendment of the Constitution or under the Civil Rights Act. Therefore citing protection of a person in the United States to life, liberty or property, or equal protection under the law, could not be used to prosecute an abortion. The case of *Roe v Wade* came before the United States Supreme Court in 1973. Jane Roe, a pseudonym for the plaintiff in the case, Norma Mc Corvey, had been in reform school as a teenager and later suffered as a battered wife. While seeking a divorce, Norma had put two of her three children up for adoption. When she became pregnant again, her search for an abortionist led instead to attorney Sarah Weddington, who was already on a mission to overturn abortion laws. Sarah Weddington took Norma McCorvey's case on legal and medical grounds. She won the case, arguing that Norma had been denied a medically safe abortion. In rendering its interpretation, the Court applied the rights of *citizens* to the Fourteenth Amendment as the legal basis for abortion. The *Roe v Wade* decision made an abortion by a licensed physician legal and available.

The court's decision on *Roe v Wade* was not the last word. Abortion became a leading political issue in elections after 1972. In 1974, First Lady Betty Ford spoke out in favor of the ERA and a woman's right to a legalized abortion. The *Roe v Wade* decision and the controversy over abortion which followed, brought divisiveness in church groups, women's groups, political parties and political candidates. Presidential hopefuls, congressional candidates, and presidential appointees to the Supreme Court were scrutinized for their stand on abortion. Voters themselves divided into two camps, either pro- or anti-abortion. The *Roe v Wade* decision left political schism and ongoing controversy but it meant that women would not have to resort to back alley abortionists, or attempt self-induced abortions.

But, succeeding Republican Presidential administrations opposed *Roe v Wade* and chipped away at its jurisdiction. In 1976, Illinois Congressman Henry Hyde sponsored the successful Hyde Amendment which forbids the use of Federal Medicaid money for abortions; and in 1980 the court upheld the constitutionality of the Hyde Amendment.

Vestiges of the Comstock Law endured in the United States even though the Congress had eliminated language from the law regarding contraception. In 1973, the Supreme Court ruled that the Comstock law only applied to unlawful abortions (a miscarriage is considered a legal or spontaneous abortion). Even though criminal penalties for distributing abortion information remained on the books, they were not enforced.

Women in National Politics

The seventies, hailed as the Decade for Women, was off to a roaring start as expressed in Helen Reddy's hit song, "I am woman, hear me roar," which became the anthem for the liberation movement. The year 1970 marked the fiftieth anniversary of the Anthony Amendment. In New York City, 50,000 women celebrated by marching down Fifth Avenue. Throughout the United States another 100,000 joined the Women's Strike for Equality. New members joined NOW by the thousands and the Federal government passed Affirmative Action legislation which banned sexual discrimination in the workplace. The U.S. Department of Labor issued guidelines on affirmative action hiring to all of its Federal contractors.

In 1950, New York attorney Bella Abzug had taken the case of black Mississippian Willie McGee, falsely accused of raping a white woman. She had appealed his case to the Supreme Court and won a stay of execution twice but eventually he was executed. In 1961, she founded the Women's Strike for Peace, an activist movement against the war in Vietnam, and in 1970, won a seat in Congress. No sooner had Bella arrived in Washington, D.C., than she introduced a resolution in the House calling for the complete withdrawal of U.S. troops from Southeast Asia. She founded the National Women's Political Caucus, NWPC, along with Congresswoman Shirley Chisholm and Feminists Betty Friedan and Gloria Steinem, for the express purpose of facilitating the campaigns of women running for political office. Looking back on the confidence and opportunity of the seventies, Bella Abzug noted, "We put sex discrimination provisions into everything. There was no opposition."

Mothers of Invention: Barbara Jordan and Watergate

In the 1970s, alongside the women's movement, other events vied for the nation's attention. In 1972, Shirley Chisholm sought the Democratic nomination for the Presidency but lacked the support of her party. During the 1972 Presidential Campaign, the National Democratic Committee announced that their offices in the Watergate complex in Washington, D.C., had been burglarized. Richard Nixon won reelection by a landslide and his administration stonewalled the investigation of the Watergate break-in. But the sleuthing of two reporters for *The*

Washington Post, Carl Bernstein and Bob Woodward, traced the hiring of the burglars and the subsequent coverup to the White House. In January 1973, when the burglars went on trial, events escalated. By April, Nixon had accepted the resignation of several White House staff, and in May, the Senate Committee, under the chairmanship of North Carolina Senator Sam Ervin, a constitutional specialist, began their investigation.

The following summer of 1974, the Watergate affair moved to the Judiciary Committee in the House of Representatives which opened impeachment hearings. A member of that committee, Barbara Jordan, a newly elected Democratic Congresswoman from Texas, entered the annals of history with her televised speech during the Watergate hearings, in which she analyzed the constitutional violations of the Nixon presidency. Point by point, for each violation and charge she quoted pertinent sections of the *Federalist Papers* and cited James Madison's speeches before the ratification committee. Her rationale for impeachment is considered by many one of the most insightful, well reasoned speeches ever delivered in the United States Congress.

On July 27, 1974, the House Judiciary Committee voted twenty-seven to eleven on three articles of impeachment. On August 8, Richard Nixon, having lost Republican support in the Congress, became the first president to resign from office.

Barbara Jordan, an African-American woman from modest means had first served in the legislature of her home state, representing the citizens or Harris County, Texas, from 1965 to 1972. As a National Congresswoman, she became the first black to represent a southern state in the United States Congress since the end of Reconstruction, and she was the first black woman from the South to serve as a Congresswoman. Seventy-five years earlier her great-grandfather, Edward A. Patton, a state legislator had been the last black reconstruction politician to be driven out of Texas as resurgent whites took back the system when Reconstruction ended in 1876.

Congresswoman Jordan worked for more effective worker's compensation, an expansion of the Voting Rights Act of 1965, to include Mexican-Americans, and for legislation to aid the working poor and minorities. When she delivered a keynote speech at the 1976 National Democratic Convention and nominated Jimmy Carter for President, she made the list of those being considered for Vice President.

Barbara Jordan, Democratic Congresswoman from Texas, was the first African-American to serve from the South since Reconstruction and the first black Congresswoman to represent a southern state. (Photo courtesy of the Library of Congress.)

In 1982, after retiring briefly from politics, Barbara Jordan taught at the University of Texas, holding the Johnson Centennial Chair on National Policy there. At the 1988 National Democratic Convention, Barbara Jordan, wheelchair bound and suffering from multiple sclerosis, delivered the endorsement speech for Lloyd Bentsen as the party's Vice Presidential candidate. At the Democratic Convention in 1992, Barbara Jordan gave the keynote address for the Democratic Presidential candidate, Bill Clinton. Her often-quoted speech, "The American Dream is not dead," infused the Democratic Party with energy for a victory. In 1994, she accepted her final political assignment as Chair of the new United States Immigration Commission, USIC, for the Clinton administration. Once asked how she accounted for her success as an African-American woman from a poor family, Barbara Jordan replied, "I never intended to become a run-of-the-mill person." She died of leukemia in

1996, and became the first free African-American to be buried at the Texas State Cemetery in Austin.

La Quinceanera is celebrated in Latino families. It is the custom of a young woman "coming out" on her fifteenth birthday (which is considered a critical time in her life). La Quinceanera celebration can be as costly as a wedding. The tradition of La Quinceanera has roots in indigenous Mexican culture, which marked the onset of menses as a rite of passage. It can also be traced to Spanish Colonial rule. At the Viceroy's court in Mexico City, eligible young women were formally presented when they came of age.

La Soldadera Reincarnada—"Una Mujer es Una Soldada Valiente!"[1]

Early evidence of a women's movement within the Mexican-American community could be seen in the prolific publications of feminist writers and poets, and the influence of the Latino Press, in newspapers such as *El Grito, Encuentro Femenil, Regeneración*, and *El Chicano*. But Latina feminists had a number of cultural obstacles to overcome. In the 1970s, during the *Chicana* Movement, i.e. the Latina Women's Rights crusade, the infamy of *Malinali* was revived. Latinas who addressed women's liberation linked their condition to the time-worn association with the historical *La Malinche* (regarded as a traitor of her people and sometimes referred to in literature as the Mexican Eve.) She served as a reminder of the appalling consequences of collaboration with Euro-Americans. According to scholar Carlos Fuentes, ever since *La Malinche's* betrayal, Mexican women had suffered the double curse of Eve and *La Malinche.* Historian Ramon Gutierrez points out the more obvious problem for Latinas: the reaction of the Latino. In the wake of a women's liberation movement in the sixties and seventies, Latinos, much like their counterparts, Euro-American males, felt threatened by the newfound assertiveness of women. Gutierrez states, "Initially the men regarded the feminist critique as an assault on their Mexican cultural past, on their power, and by implication on their virility." By promoting women's rights, Latinas also faced the resistance of male authority and the disapproval of their community.

As Professor Vickie Ruiz points out in *From Out of the Shadows, Mexican Women in Twentieth Century America,* Latinas have more affinity with their own ethnic group than with Anglo women. Within their own community, the Civil Rights Movement had mobilized all Latinos, both males and females. But, if Latinas joined Anglo liberationists, they might be seen as rebels, or worse, mirror *La Malinche*; they might be called traitors. This dilemma split Latinas into two groups—the loyalists and the feminists. The loyalists advocated maintaining the political status quo in terms of their domestic role and faithfulness to husbands and family, but the feminists were in a quandary. How could they simultaneously identify themselves with civil rights and women's rights and maintain their cultural integrity? To make feminism more acceptable in their community, Latina feminist poets reincarnated the *virago,* or heroic woman, *La Soldadera*, as their icon. Feminists hoped to inspire a new direction for Latina Feminism, drawing on the brave female warriors who had fought beside male soldiers in the Mexican Revolution. If feminists could identify their struggle with *La Raza*, they might avoid being compared with Anglo liberationists, "the cold, frigid, *gringa*," (as white feminists were stereotyped) or perceived as traitors, because the revolutionary La Soldadera represented and celebrated women who had fought for the entire community.

The effort of Latina feminists, or *feministas*, who tried to straddle their own movement

1. The reincarnated female warrior—a woman is a valiant soldier!

and the greater cause of Latino civil rights, was a tightrope walk. *Feminista* Marta Cotera observed that if Latinas wished to be remain part of their community working in organizations such as *La Raza Unida* (the People United), they could not be the least bit controversial, argumentative or assertive for women's rights. They had to prioritize their loyalty to *La Raza Unida.* One woman who got caught in the middle was Ana Nieto Gomez, a professor at California State University at Northridge. As Vickie Ruiz points out, Professor Nieto promoted *la soldadera* as the historic link for *Chicana* liberation. For her openly *Chicana* feminist position, she was silenced. While on the faculty at California State University, she received physical and verbal threats for her outspoken feminist ideas and was eventually terminated from her academic post, but maintained her high activist profile.

In 1971, *La Conferencia de Mujeres Por La Raza*, also known as the National Chicana Conference, met in Houston, Texas, to address a feminist agenda. It was the first interstate assembly of Mexican-American feminists organized in the United States. In some ways, their views were more radical than those of Anglo liberationists. Their platform included issues such as free legal abortions, birth control, programs for higher education, the identification of the Roman Catholic Church as an oppressive institution, a call for companionate marriages, and improved child care for working mothers and activists. In conference discussions, these issues proved to be not only too radical but also very divisive, and an estimated half of the delegates, about 300, who had urged conference officials to focus on racism, not sexism, walked out. Betita Martínez, one of the feminist protestors, criticized the meeting's failure to focus on poor or working-class women.

Working for an Equal Rights Amendment

Since 1879, twenty states had added equal rights amendments to their state constitutions, those included—Alaska, California, Colorado, Connecticut, Florida, Hawaii, Illinois, Iowa, Louisiana, Maryland, Massachusetts, Montana, New Hampshire, New Mexico, Pennsylvania, Texas, Utah, Virginia, Washington, and Wyoming. All of these state level amendments prohibited discrimination based on sex. Thirteen of the state level amendments also prohibited discrimination based on race, national origin, or creed—and three of them went so far as to prohibit discrimination based on a physical handicap.

The ratification of the Nineteenth Amendment had guaranteed American women the right to vote, but suffragist Alice Paul insisted that this right alone would not end legal discrimination based upon gender. In 1920, Alice Paul read her draft of an Equal Rights Amendment, which she named the "Lucretia Mott Amendment," at the celebration of the seventy-second anniversary of the 1848 Seneca Falls Conference. The National Women's Party petitioned the Congress for an ERA proposal, and Senator Charles Curtis and Representative Daniel R. Anthony, Jr.—both Republicans from Kansas—introduced it for the first time as Senate Joint Resolution No. 21 on December 10, 1923, and as House Joint Resolution No. 75 on December 13, 1923, respectively. It was never voted on. Although members of Congress introduced an Equal Rights Amendment in every session of Congress between 1923 and 1970, none ever reached the floor of either the Senate or the House of Representatives for a vote, because it was usually "bottled up" in committee.

However, forty-eight years later, on October 12, 1971, Congresswoman Martha Griffiths achieved success on Capitol Hill with her House Joint Resolution No. 208, which was adopted by the House of Representatives with a vote of 354 yeas, twenty-four nays and fifty-one not voting. Congresswoman Griffiths' joint resolution, an equal rights amendment, was then adopted by the Senate on March 22, 1972, with a vote of eighty-four yeas, eight nays and seven not voting. The ERA was finally presented by the 92nd Congress to the state legislatures and the ratification process was off and running.

Reception to the ERA

Members of the 92nd Congress who opposed the ERA were a mix of politicians that included many conservatives and a few liberals. There was mixed reception to the ERA in the state legislatures as well. Although ratification had momentum in 1972 and 1973, gaining thirty states, it slowed considerably with only three ratifications during 1974, just one in 1975, none at all in 1976, and only one in 1977. The 92nd Congress had set a seven-year time limit for the Amendment's ratification, but by the end of that deadline on March 22, 1979, a total of thirty-five of the required thirty-eight states had ratified it. Also, as of that date, four of those thirty-five states subsequently adopted resolutions to *rescind* their earlier ratifications and a fifth state adopted a resolution declaring that its earlier approval of the ERA would not extend beyond March 22, 1979.

The Illinois Senate voted to ratify the ERA in May of 1972, with a tally of thirty to twenty-one; and the House of Representatives voted to ratify the ERA on May 1, 1975, with a tally of 113 to 62.[2] At various times, votes were conducted in both chambers of the Illinois General Assembly on the question of ratifying the ERA and while most members voted *in favor of* ratification the result would often be less than the **three-fifths supermajority vote**—a requirement that existed in Illinois when those votes were cast.

In the State of Louisiana, the Senate voted to ratify the ERA on June 7, 1972, with a tally of twenty-five to thirteen. The Missouri House of Representatives voted to ratify the ERA on February 7, 1975, with a tally of eighty-two to seventy-five. The Nevada Assembly voted to ratify the ERA on February 17, 1975, with a tally of twenty-seven to thirteen; and the Nevada Senate voted to ratify the ERA on February 8, 1977, with a tally of eleven to ten. In North Carolina, the House of Representatives voted to ratify the ERA on February 9, 1977, with a tally of sixty-one to fifty-five. Oklahoma's Senate voted to ratify the ERA on March 23, 1972, by a Voice Vote. In South Carolina, the House of Representatives voted to ratify the ERA on March 22, 1972, with a tally of eighty-three to zero.

The voting pattern broke down as follows: **Idaho** had ratified the ERA on March 24, 1972, by approving Senate Joint Resolution No. 133, and then adopted House Concurrent Resolution No. 10 on February 8, 1977, to rescind that ratification. **Kentucky**, which ratified the ERA on June 26, 1972, by approving House (Joint) Resolution No. 2, then adopted House (Joint) Resolution No. 20 on March 17, 1978, to rescind that ratification; there is some speculation about Kentucky's rescission because the rescinding resolution was vetoed by the Lieutenant Governor, who was acting as Governor in the Governor's absence. **Nebraska**, which had ratified the ERA on March 29, 1972, by approving the erroneously-worded Legislative Resolution No. 83, then approved the correctly-worded Legislative Resolution No. 86. Nebraska lawmakers then adopted Legislative Resolution No. 9 on March 15, 1973, to rescind only the aforementioned Legislative Resolution No. 83. **Tennessee** ratified the ERA on April 4, 1972, by approving House Joint Resolution No. 371, and then adopted Senate Joint Resolution No. 29 on April 23, 1974, to rescind that ratification.

Constitutional Debates and Questions

A constitutional debate ensued among scholars and some believed that a state legislature *could not* rescind prior ratification of a proposed Federal Constitutional Amendment. An 1868 Congressional precedent (not a judicial precedent), had established procedures for irregularities involving the ratification of the Fourteenth Amendment.[3] In the specific case of South Dakota, its lawmakers ratified the ERA on February 5, 1973, by approving Senate Joint Resolution No. 1; then South Dakota legislators adopted Senate Joint Resolution No. 2 on March 1, 1979, but stipulated that the ERA's opportunity for ratification—by any state of the Union—would expire on March 22, 1979; furthermore, Senate Joint Resolution No. 2 made clear that South Dakota's own ratification would only be valid up until March 22, 1979, and that any activities transpiring after that date would be considered by South Dakota to be null and void.

Adding substance to the legal debate on ratification, Ruth Bader Ginsburg co-authored in

2. The Illinois Legislature voted again on May 21, 2003, with a tally of 76 to 41.
3. See Article V of the United States Constitution in Appendix A.

1977 (along with 16 other legal experts), the report entitled *Sex Bias in the U.S. Code.* This was published in 1977, by the U.S. Commission on Civil Rights, prior to Ruth Bader Ginsburg becoming a Federal judge, and intended to show how the proposed ERA (for which Ginsburg was an aggressive advocate) would change Federal laws to make them gender-neutral and to "eliminate sex-discriminatory provisions."

Pros and Cons on ERA

From 1970 to 1982, efforts for the ERA ratification took much of the energy of the Feminist Movement. Although First Ladies Betty Ford and Roslyn Carter publicly endorsed the ERA, the political tide changed direction in the late seventies and early eighties. The Republican Party withdrew its earlier support for the ERA and the most prominent ERA opposition leader, Phyllis Schlafly, a conservative Republican and successful attorney in her own right (who preached motherhood and domesticity for other women), organized the STOP ERA Campaign.

Joining the STOP ERA bandwagon, televangelist singer Anita Bryant was known for her successful campaign to remove an ordinance in Dade County, Florida, which had banned discrimination against gays in housing and job hiring. Phyllis Schlafly had also gathered support from Catholics, Mormons, and the insurance lobby. Opposition to the ERA was a vested interest for the insurance industry which faced significant financial loss if more equitable insurance rates were enforced. Phyllis Schlafly's campaign used fear and distortion, arguing that if the ERA passed, women would lose their right to financial support by their husbands and would be forced to seek employment outside the home to support their families. The truth of the matter was that women legally had no right to financial support anyway, a fact Phyllis Schlafly had never disclosed. In an intact marital relationship, a court would have no reason to intervene on a woman's behalf. Phyllis Schlafly also remonstrated against the possible use of unisex bathrooms (those marked "restroom" which were commonplace then and now), and opponents argued that the ERA passage would have far-reaching implications, obliterating traditional distinctions between the sexes. ERA opponents claimed that women would be required to register for the Selective Service System (the draft) just as men did, and would have to serve in combat just as men had.

Opponents went on to assert that the ERA would also remove laws that specially protect women, such as labor laws in heavy industry. Some states, such as Connecticut and New Mexico, had even ordered the use of tax monies in the case of "medically necessary" abortions, based upon state ERAs, under the theory that women must have health care every bit as comprehensive as that accorded to men. (Interestingly, Alice Paul, author of the original ERA, was an opponent of abortion and described the procedure as "the ultimate exploitation of women.")

According to its critics, the ERA would grant more power to Congress and to the Federal Courts, a stance unpopular at a time when public opposition to expanded Federal government authority—and Federal judicial activism in particular—was growing. Opponents, and even most supporters of the ERA, agreed that if freshly re-proposed by Congress, the ERA would have to start from scratch and would need to gain state ratifications all over again—the state approvals achieved during the 1970s being non-transferable.

Other critics feared that the courts could rule that the ERA would mandate the recognition of same-sex marriage. Some critics who maintained that the ERA would require the integration of single-sex schools, sports teams or even restrooms, pointed to a decision by a court in the State of Washington which ordered a fraternal civic organization to admit women based upon the ERA within its state constitution. Finally, some opponents of the ERA contended that the amendment simply was not necessary, and that other provisions of the Constitution—and various rulings by the Supreme Court—provided sufficient support for equal rights for both genders.

Supporters of the amendment characterized many of the anti's arguments as "scare tactics" designed to obscure the real advantages of a constitutional guarantee of equal rights for men and women. ERA supporters asserted that the concerns opponents raised about the ERA were either without merit, or were separate issues which the ERA would not affect. For example, ERA advocates pointed out that the assertion that the amendment would *require* women to register for the draft ignored the fact that, *under Article I of the Constitution, Congress has always had the power to draft women* [emphasis mine]. In response, opponents noted Congress having the power to draft women, but choosing not to, is different from Congress not having the power.

Extension and Countdown of the Ratification Deadline

In the heat of debate, Eleanor Smeal, President of NOW, realized it was crucial to buy time for ratification and persuaded Congress to extend the deadline by thirty-nine months. In 1978—as the 1979 deadline approached—the 95th Congress adopted House Joint Resolution No. 638, introduced by Representative Elizabeth Holtzman of New York, to extend the ERA's ratification deadline to June 30, 1982.

In the meantime, 2,000 women of the International Women's Year Commission met in Houston, Texas, in September of 1977, with a program focused on women's concerns, such as: abortion, child care facilities, gay rights, the ERA, rape, pornography, domestic violence and crimes against women, as well economic inequities for women in the workplace. The STOP ERA, led by Phyllis Schlafly, held a conference that same weekend in Houston entitled Pro Life, Pro Family. Schlafly appointed staff to gather reports and position papers from the women's conference and then sent these to legislators in states which had not yet ratified the ERA.

As Ronald Reagan took office in January 1981, he became the first president opposed to an equal rights amendment for women. The National Organization of Women organized "ERA YES Inaugural Watch" and 40,000 ERA supporters reminded the new president of the overwhelming pro-ERA sentiments in the nation. In April, NOW sent feminist missionaries to Utah, headquarters of the Mormon Church and the heart of the ERA opposition, and staged a door-to-door campaign; and in June, NOW announced that former First Lady, Betty Ford and actor Alan Alda would serve as co-chairs of NOW's ERA Countdown Campaign activities.

On June 30, 1981, the National Organization of Women held organized countdown rallies in over 180 cities to draw attention to the ERA deadline of June 30, 1982, and to dramatize the wide support for the ERA. In October, NOW staged the first nationwide advertising campaign for ratification of the Equal Rights Amendment. It included television spots which focused on sex discrimination and were intended to activate the vast majority of people who supported the ERA. On December 23, 1981, the United States District Court ruled, in the case of *State of Idaho, et al. v Freeman, et al.*, that the extension deadline for the ERA was unconstitutional and, further, that a state legislature may indeed rescind a prior ratification of a proposed amendment to the Federal Constitution. This signified the first time in United States History that an Act of Congress relating to the Constitutional amending process was declared unconstitutional by a Federal Court. NOW appealed the ruling to the Supreme Court and asked for an expedited hearing. Just two weeks later, in January 1982, the Supreme Court, vindicated NOW's position and granted a unanimous stay which prohibited the enforcement of the District Court's decision. This was a rare instance and the court agreed to hear NOW's appeal on the merits of the case at a later date. The Supreme Court opinion negated any legal effect of the District Court decision and removed any uncertainty and confusion that the ruling had placed over the ratification debate in the states.

The Grassroots Group of Second-Class Citizens and the Women's Hunger Fast for Justice

To promote ratification of the ERA, activists all over the country engaged in lobbying for its success. Politicizing the ERA included, among other things, petition gathering, speaking on television and radio programs and staging parades and protests. Political wisdom indicated that states which had ratified the Nineteenth Amendment would support the ERA. This meant that the stronghold of male prerogative, the

South, would maintain its traditional stance of opposition to women's rights. In the final struggle, there were fifteen states which had not yet ratified and of those, Illinois looked like the most likely prospect for approval.

In December 1981, with the deadline for ratification ticking away, a group of women in Champaign County, Illinois, known as the Grassroots Group of Second-Class Citizens, which consisted of friends and coworkers already involved locally in various feminist and lesbian organizations, began to mobilize. They believed that the slow momentum for ratification was partly due to a lack of direct action. Local groups throughout the United States, such as the Congressional Union (later known as A Group of Women), had been carrying out direct actions for the ERA since 1980, but the media had not headlined their efforts. This had impeded larger unified efforts, simply because groups were unaware of each others' existence. Perhaps this is hard to imagine, but bear in mind that twenty years ago, telecommunication such as the Internet and e-mail were not as expansive and were underutilized. From our vantage point, it is also well to consider who determines what is newsworthy, and what is broadcast. Decisions on what to print and what to broadcast are as restrictive today (if not more so) than twenty years ago, since control of the media has narrowed to a smaller and more conservative monopoly.

Assessing the climate for approval of the ERA in Illinois, things looked favorable for ratification. Sixty-seven percent of the electorate, legislators (mostly Democrats) and Republican Governor James R. Thompson all favored the ERA. As noted above, on several occasions, each branch of the legislature had voted by simple majority for the ERA. Throughout the state, churches, labor unions and citizens' groups were campaigning for passage of the ERA. But defying all logic, the legislature agreed to the three-fifths majority rule.

On Tuesday May 18th, 1982, seven women—Sonia Johnson, Sister Maureen Fiedler, Dina Bachelor, Mary Barnes, Shirley Wallace, Mary Ann Beall, and Zoe Ann Nicholson—gathered in Springfield, Illinois, to participate in a hunger fast for the ratification of the ERA. In their attempt to "turn the hearts of lawmakers to fulfill the Constitution's 200-year-old promise of equal justice under the law," the women would sit quietly every day of the fast in the Rotunda of the Illinois State Capitol.

As the June 30, 1982 ratification deadline got closer, the Grassroots Group of Second-Class Citizens borrowed tactics from the suffrage, labor, civil rights, and anti-war movements and came to Springfield, Illinois. Grassroots committed fifteen acts of civil disobedience in all and disrupted the Illinois State Legislature twice. In one demonstration, which extended into a four day occupation of the State Capitol at Springfield, they held a "chain-in" at the doors of the Senate; and on June 16th, Grassroots activists took over the floor of the Illinois House of Representatives, positioned themselves at the Speaker's podium, and forced the Chamber to adjourn early. Newspapers reported that this had so angered several lawmakers who had favored ratification that they threatened to change their votes because of the protest. Nevertheless, Grassroots continued to demonstrate, staging sit-ins at the offices of the Governor and Speaker of the House and another chain-in at the Governor's office door.

Meanwhile, during the thirty-five-day fast, the seven fasters endured death threats, harassment, and physical assault which included attempts by several onlookers to burn them with cigarettes. The fasting women held press conferences and the media covered every day of the fast. Dick Gregory, a peace activist joined the fasting women. In addition, Phyllis Schlafly's STOP ERA group came out in full force to disrupt the seven women's silent protest.

On June 22, 1982 Illinois voted: 103 for the ERA and 72 against; the vote came four votes short of the three-fifths majority required according to the Illinois Legislatures' rules for ratification. The day before, the Florida House had approved the ERA in a vote of sixty yes, fifty-eight no, but a few hours later the Florida Senate voted NO on the ERA with twenty-two nays to sixteen ayes. Ironically, the only favorable vote between the original deadline of March 22, 1979, and the revised June 30, 1982, expiration date had been in a *southern state* in the Florida House of Representatives on June 21, 1982.

As soon as the votes were counted in the Illinois Senate (which had voted down the ERA), the Grassroots Group of Second-Class Citizen/activists wrote the names of the governor and the anti-ERA legislators in blood on the marble floors in front of the legislative chambers. The blood was meant to symbolize the death of the ERA and the blood of women who suffered and would continue to suffer without legal equality.

To stop the ratification of the Equal Rights Amendment protesters demonstrate in front of the White House in 1977. (Photo courtesy of the Library of Congress.)

By the extended deadline, June 30, 1982, ratification of the ERA had failed a frustrating three states short of the 38 necessary for a three-fourths majority. After 1977, no additional state had approved and several had rescinded their yes votes. ERA supporters pledged, "We'll Remember in November." Sonia Johnson, who addressed the press shortly after the Illinois vote, stated,

> We won't ever work in their system again. We won't ever vote for them again. We will vote for women who put the women's agenda first. We will not forget who voted against women. Don't let Bush, Thompson, Ryan, and Etheredge off the hook. Both parties care only about the corporate agenda.

At a news conference, Eleanor Smeal, President of NOW, blamed the defeat of the ERA on the Republican Party, which she believed led the attack on equal rights for women. She believed that Democrats, too, were responsible because they had failed to put the ERA, "high on their agenda." Large corporations, and Chambers of Commerce were absent from the fight, but the worst offenders, Eleanor Smeal said, were insurance companies who overcharged older women. She summarized, saying, "In the final analysis, we were begging men for our rights. It is an outrage that in 1982, this nation could proclaim that women are not equal."

An analysis of the ERA vote in four key states—Florida, Illinois, North Carolina and Oklahoma—shows that the Republicans deserted the ERA, and Democratic support was not strong enough to pass the amendment; the analysis makes clear that the single most obvious problem was the gender and racial imbalance in the legislatures. While more than two-thirds of the women and all of the African-Americans in the targeted legislatures cast pro-ERA votes in 1982, less than 50 percent of the white men did so. A number of other factors influenced the outcome.

1. The failure of the feminists to educate and recruit the "ordinary housewife" (a tactic mastered effectively by STOP ERA).
2. The polarization of voters after *Roe v Wade* made abortion a political issue.
3. Phyllis Schlafly's well-timed strategy at the 1977 Houston Campaign.
4. The ratification process itself was problematic as it required a three-fourths vote.
5. Although women were the popular majority, they had remained a political minority.
6. The feminist backers of ERA were perceived by the great majority of women as extremists and radicals.

Deborah L. Rhode, in *Justice and Gender: Sex Discrimination and the Law,* suggested that the sixth point was the greatest factor in its failure. She argued that many American homemakers found it easier to reject the messengers of feminism, than to examine the message, because it was simply too painful to look at their own tenuous position in American society. Many believed that the Civil Rights legislation and the Supreme Court's articulation of equal protection language in the Fourteenth Amendment would strike down sex bias in a number of decisions. Thus, the need for an ERA seemed less critical. Since the Civil Rights Act banned discrimination and women had legal redress in its Entitlement clauses, an ERA seemed unnecessary.

Reflecting on the failure in Illinois, grassroots activist, Mary Lee Sargent, stated that,

> Throughout the month, our public statements and press releases emphasized that we had two major purposes in our actions: pressuring the legislature to ratify the ERA and promoting a new wave of militancy in U.S. feminism [sic].

Rally of activists at the Illinois State Capitol features the seven fasters in back row, from left to right: Zoe Nicholson, Dina Bachelor, Shirley Wallace (in wheelchair), Sister Maureen Fiedler's empty chair, Mary Ann Beall, Mary Barnes, and Sonia Johnson (in wheelchair).

> Although our direct action campaign did not obtain ratification of the ERA in Illinois or nationally, our work was powerful and achieved results that we did not anticipate when we began. Because these events were reported in the national media on a daily basis and later made history by being reproduced in encyclopedias and other pictorial sources, we [had] focused attention on the issues involved in the ERA and demonstrated the courage and dedication of women in the struggle for equality.

Six of the seven fasters in the grocery store stocking up on baby food at the end of their thirty-seven-day ordeal

Conclusion

Building on the populist surge of Civil Rights, AIM and the Chicano Movements of the sixties, the Women's Liberation Movement, also known as the Second Wave of Feminism, reached a crescendo in the late seventies. The future looked promising as Bella Abzug, Shirley Chisholm, Barbara Jordan and others assumed national leadership and took their places in Congress. It seemed that full equality under the law in the form of an Equal Rights Amendment to the Constitution was a predictable victory. But in 1982, with the failure of the ERA three states short of ratification, the Second Wave came to a crashing halt. The opposition, which organized rather late in the game, had used scare tactics which were both negative and effective. However, through the articulation and enforcement of the Civil Rights Act of 1964, specifically Section 703, and through Affirmative Action, individuals could bring discrimination cases to the courts.

One month after the defeat of the ERA ratification, it was officially reintroduced in the United States Congress—in July of 1982—but the U.S. House of Representatives failed to pass the amendment by a vote of 278 for the ERA and 147 against it, only 6 votes short of the required two-thirds majority for passage. Party support for the ERA was as follows: 30 percent of the Republicans and 85 percent of the Democrats voted yes.

Few people realized at the time, that an amendment for equality of rights under the laws regardless of one's gender, would not become part of the American Constitution in the twentieth century. But when the protest ended at the Illinois State Capitol on June 23, 1982, one of the fasters, Sister Maureen Fiedler, predicted that, "if the ERA does not pass now, we won't see it again, perhaps in this century." Although the ERA has been reintroduced into each session of the Congress, it has been held up in Committee each time.

Chapter 25
New Directions
Where Do We Go from Here?

Key Topics

The Third Wave of Feminism
Women in Politics
Sexual Harassment
Women and Education

Chronology

1989 - *Webster v Reproductive Health Services*
1991- Thomas -Hill Controversy
1993- President Clinton rescinds Gag rule
1996 - Madeleine Albright first woman appointed Secretary of State
2007- Nancy Pelosi, first woman Speaker of the House of Representatives

Introduction

This study of women in the United States concludes with the contemporary era or what is called the Postmodernist phase. This phase of the movement known as the Third Wave began after the failure of the ERA in 1982 and persists to the present. In the Third Wave, feminists have struggled to define their goals within a more diverse culture. While the younger generation of women have benefited from the gains of the movement, they have often negated feminism. Finding their own way, they express their womanhood within the discourse of a counter culture and a postmodernist world. A look at the attributes of Postmodernism is important in understanding current trends in the feminist movement.

Since 1982, the proposal of an Equal Rights Amendment, ERA continues to elude feminists who campaign for that constitutional reform. The lack of an equal rights amendment has punctuated the need for an organized, focused and concerted effort within the woman's movement.

Post ERA Feminist Protests

After the ERA failed to ratify in 1982, one of the seven Illinois fasters, Zoe Ann Nicholson, described the sentiment of the moment,

> It seemed as if the Women's Movement fell apart too. When no one lost an election in November because they voted against the ERA, the whole thing was just too much. The local NOW chapter began to fade. I put together a lecture with slides about Springfield and could not create any interest. I think it was all too painful. No one wanted to hear about it. They just wanted to put it in the past.

Members of the Grassroots Group of Second-Class Citizens holding a Banner. Mary Lee Sargent is the standard bearer on the left.

Grassroots activists such as Mary Lee Sargent began the task of mobilizing and rededicating themselves to direct action. In August of 1983, at a Woman Gathering (a meeting of feminists who combined political activism with women's spirituality), participants brainstormed the idea to take their Champaign, Illinois organization to a national group, and chose the name Women Rising in Resistance (WRR). This organization evolved into a network of affinity groups and individual activists who create direct action demonstrations for lesbian/feminist/womanist/pacifist/radical causes and issues. According to Professor Sargent, "Direct action can be seen as theater dramatizing issues and raising awareness, and is used as a means to energize and embolden supporters." Another objective of WRR was to educate women about the need for participation in direct action.

Other women's groups, either separately or in concert with WRR, carried out dozens of direct actions such as the witch trials of Halloween of 1983-1986, to try men and corporations guilty of crimes against women, children, and the poor. During the 1984 presidential campaign, activist/resisters plagued Reagan-Bush campaign headquarters with sit-ins and door blockings. In South Hadley and Amherst, Massachusetts, an affinity group called Women of Faith used the WRR name and blocked the doors and gates of nuclear weapons industries and nuclear submarine launching sites.

In Champaign, Illinois, WRR disrupted the lavish open house of a local newspaper which refused to publish advertising for lesbian/gay events. The Sister Resisters in New York City barred the doors of the New York and American Stock Exchanges on Women's Equality Day in August of 1985, to protest the corporate abuse of women and the woman's image. The National Rampage against Penthouse used WRR's name and logo in its protest at pornography outlets in more than fifty cities, which resulted in over one-hundred arrests of activists. The Sisters of Justice in Columbus, Ohio, under the banner of the WRR aimed at ending violence against women in demonstrations which involved dismantling a pornography store in Columbus in May of 1986.

Members of the Grassroots Group of Second-Class Citizens staging a sit-in, in front of the Speaker of the House's Office at Illinois State Capitol Building in Springfield.

Resisters regularly spray painted pornographic book stores, military bases and the headquarters of corporations involved in the nuclear weapons industry. Sisters of the California WRR confronted perpetrators of rape and sexual abuse. But in St. Louis, Missouri, resisters launched one of the most dramatic and sustained series of actions carried out by an affinity group in the network. On three successive Sunday nights in the fall of 1985, approximately 120 chanting protestors encircled the home of a trial court judge who had sentenced *to only two years probation a man found guilty of repeatedly raping an eight-year-old girl. [Emphasis mine.]*

In 1985 and 1986, the WRR network organized the national event—Women Take Liberty in '86. On the one hundredth anniversary of the dedication of the Statue of Liberty, WRR claimed the colossal female image on behalf of women and women's causes and protested the corporate and governmental abuse of the symbol of Lady Liberty. Approximately 300 women occupied the circular stairway inside the Statue for an hour singing an anthem of the women's peace movement, Naomi Littlebear's "You Can't Kill the Spirit." In defiance of the National Park Service's regulations, several affinity groups also draped banners, including a forty-foot-long *Women Take Liberty* banner, on the pedestal of the Statue. Other activities included hourly encirclements of the Statue, passing a petition demanding that the U.S. government give the monument to women to compensate for failure to pass the ERA; they also held a rally at Liberty State Park.

As a result of all these efforts, the WRR extended to a network of approximately 1,500 individuals and affinity groups, which included Lesbians Rising in Resistance and Grandmothers Rising in Resistance.

A major commitment of WRR has been the political education of women about the necessity of direct action. In the conservative 1980s, supporters of lesbian/feminist causes were often unaware that the rights and choices women enjoy were won by a combination of tactics, including direct action and long, hard fought campaigns.

Despite these kinds of protests and organizing, the female population remained an underrepresented popular majority and thus a political minority. The recent national political shift to a predominantly ultraconservative agenda threatens the *Roe v Wade* decision and the quality of life for women. The state of women's safety and legal protection has not changed appreciably since feminists first campaigned for equal rights. One characteristic of the problem is that issues and concerns for women have never held public attention for long. They are usually given brief attention often stirred by some sensational media event and then fade into the background. Several of the following cases illustrate this point.

The Thomas-Hill Controversy

In 1991, when Supreme Court Justice Thurgood Marshall retired from the bench, Republican President George Bush, Sr. nominated Clarence Thomas, an African-American, because this nominee would echo the conservative Republican ideology of the Court. NOW and other women's groups voiced concern about Thomas' lack of legal experience and that he would rule against legal abortion. During Senate deliberation on his nomination, a University of Oklahoma Law Professor, Anita Hill, testified that Clarence Thomas had sexually harassed her when he was head of the Equal Employment Opportunities Commission, the EEOC where she had worked. She described how Thomas used inappropriate language, and discussed sexual acts and pornographic films. When Thomas testified, he retorted her allegations as an attempt by the Democratic opposition to conduct, "a high tech lynching for uppity blacks." Thomas' remark was ironic, given that he had previously chided African-Americans for using race as a *crutch.* In an interview some years later, Anita Hill said, "I think he [said] it because he knew how effective it would be."

Anita Hill also explained that the way in which the hearings were structured, "the hearings were really about Thomas' race and my gender." Speaking about the hearings, she stated, "It was as if I had no race, or that my race wasn't significant in the assessments that people made about the truthfulness of my statements." Professor Hill questioned how people would have reacted, "if she had been white, blond-haired and blue-eyed." She cited the example of Strom

Thurmond, a conservative Southern Republican who had voted against the Civil Rights Act in 1964, partly due to concerns about the "mixing of races." Anita Hill added, "I do not think Strom Thurmond would have embraced Clarence Thomas so readily if his accuser had been a white female." But in reality Anita Hill believed that her race and Thomas' gender were relevant because Thomas was operating in an arena where gender meant everything. As she said, "The whole structure of power in the city of Washington seems to center around powerful men making these decisions and using sex as one of the perks of becoming powerful."

Law professor, Dr. Anita Hill who was summoned in 1991 to testify at the Senate hearings to review the nomination of Clarence Thomas for the Supreme Court (photo courtesy of Brandeis University)

The Thomas- Hill Controversy created a media frenzy focused on "he said, she said." In the end, the Senate voted fifty-two-forty-eight, for Clarence Thomas' nomination. The public assumed that after her week of testimony, Anita Hill's life would return to normal and that she would resume her job at the University of Oklahoma.[1] However, she became the subject of intense scrutiny when Congress passed a resolution to investigate the leak of an FBI interview with her about Thomas. Anita Hill's phone records were subpoenaed and family members were questioned in a months-long investigation. Politicians in Oklahoma called for her resignation from the University.

Those who opposed Thomas and believed Anita Hill saw his life-term seat on the court as defeat. However, the Thomas-Hill Controversy did raise national awareness of sexual harassment in the workplace and between 1991 and 1996 the EEOC reported that claims to their agency of sexual harassment had doubled. In that same period, awards to victims of sexual harassment quadrupled from $7.7 million to $27.8 million. Since Clarence Thomas' appointment to the Supreme Court, there have been significant strides in the Court's interpretation of sexual harassment laws. The Court now recognizes that sexual harassment in the workplace is cause for legal action, but it has resisted drawing distinct parameters in defining harassment and instead has allowed decisions to be made on a case by case basis. As Anita Hill explains, "There is a real understanding that this is a cultural problem and that we have to figure out, in a particular context, what in fact is going to be a violation of the law, but whether that trend will continue remains to be seen."

With regard to Clarence Thomas' role as a conservative Republican on the court, Anita Hill has spoken in terms of the future. Thomas' close following of Associate Justice Antonin Scalia's opinions could jeopardize advances made in civil rights and women's rights.

Women in Politics

Political analysts interpreted the increased involvement of women in politics as a direct reaction to the appointment of Clarence Thomas to the Supreme Court. The year 1992, heralded as the "Year of the Woman" recorded a whopping eleven women campaigning for Senate seats; five of them were elected. In the House of Representatives, twenty-four newly elected women took seats. These were not overwhelming victories as women, the popular majority, remained the political minority and the female

1. Professor Anita Hill left the University of Oklahoma and now teaches social policy, law and women's studies in the Heller School for Social Policy and Management at Brandeis University.

population was deficiently underrepresented in government. In the Senate alone, male legislators dominated with a 98 percent majority. Congressional membership of the 108th Congress included sixty-three women serving in the House of Representatives and fourteen in the Senate. If those numbers look promising, consider that women are the majority in the United States, comprising 52 percent of the total population, but women only make up 15 percent of the United States Congress. In the political arena, women have a long way to go. While there are more women taking seats in Congress and in state legislatures, overall the female population remains grossly underrepresented in government.

However, having noted the disparity between population and popular representation, it is also important to examine the small gains women have made. Sandra Day O'Connor, a conservative choice of President Ronald Reagan in 1981, was the first woman appointed to the Supreme Court in a unanimous senate vote. Ruth Bader Ginsburg, the liberal choice of President Clinton, was the second woman to serve on the Federal Supreme Court. Madeleine Albright, the first female Secretary of State, was appointed by President Clinton, and in the Bush administration, Condoleeza Rice ranked as the first black woman appointed as Secretary of State. Secretary Rice had formerly served as National Security Advisor to President George Bush, Jr. She worked in National Security Affairs with Colin Powell, the first black man appointed as Secretary of State.

President Barack Obama appointed Senator Hilary Rodham Clinton as Secretary of State. She became the third woman in succession to serve in that Cabinet post since Madeleine Albright.

Will a woman ever become president of the United States? Since 1972 several women have run in national elections. In 1972 Congresswoman Shirley Chisholm (Democrat, New York) ran a national campaign for her party's nomination for the presidential candidacy. Geraldine Ferraro (Democrat, New York) was the vice-presidential candidate for her party in 1984.[2]

Women are now serious contenders as presidential candidates. Elizabeth Dole (Republican, North Carolina) sought her party's nomination for president in 2000. Condoleeza Rice has received constant media pressure to announce her campaign for president and Senator Kay Bailey Hutchison (Republican, Texas) has been courted by the press as well. Voters in the 2008 presidential election faced unique canidate choices between a woman, Senator Hilary Rodham Clinton, an American of African descent, Senator Barack Obama, and a Mormon, former Governor Mitt Romney.[3] According to polls taken by Gallup and the Christian Science Monitor, American voters are more reluctant to elect a Mormon male than they are to vote for a female or a male of African descent for President.

In the 109th Congress, Nancy Pelosi (Democrat, California) made history as the first female to become Speaker of the House[4]. In the House of Representatives, 109th Congress, 67 women, or 16.1 percent, held seats of the total 435 members[5]. In addition, there were three female delegates elected to the House to represent Guam, the Virgin Islands, and Washington, D.C.; however, these are non-voting regions.

---

2. Among these three candidates Geraldine Ferraro was the only woman nominated by a national party convention as their vice presidential choice. She campaigned on the ticket with Walter Mondale, the presidential hopeful in 1984.
3. Senator Hilary Rodham Clinton, former first lady from 1992-2000.
4. The Speaker of the House is second in line of succession to the presidency after the vice-president.
5. The founding fathers created the House of Representatives as the popular branch and therefore more democratic assembly with representation based upon population. With a total of 435 delegates, and only sixty-seven women as voting members this body does not reflect the population it represents.

Women serving in the United States Senate in the 112th Congress*

Kelly Ayotte, Republican, New Hamphire

Barbara Boxer, Democrat, California

Maria Cantwell, Democrat Washington

Susan Collins, Republican, Maine

Diane Feinstein, Democrat, California

Kristen Gillibrand, Democrat, New York

Kay Hagan, Democrat, North Carolina

Kay Bailey Hutchison, Republican, Texas

Amy Klobuchar, Democrat, Minnesota

Mary Landrieu, Democrat, Louisiana

Claire McCaskill, Democrat, Missouri

Barbara Mikulski, Democrat, Maryland

Lisa Murkowski, Republican, Alaska

Patty Murray, Democrat, Washington

Jeanne Shaheen, Democrat, New Hamphire

Olympia Jean Snowe, Republican Maine

Debbie Stabenow, Democrat, Michigan

*see the appendix for list of women serving in the House of Representatives, of the 112th Congress

The Tailhook Scandal

Although the visibility of women in the military has increased steadily since the American Revolutionary War, their status today remains ambiguous; women comprise nearly 15 percent of military personnel, with 32,000 serving in the Armed Forces, but inequities in terms of promotion, pension and discrimination toward female military personnel and cases of blatant discrimination, harassment and/or molestation continue.

One such example is an event which occurred in September 1991 at the 35th annual symposium of the Tailhook Association a fraternal organization of members of the Armed Forces assigned to Aircraft Carriers, promoted a two-day debrief on Navy and Marine Corps aviation in Operation Desert Storm. It was the largest such meeting yet held, with some 4,000 attendees: active, reserve, and retired personnel convening in Las Vegas, Nevada. According to a Department of Defense report, eighty-three women and seven men stated that they had been victims of sexual assault and harassment during the meeting. There were reports of rape, sexual molestation, indecent exposure, sexual harassment and conduct unbecoming of officers of the United States Armed Forces.

On October 29, 1991, The United States Department of the Navy, possibly responding to political pressure and well before the completion of any investigations, terminated all ties to the Tailhook Association. At the insistence of Congresswoman Pat Shroeder, a series of official investigations was conducted, but all were widely criticized official cover-ups by senior Navy and civilian officials. In total, 119 Navy and 21 Marine Corps officers were referred by Pentagon investigators for possible disciplinary actions. They were cited for incidents of assault, indecent exposure, conduct unbecoming an officer, or failure to act in a proper leadership capacity while at Tailhook '91. Furthermore, fifty-one individuals were found to have made false statements during the investigation but none of these 140 cases ever went to trial. Approximately half were dropped for lack of evidence. With regard to the most celebrated case in the Tailhook scandal, the Marine Corps dropped all charges against the Marine captain charged with sexual molestation by Lieutenant Paula Coughlin. The Corps decided there was not enough evidence to proceed with a court-martial against the captain and that Coughlin had misidentified her assailant. The issues were never quite settled, and as late as 2002, the chairman of the Tailhook investigation spoke of the *alleged misconduct* [emphasis mine] that occurred.

Sexual Harassment

Charges of sexual harassment and misconduct point to the highest offices of government. During the Clinton administration, the President was charged by Paula Jones with sexual harassment, and his liaison with White House intern Monica Lewinsky brought more sexual scandal and a move toward impeachment. In 1995, after multiple charges of sexual harassment and a Congressional investigation, Senator Robert Packwood of Oregon resigned from office. Sexual harassment persists for the most part unchecked in government, industry and other institutions because the perpetrators, in many cases, are the employers themselves who can intimidate or threaten their female employees with termination. Courts have considered numerous cases in which the plaintiff was intimidated, harassed, or physically molested. In circumstances such as the stalking case of Kerry Ellison, an employee of the Federal Internal Revenue Service (Ellison v Brady, 1991), the Ninth Circuit Court ruled that the defendant created a hostile work environment. More recent government reports suggest that at least 42 percent of all female employees experience some type of harassment in the workplace.

Disclosure of sexual harassment, sexual misconduct, even rape by male public officials in high places increases and continues to make the headlines. The frequency and regularity of these misdemeanors and crimes against women serves to illustrate how the more things change the more they stay the same.

Domestic Violence

According to Bureau of Justice Statistics, in 1993, approximately 575,000 men were arrested for committing violence against women, and during the following year, 21 percent of all violent crimes against women were committed by someone they knew personally. In 1994, domestic violence and wife battering topics became a media frenzy in response to the murder of Nicole Brown Simpson, the ex-wife of athlete and celebrity O.J. Simpson. In the ensuing trial, court spectators and television viewers heard the voice of the victim, Nicole Brown Simpson, making 9-1-1 calls as her former husband, O.J. Simpson was forcibly gaining entry to her home. Family members testified on past physical abuse and Nicole Simpson had left photos of herself showing proof of one severe beating. O.J. Simpson was acquitted after the jury deliberated less than four hours.

Women's Bodies, Women's Rights

When considering health concerns, women now have access to birth control and can obtain an abortion. They are no longer forced to accept a radical mastectomy as the only means to fight breast cancer. Although women chiefly remain the responsible partner for birth control and for protection from sexually transmitted diseases, they receive inferior and discriminatory treatment from health insurance companies. Some companies will fund Viagra, for example, but not birth control and defend this policy under the criteria of approving only drugs which sustain life! In addition, drug protocols in pharmaceutical research are based on male, **not** female, physiology.

The tenuous predicament of women owning their reproductive rights has had its ups and downs. President Reagan altered abortion policy in 1984, stating that family planning organizations in foreign countries could not receive aid from the United States if they performed abortions or dispensed abortion information. The Regan Administration issued a gag rule, which further limited abortions by prohibiting doctors and health counselors in medical facilities from receiving Federal funding for giving abortion information or dispensing abortion referrals for patients. In 1986, Randall Terry put together an organization known as Operation Rescue, for the purpose of blockading clinics where abortions were performed. In 1989, in the Supreme Court Case *Webster v Reproductive Health Services*, the judges ruled that states could regulate access to abortion. In 1991, the Supreme Court ruling upheld the *Roe v Wade* decision but maintained the restriction on abortion cases, spelled out by the Reagan Gag Rule.

When President Bill Clinton took office in 1993, he rescinded Reagan's gag rule on family planning clinics, and he appointed Ruth

Bader Ginsburg a judge to the U. S. Supreme Court. She openly supported a women's right to have an abortion. President Clinton also lifted the restriction on importing RU-486, an abortifacient pill, into the United States. In 1993, the House of Representatives, by a vote of 255 to 178, extended the Hyde Amendment and reinforced the restriction that government funding would not be available for poor women to obtain abortions. But in 1994, the Supreme Court rendered a decision favorable to abortion clinics. In the majority decision, the justices stated that abortion clinics could take violent antiabortion groups to court and sue them for damages. It also ruled that anti-abortion protesters could not restrict access to family planning or abortion clinics.

Citizen action became more polarized on the abortion issue when, in 1993, Dr. David Gunn, a physician in Pensacola, Florida, who performed legal abortions was murdered during a protest billed as a Pro-Life demonstration. Another doctor was shot, but not fatally, outside a clinic in Wichita, Kansas. In 1994, again in Pensacola, Drs. John Britton and James H. Barrett were murdered while entering an abortion clinic.

Discrimination and Equal Rights

The struggle for gay rights continues. State laws ban same-sex marriages and political conservatives and right wing groups fight to defeat legislation for Gay Civil Rights. Furthermore, the extent to which the opposition would go was clear in 1980, when California legislator John Briggs sponsored a ballot initiative which would have forbid homosexuals from working in any public school system in the state. It took the concerted effort of the gay community to defeat the proposition. A campaign in Colorado which presented an initiative for gay rights was soundly defeated. For gays in modern America, coming out involves serious risk taking. It often results in the alienation of families, expulsion from the military, loss of one's job, social ostracism or even worse, physical violence.

Individuals feel fragmented in terms of isolation and alienation in an American society characterized more and more by cultural diversity. It has become more difficult to find one's place, identity and sense of belonging. Concepts of liberation change from one group to another. Each has had a different experience and therefore frames a different discourse. This has been especially critical for *Chicana* lesbians who are actively involved in the Latina feminist struggle. Latina feminist lesbian activist Gloria Anzaldua, in *Borderlands/La Frontera: The New Mestiza,* expressed the anguish of the *Chicana* lesbian's nebulous and ambivalent status. While trying to negotiate their space in an alien society, they are also aware of the common bond and universal place they share with all women.

> As a *mestiza*, I have no country, my homeland cast me out; yet all countries are mine, because I am every woman's sister or potential lover. As a lesbian, I have no race, my own people disclaim me: but I am all races because there is the queer of me in all races.

Carla Trujillo, Emma Perez and other lesbians in the Latina community have articulated their group's perspective. Obviously, they do not see the women's movement as a plea to get men to do the housework. Their concept of liberation comes from a different experience and has a different context. They are more concerned with the repressive atmosphere within their community which tries to foist a heterosexual lifestyle on everyone, what Carla Trujillo typifies as "the controlling forces of compulsory heterosexuality." In their context, Latina lesbians have created a different women's movement in which they seek a voice, a safe haven in their community, and their right to a place in the profession of their choosing. One such visionary scholar, Yolanda Chavez Leyva, has established the first Latina lesbian archival holdings at the University of Arizona.

Elizabeth Cady Stanton, Susan B. Anthony, Ernestine Rose and others had worked for married women's rights to property, and child custody in the case of divorce. In the past, abused women seldom had legal or financial means to seek a divorce. If they did, they lost custody or the right to see their children. Things have not changed appreciably. Presently men who seek child custody win an average of seventy percent [emphasis mine] of the cases.

The Civil Rights Act mandates that athletic scholarships and programs for males and females are to be distributed equitably, yet girl's and women's sports are ranked second-class and are still severely underfunded.

It was not until 1993, when Connie Chung joined Dan Rather on the CBS Evening News that an Asian-American woman became a top television news anchor on a major network. In 1971, Connie Chung had been hired by CBS to cover the news on Capitol Hill during the McGovern campaign and then the Watergate investigation. It had taken more than twenty years for her to move up, but she did not stay in the top anchor post very long. She was dismissed from her post on CBS after a controversial interview with the mother of former Congressman Newt Gingrich. After her dismissal, Connie Chung reflected on the inequities in hiring female television news reporters stating, "I'll know women have succeeded in TV news when there's a woman on the air who looks like David Brinkley."

Clio's Corner - How Does Feminism Fit into a Postmodernist Society?

In the Third Wave, the most recent phase of the Women's Movement, feminists have struggled to define their goals within a more diverse culture. While the younger generation of women have benefited from the gains of the movement, they have often negated feminism. Finding their own way, they express womanhood within the discourse of a postmodernist counterculture.

The postmodernist world, defined largely by French philosopher and literary theorist Jean-Francois Lyotard in *The Postmodernist Condition: A Report on Knowledge,* disputes broad claims and rejects grand theories about society, historical progress, the knowability of everything through science, the possibility of absolute freedom and the universality of the human condition. Lyotard's postmodernism interprets individuals living in a society much more acutely aware of differences, of injustices and the incompatibility of each one's own beliefs and desires. It is a world made up of myriad communities, of multicultural diversity.

These attributes of postmodernism are important in understanding the current trends in the feminist movement. Looking at the present milieu, postmodernists such as Lyotard observe that order and the rigid structures of the past have been replaced with disorder, skepticism and manipulation. In comparison to the past, there is a sense of disarray with what had been the socially prescribed gender roles—what constituted masculine and feminine dress and behavior, for example—have been challenged or altered. Entertainers such as Lady Gaga define feminism in their own terms. What had been previously regarded as dysfunctional and counterculture, such as cross-dressing or transvestism is embraced as part of the new American culture. As in the past, so in the postmodern world, fashion and art are indicators of change.

Postmodernist symbols are irreverent and everywhere, displaying obsession with, for example, violence and vampires, gothic styles and discordant music. Young people, inspired by rock stars, fashionistas or film celebrities, have adopted this counterculture wholeheartedly with tattooing, body piercing, shaved heads, wearing animal print motifs and ethnic styles, dyeing their hair unnatural colors and styling it into grotesque shapes and textures. One of the most successful celebrities purveying postmodernist hype is Louise Veronica Ciccone, better known as Madonna. Over the course of several decades, this superstar has recreated herself for each new generation. In the postmodernist mode, she defies convention and tradition. In Madonna videos, for example, anything goes—men wear bras, virgins are whores and sluts are virgins. She has deconstructed the female image right down to her stage name, Madonna, robbing it of its sacred meaning.

What does the present Feminist Movement, contained within a postmodernist structure, suggest now for the Movement's third wave? According to Jennifer Baumgardner and Amy Richards in, *Manifesta, young women, feminism and the future,* [sic], "Although the present generation has benefited from the First and Second Wave of Feminism, they have not identified with feminism because they lack their own declaration or mission statement, a *Manifesta.*" They propose the following thirteen points as objectives for the Third Wave of the Women's Movement.

1. To promote a voting block of women in the age range from 18-40 years.

2. To support a woman's right to have or not to have a child.

3. To fight for reproductive rights, including the right to birth control, the rights of poor and lesbian women to have children and for the rights of gay couples to adopt.

4. To end the double standard in sex and sexual health care.

5. To educate and pass on the legacy of women's history and women's culture in school curricula.

6. To defend the presence and power of lesbian and bisexual women, to promote their place and history in the women's movement

7. To practice autokeonomy, i.e. activism and self in community as a link, not a choice.

8. To advocate women's equal access to health care.

9. To support women's opportunities to serve in the military and enjoy equal benefits of income, promotion and pension.

10. To liberate women from sexual harassment and violence.

11. To bring about a more responsive workplace to address the employees' needs.

12. To recognize and respect the differing values and goals among feminists.

13. To work for the passage of the Equal Rights Amendment.

Women and Education

In the workplace, the glass ceiling defines an invisible barrier which still exists and prevents women from moving up the corporate ladder; seemingly, they can peer through the glass and see the top but cannot reach it. While this metaphor does describe present circumstance for many women, it is important for us to get some perspective on the problem by calling to mind the condition of women from our earlier history. Before the eighteenth century, we find very few women who could read, write or, as much as sign their name. From our study of women's history we have seen that one of the longest struggles for American women has been to get an education. We have highlighted certain brave and notable women who broke ground in the fields of medicine, law, and education. Today we mark our progress more substantially not by citing a few individuals but by looking at our entire gender.

Women now surpass men in completing secondary and post-secondary education; thus, the gender gap is almost completely reversed. In 2006, 10.3 percent of males and 8.3 percent of females dropped out of high school. In 2005/2006, women earned 62 percent of Associate's degrees, 58 percent of Bachelor's degrees, 60.0 percent of Master's degrees, and 48.9 percent of Doctorates. Projections for 2016-2017, women are expected to earn 64.2 percent of Associate's degrees, 59.9 percent of Bachelor's degrees, 62.9 percent of Master's degrees, and 55.5 percent of Doctorates. More women with graduate degrees will translate into more women in the professions of education, law and medicine.

Looking at changes as early as 1990, we see that the educational attainment of all races increased with the gap between African Americans and non-Hispanic whites *decreasing*. While overall success in completing a college degree is improving for women of all groups some severe disparities remain especially among those with a Bachelor's degree or higher. Asian Americans have the highest educational attainment of any race, followed by whites who had a higher percentage of high school graduates but a lower percentage of college graduates. Persons identifying as Hispanic *or Latino*, without regard to race, had the lowest educational attainment[6]. The gap was the largest between foreign-born Asian Americans, over half (50.1 percent) of whom had a Bachelor's degree or higher and foreign-born Hispanics, 9.8 percent of whom had a four-year college degree. Hispanics and *Latinos* also trailed far behind in terms of graduating from high school; it was the only major group for which high school graduates constituted less than eighty percent of the population. This disparity can be partially explained by immigration i.e. the influx of uneducated foreign-born Hispanic Americans who have not been offered the chance to complete secondary education in their home country and/or who have not completed secondary education in the United States. In recent studies, nearly half (49.8 percent) of Asian Americans, nearly a third (30 percent) of non-Hispanic Whites, 17.3 percent of non-Hispanic Blacks, and just over a tenth (11.4 percent) of Hispanics or *Latinos* achieved a four-year college degree. The same differences *decrease* significantly at the high school level with 89.4 percent of non-Hispanic whites, 87.6 percent of Asian Americans, 80.0 percent of African Americans, and only 57 percent of Hispanics or *Latinos* having graduated from high school.

Mothers of Invention: Martha Stewart, Reinventing Domesticity

Martha Stewart a multimedia personality who promotes domesticity and sells products for the American Home is indeed a household name herself. The founder of Martha Stewart Living Omnimedia, she is a successful American businesswoman, media personality, author, and magazine publisher. Taking on a number of business ventures, including publishing, broadcasting, and merchandising her activities range from a syndicated talk show, *Martha*, which is broadcast throughout the world, numerous bestselling books, and publications such as *Martha Stewart Living magazine*.

She was raised in a middle class Polish-American family one of five children in Nutley, New Jersey. Her mother, Martha Ruszkowski Kostyra taught her to cook and bake and her father Edward Kostyra passed on his zest for gardening to her. She majored in Art History at Barnard College and as a student took up modeling. In 1961 she married Andrew Stewart, a law student at Yale. Martha entered the business world as a stockbroker on Wall Street but found her niche in 1973 when she began restoring her 1805 farmhouse. Three years later she started a catering business in her basement with a friend and the project took off.

Her first book, *Entertaining* made the New York Times best seller list and Entertaining became the first best selling cookbook since Julia Child and Simone Beck's *Mastering the Art of French Cooking*, which had been released some twenty years earlier. Although Entertaining was actually ghost written by Elizabeth Hawes, Martha Stewart's success with the book led to the publication of many more including: *Martha Stewart's Quick Cook* (1983), *Martha Stewart's Hors D'oeuvres* (1984), *Martha Stewart's Pies &Tarts* (1985), *Weddings* (1987), *The Wedding Planner* (1988), *Martha Stewart's Quick Cook Menus* (1988), and *Martha Stewart's Christmas* (1989). These books and her television holiday specials made Martha Stewart a trademark. On the cover of the May 1995 issue, New York Magazine headlined her "the definitive American woman of our time".

In 2004, news of Martha Stewart's insider trading of ImClone stock shocked the American public. She was convicted and served five months in a West Virginia federal prison camp. Although media hype widely speculated that the scandal would topple her empire, Stewart began a comeback in 2005, and her company returned to profitability the following year. Since then she has continued to branch out into new business and media ventures. In 2006 Martha Stewart's daily talk show was nominated in six categories for the 33rd Daytime Emmy Awards including Best Host and Best Show.

---

6. Group noted as *Latino* would include both males and females (*Latinas*) and we cite more specific figures for *Latinas* in higher education in this chapter, see the table for *Percent of Women with a college education by ethnic group*.

Conclusion

What progress have women made toward equal rights? The Feminist Movement is now in its third phase and obviously, there is still much to be done to improve the lot of all women. In assessing the state of the women's movement, historical comparisons are useful and hold out reasons to be optimistic. Jennifer Baumgardner and Amy Richards describe what it was like for females in American society just forty years ago.

> In high school, the principal is a man. Girls have physical education class and play half-court basketball, but not soccer, track, or cross country; nor do they have any varsity sport teams. The only prestigious physical activity for girls is cheerleading. Most girls don't take calculus or physics; they plan dances and decorate the gym. Even when girls get better grades than their male counterparts, they are half as likely to qualify for a National Merit Scholarship because many of the test questions favor boys.

Forty years ago, the greatest source of scholarship money was the Miss America Pageant. Lesbians were seldom out except at certain bars, usually those operated by organized crime. Newspaper classified ads listed job openings as "Help Wanted Male" and "Help Wanted Female." If women went to college, they pursued higher education to get an "MRS. not a B.S." and the standard joke about a woman's place in society was "barefoot, pregnant and on the edge of town."

Since the early colonial period, women were assigned a gendered space—the confines of the home and its environs. A woman's body occupied a restricted, socially defined compass. How far have women come in the last 400 years? Has the feminist movement brought progress? Women can vote, go to court, obtain a divorce, seek custody of their children, use their own name, join the military, sit on a jury, and appeal inequities in the workplace.

Demographic changes in the American population will affect social change. The Latino population in particular is growing rapidly in the United States, from 25 million in the 1990 Federal Census to 32.8 million in the year 2000. People of Mexican origin comprise just over 66 percent of the Latino population in the country. But twenty-three percent of Mexican-American families live in poverty, and the percentage for Latinas caps higher at twenty-eight percent. Professor Vicki Ruiz shows that as of 1993, in the United States, 51 percent of the Latinas who worked for wages were grossly underpaid. For every dollar earned by a Euro-American man, a female Mexican laborer in Texas earned 46 cents; in New Mexico, 55 cents.

While it is essential for all women to improve their economic status, it is especially important for Latinas to do so. After completing one year of high school, 70 percent of Latinas drop out. Lacking a basic high school diploma, at age thirty-five these women find themselves among the least employed and lowest paid people in the American labor force. It is not surprising then that forty percent are unemployed. Consequently, Latinas are relegated to lower service jobs and paid menial wages.

Poverty among all women is growing at an alarming rate. The feminization of poverty stretches across ethnic and racial boundaries. Figures reported by the U.S. Bureau of Labor Statistics continue to show that in the African-American community, sixty-seven percent of the women work outside the home for wages but their median income does not equal half of the income of white families. Poverty increases in old age. Based upon Bureau of Statistics figures, demographers predict that *one out of every four women* in America can anticipate poverty in their declining years. Minority women comprise a significant portion of poor elderly females. (In the Latino community, twenty-five percent of the senior citizens live in poverty.)

Considering the scale of poverty among women, education remains the critical difference between the haves and the have-nots. Women from ethnic minority groups lack the education and training necessary to improve their lives and to ensure comfort and security in their old age.

Political activism is crucial for women to achieve full benefit of their civil rights. Feminists have campaigned tirelessly for a better standard of living for women and children. This social malaise continues to affect women and children most severely. Domestic violence kills women and children. There are eleven million children in the United States without health care. Statistics continue to emphasize the number of reported rapes rather than the preponderance of male rapists. Sexual harassment in the workplace thrives. All things being the same in a job position, for every dollar a man earns, a woman earns seventy cents.

Since the defeat of the ERA in 1982, an Equal Rights Amendment has been proposed at every convening Congress in the hopes that someday women (the majority of Americans) will be guaranteed their rights by the Constitution.

Each decade, dominating conservatives diminish the *Roe v Wade* decision and erode women's reproductive rights with more Federal laws. The statistics on rape, domestic violence, employment, health care and poverty remind us that there has not been much progress in ensuring a safe and equitable place for women in America. Women face significant challenges and longstanding problems. There is much to be done in order to make American society a place where everyone matters. But, as Anthropologist Margaret Mead once said, "Never doubt that a small group of thoughtful committed citizens can change the world; indeed, it's the only thing that ever has."

APPENDIXES

Appendix A. The Constitution of the United States of America

(The Constitution of the United States and its twenty-seven amendments, our public documents, are housed in the National Archives and Records Administration in Washington, D.C.)

We the People of the United States, in Order to form a more perfect Union, establish Justice, insure domestic Tranquility, provide for the common defense, promote the general Welfare, and secure the Blessings of Liberty to ourselves and our Posterity, do ordain and establish this Constitution for the United States of America.

Article. I.

Section 1.
All legislative Powers herein granted shall be vested in a Congress of the United States, which shall consist of a Senate and House of Representatives.

Section. 2.
Clause 1: The House of Representatives shall be composed of Members chosen every second Year by the People of the several States, and the Electors in each State shall have the Qualifications requisite for Electors of the most numerous Branch of the State Legislature.
Clause 2: No Person shall be a Representative who shall not have attained to the Age of twenty five Years, and been seven Years a Citizen of the United States, and who shall not, when elected, be an Inhabitant of that State in which he shall be chosen.
Clause 3: Representatives and direct Taxes shall be apportioned among the several States which may be included within this Union, according to their respective Numbers, which shall be determined by adding to the whole Number of free Persons, including those bound to Service for a Term of Years, and excluding Indians not taxed, three fifths of all other Persons. The actual Enumeration shall be made within three Years after the first Meeting of the Congress of the United States, and within every subsequent Term of ten Years, in such Manner as they shall by Law direct. The Number of Representatives shall not exceed one for every thirty Thousand, but each State shall have at Least one Representative; and until such enumeration shall be made, the State of New Hampshire shall be entitled to choose three, Massachusetts eight, Rhode-Island and Providence Plantations one, Connecticut five, New-York six, New Jersey four, Pennsylvania eight, Delaware one, Maryland six, Virginia ten, North Carolina five, South Carolina five, and Georgia three.
Clause 4: When vacancies happen in the Representation from any State, the Executive Authority thereof shall issue Writs of Election to fill such Vacancies.
Clause 5: The House of Representatives shall choose their Speaker and other Officers; and shall have the sole Power of Impeachment.

Section. 3.
Clause 1: The Senate of the United States shall be composed of two Senators from each State, chosen by the Legislature thereof, for six Years; and each Senator shall have one Vote.
Clause 2: Immediately after they shall be assembled in Consequence of the first Election, they shall be divided as equally as may be into three Classes. The Seats of the Senators of the first Class shall be vacated at the Expiration of the second Year, of the second Class at the Expiration of the fourth Year, and of the third Class at the Expiration of the sixth Year, so that one third may be chosen every second Year; and if Vacancies happen by Resignation, or otherwise, during the Recess of the Legislature of any State, the Executive thereof may make temporary Appointments until the next Meeting of the Legislature, which shall then fill such Vacancies.

Clause 3: No Person shall be a Senator who shall not have attained to the Age of thirty Years, and been nine Years a Citizen of the United States, and who shall not, when elected, be an Inhabitant of that State for which he shall be chosen.
Clause 4: The Vice President of the United States shall be President of the Senate, but shall have no Vote, unless they be equally divided.
Clause 5: The Senate shall choose their other Officers, and also a President pro tempore, in the Absence of the Vice President, or when he shall exercise the Office of President of the United States.
Clause 6: The Senate shall have the sole Power to try all Impeachments. When sitting for that Purpose, they shall be on Oath or Affirmation. When the President of the United States is tried, the Chief Justice shall preside: And no Person shall be convicted without the Concurrence of two thirds of the Members present.
Clause 7: Judgment in Cases of Impeachment shall not extend further than to removal from Office, and disqualification to hold and enjoy any Office of honor, Trust or Profit under the United States: but the Party convicted shall nevertheless be liable and subject to Indictment, Trial, Judgment and Punishment, according to Law.

Section. 4.
Clause 1: The Times, Places and Manner of holding Elections for Senators and Representatives, shall be prescribed in each State by the Legislature thereof; but the Congress may at any time by Law make or alter such Regulations, except as to the Places of choosing Senators.
Clause 2: The Congress shall assemble at least once in every Year, and such Meeting shall be on the first Monday in December, unless they shall by law appoint a different Day.

Section. 5.
Clause 1: Each House shall be the Judge of the Elections, Returns and Qualifications of its own Members, and a Majority of each shall constitute a Quorum to do Business; but a smaller Number may adjourn from day to day, and may be authorized to compel the Attendance of absent Members, in such Manner, and under such Penalties as each House may provide.
Clause 2: Each House may determine the Rules of its Proceedings, punish its Members for disorderly Behavior, and, with the Concurrence of two thirds, expel a Member.
Clause 3: Each House shall keep a Journal of its Proceedings, and from time to time publish the same, excepting such Parts as may in their judgment require secrecy; and the Yeas and Nays of the Members of either House on any question shall, at the Desire of one fifth of those Present, be entered on the Journal.
Clause 4: Neither House, during the Session of Congress, shall, without the Consent of the other, adjourn for more than three days, nor to any other Place than that in which the two Houses shall be sitting.

Section. 6.
Clause 1: The Senators and Representatives shall receive a Compensation for their Services, to be ascertained by Law, and paid out of the Treasury of the United States. They shall in all Cases, except Treason, Felony and Breach of the Peace, be privileged from Arrest during their Attendance at the Session of their respective Houses, and in going to and returning from the same; and for any Speech or Debate in either House, they shall not be questioned in any other Place.
Clause 2: No Senator or Representative shall, during the Time for which he was elected, be appointed to any civil Office under the Authority of the United States, which shall have been created, or the Emoluments whereof shall have been increased during such time; and no Person holding any Office under the United States, shall be a Member of either House during his Continuance in Office.

Section. 7.
Clause 1: All Bills for raising Revenue shall originate in the House of Representatives; but the Senate may propose or concur with Amendments as on other Bills.
Clause 2: Every Bill which shall have passed the House of Representatives and the Senate, shall, before it become a Law, be presented to the President of the United States; If he approve he shall sign it, but if not he shall return it, with his Objections to that House in which it shall have originated, who shall enter the Objections at large on their Journal, and proceed to reconsider it. If after such Reconsideration two thirds of that House shall agree to pass the Bill, it shall be sent, together with the Objections, to the other House, by which it shall likewise be reconsidered, and if approved by two thirds of that House, it shall become a Law. But in all such Cases the Votes of both Houses shall be determined by yeas and Nays, and the Names of the Persons voting for and against the Bill shall be entered on the Journal of each House respectively. If any Bill shall not be returned by the President within ten Days (Sundays excepted) after it shall have been presented to him, the same shall be a Law, in like Manner as if he had signed it, unless the Congress by their Adjournment prevent its Return, in which Case it shall not be a Law.
Clause 3: Every Order, Resolution, or Vote to which the Concurrence of the Senate and House of Representatives may be necessary (except on a question of Adjournment) shall be presented to the President of the United States; and before the Same shall take Effect, shall be approved by him, or being disapproved by him, shall be re-passed by two thirds of the Senate and House of Representatives, according to the Rules and Limitations prescribed in the Case of a Bill.

Section. 8.
Clause 1: The Congress shall have Power To lay and collect Taxes, Duties, Imposts and Excises, to pay the Debts and provide for the common Defense and general Welfare of the United States; but all Duties, Imposts and Excises shall be uniform throughout the United States;
Clause 2: To borrow Money on the credit of the United States;
Clause 3: To regulate Commerce with foreign Nations, and among the several States, and with the Indian Tribes;
Clause 4: To establish an uniform Rule of Naturalization, and uniform laws on the subject of Bankruptcies throughout the United States;
Clause 5: To coin Money, regulate the Value thereof, and of foreign Coin, and fix the Standard of Weights and Measures;
Clause 6: To provide for the Punishment of counterfeiting the Securities and current Coin of the United States;
Clause 7: To establish Post Offices and post Roads;
Clause 8: To promote the Progress of Science and useful Arts, by securing for limited Times to Authors and Inventors the exclusive Right to their respective Writings and Discoveries;
Clause 9: To constitute Tribunals inferior to the Supreme Court;
Clause 10: To define and punish Piracies and Felonies committed on the high Seas, and Offences against the Law of Nations;
Clause 11: To declare War, grant Letters of Marque and Reprisal, and make Rules concerning Captures on Land and Water;
Clause 12: To raise and support Armies, but no Appropriation of Money to that Use shall be for a longer Term than two Years;
Clause 13: To provide and maintain a Navy;
Clause 14: To make Rules for the Government and Regulation of the land and naval Forces;
Clause 15: To provide for calling forth the Militia to execute the Laws of the Union, suppress Insurrections and repel Invasions;
Clause 16: To provide for organizing, arming, and disciplining, the Militia, and for governing such Part of them as may be employed in the Service of the United States, reserving to the States respec-

tively, the Appointment of the Officers, and the Authority of training the Militia according to the discipline prescribed by Congress;
Clause 17: To exercise exclusive Legislation in all Cases whatsoever, over such District (not exceeding ten Miles square) as may, by session of particular States, and the Acceptance of Congress, become the Seat of the Government of the United States, and to exercise like Authority over all Places purchased by the Consent of the Legislature of the State in which the Same shall be, for the Erection of Forts, Magazines, Arsenals, dock-Yards, and other needful Buildings;--And
Clause 18: To make all Laws which shall be necessary and proper for carrying into Execution the foregoing Powers, and all other Powers vested by this Constitution in the Government of the United States, or in any Department or Officer thereof.

Section. 9.
Clause 1: The Migration or Importation of such Persons as any of the States now existing shall think proper to admit, shall not be prohibited by the Congress prior to the Year one thousand eight hundred and eight, but a Tax or duty may be imposed on such Importation, not exceeding ten dollars for each Person.
Clause 2: The Privilege of the Writ of Habeas Corpus shall not be suspended, unless when in Cases of Rebellion or Invasion the public Safety may require it.
Clause 3: No Bill of Attainder or ex post facto Law shall be passed.
Clause 4: No Capitation, or other direct, Tax shall be laid, unless in Proportion to the Census or Enumeration herein before directed to be taken.
Clause 5: No Tax or Duty shall be laid on Articles exported from any State.
Clause 6: No Preference shall be given by any Regulation of Commerce or Revenue to the Ports of one State over those of another: nor shall Vessels bound to, or from, one State, be obliged to enter, clear, or pay Duties in another.
Clause 7: No Money shall be drawn from the Treasury, but in Consequence of Appropriations made by Law; and a regular Statement and Account of the Receipts and Expenditures of all public Money shall be published from time to time.
Clause 8: No Title of Nobility shall be granted by the United States: And no Person holding any Office of Profit or Trust under them, shall, without the Consent of the Congress, accept of any present, Emolument, Office, or Title, of any kind whatever, from any King, Prince, or foreign State.

Section. 10.
Clause 1: No State shall enter into any Treaty, Alliance, or Confederation; grant Letters of Marque and Reprisal; coin Money; emit Bills of Credit; make any Thing but gold and silver Coin a Tender in Payment of Debts; pass any Bill of Attainder, ex post facto Law, or Law impairing the Obligation of Contracts, or grant any Title of Nobility.
Clause 2: No State shall, without the Consent of the Congress, lay any Imposts or Duties on Imports or Exports, except what may be absolutely necessary for executing it's inspection Laws: and the net Produce of all Duties and Imposts, laid by any State on Imports or Exports, shall be for the Use of the Treasury of the United States; and all such Laws shall be subject to the revision and control of the Congress.
Clause 3: No State shall, without the Consent of Congress, lay any Duty of Tonnage, keep Troops, or Ships of War in time of Peace, enter into any Agreement or Compact with another State, or with a foreign Power, or engage in War, unless actually invaded, or in such imminent Danger as will not admit of delay.

Article. II.

Section. 1.

Clause 1: The executive Power shall be vested in a President of the United States of America. He shall hold his Office during the Term of four Years, and, together with the Vice President, chosen for the same Term, be elected, as follows

Clause 2: Each State shall appoint, in such Manner as the Legislature thereof may direct, a Number of Electors, equal to the whole Number of Senators and Representatives to which the State may be entitled in the Congress: but no Senator or Representative, or Person holding an Office of Trust or Profit under the United States, shall be appointed an Elector.

Clause 3: The Electors shall meet in their respective States, and vote by Ballot for two Persons, of whom one at least shall not be an Inhabitant of the same State with themselves. And they shall make a List of all the Persons voted for, and of the Number of Votes for each; which List they shall sign and certify, and transmit sealed to the Seat of the Government of the United States, directed to the President of the Senate. The President of the Senate shall, in the Presence of the Senate and House of Representatives, open all the Certificates, and the Votes shall then be counted. The Person having the greatest Number of Votes shall be the President, if such Number be a Majority of the whole Number of Electors appointed; and if there be more than one who have such Majority, and have an equal Number of Votes, then the House of Representatives shall immediately choose by Ballot one of them for President; and if no Person have a Majority, then from the five highest on the List the said House shall in like Manner choose the President. But in choosing the President, the Votes shall be taken by States, the Representation from each State having one Vote; a quorum for this Purpose shall consist of a Member or Members from two thirds of the States, and a Majority of all the States shall be necessary to a Choice. In every Case, after the Choice of the President, the Person having the greatest Number of Votes of the Electors shall be the Vice President. But if there should remain two or more who have equal Votes, the Senate shall choose from them by Ballot the Vice President.

Clause 4: The Congress may determine the Time of choosing the Electors, and the Day on which they shall give their Votes; which Day shall be the same throughout the United States.

Clause 5: No Person except a natural born Citizen, or a Citizen of the United States, at the time of the Adoption of this Constitution, shall be eligible to the Office of President; neither shall any Person be eligible to that Office who shall not have attained to the Age of thirty five Years, and been fourteen Years a Resident within the United States.

Clause 6: In Case of the Removal of the President from Office, or of his Death, Resignation, or Inability to discharge the Powers and Duties of the said Office, *(See Note 9)* the Same shall devolve on the Vice President, and the Congress may by Law provide for the Case of Removal, Death, Resignation or Inability, both of the President and Vice President, declaring what Officer shall then act as President, and such Officer shall act accordingly, until the Disability be removed, or a President shall be elected.

Clause 7: The President shall, at stated Times, receive for his Services, a Compensation, which shall neither be increased nor diminished during the period for which he shall have been elected, and he shall not receive within that Period any other Emolument from the United States, or any of them.

Clause 8: Before he enter on the Execution of his Office, he shall take the following Oath or Affirmation: "I do solemnly swear (or affirm) that I will faithfully execute the Office of President of the United States, and will to the best of my Ability, preserve, protect and defend the Constitution of the United States."

Section. 2.

Clause 1: The President shall be Commander in Chief of the Army and Navy of the United States, and of the Militia of the several States, when called into the actual Service of the United States; he may require the Opinion, in writing, of the principal Officer in each of the executive Departments, upon

any Subject relating to the Duties of their respective Offices, and he shall have Power to grant Reprieves and Pardons for Offenses against the United States, except in Cases of Impeachment.
Clause 2: He shall have Power, by and with the Advice and Consent of the Senate, to make Treaties, provided two thirds of the Senators present concur; and he shall nominate, and by and with the Advice and Consent of the Senate, shall appoint Ambassadors, other public Ministers and Consuls, Judges of the supreme Court, and all other Officers of the United States, whose Appointments are not herein otherwise provided for, and which shall be established by Law: but the Congress may by Law vest the Appointment of such inferior Officers, as they think proper, in the President alone, in the Courts of Law, or in the Heads of Departments.
Clause 3: The President shall have Power to fill up all Vacancies that may happen during the Recess of the Senate, by granting Commissions which shall expire at the End of their next Session.

Section. 3.
He shall from time to time give to the Congress Information of the State of the Union, and recommend to their Consideration such Measures as he shall judge necessary and expedient; he may, on extraordinary Occasions, convene both Houses, or either of them, and in Case of Disagreement between them, with Respect to the Time of Adjournment, he may adjourn them to such Time as he shall think proper; he shall receive Ambassadors and other public Ministers; he shall take Care that the Laws be faithfully executed, and shall Commission all the Officers of the United States.

Section. 4.
The President, Vice President and all civil Officers of the United States, shall be removed from Office on Impeachment for, and Conviction of, Treason, Bribery, or other high Crimes and Misdemeanors.

Article. III.

Section. 1.
The judicial Power of the United States shall be vested in one Supreme Court and in such inferior Courts as the Congress may from time to time ordain and establish. The Judges, both of the supreme and inferior Courts, shall hold their Offices during good Behavior, and shall, at stated Times, receive for their Services, a Compensation, which shall not be diminished during their Continuance in Office.

Section. 2.
Clause 1: The judicial Power shall extend to all Cases, in Law and Equity, arising under this Constitution, the Laws of the United States, and Treaties made, or which shall be made, under their Authority; to all Cases affecting Ambassadors, other public Ministers and Consuls; to all Cases of admiralty and maritime Jurisdiction; to Controversies to which the United States shall be a Party; to Controversies between two or more States; between a State and Citizens of another State; between Citizens of different States, between Citizens of the same State claiming Lands under Grants of different States, and between a State, or the Citizens thereof, and foreign States, Citizens or Subjects.
Clause 2: In all Cases affecting Ambassadors, other public Ministers and Consuls, and those in which a State shall be Party, the Supreme Court shall have original Jurisdiction. In all the other Cases before mentioned, the Supreme Court shall have appellate Jurisdiction, both as to Law and Fact, with such Exceptions, and under such Regulations as the Congress shall make.
Clause 3: The Trial of all Crimes, except in Cases of Impeachment, shall be by Jury; and such Trial shall be held in the State where the said Crimes shall have been committed; but when not committed within any State, the Trial shall be at such Place or Places as the Congress may by Law have directed.

Section. 3.
Clause 1: Treason against the United States shall consist only in levying War against them, or in adhering to their Enemies, giving them Aid and Comfort. No Person shall be convicted of Treason unless on the Testimony of two Witnesses to the same overt Act, or on Confession in open Court.
Clause 2: The Congress shall have Power to declare the Punishment of Treason, but no Attainder of Treason shall work Corruption of Blood, or Forfeiture except during the Life of the Person attainted.

Article. IV.

Section. 1.
Full Faith and Credit shall be given in each State to the public Acts, Records, and judicial Proceedings of every other State. And the Congress may by general Laws prescribe the Manner in which such Acts, Records and Proceedings shall be proved, and the Effect thereof.

Section. 2.
Clause 1: The Citizens of each State shall be entitled to all Privileges and Immunities of Citizens in the several States.
Clause 2: A Person charged in any State with Treason, Felony, or other Crime, who shall flee from Justice, and be found in another State, shall on Demand of the executive Authority of the State from which he fled, be delivered up, to be removed to the State having Jurisdiction of the Crime.
Clause 3: No Person held to Service or Labor in one State, under the Laws thereof, escaping into another, shall, in Consequence of any Law or Regulation therein, be discharged from such Service or Labor, but shall be delivered up on Claim of the Party to whom such Service or Labor may be due.

Section. 3.
Clause 1: New States may be admitted by the Congress into this Union; but no new State shall be formed or erected within the Jurisdiction of any other State; nor any State be formed by the Junction of two or more States, or Parts of States, without the Consent of the Legislatures of the States concerned as well as of the Congress.
Clause 2: The Congress shall have Power to dispose of and make all needful Rules and Regulations respecting the Territory or other Property belonging to the United States; and nothing in this Constitution shall be so construed as to Prejudice any Claims of the United States, or of any particular State.

Section. 4.
The United States shall guarantee to every State in this Union a Republican Form of Government, and shall protect each of them against Invasion; and on Application of the Legislature, or of the Executive (when the Legislature cannot be convened) against domestic Violence.

Article. V.

The Congress, whenever two thirds of both Houses shall deem it necessary, shall propose Amendments to this Constitution, or, on the Application of the Legislatures of two thirds of the several States, shall call a Convention for proposing Amendments, which, in either Case, shall be valid to all Intents and Purposes, as Part of this Constitution, when ratified by the Legislatures of three fourths of the several States, or by Conventions in three fourths thereof, as the one or the other Mode of Ratification may be proposed by the Congress; Provided that no Amendment which may be made prior to the Year One thousand eight hundred and eight shall in any Manner affect the first and fourth Clauses in the Ninth Section of the first Article; and that no State, without its Consent, shall be deprived of its equal Suffrage in the Senate.

Article. VI.

Clause 1: All Debts contracted and Engagements entered into, before the Adoption of this Constitution, shall be as valid against the United States under this Constitution, as under the Confederation.
Clause 2: This Constitution, and the Laws of the United States which shall be made in Pursuance thereof; and all Treaties made, or which shall be made, under the Authority of the United States, shall be the supreme Law of the Land; and the Judges in every State shall be bound thereby, any Thing in the Constitution or Laws of any State to the Contrary notwithstanding.
Clause 3: The Senators and Representatives before mentioned, and the Members of the several State Legislatures, and all executive and judicial Officers, both of the United States and of the several States, shall be bound by Oath or Affirmation, to support this Constitution; but no religious Test shall ever be required as a Qualification to any Office or public Trust under the United States.

Article. VII.

The Ratification of the Conventions of nine States shall be sufficient for the Establishment of this Constitution between the States so ratifying the same. Done in Convention by the Unanimous Consent of the States present the Seventeenth Day of September in the Year of our Lord one thousand seven hundred and Eighty seven and of the Independence of the United States of America the Twelfth. In witness whereof We have hereunto subscribed our Names.

Geo.Washington, President and deputy from Virginia
[Signed also by the deputies of twelve States.]

Delaware
Geo. Read
Gunning Bedford Jr.
John Dickinson
Richard Bassett
Jacob Broom

North Carolina
William Blount
Rich D. Dobbs Spaight
Hugh Williamson

Georgia
William Few
Abraham Baldwin

New Hampshire
John Langdon
Nicholas Gilman

Connecticut
William Samual Johnson
Roger Sherman

New York
Alexander Hamilton

Pennsylvania
B. Franklin
Thomas Mifflin
Robert Morris
George Clymer
Thomas Fitzsimons
Jared Ingersoll
James Wilson
Governor Morris
Attest William Jackson Secretary

Maryland
James McHenry
Daniel of St. Thomas-Jenifer
Daniel Carroll

Virginia
John Blair
James Madison Jr.

North Carolina
J. Rutledge
Charles Cotesworth Pinckney
Charles Pinckney
Pierce Butler

Massachusetts
Nathaniel Gorham
Rufus King

New Jersey
William Livingston
David Brearley
William Paterson
Jonathan Dayton

Amendments to the Constitution

Amedment I. Freedom of Religion, Press, Expression

Congress shall make no law respecting an establishment of religion, or prohibiting the free exercise thereof; or abridging the freedom of speech, or of the press; or the right of the people peaceably to assemble, and to petition the Government for a redress of grievances.

Amendment II. Right to Bear Arms

A well regulated Militia, being necessary to the security of a free State the right of the people to keep and bear Arms, shall not be infringed.

Amendment III. Quartering of Soldiers

No Soldier shall, in time of peace be quartered in any house, without the consent of the Owner, nor in time of war, but in a manner to be prescribed by law.

Amendment IV. Search and Seizure

The right of the people to be secure in their persons, houses, papers, and effects, against unreasonable searches and seizures, shall not be violated, and no Warrants shall issue, but upon probable cause, supported by Oath or affirmation, and particularly describing the place to be searched, and the persons or things to be seized.

Amendment V. Trial and Punishment, Compensation for Takings

No person shall be held to answer for a capital, or otherwise infamous crime, unless on a presentment or indictment of a Grand Jury, except in cases arising in the land or naval forces, or in the Militia, when in actual service in time of War or public danger; nor shall any person be subject for the same offence to be twice put in jeopardy of life or limb; nor shall be compelled in any criminal case to be a witness against himself, nor be deprived of life, liberty, or property, without due process of law; nor shall private property be taken for public use, without just compensation.

Amendment VI. Right to Speedy Trial, Confrontation of Witnesses

In all criminal prosecutions, the accused shall enjoy the right to a speedy and public trial, by an impartial jury of the State and district wherein the crime shall have been committed, which district shall have been previously ascertained by law, and to be informed of the nature and cause of the accusation; to be confronted with the witnesses against him; to have compulsory process for obtaining witnesses in his favor, and to have the Assistance of Counsel for his defense.

Amendment VII. Trial by Jury in Civil Cases

In Suits at common law, where the value in controversy shall exceed twenty dollars, the right of trial by jury shall be preserved, and no fact tried by a jury, shall be otherwise re-examined in any Court of the United States, than according to the rules of the common law.

Amendment VIII. Cruel and Unusual Punishment

Excessive bail shall not be required, nor excessive fines imposed, nor cruel and unusual punishments inflicted.

Amendment IX. Construction of Constitution

The enumeration in the Constitution, of certain rights, shall not be construed to deny or disparage others retained by the people.

Amendment X. Powers of the States and People

The powers not delegated to the United States by the Constitution, nor prohibited by it to the States, are reserved to the States respectively, or to the people.

Amendment XI. Judicial Limits

The Judicial power of the United States shall not be construed to extend to any suit in law or equity, commenced or prosecuted against one of the United States by Citizens of another State, or by Citizens or Subjects of any Foreign State.

Amendment XII. Choosing the President, Vice President

The Electors shall meet in their respective states, and vote by ballot for President and Vice-President, one of whom, at least, shall not be an inhabitant of the same state with themselves; they shall name in their ballots the person voted for as President, and in distinct ballots the person voted for as Vice-President, and they shall make distinct lists of all persons voted for as President, and of all persons voted for as Vice-President, and of the number of votes for each, which lists they shall sign and certify, and transmit sealed to the seat of the government of the United States, directed to the President of the Senate;The President of the Senate shall, in the presence of the Senate and House of Representatives, open all the certificates and the votes shall then be counted; The person having the greatest number of votes for President, shall be the President, if such number be a majority of the whole number of Electors appointed; and if no person have such majority, then from the persons having the highest numbers not exceeding three on the list of those voted for as President, the House of Representatives shall choose immediately, by ballot, the President. But in choosing the President, the votes shall be taken by states, the representation from each state having one vote; a quorum for this purpose shall consist of a member or members from two-thirds of the States and a majority of all the states shall be necessary to a choice. And if the House of Representatives shall not choose a President whenever the right of choice shall devolve upon them, before the fourth day of March next following, then the Vice-President shall act as President, as in the case of the death or other constitutional disability of the President. The person having the greatest number of votes as Vice-President, shall be the Vice-President, if such number be a majority of the whole number of Electors appointed, and if no person have a majority, then from the two highest numbers on the list, the Senate shall choose the Vice-President; a quorum for the purpose shall consist of two-thirds of the whole number of Senators, and a majority of the whole number shall be necessary to a choice. But no person constitutionally ineligible to the office of President shall be eligible to that of Vice-President of the United States.

Amendment XIII. Slavery Abolished

Section 1. Neither slavery nor involuntary servitude, except as a punishment for crime whereof the party shall have been duly convicted, shall exist within the United States, or any place subject to their jurisdiction.

Section 2. Congress shall have power to enforce this article by appropriate legislation.

Amendment XIV. Citizenship Rights

Section 1. All persons born or naturalized in the United States, and subject to the jurisdiction thereof, are citizens of the United States and of the State wherein they reside. No State shall make or enforce any law which shall abridge the privileges or immunities of citizens of the United States; nor shall any State deprive any person of life, liberty, or property, without due process of law; nor deny to any person within its jurisdiction the equal protection of the laws.

Section 2. Representatives shall be apportioned among the several States according to their respective numbers, counting the whole number of persons in each State, excluding Indians not taxed. But when the right to vote at any election for the choice of electors for President and Vice-President of the United States, Representatives in Congress, the Executive and Judicial officers of a State, or the members of the Legislature thereof, is denied to any of the male inhabitants of such State, being twenty-one years of age, and citizens of the United States, or in any way abridged, except for participation in rebellion, or other crime, the basis of representation therein shall be reduced in the proportion which the number of such male citizens shall bear to the whole number of male citizens twenty-one years of age in such State.

Section 3. No person shall be a Senator or Representative in Congress, or elector of President and Vice-President, or hold any office, civil or military, under the United States, or under any State, who, having previously taken an oath, as a member of Congress, or as an officer of the United States, or as a member of any State legislature, or as an executive or judicial officer of any State, to support the Constitution of the United States, shall have engaged in insurrection or rebellion against the same, or given aid or comfort to the enemies thereof. But Congress may by a vote of two-thirds of each House, remove such disability.

Section 4. The validity of the public debt of the United States, authorized by law, including debts incurred for payment of pensions and bounties for services in suppressing insurrection or rebellion, shall not be questioned. But neither the United States nor any State shall assume or pay any debt or obligation incurred in aid of insurrection or rebellion against the United States, or any claim for the loss or emancipation of any slave; but all such debts, obligations and claims shall be held illegal and void.

Section 5. The Congress shall have power to enforce, by appropriate legislation, the provisions of this article.

Amendment XV. Race No Bar to Vote

Section 1. The right of citizens of the United States to vote shall not be denied or abridged by the United States or by any State on account of race, color, or previous condition of servitude.

Section 2. The Congress shall have power to enforce this article by appropriate legislation.

Amendment XVI. Status of Income Tax Clarified

The Congress shall have power to lay and collect taxes on incomes, from whatever source derived, without apportionment among the several States, and without regard to any census or enumeration.

Amendment XVII. Senators Elected by Popular Vote

The Senate of the United States shall be composed of two Senators from each State, elected by the people thereof, for six years; and each Senator shall have one vote. The electors in each State shall have the qualifications requisite for electors of the most numerous branch of the State legislatures.

When vacancies happen in the representation of any State in the Senate, the executive authority of such State shall issue writs of election to fill such vacancies: Provided, that the legislature of any State

may empower the executive thereof to make temporary appointments until the people fill the vacancies by election as the legislature may direct.
This amendment shall not be so construed as to affect the election or term of any Senator chosen before it becomes valid as part of the Constitution.

Amendment XVIII. Liquor Abolished

Section 1. After one year from the ratification of this article the manufacture, sale, or transportation of intoxicating liquors within, the importation thereof into, or the exportation thereof from the United States and all territory subject to the jurisdiction thereof for beverage purposes is hereby prohibited.
Section. 2. The Congress and the several States shall have concurrent power to enforce this article by appropriate legislation.
Section. 3. This article shall be inoperative unless it shall have been ratified as an amendment to the Constitution by the legislatures of the several States, as provided in the Constitution, within seven years from the date of the submission hereof to the States by the Congress.

Amendment XIX. Women's Suffrage

The right of citizens of the United States to vote shall not be denied or abridged by the United States or by any State on account of sex.
Congress shall have power to enforce this article by appropriate legislation.

[Proposal and Ratification of the Susan B. Anthony Amendment
The nineteenth amendment to the Constitution of the United States was proposed to the legislatures of the several States by the Sixty-sixth Congress, on the 4th of June, 1919, and was declared, in a proclamation of the Secretary of State, dated the 26th of August, 1920, to have been ratified by the legislatures of 36 of the 48 States. The dates of ratification were: Illinois, June 10, 1919 (and that State readopted its resolution of ratification June 17, 1919); Michigan, June 10, 1919; Wisconsin, June 10, 1919; Kansas, June 16, 1919; New York, June 16, 1919; Ohio, June 16, 1919; Pennsylvania, June 24, 1919; Massachusetts, June 25, 1919; Texas, June 28, 1919; Iowa, July 2, 1919; Missouri, July 3, 1919; Arkansas, July 28, 1919; Montana, August 2, 1919; Nebraska, August 2, 1919; Minnesota, September 8, 1919; New Hampshire, September 10, 1919; Utah, October 2, 1919; California, November 1, 1919; Maine, November 5, 1919; North Dakota, December 1, 1919; South Dakota, December 4, 1919; Colorado, December 15, 1919; Kentucky, January 6, 1920; Rhode Island, January 6, 1920; Oregon, January 13, 1920; Indiana, January 16, 1920; Wyoming, January 27, 1920; Nevada, February 7, 1920; New Jersey, February 9, 1920; Idaho, February 11, 1920; Arizona, February 12, 1920; New Mexico, February 21, 1920; Oklahoma, February 28, 1920; West Virginia, March 10, 1920; Washington, March 22, 1920; Tennessee, August 18, 1920.
Ratification was completed on August 18, 1920.
The amendment was subsequently ratified by Connecticut on September 14, 1920 (and that State reaffirmed on September 21, 1920); Vermont, February 8, 1921; Delaware, March 6, 1923 (after having rejected it on June 2, 1920); Maryland, March 29, 1941 (after having rejected it on February 24, 1920, ratification certified on February 25, 1958); Virginia, February 21, 1952 (after having rejected it on February 12, 1920); Alabama, September 8, 1953 (after having rejected it on September 22, 1919); Florida, May 13, 1969; South Carolina, July 1, 1969 (after having rejected it on January 28, 1920, ratification certified on August 22, 1973); Georgia, February 20, 1970 (after having rejected it on July 24, 1919); Louisiana, June 11, 1970 (after having rejected it on July 1, 1920); North Carolina, May 6, 1971; Mississippi, March 22, 1984 (after having rejected it on March 29, 1920).]

Amendment XX. Presidential, Congressional Terms

Section 1. The terms of the President and Vice President shall end at noon on the 20th day of January, and the terms of Senators and Representatives at noon on the 3d day of January, of the years in which such terms would have ended if this article had not been ratified; and the terms of their successors shall then begin.
Section. 2. The Congress shall assemble at least once in every year, and such meeting shall begin at noon on the 3d day of January, unless they shall by law appoint a different day.
Section. 3. If, at the time fixed for the beginning of the term of the President, the President elect shall have died, the Vice President elect shall become President. If a President shall not have been chosen before the time fixed for the beginning of his term, or if the President elect shall have failed to qualify, then the Vice President elect shall act as President until a President shall have qualified; and the Congress may by law provide for the case wherein neither a President elect nor a Vice President elect shall have qualified, declaring who shall then act as President, or the manner in which one who is to act shall be selected, and such person shall act accordingly until a President or Vice President shall have qualified.
Section. 4. The Congress may by law provide for the case of the death of any of the persons from whom the House of Representatives may choose a President whenever the right of choice shall have devolved upon them, and for the case of the death of any of the persons from whom the Senate may choose a Vice President whenever the right of choice shall have devolved upon them.
Section. 5. Sections 1 and 2 shall take effect on the 15th day of October following the ratification of this article.
Section. 6. This article shall be inoperative unless it shall have been ratified as an amendment to the Constitution by the legislatures of three-fourths of the several States within seven years from the date of its submission to the states by Congress.

Amendment XXI. Amendment XVIII Repealed

Section 1. The eighteenth article of amendment to the Constitution of the United States is hereby repealed.
Section 2. The transportation or importation into any State, Territory, or possession of the United States for delivery or use therein of intoxicating liquors, in violation of the laws thereof, is hereby prohibited.
Section 3. This article shall be inoperative unless it shall have been ratified as an amendment to the Constitution by conventions in the several States, as provided in the Constitution, within seven years from the date of the submission hereof to the States by the Congress.

Amendment XXII. Presidential Term Limits

Section 1. No person shall be elected to the office of the President more than twice, and no person who has held the office of President, or acted as President, for more than two years of a term to which some other person was elected President shall be elected to the office of the President more than once. But this article shall not apply to any person holding the office of President when this article was proposed by the Congress, and shall not prevent any person who may be holding the office of President, or acting as President, during the term within which this article becomes operative from holding the office of President or acting as President during the remainder of such term.
Section 2. This article shall be inoperative unless it shall have been ratified as an amendment to the Constitution by the legislatures of three-fourths of the several states within seven years from the date of its submission to the states by the Congress.

Amendment XXIII. Presidential Vote for District of Columbia

Section 1. The District constituting the seat of government of the United States shall appoint in such manner as the Congress may direct:
A number of electors of President and Vice President equal to the whole number of Senators and Representatives in Congress to which the District would be entitled if it were a state, but in no event more than the least populous state; they shall be in addition to those appointed by the states, but they shall be considered, for the purposes of the election of President and Vice President, to be electors appointed by a state; and they shall meet in the District and perform such duties as provided by the twelfth article of amendment.
Section 2. The Congress shall have power to enforce this article by appropriate legislation.

Amendment XXIV. Poll Taxes Barred

Section 1. The right of citizens of the United States to vote in any primary or other election for President or Vice President, for electors for President or Vice President, or for Senator or Representative in Congress, shall not be denied or abridged by the United States or any state by reason of failure to pay any poll tax or other tax.
Section 2. The Congress shall have power to enforce this article by appropriate legislation.

Amendment XXV. Presidential Disability and Succession

Section 1. In case of the removal of the President from office or of his death or resignation, the Vice President shall become President.
Section 2. Whenever there is a vacancy in the office of the Vice President, the President shall nominate a Vice President who shall take office upon confirmation by a majority vote of both Houses of Congress.
Section 3. Whenever the President transmits to the President pro tempore of the Senate and the Speaker of the House of Representatives his written declaration that he is unable to discharge the powers and duties of his office, and until he transmits to them a written declaration to the contrary, such powers and duties shall be discharged by the Vice President as Acting President.
Section 4. Whenever the Vice President and a majority of either the principal officers of the executive departments or of such other body as Congress may by law provide, transmit to the President pro tempore of the Senate and the Speaker of the House of Representatives their written declaration that the President is unable to discharge the powers and duties of his office, the Vice President shall immediately assume the powers and duties of the office as Acting President.

Thereafter, when the President transmits to the President pro tempore of the Senate and the Speaker of the House of Representatives his written declaration that no inability exists, he shall resume the powers and duties of his office unless the Vice President and a majority of either the principal officers of the executive department or of such other body as Congress may by law provide, transmit within four days to the President pro tempore of the Senate and the Speaker of the House of Representatives their written declaration that the President is unable to discharge the powers and duties of his office. Thereupon Congress shall decide the issue, assembling within forty-eight hours for that purpose if not in session. If the Congress, within twenty-one days after receipt of the latter written declaration, or, if Congress is not in session, within twenty-one days after Congress is required to assemble, determines by two-thirds vote of both Houses that the President is unable to discharge the powers and duties of his office, the Vice President shall continue to discharge the same as Acting President; otherwise, the President shall resume the powers and duties of his office.

Amendment XXVI. Voting Age Set to 18 Years

Section 1. The right of citizens of the United States, who are 18 years of age or older, to vote, shall not be denied or abridged by the United States or any state on account of age.
Section 2. The Congress shall have the power to enforce this article by appropriate legislation.

Amendment XXVII. Limiting Congressional Pay Increases

No law varying the compensation for the services of the Senators and Representatives shall take effect until an election of Representatives shall have intervened.

Appendix B. The Seneca Falls Declaration of Sentiments and Resolutions

July 19, 1848

When, in the course of human events, it becomes necessary for one portion of the family of man to assume among the people of the earth a position different from that which they have hitherto occupied, but one to which the laws of nature and of nature's God entitle them, a decent respect to the opinions of mankind requires that they should declare the causes that impel them to such a course.

We hold these truths to be self-evident: that all men and women are created equal; that they are endowed by their Creator with certain inalienable rights; that among these are life, liberty, and the pursuit of happiness; that to secure these rights governments are instituted, deriving their just powers from the consent of the governed. Whenever any form of government becomes destructive of these ends, it is the right of those who suffer from it to refuse allegiance to it, and to insist upon the institution of a new government, laying its foundation on such principles, and organizing its powers in such form, as to them shall seem most likely to effect their safety and happiness. Prudence, indeed, will dictate that governments long established should not be changed for light and transient causes; and accordingly all experience hath shown that mankind are more disposed to suffer while evils are sufferable, than to right themselves by abolishing the forms to which they are accustomed. But when a long train of abuses and usurpations, pursuing invariably the same object, evinces a design to reduce them under absolute despotism, it is their duty to throw off such government, and to provide new guards for their future security. Such has been the patient sufferance of the women under this government, and such is now the necessity which constrains them to demand the equal station to which they are entitled.

The history of mankind is a history of repeated injuries and usurpations on the part of man toward woman, having in direct object the establishment of an absolute tyranny over her. To prove this, let facts be submitted to a candid world.

He has never permitted her to exercise her inalienable right to the elective franchise.

He has compelled her to submit to laws, in the formation of which she had no voice.

He has withheld from her rights which are given to the most ignorant and degraded men both natives and foreigners.

Having deprived her of this first right of a citizen, the elective franchise, thereby leaving her without representation in the halls of legislation, he has oppressed her on all sides.

He has made her, if married, in the eye of the law, civilly dead.

He has taken from her all right in property, even to the wages she earns.

He has made her, morally, an irresponsible being, as she can commit many crimes with impunity, provided they be done in the presence of her husband. In the covenant of marriage, she is compelled to promise obedience to her husband, he becoming, to all intents and purposes, her master—the law giving him power to deprive her of her liberty, and to administer chastisement.

He has so framed the laws of divorce, as to what shall be the proper causes, and in case of separation, to whom the guardianship of the children shall be given, as to be wholly regardless of the happiness of women—the law, in all cases, going upon a false supposition of the supremacy of man, and giving all power into his hands.

After depriving her of all rights as a married woman, if single, and the owner of property, he has taxed her to support a government which recognizes her only when her property can be made profitable to it.

He has monopolized nearly all the profitable employments, and from those she is permitted to follow, she receives but a scanty remuneration. He closes against her all the avenues to wealth and distinction which he considers most honorable to himself. As a teacher of theology, medicine, or law, she is not known.

He has denied her the facilities for obtaining a thorough education, all colleges being closed against her.

He allows her in Church, as well as State, but a subordinate position, claiming Apostolic authority for her exclusion from the ministry, and, with some exceptions, from any public participation in the affairs of the Church.

He has created a false public sentiment by giving to the world a different code of morals for men and women, by which moral delinquencies which exclude women from society, are not only tolerated, but deemed of little account in man.

He has usurped the prerogative of Jehovah himself, claiming it as his right to assign for her a sphere of action, when that belongs to her conscience and to her God.

He has endeavored, in every way that he could, to destroy her confidence in her own powers, to lessen her self-respect and to make her willing to lead a dependent and abject life.

Now, in view of this entire disfranchisement of one-half the people of this country, their social and religious degradation—in view of the unjust laws above mentioned, and because women do feel themselves aggrieved, oppressed, and fraudulently deprived of their most sacred rights, we insist that they have immediate admission to all the rights and privilege which belong to them as citizens of the United States.

In entering upon the great work before us, we anticipate no small amount of misconception, misrepresentation, and ridicule; but we shall use every instrumentality within our power to affect our object. We shall employ agents, circulate tracts, petition the State and National legislatures, and endeavor to enlist the pulpit and the press in our behalf. We hope this Convention will be followed by a series of Conventions embracing every part of the country.

2. RESOLUTIONS

WHEREAS, the great precept of nature is conceded to be, that "man shall pursue his own true and substantial happiness." Blackstone in his Commentaries remarks, that this law of Nature being coeval with mankind, and dictated by God himself, is of course superior in obligation to any other. It is binding over all the globe, in all countries and at all times; no human laws are of any validity if contrary to this, and such of them as are valid, derive all their force, and all their validity, and all their authority, mediately and immediately, from this original, therefore,

Resolved, that all laws which prevent woman from occupying such a station in society as her conscience shall dictate, or which place her in a position inferior to that of man, are contrary to the great precept of nature, and therefore of no force or authority.

Resolved, that woman is man's equal—was intended to be so by the Creator, and the highest good of the race demands that she should be recognized as such.

Resolved, that the women of this country ought to be enlightened in regard to the laws under which they live, that they may no longer publish their degradation by declaring themselves satisfied with their present position, nor their ignorance, by asserting that they have all the rights they want.

Resolved, that inasmuch as man, while claiming for himself intellectual superiority, does accord to woman moral superiority, it is pre-eminently his duty to encourage her to speak and teach, as she has an opportunity, in all religious assemblies.

Resolved, that the same amount of virtue, delicacy, and refinement of behavior that is required of woman in the social state, should also be required of man, and the same transgressions should be visited with equal severity on both man and woman.

Resolved, that the objection of indelicacy and impropriety, which is so often brought against woman when she addresses a public audience, comes with a very ill-grace from those who encourage, by their attendance, her appearance on the stage, in the concert, or in feats of the circus.

Resolved, that woman has too long rested satisfied in the circumscribed limits which corrupt customs and a perverted application of the Scriptures have marked out for her, and that it is time she should move in the enlarged sphere which her great Creator has assigned her.

Resolved, that it is the duty of the women of this country to secure to themselves their sacred right to the elective franchise.

Resolved, that the equality of human rights results necessarily from the fact of the identity of the race in capabilities and responsibilities.

Resolved, that the speedy success of our cause depends upon the zealous and untiring efforts of both men and women, for the overthrow of the monopoly of the pulpit, and for the securing to women an equal participation with men in the various trades, professions, and commerce.

Resolved, therefore, that, being invested by the creator with the same capabilities, and the same consciousness of responsibility for their exercise, it is demonstrably the right and duty of woman, equally with man, to promote every righteous cause by every righteous means; and especially in regard to the great subjects of morals and religion, it is self-evidently her right to participate with her brother in teaching them, both in private and in public, by writing and by speaking, by any instrumentalities proper to be used, and in any assemblies proper to be held; and this being a self-evident truth growing out of the divinely implanted principles of human nature, any custom or authority adverse to it, whether modern or wearing the hoary sanction of antiquity, is to be regarded as a self evident falsehood, and at war with mankind.

Firmly relying upon the final triumph of the Right and the True, we do this day affix our **signatures to this declaration**:

Lucretia Mott, Harriet Cady Eaton, Margaret Pryor, Elizabeth Cady Stanton, Eunice Newton Foote, Mary Ann McClintock, Margaret Schooley, Martha C. Wright, Jane C. Hunt, Amy Post, Catharine F. Stebbins, Mary Ann Frink, Lydia Mount, Delia Mathews, Catharine C. Paine, Elizabeth W. McClintock, Malvina Seymour, Phebe Mosher, Catharine Shaw, Deborah Scott, Sarah Hallowell, Mary McClintock, Mary Gilbert, Sophrone Tayor, Cynthia Davis, Hannah Plant, Lucy Jones, Sarah Whitney, Mary H. Hallowell, Elizabeth Conklin, Sally Pitcher, Mary Conklin, Susan Quinn, Mary S.

Mirror, Phebe King, Julia Ann Drake, Charlotte Woodard, Martha Underhill, Dorothy Mathews, Eunice Barker, Sarah R. Woods, Lydia Gild, Sarah Hoffman, Elizabeth Leslie, Martha Ridley, Rachel D. Bonnel, Betsey Tewksbury, Rhoda Palmer, Margaret Jenkins, Cynthia Fuller, Mary Martin, P. A. Culvert, Susan R. Doty, Rebecca Race, Sarah A. Mosher, Mary E. Vail, Lucy Spalding, Lavinia Latham, Sarah Smith, Eliza Martin, Maria E. Wilbur, Elizabeth D. Smith, Caroline Barker, Ann Porter, Experience Gibbs, Antoinette E. Segur, Hannah J. Latham, Sarah Sisson.

The following are the names of the gentlemen present in favor of the movement:

Richard P. Hunt, Samuel D. Tillman, Justin Williams, Elisha Foote, Frederick Douglass, Henry W. Seymour, Henry Seymour, David Salding, William G. Barker, Elias J. Doty, John Jones, William S. Dell, James Mott, William Burroughs, Robert Smalldridge, Jacob Matthews, Charles L. Hoskins, Thomas McClintock, Saron Phillips, Jacob Chamberlain, Jonathan Metcalf, Nathan J. Milliken, S. E. Woodworth, Edward F. Underhill, George W. Pryor, Joel Bunker, Isaac Van Tassel, Thomas Dell, E. W. Capron, Stephen Shear, Henry Hatley, Azaliah Schooley.

NOTE: reprinted from the work of Susan B. Anthony, Elizabeth Cady Stanton and Matilda Joslyn Gage, eds., *History of Woman Suffrage*. Rochester, N.Y.: S.B. Anthony

Appendix C. Section 703 of the Civil Rights Act of 1964

DISCRIMINATION BECAUSE OF RACE, COLOR, RELIGION, SEX, OR NATIONAL ORIGIN
SEC. 703. (a) It shall be an unlawful employment practice for an employer--
(1) to fail or refuse to hire or to discharge any individual, or otherwise to discriminate against any individual with respect to his compensation, terms, conditions, or privileges of employment, because of such individual's race, color, religion, sex, or national origin; or
(2) to limit, segregate, or classify his employees in any way which would deprive or tend to deprive any individual of employment opportunities or otherwise adversely affect his status as an employee, because of such individual's race, color, religion, sex, or national origin.
(b) It shall be an unlawful employment practice for an employment agency to fail or refuse to refer for employment, or otherwise to discriminate against, any individual because of his race, color, religion, sex, or national origin, or to classify or refer for employment any individual on the basis of his race, color, religion, sex, or national origin.
(c) It shall be an unlawful employment practice for a labor organization--
(1) to exclude or to expel from its membership, or otherwise to discriminate against, any individual because of his race, color, religion, sex, or national origin;
(2) to limit, segregate, or classify its membership, or to classify or fail or refuse to refer for employment any individual, in any way which would deprive or tend to deprive any individual of employment opportunities, or would limit such employment opportunities or otherwise adversely affect his status as an employee or as an applicant for employment, because of such individual's race, color, religion, sex, or national origin; or
(3) to cause or attempt to cause an employer to discriminate against an individual in violation of this section.
(d) It shall be an unlawful employment practice for any employer, labor organization, or joint labor-management committee controlling apprenticeship or other training or retraining, including on-the-job training programs to discriminate against any individual because of his race, color, religion, sex, or national origin in admission to, or employment in, any program established to provide apprenticeship or other training.
(e) Notwithstanding any other provision of this title, (1) it shall not be an unlawful employment practice for an employer to hire and employ employees, for an employment agency to classify, or refer for employment any individual, for a labor organization to classify its membership or to classify or refer

for employment any individual, or for an employer, labor organization, or joint labor-management committee controlling apprenticeship or other training or retraining programs to admit or employ any individual in any such program, on the basis of his religion, sex, or national origin in those certain instances where religion, sex, or national origin is a bona fide occupational qualification reasonably necessary to the normal operation of that particular business or enterprise, and (2) it shall not be an unlawful employment practice for a school, college, university, or other educational institution or institution of learning to hire and employ employees of a particular religion if such school, college, university, or other educational institution or institution of learning is, in whole or in substantial part, owned, supported, controlled, or managed by a particular religion or by a particular religious corporation, association, or society, or if the curriculum of such school, college, university, or other educational institution or institution of learning is directed toward the propagation of a particular religion.

(f) As used in this title, the phrase "unlawful employment practice" shall not be deemed to include any action or measure taken by an employer, labor organization, joint labor-management committee, or employment agency with respect to an individual who is a member of the Communist Party of the United States or of any other organization required to register as a Communist-action or Communist-front organization by final order of the Subversive Activities Control Board pursuant to the Subversive Activities Control Act of 1950.

(g) Notwithstanding any other provision of this title, it shall not be an unlawful employment practice for an employer to fail or refuse to hire and employ any individual for any position, for an employer to discharge any individual from any position, or for an employment agency to fail or refuse to refer any individual for employment in any position, or for a labor organization to fail or refuse to refer any individual for employment in any position, if–

(1) the occupancy of such position, or access to the premises in or upon which any part of the duties of such position is performed or is to be performed, is subject to any requirement imposed in the interest of the national security of the United States under any security program in effect pursuant to or administered under any statute of the United States or any Executive order of the President; and

(2) such individual has not fulfilled or has ceased to fulfill that requirement.

(h) Notwithstanding any other provision of this title, it shall not be an unlawful employment practice for an employer to apply different standards of compensation, or different terms, conditions, or privileges of employment pursuant to a bona fide seniority or merit system, or a system which measures earnings by quantity or quality of production or to employees who work in different locations, provided that such differences are not the result of an intention to discriminate because of race, color, religion, sex, or national origin, nor shall it be an unlawful employment practice for an employer to give and to act upon the results of any professionally developed ability test provided that such test, its administration or action upon the results is not designed, intended or used to discriminate because of race, color, religion, sex or national origin. It shall not be an unlawful employment practice under this title for any employer to differentiate upon the basis of sex in determining the amount of the wages or compensation paid or to be paid to employees of such employer if such differentiation is authorized by the provisions of section 6(d) of the Fair Labor Standards Act of 1938, as amended (29 U.S.C. 206(d)).

(i) Nothing contained in this title shall apply to any business or enterprise on or near an Indian reservation with respect to any publicly announced employment practice of such business or enterprise under which a preferential treatment is given to any individual because he is an Indian living on or near a reservation.

(j) Nothing contained in this title shall be interpreted to require any employer, employment agency, labor organization, or joint labor-management committee subject to this title to grant preferential treatment to any individual or to any group because of the race, color, religion, sex, or national origin of such individual or group on account of an imbalance which may exist with respect to the total number or percentage of persons of any race, color, religion, sex, or national origin employed by any employer, referred or classified for employment by any employment agency or labor organization, admitted to membership or classified by any labor organization, or admitted to, or employed in, any apprenticeship or other training program, in comparison with the total number or percentage of persons of such race, color, religion, sex, or national origin in any community, State, section, or other area, or in the available work force in any community, State, section, or other area.

OTHER UNLAWFUL EMPLOYMENT PRACTICES

SEC. 704. (a) It shall be an unlawful employment practice for an employer to discriminate against any of his employees or applicants for employment, for an employment agency to discriminate against any individual, or for a labor organization to discriminate against any member thereof or applicant for membership, because he has opposed, any practice made an unlawful employment practice by this title, or because he has made a charge, testified, assisted, or participated in any manner in an investigation, proceeding, or hearing under this title.

(b) It shall be an unlawful employment practice for an employer, labor organization, or employment agency to print or publish or cause to be printed or published any notice or advertisement relating to employment by such an employer or membership in or any classification or referral for employment by such a labor organization, or relating to any classification or referral for employment by such an employment agency, indicating any preference, limitation, specification, or discrimination, based on race, color, religion, sex, or national origin, except that such a notice or advertisement may indicate a preference, limitation, specification, or discrimination based on religion, sex, or national origin when religion, sex, or national origin is a bona fide occupational qualification for employment.

EQUAL EMPLOYMENT OPPORTUNITY COMMISSION

SEC. 705. (a) There is hereby created a Commission to be known as the Equal Employment Opportunity Commission, which shall be composed of five members, not more than three of whom shall be members of the same political party, who shall be appointed by the President by and with the advice and consent of the Senate. One of the original members shall be appointed for a term of one year, one for a term of two years, one for a term of three years, one for a term of four years, and one for a term of five years, beginning from the date of enactment of this title, but their successors shall be appointed for terms of five years each, except that any individual chosen to fill a vacancy shall be appointed only for the unexpired term of the member whom he shall succeed. The President shall designate one member to serve as Chairman of the Commission, and one member to serve as Vice Chairman. The Chairman shall be responsible on behalf of the Commission for the administrative operations of the Commission, and shall appoint, in accordance with the civil service laws, such officers, agents, attorneys, and employees as it deems necessary to assist it in the performance of its functions and to fix their compensation in accordance with the Classification Act of 1949, as amended. The Vice Chairman shall act as Chairman in the absence or disability of the Chairman or in the event of a vacancy in that office.

(b) A vacancy in the Commission shall not impair the right of the remaining members to exercise all the powers of the Commission and three members thereof shall constitute a quorum.

(c) The Commission shall have an official seal which shall be judicially noticed.

(d) The Commission shall at the close of each fiscal year report to the Congress and to the President concerning the action it has taken; the names, salaries, and duties of all individuals in its employ and the moneys it has disbursed; and shall make such further reports on the cause of and means of eliminating discrimination and such recommendations for further legislation as may appear desirable.

(e) The Federal Executive Pay Act of 1956, as amended (5 U.S.C. 2201-2209), is further amended--

(1) by adding to section 105 thereof (5 U.S.C. 2204) the following clause:

"(32) Chairman, Equal Employment Opportunity Commission"; and

(2) by adding to clause (45) of section 106(a) thereof (5 U.S.C. 2205(a)) the following: "Equal Employment Opportunity Commission (4)."

(f) The principal office of the Commission shall be in or near the District of Columbia, but it may meet or exercise any or all its powers at any other place. The Commission may establish such regional or State offices as it deems necessary to accomplish the purpose of this title.
(g) The Commission shall have power--
(1) to cooperate with and, with their consent, utilize regional, State, local, and other agencies, both public and private, and individuals;
(2) to pay to witnesses whose depositions are taken or who are summoned before the Commission or any of its agents the same witness and mileage fees as are paid to witnesses in the courts of the United States;
(3) to furnish to persons subject to this title such technical assistance as they may request to further their compliance with this title or an order issued there under;
(4) upon the request of (i) any employer, whose employees or some of them, or (ii) any labor organization, whose members or some of them, refuse or threaten to refuse to cooperate in effectuating the provisions of this title, to assist in such effectuation by conciliation or such other remedial action as is provided by this title;
(5) to make such technical studies as are appropriate to effectuate the purposes and policies of this title and to make the results of such studies available to the public;
(6) to refer matters to the Attorney General with recommendations for intervention in a civil action brought by an aggrieved party under section 706, or for the institution of a civil action by the Attorney General under section 707, and to advise, consult, and assist the Attorney General on such matters.
(h) Attorneys appointed under this section may, at the direction of the Commission, appear for and represent the Commission in any case in court.
(i) The Commission shall, in any of its educational or promotional activities, cooperate with other departments and agencies in the performance of such educational and promotional activities.
(j) All officers, agents, attorneys, and employees of the Commission shall be subject to the provisions of section 9 of the Act of August 2, 1939, as amended (the Hatch Act), notwithstanding any exemption contained in such section.

PREVENTION OF UNLAWFUL EMPLOYMENT PRACTICES

SEC. 706. (a) Whenever it is charged in writing under oath by a person claiming to be aggrieved, or a written charge has been filed by a member of the Commission where he has reasonable cause to believe a violation of this title has occurred (and such charge sets forth the facts upon which it is based) that an employer, employment agency, or labor organization has engaged in an unlawful employment practice, the Commission shall furnish such employer, employment agency, or labor organization (hereinafter referred to as the "respondent") with a copy of such charge and shall make an investigation of such charge, provided that such charge shall not be made public by the Commission. If the Commission shall determine, after such investigation, that there is reasonable cause to believe that the charge is true, the Commission shall endeavor to eliminate any such alleged unlawful employment practice by informal methods of conference, conciliation, and persuasion. Nothing said or done during and as a part of such endeavors may be made public by the Commission without the written consent of the parties, or used as evidence in a subsequent proceeding. Any officer or employee of the Commission, who shall make public in any manner whatever any information in violation of this subsection shall be deemed guilty of a misdemeanor and upon conviction thereof shall be fined not more than $1,000 or imprisoned not more than one year.
(b) In the case of an alleged unlawful employment practice occurring in a State, or political subdivision of a State, which has a State or local law prohibiting the unlawful employment practice alleged and establishing or authorizing a State or local authority to grant or seek relief from such practice or to institute criminal proceedings with respect thereto upon receiving notice thereof, no charge may be filed under subsection (a) by the person aggrieved before the expiration of sixty days after proceedings have been commenced under the State or local law, unless such proceedings have been earlier

terminated, provided that such sixty-day period shall be extended to one hundred and twenty days during the first year after the effective date of such State or local law. If any requirement for the commencement of such proceedings is imposed by a State or local authority other than a requirement of the filing of a written and signed statement of the facts upon which the proceeding is based, the proceeding shall be deemed to have been commenced for the purposes of this subsection at the time such statement is sent by registered mail to the appropriate State or local authority.

(c) In the case of any charge filed by a member of the Commission alleging an unlawful employment practice occurring in a State or political subdivision of a State, which has a State or local law prohibiting the practice alleged and establishing or authorizing a State or local authority to grant or seek relief from such practice or to institute criminal proceedings with respect thereto upon receiving notice thereof, the Commission shall, before taking any action with respect to such charge, notify the appropriate State or local officials and, upon request, afford them a reasonable time, but not less than sixty days (provided that such sixty-day period shall be extended to one hundred and twenty days during the first year after the effective day of such State or local law), unless a shorter period is requested, to act under such State or local law to remedy the practice alleged.

(d) A charge under subsection (a) shall be filed within ninety days after the alleged unlawful employment practice occurred, except that in the case of an unlawful employment practice with respect to which the person aggrieved has followed the procedure set out in subsection (b), such charge shall be filed by the person aggrieved within two hundred and ten days after the alleged unlawful employment practice occurred, or within thirty days after receiving notice that the State or local agency has terminated the proceedings under the State or local, law, whichever is earlier, and a copy of such charge shall be filed by the Commission with the State or local agency.

(e) If within thirty days after a charge is filed with the Commission or within thirty days after expiration of any period of reference under subsection (c) (except that in either case such period may be extended to not more than sixty days upon a determination by the Commission that further efforts to secure voluntary compliance are warranted), the Commission has been unable to obtain voluntary compliance with this title, the Commission shall so notify the person aggrieved and a civil action may, within thirty days thereafter, be brought against the respondent named in the charge (1) by the person claiming to be aggrieved, or (2) if such charge was filed by a member of the Commission, by any person whom the charge alleges was aggrieved by the alleged unlawful employment practice. Upon application by the complainant and in such circumstances as the court may deem just, the court may appoint an attorney for such complainant and may authorize the commencement of the action without the payment of fees, costs, or security. Upon timely application, the court may, in its discretion, permit the Attorney General to intervene in such civil action if he certifies that the case is of general public importance. Upon request, the court may, in its discretion, stay further proceedings for not more than sixty days pending the termination of State or local proceedings described in subsection (b) or the efforts of the Commission to obtain voluntary compliance.

(f) Each United States district court and each United States court of a place subject to the jurisdiction of the United States shall have jurisdiction of actions brought under this title. Such an action may be brought in any judicial district in the State in which the unlawful employment practice is alleged to have been committed, in the judicial district in which the employment records relevant to such practice are maintained and administered, or in the judicial district in which the plaintiff would have worked but for the alleged unlawful employment practice, but if the respondent is not found within any such district, such an action may be brought within the judicial district in which the respondent has his principal office. For purposes of sections 1404 and 1406 of title 28 of the United States Code, the judicial district in which the respondent has his principal office shall in all cases be considered a district in which the action might have been brought.

(g) If the court finds that the respondent has intentionally engaged in or is intentionally engaging in an unlawful employment practice charged in the complaint, the court may enjoin the respondent from engaging in such unlawful employment practice, and order such affirmative action as may be appro-

priate, which may include reinstatement or hiring of employees, with or without back pay (payable by the employer, employment agency, or labor organization, as the case may be, responsible for the unlawful employment practice). Interim earnings or amounts earnable with reasonable diligence by the person or persons discriminated against shall operate to reduce the back pay otherwise allowable. No order of the court shall require the admission or reinstatement of an individual as a member of a union or the hiring, reinstatement, or promotion of an individual as an employee, or the payment to him of any back pay, if such individual was refused admission, suspended, or expelled or was refused employment or advancement or was suspended or discharged for any reason other than discrimination on account of race, color, religion, sex or national origin or in violation of section 704(a).
(h) The provisions of the Act entitled "An Act to amend the Judicial Code and to define and limit the jurisdiction of courts sitting in equity, and for other purposes," approved March 23, 1932 (29 U.S.C. 101-115), shall not apply with respect to civil actions brought under this section.
(i) In any case in which an employer, employment agency, or labor organization fails to comply with an order of a court issued in a civil action brought under subsection (e), the Commission may commence proceedings to compel compliance with such order.
(j) Any civil action brought under subsection (e) and any proceedings brought under subsection (i) shall be subject to appeal as provided in sections 1291 and 1292, title 28, United States Code.
(k) In any action or proceeding under this title the court, in its discretion, may allow the prevailing party, other than the Commission or the United States, a reasonable attorney's fee as part of the costs, and the Commission and the United States shall be liable for costs the same as a private person.

Appendix D. Women Serving in the House of Representatives of the 112th Congress

Sandra (Sandy) Adams (Republican, FL)
Michele Bachmann (Republican, MN)
Tammy Baldwin (Democrat, WI)
Karen Bass (Democrat, CA)
Shelley Berkley (Democrat, NV)
Judy Borg Biggert (Republican, IL)
Diane Black (Republican, TN)
Marsha Blackburn (Republican, TN)
Mary Bono Mack (Republican, CA)
Madeleine Z. Bordallo (Democrat, GU)
Corrine Brown (Democrat, FL)
Ann Marie Buerkle (Republican, NY)
Shelley Moore Capito (Republican, WV)
Lois Capps (Democrat, CA)
Kathy Castor (Democrat, FL)
Donna M. Christensen (Democrat, VI)
Judy Chu (Democrat, CA)
Yvette D. Clarke (Democrat, NY)
Susan A. Davis (Democrat, CA)
Diana L. DeGette (Democrat, CO)
Rosa DeLauro (Democrat, CT)
Donna F. Edwards (Democrat, MD)
Renee Ellmers (Republican, NC)
Jo Ann Emerson (Republican, MO)
Anna Georges Eshoo (Democrat, CA)
Virginia Foxx (Republican, NC)

Marcia L. Fudge (Democrat, OH)
Gabrielle Giffords (Democrat, AZ)
Kay Granger (Republican, TX)
Colleen Hanabusa (Democrat, HI)
Jane F. Harman (Democrat, CA) resigned from office February 28, 2011
Vicky Hartzler (Republican, MO)
Nan Hayworth (Republican, NY)
Jaime Herrera Beutler (Republican, WA)
Mazie Hirono (Democrat, HI)
Kathleen C. Hochul (Democrat, NY)
Sheila Jackson Lee (Democrat, TX)
Lynn Jenkins (Republican, KS)
Eddie Bernice Johnson (Democrat, TX)
Marcia C. (Marcy) Kaptur (Democrat, OH)
Barbara Lee (Democrat, CA)
Zoe Lofgren (Democrat, CA)
Nita M. Lowey (Democrat, NY)
Cynthia M. Lummis (Republican, WY)
Carolyn B. Maloney (Democrat, NY)
Doris Matsui (Democrat, CA)
Carolyn McCarthy (Democrat, NY)
Betty McCollum (Democrat, MN)
Cathy McMorris Rodgers (Republican, WA)
Candice Miller (Republican, MI)
Gwen Moore (Democrat, WI)
Sue Myrick (Republican, NC)
Grace Napolitano (Democrat, CA)
Kristi Noem (Republican, SD)
Eleanor Holmes Norton (Democrat, DC)
Nancy Pelosi (Democrat, CA)
Chellie Pingree (Democrat, ME)
Laura Richardson (Democrat, CA)
Martha Roby (Republican, AL)
Ileana Ros-Lehtinen (Republican, FL)
Lucille Roybal-Allard (Democrat, CA)
Linda T. Sánchez (Democrat, CA)
Loretta Sanchez (Democrat, CA)
Janice Schakowsky (Democrat, IL)
Jean Schmidt (Republican, OH)
Allyson Schwartz (Democrat, PA)
Terri Sewell (Democrat, AL)
Louise M. Slaughter (Democrat, NY)
Jackie Speier (Democrat, CA)
Betty Sutton (Democrat, OH)
Nicola S. (Niki) Tsongas (Democrat, MA)
Nydia M. Velázquez (Democrat, NY)
Debbie Wasserman Schultz (Democrat, FL)
Maxine Waters (Democrat, CA)
Frederica Wilson (Democrat, FL)
Lynn C. Woolsey (Democrat, CA)

BIBLIOGRAPHY

A. Primary Sources:

Bank, Mirra. *Anonymous Was a Woman*. New York: St. Martin's Press, 1979.

Beecher, Catherine, and Harriet Beecher Stowe, *The American Woman's Home or the Principles of Domestic Science*. Hartford: Stowe-Day Foundation, 1991.

Better Homes and Gardens, eds. *The Better Homes and Gardens, Heritage Cook Book*. New York: Meredith Publishing, 1975.

Boyer, Paul and Stephen Nissenbaum. *Salem Witchcraft Papers, Three Volumes*. New York, 1977.

Boyer, Richard and Geoffrey Spurling. *Colonial Lives. Documents in Latin American History, 1550-1850*. New York: Oxford Press, 2000.

Burr, G.L. ed. *Narratives of the Witchcraft Cases. 1648-1706*. New York, 1914, & 1968 editions.

Chase-Smith, Margaret. *Declaration of Conscience*. William C. Lewis, Jr. ed. New York: Doubleday, 1953.

Clinton, Catherine, ed. *Fanny Kemble's Journals*. Cambridge: Harvard University Press, 2000.

Dulany, Daniel. *Lucy Larcom: Life, Letters, and Diary*. 1894.

East, Charles, ed. *Sarah Morgan, The Civil War Diary of a Southern Woman*. New York: Simon and Schuster, 1991.

Fairchild, Helen, RN. *The Letters of Helen Fairchild,* Printed with Permission of Nelle Fairchild Rote. 2000.

Gordon, Ann D., ed. *The Selected Papers of Elizabeth Cady Stanton and Susan B. Anthony. Volume I, In the School of Anti-Slavery, 1840-1856*. New Brunswick: Rutgers University Press, l997.

Gorn, Elliott J., ed. *The McGuffey Readers, Selections from the 1879 Edition*. Boston: Bedford, 1998.

Hewitt, Nancy, ed. *Women Families and Communities, Reading in American History, Volume One: to 1877. Volume Two from 1865*. Glenview, IL: Little Brown, 1990.

Holbrook, Harriet Ravenel, ed. *Journals and Letters of Eliza Lucas Pinckney.*1850.

Mann, Hermann. *The Female Review or Memories of an American Lady*. Dedham: Heaton, 1797.

Markman, Marsha, ed., et al. *Writing Women's Lives, American Women's History through Letters and Diaries*. St. James: Brandywine Press, 1999.

The National Archives. *Revolutionary Pensions and Bounty Land Warrants, Series M804*. The National Archives Microfilm edition, the pension application of Deborah Samson Gannett reel# 1045, reel number 2095, file # W-8566. Washington,D.C.: The National Archives and Records Administration.

Nicholson, Zoe. *The Hungry Heart, One Woman's Search for Justice*. Newport Beach: Lune-Soleil Press, 2004.

Pinckney, Elise and Marvin Zahniser, eds., *The Letterbook of Eliza Lucas Pinckney, 1739-1762*. Chapel Hill: University Press, 1972.

Ravenel, Harriet Horry. *Eliza Pinckney*, 1896.

Roosevelt, Eleanor. *My Day*. September 9, 1941. United Feature Syndicate.

Skinner, Ellen. *Primary Sources in American History, Women and the National Experience*. New York: Addison-Wesley Longmans, 1996.

South Carolina Historical Society. *Letters of Eliza Lucas Pinckney*, 1739-1762.

Sterne, Madeleine, ed. *The Victoria Woodhull Reader. We the Women*. 1963.

Tyree, Marion Cabell. *Housekeeping in Old Virginia*. Louisville: John P. Morton, & Company, 1879.

United States Department of Labor, Office of the Assistant Secretary for Policy. *The Department in the New Deal and World War II 1933-1945.* Washington, D.C.: United States Department of Labor.

Ware, Susan. *Modern American Women, A Documentary History.* New York: McGraw-Hill, 1997.

Warren, Mercy Otis. *History of the Rise Progress and Termination of the American Revolution, Volume I and II.* Lester Cohen, ed. Indianapolis: Liberty Fund, 1989.

White, Annie R. *Polite Society at Home and Abroad, A Complete Compendium of Information Upon All Topics Classified Under the Head of Etiquette.* Chicago: L. P. Miller and Company.

Woloch, Nancy. *Early American Women, A Documentary History, 1600-1900.* New York: McGraw-Hill, 1997.

Woodhull, Victoria C. *Speech of Victoria C. Woodhull on the Great Political Issue of Constitutional Equality, Together with her Secession Speech*, 1871.

Woodward, C. Vann and Elisabeth Muhlenfeld. *The Private Mary Chestnut: The Unpublished Civil War Diaries.* New York: Oxford, 1984.

B. Reference Works

Magill, Frank N. *Great Lives from History, American Women Series, Five Volumes*. Pasadena, CA: Salem Press, 1995.

Olsen, Kirsten. *Remember the Ladies, A Woman's Book of Days*. New York: Main Street, 1988.

O'Neill, Lois D. *The Women's Book of World Records and Achievements*.

Warner, Carolyn. *Treasury of Women's Quotations*. Englewood Cliffs: Prentice-Hall, 1992.

United States Bureau of Statistics. *Records of the Department of Labor.* Washington, D.C.: Federal Census Records, 1792-2000.

Webster, Merriam Inc. *Webster's Dictionary of American Women*. New York: Smithmark, 1980.

C. Women in Colonial History

Barker-Benfield, G. J. and Catherine Clinton. *Portraits of American Women, From Settlement to the Civil War. Volume I.* New York: St Martin's Press, 1991.

Bender, David L., et al. *Puritanism Opposing Viewpoints. American History Series*. San Diego: Greenhaven Press, 1994.

De La Cruz, Sor Juana Ines. *A Sor Juana Anthology.* Alan S. Trueblood, trans. Cambridge: Harvard University Press, 1980.

Fischer, David Hackett. *Growing Old in America*. New York: Oxford, 1978.

Goodfriend, Joyce D. *Before the Melting Pot: Society and Culture in Colonial New York City, 1664-1730.* Princeton: Princeton University Press, 1992.

Greer, Allan, ed. *The Jesuit Relations, Natives and Missionaries in Seventeenth Century North America.* The Bedford Series on History and Culture. Boston: Bedford Books, 1997.

Gundersen, Joan R. *To Be Useful to the World: Women in Revolutionary America, 1740-1790.* New York: Twayne Publishers, 1996.

Hulton, Paul., ed. *America 1585: The Complete Drawings of John White*. Chapel Hill: University of North Carolina Press, 1984.

Larkin, Jack. *The Reshaping of Everyday Life, 1790- 1840.* New York: Harper Perennial, 1988.

Noble, David Grant. *Santa Fe, History of an Ancient City.* Santa Fe: SAR Press, 1989.

Ransome, David R. "Wives for Virginia," Williamsburg: *The William & Mary Quarterly, 1990: 3-18.*

Salinger, Sharon V. *Taverns and Drinking in Early America.* Baltimore: Johns Hopkins University Press, 2002.
To Serve Well and Faithfully: Labor and Indentured Servants in Pennsylvania 1682-1800. Bowie, MD: Heritage Books, 2000.

Spruill, Julia Cherry. *Women's Life and Work in the Southern Colonies*. New York: W. W. Norton, 1938.

Treckel Paula A. *To Comfort the Heart, Women in Seventeenth Century America.* New York: Twayne Publishers, 1996.

D. The Salem Witch Trials

Boyer, Paul, and Stephen Nissenbaum. *Salem Possessed: The Social Origins of Witchcraft.* Cambridge: University Press, 1974.

Burr, G. L., ed. *Narratives of the Witchcraft Cases. 1648-1706.* New York: 1914, & 1968 editions.

Caporael, Linda R. "Ergotism: The Satan Loosed in Salem?" *Science* 192 (1976) pp. 21-26.

Carlson, Laurie Winn. *A Fever in Salem: A New Interpretation of the New England Witch Trials.* Chicago: Ivan R. Dee, 1999.

Demos, John. *Entertaining Satan*. Boston: Oxford University Press, 1982.

Karlsen, Carol F. *The Devil in the Shape of a Woman, Witchcraft in Colonial New England.* New York: W.W. Norton, 1987.

Maddox, James Robert, ed. *American History Volume I, Annual editions*. Guilford, Dushkin, 1981. Robbins, Peggy. "The Devil in Salem."

Matossian, Mary Kilbourne. *Poisons of the Past: Molds, Epidemics and History.* New Haven: Yale University Press, 1989.

Salem Witchcraft Papers, Three Volumes, New York, 1977.

E. Women in the Revolutionary Era and the New Republic

Barker-Benfield, G. L., and Catherine Clinton, ed. *Portraits of American Women: Volume I, From Settlement to the Civil War. Volume II, From the Civil War to the Present.* New York: St. Martin's Press, 1991.

Blumenthal, Walter Hart. *Women Camp Followers of the American Revolution*. 1952.

Boydston, Jeanne. *Home and Work, Housework and Wages and Ideology of Labor in the Early Republic.* New York: Oxford, 1990.

Clement, Priscilla F. *Growing Pains, Children in the Industrial Age. Twayne's History of American Childhood Series*. New York: Twayne, 1997.

Coburn, Carol, and Martha Smith. *Spirited Lives, How Nuns Shaped Catholic Culture and American Life. 1836-1920*. Chapel Hill: University of North Carolina Press, 1999.

Cohen, Patricia Cline. *The Murder of Helen Jewett*. New York: Vintage Books, 1999.

Cott, Nancy. *Bonds of Womanhood.* New Haven: Yale University Press, 1977.

Eisler, Benita, ed. *The Lowell Offering, Writings by New England Mill Women*. New York: Harper Row, 1977.

Ellet, Elizabeth. *The Women of the American Revolution, Three Volumes*. Williamstown, MA: Corner House Publications, 1980.

Evans, Elizabeth. *Weathering the Storm, Women of the American Revolution*. New York: Charles Scribners' Sons, 1975.

Fern, Fanny. *Ruth Hall A Domestic Tale of the Present Time*. New York: Penguin, 1997.

Giffoyle, Timothy J. *City of Eros, New York City, Prostitution, and the Commercialization of Sex, 1790-1920.* New York: W. W. Norton, 1992.

Grossberg, Michael. *Governing the Hearth, Law and Family in Nineteenth Century America.* Chapel Hill: University of North Carolina Press, 1985.

Gundersen, Joan. *To Be Useful to the World, Women in Revolutionary America, 1740-1790.* New York: Twayne,

Hoffman, Ronald and Peter Albert, eds., *Women in the Age of the American Revolution.* Charlottesville: University of Virginia Press, 1989.

Johnson, Paul E. *A Shopkeeper's Millennium, Society and Revivals in Rochester, New York, 1815-1837.* New York: Hill and Wang, 1978.

Kerber, Linda. *Women of the Republic.* Chapel Hill: University Press, 1980.

"The Lady and the Mill Girl: Changes in the Status of Women in the Age of Jackson," *Mid Continent American Studies Journal.* (October 1969) p. 10.

Larkin, Jack. *The Reshaping of Everyday Life, 1790-1840.* New York: Harper Collins, 1988.

Lerner, Gerda. *The Majority Finds Its Past: Placing Women in American History*; *Black Women in White America: A Documentary History*; *The Female Experience: An American Documentary*; and *An Overview of American Women's History.*

Mason, Julian, ed. *The Poems of Phillis Wheatley: Revised and Enlarged Edition.* Chapel Hill: University of North Carolina Press, 1989.

Norton, Mary Beth. *Liberty's Daughters.* Boston: Little, Brown, 1980.

"Politics and Public Culture: The Revolutionary War Pension Act of 1818." *Journal of the Early Republic*, 8:139-158, 1988.

Resch, John P. "Federal Welfare for Revolutionary War Veterans." *The Social Science Review.* June 1982, 171-195.

Rowson, Susanna Haswell. *Charlotte Temple.* Cathy N. Davidson, ed. New York: Oxford, 1986.

Spruill, Julia Cherry. *Women's Life and Work in the Southern Colonies.* New York: W. W. Norton and Company, 1938.

Srebnick, Amy Gilman. *The Mysterious Death of Mary Rogers, Sex and Culture in Nineteenth Century New York.* Boston: Oxford University Press, 1995.

Teipe, Emily. *America's First Veterans and the Revolutionary War Pensions.* New York: Edwin Mellen Press, 2002.

"Mercy Otis Warren," *Great Lives from History, American Women Series*, Vol.V, Frank Magill, ed. pp. 1845-1849.

A Woman's Journal, Reading and Writing on Feminist Themes in Women's Studies. Emily Teipe, ed. New York: McGraw-Hill, 2001.

Visser, Margaret. *The Rituals of Dinner: The Origins, Evolution, Eccentricities and Meaning of Table Manners.* New York: Penguin, 1991.

Welter, Barbara. "The Cult of True Womanhood: 1820-1860." *American Quarterly*, Summer, 1966, pp. 151-174.

Wyatt-Brown, Betram. *Southern Honor, Ethics and Behavior in the Old South.* New York: Oxford Press, 1982.

F. Women in Reform and the Women's Movement

Bernard, Virginia and Elizabeth Fox-Genovese, eds. *The Birth of American Feminism, The Seneca Falls Woman's Convention of 1848.* St. James, New York: Brandywine Press, 1997.

Buechler, Steven. *Women's Movements in the United States.* New Brunswick, Rutgers University Press, 1990.

DuBois, Ellen Carol. *Feminism and Suffrage: The Emergence of an Independent Women's Movement in America, 1848-1869.* New York: Cornell University Press, 1978.

The Elizabeth Cady Stanton - Susan B. Anthony Reader. Boston: Northeastern University Press, 1992.

ERA Task Force. National Council of Women's Organizations. The Alice Paul Foundation, 1998.

Flexner, Eleanor. *A Century of Struggle: The Women's Rights Movement in the United States.*New York: Atheneum, 1974.

Francis, Roberta W. *The Equal Rights Amendment: Unfinished Business for the Constitution.*

Goldsmith, Barbara. *Other Powers: The Age of Suffrage, Spiritualism, and the Scandalous Victoria Woodhull.* New York: Harper Perennial, 1998

Harrison, Patricia Greenwood. *Connecting Links, the British and American Suffrage Movements, 1900-1914.* London: Greenwood Press, 2000.

Isenberg, Nancy. *Sex and Citizenship in Antebellum America.* Chapel Hill: University of North Carolina Press, 1998.

Kraditor, Aileen S. *The Ideas of the Woman Suffrage Movement, 1890-1920.* New York: W. W. Norton, 1981.

McClymer, John. This High and Holy Moment, The First National Woman's Rights Convention, Worcester, MA, 1850. New York: Harcourt, 1999.

Stanton, Elizabeth Cady. *Eighty Years and More: Reminiscences 1815-1897.* Boston: Northeastern University Press, 1993.

Stanton, Elizabeth Cady, Susan B. Anthony, et al. *History of Woman Suffrage, Vols. 1-3.* New York: Fowler & Wells, 1884.

Ward, Geoffrey. *Not for Ourselves Alone: The Story of Elizabeth Cady Stanton and Susan B. Anthony.* New York: Alfred Knopf, 1999.

Wheeler, Marjorie Spruill, ed. *One Woman, One Vote: Rediscovering the Woman Suffrage Movement.* Troutdale: Newsage Press, 1995.

The Women's Rights Movement: Opposing Viewpoints. The American History Series. San Diego: Greenhaven Press, 1996

G. Women and the Civil War

Brownmiller, Susan. *Against Our Will: Men, Women and Rape.* New York: Simon & Schuster, 1975

Chang, Ina. *A Separate Battle: Women and the Civil War.* New York: Scholastic Inc. 1991

Cooper, Helen, ed., et al. *Arms and the Woman: War, Gender, and Literary Representation.* Chapel Hill: University of North Carolina Press, 1989.

De Pauw, Linda Grant. *Battle Cries and Lullabies.* Norman: University of Oklahoma Press, 1998.

Faragher, John Mack. "The Midwest Farm Family at Mid Century," in Hewitt, Nancy A., ed., *Women, Families and Communities, Volume One: to 1877.* New York: Scott Foresman Company, 1990.

Green, Harvey. *The Light of the Home: An Intimate View of the Lives of Women in Victorian America.* New York: Pantheon Books, 1983.

Leonard, Elizabeth D. *Yankee Women: Gender Battles in the Civil War.* New York: W. W. Norton, 1994.

Mitchell, Reid. *The Vacant Chair: The Northern Soldier Leaves Home.* New York: Oxford University Press, 1993.

Schultz, Jane. "A Mute Fury: Southern Women's Diaries of Sherman's March to the Sea, 1864-1865," in *Arms and the Woman: War, Gender, and Literary Representation*, Ward, Geoffrey, et al. *The Civil War, An Illustrated History.* New York: Alfred Knopf, 1990.

H. Women in the Twentieth and Twenty-First Centuries

Armor, John and Peter Wright. *Manzanar.* New York: Random House, 1988.

Baumgardner, Jennifer and Amy Richards. *Manifesta; Young Women, Feminism and the Future.* New York: Farrar, Straus, and Giroux, 2000.

Blee, Kathleen. *Women of the Klan: Racism and Gender in the 1920s.* Berkeley: University of California Press, 1991.

Brumberg, Joan Jacobs. *The Body Project: An Intimate History of American Girls.* New York: Random House, 1997.

Bushman, Claudia and Richard. *Mormons in America. Religion in American Life Series.* New York: Oxford Press, 1999.

Daniel, Robert L. *American Women in the 20th Century: The Festival of Life.* Boston: Harcourt, Brace Jovanovitch, 1986.

Deffner, Elizabeth. "Nursing in the Military."*Fullerton News Tribune.* May 23, 2002.

French, Marilyn. *The War Against Women.* New York: Summit Books, 1992.

Hillis, Marjorie. *Live Alone and Like It. A Guide for the Extra Woman, Sixth edition.* New York: Bobs-Merrill, 1936.

Ingraham, Chrys. *White Weddings: Romancing Heterosexuality in Popular Culture.* London: Rutledge, 1999.

Joy, Leonard. "Yes, My Darling Daughter." Recorded by Dinah Shore. Music Match Video, 1939.

Noble, Antoinette C. "Masaye Nakamura's Personal Story." *Organization of American Historians Magazine of History.* Spring 2002. 16:3, 37-40.

Ruiz, Vickie L. *From Out of the Shadows: Mexican Women in the Twentieth Century,* New York: Oxford. University Press, 1998.

Steinem, Gloria. *Outrageous Acts and Everyday Rebellions.* Second Edition. New York: Henry Holt and Company, 1995.

Swisher, Karin, ed. *At Issue: Domestic Violence.* New York: Greenhaven Press, 1996.

Swisher, Karin, ed. *At Issue: What is Sexual Harassment?* New York: Greenhaven Press, 1996.

Tavris, Carol. *The Mismeasure of Woman.* New York: Simon & Schuster, 1992.

Teipe, Emily. "Aileen Clarke Hernandez," in *Great Lives from Histor:, American Women Series, Volume III,* Frank Magill, ed. pp. 872-876.

Walker, Nancy A. ed. *Women's Magazines, 1940-1960: Gender Roles and the Popular Press.* Boston: Bedford, St. Martins. 1998.

I. Women's Health

Green, Harvey. *The Light of the Home, An Intimate View of the Lives of Women in Victorian America.* New York: Pantheon Books, 1983.

Herndl, Diane Price. *Invalid Women, Figuring Feminine Illness in American Fiction and Culture, 1840-1940.* Chapel Hill: University of North Carolina Press, 1993.

Leavitt, Judith Walzer. *Brought to Bed: Childbearing in America, 1750-1950.* Boston: Oxford Press, 1986.

McGregor, Deborah Kuhn Mc Gregor. *From Midwives to Medicine: The Birth of American Gynecology.* Piscataway, New Jersey: Rutgers University Press, 1998.

Morantz, Regina, and Sue Zschoche, "Professionalism, Feminism and Gender Roles: A Comparative Study of Nineteenth Century Medical Therapeutics," in Journal of American Medical History, vol. 67, no. 3, (December 198), 568-588.

Morantz-Sanchez, Regina. *Conduct Unbecoming a Woman, Medicine on Trial in Turn-of-the-Century Brooklyn.* New York: Oxford Press, 1999.

More, Ellen S. *Restoring the Balance: Women Physicians and the Profession of Medicine, 1850-1995.* Cambridge: Harvard University Press, 1999.

Riddle, John M. *Eve's Herbs: A History of Contraception and Abortion in the West.* Cambridge: Harvard University Press, 1999.

Rorabaugh, W. J. *The Alcoholic Republic: An American Tradition.* New York: Oxford University Press, 1979.

Smith-Rosenberg, Carroll. *Disorderly Conduct: Visions of Gender in Victorian America.* New York: Oxford Press, 1985.

Stage, Sarah. *Female Complaints: Lydia Pinkham and the Business of Women's Medicine.* New York: W. W. Norton, 1979.

Sutcliffe, Jenny Dr., Nancy Duin, et al. *A History of Medicine.* New York: Barnes & Noble, 1992.

Sympathy and Science: Women Physicians in American Medicine. New York: Oxford Press, 1985.

J. Autobiographies and Biographies

Addams, Jane. *Twenty Years at Hull House.* New York: American Library. 1955.

Addams, Jane. *My Second Twenty Years at Hull House.* New York: American Library. 1950

Anthony, Carl S. *First Ladies: The Saga of the President's Wives and their Power, 1789-1961.* New York: Quill, 1990.

Barker-Benfield, G. J., and Catherine Clinton. *Portraits of American Women: From Settlement to the Civil War. Volume I.* New York: St Martin's Press, 1991.

Baxandall, Rosalyn Fraad. *Words on Fire: The Life and Writing of Elizabeth Gurley Flynn.* New Brunswick: Rutgers University Press, 1987.

Davis, Allen F. *American Heroine: The Life and Legend of Jane Addams.* New York: Oxford University Press, 1972.

Dirvin, Joseph. *Mrs Seton: Foundress of the American Sisters of Charity.* New York, 1975.

Flynn, Elizabeth Gurley. *I Speak my Own Piece: Autobiography of "The Rebel Girl."* New York: 1973.

Gilman, Charlotte Perkins. *The Living of Charlotte Perkins Gilman: An Autobiography.* New York, 1935.

Goldman, Emma. *Living My Life.* New York: Dover, 1969.

Graham, S. *The Story of Phillis Wheatley.* New York: Washington Square Press, 1949.

Griffith, Elisabeth. *In Her Own Right: The Life of Elizabeth Cady Stanton.* New York: Oxford Press, 1984.

Jones, Mary Harris. *The Autobiography of Mother Jones. Third edition.* Chicago: Charles Kerr Publishing, 1976.

Kornfeld, Eve. *Margaret Fuller: A Brief Biography with Documents.* Boston: Bedford Books, 1997.

Magill, Frank. ed. *Great Lives from History, American Women Series. Volumes I-V.* Pasadena, CA: Salem Press, 1995.

Malloy, Louise. *The Life Story of Mother Seton.* Baltimore: 1924.

Melville, Annabelle. *Elizabeth Bayley Seton.* New York: Scribner's, 1962.

Painter, Nell Irvin. *Sojourner Truth: A Life, A Symbol.* New York: W.W. Norton, 1996.

Ravenel, Harriet Horry. *Eliza Pinckney*, 1896.Addams, Jane. *Twenty Years at Hull-House. New York:* American Library, 1961.,

Skemp, Sheila. *Judith Sargent Murray: ABrief Biography with Documents*. Boston: Bedford Books, 1998.

Underhill, Lois Beachy. *The Woman Who Ran for President: the Many Lives of Victoria Woodhull.* New York: Bridgeworks Publishing Company, 1995.

Vorse, Mary Heaton. *A Footnote to Folly.* New York, 1935.

Wadsworth, Ginger. *Julia Morgan: Architect of Dreams*. Minneapolis: Lerner Publications, 1990.

Wald, Lillian. *The House on Henry Street.* New York: Dover, 1969.

Wallace, Irving. *The Square Pegs*. 1957

Ward, Martha C. *A Sounding of Women, Autobiographies from Unexpected Places*. New York: Allyn & Bacon, 1998.

White, Charles I. *The Life of Elizabeth Ann Seton*. Baltimore: 1853.

K. Surveys of Women's History

Barker-Benfield, G. J., and Catherine Clinton. *Portraits of American Women: From Settlement to the Civil War. Volume I.* New York: St Martin's Press, 1991.

Cott, Nancy F. ed. *No Small Courage: A History of Women in the United States*. Boston: Oxford Press, 2000.

Duby, Georges, and Michelle Perrot. *A History of Women in the West*. Boston: Belknap Harvard, 1993.

Jones, Constance. *1001 Things Everyone Should Know About Women's History.* New York: Doubleday, 1998.

Lerner, Gerda. *The Creation of Patriarchy.* Boston: Oxford University Press, 1986.

Mills, Kay. *From Pocohontas to Power Suits: Everything You Need to Know about Women's History in America*. New York: Plume-Penguin Books, 1995.

Norton, Mary Beth, ed., *Major Problems in American Women's History.* Boston: D. C. Heath Company, 1989.

Rowbotham, Sheila. *A Century of Women*. London: Penguin Books, 1999.

Sanders, Beverly. *Women in American History, Books One-Four,* American Federation of Teachers. Washington, D.C.: U. S. Office of Education, 1979.

Smith, Page. *Daughters of the Promised Land: Women in American History.* Boston: Little, Brown, 1970.

Sochen, June. *Herstory, A Woman's View of American History.* New York: Alfred Publishing, 1974.

L. Survey Texts of American History

Divine, Robert., et. al. *American Past & Present, Fifth edition, Volume I to 1877.* New York: Longmans, 1999.

Haynes, Keen. *A History of Latin America, Sixth edition.* New York: Houghton Mifflin, 2000.

Henretta, James A., et al. *America's History, Fourth edition*. Boston: Bedford-St. Martin's, 2000.

Jordan, Winthrop, and Leon Litwack. *The United States, Seventh edition*. Englewood Cliffs, NJ: Prentice Hall, 1990.

M. Women of Color History, Slave History and Ethnic History

Acuna, Rodolfo. *Occupied America: A History of Chicanos. Fourth edition*. New York: Addison-Wesley Longmans, 2000.

De La Cruz, Sor Juana Ines. *A Sor Juana Anthology.* Alan S. Trueblood, trans. Cambridge: Harvard University Press, 1980.

Eltis, David. *Economic Growth and the Ending of the Transatlantic Slave Trade*. New York: Oxford University Press, 1987.

Gonzalez, Deena J. *Refusing the Favor: the Spanish-Mexican Women of Santa Fe, 1820-1880.* New York: Oxford Press, 1999.

Haynes, Keen. *A History of Latin America, Sixth Edition*. New York: Houghton Mifflin, 2000.

Nash, Gary B. "The Hidden History of Mestizo America." Presidential Address, Organization of American Historians, Washington, D.C., March 31, 1995. Reprinted in *The Journal of American History.* 82:3. December 1995, 941-962.

Ruiz, Vickie L. *From Out of the Shadows: Mexican Women in the Twentieth Century.* New York: Oxford University Press, 1998.

Shoemaker, Nancy. *Negotiators of Change: Historical Perspectives on Native American Women*. New York: Routledge Press, 1995.

Talbot, Margaret. "Sacagawea." *National Geographic*, 203:2. February, 2002, 68-85.

Tobin, Jacqueline, and Raymond Dobard. *Hidden in Plain View: A Secret Story of Quilts and the Underground Railroad.* New York: Doubleday, 1999.

White, Deborah Gray. *Arn'tia Woman? Female Slaves in the Plantation South*. New York: W. W. Norton Company, 1985.

N. Women in the West

Acuna, Rodolfo. *Occupied America: A History of Chicanos. Fourth edition*. New York: Addison-Wesley Longmans, 2000.

Butruille, Susan G. *Women's Voices From the Oregon Trail.* Boise: Tamarack Books, 1993.

Faragher, John Mack. "The Midwest Farm Family at Mid Century," in Hewitt, Nancy A. ed. *Women, Families and Communities, Volume One: to 1877.* New York: Scott Foresman Company, 1990.

Gonzalez, Deena J. *Refusing the Favor: the Spanish-Mexican Women of Santa Fe, 1820-1880.* New York: Oxford Press, 1999.

Levy, Jo Ann. *They Saw the Elephant: Women in the California Gold Rush*. Norman: University of Oklahoma Press, 1990.

Miller, Robert.*The Story of Stagecoach Mary Fields*. New York: Silver Burdett Press, 1995.

Reiter, Joan Swallow. *Women of the Old West*. Alexandria: Time-Life, Inc. 1979.

Ruiz, Vickie L. *From Out of the Shadows: Mexican Women in the Twentieth Century.* New York: Oxford University Press, 1998.

Talbot, Margaret. "Sacagawea. "*National Geographic*, 203:2. February, 2002, 68-85.

INDEX

A

B

C

D

E

F

G

H

I

J

K

L

M

N

O

P

Q

R

S

T

U

V

W

Y

Z